P9-CRP-531

PIECES OF

THE

PERSONALITY

PUZZLE

READINGS IN THEORY AND RESEARCH
FOURTH EDITION

David C. Funder

UNIVERSITY OF CALIFORNIA, RIVERSIDE

Daniel J. Ozer

UNIVERSITY OF CALIFORNIA, RIVERSIDE

W · W · NORTON & COMPANY

NEW YORK · LONDON

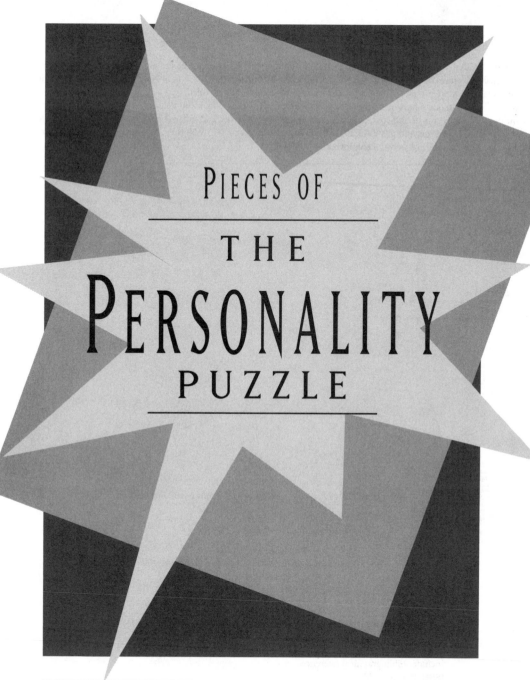

Pieces of

THE

PERSONALITY

PUZZLE

READINGS IN THEORY AND RESEARCH
FOURTH EDITION

W. W. Norton & Company has been independent since its founding in 1923, when William Warder Norton and Mary D. Herter Norton first published lectures delivered at the People's Institute, the adult education division of New York City's Cooper Union. The Nortons soon expanded their program beyond the Institute, publishing books by celebrated academics from America and abroad. By mid-century, the two major pillars of Norton's publishing program—trade books and college texts—were firmly established. In the 1950s, the Norton family transferred control of the company to its employees, and today—with a staff of four hundred and a comparable number of trade, college, and professional titles published each year—W. W. Norton & Company stands as the largest and oldest publishing house owned wholly by its employees.

Copyright © 2007, 2004, 2001, 1997 by W. W. Norton & Company, Inc.

All rights reserved
Printed in the United States of America

Composition by Matrix.
Manufacturing by R. R. Donnelley & Sons—Crawfordsville.
Book design by Joan Greenfield.
Production manager: Ben Reynolds.

Library of Congress Cataloging-in-Publication Data
Pieces of the personality puzzle : readings in theory and research / [edited by] David C. Funder,
Daniel J. Ozer.— 4th ed.
   p. cm.
Includes bibliographical references.
ISBN-10 0-393-93035-1
ISBN-13 978-0-393-93035-1
1. Personality. I. Funder, David Charles. II. Ozer, Daniel J.

W. W. Norton & Company, Inc., 500 Fifth Avenue, New York, N.Y. 10110
www.wwnorton.com

W. W. Norton & Company Ltd., Castle House,
75/76 Wells Street, London W1T 3QT

1   2   3   4   5   6   7   8   9   0

CONTENTS

Part III

Biological Approaches to Personality 107

Part IV

The Psychoanalytic Approach to Personality 179

Part V

Humanistic Approach to Personality   233

Part VI

Cross-Cultural Approaches to Personality   299

Part VII

Process Approaches to Personality: Learning, Motivation, and the Self   353

PREFACE

Theory and research in personality psychology address the ways in which people are different from one another, the relations between body and mind, how people think (consciously and unconsciously), what people want (consciously and unconsciously), and what people do. Personality is the broadest, most all-encompassing part of psychology.

This breadth of relevance is personality psychology's greatest attraction, but it also makes good work in this field difficult to do. Nearly all personality psychologists have therefore chosen to limit their approach in some way, by focusing on particular phenomena they deem of special interest, and more or less neglecting everything else. A group of psychologists who focus on the same basic phenomena could be said to be working within the same "paradigm," or following the same "basic approach."

The articles in this reader are organized by the basic approaches they follow. The first section presents articles that describe and discuss the research methods used by personality psychologists. The second section includes articles relevant to the trait approach, the approach that concentrates on the conceptualization and measurement of individual differences in personality. The third section presents articles that follow the biological approach and attempt to connect the biology of the body and nervous system with the processes of emotion, thought, and behavior. The fourth section presents classic and modern research from the psychoanalytic approach, which considers (among other things) unconscious processes of the mind based, ultimately, on the writings of Sigmund Freud. The fifth section presents some examples from the humanistic approach, which focuses on experience, free will, and the meaning of life, and in recent years has branched into a "positive psychology" movement that tries to find and enhance happiness and the good things in life. Articles in the sixth section consider the constancy and variability of personality across different cultures. Articles in the seventh section trace the way the behavioristic approach developed into social learning theory and the modern social-cognitive approaches to personality that address topics including thinking, motivation, and the self.

There is no substitute for reading original work in a field to appreciate its content and its style. But assembling a reader such as this does entail certain difficulties and requires strategic choices. As the editors we chose, first of all, to be representative rather than exhaustive in our coverage of the domain of personality psychology. While we believe the most important areas of personality are represented by an exemplar or two in what follows, no topic is truly covered in depth. We hope readers who become seriously interested will use the reference sections that follow each article to guide their further reading.

A second choice was to search for articles most likely to be interesting to an audience that does *not* consist of professionally trained psychologists. At the same time, we tried to ensure that many of the most prominent personality psychologists of this century were represented. In some cases, this meant selecting a prominent psychologist's most accessible—rather than by some definition most "important"—writing.

A third decision—made reluctantly—was to excerpt nearly all of these articles. Most of the articles that follow are, in their original form, much longer. We tried to be judicious in our editing. We removed passages that would be uninformative to a non-professional reader, digressions, and treatments of issues beside the main point of each article. We have marked all changes to the original text; three asterisks centered on a blank line mark the omission of a complete paragraph or section, while three asterisks run into the text indicate that sentences within that paragraph have been omitted.

We probably should mention here one other thing that a reader might notice. Prior to about 1970, it was conventional to use the pronoun "he" to refer to both males and females. This practice is followed in some of the older selections in this volume, and we have left them intact. Current guidelines of the American Psychological Association (APA, 2001) require that "he or she" or similar inclusive constructions be used.

Most articles have footnotes. A few of these are by the original authors (we have indicated which these are), but we deleted most author footnotes. We added many footnotes of our own. These define bits of jargon, explain references to other research, and—when we couldn't help ourselves—provide editorial commentary.

Each section begins with an introduction that describes the articles to follow and lays out their sequence. Each article is preceded by a brief essay outlining what we see as its take-home message and some issues we believe readers should consider.

Though it is divided into seven rather than six parts, the reader follows the same organization as Funder's (2007) textbook, *The Personality Puzzle* (4th ed.), and some of the research referred to in that book will be found here. However, one does not need to use that text to use this reader; the two books are largely independent and this reader was designed to be useful in conjunction with almost any textbook—or even by itself. The reader includes representative writings in method, theory, and research—the three staples of any good personality course.

Changes in the Fourth Edition

Roughly a third of the articles are new to the Fourth Edition. In particular, research in the biological, cross-cultural, and cognitive approaches to personality is so active and changing so rapidly that we felt compelled to add new and up-to-date examples of research in those fields. We have also added other articles we thought illustrated important and interesting aspects of the various approaches to personality psychology, and removed some articles that appeared seldom to be assigned to students or that have simply become out-of-date.

ACKNOWLEDGMENTS

Many individuals assisted this project in a number of ways. For the First Edition, useful suggestions were provided by Jana Spain of Highpoint University, Susan Krauss Whitbourne of the University of Massachusetts (Amherst), Andrew J. Tomarken of Vanderbilt University, and Brian C. Hayden of Brown University. As we prepared the Second, Third, and Fourth Editions, we prowled many Web sites of courses around the world that used this book, trying to learn which chapters were really being assigned for students to read, and also received informal advice from many colleagues. We made adjustments accordingly in the Fourth Edition and thank the instructors who used this book for their explicit and implicit guidance.

For the First Edition, Liz Suhay of W. W. Norton assembled the manuscript and gathered copyright permissions, and April Lange, the editor, was an important source of organization and guidance. For the Second Edition, Mary Babcock copyedited and organized the manuscript, Anne Hellman copyedited the Third, and Lynne Cannon Menges copyedited the Fourth. The original idea for a book of readings to accompany Funder's *Personality Puzzle* came from Don Fusting, a former Norton editor. We are grateful to all these individuals, and also to the authors who graciously and generously allowed us to edit and reproduce their work.

Pieces of

The

Personality

Puzzle

Readings in Theory and Research
Fourth Edition

PART I

Research Methods

How do you learn something that nobody has ever known before? This is the question of "research methods," the strategies and techniques that are used to obtain new knowledge. The knowledge of interest for personality psychology is knowledge about people, so for this field the question of research methods translates into a concern with the ways in which one can learn more about a person. These include techniques for measuring an individual's personality traits as well as his or her thoughts, motivations, emotions, and goals.

Personality psychologists have a long tradition of being particularly interested in and sophisticated about research methods. Over the years, they have developed new sources of data, invented innovative statistical techniques, and even provided some important advances in the philosophy of science. The selections in this section address some critical issues that arise when considering the methods one might use to learn more about people.

The opening selection, by Dan McAdams, asks, "What do we know when we know a person?" The article presents an introduction to and comparison of the various conceptual units—ranging from traits to the holistic meaning of life—that personality psychologists have used to describe and understand people.

The second selection, by Robert Rosenthal and Donald Rubin, concerns a particular statistic that is unavoidable by any reader of personality research—the correlation coefficient. Despite its ubiquity, this statistic is frequently misunderstood, and in particular, the effects it describes are often underestimated. For example, if someone tells you they have obtained a correlation between a trait and behavior equal to .32, is this big or little? For reasons Rosenthal and Rubin explain, the answer is "pretty big."

The third selection is one of the unquestioned, all-time classics of psychological methodology, and absolutely required reading for any psychologist. The article by Lee Cronbach and Paul Meehl concerns "construct validity," or the issue of how one determines whether a test of personality (or any other attribute) really measures what it is supposed to.

Personality psychology is now moving away from its former nearly exclusive reliance on self-report personality assessments, to include other methods such as online coding of videotaped behavior. In the final selection, Samuel Gosling and his colleagues demonstrate how a comparison between self-reports and observers' reports of behavior can illustrate not only the relative validity of each kind of data but also interesting psychological processes, such as self-enhancement, that produce discrepancies.

WHAT DO WE KNOW WHEN WE KNOW A PERSON?

Dan P. McAdams

Personality psychology is all about understanding individuals better. In this first selection, the personality psychologist Dan McAdams asks one of the fundamental questions about this enterprise, which is: when we learn about a person, what is it we learn? He begins by describing the kind of personality psychology that nonpsychologists (or psychologists when off duty) frequently practice: discussing an individual that one has just met. In such discussions, the individual is often considered at several different levels, ranging from surface descriptions of behavior to inferences about deeper motivations.

The challenge for professional personality psychologists, McAdams argues, is to become at least as sophisticated as amateur psychologists by taking into account aspects of individuals at multiple levels. In his own work, McAdams collects life stories and tries to understand individuals in holistic terms. He is a critic of the more dominant approach, which characterizes individuals in terms of their personality traits. However, in this well-balanced article we see McAdams attempt to integrate the various levels of personality description into a complete portrait of what we know when we know a person.

From *Journal of Personality*, 63, 365–396, 1995.

One of the great social rituals in the lives of middle-class American families is "the drive home." The ritual comes in many different forms, but the idealized scene that I am now envisioning involves my wife and me leaving the dinner party sometime around midnight, getting into our car, and, finding nothing worth listening to on the radio, beginning our traditional post-party postmortem. Summoning up all of the personological wisdom and nuance I can muster at the moment, I may start off with something like,

"He was really an ass." Or adopting the more "relational" mode that psychologists such as Gilligan (1982) insist comes more naturally to women than men, my wife may say something like, "I can't believe they stay married to each other." It's often easier to begin with the cheap shots. As the conversation develops, however, our attributions become more detailed and more interesting. We talk about people we liked as well as those we found offensive. There is often a single character who stands out from the party—the person we found most intriguing, perhaps; or the one who seemed most troubled; maybe the one we would like to get to know much better in the future. In the scene I am imagining, let us call that person "Lynn" and let us consider what my wife and I might say about her as we drive home in the dark.

I sat next to Lynn at dinner. For the first 15 minutes, she dominated the conversation at our end of the table with her account of her recent trip to Mexico where she was doing research for an article to appear in a national magazine. Most of the people at the party knew that Lynn is a free-lance writer whose projects have taken her around the world, and they asked her many questions about her work and her travels. Early on, I felt awkward and intimidated in Lynn's presence. I have never been to Mexico; I was not familiar with her articles; I felt I couldn't keep up with the fast tempo of her account, how she moved quickly from one exotic tale to another. Add to this the fact that she is a strikingly attractive woman, about 40 years old with jet black hair, dark eyes, a seemingly flawless complexion, clothing both flamboyant and tasteful, and one might be able to sympathize with my initial feeling that she was, in a sense, "just too much."

My wife formed a similar first impression earlier in the evening when she engaged Lynn in a lengthy conversation on the patio. But she ended up feeling much more positive about Lynn as they shared stories of their childhoods. My wife mentioned that she was born in Tokyo during the time her parents were Lutheran missionaries in Japan. Lynn remarked that she had great admiration for missionaries "because they really believe in something." Then she remarked: "I've never really believed in anything very strongly, nothing to get real passionate about. Neither did my parents, except for believing in us kids. They probably believed in us kids too much." My wife immediately warmed up to Lynn for this disarmingly intimate comment. It was not clear exactly what she meant, but Lynn seemed more vulnerable now, and more mysterious.

I eventually warmed up to Lynn, too. As she and I talked about politics and our jobs, she seemed less brash and domineering than before. She seemed genuinely interested in my work as a personality psychologist who, among other things, collects people's life stories. She had been a psychology major in college. And lately she had been reading a great many popular psychology books on such things as Jungian archetypes, the "child within," and "addictions to love." As a serious researcher and theorist, I must confess that I have something of a visceral prejudice against many of these self-help, "New Age" books. Still, I resisted the urge to scoff at her reading list and ended up enjoying our conversation very much. I did notice, though, that Lynn filled her wine glass about twice as often as I did mine. She never made eye contact with her husband, who was sitting directly across the table from her, and twice she said something sarcastic in response to a story he was telling.

Over the course of the evening, my wife and I learned many other things about Lynn. On our drive home we noted the following:

1. Lynn was married once before and has two children by her first husband.
2. The children, now teenagers, currently live with her first husband rather than with her; she didn't say how often she sees them.
3. Lynn doesn't seem to like President Clinton and is very critical of his excessively "liberal" policies; but she admires his wife, Hillary, who arguably is more liberal in her views; we couldn't pin a label of conservative or liberal to Lynn because she seemed to contradict herself on political topics.
4. Lynn hates jogging and rarely exercises; she claims to eat a lot of "junk food"; she ate very little food at dinner.
5. Lynn says she is an atheist.
6. Over the course of the evening, Lynn's elegant demeanor and refined speech style seemed to give way to a certain crudeness; shortly before we left, my wife heard her telling an off-color joke, and I noticed that

she seemed to lapse into a street-smart Chicago dialect that one often associates with growing up in the toughest neighborhoods.

As we compared our notes on Lynn during the drive home, my wife and I realized that we learned a great deal about Lynn during the evening, and that we were eager to learn more. But what is it that we thought we now knew about her? And what would we need to know to know her better? In our social ritual, my wife and I were enjoying the rather playful exercise of trying to make sense of persons. In the professional enterprise of personality psychology, however, making sense of persons is or should be the very raison d'être of the discipline. From the time of Allport (1937) and Murray (1938), through the anxious days of the "situationist" critique (Bowers, 1973; Mischel, 1968), and up to the present, upbeat period wherein we celebrate traits[1] (John, 1990; Wiggins, 1996) while we offer a sparkling array of new methods and models for personality inquiry (see, for example, McAdams, 1994a; Ozer & Reise, 1994; Revelle, 1995), making sense of persons was and is fundamentally what personality psychologists are supposed to do, in the lab, in the office, even on the drive home. But how should we do it?

Making Sense of Persons

* * *

Since the time of Allport, Cattell, and Murray, personality psychologists have offered a number of different schemes for describing persons. For example, McClelland (1951) proposed that an adequate account of personality requires assessments of stylistic traits (e.g., extraversion, friendliness), cognitive schemes (e.g., personal constructs, values, frames), and dynamic motives (e.g., the need for achievement, power motivation). In the wake of Mischel's (1968) critique of personality dispositions, many personality psychologists eschewed broadband constructs such as traits and motives in favor of more domain-specific variables, like "encoding strategies," "self-regulatory systems and plans," and other "cognitive social learning person variables" (Mischel, 1973). By contrast, the 1980s and 1990s have witnessed a strong comeback for the concept of the broad, dispositional trait, culminating in what many have argued is a consensus around the five-factor model of personality traits (Digman, 1990; Goldberg, 1993; McCrae & Costa, 1996). Personality psychologists such as A. H. Buss (1989) have essentially proclaimed that personality is *traits* and only traits. Others are less sanguine, however, about the ability of the Big Five trait taxonomy in particular and the concept of trait in general to provide all or even most of the right stuff for personality inquiry (Block, 1995; Briggs, 1989; Emmons, 1993; McAdams, 1992, 1994b; Pervin, 1994).

Despite the current popularity of the trait concept, I submit that I will never be able to render Lynn "knowable" by relying solely on a description of her personality traits. At the same time, a description that failed to consider traits would be equally inadequate. Trait descriptions are essential both for social rituals like the post-party post-mortem and for adequate personological inquiry. A person cannot be known without knowing traits. But knowing traits is not enough. Persons should be described on at least *three separate* and, at best, *loosely related levels* of functioning. The three may be viewed as levels of comprehending *individuality* amidst otherness—how the person is similar to and different from *some* (but not all) other persons. Each level offers categories and frameworks for organizing *individual differences* among persons. Dispositional traits comprise the first level in this scheme—the level that deals primarily with what I have called (McAdams, 1992, 1994b) a "psychology of the stranger."

[1]The reference here is to the "person-situation debate" that dominated personality psychology from 1968 to 1988. The debate was about whether the most important causes of behavior were properties of people or of the situations they find themselves in. The "situationist" viewpoint was that situations were more important. As McAdams notes, the eventual resolution of this controversy reaffirmed the importance—but not all-importance—of stable individual differences in personality (traits) as important determinants of behavior.

The Power of Traits

Dispositional traits are those relatively nonconditional, relatively decontextualized, generally linear, and implicitly comparative dimensions of personality that go by such titles as "extraversion," "dominance," and "neuroticism." One of the first things both I and my wife noticed about Lynn was her social dominance. She talked loudly and fast; she held people's attention when she described her adventures; she effectively controlled the conversation in the large group. Along with her striking appearance, social dominance appeared early on as one of her salient characteristics. Other behavioral signs also suggested an elevated rating on the trait of neuroticism, though these might also indicate the situationally specific anxiety she may have been experiencing in her relationship with the man who accompanied her to the party. According to contemporary norms for dinner parties of this kind, she seemed to drink a bit too much. Her moods shifted rather dramatically over the course of the evening. While she remained socially dominant, she seemed to become more and more nervous as the night wore on. The interjection of her off-color joke and the street dialect stretched slightly the bounds of propriety one expects on such occasions, though not to an alarming extent. In a summary way, then, one might describe Lynn, as she became known during the dinner party, as socially dominant, extraverted, entertaining, dramatic, moody, slightly anxious, intelligent, and introspective. These adjectives describe part of her dispositional signature.

How useful are these trait descriptions? Given that my wife's and my observations were limited to one behavioral setting (the party), we do not have enough systematic data to say how accurate our descriptions are. However, if further systematic observation were to bear out this initial description—say, Lynn were observed in many settings; say, peers rated her on trait dimensions; say, she completed standard trait questionnaires such as the Personality Research Form (Jackson, 1974) or the NEO Personality Inventory (Costa & McCrae, 1985)—then trait descriptions like these, wherein the individual is rated on a series of linear and noncontingent behavior dimensions, prove very useful indeed.

* * *

The Problem with Traits

It is easy to criticize the concept of trait. Trait formulations proposed by Allport (1937), Cattell (1957), Guilford (1959), Eysenck (1967), Jackson (1974), Tellegen (1982), Hogan (1986), and advocates of the Big Five have been called superficial, reductionistic, atheoretical, and even imperialistic. Traits are mere labels, it is said again and again. Traits don't explain anything. Traits lack precision. Traits disregard the environment. Traits apply only to score distributions in groups, not to the individual person (e.g., Lamiell, 1987). I believe that there is some validity in some of these traditional claims but that traits nonetheless provide invaluable information about persons. I believe that many critics expect too much of traits. Yet, those trait enthusiasts (e.g., A. H. Buss, 1989; Digman, 1990; Goldberg, 1993) who equate personality with traits in general, and with the Big Five in particular, are also claiming too much.

Goldberg (1981) contended that the English language includes five clusters of trait-related terms—the Big Five—because personality characteristics encoded in these terms have proved especially salient in human interpersonal perception, especially when it comes to the perennial and evolutionary crucial task of sizing up a stranger. I think Goldberg was more right than many trait enthusiasts would like him to be. Reliable and valid trait ratings provide an excellent "first read" on a person by offering estimates of a person's relative standing on a delimited series of general and linear dimensions of proven social significance. This is indeed crucial information in the evaluation of strangers and others about whom we know very little. It is the kind of information that strangers quickly glean from one another as they size one another up and anticipate future interactions. It did not take long for me to conclude that Lynn was high on certain aspects of Extraversion and moderately high on Neuroticism.

What makes trait information like this so valuable is that it is comparative and relatively nonconditional. A highly extraverted person is generally more extraverted than most other people (comparative) and tends to be extraverted in a wide variety of settings (nonconditional), although by no means in all.

Consider, furthermore, the phenomenology of traditional trait assessment in personality psychology. In rating one's own or another's traits on a typical paper-and-pencil measure, the rater/subject must adopt an observational stance in which the target of the rating becomes an object of comparison on a series of linear and only vaguely conditional dimensions (McAdams, 1994c). Thus, if I were to rate Lynn, or if Lynn were to rate herself, on the Extraversion-keyed personality item "I am not a cheerful optimist" (from the NEO), I (or Lynn) would be judging the extent of Lynn's own "cheerful optimism" in comparison to the cheerful optimism of people I (or she) know or have heard about, or perhaps even an assumed average level of cheerful optimism of the rest of humankind. Ratings like these must have a social referent if they are to be meaningful. The end result of my (or her) ratings is a determination of the extent to which Lynn is seen as more or less extraverted across a wide variety of situations, conditions, and contexts, and compared to other people in general. There is, therefore, no place in trait assessment for what Thorne (1989) calls the conditional patterns of personality (see also Wright & Mischel, 1987). Here are some examples of conditional patterns: "My dominance shows when my competence is threatened; I fall apart when people try to comfort me; I talk most when I am nervous" (Thorne, 1989, p. 149). But to make traits into conditional statements is to rob them of their power as nonconditional indicators of general trends.

The two most valuable features of trait description—its comparative and nonconditional qualities—double as its two greatest limitations as well.[2]

As persons come to know one another better, they seek and obtain information that is both noncomparative and highly conditional, contingent, and contextualized. They move beyond the mindset of comparing individuals on linear dimensions. In a sense, they move beyond traits to construct a more detailed and nuanced portrait of personality, so that the stranger can become more fully known. New information is then integrated with the trait profile to give a fuller picture. My wife and I began to move beyond traits on the drive home. As a first read, Lynn seemed socially dominant (Extraversion) and mildly neurotic (Neuroticism). I would also give her a high rating on Openness to Experience; I would say that Agreeableness was probably medium; I would say that Conscientiousness was low to medium, though I do not feel that I received much trait-relevant information on Conscientiousness. Beyond these traits, however, Lynn professed a confusing set of political beliefs: She claimed to be rather conservative but was a big fan of Hillary Clinton; she scorned government for meddling in citizens' private affairs and said she paid too much in taxes to support wasteful social programs, while at the same time she claimed to be a pacifist and to have great compassion for poor people and those who could not obtain health insurance. Beyond traits, Lynn claimed to be an atheist but expressed great admiration for missionaries. Beyond traits, Lynn appeared to be having problems in intimate relationships; she wished she could believe in something; she enjoyed her work as a freelance writer; she was a good listener one on one but not in the large group; she expressed strong interest in New Age psychology; she seemed to think her parents invested too much faith in her and in her siblings. To know Lynn well, to know her more fully than one would know a stranger, one must be privy to information that does not fit trait categories, information that is exquisitely conditional and contextualized.

Going beyond Traits: Time, Place, and Role

There is a vast and largely unmapped domain in personality wherein reside such constructs as

---

[2]This observation provides an example of Funder's First Law, which states that great strengths are often great weaknesses and, surprisingly often, the opposite is also true (Funder, 2007).

motives (McClelland, 1961), values (Rokeach, 1973), defense mechanisms (Cramer, 1991), coping styles (Lazarus, 1991), developmental issues and concerns (Erikson, 1963; Havighurst, 1972), personal strivings (Emmons, 1986), personal projects (Little, 1989), current concerns (Klinger, 1977), life tasks (Cantor & Kihlstrom, 1987), attachment styles (Hazan & Shaver, 1990), conditional patterns (Thorne, 1989), core conflictual relationship themes (Luborsky & Crits-Christoph, 1991), patterns of self-with-other, domain-specific skills and talents (Gardner, 1993), strategies and tactics (D. M. Buss, 1991), and many more personality variables that are both linked to behavior (Cantor, 1990) and important for the full description of the person (McAdams, 1994a). This assorted collection of constructs makes up a second level of personality, to which I give the generic and doubtlessly inadequate label of *personal concerns.* Compared with dispositional traits, personal concerns are typically couched in motivational, developmental, or strategic terms. They speak to what people want, often during particular periods in their lives or within particular domains of action, and what life methods people use (strategies, plans, defenses, and so on) in order to get what they want or avoid getting what they don't want over time, in particular places, and/or with respect to particular roles.

What primarily differentiates, then, personal concerns from dispositional traits is the contextualization of the former within time, place, and/or role. Time is perhaps the most ubiquitous context. In their studies of the "intimacy life task" among young adults, Cantor, Acker, and Cook-Flanagan (1992) focus on "those tasks that individuals see as personally important and time consuming at particular times in their lives" (p. 644). In their studies of generativity across the adult life span, McAdams, de St. Aubin, and Logan (1993) focus on a cluster of concern, belief, commitment, and action oriented toward providing for the well-being of the next generation, a cluster that appears to peak in salience around middle age. Intimacy and generativity must be contextualized in the temporal life span if they are to be properly understood. By contrast, the traits of Extraversion and

Agreeableness are easily defined and understood outside of time. They are not linked to developmental stages, phases, or seasons.

The temporal context also distinguishes traits on the one hand from motives and goals on the other. Motives, goals, strivings, and plans are defined in terms of future ends. A person high in power motivation wants, desires, strives for power—having impact on others is the desired end state, the temporal goal (Winter, 1973). To have a strong motive, goal, striving, or plan is to orient oneself in a particular way in time. The same cannot be readily assumed with traits. Extraversion is not naturally conceived in goal-directed terms. It is not necessary for the viability of the concept of extraversion that an extraverted person strive to obtain a particular goal in time, although of course such a person may do so. Extraverted people simply *are* extraverted; whether they try to be or not is irrelevant. The case is even clearer for neuroticism, for the commonsense assumption here is that highly neurotic people do not strive to be neurotic over time. They simply are neurotic. While dispositional traits may have motivational properties (Allport, 1937; McCrae & Costa, 1996), traits do not exist in time in the same way that motives, strivings, goals, and plans are temporally contextualized. To put it another way, I cannot understand Lynn's life in time when I merely consider her dispositional traits. Developmental and motivational constructs, by contrast, begin to provide me with the temporal context, the life embedded in and evolving over time.

Contextualization of behavior in place was a major theme of the situationist critique in the 1970s (Frederiksen, 1972; Magnusson, 1971). The situationists argued that behavior is by and large local rather than general, subject to the norms and expectations of a given social place or space. Attempts to formulate taxonomies of situations have frequently involved delineating the physical and interpersonal features of certain kinds of prototypical behavioral settings and social environments, like "church," "football game," "classroom," and "party" (Cantor, Mischel, & Schwartz, 1982; Krahe, 1992; Moos, 1973). Certain domain-specific skills, competencies, attitudes, and schemas are examples of personality variables contextualized in place. For example, Lynn is both a very good listener in one-on-one conversations, especially when the topic concerns psychology, and an extremely effective storyteller in large groups, especially when she is talking about travel. When she is angry with her husband in a social setting, she drinks too much. The latter is an example of a conditional pattern (Thorne, 1989) or perhaps a very simple personal script. Some varieties of personal scripts and conditional patterns are contextualized in place and space: "When I am at home, I am unable to relax"; "When the weather is hot, I think about how miserable I was as a child, growing up in St. Louis"; "If I am lost in Chicago, I never ask for directions." To know a person well, it is not necessary to have information about all of the different personal scripts and conditional patterns that prevail in all of the different behavioral settings he or she will encounter. Instead, the personologist should seek information on the most salient settings and environments that make up the ecology of a person's life and investigate the most influential, most common, or most problematic personal scripts and conditional patterns that appear within that ecology (Demorest & Alexander, 1992).

Another major context in personality is social role. Certain strivings, tasks, strategies, defense mechanisms, competencies, values, interests, and styles may be role-specific. For example, Lynn may employ the defense mechanism of rationalization to cope with her anxiety about the setbacks she has experienced in her role as a mother. In her role as a writer, she may excel in expressing herself in a laconic, Hemingway-like style (role competence, skill) and she may strive to win certain journalistic awards or to make more money than her husband (motivation, striving). In the role of student/learner, she is fascinated with New Age psychology (interests). In the role of daughter, she manifests an insecure attachment style, especially with her mother, and this style seems to carry over to her relationships with men (role of lover/spouse) but not with women (role of friend). Ogilvie (Ogilvie & Ashmore, 1991) has developed a new approach

to personality assessment that matches personality descriptors with significant persons in one's life, resulting in an organization of self-with-other constructs. It would appear that some of the more significant self-with-other constellations in a person's life are those associated with important social roles. Like social places, not all social roles are equally important in a person's life. Among the most salient in the lives of many American men and women are the roles of spouse/lover, son/daughter, parent, sibling, worker/provider, and citizen.

* * *

There is no compelling reason to believe that the language of nonconditional and decontextualized dispositions should work well to describe constructs that are situated in time, place, and role. Consistent with this supposition, Kaiser and Ozer (under review) found that personal goals, or what they term "motivational units," do not map onto the five-factor structure demonstrated for traits. Instead, their study suggests that the structure of personal goals may be more appropriately conceptualized in terms of various content domains (e.g., work, social). It seems reasonable, therefore, to begin with the assumption that an adequate description of a person should bring together contrasting and complementary attributional schemes, integrating dispositional insights with those obtained from personal concerns. To know Lynn well is to be able to describe her in ways that go significantly beyond the language of traits. This is not to suggest that Levels I and II are or must be completely unrelated to each other, that Lynn's extraversion, for example, has nothing to do with her personal career strivings. In personality psychology, linkages between constructs at these different levels should and will be investigated in research. But the linkages, if they indeed exist, should be established empirically rather than assumed by theorists to be true.

What Is Missing?

As we move from Level I to Level II, we move from the psychology of the stranger to a more detailed and nuanced description of a flesh-and-blood, in-the-world person, striving to do things over time, situated in place and role, expressing herself or himself in and through strategies, tactics, plans, and goals. In Lynn's case, we begin our very provisional sketch with nonconditional attributions suggesting a high level of extraversion and moderately high neuroticism and we move to more contingent statements suggesting that she seems insecurely attached to her parents and her husband, strives for power and recognition in her career, wants desperately to believe in something but as yet has not found it in religion or in spirituality, holds strong but seemingly contradictory beliefs about politics and public service, employs the defense of rationalization to cope with the frustration she feels in her role as mother, has interests that tend toward books and ideas rather than physical health and fitness, loves to travel, is a good listener one on one but not in groups, is a skilled writer, is a good storyteller, tells stories that are rambling and dramatic. If we were to continue a relationship with Lynn, we would learn more and more about her. We would find that some of our initial suppositions were naive, or even plain wrong. We would obtain much more information on her traits, enabling us to obtain a clearer and more accurate dispositional signature. We would learn more about the contextualized constructs of her personality, about how she functions in time, place, and role. Filling in more and more information in Levels I and II, we might get to know Lynn very well.

But I submit that, as Westerners living in this modern age, we would not know Lynn "well enough" until we moved beyond dispositional traits and personal concerns to a third level of personality. Relatedly, should Lynn think of herself only in Level I and Level II terms, then she, too, as a Western, middle-class adult living in the last years of the 20th century, would not know herself "well enough" to comprehend her own identity. The problem of identity is the problem of overall unity and purpose in human lives (McAdams, 1985). It is a problem that has come to preoccupy men and women in Western democracies during the past

200 years (Baumeister, 1986; Langbaum, 1982). It is not generally a problem for children, though there are some exceptions. It is probably not as salient a problem for many non-Western societies that put less of a premium on individualism and articulating the autonomous adult self, although it is a problem in many of these societies. It is not equally problematic for all contemporary American adults. Nonetheless, identity is likely to be a problem for Lynn, for virtually all people attending that dinner party or reading this article, and for most contemporary Americans and Western Europeans who at one time or another in their adult lives have found the question "Who am I?" to be worth asking, pondering, and worth working on.

Modern and postmodern democratic societies do not explicitly tell adults who they should be. At the same time, however, these societies insist that an adult should be someone who both fits in and is unique (Bellah, Madsen, Sullivan, Swidler, & Tipton, 1985). The self should be defined so that it is both separate and connected, individuated and integrated at the same time. These kinds of selves do not exist in prepackaged, readily assimilated form. They are not passed down from one generation to the next, as they were perhaps in simpler times. Rather, selves must be made or discovered as people become what they are to become in time. The selves that we make before we reach late adolescence and adulthood are, among other things, "lists" of characteristics to be found in Levels I and II of personality. My 8-year-old daughter, Amanda, sees herself as relatively shy (low Extraversion) and very caring and warm (high Agreeableness); she knows she is a good ice skater (domain-specific skill); she loves amusement parks (interests); and she has strong feelings of love and resentment toward her older sister (ambivalent attachment style, though she wouldn't call it that). I hazard to guess that these are a few items in a long list of things, including many that are not in the realm of personality proper ("I live in a white house"; "I go to Central School"), that make up Amanda's self-concept. A list of attributes from Levels I and II is not, however, an identity. Then again, Amanda is too young to have an identity because she is probably not able to experience unity and purpose as problematic in her life. Therefore, one can know Amanda very well by sticking to Levels I and II.

But not so for Lynn. As a contemporary adult, Lynn most likely can understand and appreciate, more or less, the problem of unity and purpose in her life. While the question of "Who am I?" may seem silly or obvious to Amanda, Lynn is likely to see the question as potentially problematic, challenging, interesting, ego-involving, and so on. For reasons that are no doubt physiological and cognitive, as well as social and cultural, it is in late adolescence and young adulthood that many contemporary Westerners come to believe that the self must or should be constructed and told in a manner that integrates the disparate roles they play, incorporates their many different values and skills, and organizes into a meaningful temporal pattern their reconstructed past, perceived present, and anticipated future (Breger, 1974; Erikson, 1959; McAdams, 1985). The challenge of identity demands that the Western adult construct a telling of the self that synthesizes synchronic and diachronic elements in such a way as to suggest that (*a*) despite its many facets the self is coherent and unified and (*b*) despite the many changes that attend the passage of time, the self of the past led up to or set the stage for the self of the present, which in turn will lead up to or set the stage for the self of the future (McAdams, 1990, 1993).

What form does such a construction take? A growing number of theorists believe that the only conceivable form for a unified and purposeful telling of a life is the story (Bruner, 1990; Charme, 1984; Cohler, 1982, 1994; Hermans & Kempen, 1993; Howard, 1991; Kotre, 1984; Linde, 1990; MacIntyre, 1984; Polkinghorne, 1988). In my own theoretical and empirical work, I have argued that identity is itself an internalized and evolving life story, or personal myth (McAdams, 1984, 1985, 1990, 1993, 1996). Contemporary adults create identity in their lives to the extent that the self can be told in a coherent, followable, and vivifying narrative that integrates the person into society in a productive and generative way and provides the person with a purposeful self-history that explains

how the self of yesterday became the self of today and will become the anticipated self of tomorrow. Level III in personality, therefore, is the level of identity as a life story. Without exploring this third level, the personologist can never understand how and to what extent the person is able to find unity, purpose, and meaning in life. Thus what is missing so far from our consideration of Lynn is her very identity.

Misunderstandings About Level III

Lynn's identity is an inner story, a narration of the self that she continues to author and revise over time to make sense, for herself and others, of her own life in time. It is a story, or perhaps a collection of related stories, that Lynn continues to fashion to specify who she is and how she fits into the adult world. Incorporating beginning, middle, and anticipated ending, Lynn's story tells how she came to be, where she has been and where she may be going, and who she will become (Hankiss, 1981). Lynn continues to create and revise the story across her adult years as she and her changing social world negotiate niches, places, opportunities, and positions within which she can live, and live meaningfully.

What is Lynn's story about? The dinner party provided my wife and me with ample material to begin talking about Lynn's personality from the perspectives of Levels I and II. But life-story information is typically more difficult to obtain in a casual social setting. Even after strangers have sized each other up on dispositional traits and even after they have begun to learn a little bit about each others' goals, plans, defenses, strategies, and domain-specific skills, they typically have little to say about the other person's identity. By contrast, when people have been involved in long-term intensive relationships with each other, they may know a great deal about each others' stories, about how the friend or lover (or psychotherapy client) makes sense of his or her own life in narrative terms. They have shared many stories with each other; they have observed each other's behavior in many different situations; they have come to see how the other person sees life, indeed, how the other sees his or her own life organized with purpose in time.

Without that kind of intimate relationship with Lynn, my wife and I could say little of substance about how Lynn creates identity in her life. We left the party with but a few promising hints or leads as to what her story might be about. For example, we were both struck by her enigmatic comment about passionate belief. Why did she suggest that her parents believed too strongly in her and in her siblings? Shouldn't parents believe in their children? Has she disappointed her parents in a deep way, such that their initial belief in their children was proven untenable? Does her inability to believe passionately in things extend to her own children as well? It is perhaps odd that her ex-husband has custody of their children; how is this related to the narrative she has developed about her family and her beliefs? And what might one make of that last incident at the party, when Lynn seemed to lapse into a different mode of talking, indicative perhaps of a different persona, a different public self, maybe a different "character" or "imago" (McAdams, 1984) in her life story? One can imagine many different kinds of stories that Lynn might create to make sense of her own life— adventure stories that incorporate her exotic travels and her considerable success; tragic stories that tell of failed love and lost children; stories in which the protagonist searches far and wide for something to believe in; stories in which early disappointments lead to cynicism, hard-heartedness, despair, or maybe even hope. We do not know Lynn well enough yet to know what kinds of stories she has been working on. Until we can talk with some authority both to her and about her in the narrative language of Level III, we cannot say that we know her well at all. On the drive home, my wife and I know Lynn a little better than we might know a stranger. Our desire to know her much better than we know her now is, in large part, our desire to know her story. And were we to get to know her better and come to feel a bond of intimacy with her, we would want her to know our stories, too (McAdams, 1989).

* * *

References

Allport, G. W. (1937). *Personality: A psychological interpretation.* New York: Holt, Rinehart & Winston.

Baumeister, R. F. (1986). *Identity: Cultural change and the struggle for self.* New York: Oxford University Press.

Bellah, R. N., Madsen, R., Sullivan, W. M., Swidler, A., & Tipton, S. M. (1985). *Habits of the heart.* Berkeley: University of California Press.

Block, J. (1995). A contrarian view of the five-factor approach to personality description. *Psychological Bulletin.*

Bowers, K. S. (1973). Situationism in psychology: An analysis and critique. *Psychological Review, 80,* 307–336.

Breger, L. (1974). *From instinct to identity: The development of personality.* Englewood Cliffs, NJ: Prentice-Hall.

Briggs, S. R. (1989). The optimal level of measurement for personality constructs. In D. M. Buss & N. Cantor (Eds.), *Personality psychology: Recent trends and emerging directions* (pp. 246–260). New York: Springer-Verlag.

Bruner, J. S. (1990). *Acts of meaning.* Cambridge, MA: Harvard University Press.

Buss, A. H. (1989). Personality as traits. *American Psychologist, 44,* 1378–1388.

Buss, D. M. (1991). Evolutionary personality psychology. In M. R. Rosenzweig & L. W. Porter (Eds.), *Annual review of psychology* (Vol. 42, pp. 459–491). Palo Alto, CA: Annual Reviews.

Cantor, N. (1990). From thought to behavior: "Having" and "doing" in the study of personality and cognition. *American Psychologist, 45,* 735–750.

Cantor, N., Acker, M., & Cook-Flanagan, C. (1992). Conflict and preoccupation in the intimacy life task. *Journal of Personality and Social Psychology, 63,* 644–655.

Cantor, N., & Kihlstrom, J. F. (1987). *Personality and social intelligence.* Englewood Cliffs, NJ: Prentice-Hall.

Cantor, N., Mischel, W., & Schwartz, J. C. (1982). A prototype analysis of psychological situations. *Cognitive Psychology, 14,* 45–77.

Cattell, R. B. (1957). *Personality and motivation structure and measurement.* New York: Harcourt, Brace & World.

Charme, S. T. (1984). *Meaning and myth in the study of lives: A Sartrean perspective.* Philadelphia: University of Pennsylvania Press.

Cohler, B. J. (1982). Personal narrative and the life course. In P. Baltes & O. G. Brim, Jr. (Eds.), *Life span development and behavior* (Vol. 4, pp. 205–241). New York: Academic Press.

Cohler, B. J. (1994, June). *Studying older lives: Reciprocal acts of telling and listening.* Paper presented at annual meeting of the Society for Personology, Ann Arbor.

Costa, P. T., Jr., & McCrae, R. R. (1985). *The NEO Personality Inventory.* Odessa, FL: Psychological Assessment Resources.

Cramer, P. (1991). *The development of defense mechanisms.* New York: Springer-Verlag.

Demorest, A. P., & Alexander, I. E. (1992). Affective scripts as organizers of personal experience. *Journal of Personality, 60,* 645–663.

Digman, J. M. (1990). Personality structure: Emergence of the five-factor model. In M. R. Rosenzweig & L. W. Porter (Eds.), *Annual review of psychology* (Vol. 41, pp. 417–440). Palo Alto, CA: Annual Reviews.

Emmons, R. A. (1986). Personal strivings: An approach to personality and subjective well-being. *Journal of Personality and Social Psychology, 51,* 1058–1068.

Emmons, R. A. (1993). Current status of the motive concept. In K. H. Craik, R. Hogan, & R. N. Wolfe (Eds.), *Fifty years of personality psychology* (pp. 187–196). New York: Plenum.

Erikson, E. H. (1959). Identity and the life cycle: Selected papers. *Psychological Issues, 1*(1), 5–165.

Erikson, E. H. (1963). *Childhood and society* (2nd ed.). New York: Norton.

Eysenck, H. J. (1967). *The biological basis of personality.* Springfield, IL: Thomas.

Frederiksen, N. (1972). Toward a taxonomy of situations. *American Psychologist, 27,* 114–123.

Gardner, H. (1993). *Creating minds.* New York: Basic Books.

Gilligan, C. (1982). *In a different voice.* Cambridge, MA: Harvard University Press.

Goldberg, L. R. (1981). Language and individual differences: The search for universals in personality lexicons. In L. Wheeler (Ed.), *Review of personality and social psychology* (Vol. 2, pp. 141–166). Beverly Hills: Sage.

Goldberg, L. R. (1993). The structure of phenotypic personality traits. *American Psychologist, 48,* 26–34.

Guilford, J. P. (1959). *Personality.* New York: McGraw-Hill.

Hankiss, A. (1981). On the mythological rearranging of one's life history. In D. Bertaux (Ed.), *Biography and society: The life history approach in the social sciences* (pp. 203–209). Beverly Hills: Sage.

Havighurst, R. J. (1972). *Developmental tasks and education* (3rd ed.). New York: McKay.

Hazan, C., & Shaver, P. (1990). Love and work: An attachment-theoretical perspective. *Journal of Personality and Social Psychology, 59,* 270–280.

Hermans, H. J. M., & Kempen, H. J. G. (1993). *The dialogical self.* New York: Academic Press.

Hogan, R. (1986). *Hogan Personality Inventory manual.* Minneapolis: National Computer Systems.

Howard, G. S. (1991). Culture tales: A narrative approach to thinking, cross-cultural psychology, and psychotherapy. *American Psychologist, 46,* 187–197.

Jackson, D. N. (1974). *The Personality Research Form.* Port Huron, MI: Research Psychologists Press.

John, O. P. (1990). The "Big Five" factor taxonomy: Dimensions of personality in the natural language and in questionnaires. In L. Pervin (Ed.), *Handbook of personality theory and research* (pp. 66–100). New York: Guilford.

Kaiser, R. T., & Ozer, D. J. (under review). The structure of personal goals and their relation to personality traits. Manuscript under editorial review.

Klinger, E. (1977). *Meaning and void.* Minneapolis: University of Minnesota Press.

Kotre, J. (1984). *Outliving the self: Generativity and the interpretation of lives.* Baltimore: Johns Hopkins University Press.

Krahe, B. (1992). *Personality and social psychology: Toward a synthesis.* London: Sage.

Lamiell, J. T. (1987). *The psychology of personality: An epistemological inquiry.* New York: Columbia University Press.

Langbaum, R. (1982). *The mysteries of identity: A theme in modern literature.* Chicago: University of Chicago Press.

Lazarus, R. J. (1991). *Emotion and adaptation.* New York: Oxford University Press.

Linde, C. (1990). *Life stories: The creation of coherence* (Monograph No. IRL90-0001). Palo Alto, CA: Institute for Research on Learning.

Little, B. R. (1989). Personal projects analysis: Trivial pursuits, magnificent obsessions, and the search for coherence. In D. M. Buss & N. Cantor (Eds.), *Personality psychology: Recent trends and emerging directions* (pp. 15–31). New York: Springer-Verlag.

Loevinger, J. (1976). *Ego development.* San Francisco: Jossey-Bass.

Luborsky, L., & Crits-Christoph, P. (1991). *Understanding transference: The core conflictual relationship theme method.* New York: Basic Books.

MacIntyre, A. (1984). *After virtue.* Notre Dame: University of Notre Dame Press.

Magnusson, D. (1971). An analysis of situational dimensions. *Perceptual and Motor Skills, 32,* 851–867.

McAdams, D. P. (1984). Love, power, and images of the self. In C. Z. Malatesta & C. E. Izard (Eds.), *Emotion in adult development* (pp. 159–174). Beverly Hills: Sage.

McAdams, D. P. (1985). *Power, intimacy, and the life story: Personological inquiries into identity.* New York: Guilford.

McAdams, D. P. (1989). *Intimacy: The need to be close.* New York: Doubleday.

McAdams, D. P. (1990). Unity and purpose in human lives: The emergence of identity as a life story. In A. I. Rabin, R. A. Zucker, R. A. Emmons, & S. Frank (Eds.), *Studying persons and lives* (pp. 148–200). New York: Springer.

McAdams, D. P. (1992). The five-factor model in personality: A critical appraisal. *Journal of Personality, 60,* 329–361.

McAdams, D. P. (1993). *The stories we live by: Personal myths and the making of the self.* New York: Morrow.

McAdams, D. P. (1994a). *The person: An introduction to personality psychology* (2nd ed.). Fort Worth: Harcourt Brace.

McAdams, D. P. (1994b). A psychology of the stranger. *Psychological Inquiry, 5,* 145–148.

McAdams, D. P. (1994c). Can personality change? Levels of stability and growth in personality across the life span. In T. F. Heatherton & J. L. Weinberger (Eds.), *Can personality change?* (pp. 299–314). Washington, DC: American Psychological Association.

McAdams, D. P. (1996). Narrating the self in adulthood. In J. Birren, G. Kenyon, J. E. Ruth, J. J. F. Schroots, & T. Svensson (Eds.), *Aging and biography: Explorations in adult development.* New York: Springer.

McAdams, D. P., de St. Aubin, E., & Logan, R. L. (1993). Generativity among young, midlife, and older adults. *Psychology and Aging, 8,* 221–230.

McClelland, D. C. (1951). *Personality.* New York: Holt, Rinehart & Winston.

McClelland, D. C. (1961). *The achieving society.* New York: D. Van Nostrand.

McCrae, R. R., & Costa, P. T., Jr. (1996). Toward a new generation of personality theories: Theoretical contexts for the five-factor model. In J. S. Wiggins (Ed.), *The five-factor model of personality.* New York: Guilford.

Mischel, W. (1968). *Personality and assessment.* New York: Wiley.

Mischel, W. (1973). Toward a cognitive social-learning reconceptualization of personality. *Psychological Review, 80,* 252–283.

Moos, R. H. (1973). Conceptualization of human environments. *American Psychologist, 28,* 652–665.

Murray, H. A. (1938). *Explorations in personality.* New York: Oxford University Press.

Ogilvie, D. M., & Ashmore, R. D. (1991). Self-with-other representation as units of analysis in self-concept research. In R. A. Curtis (Ed.), *The relational self: Theoretical convergences in psychoanalysis and social psychology* (pp. 282–314). New York: Guilford.

Ozer, D. J., & Reise, S. P. (1994). Personality assessment. In L. W. Porter & M. R. Rosenzweig (Eds.), *Annual review of psychology* (Vol. 45, pp. 357–388). Palo Alto, CA: Annual Reviews.

Pervin, L. (1994). A critical analysis of current trait theory. *Psychological Inquiry, 5,* 103–113.

Polkinghorne, D. (1988). *Narrative knowing and the human sciences.* Albany, NY: SUNY Press.

Revelle, W. (1995). Personality processes. In L. W. Porter & M. R. Rosenzweig (Eds.), *Annual review of psychology* (Vol. 46, pp. 295–328). Palo Alto, CA: Annual Reviews.

Rokeach, M. (1973). *The nature of human values.* New York: Free Press.

Tellegen, A. (1982). *Brief manual for the Differential Personality Questionnaire.* Unpublished manuscript, University of Minnesota.

Thorne, A. (1989). Conditional patterns, transference, and the coherence of personality across time. In D. M. Buss & N. Cantor (Eds.), *Personality psychology: Recent trends and emerging directions* (pp. 149–159). New York: Springer.

Wiggins, J. S. (Ed.). (1996). *The five-factor model of personality.* New York: Guilford.

Winter, D. G. (1973). *The power motive.* New York: Free Press.

Wright, J. C., & Mischel, W. (1987). A conditional approach to dispositional constructs: The local predictability of social behavior. *Journal of Personality and Social Psychology, 53,* 1159–1177.

A SIMPLE, GENERAL-PURPOSE DISPLAY OF MAGNITUDE OF EXPERIMENTAL EFFECT

Robert Rosenthal and Donald B. Rubin

The most widely used statistic in personality psychology, the correlation coefficient, has been the source of considerable, needless confusion. An r of 1 (or −1) means that two variables are perfectly correlated, and an r of 0 means they are not correlated at all. But how should we interpret the r's in between, as most are?

Confusion has been engendered by a commonly taught practice of squaring correlations to yield the "percentage of variance explained" by the relationship. While this phrase sounds rather close to what one would want to know, it causes people to interpret correlations of .32, for example, as "explaining only 10% of the variance" (because .32 squared is about .10), which leaves 90% "unexplained." This does not make it sound like much has been accomplished.

In the next selection, psychologist Robert Rosenthal and statistician Donald Rubin team up to explain why this common calculation is misleading. In particular, they believe it causes strong effects, such as those indexed by correlations between .30 and .40, to seem smaller than they are. They introduce a simple technique of their own invention for illustrating the real size and importance of correlations. The "binomial effect size display" (BESD) allows correlation coefficients to be interpreted in terms of the percentage of correct classification or effective treatment they represent.

The basic calculation is even simpler than this article may make it sound. Look at Table 1 and assume an r of 0. This would yield an entry of 50 in each of the four cells. To see what a correlation of .32 looks like, divide 32 by 2, which gives you 16. Add the 16 to 50 and put this 66 in the upper-left and lower-right cells. Now subtract 16 from 50 and put 34 in the lower-left and upper-right cells. The rows and columns still each add up to 100, but now show what r = .32 looks like. It's easy! And it shows that a correlation between a treatment and an outcome, or between a predictor and a criterion, of a size of .32 would give you the right result almost twice as often as the wrong result.

The BESD is particularly important for personality psychology because most of the strongest relations between traits or between traits and behaviors are found to yield correlations between about .30 and .40. Rosenthal and Rubin show us that this means the prediction of one trait from another, or of a behavior on the basis of a trait, is usually more than twice as likely to be right as it is to be wrong.

From *Journal of Educational Psychology, 74*, 166–169, 1982.

* * *

Traditionally, behavioral researchers have concentrated on reporting significance levels of experimental effects. Recent years, however, have shown a welcome increase in emphasis on reporting the magnitude of experimental effects obtained (Cohen, 1977; Fleiss, 1969; Friedman, 1968; Glass, 1976; Hays, 1973; Rosenthal, 1978; Rosenthal & Rubin, 1978; Smith & Glass, 1977).

Despite the growing awareness of the importance of estimating sizes of effects along with estimating the more conventional levels of significance, there is a problem in interpreting various effect size estimators such as the Pearson r. For example, we found experienced behavioral researchers and experienced statisticians quite surprised when we showed them that the Pearson r of .32 associated with a coefficient of determination (r^2) of only .10 was the correlational equivalent of increasing a success rate from 34% to 66% by means of an experimental treatment procedure; for example, these values could mean that a death rate under the control condition is 66% but is only 34% under the experimental condition. We believe (Rosenthal & Rubin, 1979) that there may be a widespread tendency to underestimate the importance of the effects of behavioral (and biomedical) interventions (Mayo, 1978; Rimland, 1979) simply because they are often associated with what are thought to be low values of r^2.

The purpose of the present article is to introduce an intuitively appealing general purpose effect size display whose interpretation is perfectly transparent: the binomial effect size display (BESD). In no sense do we claim to have resolved the differences and controversies surrounding the use of various effect size estimators (e.g., Appelbaum & Cramer, 1974). Our display is useful because it is (a) easily understood by researchers, students, and lay persons; (b) applicable in a wide variety of contexts; and (c) conveniently computed.

The question addressed by BESD is: What is the effect on the success rate (e.g., survival rate, cure rate, improvement rate, selection rate, etc.) of the institution of a certain treatment procedure? It displays the change in success rate (e.g., survival rate, cure rate, improvement rate, selection rate, etc.) attributable to a certain treatment procedure. An example shows the appeal of our procedure.

In their meta-analysis of psychotherapy outcome studies, Smith and Glass (1977) summarized the results of some 400 studies. An eminent critic stated that the results of their analysis sounded the "death knell" for psychotherapy because of the modest size of the effect (Rimland, 1979). This modest effect size was calculated to be equivalent to an r of .32 accounting for "only 10% of the variance" (p. 192).

Table 1 is the BESD corresponding to an r of .32 or an r^2 of .10. The table shows clearly that it is absurd to label as "modest indeed" (Rimland, 1979, p. 192) an effect size equivalent to increasing the success rate from 34% to 66% (e.g., reducing a death rate from 66% to 34%).

Table 2 shows systematically the increase in success rates associated with various values of r^2 and r. Even so small an r as .20, accounting for only 4% of the variance, is associated with an increase in success rate from 40% to 60%, such as a reduction in death rate from 60% to 40%. The last column of Table 2 shows that the difference

TABLE 1

THE BINOMIAL EFFECT SIZE DISPLAY: AN EXAMPLE "ACCOUNTING FOR ONLY 10% OF THE VARIANCE"

Condition	Alive	Dead	Σ
Treatment	66	34	100
Control	34	66	100
Σ	100	100	200

TABLE 2

BINOMIAL EFFECT SIZE DISPLAYS: CORRESPONDING TO VARIOUS VALUES OF r^2 AND r

		Success rate increased		
r^2	r	From	To	Difference in success rates
.01	.10	.45	.55	.10
.04	.20	.40	.60	.20
.09	.30	.35	.65	.30
.16	.40	.30	.70	.40
.25	.50	.25	.75	.50
.36	.60	.20	.80	.60
.49	.70	.15	.85	.70
.64	.80	.10	.90	.80
.81	.90	.05	.95	.90
1.00	1.00	.00	1.00	1.00

TABLE 3

COMPUTATION OF r FROM COMMON TEST STATISTICS

Test statistic	r[a] given by
t	$\sqrt{\dfrac{t^2}{t^2 + df}}$
F[b]	$\sqrt{\dfrac{F}{F + df\,(\text{error})}}$
χ^2,[c]	$\sqrt{\dfrac{\chi^2}{N}}$

[a] The sign of r should be positive if the experimental group is superior to the control group and negative if the control group is superior to the experimental group.
[b] Used only when df for numerator = 1 as in the comparison of two group means or any other contrast.
[c] Used only when df for χ^2 = 1.

in success rates is identical to r. Consequently the experimental success rate in the BESD is computed as $.50 + r/2$, whereas the control group success rate is computed as $.50 - r/2$. Cohen (1965) and Friedman (1968) have useful discussions of computing the r associated with a variety of test statistics, and Table 3 gives the three most frequently used equivalences.

We propose that the reporting of effect sizes can be made more intuitive and more informative by using the BESD. It is our belief that the use of the BESD to display the increase in success rate due to treatment will more clearly convey the real world importance of treatment effects than do the commonly used descriptions of effect size based on the proportion of variance accounted for. The BESD is most appropriate when the variances within the two conditions are similar, as they are assumed to be whenever we compute the usual t test.

It might appear that the BESD can be employed only when the outcome variable is dichotomous and the mean outcome in one group is the same amount above .5 as the mean outcome in the other group is below .5. Actually, the BESD is often a realistic representation of the size of treatment effect when the variances of the outcome variable are approximately the same in the two approximately equal sized groups, as is commonly the case in educational and psychological studies.

*   *   *

References

Appelbaum, M. I., & Cramer, E. M. (1974). The only game in town. *Contemporary Psychology, 19*, 406–407.

Cohen, J. (1965). Some statistical issues in psychological research. In B. B. Wolman (Ed.), *Handbook of clinical psychology.* New York: McGraw-Hill.

Cohen, J. (1977). *Statistical power analysis for the behavioral sciences* (Rev. ed.). New York: Academic Press.

Fleiss, J. L. (1969). Estimating the magnitude of experimental effects. *Psychological Bulletin, 72*, 273–276.

Friedman, H. (1968). Magnitude of experimental effect and a table for its rapid estimation. *Psychological Bulletin, 70*, 245–251.

Glass, G. V. (1976, April). *Primary, secondary, and meta-analysis of research.* Paper presented at the meeting of the American Educational Research Association, San Francisco.

Hays, W. L. (1973). *Statistics for the social sciences* (2nd ed.). New York: Holt, Rinehart & Winston.

Mayo, R. J. (1978). Statistical considerations in analyzing the results of a collection of experiments. *The Behavioral and Brain Sciences, 3,* 400–401.

Rimland, B. (1979). Death knell for psychotherapy? *American Psychologist, 34,* 192.

Rosenthal, R. (1978). Combining results of independent studies. *Psychological Bulletin, 85,* 185–193.

Rosenthal, R., & Rubin, D. B. (1978). Interpersonal expectancy effects: The first 345 studies. *The Behavioral and Brain Sciences, 3,* 377–386.

Rosenthal, R., & Rubin, D. B. (1979). A note on percent variance explained as a measure of the importance of effects. *Journal of Applied Social Psychology, 9,* 395–396.

Smith, M. L., & Glass, G. V. (1977). Meta-analysis of psychotherapy outcome studies. *American Psychologist, 32,* 752–760.

CONSTRUCT VALIDITY IN PSYCHOLOGICAL TESTS

Lee J. Cronbach and Paul E. Meehl

Lee Cronbach and Paul Meehl are two of the most prominent methodologists in the history of psychology. In the following classic selection, they team up to address the knotty question of "construct validity," which is, how do you know whether a test—such as a personality test—really measures what it is supposed to measure? As is mentioned in the opening paragraphs, the article was occasioned by concerns in the mid-1950s over the proper way to establish the validity of a test. This issue generated political heat both within and outside the American Psychological Association, the professional organization of many psychologists, because the tests that people take often have consequences. They are used for selection in education and employment, for example. Thus, the degree to which a test is valid is more than an academic issue. Its resolution has real consequences for real people.

This article is a fairly difficult piece, but worth some effort. Psychologists who have been doing research for years can reread this article and learn something important that escaped them on previous readings. The essential points to glean from this article are that no single study or one source of data will ever sufficiently explain any important aspect of personality, and that psychological theory plays an essential role in developing an understanding of what any measure of personality really means. Multiple methods must always be employed, and the validation of a test will emerge only gradually from an examination of how different methods produce results that are sometimes the same and sometimes different. The present excerpt concludes with the important observation that the aim of construct validation is not to conclude that a test is "valid," but rather to assess its degree of validity for various purposes.

From *Psychological Bulletin, 52,* 281–302, 1955.

Validation of psychological tests has not yet been adequately conceptualized, as the APA Committee on Psychological Tests learned when it undertook (1950–54) to specify what quali-ties should be investigated before a test is published. In order to make coherent recommendations the Committee found it necessary to distinguish four types of validity, established by different types of research and requiring different interpretation. The chief innovation in the Committee's report was the term *construct validity*. This idea was first formulated by a subcommittee (Meehl and R. C. Challman) studying how proposed recommendations would apply to projective techniques, and later modified and clarified by the entire Committee (Bordin, Challman, Conrad, Humphreys, Super, and the present writers). The statements agreed upon by the Committee (and by committees of two other associations) were published in the *Technical Recommendations* (American Psychological Association, 1954). The present interpretation of construct validity is not "official" and deals with some areas where the Committee would probably not be unanimous. The present writers are solely responsible for this attempt to explain the concept and elaborate its implications.

Identification of construct validity was not an isolated development. Writers on validity during the preceding decade had shown a great deal of dissatisfaction with conventional notions of validity, and introduced new terms and ideas, but the resulting aggregation of types of validity seems only to have stirred the muddy waters. Portions of the distinctions we shall discuss are implicit in Jenkins's (1946) paper, Gulliksen (1950), Good-enough's (1950) distinction between tests as "signs" and "samples," Cronbach's (1949) separation of "logical" and "empirical" validity, Guilford's (1946) "factorial validity," and Mosier's (1947, 1951) papers on "face validity" and "validity generalization." Helen Peak (1953) comes close to an explicit statement of construct validity as we shall present it.

Four Types of Validation

The categories into which the *Recommendations* divide validity studies are: predictive validity, concurrent validity, content validity, and construct validity. The first two of these may be considered together as *criterion-oriented* validation procedures.

The pattern of a criterion-oriented study is familiar. The investigator is primarily interested in some criterion which he wishes to predict. He administers the test, obtains an independent criterion measure on the same subjects, and computes a correlation. If the criterion is obtained some time after the test is given, he is studying *predictive validity*. If the test score and criterion score are determined at essentially the same time, he is studying *concurrent validity*. Concurrent validity is studied when one test is proposed as a substitute for another (for example, when a multiple-choice form of spelling test is substituted for taking dictation), or a test is shown to correlate with some contemporary criterion (e.g., psychiatric diagnosis).

Content validity is established by showing that the test items are a sample of a universe in which the investigator is interested. Content validity is ordinarily to be established deductively, by defining a universe of items and sampling systematically within this universe to establish the test.

Construct validation is involved whenever a test is to be interpreted as a measure of some attribute or quality which is not "operationally defined." The problem faced by the investigator is, "What constructs account for variance in test performance?" Construct validity calls for no new scientific approach. Much current research on tests of personality (Child, 1954) is construct validation, usually without the benefit of a clear formulation of this process.

Construct validity is not to be identified solely by particular investigative procedures, but by the orientation of the investigator. Criterion-oriented validity, as Bechtoldt emphasizes (1951, p. 1245), "involves the *acceptance* of a set of operations as an adequate definition of whatever is to be measured." When an investigator believes that no criterion available in him is fully valid, he perforce becomes interested in construct validity because this is the only way to avoid the "infinite frustration" of relating every criterion to some more ultimate standard (Gaylord, unpublished manuscript). In content validation, *acceptance* of the universe of content as defining the variable to be measured is essential. Construct validity must be investigated whenever no criterion or universe of content is accepted as entirely adequate to define the quality to be measured. Determining what psychological constructs account for test performance is desirable for almost any test. Thus, although the MMPI was originally established on the basis of empirical discrimination between patient groups and so-called normals (concurrent validity), continuing research has tried to provide a basis for describing the personality associated with each score pattern. Such interpretations permit the clinician to predict performance with respect to criteria which have not yet been employed in empirical validation studies (cf. Meehl, 1954, pp. 49–50, 110–111).

We can distinguish among the four types of validity by noting that each involves a different emphasis on the criterion. In predictive or concurrent validity, the criterion behavior is of concern to the tester, and he may have no concern whatsoever with the type of behavior exhibited in the test. (An employer does not care if a worker can manipulate blocks, but the score on the block test may predict something he cares about.) Content validity is studied when the tester *is* concerned with the type of behavior involved in the test performance. Indeed, if the test is a work sample, the behavior represented in the test may be an end in itself. Construct validity is ordinarily studied when the tester has no definite criterion measure of the quality with which he is concerned, and must use indirect measures. Here the trait or quality underlying the test is of central importance, rather than either the test behavior or the scores on the criteria (APA, 1954, p. 14).

Construct validation is important at times for every sort of psychological test: aptitude, achievement, interests, and so on. Thurstone's statement is interesting in this connection:

In the field of intelligence tests, it used to be common to define validity as the correlation between a test score and some outside criterion. We have reached a stage of sophistication where the test-criterion correlation is too coarse. It is obsolete. If we attempted to ascertain the validity of a test for the second space-factor, for example, we would have to get judges [to] make reliable judgments about people as to this factor. Ordinarily their [the available judges'] ratings would be of no value as a criterion. Consequently, validity studies in the cognitive functions now depend on criteria of internal consistency . . . (Thurstone, 1952, p. 3).

Construct validity would be involved in answering such questions as: To what extent is this test of intelligence culture-free? Does this test of "interpretation of data" measure reading ability, quantitative reasoning, or response sets? How does a person with A in Strong Accountant, and B in Strong CPA, differ from a person who has these scores reversed?

Example of construct validation procedure. Suppose measure X correlates .50 with Y, the amount of palmar sweating induced when we tell a student that he has failed a Psychology I exam. Predictive validity of X for Y is adequately described by the coefficient, and a statement of the experimental and sampling conditions. If someone were to ask, "Isn't there perhaps another way to interpret this correlation?" or "What other kinds of evidence can you bring to support your interpretation?" we would hardly understand what he was asking because no interpretation has been made. These questions become relevant when the correlation is advanced as evidence that "test X measures anxiety proneness." Alternative interpretations are possible; e.g., perhaps the test measures "academic aspiration," in which case we will expect different results if we induce palmar sweating by economic threat. It is then reasonable to inquire about other *kinds* of evidence.

Add these facts from further studies: Test X correlates .45 with fraternity brothers' ratings on "tenseness." Test X correlates .55 with amount of intellectual inefficiency induced by painful electric shock, and .68 with the Taylor Anxiety scale. Mean X score decreases among four diagnosed groups in this order: anxiety state, reactive depression, "normal," and psychopathic personality. And palmar sweat under threat of failure in Psychology I correlates .60 with threat of failure in mathematics. Negative results eliminate competing explanations of the X score; thus, findings of negligible correlations between X and social class, vocational aim, and value-orientation make it fairly safe to reject the suggestion that X measures "academic aspiration." We can have substantial confidence that X does measure anxiety proneness if the current theory of anxiety can embrace the variates which yield positive correlations, and does not predict correlations where we found none.

* * *

The Relation of Constructs to "Criteria"

CRITICAL VIEW OF THE CRITERION IMPLIED An unquestionable criterion may be found in a practical operation, or may be established as a consequence of an operational definition. Typically, however, the psychologist is unwilling to use the directly operational approach because he is interested in building theory about a generalized construct. A theorist trying to relate behavior to "hunger" almost certainly invests that term with meanings other than the operation "elapsed-time-since-feeding." If he is concerned with hunger as a tissue need, he will not accept time lapse as *equivalent* to his construct because it fails to consider, among other things, energy expenditure of the animal.

In some situations the criterion is no more valid than the test. Suppose, for example, that we want to know if counting the dots on Bender-Gestalt figure five indicates "compulsive rigidity," and take psychiatric ratings on this trait as a criterion. Even a conventional report on the resulting correlation will say something about the extent and intensity of the psychiatrist's contacts and should describe his qualifications (e.g., diplomate status? analyzed?).

Why report these facts? Because data are needed to indicate whether the criterion is any good. "Compulsive rigidity" is not really intended to mean "social stimulus value to psychiatrists." The implied trait involves a range of behavior-dispositions which may be very imperfectly sampled by the psychiatrist. Suppose dot-counting does not occur in a particular patient and yet we find that the psychiatrist has rated him as "rigid." When questioned the psychiatrist tells us that the patient was a rather easy, free-wheeling sort: however, the patient *did* lean over to straighten out a skewed desk blotter, and this, viewed against cer-

tain other facts, tipped the scale in favor of a "rigid" rating. On the face of it, counting Bender dots may be just as good (or poor) a sample of the compulsive-rigidity domain as straightening desk blotters is.

Suppose, to extend our example, we have four tests on the "predictor" side, over against the psychiatrist's "criterion," and find generally positive correlations among the five variables. Surely it is artificial and arbitrary to impose the "test-should-predict-criterion" pattern on such data. The psychiatrist samples verbal content, expressive pattern, voice, posture, etc. Our proper conclusion is that, from this evidence, the four tests and the psychiatrist all assess some common factor.

The asymmetry between the "test" and the so-designated "criterion" arises only because the terminology of predictive validity has become a commonplace in test analysis. In this study where a construct is the central concern, any distinction between the merit of the test and criterion variables would be justified only if it had already been shown that the psychiatrist's theory and operations were excellent measures of the attribute.

Inadequacy of Validation in Terms of Specific Criteria

The proposal to validate constructual interpretations of tests runs counter to suggestions of some others. Spiker and McCandless (1954) favor an operational approach. Validation is replaced by compiling statements as to how strongly the test predicts other observed variables of interest. To avoid requiring that each new variable be investigated completely by itself, they allow two variables to collapse into one whenever the properties of the operationally defined measures are the same: "If a new test is demonstrated to predict the scores on an older, well-established test, then an evaluation of the predictive power of the older test may be used for the new one." But accurate inferences are possible only if the two tests correlate so highly that there is negligible reliable variance in either test, independent of the other. Where the correspondence is less close, one must either retain all the separate variables operationally defined or embark on construct validation.

The practical user of tests must rely on constructs of some generality to make predictions about new situations. Test X could be used to predict palmar sweating in the face of failure without invoking any construct, but a counselor is more likely to be asked to forecast behavior in diverse or even unique situations for which the correlation of test X is unknown. Significant predictions rely on knowledge accumulated around the generalized construct of anxiety. The "Technical Recommendations" state:

> It is ordinarily necessary to evaluate construct validity by integrating evidence from many different sources. The problem of construct validation becomes especially acute in the clinical field since for many of the constructs dealt with it is not a question of finding an imperfect criterion but of finding any criterion at all. The psychologist interested in construct validity for clinical devices is concerned with making an estimate of a hypothetical internal process, factor, system, structure, or state and cannot expect to find a clear unitary behavioral criterion. An attempt to identify any one criterion measure or any composite as *the* criterion aimed at is, however, usually unwarranted (APA, 1954, pp. 14–15).

This appears to conflict with arguments for specific criteria prominent at places in the testing literature. Thus Anastasi (1950) makes many statements of the latter character: "It is only as a measure of a specifically defined criterion that a test can be objectively validated at all . . . To claim that a test measures anything over and above its criterion is pure speculation" (p. 67). Yet elsewhere this article supports construct validation. Tests can be profitably interpreted if we "know the relationships between the tested behavior . . . and other behavior samples, none of these behavior samples necessarily occupying the preeminent position of a criterion" (p. 75). Factor analysis with several partial criteria might be used to study whether a test measures a postulated "general learning ability." If the data demonstrate specificity of ability instead, such specificity is "useful in its own right in advancing our knowledge of behavior; it should

not be construed as a weakness of the tests" (p. 75).

We depart from Anastasi at two points. She writes, "The validity of a psychological test should not be confused with an analysis of the factors which determine the behavior under consideration." We, however, regard such analysis as a most important type of validation. Second, she refers to "the will-o'-the-wisp of psychological processes which are distinct from performance" (Anastasi, 1950, p. 77). While we agree that psychological processes are elusive, we are sympathetic to attempts to formulate and clarify constructs which are evidenced by performance but distinct from it. Surely an inductive inference based on a pattern of correlations cannot be dismissed as "pure speculation."

SPECIFIC CRITERIA USED TEMPORARILY: THE "BOOTSTRAPS" EFFECT

Even when a test is constructed on the basis of a specific criterion, it may ultimately be judged to have greater construct validity than the criterion. We start with a vague concept which we associate with certain observations. We then discover empirically that these observations covary with some other observation which possesses greater reliability or is more intimately correlated with relevant experimental changes than is the original measure, or both. For example, the notion of temperature arises because some objects feel hotter to the touch than others. The expansion of a mercury column does not have face validity as an index of hotness. But it turns out that (a) there is a statistical relation between expansion and sensed temperature; (b) observers employ the mercury method with good interobserver agreement; (c) the regularity of observed relations is increased by using the thermometer (e.g., melting points of samples of the same material vary little on the thermometer; we obtain nearly linear relations between mercury measures and pressure of a gas). Finally, (d) a theoretical structure involving unobservable microevents—the kinetic theory—is worked out which explains the relation of mercury expansion to heat. This whole process of conceptual enrichment begins with what in retrospect we see as an extremely fallible "criterion"—the human temperature sense. That original criterion has now been relegated to a peripheral position. We have lifted ourselves by our bootstraps, but in a legitimate and fruitful way.

Similarly, the Binet scale was first valued because children's scores tended to agree with judgments by schoolteachers. If it had not shown this agreement, it would have been discarded along with reaction time and the other measures of ability previously tried. Teacher judgments once constituted the criterion against which the individual intelligence test was validated. But if today a child's IQ is 135 and three of his teachers complain about how stupid he is, we do not conclude that the test has failed. Quite to the contrary, if no error in test procedure can be argued, we treat the test score as a valid statement about an important quality, and define our task as that of finding out what other variables—personality, study skills, etc.—modify achievement or distort teacher judgment.

Experimentation to Investigate Construct Validity

VALIDATION PROCEDURES We can use many methods in construct validation. Attention should particularly be drawn to Macfarlane's survey of these methods as they apply to projective devices (Macfarlane, 1942).

Group differences. If our understanding of a construct leads us to expect two groups to differ on the test, this expectation may be tested directly. Thus Thurstone and Chave validated the Scale for Measuring Attitude Toward the Church by showing score differences between church members and nonchurchgoers. Churchgoing is not *the* criterion of attitude, for the purpose of the test is to measure something other than the crude sociological fact of church attendance; on the other hand, failure to find a difference would have seriously challenged the test.

Only coarse correspondence between test and group designation is expected. Too great a corre-

spondence between the two would indicate that the test is to some degree invalid, because members of the groups are expected to overlap on the test. Intelligence test items are selected initially on the basis of a correspondence to age, but an item that correlates .95 with age in an elementary school sample would surely be suspect.

Correlation matrices and factor analysis. If two tests are presumed to measure the same construct, a correlation between them is predicted. (An exception is noted where some second attribute has positive loading in the first test and negative loading in the second test; then a low correlation is expected. This is a testable interpretation provided an external measure of either the first or the second variable exists.) If the obtained correlation departs from the expectation, however, there is no way to know whether the fault lies in test A, test B, or the formulation of the construct. A matrix of intercorrelations often points out profitable ways of dividing the construct into more meaningful parts, factor analysis being a useful computational method in such studies.

Guilford (1948) has discussed the place of factor analysis in construct validation. His statements may be extracted as follows:

"The personnel psychologist wishes to know 'why his tests are valid.' He can place tests and practical criteria in a matrix and factor it to identify 'real dimensions of human personality.' A factorial description is exact and stable; it is economical in explanation; it leads to the creation of pure tests which can be combined to predict complex behaviors." It is clear that factors here function as constructs. Eysenck (1950) in his "criterion analysis," goes further than Guilford and shows that factoring can be used explicitly to test hypotheses about constructs.

Factors may or may not be weighted with surplus meaning. Certainly when they are regarded as "real dimensions" a great deal of surplus meaning is implied, and the interpreter must shoulder a substantial burden of proof. The alternative view is to regard factors as defining a working reference frame, located in a convenient manner in the "space" defined by all behaviors of a given type. Which set of factors from a given matrix is "most useful" will depend partly on predilections, but in essence the best construct is the one around which we can build the greatest number of inferences, in the most direct fashion.

Studies of internal structure. For many constructs, evidence of homogeneity within the test is relevant in judging validity. If a trait such as *dominance* is hypothesized, and the items inquire about behaviors subsumed under this label, then the hypothesis appears to require that these items be generally intercorrelated. Even low correlations, if consistent, would support the argument that people may be fruitfully described in terms of a generalized tendency to dominate or not dominate. The general quality would have power to predict behavior in a variety of situations represented by the specific items. Item-test correlations and certain reliability formulas describe internal consistency.

It is unwise to list uninterpreted data of this sort under the heading "validity" in test manuals, as some authors have done. High internal consistency may *lower* validity. Only if the underlying theory of the trait being measured calls for high item intercorrelations do the correlations support construct validity. Negative item-test correlations may support construct validity, provided that the items with negative correlations are believed irrelevant to the postulated construct and serve as suppressor variables (Horst, 1941, pp. 431–436; Meehl, 1945).

Study of distinctive subgroups of items within a test may set an upper limit to construct validity by showing that irrelevant elements influence scores. Thus a study of the PMA space tests shows that variance can be partially accounted for by a response set, tendency to mark many figures as similar (Cronbach, 1950). An internal factor analysis of the PEA Interpretation of Data Test shows that in addition to measuring reasoning skills, the test score is strongly influenced by a tendency to say "probably true" rather than "certainly true," regardless of item content (Damrin, 1952). On the other hand, a study of item groupings in the DAT

Mechanical Comprehension Test permitted rejection of the hypothesis that knowledge about specific topics such as gears made a substantial contribution to scores (Cronbach, 1951).

Studies of change over occasions. The stability of test scores ("retest reliability," Cattell's "N-technique") may be relevant to construct validation. Whether a high degree of stability is encouraging or discouraging for the proposed interpretation depends upon the theory defining the construct.

More powerful than the retest after uncontrolled intervening experiences is the retest with experimental intervention. If a transient influence swings test scores over a wide range, there are definite limits on the extent to which a test result can be interpreted as reflecting the typical behavior of the individual. These are examples of experiments which have indicated upper limits to test validity: studies of differences associated with the examiner in projective testing, of change of score under alternative directions ("tell the truth" vs. "make yourself look good to an employer"), and of coachability of mental tests. We may recall Gulliksen's (1950) distinction: When the coaching is of a sort that improves the pupil's intellectual functioning in school, the test which is affected by the coaching has validity as a measure of intellectual functioning; if the coaching improves test taking but not school performance, the test which responds to the coaching has poor validity as a measure of this construct.

Sometimes, where differences between individuals are difficult to assess by any means other than the test, the experimenter validates by determining whether the test can detect induced intraindividual differences. One might hypothesize that the Zeigarnik effect is a measure of ego involvement, i.e., that with ego involvement there is more recall of incomplete tasks. To support such an interpretation, the investigator will try to induce ego involvement on some task by appropriate directions and compare subjects' recall with their recall for tasks where there was a contrary induction. Sometimes the intervention is drastic. Porteus (1950) finds that brain-operated patients show disruption of performance on his maze, but do not show impaired performance on conventional verbal tests and argues therefrom that his test is a better measure of planfulness.

Studies of process. One of the best ways of determining informally what accounts for variability on a test is the observation of the person's process of performance. If it is supposed, for example, that a test measures mathematical competence, and yet observation of students' errors shows that erroneous reading of the question is common, the implications of a low score are altered. Lucas (1953) in this way showed that the Navy Relative Movement Test, an aptitude test, actually involved two different abilities: spatial visualization and mathematical reasoning.

Mathematical analysis of scoring procedures may provide important negative evidence on construct validity. A recent analysis of "empathy" tests is perhaps worth citing (Cronbach, 1955). "Empathy" has been operationally defined in many studies by the ability of a judge to predict what responses will be given on some questionnaire by a subject he has observed briefly. A mathematical argument has shown, however, that the scores depend on several attributes of the judge which enter into his perception of *any* individual, and that they therefore cannot be interpreted as evidence of his ability to interpret cues offered by particular others, or his intuition.

THE NUMERICAL ESTIMATE OF CONSTRUCT VALIDITY There is an understandable tendency to seek a "construct validity coefficient." A numerical statement of the degree of construct validity would be a statement of the proportion of the test score variance that is attributable to the construct variable. This numerical estimate can sometimes be arrived at by a factor analysis, but since present methods of factor analysis are based on linear relations, more general methods will ultimately be needed to deal with many quantitative problems of construct validation.

Rarely will it be possible to estimate definite "construct saturations," because no factor corresponding closely to the construct will be available. One can only hope to set upper and lower bounds to the "loading." If "creativity" is defined as something independent of knowledge, then a correlation of .40 between a presumed test of creativity and a test of arithmetic knowledge would indicate that at least 16 per cent of the reliable test variance is irrelevant to creativity as defined. Laboratory performance on problems such as Maier's "hat-rack" would scarcely be an ideal measure of creativity, but it would be somewhat relevant. If its correlation with the test is .60, this permits a tentative estimate of 36 per cent as a lower bound. (The estimate is tentative because the test might overlap with the irrelevant portion of the laboratory measure.) The saturation seems to lie between 36 and 84 per cent; a cumulation of studies would provide better limits.

It should be particularly noted that rejecting the null hypothesis does not finish the job of construct validation (Kelly, 1954, p. 284). The problem is not to conclude that the test "is valid" for measuring the construct variable. The task is to state as definitely as possible the degree of validity the test is presumed to have.

* * *

References

American Psychological Association (1954). Technical recommendations for psychological tests and diagnostic techniques. *Psychological Bulletin Supplement, 51, Part 2*, 1–38.

Anastasi, A. (1950). The concept of validity in the interpretation of test scores. *Educational and Psychological Measurement, 10*, 67–78.

Bechtoldt, H. P. (1951). Selection. In S. S. Stevens (Ed.), *Handbook of experimental psychology* (pp. 1237–1267). New York: Wiley.

Child, I. L. (1954). Personality. *Annual Review of Psychology, 5*, 149–171.

Cronbach, L. J. (1949). *Essentials of psychological testing.* New York: Harper.

Cronbach, L. J. (1950). Further evidence on response sets and test design. *Educational and Psychological Measurement, 10*, 3–31.

Cronbach, L. J. (1951). Coefficient alpha and the internal structure of tests. *Psychometrika, 16*, 297–335.

Cronbach, L. J. (1955). Processes affecting scores on "understanding of others" and "assumed similarity." *Psychology Bulletin, 52*, 177–193.

Damrin, Dora E. (1952). A comparative study of information derived from a diagnostic problem-solving test by logical and factorial methods of scoring. Unpublished doctor's dissertation, University of Illinois.

Eysenck, H. J. (1950). Criterion analysis—an application of the hypothetico-deductive method in factor analysis. *Psychology Review, 57,* 38–53.

Gaylord, R. H. Conceptual consistency and criterion equivalence: a dual approach to criterion analysis. Unpublished manuscript (PRB Research Note No. 17). Copies obtainable from ASTIA-DSC, AD-21 440.

Goodenough, F. L. (1950). *Mental testing.* New York: Rinehart.

Guilford, J. P. (1946). New standards for test evaluation. *Educational and Psychological Measurement, 6,* 427–439.

Guilford, J. P. (1948). Factor analysis in a test-development program. *Psychology Review, 55,* 79–94.

Gulliksen, H. (1950). Intrinsic validity. *American Psychologist, 5,* 511–517.

Horst, P. (1941). The prediction of personal adjustment. *Social Science Research Council Bulletin,* No. 48.

Jenkins, J. G. (1946). Validity for what? *Journal of Consulting Psychology, 10,* 93–98.

Kelly, E. L. (1954). Theory and techniques of assessment. *Annual Review of Psychology, 5,* 281–311.

Lucas, C. M. (1953). Analysis of the relative movement test by a method of individual interviews. *Bureau Naval Personnel Res. Rep.,* Contract Nonr-694 (00), NR 151-13, Educational Testing Service, March 1953.

Macfarlane, J. W. (1942). Problems of validation inherent in projective methods. *American Journal of Orthopsychiatry, 12,* 405–410.

Meehl, P. E. (1945). A simple algebraic development of Horat's suppressor variables. *American Journal of Psychology, 58,* 550–554.

Meehl, P. E. (1954). *Clinical vs. statistical prediction.* Minneapolis: University of Minnesota Press.

Mosier, C. I. (1947). A critical examination of the concepts of face validity. *Educational and Psychological Measurement, 7,* 191–205.

Mosier, C. I. (1951). Problems and designs of cross-validation. *Educational and Psychological Measurement, 11,* 5–12.

Peak, H. (1953). Problems of objective observation. In L. Festinger and D. Katz (Eds.), *Research methods in the behavioral sciences* (pp. 243–300). New York: Dryden Press.

Porteus, S. D. (1950). *The Porteus maze test and intelligence.* Palo Alto: Pacific Books.

Spiker, C. C., & McCandless, B. R. (1954). The concept of intelligence and the philosophy of science. *Psychology Review, 61,* 255–267.

Thurstone, L. L. (1952). The criterion problem in personality research. *Psychometric Laboratory Report,* No. 78. Chicago: University of Chicago.

Do People Know How They Behave? Self-Reported Act Frequencies Compared with On-line Codings by Observers

Samuel D. Gosling, Oliver P. John, Kenneth H. Craik, and Richard W. Robins

Self-reports of personality and behavior are by far the most commonly used method of personality assessment. As we saw in the earlier selection by McAdams, however, other methods are available as well. One particularly interesting possibility is to observe directly the behavior of research participants and record on videotape what they do. The use of such a method immediately raises interesting questions such as, What is the relationship between behavior as recorded on-line and behavior as reported by the person being observed?

This selection reports data that address this question directly, comparing self-reports of behavior with counts of these same behaviors as recorded on videotaped interactions. As the data quickly reveal, such a comparison raises issues that go beyond a mere methodological comparison of self-reports and observers' ratings. Some of the discrepancies illustrate interesting psychological processes such as self-enhancement (striving to appear in a more favorable light than is objectively justifiable) and personality traits such as narcissism (the disposition to habitually practice self-enhancement).

Which illustrates a still broader point: Discrepancies between sources of data about personality often are more than merely errors to be explained away. They can be clues to interesting and important psychological processes that deserve research attention.

From *Journal of Personality and Social Psychology, 74*, 1397–1349, 1998.

"You interrupted my mother at least three times this morning" exclaims Roger. "That's not true," responds Julia, "I only interrupted her *once*!" And so the discussion continues.

Disagreements about who did and did not do what are commonplace in social interactions. When such disagreements arise, whom should we believe? Perhaps Julia was distorting the truth to paint a favorable picture of herself. Alternatively, Roger may remember that Julia interrupted his mother, when really the conversation was interrupted by a telephone call; or perhaps Julia was so caught up with what she was trying to say that she did not notice that Roger's mother had not finished speaking. When caught in such situations, many of us, convinced that we are right, wish that somehow past events had been recorded on videotape so that we could triumphantly rewind the tape and reveal the veracity of our own reports. Unfortunately, in everyday life, no such video is available.

In the present study, however, we compared individuals' reports of their behavior with observer codings of their behavior from videotapes. Specifically, participants interacted in a 40-min group-discussion task and then reported how frequently they had performed a set of acts. Observers later coded (from videotapes) the frequency with which each participant had performed each act. Thus, this design allowed us to compare retrospective act frequency reports by the self with on-line act frequency codings by observers.[1] Specifically, we examined whether individuals can accurately report how they behaved in a specific situation, and when and why their reports are discrepant from observer codings of their behavior. Understanding the processes that lead to accurate judgments about act performances is fundamental to the study of social perception.

*   *   *

The present research examined the following questions. First, to what extent do people agree about how often an act occurred? For example, do Julia's self-reports of her behavior agree with Roger's reports of her behavior, and will Roger agree with other observers about Julia's behavior? Second, what makes an act easy to judge? That is, are there some attributes or properties intrinsic to a given act that influence the degree to which both self and observer agree about its occurrence?

Third, do people accurately report what they did in a particular situation? For example, did Julia really interrupt Roger's mother only once? Fourth, are self-reports of specific acts biased by a motive to self-enhance, and are some individuals more likely to self-enhance than others? For example, does Julia tend to exaggerate her desirable behaviors?

The present research builds on recent investigations of the determinants of agreement and accuracy in personality judgments. For example, John and Robins (1993, 1994) and Kenny (1994) found observer–observer agreement in trait judgments to be consistently higher than self–observer agreement. Furthermore, Funder and Colvin (1988) and John and Robins (1993) found trait properties, such as observability, social desirability, and location within the five-factor model (FFM) of personality structure (John, 1990), to be related to observer–observer and self–observer agreement in trait judgments. Finally, John and Robins (1994) found that self-judgments at the trait level are influenced by self-enhancement bias, which in turn is associated with individual variations in narcissism. Ozer and Buss (1991) have begun to address issues of this kind at the level of act frequency reports. They showed, for example, that agreement between retrospective observer and self act frequency reports is higher for acts associated with Extraversion but lower for acts associated with Agreeableness.

The present study extends this line of inquiry by examining determinants of agreement and accuracy using on-line act reports by observers and retrospective act reports by the self. On-line observer reports warrant study because in aggregated form they represent an important criterion for act occurrence. Retrospective self-reports warrant study because the self is an ever-present monitor of act occurrence and because the self enjoys a distinctive and, in certain respects, privileged vantage point for interpreting the nature of acts as they are performed. At the same time, however, self-reports are vulnerable to self-enhancement and other biases. Below we formulate hypotheses based on self-concept theory and previous research in the act and trait domains.

---

[1]By *on-line codings*, we mean that observers coded and recorded acts as they occurred rather than relying on memory.—Authors

How Well Do People Agree About How Often an Act Occurred?

Two types of agreement can be distinguished: agreement between observers (observer–observer agreement) and agreement between observers and the targets' own self-reports of their behavior (self–observer agreement). Bem (1967, 1972) and other cognitive-informational self-theorists have argued that individuals perceive their own behavior in much the same way as external observers do: the way individuals perceive themselves should, therefore, correspond closely with the way they are perceived by others. This view suggests that self and observer reports of act frequencies should show substantial convergence, especially when the reports concern an interaction situation that is brief and clearly delimited.

In contrast, studies of global trait judgments (Funder & Colvin, 1997; John & Robins, 1993; Kenny, 1994) and evaluations of task performance (John & Robins, 1994) have shown that the self is a unique judge: Self-judgments tend to agree less with observer judgments than observers agree with each other. On the basis of this research, we predicted that self–observer agreement on act frequency reports would be lower than observer–observer agreement (Hypothesis 1).

Do Acts Differ in How Much Individuals Agree About Act Frequencies?

What makes an act easy to judge? To address this question, Ozer and Buss (1991) asked spouses to report how frequently they had performed a set of acts over the previous 3 months. Agreement between spouses varied across acts and depended on a number of properties of the acts. For example, spouses showed relatively high levels of agreement about acts related to Extraversion (e.g., "I danced in front of a crowd") but relatively little agreement about acts related to Agreeableness (e.g., "I let someone cut into the parking space I was waiting for"). The Ozer and Buss study provides insights into act properties that might moderate interjudge agreement. Several studies have identified properties of traits that influence agreement, including the observability of trait-relevant behaviors, the social desirability of the trait, and the Big Five content domain of the trait judged. If acts are indeed the building blocks of personality, then the properties affecting agreement about traits may also affect agreement about acts, and findings for acts should therefore parallel those for traits.

Thus, drawing on trait research, we made the following predictions about acts. First, we predicted higher observer–observer and self–observer agreement for acts that are easily observed (Funder & Dobroth, 1987; John & Robins, 1993; Kenrick & Stringfield, 1980; Ozer & Buss, 1991) (Hypothesis 2a). Some acts refer to psychological events or processes within the mind of the actor that may not be directly observable (e.g., "I appeared cooperative in order to get my way"), whereas other acts are more easily observed from an external vantage point (e.g., "I sat at the head of the table"). Highly observable acts will be more salient to observers (who focus on visible behaviors) than to the self-perceiver, for whom internal experiences (e.g., intentions and motives) are also available (Funder, 1980). Whereas observable behavior is, in principle, available to both observer and self, less observable aspects of an act (such as intentions) are available primarily to the self and are potentially more salient than observable aspects of the act (Robins & John, 1997b; White & Younger, 1988). Thus, it seems unlikely that all acts can be coded with high reliability by even the most conscientious observers.

Second, we predicted higher agreement for acts that occur frequently (Funder & Colvin, 1991; Ozer & Buss, 1991) (Hypothesis 2b). If an act has a low base rate of occurrence, then observers are more likely to miss it over the course of an interaction. Moreover, on psychometric grounds, low base-rate acts will have less variance across targets, which will tend to reduce correlations between observers. Both observability and base rate involve informational factors that might limit agreement about act performances.

We also expected motivational factors to play a role. In particular, we predicted that agreement would be related to the social desirability of the act (Hypothesis 2c). However, trait research provides conflicting evidence about whether this relation will be linear or curvilinear. That is, Funder and Colvin (1988) and Hayes and Dunning (1997) found a positive linear relation, with higher agreement for more desirable traits. In contrast, the two studies reported by John and Robins (1993) showed a curvilinear relation, with higher agreement for evaluatively neutral traits and lower agreement for evaluatively extreme traits (either highly undesirable or highly desirable). The present study will examine the effects of desirability and evaluativeness on agreement in the act domain.

Fourth, extrapolating from earlier findings, we predicted higher agreement for acts related to Extraversion (Funder & Colvin, 1988; John & Robins, 1993; Kenny, 1994; Norman & Goldberg, 1966; Ozer & Buss, 1991) and lower agreement for acts related to Agreeableness (John & Robins, 1993) (Hypothesis 2d).

How Accurate Are Self-Reports of Act Frequency?

The accuracy of self-perception has been a long-standing concern in psychology (see Robins & John, 1997a, for a review). Many theorists are less than sanguine about the ability of people to perceive their behavior objectively. Hogan (1996), for example, spoke of the "inevitability of human self-deception" (p. 165), and Thorne (1989) observed that "due to self-deception, selective inattention, repression, or whatever one wishes to call lack of self-enlightenment, self-views may be less accurate than outsiders' views" (p. 157).

Assessing the accuracy of self-reports requires a criterion—a measure of "reality" against which self-perceptions can be compared. Given the absence of a single objective standard for evaluating the accuracy of global personality traits, the social consensus (i.e., aggregated trait ratings by others) has often been used as an accuracy crite-

rion (e.g., Funder, 1995; Hofstee, 1994; Norman & Goldberg, 1966; Robins & John, 1997a). For example, much research on the accuracy of self-reports has compared self-ratings with judgments provided by peers (John & Robins, 1994; Kolar, Funder, & Colvin, 1996). However, some researchers have been skeptical of reports by such informants and have instead emphasized the need for direct behavioral observation (e.g., Kenny, 1994, p. 136). Hence, the present research focused on observer codings of act frequencies from videotapes in a specific interaction task. These codings provide a more objective measure of the behavioral reality in the task and can therefore serve as a criterion to evaluate accuracy and bias in self-reports of behavior in this task (Funder, 1995; Kenny, 1994; Robins & John, 1997b). We expected self-reported act frequencies to reflect, at least in part, the observed "reality" of participants' behavioral conduct. Thus, we predicted that the self-reports would show levels of accuracy similar to those found in trait research (Hypothesis 3). However, we did not expect the accuracy correlations to be uniformly high, so we also examined the properties of acts that might explain why accuracy is higher for some behaviors than for others.

Are Self-Reports of Act Frequency Biased?

Do individuals overreport socially desirable acts to enhance their self-views? Most self-concept theorists assume that people are motivated to maintain and enhance their feelings of self-worth (e.g., Allport, 1937; Greenwald, 1980; James, 1890; Rogers, 1959; Tesser, 1988). According to Taylor and Brown (1988, 1994) and others, most individuals have "positive illusions" about themselves, presumably stemming from the basic motive toward self-enhancement. Several studies have examined positive illusions by comparing self-reports to observer ratings of global personality traits, such as friendly and outgoing (Campbell & Fehr, 1990; Colvin, Block, & Funder, 1995; Lewinsohn, Mischel, Chaplin, & Barton, 1980). This research on trait ratings shows that, on average, individuals perceive themselves somewhat more positively than they are perceived by others. If these positive illusions extend to perceptions of specific behaviors, then we would also expect individuals to show a self-enhancement bias in their act reports.

* * *

Illusory self-enhancement is sometimes described as if it is present in all normal, psychologically healthy individuals: Taylor (1989) concluded that "normal human thought is marked not by accuracy but by positive self-enhancing illusions" (p. 7); Paulhus and Reid (1991) emphasized that "the healthy person is prone to self-deceptive positivity" (p. 307); and Greenwald and Pratkanis (1984) believed that self-enhancing biases pervade the "self-knowledge of the average normal adult of (at least) North American culture" (p. 139). However, John and Robins (1994) found self-enhancement bias in only 60% of their participants who evaluated their performance in a group discussion task more positively than did a group of independent observers. This finding raises the question of whether some individuals are particularly prone to positive illusions. As noted by John and Robins, the most theoretically relevant construct is narcissism. The *Diagnostic and Statistical Manual of Mental Disorders* (4th ed.; *DSM-IV*) criteria for the narcissistic personality include a grandiose sense of self-importance, a tendency to exaggerate accomplishments and talents, and an expectation to be recognized as "extraordinary" even without appropriate accomplishments (American Psychiatric Association, 1994). Research suggests that narcissistic individuals respond to threats to their self-worth by perceiving themselves more positively than is justified (Gabriel, Critelli, & Ee, 1994; John & Robins, 1994) and by denigrating others (Morf & Rhodewalt, 1993). Narcissists may be particularly prone to positively distorted self-evaluations because their inflated sense of self-importance is easily threatened. Thus, we predicted that narcissistic individuals will show more self-enhancement bias than non-narcissistic individuals in their act frequency self-reports (Hypothesis 4).

Method

PARTICIPANTS Ninety Masters of Business Administration (MBA) students (41 women, 49 men) volunteered to participate in a personality and managerial assessment program. Because of technical problems, the videotapes of 2 participants were unusable; thus, the final N was 88. Their median age was 29 years, and on average they had more than 3 years of postcollege work experience. We collected data from two samples: 54 participants (26 women) in Sample 1 and 36 participants (15 women) in Sample 2.

GROUP DISCUSSION TASK The group discussion task we used is a standardized exercise commonly used to assess managerial performance (e.g., Howard & Bray, 1988; Thornton & Byham, 1982). The task simulates a committee meeting in a large organization. Participants were randomly assigned to mixed-sex groups, with 6 members in each. Participants were told that the purpose of the meeting was to allocate a fixed amount of money to 6 candidates for a merit bonus. Each participant was assigned the role of supervisor of one candidate and was instructed to present a case for that candidate at the meeting; participants were seated at a round table and no leader was assigned. Participants received a realistic written summary of the employment backgrounds of all candidates, including salary, biographical information, and appraisals of prior job performance, and were given 10 min to review this information. They were instructed to start the meeting by each giving a 3- to 5-min presentation on the relative merits of their candidate. The groups had 40 min to reach consensus on how to allocate the merit bonuses. Instructions emphasized two goals: (a) obtain a large bonus for the candidate they represented and (b) help the group achieve a fair overall allocation of the bonus money. Thus, effective performance required behaviors that promoted the achievement of both goals. To permit subsequent coding of act frequencies, the task was videotaped with cameras mounted unobtrusively on the walls and focused on each participant's face and upper body.

SELECTION OF ACTS   We studied a total of 34 acts (20 acts in Sample 1 and 14 acts in Sample 2). * * * We selected 20 acts * * * that seemed likely to occur in our task (e.g., "Target issued orders that got the group organized"). In Sample 2, five psychologists familiar with the group discussion task generated a second set of 14 acts that refer to easily observable behaviors and occur often in this task (e.g., "Target outlined a set of criteria for determining how to allocate the money").

SELF-REPORTS OF ACT FREQUENCY   Immediately after completing the task, participants reported how frequently they had performed each act during the group discussion. The acts were worded in the first person (e.g., "I persuaded the others to accept my opinion on the issue"). * * * We used a 4-point scale referring to the actual frequency of acts performed (0 = not at all, 1 = once, 2 = two or three times, 3 = more than three times).

VIDEO-BASED OBSERVER CODINGS OF ACT FREQUENCY   In Sample 1, four observers viewed the videotaped behavior of each participant and coded the frequencies of each of the 20 acts. In Sample 2, a second set of four observers coded the additional 14 acts for each participant. Both sets of observers were students at the same university but unacquainted with the videotaped participants. Acts were worded in the third person (e.g., "Target persuaded the others to accept his/her opinion on the issue"). Before viewing the videotapes, the observers watched four practice videotapes (which were not used in this research) to familiarize themselves with typical behavioral repertoires and the way the acts were manifested in the task.

 * * * The four observers coded participants' act frequencies with reasonable reliability; across the 34 acts, the average coefficient alpha reliability of the composited ratings was .69 (SD = .29).[2]

INDEPENDENT VARIABLES: PROPERTIES OF ACTS   For each of the 34 acts, we measured four properties hypothesized to influence interjudge agreement and accuracy and bias in self-reported act frequencies.

Observability. Two facets of observability were rated by eight judges who were familiar with the group discussion task: Noticeability was defined by how well the act stands out from the stream of behavior (α = .89), and high inferential content was the degree of inference about internal thoughts and motivations required for an observer to be sure that the act has occurred (α = .96).[3] * * * We standardized both variables, reverse scored high inferential content, and combined the two ratings into one overall measure of observability. The most observable act was "Target reminded the group of their time limit"; the least observable act was "Target took the opposite point of view just to be contrary."

Social desirability. Using a 9-point scale (Hampson, Goldberg, & John, 1987), the judges also rated how socially desirable it was to perform each act in the group discussion. The mean ratings were used as an index of each act's desirability (α = .94). The most desirable act was "Target settled the dispute among other members of the group"; the least desirable act was "Target yelled at someone." Evaluativeness was measured by folding the 9-point scale such that 1 and 9 were recoded as 4, 2 and 8 were recoded as 3, and so on.

Base rate. The base rate of an act was the number of times the act was performed by any participant, on

---

[2]"Reliability" in this context refers to the statistical stability of the averaged observers' ratings. This number is higher to the degree that (a) the different observers agree in their ratings and (b) there is a large number of observers. With four observers being averaged here, a

composite reliability of .69 is good but not excellent. Other reliabilities reported later (e.g., of act properties) were higher, as you will see.

[3]The Greek letter α is a conventional label for the reliability (stability) of a personality scale. A scale is more reliable to the degree that (a) its items correlate with each other and (b) it has more items. Reliability in this sense is a necessary but not sufficient condition for validity.

the basis of the observer codings. This index was computed separately for each observer and then composited; the mean alpha (averaged across the two sets of observers) was .83. The act with the highest base rate was "Target expressed her/his agreement with a point being made by another member of the group"; the act with the lowest base rate was "Target monopolized the conversation." * * *

Big Five personality domain. Acts in the group discussion task tend to be overt behaviors that are either interpersonal (e.g., negotiation and persuasion) or task-oriented (setting goals and organizing group activities; Bass, 1954). In terms of the Big Five personality domains, the interpersonal domains of Extraversion and Agreeableness and the task-focused domain of Conscientiousness were most relevant. In contrast, the other two Big Five domains (Neuroticism, Openness to Experience) refer primarily to an individual's covert experiences. Three expert judges rated the prototypicality of each act for each of the Big Five domains, with low ratings indicating the act was unrelated to that Big Five domain and high ratings indicating the act was highly related to either high or low pole. For example, the Extraversion rating for each act ranged from 0 (*act is unrelated to Extraversion or Introversion*) to 4 (*act is extremely prototypical of Extraversion or Introversion*). The alpha reliabilities of their composite judgments were high for Extraversion (.81), Agreeableness (.86), and Conscientiousness (.88) and somewhat lower for Neuroticism (.67) and Openness to Experience (.62). There were no prototypical examples of the Neuroticism and Openness to Experience domains. All acts had their highest mean prototypicality values on Extraversion, Agreeableness, or Conscientiousness, and therefore only these three Big Five domains will be examined in our analyses. "Target laughed out loud" was the most proto-typical act for the Extraversion domain, "Target took the opposite point of view just to be contrary" for (low) Agreeableness, and "Target reminded the group of their time limit" for Conscientiousness. We used these continuous prototypicality ratings in our correlational analyses. * * *

NARCISSISM We used the 33-item version of the Narcissistic Personality Inventory (NPI; $\alpha = 70$; Raskin & Terry, 1988) to assess participants' level of narcissism. The NPI is the best validated self-report measure of overt narcissism for nonclinical populations (Raskin & Terry, 1988; see also Hendin & Cheek, 1997) and has been shown to predict psychologists' ratings of narcissism (e.g., John & Robins, 1994).

DEPENDENT VARIABLES

Interjudge agreement: Observer–observer and self–observer agreement. To assess how much the observers agreed about the frequency of each act, we computed the correlation (across participants) between each pair of observers' video-based codings. We then averaged the resulting six pairwise observer–observer correlations. This index reflects the average observer–observer agreement for each act.

To assess how much self and observer agreed about the frequency of each act, we computed the correlation (across participants) between the self-reports and video-based codings by each of the four observers. We then averaged the resulting four dyadic self–observer correlations. This index reflects the average agreement between self and a single observer and is therefore directly comparable to the dyadic observer–observer agreement index.

Accuracy and bias in self-reported acts. To assess accuracy and bias, we used the aggregated video-based observer codings as a behavior-based criterion measure of act frequency. Accuracy was defined by the correlation (computed across participants) between self-reports of act frequency and the observer criterion for act frequency. Bias was defined by the discrepancy between each participant's self-report and the observer criterion; positive values indicate that participants overreported how frequently they performed the act, and negative values indicate they underreported how frequently they performed the act. Bias can be computed both at the aggregate level (i.e., do individuals, on average, overreport or underreport some acts more than others?) and at the level of the individual person (i.e., do some persons overreport or underreport an act more than others?). Both accuracy and bias were computed separately for each act.

The dependent variables were computed separately for the acts in each sample. However, because the findings were similar in both samples, analyses across acts used the whole set of 34 acts.

Results and Discussion

DO OBSERVERS AGREE MORE WITH EACH OTHER THAN THEY DO WITH THE SELF?
We first tested Hypothesis 1, which predicts that observer–observer agreement would be higher than self–observer agreement. Across the 34 acts, observer–observer agreement ($M = .40$, $SD = .25$) was significantly higher than self–observer agreement ($M = .19$, $SD = .19$), as shown by a t-test for paired samples, $t(33) = 5.2$, $p < .001$, one-tailed.[4] This effect held for 83% of the acts. In short, two observers generally agreed more about an act's frequency than did the self and an observer. * * *

We also found that acts eliciting high levels of observer–observer agreement also tended to elicit high self–observer agreement; the correlation between the two agreement indices across the 34 acts was .65, closely replicating the .64 value reported by John and Robins (1993) for trait ratings. In other words, when two observers agree about an act (or a trait), self and observer are also likely to agree.

WHAT MAKES AN ACT EASY TO JUDGE? EFFECTS OF OBSERVABILITY, SOCIAL DESIRABILITY, BASE RATE, AND BIG FIVE DOMAIN
The level of agreement varied substantially across acts, ranging

---

[4]M is the mean and SD is the standard deviation. The p-level reported implies that a difference of the size found would occur less than 1 time in 1,000 if there really is no difference between the two kinds of agreement.

from −.08 to .88 for observer–observer agreement, and from −.12 to .62 for self–observer agreement. Why are some acts judged more consensually than others? To address this question, we correlated the act properties with observer–observer and self–observer agreement across the 34 acts. These across-act correlation coefficients are given in Table 1. As predicted by Hypotheses 2a, 2b, and 2c, observability, social desirability, and base rate of the acts were all positively and substantially correlated with both observer–observer and self–observer agreement. The observability effect is consistent with Ozer and Buss's (1991) research on acts, as well as with Funder and Dobroth's (1987) and John and Robins's (1993) research on traits. The positive linear relation between social desirability and agreement is consistent with Funder and Dobroth (1987) and Hayes and Dunning (1997). However, we did not find the evaluativeness effect reported by John and

---

TABLE 1

CORRELATIONS BETWEEN ACT PROPERTIES AND INTERJUDGE AGREEMENT ON ACT FREQUENCY REPORTS (COMPUTED ACROSS THE 34 ACTS)

Act properties	Observer–observer agreement	Self–observer agreement
Observability	.38*	.34*
Base rate	.44*	.35*
Desirability	.52*	.46*
Evaluativeness	−.14	−.06
Prototypicality for Big Five domain		
Extraversion	.08	.32*
Agreeableness	−.27†	−.51*
Conscientiousness	.20	.38*

Note. Numbers in this table are correlations computed across the 34 acts. For example, the correlation of .38 between observability and observer–observer agreement indicates that more observable acts tended to elicit higher levels of agreement than less observable acts. Similarly, the correlation of −.51 between Agreeableness and self–observer agreement indicates that acts from the Agreeableness domain (i.e., prototypical examples of either Agreeableness or Disagreeableness) tended to elicit lower levels of self–observer agreement than acts unrelated to Agreeableness.
†$p < .10$ (marginally significant). *$p < .05$.

TABLE 2

THE 12 MOST RELIABLY CODED ACTS (α > .80) RANKED BY THEIR SELF-OBSERVER VALIDITY

Act	Big Five domain	Self-observer validity
Told joke to lighten tense moment	E	.72
Made humorous remark	E	.60
Took charge of things at the meeting	E	.57
Laughed out loud	E	.52
Outlined set of steps thought group should follow	C	.45
Pointed out the distinction between a merit bonus and salary increase	C	.45
Reminded group of time limit	C	.41
Said was willing to lower the money recommending for our candidate	A	.32
Expressed agreement with another group member	A	.31
Pointed out possible effects on employee morale	A	.08
Interrupted someone else	A	.07
Suggested they give some money to every candidate	A	.03
M		.40
SD		.26

Note. The act descriptions have been slightly abbreviated. All acts are desirable (i.e., rated above 6 on the 9-point social desirability scale) except "Interrupted someone else," which was undesirable (mean desirability = 2.8), and "Laughed out loud," which was relatively neutral (mean desirability = 5.6). E = Extraversion; A = Agreeableness; C = Conscientiousness.

Robins, who found that both extremely negative and extremely positive traits elicit lower levels of agreement. In summary, acts that were observable, desirable, and occurred relatively frequently were judged with relatively more agreement than acts that were difficult to observe, undesirable, and relatively infrequent.

Table 2 also shows the correlation between Big Five content domain and interjudge agreement. These correlations are generally consistent with Hypothesis 2d. Self–observer agreement correlated positively with act prototypicality for both Extraversion and Conscientiousness and negatively with prototypicality for Agreeableness, indicating that self–observer agreement was higher for acts from the Extraversion and Conscientiousness domains and lower for acts from the Agreeableness domain. The same pattern was found for observer–observer agreement, but the correlations did not reach conventional levels of significance. These findings are generally consistent with previous research in both the act and trait domains. However, there were two

differences. First, we did not find the Extraversion effect for observer–observer agreement found in several previous studies (e.g., John & Robins, 1993; Kenny, 1994). Second, we found a Conscientiousness effect for self–observer agreement that has not been found in previous research.

* * *

HOW ACCURATE ARE SELF-REPORTS OF ACT FREQUENCY? To examine accuracy, we correlated the self-reported act frequencies with the aggregated observer codings. Across all 34 acts, the mean correlation was .24 (SD = .26). However, this value underestimates the accuracy of the self-reports because for some acts the video-based observer codings were not highly reliable. Thus, as a fairer test, we considered only those 12 acts that observers coded with high reliability (i.e., those with an alpha above .80). Consistent with Hypothesis 3, the self-reports showed a significant level of accuracy, with a mean correlation of .40 (SD = .26; see Table 2).

However, the accuracy correlations varied considerably even within this subset of highly reliable acts, ranging from a high of .72 to a low of .03. Table 2 presents the Big Five classifications of these 12 acts. The 4 acts with the highest accuracy correlations (mean $r = .61$) were all from the Extraversion domain, whereas the 5 acts with the lowest accuracy correlations (mean $r = .16$) were all from the Agreeableness domain; the 3 Conscientiousness acts fell in between, with a mean r of .44.

* * *

Individual Differences in Self-Enhancement
Bias * * * Now we turn to the question of whether certain kinds of individuals give biased reports of their behavior. To establish the existence of such individual differences, we examined for each desirable act the percentage of individuals whose self-reported act frequencies were greater than, less than, and the same as the observer codings. Averaging the percentages across the 15 desirable acts, 57% of the participants overreported (i.e., showed self-enhancement bias), 24% underreported (i.e., self-diminishment bias), and 19% were exactly accurate. That is, 43% of the participants failed to show the general self-enhancement effect (Taylor & Brown, 1988). Clearly, then, individuals show substantial differences in self-perception bias, suggesting that the self-enhancement tendency should not be treated as a general law of social behavior (John & Robins, 1994).

To test the prediction that narcissism will predict these individual differences in self-enhancement, we computed a self-enhancement index based on the degree to which participants overreported their desirable acts plus the degree to which they underreported their undesirable acts. Consistent with Hypothesis 4, the NPI correlated .27 ($p < .05$) with this self-enhancement index. Analyses of individual acts revealed that narcissists were particularly inclined to overreport desirable acts such as "I took charge of things at the meeting" and "I made an argument that changed another person's mind." The tendency for narcissistic individuals to exaggerate the frequency with which they performed desirable acts provides further support for the link between narcissism and positive illusions about the self (John & Robins, 1994).

General Discussion

This research addressed a fundamental question about self-perception: Do people know how they acted in a particular situation? We compared individuals' reports of how frequently they performed a set of acts with observer codings of their behavior from videotapes. We found that for some acts there is a clear consensus about how often the act occurred whereas for other acts individuals simply do not agree. We explored several factors that might account for these differences and found that individuals tend to agree about acts that are observable, desirable, frequently occurring, and are from the Extraversion and Conscientiousness (rather than the Agreeableness) domains. We also examined how accurately people report on their behavior and whether their reports are positively biased. We found that individuals' recollections of their behavior showed some correspondence with codings of their behavior, but the degree of correspondence varied systematically across acts. Finally, we found a general tendency toward self-enhancement bias in the act self-reports, but the degree of bias depended on both the individual act and the individual person. Specifically, self-enhancement was greatest for acts that were highly desirable and difficult to observe and for persons who were particularly narcissistic.

What can these findings tell us about the disagreement between Julia and Roger regarding how many times she had interrupted his mother that morning? First, we can expect less agreement between self and other, Julia and Roger, than between Roger and another observer. Second, however, for both Julia and Roger, the amount of agreement will depend on the specific act being monitored; we would expect relatively low agreement because "interrupting another person" is an undesirable and disagreeable act. Third, given that act self-reports are susceptible to self-enhancement bias, we would expect Julia to underestimate how often she had in fact interrupted Roger's mother, especially if she has narcissistic tendencies. In short, our analysis suggests that their disagreement may resist easy resolution.

We now move beyond the rather specific context of Julia and Roger's disagreement and turn to the wider implications of the findings. * * *

COMPARISON OF ACT AND TRAIT RESEARCH ON AGREEMENT AND ACCURACY

* * *

* * * There appear to be both similarities and differences between agreement on acts and agreement on traits. Clearly, an important avenue for future research concerns the psychological roots of these similarities and differences. Such research will need to take into account differences in the way act and trait judgments are made. One might expect judges to agree more about acts than about general personality traits because many acts are directly observable (Buss & Craik, 1980, 1983; Kenny, 1994), whereas traits represent summary impressions of multiple-act occurrences. Thus, trait inferences require first perceiving specific behaviors and then abstracting them into trait ascriptions. On the other hand, agreement may be higher for traits because trait inferences are typically based on a diverse set of relevant behavioral episodes. The broader observational base of traits means that observers are less likely to miss all of the many trait-relevant behaviors than they are to miss a specific performance of a single act. For example, it would be perfectly plausible for some judges to miss an instance of the specific act of "interrupting someone." It is less plausible that a judge will miss all disagreeable behaviors in the situation (including, among others, "interrupting someone," "loudly correcting someone's mistake," and "insisting on having the last word"). The present findings indicate higher observer–observer agreement for acts than for trait ratings by peers, thus suggesting that the greater observability of acts may outweigh the greater breadth of traits in determining agreement among observers.

In addition, act and trait reports may dif-
fer because they derive from two different forms of memory. Specific behaviors are encoded in episodic memory whereas representations of traits are encoded in semantic memory (Klein & Loftus, 1993). Consequently, judgments about acts require recall of specific behavioral instances (i.e., episodic memory) and are likely to proceed through a different cognitive process than judgments about traits, which require retrieval of abstract, generalized information about a person (i.e., semantic memory). One implication of this distinction is that self-perception bias may occur either at the initial stage of encoding behavior into episodic memory or at the stage when memories of specific acts are generalized into semantic knowledge as trait representations (e.g., by selectively attending to desirable episodic memories). The present findings imply the former—that act perceptions themselves are biased. Thus, self-judgments about traits may be biased just because self-judgments about acts are biased. Clearly, however, our findings do not exclude the possibility that bias also exists when semantic knowledge about the self is formed. In summary, understanding the processes by which perceptions of act occurrences are translated into trait judgments will help elucidate the factors that cause accuracy and bias in personality impressions.

* * *

IMPLICATIONS FOR ACT-BASED TRAIT ASSESSMENT The present study has some implications for the feasibility and practice of act-based personality assessment using both on-line and retrospective act frequency reports. Our findings for on-line act reports showed levels of interobserver agreement that were reasonably high for the majority of acts, and, indeed, slightly higher than that obtained for trait ratings. These results support the feasibility of this fundamental mode of act-based trait assessment. Furthermore, Borkenau and Ostendorf (1987) studied a situation similar to that used in this research and found substantial accuracy for retrospective observer act reports. Finally, it is important to keep in mind that our findings focus on reports of single acts and do not benefit from aggregation across acts. Thus, reliability and validity of both on-line observer and retrospective self-reports would be substantially higher for the multiple-act indices advocated by the AFA (Cheek, 1982).

However, the present findings suggest some limitations of retrospective self-reports as surrogates for on-line codings of act frequency. Although we found some degree of correspondence between self-reports and aggregated on-line act reports by observers, the more salient finding was the great variability in self–observer agreement across acts. For some acts, self-reports appear to correspond with the on-line observer codings (i.e., Extraversion) but for other acts self-reports do not (i.e., Agreeableness). Furthermore, our results indicate that the operation of self-enhancement bias, previously found for trait ratings, cannot be avoided at the act report level. Finally, unlike observer reports, self-reports of acts have the intrinsic limitation that aggregation across "multiple selves" is not possible (Hofstee, 1994).

∗   ∗   ∗

The present findings suggest that some practical challenges remain to be overcome to fully implement the AFA and realize its envisioned theoretical potential. For example, valid retrospective self-reports are difficult to obtain for acts related to Agreeableness, results consistent with those reported by Ozer and Buss (1991). These findings for acts parallel those for trait ratings, thus indicating that the problem may reside not with act monitoring per se but rather with the distinctiveness of self–other perspectives in this behavioral domain. Thus, the implications of these findings pertain not just to AFA assessment methods but more generally to method effects in construct validation (e.g., Ozer, 1989). In particular, researchers should specify what kinds of method effects should be expected given the conceptual definition of the particular trait construct in question.

∗   ∗   ∗

In conclusion, a greater understanding of when and why individuals can accurately report what they and others did in a situation should be the goal of further psychological research. Not only can such research inform studies that use observer and self-report methods, but it can also illuminate the processes that underlie disagreements in such domains as romantic relationships, conflict resolution, and negotiation.

References

Allport, G. W. (1937). *Personality: A psychological interpretation.* New York: Holt.

American Psychiatric Association. (1994). *Diagnostic and statistical manual of mental disorders* (4th ed.). Washington, DC: Author.

Bass, B. (1954). The leaderless group discussion. *Psychological Bulletin, 51,* 465–492.

Bem, D. J. (1967). Self-perception: An alternative interpretation of cognitive dissonance phenomena. *Psychological Review, 74,* 183–200.

Bem, D. J. (1972). Self-perception theory. In L. Berkowitz (Ed.), *Advances in experimental social psychology* (Vol. 6, pp. 1–62). New York: Academic Press.

Borkenau, P., & Ostendorf, F. (1987). Retrospective estimates of act frequencies: How accurately do they reflect reality? *Journal of Personality and Social Psychology, 52,* 626–638.

Buss, D. M., & Craik, K. H. (1980). The frequency concept of disposition: Dominance and prototypically dominant acts. *Journal of Personality, 48,* 379–392.

Buss, D. M., & Craik, K. H. (1983). The act frequency approach to personality. *Psychological Review, 90,* 105–126.

Campbell, J. D., & Fehr, B. (1990). Self-esteem and perceptions of conveyed impressions: Is negative affectivity associated with greater realism? *Journal of Personality and Social Psychology, 58,* 122–133.

Cheek, J. M. (1982). Aggregation, moderator variables, and the validity of personality tests: A peer rating study. *Journal of Personality and Social Psychology, 43,* 1254–1269.

Colvin, C. R., Block, J., & Funder, D. C. (1995). Overly positive self-evaluations and personality: Negative implications for mental health. *Journal of Personality and Social Psychology, 68,* 1152–1162.

Funder, D. C. (1980). On seeing ourselves as others see us: Self–other agreement and discrepancy in personality ratings. *Journal of Personality, 48,* 473–493.

Funder, D. C. (1995). On the accuracy of personality judgment: A realistic approach. *Psychological Review, 102,* 652–670.

Funder, D. C., & Colvin, C. R. (1988). Friends and strangers: Acquaintanceship, agreement, and the accuracy of personality judgment. *Journal of Personality and Social Psychology, 55,* 149–158.

Funder, D. C., & Colvin, C. R. (1991). Explorations in behavioral consistency: Properties of persons, situations, and behaviors. *Journal of Personality and Social Psychology, 60,* 773–794.

Funder, D. C., & Colvin, C. R. (1997). Congruence of self and others' judgments of personality. In R. Hogan, J. A. Johnson, & S. R. Briggs (Eds.), *Handbook of personality psychology* (pp. 617–647). New York: Academic Press.

Funder, D. C., & Dobroth, K. M. (1987). Differences between traits: Properties associated with interjudge agreement. *Journal of Personality and Social Psychology, 52*, 409–418.

Gabriel, M. T., Critelli, J. W., & Ee, J. S. (1994). Narcissistic illusions in self-evaluations of intelligence and attractiveness. *Journal of Personality, 62*, 143–155.

Greenwald, A. G. (1980). The totalitarian ego: Fabrication and revision of personal history. *American Psychologist, 35*, 603–618.

Greenwald, A. G., & Pratkanis, A. R. (1984). The self. In R. S. Wyer & T. K. Srull (Eds.), *Handbook of social cognition* (Vol. 3, pp. 129–178). Hillsdale, NJ: Erlbraum.

Hampson, S. E., Goldberg, L. R., & John, O. P. (1987). Category-breadth and social-desirability values for 573 personality terms. *European Journal of Personality, 1*, 241– 258.

Hayes, A. F., & Dunning, D. (1997). Construal processes and trait ambiguity: Implications for self–peer agreement in personality judgment. *Journal of Personality and Social Psychology, 72*, 664–677.

Hendin, H. M., & Cheek, J. M. (1997). Assessing hypersensitive narcissism: A reexamination of Murray's Narcissism scale. *Journal of Research in Personality, 31*, 588–599.

Hofstee, W. K. B. (1994). Who should own the definition of personality? *European Journal of Personality, 8*, 149–162.

Hogan, R. (1996). A socioanalytic perspective on the five-factor model. In J. S. Wiggins (Ed.), *The five-factor model of personality: Theoretical perspectives* (pp. 163–179). New York: Guilford Press.

Howard, A., & Bray, D. W. (1988). *Managerial lives in transition: Advancing age and changing times.* New York: Guilford Press.

James, W. (1890). *The principles of psychology.* Cambridge, MA: Harvard University.

John, O. P. (1990). The "Big Five" factor taxonomy: Dimensions of personality in the natural language and in questionnaires. In L. A. Pervin (Ed.), *Handbook of personality: Theory and research* (pp. 66–100). New York: Guilford Press.

John, O. P., & Robins, R. W. (1993). Determinants of interjudge agreement on personality traits: The Big Five domains, observability, evaluativeness, and the unique perspective of the self. *Journal of Personality, 61*, 521–551.

John, O. P., & Robins, R. W. (1994). Accuracy and bias in self-perception: Individual differences in self-enhancement and the role of narcissism. *Journal of Personality and Social Psychology, 66*, 206–219.

Kenny, D. A. (1994). *Interpersonal perception: A social relations analysis.* New York: Guilford Press.

Kenrick, D. T., & Stringfield, D. O. (1980). Personality traits and the eye of the beholder: Crossing some traditional philosophical boundaries in the search for consistency in all of the people. *Psychological Review, 87*, 88–104.

Klein, S. B., & Loftus, J. (1993). The mental representation of trait and autobiographical knowledge about the self. In T. K. Srull & R. S. Wyer, Jr. (Eds.), *Advances in social cognition* (Vol. 5, pp. 1–49). Hillsdale, NJ: Erlbaum.

Kolar, D. W., Funder, D. C., & Colvin, C. R. (1996). Comparing the accuracy of personality judgments by the self and knowledgeable others. *Journal of Personality, 64*, 311–337.

Lewinsohn, P. M., Mischel, W., Chaplin, W., & Barton, R. (1980). Social competence and depression: The role of illusory self-perceptions. *Journal of Abnormal Psychology, 89*, 203–212.

Morf, C. C., & Rhodewalt, F. (1993). Narcissism and self-evaluation maintenance: Explorations in object relations. *Personality and Social Psychology Bulletin, 19*, 668–676.

Norman, W. T., & Goldberg, L. R. (1966). Raters, ratees, and randomness in personality structure. *Journal of Personality and Social Psychology, 4*, 681–691.

Ozer, D. J. (1989). Construct validity in personality assessment. In D. M. Buss & N. Cantor (Eds.), *Personality psychology: Recent trends and emerging directions* (pp. 224–234). New York: Springer-Verlag.

Ozer, D. J., & Buss, D. M. (1991). Two views of behavior: Agreement and disagreement among marital partners. In D. J. Ozer, J. M. Healy, Jr., & A. J. Stewart (Eds.), *Perspectives in personality* (Vol. 3, pp. 91–106). London: Jessica Kingsley.

Paulhus, D. L., & Reid, D. B. (1991). Enhancement and denial in socially desirable responding. *Journal of Personality and Social Psychology, 60*, 307–317.

Raskin, R., & Terry, H. (1988). A principal-components analysis of the Narcissistic Personality Inventory and some further evidence of its construct validity. *Journal of Personality and Social Psychology, 54*, 890–902.

Robins, R. W., & John, O. P. (1997a). The quest for self-insight: Theory and research on accuracy and bias in self-perception. In R. Hogan, J. Johnson, & S. Briggs (Eds.), *Handbook of personality psychology* (pp. 649–679). New York: Academic Press.

Robins, R. W., & John, O. P. (1997b). Self-perception, visual perspective, and narcissism: Is seeing believing? *Psychological Science, 8*, 37–42.

Rogers, C. R. (1959). A theory of therapy, personality, and interpersonal relations, developed in the client-centered framework. In S. Koch (Ed.), *Psychology: A study of a science* (Vol. 3, pp. 185–256). New York: McGraw-Hill.

Taylor, S. E. (1989). *Positive illusions: Creative self-deception and the healthy mind.* New York: Basic Books.

Taylor, S. E., & Brown, J. (1988). Illusion and well-being: A social psychological perspective on mental health. *Psychological Bulletin, 103*, 193–210.

Taylor, S. E., & Brown, J. (1994). Positive illusions and well-being revisited: Separating fact from fiction. *Psychological Bulletin, 116*, 21–27.

Tesser, A. (1988). Toward a self-evaluation maintenance model of social behavior. In L. Berkowitz (Ed.), *Advances in experimental social psychology* (Vol. 21, pp. 181–227). New York: Academic Press.

Thorne, A. (1989). Conditional patterns, transference, and the coherence of personality across time. In D. M. Buss & N. Cantor (Eds.), *Personality psychology: Recent trends and emerging directions* (pp. 149–159). New York: Springer-Verlag.

Thornton, G. C., & Byham, W. C. (1982). *Assessment centers and managerial performance.* San Diego, CA: Academic Press.

White, P. A., & Younger, D. (1988). Differences in the ascription of transient internal states to self and other. *Journal of Experimental Social Psychology, 24*, 292–309.

PART II

The Trait Approach to Personality

People are not all the same. They think differently, feel differently, and act differently. This raises an important question: What is the best way to describe enduring psychological differences among persons? The purpose of the trait approach to personality psychology is to attempt to answer this question. The ordinary language of personality—found in any dictionary—consists of terms like "sociable" and "anxious" and "dominant." The goal of many researchers who follow the trait approach is to transform this everyday language into a scientifically valid technology for describing individual differences in personality that can be used for predicting a person's behavior and, more importantly, for understanding what he or she does and feels.

This section begins with a consideration of basic theoretical issues in the study of personality. Gordon Allport, widely recognized as the founder of modern personality psychology, describes what he thinks a personality trait is and why traits are important. The second selection is an excerpt from a book by Walter Mischel that was widely read as a frontal assault on the very existence of personality. Although Allport anticipated many of Mischel's criticisms, the book had a widespread impact and triggered a heated controversy that filled pages in the psychological literature for years. The third selection, by Douglas Kenrick and David Funder, sums up the lessons learned from the controversy over the existence of personality, which include not just the conclusion that "traits exist," but also concern the circumstances under which personality is most likely to be clearly seen.

The fourth selection, by Robert McCrae and Paul Costa Jr., argues that a wide swathe of the personality domain is encompassed by five broad traits (extraversion, openness, agreeableness, and conscientiousness), and they suggest that these traits describe the "basic tendencies" that underlie all of human personality. The fifth and final selection employs these "big five" traits to organize a review of research documenting relations between personality traits and important life outcomes. The simple but important conclusion is that people will always study and be interested in personality, because personality matters.

WHAT IS A TRAIT OF PERSONALITY?

Gordon W. Allport

Our first selection is a classic theoretical statement by the original and still perhaps most important trait theorist. What Sigmund Freud is to psychoanalysis, Gordon Allport is—almost—to trait psychology.

In this selection, Allport offers one of the earliest—and still one of the best— psychological definitions of a personality trait. This article was written for a conference held in 1929, when the modern field of personality psychology was just beginning to be formed. Allport's fundamental contribution, in efforts like this paper, was to take the study of normal variations in personality out of the exclusive hands of novelists, dramatists, theologians, and philosophers and to begin to transform it into a scientific discipline.

Especially considering how old this article is, it is remarkable to observe how many modern issues it anticipates, and how cogently it addresses them. These issues include the person-situation debate (see the upcoming selection by Mischel), the issue of whether a trait is a cause or just a summary of behavior (Allport says it is a cause), and the distinction between focusing on how traits are structured within a single individual (now called the "idiographic approach") and focusing on how traits distinguish between people (now called the "nomothetic approach"). More than 70 years after it was written, this article still has much to say to the modern field of personality psychology.

From *Journal of Abnormal and Social Psychology, 25,* 368–372, 1931.

At the heart of all investigation of personality lies the puzzling problem of the nature of the unit or element which is the carrier of the distinctive behavior of a man. *Reflexes* and *habits* are too specific in reference, and connote constancy rather than consistency in behavior; *attitudes* are ill-defined, and as employed by various writers refer to determining tendencies that range in inclusiveness from the *Aufgabe* to the *Weltan-schauung*;[1] *dispositions* and *tendencies* are even less definitive. But *traits*, although appropriated by all manner of writers for all manner of purposes, may still be salvaged, I think, and limited in their refer-

[1]With these German words, Allport is describing the range from the specific tasks an individual must perform (*Aufgabe*) to his or her entire view of the world (*Weltanschauung*).

ence to a certain definite conception of a generalized response-unit in which resides the distinctive quality of behavior that reflects personality. Foes as well as friends of the doctrine of traits will gain from a more consistent use of the term.

The doctrine itself has never been explicitly stated. It is my purpose with the aid of eight criteria to define *trait*, and to state the logic and some of the evidence for the admission of this concept to good standing in psychology.

1. A trait has more than nominal existence. A trait may be said to have the same kind of existence that a habit of a complex order has. Habits of a complex, or higher, order have long been accepted as household facts in psychology. There is no reason to believe that the mechanism which produces such habits (integration, *Gestaltung*, or whatever it may be) stops short of producing the more generalized habits which are here called traits of personality.

2. A trait is more generalized than a habit. Within a personality there are, of course, many independent habits; but there is also so much integration, organization, and coherence among habits that we have no choice but to recognize great systems of interdependent habits. If the habit of brushing one's teeth can be shown, statistically or genetically, to be unrelated to the habit of dominating a tradesman, there can be no question of a common trait involving both these habits; but if the habit of dominating a tradesman can be shown, statistically or genetically, to be related to the habit of bluffing one's way past guards, there is the presumption that a common trait of personality exists which includes these two habits. Traits may conceivably embrace anywhere from two habits to a legion of habits. In this way, there may be said to be major, widely extensified traits and minor, less generalized traits in a given personality.

3. A trait is dynamic, or at least determinative. It is not the stimulus that is the crucial determinant in behavior that expresses personality; it is the trait itself that is decisive. Once formed a trait seems to

have the capacity of directing responses to stimuli into characteristic channels. This emphasis upon the dynamic nature of traits, ascribing to them a capacity for guiding the specific response, is variously recognized by many writers. The principle is nothing more than that which has been subscribed to in various connections by Woodworth, Prince, Sherrington, Coghill, Kurt Lewin, Troland, Lloyd Morgan, Thurstone, Bentley, Stern, and others.[2] From this general point of view traits might be called "derived drives" or "derived motives." Whatever they are called they may be regarded as playing a motivating role in each act, thus endowing the separate adjustments of the individual to specific stimuli with that *adverbial* quality that is the very essence of personality.

* * *

4. The existence of a trait may be established empirically or statistically. In order to know that a person has a *habit* it is necessary to have evidence of repeated reactions of a constant type. Similarly in order to know that an individual has a trait it is necessary to have evidence of repeated reactions which, though not necessarily constant in type, seem none the less to be consistently a function of the same underlying determinant. If this evidence is gathered casually by mere observation of the subject or through the reading of a case history or biography, it may be called empirical evidence.

More exactly, of course, the existence of a trait may be established with the aid of statistical techniques that determine the degree of coherence among the separate responses. Although this employment of statistical aid is highly desirable, it is not necessary to wait for such evidence before speaking of traits, any more than it would be necessary to refrain from speaking of the habit of biting fingernails until the exact frequency of the occurrence is known. Statistical methods are at present better suited to intellective than to conative

---

[2]This is an all-star list of important psychologists and scientists at the time this article was written. Of these, Kurt Lewin and Allport himself had the most lasting influence on personality psychology.

functions, and it is with the latter that we are chiefly concerned in our studies of personality.[3]

5. Traits are only relatively independent of each other. The investigator desires, of course, to discover what the fundamental traits of personality are, that is to say, what broad trends in behavior do exist independently of one another. Actually with the test methods and correlational procedures in use, completely independent variation is seldom found. In one study expansion correlated with extroversion to the extent of +.39, ascendance with conservatism, +.22, and humor with insight, +.83, and so on. This overlap may be due to several factors, the most obvious being the tendency of the organism to react in an integrated fashion, so that when concrete acts are observed or tested they reflect not only the trait under examination, but also simultaneously other traits; several traits may thus converge into a final common path. It seems safe, therefore, to predict that traits can never be completely isolated for study, since they never show more than a relative independence of one another.

In the instance just cited, it is doubtful whether humor and insight (provided their close relationship is verified in subsequent studies) represent distinct traits. In the future perhaps it may be possible to agree upon a certain magnitude of correlation below which it will be acceptable to speak of *separate* traits, and above which *one* trait only will be recognized. If one trait only is indicated it will presumably represent a broadly generalized disposition. For example, if humor and insight cannot be established as independent traits, it will be necessary to recognize a more inclusive trait, and name it perhaps "sense of proportion."

6. A trait of personality, psychologically considered, is not the same as moral quality. A trait of personality may or may not coincide with some well-defined, conventional, social concept. Extroversion, ascendance, social participation, and insight are free from preconceived moral significance, largely because each is a word newly coined or adapted to fit a psychological discovery. It would be ideal if we could in this way find our traits first and then name them. But honesty, loyalty, neatness, and tact, though encrusted with social significance, *may* likewise represent true traits of personality. The danger is that in devising scales for their measurement we may be bound by the conventional meanings, and thus be led away from the precise integration as it exists in a given individual. Where possible it would be well for us to find our traits first, and then seek devaluated terms with which to characterize our discoveries.

7. Acts, and even habits, that are inconsistent with a trait are not proof of the non-existence of the trait. The objection most often considered fatal to the doctrine of traits has been illustrated as follows: "An individual may be habitually neat with respect to his person, and characteristically slovenly in his handwriting or the care of his desk."[4]

In the first place this observation fails to state that there are cases frequently met where a constant level of neatness is maintained in all of a person's acts, giving unmistakable empirical evidence that the trait of neatness is, in some people at least, thoroughly and permanently integrated. All people must not be expected to show the same degree of integration in respect to a given trait. *What is a major trait in one personality may be a minor trait, or even nonexistent in another personality.*[5]

---

[3]"Conative functions" here refer to motivation; at the time this was written, statistical methods of psychological measurement (psychometrics) had been used exclusively for the measurement of intellectual skills, not motivation or personality. Over the following decades, this situation changed and psychometrics became a foundation of modern personality psychology.

[4]This comment anticipates the "person-situation" debate that flared up in 1968, almost 40 years later, with the publication of a book by Walter Mischel (excerpted in the following selection). Interestingly, the inconsistency of neatness, almost exactly as Allport here describes it, *was* used as an argument against the doctrine of traits in an even later article by Mischel and Peake (1982).

[5]This comment—that not all traits apply to all people— was developed into an important article many years later by the psychologists Daryl Bem and Andrea Allen (1974).

In the second place, we must concede that there may be opposed integrations, i.e., contradictory traits, in a single personality. The same individual may have a trait *both* of neatness *and* of carelessness, of ascendance *and* submission, although frequently of unequal strength.

In the third place there are in every personality instances of acts that are unrelated to existent traits, the product of the stimulus and of the attitude of the moment. Even the characteristically neat person may become careless in his haste to catch a train.

But to say that not all of a person's acts reflect some higher integration is not to say that no such higher integrations exist.

8. A trait may be viewed either in the light of the personality which contains it, or in the light of its distribution in the population at large. Each trait has both its unique and its universal aspect. In its unique aspect, the trait takes its significance entirely from the role it plays in the personality as a whole. In its universal aspect, the trait is arbitrarily isolated for study, and a comparison is made between individuals in respect to it. From this second point of view traits merely extend the familiar field of the psychology of individual differences.

There may be relatively few traits, a few hundred perhaps, that are universal enough to be scaled in the population at large; whereas there may be in a single personality a thousand traits distinguishable to a discerning observer. For this reason, after a scientific schedule of universal traits is compiled, there will still be the field of *artistic* endeavor for psychologists in apprehending correctly the subtle and unique traits peculiar to one personality alone, and in discovering the *pattern* which obtains *between* these traits in the same personality.

CONSISTENCY AND SPECIFICITY IN BEHAVIOR

Walter Mischel

The "book that launched a thousand rebuttals" is Walter Mischel's Personality
and Assessment *(1968). This book, widely perceived as an all-out frontal assault
on the existence of personality traits and the viability of personality psychology,
touched off the "person-situation debate," which lasted 20 years. Put briefly, the
debate was over this issue: For determining what an individual does, which is
more important, stable aspects of his or her personality, or the situation he or she
happens to be in at the time? You have already seen that Allport's view, which is
the traditional view of the trait approach, is that personality is an important
determinant of behavior. Mischel's view is that people act very differently in different situations, to the point that characterizing them in terms of broad personality
traits may be neither meaningful nor useful.*

*The next selection is drawn from one of the key chapters of Mischel's book. In
it, Mischel argues that inconsistency in behavior is the rule rather than the exception. He surveys, very briefly, a large number of studies that attempted to find
strong relationships between what individuals did in one situation and what they
did in another. In Mischel's view, such studies generally have failed. Specifically,
Mischel assumes that if the relationship between behaviors in two different situations yields a correlation coefficient of less than about .30, not enough of the variance in behavior has been explained to make it useful to assume that both
behaviors are affected by the same underlying personality trait. Of course, the
selection by Rosenthal and Rubin in Part I provides a different—and more optimistic—interpretation of a correlation of about .30.*

*Although the field of personality and what Allport called the "doctrine of
traits" ultimately survived the Mischelian onslaught, the book and this chapter
remain important landmarks in the recent history of personality psychology. First,
the ideas presented in this chapter had a powerful effect on the viewpoint of many
psychologists within and outside the field of personality, an effect that more than
35 years later has still not dissipated. To this day, a surprising number of psychologists "don't believe in personality." Second and even more important, with the
words you are about to read Mischel forced the field of personality into an agoniz-
ing reappraisal of some of its most basic and cherished assumptions. Although*

these assumptions can be said to have survived, their close reexamination was, on the whole, potentially beneficial for our understanding of personality (see the following selection by Kenrick and Funder).

From *Personality and Assessment* (New York: Wiley, 1968), pp. 13–39.

For more than 50 years personality psychologists have tried to measure traits and states in order to discover personality structure and dynamics. There has been an enormous effort to investigate the reliability and, more recently, the validity of the results. This chapter examines some of the evidence for the assumption of generalized personality traits and states. Empirically, the generality of a trait is established by the associations found among trait indicators. The evidence consists of obtained correlations between behaviors measured across similar situations. Data that demonstrate strong generality in the behavior of the same person across many situations are critical for trait and state personality theories; the construct of personality itself rests on the belief that individual behavioral consistencies exist widely and account for much of the variance in behavior. Most definitions of personality hinge on the assumption that an individual's behavior is consistent across many stimulus conditions (e.g., Sanford, 1963).

Data on the generality-specificity of behavior usually fall under the rubric of "reliability" and are separated from "validity" evidence. This distinction between reliability and validity is not very sharp. Both reliability and validity are established by demonstrating relations between responses to various stimulus conditions. The stimulus conditions are the particular measures and settings used to sample responses. *Reliability* concerns the congruence among responses measured under maximally *similar* stimulus conditions (Campbell, 1960; Campbell & Fiske, 1959). *Validity*, in contradistinction to reliability, requires convergence between

responses to maximally *different*, independent stimulus conditions or measures.[1] The distinction between reliability and validity research depends chiefly on judgments about the degree of similarity among the stimuli used to evoke responses with the particular eliciting techniques or tests employed. For example, correlations among two similar tests, or of two forms of one test, or of the same test administered to the same person on different occasions, all are taken as reliability evidence; correlations among more dissimilar tests, on the other hand, are interpreted as validity data. This chapter is concerned mainly with reliability evidence and evaluates the behavioral consistencies obtained under relatively similar stimulus conditions. We shall look at several kinds of data, first examining the consistency of intellectual varia- bles and then turning to measures of personality. Throughout this chapter some of the empirical evidence for the cross-situational generality of behavior will be reviewed in order to assess more concretely the appropriateness of the trait assumptions which have had such a marked impact on the field.

* * *

---

[1] Our reading of Cronbach and Meehl (see Part I) suggests that validity implies something much more than, and sometimes much different from, this simple characterization. Validity concerns the convergence between patterns of data that are theoretically predicted and those that are empirically obtained. The patterns are not necessarily simple consistency of the sort Mischel describes.

Personality Variables

*   *   *

Personality variables have been examined thoroughly to determine individual consistencies with respect to particular dimensions or dispositions. The following personality dimensions are representative of those attracting most theoretical and research interest during the last decade, and some of the evidence for their consistency is examined. It will become apparent rapidly that the generality of these dispositions usually is far less than that found for cognitive and intellectual variables.[2]

ATTITUDES TOWARD AUTHORITY AND PEERS   The belief that an individual has generalized attitudes toward classes of persons pervades clinical, diagnostic, and research practice. This belief is reflected in the common assumption that problems of sibling rivalry repeat themselves in peer relations, and that attitudes toward parental figures are mirrored in reactions to diverse authority figures throughout life and toward the psychotherapist in particular. Psychologists of many theoretical orientations often agree that persons develop highly generalized attitudes toward authority. Freud, Piaget, and Rogers, among others, all posit that reactions toward authority originate in the family situation and manifest themselves as broadly generalized attitudes expressed in many contexts toward superiors in later social situations. As Piaget puts it:

> Day to day observation and psycho-analytic experience show that the first personal schemas are afterward generalised and applied to many people. According as the first inter-individual experiences of the child who is just learning to speak are connected with a father who is understanding or dominating, loving or cruel, etc., the child will tend (even throughout life if these relationships have influenced his whole youth) to assimilate all other individuals to this father schema. (Piaget, 1951, p. 207)

These assumptions have been subjected to a rare and extensive test by Burwen and Campbell (1957). Burwen and Campbell studied a large sample of Air Force personnel by means of interviews, TAT,[3] description of self and others, judgments of photos, and autobiographical inventories, as well as an attitude survey and sociometric questionnaire.[4] Through each of these techniques, where possible, attitudes were scored toward own father, symbolic authority (e.g., in responses to pictures of older persons on the TAT), immediate boss, immediate peers, and symbolic peers. The topics or attitude objects and the measures for scoring attitudes toward authority on each are summarized below:

Topic	Measures
Father	Interview; description of self and others; autobiographical inventory
Symbolic authority	Interview; TAT (scored globally); TAT (scored objectively); judgments of photos (of older persons); attitude survey
Boss	Interview; description of self and others; autobiographical inventory; sociometric questionnaire

Similar measures were used to score attitudes toward real and symbolic peers.

The interjudge reliability of all ratings on each instrument was adequately high, and scores were available on twenty variables. Their intercorrelations revealed, first of all, the major impact of stimulus similarity or "method variance": for

---

[2]In a section of this chapter that has been omitted, Mischel acknowledged that cognitive and intellectual variables, such as IQ and cognitive style, are relatively consistent over time and across situations.

[3]The TAT is the Thematic Apperception Test, in which a person looks at a picture (e.g., of a person working at a desk) and makes up a story about what is going on. This story can then be scored in various ways, most commonly as to the motivations that it reveals.

[4]A sociometric questionnaire is one in which members of a group are asked about their impressions of or feelings about one another.

TABLE 1

MEAN CORRELATIONS AMONG ATTITUDES MEASURED BY DIFFERENT METHODS

Attitude toward		F	SA	B	P	SP
Father	F	.35	.12	.03	.06	.08
Symbolic authority	SA		.15	.08	.10	.06
Boss	B			.09	.13	.03
Peer	P				.22	.07
Symbolic peer	SP					.01

(Adapted from Burwen & Campbell, 1957, p . 26.)

three quarters of all the variables the highest correlations occurred between measures of different attitudes based on the *same* instrument. When these method-produced correlations were disregarded, there was little evidence for generality of attitudes either toward authority or toward peers. Attitudes toward father, symbolic authority, and boss were no more highly correlated with each other than they were with attitudes toward real or symbolic peers, and all correlations tended to be low.

Table 1 shows the average of transformed correlations between attitude topics, eliminating those based on the same instrument. Of the correlations between different measures of attitude toward a *single* type of authority figure, only among attitudes toward father and among attitudes toward peers are there any indications that independent methods tap a specific attitude focus at least to some extent. Even these associations among different measures of attitudes toward the same type of authority were very modest, being .35 for father and .22 for peers. Attitude toward *different* types of authority figures showed no consistency at all. For example, attitude toward one's father correlated .03 with attitude toward one's boss. The authors appropriately concluded that:

> Evidence for a generalized attitude toward authority which encompasses attitudes toward father, symbolic authority, and boss is totally negative, suggesting the need for reconsideration of the applicability of commonly held theory in this area. (Burwen & Campbell, 1957, p. 31)

MORAL BEHAVIOR Psychodynamic theory has emphasized the role of the "superego" as an internalized moral agency that has a critical role in the regulation of all forms of conduct and in the control of impulses. Theorizing regarding the superego has focused on the way in which authority figures and their values become "incorporated" during the course of socialization. It has been assumed that as a result of this process the child adopts parental standards and controls as his own. There is no doubt that in the course of development most children acquire the capacity to regulate, judge, and monitor their own behavior even in the absence of external constraints and authorities. An important theoretical issue, however, is the consistency of these self-regulated patterns of conduct and self-control.

In the extraordinarily extensive and sophisticated Character Education Inquiry, more than thirty years ago,[5] thousands of children were exposed to various situations in which they could cheat, lie, and steal in diverse settings, including the home, party games, and athletic contexts (Hartshorne & May, 1928; Hartshorne, May, & Shuttleworth, 1930).

Although moral conduct was relatively inconsistent, the children showed substantial consistency in their self-reported opinions and thoughts about moral issues elicited on paper-and-pencil tests

---

[5]That is, more than 30 years before this book was published in 1968.

administered in the classroom. High correlations also were found between various forms of these paper-and-pencil tests. However, if children took alternate equivalent forms of the same tests in diverse social settings—such as at home, in Sunday school, at club meetings, as well as in the classroom—the correlations of their scores among situations were reduced to about .40. The investigators concluded that children vary their opinions to "suit the situation" (Hartshorne, May, & Shuttleworth, 1930, p. 108) and do not have a generalized code of morals.

The specificity of responses, and their dependence on the exact particulars of the evoking situation, was keenly noted by Hartshorne and May (1928). For example:

> . . . even such slight changes in the situation as between crossing out A's and putting dots in squares are sufficient to alter the amount of deception both in individuals and in groups. (p. 382)

To illustrate further from their data, copying from an answer key on one test correlated .696 with copying from a key on another test, and cheating by adding on scores from a speed test correlated .440 with adding on scores on another speed test. However, copying from a key on one test correlated only .292 with adding on scores. Moreover, the average intercorrelations among four classroom tests was only .256 (Hartshorne & May, 1928, p. 383). The more the situation changed the lower the correlations became. The average correlation between four classroom tests and two out-of-classroom tests (contests and stealing) was .167. The lying test given in the classroom averaged .234 with the other classroom tests but only .061 with the two out-of-classroom deception tests (p. 384).

* * *

The observations that Hartshorne and May reported for the relative specificity of moral behavior accurately foreshadowed the findings that emerged from later research on other behavioral consistencies. Response specificity of the kind emphasized by Hartshorne and May is also reflected, for example, in the finding that questionnaires dealing with attitudes and hypothetical matters may correlate with other questionnaires but are less likely to relate to non-self-report behavior (Mischel, 1962). In one study, children were asked questions about whether or not they would postpone immediate smaller rewards for the sake of larger but delayed outcomes in hypothetical situations. Their answers in these hypothetical delay of reward situations were found to relate to other questionnaires dealing with trust and a variety of verbally expressed attitudes. What they said, however, was unrelated to their actual delay of reward choices in real situations (Mischel, 1962). Likewise, measures eliciting direct nonverbal behavior may relate to other behavioral indices in the same domain but not to questionnaires. Thus real behavioral choices between smaller but immediately available gratifications, as opposed to larger but delayed rewards, correlated significantly with such behavioral indices as resistance to temptation, but not with self reports on questionnaires (Mischel, 1962).

Moral guilt also has been studied utilizing projective test[6] responses. For example, in a study with teenage boys (Allinsmith, 1960) moral feelings were inferred from the subjects' projective story completions in response to descriptions of various kinds of immoral actions. The findings led Allinsmith to the view that a person with a truly generalized conscience is a statistical rarity. Johnson (1962) also found that moral judgments across situations tend to be highly specific and even discrepant.

Recent research on moral behavior has concentrated on three areas: moral judgment and verbal standards of right and wrong (e.g., Kohlberg, 1963); resistance to temptation in the absence of external constraint (e.g., Aronfreed & Reber, 1965; Grinder, 1962; MacKinnon, 1938; Mischel & Gilligan, 1964); and post-transgression indices of remorse and guilt (e.g., Allinsmith, 1960; Aron-

---

[6]A projective test is one in which a subject is shown an ambiguous stimulus (e.g., an inkblot, a TAT picture) and asked for his or her interpretation. The subject's answer is assumed to be a "projection" of some aspect of his or her underlying psychology.

freed, 1961; Sears, Maccoby, & Levin, 1957; Whiting, 1959). These three areas of moral behavior turn out to be either completely independent or at best only minimally interrelated (Becker, 1964; Hoffman, 1963; Kohlberg, 1963). Within each area specificity also tends to be the rule. For example, an extensive survey of all types of reactions to transgression yielded no predictable relationships among specific types of reaction (Aronfreed, 1961). Similarly, Sears and his coworkers (1965, chapter 6) did not find consistent associations among various reactions to transgression. Thus the data on moral behavior provide no support for the widespread psychodynamic belief in a unitary intrapsychic moral agency like the superego, or for a unitary trait entity of conscience or honesty. Rather than acquiring a homogeneous conscience that determines uniformly all aspects of their self-control, people seem to develop subtler discriminations that depend on many considerations.

SEXUAL IDENTIFICATION, DEPENDENCY, AND AGGRESSION It is widely assumed in most dynamic and trait theories that people develop firm masculine or feminine identifications early in life. These stable identifications, in turn, are believed to exert pervasive effects on what the person does in many diverse situations (e.g., Kohlberg, 1966). There is, of course, no doubt that boys and girls rapidly learn about sex differences and soon recognize their own gender permanently. A much less obvious issue is the extent to which children develop highly consistent patterns of masculine or feminine "sex-typed" behavior. This question has received considerable research attention. The chief strategy has involved studying the associations among different indicators of masculine and feminine sex-typed behavior.

Dependency and aggression often serve conceptually as behavioral referents for sex typing, with boys expected to be more aggressive and girls more dependent. In dependency research, although Beller's (1955) correlations ranged from .48 to .83 for teacher ratings of five dependency components in nursery school children, it is likely that a "halo" effect spuriously inflated the teachers' ratings.[7] Mann (1959) obtained ratings of 55 two-minute observations of 41 nursery school children in free play on six kinds of dependency behavior. He found only 1 of 15 intercorrelations among components of dependency significant. Likewise, observations of nursery school children revealed that the frequencies of "affection seeking" and "approval seeking" were unrelated (Heathers, 1953).

Sears (1963) extensively studied the intercorrelations between five categories of dependency behavior in preschool girls and boys. The five categories were: *negative attention seeking*, e.g., attention getting by disruption or aggressive activity; *positive attention seeking*, as in seeking praise; nonaggressive *touching or holding*; *being near*, e.g., following a child or teacher; and *seeking reassurance*. The frequency of these behaviors was carefully and reliably scored by observing the children at nursery school with an extensive time-sampling procedure. Each child was observed in free play for a total of 7 to 10 hours. The intercorrelations among the five dependency categories for 21 boys and 19 girls are shown in Table 2. Note that only 1 of the 20 correlations reached statistical significance since for 20 degrees of freedom correlations of .423 and .537 would have been needed to reach significance at the .05 and .01 levels respectively.[8]

* * *

Some support for sex differences in the generality of particular patterns of sex-typed behaviors comes in the form of more (and stronger) intercorrelations for girls than boys on five observation measures of dependency (Sears, 1963), whereas the reverse holds for aggression, with more intercorrelations among aggression variables for boys than for girls (Lansky, Crandall, Kagan, & Baker, 1961; Sears, 1961). However, individuals discriminate sharply between situations. The specificity of aggres-

---

[7]A "halo effect" occurs when a rater's global positive or negative evaluation of a target person affects all of her or his ratings.

[8]The .05 and .01 significance levels are conventional criteria by which findings are judged not to have occurred merely by chance.

TABLE 2

INTERCORRELATIONS AMONG DEPENDENCY MEASURES[a]

Measures		I	II	III	IV	V
Negative attention	I		.06	.10	.15	.37
Reassurance	II	.24		.25	.19	.26
Positive attention	III	.23	.11		.11	.03
Touching and holding	IV	.01	.11	.16		.71
Being near	V	.03	.12	.14	.13	

(Adapted from Sears, 1963, p. 35.)
[a]Girls above diagonal, boys below.

sive behavior, for example, is documented in a study of highly aggressive boys by Bandura (1960). Parents who punished aggression in the home, but who simultaneously modeled aggressive behavior and encouraged it in their sons' peer relationships, produced boys who were nonaggressive at home but markedly aggressive at school.

RIGIDITY AND TOLERANCE FOR AMBIGUITY If individuals did develop strongly consistent character structures that channelized them in stable ways, it would be important to identify these syndromes. One of the most thoroughly studied personality patterns is the "authoritarian personality." Intolerance for ambiguity attracted considerable interest as a characteristic of the authoritarian personality (Adorno, Frenkel-Brunswik, Levinson, & Sanford, 1950), and a voluminous literature was devoted to elaborating its correlates.

Several behavioral signs have been used as the referents for intolerance for ambiguity. These signs include resistance to reversal of apparent fluctuating stimuli, early selection and adherence to one solution in perceptually ambiguous situations, seeking for certainty, rigid dichotomizing into fixed categories, premature closure, and the like. In one study, an extensive battery of tests to measure intolerance of ambiguity was designed and administered (Kenny & Ginsberg, 1958). Only 7 of the 66 correlations among intolerance of ambiguity measures reached significance and the relationship for 2 of these was opposite to the predicted direc-

tion. Moreover, the measures in the main failed to correlate with the usual questionnaire indices of authoritarianism submissiveness as elicited by a form of the California F scale.

Closely related to authoritarianism, "rigidity" is another personality dimension that has received much attention as a generalized trait (Chown, 1959; Cronbach, 1956). In one study (Applezweig, 1954), among 45 correlations between behaviors on six measures of rigidity (including arithmetic problems, Rorschach,[9] and F scale), 22 were negative, 21 were positive, and 2 were zero; only 3 of the 45 correlations were significant and 2 of these were negative. Likewise, Pervin's (1960) data on five noninventory performance measures of rigidity, including the water-jars problems, provide generally low associations and suggest that "individuals may be rigid in one area of personality functioning and not in another" and that "rigidity is not a general personality characteristic" (p. 394). The conclusion that rigidity is not a unitary trait is also supported by the modest intercorrelations between measures obtained by Wrightsman and Baumeister (1961) and by the specificity found earlier by Maher (1957).

* * *

Thus investigators frequently measure and describe a purportedly general dimension of behavior only to discover later that it has dubious

---

[9]The Rorschach is the famous projective test in which subjects are asked what they see in blots of ink.

consistency. As a result the popular dimensions of personality research often wax and wane almost like fashions. Research on the generality of the behavioral indices of personality dimensions has generated its own truisms. Over and over again the conclusions of these investigations, regardless of the specific content area, are virtually identical and predictable. The following paragraph, from Applezweig's (1954) own summary, is essentially interchangeable with those from a plethora of later researches on the generality of many different traits:

> The following conclusions appear to be justified:
> (a) There is no general factor of rigidity among a number of so-called measures of rigidity; the inter-relationships of these measures appear to vary with the nature of the tests employed and the conditions of test administration as well as behavioral determinants within S's.[10]
> (b) Scores obtained by an individual on any so-called measure of rigidity appear to be a function not only of the individual, but also of the nature of the test and the conditions of test administration. (Applezweig, 1954, p. 228)

* * *

CONDITIONABILITY Classical learning formulations place great emphasis on conditioning as a basic process in learning. Consequently psychologists with an interest in both learning and individual differences have been especially interested in studying conditionability as a personality dimension. In spite of a great deal of research, however, there is no evidence for the existence of a general factor or trait of "conditionability" in either classical or operant conditioning paradigms.

Correlations among different measures and types of conditioning tend to be low or zero (e.g., Bunt & Barendregt, 1961; Campbell, 1938; Davidson, Payne, & Sloane, 1964; Eysenck, 1965; Franks, 1956; Lovibond, 1964; Moore & Marcuse, 1945; Patterson & Hinsey, 1964). Moore and Marcuse (1945) noted many years ago that "the concept of good or poor conditioners must always be with reference to a specific response." Reviewing the literature two decades later, Eysenck (1965) points out that correlations between conditionability measures depend on specific peripheral factors (sweat glands in the hand, pain sensitivity of the cornea). He also notes that even if these sources were eliminated correlations would still be affected by situational circumstances such as the sequence and massing of stimuli, the scheduling of reinforcement, the strength of CS and UCS,[11] temporal intervals, and so on.

The evidence that learning variables like conditionability are unitary traitlike entities is no more convincing than the data for the consistency of personality traits couched in any other theoretical language. Whenever individual differences are elicited, however, the failure to demonstrate impressive reliability does not preclude the existence of extensive correlations with other response measures (e.g., Franks, 1961).

MODERATOR VARIABLES Wallach (1962) and Kogan and Wallach (1964) have called attention to the fact that "moderator variables" may influence the correlations found in research on behavioral consistency. By moderator variables Wallach and Kogan mean interactions among several variables that influence the correlations obtained between any one of the variables and other data. For example, correlations between two response patterns may be found for males, but not for females, or may even be positive for one sex but negative for the other. Thus, if the correlations between two response patterns are examined for both sexes combined, the different relations that might be obtained if each sex were taken into account separately could become obscured. Similarly, relations between two measures might be positive for children with high IQ but negative for those with low IQ. In other words, there are complex interactions

---

[10]The abbreviation S's refers to subjects (now usually called "participants").

[11]The abbreviation CS means conditioned stimulus; UCS means unconditioned stimulus. In learning experiments, the stimuli employed, of either type, may vary in intensity or strength.

so that the relations between any two variables depend on several other variables.

By analyzing their data to illuminate higher-order interactions of this kind, these investigators have been able to demonstrate significant associations among various measures of risk taking, and between risk taking and other variables. The resulting associations of course apply only to some subjects under a few conditions. This strategy of searching for interactions holds some promise. Since the interactions are obtained post hoc rather than predicted, however, considerable interpretative caution must be observed. Otherwise the analysis of the same data for many interactions provides many additional chances to obtain seemingly statistically significant results that actually monopolize on chance. That is, more "significant" associations occur by chance when more correlations are computed.

TEMPORAL STABILITY   So far, our discussion of consistency has focused on relationships among a person's behaviors across situations sampled more or less at the same time. Equally important, however, are data that examine how stable the individual's behavior remains in any one particular domain when he is reassessed at later times.

Results from the Fels Longitudinal Study give some typical examples of the stability of a person's behavior patterns over time (Kagan & Moss, 1962). The overall findings suggest some significant consistency between childhood and early adulthood ratings of achievement behavior, sex-typed activity, and spontaneity for both sexes. For certain other variables, like dependency, some consistency was found for one sex but not the other. Thus the rated dependency of girls at age six years to ten years correlated .30 with their adult dependence on family; the comparable correlation for boys was near zero. In the same longitudinal study of middle-class subjects the most highly significant positive associations were found between ratings of achievement and recognition strivings obtained at various periods of childhood and in early adulthood (Kagan & Moss, 1962; Moss & Kagan, 1961). Children who were rated as showing strong desires

for recognition also tended to be rated as more concerned with excellence and with the attainment of high self-imposed standards when they were interviewed as young adults. Some of the many correlations between achievement strivings in childhood and comparable adult preoccupation with attaining excellence were exceptionally high, in several instances reaching the .60 to .70 range.

Apart from ratings the motive or need to achieve ("n Ach") has also been studied most extensively by scoring the subject's achievement imagery in the stories he tells to selected TAT cards. For example, if the person creates stories in which the hero is studying hard for a profession and aspires and strives to improve himself and to advance in his career, the story receives high n Ach scores. This technique, developed thoroughly by McClelland and his associates (1953), has become the main index of the motive to achieve and to compete against standards of excellence. As a result considerable attention has been devoted to studying the stability of this need by comparing n Ach scores obtained from the same individuals at different times. Moss and Kagan (1961) reported a stability coefficient of .31 for their sample over a 10-year period from adolescence to adulthood. They also reported a 3-year stability coefficient of .32 for TAT achievement themes obtained at ages 8 and 11 (Kagan & Moss, 1959). However, the correlation between n Ach at age 8 and at age 14 was only .22; the correlation between n Ach at age 11 and at 14 years was a nonsignificant .16.

The stability of achievement motivation was also studied closely for shorter time intervals with other samples of people. Birney (1959) reported a coefficient of only .29 for n Ach on equivalent picture forms administered to college students within six months. He concluded that ". . . the n Ach measure is highly situational in character . . ." (p. 267). Similarly, a significant but modest coefficient of .26 was reported for a 9-week test-retest study with college students (Krumboltz & Farquhar, 1957). Higher correlations ranging from .36 to .61 have been found for shorter time intervals of 3 weeks to 5 weeks (Haber & Alpert, 1958; Morgan, 1953). Reviewing a great deal of information from many studies, Skolnick (1966a, b) reported extensive correlations between diverse adolescent and adult measures. Many correlations reached significance, especially for achievement and power imagery indices, although the associations tended to be extremely complicated and most often of modest magnitude.

Just as with consistency across situations, stability over time tends to be greatest for behaviors associated with intelligence and cognitive processes (e.g., Bloom, 1964; Gardner & Long, 1960; Kagan & Moss, 1962; Moss & Kagan, 1961). Most notably, extremely impressive stability over long time periods has been found for certain cognitive styles. Retest correlations on Witkin's rod-and-frame test (RFT), for example, were as high as .92 for time intervals of a few years (Witkin, Goodenough, & Karp, 1967). A time lapse of 14 years was the lengthiest interval sampled in their longitudinal study. Even after such a long period, the stability correlation for boys tested with the RFT at age 10 and retested at age 24 was .66. Data of this kind demonstrate genuine durability in aspects of cognitive and perceptual functioning.

A representative illustration of temporal stability comes from studies of behavior during interviews. Reasonable stability has been demonstrated for certain interaction patterns during interviews. These patterns were measured by an interaction chronograph devised to record selected temporal aspects of verbal and gestural behavior (e.g., Matarazzo, 1965; Saslow, Matarazzo, Phillips, & Matarazzo, 1957). In these studies the interviewer followed a standardized pattern of behavior, including systematic periods of "not responding," "interrupting," and other variations in style. The subject's corresponding behavior was scored on formal dimensions such as the frequency of his actions, their average duration, and the length of his silences. The results indicated that these interactions are highly stable across short time periods (such as 1-week retests) when the interviewer's behavior remains fixed. The same interactions, however, were readily and predictably modifiable by planned changes in the interviewer's behavior.

The trait-descriptive categories and personality labels with which individuals describe themselves on questionnaires and trait-rating scales seem to be especially long lasting. E. L. Kelly (1955) compared questionnaire trait self-descriptions obtained almost 20 years apart. During the years 1935–1938 several personality questionnaires were administered to 300 engaged couples, and most of them were retested with the same measures in 1954. The questionnaires included the Strong Vocational Interest Blank, the Allport-Vernon values test, and the Bernreuter personality questionnaire, among others. Self-reports of attitudes about marriage were highly unstable ($r < .10$), but the stability coefficients for self-descriptions of interests, of economic and political values, of self-confidence and sociability were high. The coefficients for these areas of self-reported traits ranged from about .45 to slightly over .60, indicating impressive stability, considering the long temporal delay between assessments.

As another example, the test-retest correlations on the California Psychological Inventory scales for high school students retested after 1 year, and for a sample of prisoners retested after a lapse of 7 to 21 days, were also high (Gough, 1957). In general, trait self-descriptions on many personality questionnaires show considerable stability (Byrne, 1966). Studies of the semantic differential also suggest that the meanings associated with semantic concepts may be fairly stable (Osgood, Suci, & Tannenbaum, 1957).

Research on the temporal stability of personal constructs evoked by Kelly's Role Construct Repertory Test (Reptest) also indicates considerable consistency in constructs over time (Bonarius, 1965). For example, a retest correlation of .79 was found for constructs after a 2-week interval (Landfield, Stern, & Fjeld, 1961). * * * Thus the trait categories people attribute to themselves and others may be relatively permanent, and may be more enduring than the behaviors to which they refer.

Implications

The data on cross-situational consistency and stability over time reviewed in this chapter merely provide representative examples from an enormous domain. The results indicate that correlations across situations tend to be highest for cognitive and intellectual functions. Moreover, behaviors sampled in closely similar situations generally yield the best correlations. Considerable stability over time has been demonstrated for some domains, and again particularly for ability and cognitive measures. Self-descriptions on trait dimensions also seem to be especially consistent even over very long periods of time.

As early as 1928 Hartshorne and May surprised psychologists by showing that the honesty or moral behavior of children is not strongly consistent across situations and measures. The Hartshorne and May data were cited extensively but did not influence psychological theorizing about the generality of traits. Similar evidence for behavioral specificity across situations has been reported over and over again for personality measures since the earliest correlational studies at the turn of the century. Considerable specificity has been found regularly even for syndromes like attitudes toward authority, or aggression and dependency, whose assumed generality has reached the status of a cliché in psychological writings.

The interpretation of all data on behavioral consistency is affected of course by the criteria selected. Consistency coefficients averaging between .30 and .40, of the kind obtained by Hartshorne and May, can be taken either as evidence for the relative specificity of the particular behaviors or as support for the presence of underlying generality. Indeed, the Hartshorne and May data have been reinterpreted as evidence for generality in children's moral behavior, at least across related situations (Burton, 1963). Similarly, McGuire (1968) reviewed data on the consistency of suggestibility, persuasibility, and conformity and concluded that each has the status of a generalized, although "weak," trait. McGuire noted the tenuousness of the evidence, since the data consisted mostly of low but positive correlations which often reached the .05 statistical confidence level, sometimes did not, and which never

accounted for more than a trivial proportion of the variance.[12]

There is nothing magical about a correlation coefficient, and its interpretation depends on many considerations. The accuracy or reliability of measurement increases with the length of the test. Since no single item is a perfect measure, adding items increases the chance that the test will elicit a more accurate sample and yield a better estimate of the person's behavior. Second, a test may be reliable at one score level but unreliable at another. That is, the accuracy of the test is not necessarily uniform for different groups of people; a test that yields reliable achievement scores for 10-year-old children may be so difficult for 7-year-olds that they are reduced to guessing on almost all items. Moreover, different items within the same test do not necessarily yield uniformly reliable information (Cronbach, 1960). The interpretation of reliability coefficients is influenced by the relative homogeneity or heterogeneity in the tested behavior range of the sample of subjects. For example, if an ability test is given to a more or less uniformly bright group of college students, very slight errors in measurement could obscure actual individual differences. Any one set of observations provides merely a sample of behavior whose meaning may be confounded by numerous errors of measurement.

These and similar statistical considerations (Cronbach, 1960) caution us to interpret the meaning of particular coefficients with care. In spite of methodological reservations, however, it is evident that the behaviors which are often construed as stable personality trait indicators actually are highly specific and depend on the details of the

---

[12]Mischel is here following the common practice of squaring a correlation to yield the percent of variance "explained" (see the selection by Rosenthal and Rubin in Part I). Thus a correlation of .30 is said to explain 9% of the variance (.30 squared being .09) and a correlation of .40 is said to explain 16% of the variance (.40 squared being .16). Mischel regards these percentages as "trivial." But recall that Rosenthal and Rubin (Part I) demonstrated that a correlation of .32 yields correct classification twice as often as incorrect classification.

evoking situations and the response mode employed to measure them.

* * *

It is important to distinguish clearly between "statistically significant" associations and equivalence. A correlation of .30 easily reaches statistical significance when the sample of subjects is sufficiently large, and suggests an association that is highly unlikely on the basis of chance. However, the same coefficient accounts for less than 10 percent of the relevant variance. Statistically significant relationships of this magnitude are sufficient to justify personality research on individual and group differences. It is equally plain that their value for making statements about an individual is severely limited. Even when statistically significant behavioral consistencies are found, and even when they replicate reliably, the relationships usually are not large enough to warrant individual assessment and treatment decisions except for certain screening and selection purposes.

It is very easy to misunderstand the meaning of the findings on behavioral consistency and specificity surveyed in this chapter. It would be a complete misinterpretation, for instance, to conclude that individual differences are unimportant.[13] To remind oneself of their pervasive role one need merely observe the differences among people's responses to almost any complex social stimulus under most supposedly uniform laboratory conditions. The real questions are not the existence of differences among individuals but rather their nature, their causes and consequences, and the utility of inferring them for particular purposes and by particular techniques.

Consistency coefficients of the kind reviewed in this chapter are only one of several types of data pertinent to an appropriate evaluation of the empirical status of the main trait and state approaches to personality. It would be premature therefore to attempt to draw conclusions at this point. Sophisticated dispositional personality theories increasingly have come to recognize that behavior tends to change with alterations in the situations in which it occurs. They note, however, that the same basic underlying disposition (or "genotype") may manifest itself behaviorally in diverse ways in different situations so that heterogeneous behaviors can be signs of the same underlying trait or state. According to this argument, the dependent person, for example, need not behave dependently in all situations; indeed his basic dependency may show itself in diverse and seemingly contradictory overt forms. Although fundamentally dependent, he may, for instance, try to appear aggressively independent under some circumstances, and even may become belligerent and hostile in other settings in efforts to deny his dependency. Similarly, and in accord with psychodynamic theorizing, seemingly diverse acts may be in the service of the same underlying motivational force. For example, a person's overtly liberal political behavior and his overt social conservativism, although apparently inconsistent, may actually both be understandable as expressions of a more fundamental motive, such as his desire to please and win approval and recognition. These arguments for basic consistencies that underlie surface diversity are theoretically defensible, but they ultimately depend, of course, on supporting empirical evidence.

* * *

References

Adorno, I. W., Frenkel-Brunswik, Else, Levinson, D. J., & Sanford, R. N. (1950). *The authoritarian personality*. New York: Harper.

Allinsmith, W. (1960). The learning of moral standards. In D. R. Miller & G. E. Swanson (Eds.), *Inner conflict and defense* (pp. 141–176). New York: Holt.

Applezweig, Dee G. (1954). Some determinants of behavioral rigidity. *Journal of Abnormal and Social Psychology, 49,* 224–228.

Aronfreed, J. (1961). The nature, variety, and social patterning of moral responses to transgression. *Journal of Abnormal and Social Psychology, 63,* 223–240.

Aronfreed, J. (1964). The origin of self-criticism. *Psychological Review, 71,* 193–218.

Aronfreed, J., & Reber, A. (1965). Internalized behavioral suppression and the timing of social punishment. *Journal of Personality and Social Psychology, 1,* 3–16.

---

[13]Despite this disclaimer, the book from which this excerpt is drawn *was* widely interpreted as arguing—even proving—that stable individual differences in personality are unimportant.

Bandura, A. (1960). Relationship of family patterns to child behavior disorders. Progress Report, U.S.P.H. Research Grant M-1734, Stanford University.

Becker, W. C. (1964). Consequences of different kinds of parental discipline. In M. L. Hoffman & Lois W. Hoffman (Eds.), *Review of child development research* (Vol. 1, pp. 169–208). New York: Russell Sage Foundation.

Beller, E. K. (1955). Dependency and independence in young children. *Journal of Genetic Psychology, 87,* 25–35.

Birney, R. C. (1959). The reliability of the achievement motive. *Journal of Abnormal and Social Psychology, 58,* 266–267.

Bloom, R. S. (1964). *Stability and change in human characteristics.* New York: Wiley.

Bonarius, J. C. J. (1965). Research in the personal construct theory of George A. Kelly: Role Construct Repertory Test and basic theory. In B. A. Maher (Ed.), *Progress in experimental personality research* (Vol. 2, pp. 1–46). New York: Academic Press.

Bunt, A. van de, & Barendregt, J. T. (1961). Inter-correlations of three measures of conditioning. In J. T. Barendregt (Ed.), *Research in psychodiagnostics.* The Hague: Mouton.

Burton, R. V. (1963). Generality of honesty reconsidered. *Psychological Review, 70,* 481–499.

Burwen, L. S., & Campbell, D. T. (1957). The generality of attitudes toward authority and nonauthority figures. *Journal of Abnormal and Social Psychology, 54,* 24–31.

Byrne, D. (1966). *An introduction to personality.* Englewood Cliffs, N. J.: Prentice-Hall.

Campbell, A. A. (1938). The interrelations of two measures of conditioning in man. *Journal of Experimental Psychology, 22,* 225–243.

Campbell, D. T. (1960). Recommendations for APA test standards regarding construct, trait, or discriminant validity. *American Psychologist, 15,* 546–553.

Campbell, D., & Fiske, D. (1959). Convergent and discriminant validation by the multitrait-multimethod matrix. *Psychological Bulletin, 56,* 81–105.

Chown, Sheila M. (1959). Rigidity—A flexible concept. *Psychological Bulletin, 56,* 195–223.

Cronbach, L. J. (1956). Assessment of individual differences. *Annual Review of Psychology, 7,* 173–196.

Cronbach, L. J. (1960). *Essentials of psychological testing* (2nd ed.) New York: Harper.

Davidson, P. O., Payne, R. W., & Sloane, R. B. (1964). Introversion, neuroticism, and conditioning. *Journal of Abnormal and Social Psychology, 68,* 136–148.

Eysenck, II. J. (1965). Extraversion and the acquisition of eyeblink and GSR conditioned responses. *Psychological Bulletin, 63,* 258–270.

Franks, C. M. (1956). Conditioning and personality: A study of normal and neurotic subjects. *Journal of Abnormal and Social Psychology, 52,* 143–150.

Franks, C. M. (1961). Conditioning and abnormal behaviour. In H. J. Eysenck (Ed.), *Handbook of abnormal psychology* (pp. 457–487). New York: Basic Books.

Gardner, R. W., & Long, R. I. (1960). The stability of cognitive controls. *Journal of Abnormal Social Psychology, 61,* 485–487.

Gough, H. G. (1957). *Manual for the California Psychological Inventory.* Palo Alto, Calif: Consulting Psychologists Press.

Grinder, R. E. (1962). Parental childrearing practices, conscience, and resistance to temptation of sixth-grade children. *Child Development, 33,* 803–820.

Haber, R. N., & Alpert, R. (1958). The role of situation and picture cues in projective measurement of the achievement motive. In J. W. Atkinson (Ed.), *Motives in fantasy, action, and society* (pp. 644–663). Princeton: Van Nostrand.

Hartshorne, H., & May, M. A. (1928). *Studies in the nature of character.* Vol. I., *Studies in deceit.* New York: Macmillan.

Hartshorne, H., May, M. A., & Shuttleworth, F. K. (1930). *Studies in the nature of character.* Vol. 3, *Studies in the organization of character.* New York: Macmillan.

Heathers, G. (1953). Emotional dependence and independence in a physical threat situation. *Child Development, 24,* 169–179.

Hoffman, M. L. (1963). Child rearing practices and moral development: Generalizations from empirical research. *Child Development, 34,* 295–318.

Kagan, J., & Moss, H. A. (1959). Stability and validity of achievement fantasy. *Journal of Abnormal and Social Psychology, 58,* 357–364.

Kagan, J., & Moss, H. A. (1962). *Birth to maturity: A study in psychological development.* New York: Wiley.

Kelly, E. L. (1955). Consistency of the adult personality. *American Psychologist, 10,* 659–681.

Kenny, D. T., & Ginsberg, Rose. (1958). The specificity of intolerance of ambiguity measures. *Journal of Abnormal and Social Psychology, 56,* 300–304.

Kogan, N., & Wallach, M. A. (1964). *Risk taking: A study in cognition and personality.* New York: Holt, Rinehart & Winston.

Kohlberg, L. (1963). The development of children's orientations toward a moral order: I. Sequence in the development of moral thought. *Vita Humana, 6,* 11–33.

Kohlberg, L. (1966). A cognitive-developmental analysis of children's sex-role concepts and attitudes. In Eleanor E. Maccoby (Ed.), *The development of sex differences* (pp. 25–55). Stanford: Stanford University Press.

Krumboltz, J. D., & Farquhar, W. W. (1957). Reliability and validity of the *n*-Achievement test. *Journal of Consulting Psychology, 21,* 226–228.

Landfield, A. W., Stern, M., & Fjeld, S. (1961). Social conceptual processes and change in students undergoing psychotherapy. *Psychological Reports, 8,* 63–68.

Lansky, L. M., Crandall, V. J., Kagan, J., & Baker, C. T. (1961). Sex differences in aggression and its correlates in middle-class adolescents. *Child Development, 32,* 45–58.

Lovibond, S. H. (1964). Personality and conditioning. In B. A. Maher (Ed.), *Progress in experimental personality research* (pp. 115–168). Vol. 1. New York: Academic Press.

MacKinnon, D. W. (1938). Violation of prohibitions. In H. A. Murray, *Explorations in personality* (pp. 491–501). New York: Oxford University Press.

Maher, B. A. (1957). Personality, problem solving, and the Einstellung effect. *Journal of Abnormal and Social Psychology, 54,* 70–74.

Mann, R. D. (1959). A review of the relationships between personality and performance in small groups. *Psychological Bulletin, 56,* 241–270.

Matarazzo, J. D. (1965). The interview. In B. B. Wolman (Ed.), *Handbook of clinical psychology* (pp. 403–450). New York: McGraw-Hill.

McClelland, D. C., Atkinson, J. W., Clark, R. A., & Lowell, E. I. (1953). *The achievement motive.* New York: Appleton-Century-Crofts.

McGuire, W. J. (1968). Personality and susceptibility to social influence. In E. F. Borgatta & W. W. Lambert (Eds.), *Handbook of personality theory and research* (pp. 1130–1187). Chicago: Rand McNally.

Mischel, W. (1962). Delay of gratification in choice situations. NIMH Progress Report, Stanford University.

Mischel, W., & Gilligan, C. (1964). Delay of gratification, motivation for the prohibited gratification, and responds to temptation. *Journal of Abnormal and Social Psychology, 69*, 411–417.

Moore, A. U., & Marcuse, F. I. (1945). Salivary, cardiac and motor indices of conditioning in two sows. *Journal of Comparative Psychology, 38*, 1–16.

Morgan, H. H. (1953). Measuring achievement motivation with "picture interpretations." *Journal of Consulting Psychology, 17*, 289–292.

Moss, H. A., & Kagan, J. (1961). Stability of achievement and recognition seeking behaviors from early childhood through adulthood. *Journal of Abnormal and Social Psychology, 62*, 504–518.

Osgood, C. E., Suci, G. J., & Tannenbaum, P. H. (1957). *The measurement of meaning.* Urbana: University of Illinois Press.

Patterson, G. R., & Hinsey, W. C. (1964). Investigations of some assumptions and characteristics of a procedure for instrumental conditioning in children. *Journal of Experimental Child Psychology, 1*, 111–122.

Pervin, L. A. (1960). Rigidity in neurosis and general personality functioning. *Journal of Abnormal and Social Psychology, 61*, 389–395.

Piaget, J. (1951). *Play, dreams, and imitation in childhood.* New York: Norton.

Sanford, N. (1963). Personality: Its place in psychology. In S. Koch (Ed.), *Psychology: A study of a science.* Vol. 5 (pp. 488–592). New York: McGraw-Hill.

Saslow, G., Matarazzo, J. D., Phillips, Jeanne S., & Matarazzo, Ruth C. (1957). Test-retest stability of interaction patterns during interviews conducted one week apart. *Journal of Abnormal and Social Psychology, 54*, 295–802.

Sears, R. R. (1961). Relation of early socialization experiences to aggression in middle childhood. *Journal of Abnormal and Social Psychology, 63*, 466–492.

Sears, R. R. (1963). Dependency motivation. In M. R. Jones (Ed.), *Nebraska symposium on motivation* (pp. 25–64). Lincoln: University of Nebraska Press.

Sears, R. R., Maccoby, Eleanor E., & Levin, H. (1957). *Patterns of child rearing.* Evanston, IL: Row, Peterson.

Sears, R. R., Rau, Lucy, & Alpert, R. (1965). *Identification and child rearing.* Stanford, CA: Stanford University Press.

Skolnick, Arlene. (1966a). Motivational imagery and behavior over twenty years. *Journal of Consulting Psychology, 30*, 463–478.

Skolnick, Arlene. (1966b). Stability and interrelations of thematic test imagery over 20 years. *Child Development, 37*, 389–396.

Wallach, M. A. (1962). Commentary: Active-analytical vs. passive-global cognitive functioning. In S. Messick & J. Ross (Eds.), *Measurement in personality and cognition* (pp. 199–215). New York: Wiley.

Whiting, J. W. M. (1959). Sorcery, sin, and the superego. A cross-cultural study of some mechanisms of social control. In M. R. Jones (Ed.), *Nebraska symposium on motivation* (pp. 174–195). Lincoln: University of Nebraska Press.

Witkin, H. A., Goodenough, D. R., & Karp, S. A. (1967). Stability of cognitive style from childhood to young adulthood. *Journal of Personality and Social Psychology, 7*, 291–300.

Wrightsman, L. S., Jr., & Baumeister, A. A. (1961). A comparison of actual and paper-and-pencil versions of the Water Jar Test of Rigidity. *Journal of Abnormal and Social Psychology, 63*, 191–198.

Profiting from Controversy: Lessons from the Person-Situation Debate

Douglas T. Kenrick and David C. Funder

When Mischel proposed that personality traits are not important, this proposal immediately ran counter to the fact that nearly everybody thinks that they are. Personality traits are not only an important topic of psychological research, but obviously a major part of the way we think and talk about people in daily life. Mischel's response to this paradox was a further proposal: that our perceptions of personality traits in ourselves and each other are cognitive illusions. This position was bolstered by the development of research in social psychology describing many errors that people make in their judgments of each other. Indeed, the tendency to see personality traits as affecting behaviors that are really due to the situation became dubbed the "fundamental attribution error" (Ross, 1977).

The following article, by the social-personality psychologist Douglas Kenrick and one of the editors of this reader, was intended to sum up the person-situation debate by directly addressing this question: Are personality traits merely illusions? The article is structured by considering seven hypotheses that range from the most to the least pessimistic about the existence and importance of personality traits. Traits are not just illusions in the eye of the beholder, Kenrick and Funder conclude, nor is their appearance the mere by-product of processes—such as discussion among peers about what somebody is like—that may have nothing to do with the personality of the person who is being described. Rather, the accumulated evidence supports the conclusion that traits are real and have a major influence on what people do.

Kenrick and Funder conclude—contrary to the opinion of some—that the person-situation controversy was good for personality psychology. It forced the reconsideration of some of the basic premises of the field in the light of new evidence and illuminated a number of ways in which the influence of personality can and cannot be validly demonstrated. For example, personality judgments of traits that are visible (such as "talkative") are more likely to be accurate than judgments of traits that are hard to see (such as "tends to fantasize"), and judgments by people who know well the people they are judging are more likely to be valid than judgments by relative strangers. These points might seem obvious in retrospect but,

Kenrick and Funder point out, it took the field of personality a surprisingly long time to realize how important they are.

Notice that this article originally appeared in 1988, exactly 20 years after the publication of Mischel's influential book. The article attempted not just to sum up the lessons learned from the person-situation controversy, but also to declare the war over. In the years since 1988, the field of personality largely has turned its attention to other issues.

From *American Psychologist, 43*, 23–34, 1988.

* * *

Whether we are acting as professional psychologists, as academic psychologists, or simply as lay psychologists engaging in everyday gossip, the assumption that people have "traits" (or enduring cross-situational consistencies in their behavior) provides a basis for many of our decisions. When a clinical or counseling psychologist uses a standard assessment battery, he or she assumes that there is some degree of traitlike consistency in pathological behavior to be measured. When an organizational psychologist designs a personnel selection procedure, he or she assumes that consistent individual differences between the applicants are there to be found. When an academic psychologist teaches a course in personality, he or she must either assume some consistency in behavior or else face a bit of existential absurdity for at least 3 hours a week. Likewise, a good portion of our courses on clinical and developmental psychology would be unimaginable unless we assumed some cross-situational consistency. Even in everyday lay psychology, our attempts to analyze the behaviors of our friends, relatives, and co-workers are riddled with assumptions about personality traits.

Despite the wide appeal of the trait assumption, personality psychologists have been entangled for some time in a debate about whether it might be based more on illusion than reality (e.g., Alker, 1972; Allport, 1966; Argyle & Little, 1972; Bem, 1972; Block, 1968, 1977; Bowers, 1973; Epstein, 1977, 1979, 1980; Fiske, 1974; Gormly &

Edelberg, 1974; Hogan, DeSoto, & Solano, 1977; Hunt, 1965; Magnusson & Endler, 1977; Mischel, 1968, 1983; West, 1983). Murmurs of the current debate could be heard more than 40 years ago (Ichheisser, 1943), but the volume increased markedly after Mischel's (1968) critique, and things have not quieted down yet (Bem, 1983; Epstein, 1983; Funder, 1983; Kenrick, 1986; Mischel, 1983; Mischel & Peake, 1982, 1983). Of late, discussants have begun to express yearning to end what some see as an endless cycle of repeating the same arguments. Mischel and Peake (1982) and Bem (1983), for instance, both use the term *déjà vu* in the titles of recent contributions, suggesting that they feel as if they have been here before. Other commentators maintain that the debate has been a "pseudo-controversy" (Carlson, 1984; Endler, 1973) that never should have occurred in the first place.

However fatiguing it may now seem to some of its erstwhile protagonists, the debate over the alleged inconsistency of personality has been more than an exercise in sophistry. In the course of the nearly two decades since Mischel's (1968) critique, a number of provocative hypotheses have been put forward, along with a host of studies to evaluate them. Platt (1964) and Popper (1959), among others, maintained that science typically progresses through the accumulation of negative information—that is, by eliminating hypotheses that data suggest are no longer tenable. From this perspective, it may be worth taking a look back at the hypotheses suggested during the consistency controversy, this time in the improved light shed by two decades of research. In this light, the debate can be seen as an intellectually stimulating chapter in the history of the discipline, replete with useful lessons for professionals who include assessment in their repertoire.

The "Pure Trait" Model and Its Alternatives

Discussions of the "person versus situation" debate traditionally begin with the "pure trait" model (Alston, 1975; Argyle & Little, 1972; Mischel, 1968): that people show powerful, unmodulated consistencies in their behavior across time and diverse situations. This position has been attacked frequently over the years. However, it is really just a "straw man," and even traditional personality researchers find it unacceptable (see, e.g., Allport, 1931, 1966; Block, 1977; Hogan et al., 1977; Jackson, 1983; Wiggins, 1973; Zuroff, 1986). Complete invariance in behavior is associated more with severe psychopathology than with "normal" behavior.

If the consensus rejects the "pure trait" position, then what can replace it? Several alternative hypotheses have been advanced over the years. These hypotheses differ with regard to four issues, which can be arranged into a logical hierarchy:

1. Consensus versus solipsism. Are traits merely idiosyncratic constructs that reside solely inside the heads of individual observers, or can observers reach agreement in applying trait terms?

2. Discriminativeness versus generality. If observers can agree with one another in ascribing traits to targets, is it simply because they apply a nondiscriminative "one size fits all" approach?

3. Behavior versus labeling. If observers can agree with one another, and can also differentiate between who is low or high on a given trait, does this occur because they really observe behavior? Or do they merely provide their judgments based on superficial stereotypes, targets' self-presentations, or other socially assigned labels?

4. Internal versus external locus of causal explanation. If observers can agree with one another and can distinguish individual differences on the basis of *actual behavior* of the people they are observing, are the causes of these consistencies located within each person or within his or her situation and role?

Each of these issues depends on the resolution of those earlier in the list. For instance, if observers cannot agree with one another about who has which traits, there is no point in going on to debate whether traits have a behavioral basis. Ultimately, assumptions about traits must pass the tests of consensus, discriminativeness, behavioral foundation, and internality. We will discuss seven hypotheses that assume that traits fail one or more of these tests. In Table 1, we list the hypotheses in terms of the four hierarchical issues just discussed. As can be seen, the hypotheses can be arranged more or less in order of their pessimism regarding the existence of (consensually verifiable, discriminative, internal) traitlike consistencies.

We will consider each hypothesis in its purest form and, for the moment, disregard the various qualifications that have sometimes been attached to each. Placing each hypothesis in bold relief allows us to assess it most clearly, and philosophers of science tell us that we learn most when hypotheses are stated in such a way as to allow disproof (e.g., Platt, 1964; Popper, 1959). Moreover, each of these hypotheses has, at some time, actually been stated in its bold form. In 1968, for instance, one social psychologist argued that

> the prevalent view that the normal behavior of individuals tends toward consistency is misconceived [and the research evidence] . . . strongly suggests that consistency, either in thought or action, does not constitute the normal state of affairs. (Gergen, 1968, pp. 305–306)

In the same year, a behavioral psychologist stated that "I, for one, look forward to the day when personality theories are regarded as historical curiosities" (Farber, 1964, p. 37).

Such extreme pessimism was clearly unwarranted. The data available now, more than two

TABLE 1

HIERARCHY OF HYPOTHESES FROM THE PERSON-SITUATION CONTROVERSY, ARRANGED FROM MOST TO LEAST PESSIMISTIC

Critical assumptions	Hypotheses
Solipsism over consensus	1. Personality is in the eye of the beholder.
Consensus without discrimination	2. Agreement between raters is an artifact of the semantic structure of the language used to describe personality. 3. Agreement is an artifact of base-rate accuracy (rater's tendency to make similar guesses about what people in general are like).
Discriminative consensus without behavioral referents	4. Differential agreement is an artifact of the shared use of invalid stereotypes. 5. Observers are in cahoots with one another; that is, their agreement results from discussion rather than accurate observation.
Differential agreement about behavior without internal traits	6. Raters see targets only within a limited range of settings and mistake situational effects for traits. 7. Compared with situational pressures, cross-situational consistencies in behavior are too weak to be important.

decades later, argue strongly against all seven of the hypotheses in Table 1. However, it would be a mistake to presume, as some personologists seem to do, that the issues raised by the "situationists" were merely diversions from the true path that can now be safely disregarded. We have learned, in the course of the debate, about a number of sources of distortion in trait judgments. These not only are of interest in their own right but are useful to personality assessment professionals, whose main goal may be to eliminate as much clutter from their path as possible.

HYPOTHESIS 1: PERSONALITY IS IN THE EYE OF THE BEHOLDER The first and most pessimistic hypothesis that must be considered is that our perceptions of personality traits in our friends, acquaintances, and selves might be largely or exclusively by-products of the limitations and flaws of human information processing. Although no personality researcher has ever advocated that personality exists solely in the head and not in the external world, social psychologists such as Gergen (1968) and behavioral analysts such as Farber (1964) have done so. Moreover, the issue lies in the logical path of any further inquiries into the origin of trait attributions.

Social psychologists have often emphasized how personality impressions can arise in the absence of supporting evidence in the real world:

Unwitting evidence provided by countless personality psychologists shows how objectively low or nonexistent covariations (between personality and behavior) can be parlayed into massive perceived covariations through a priori theories and assumptions. (Nisbett & Ross, 1980, p. 109)

The personality theorists' (and the layperson's) conviction that there are strong cross-situational consistencies in behavior may be seen as merely another instance of theory-driven covariation assessments operating in the face of contrary evidence. (Nisbett & Ross, 1980, p. 112)

Research relevant to the "eye of the beholder" hypothesis has mainly consisted of (a) demonstrations of various "errors" in the way that people process social information, or (b) claims that different judges rating the same personality rarely agree with each other or with the person being rated.

The demonstrations of error (for reviews, see Nisbett & Ross, 1980; Ross, 1977) establish that information given to subjects in laboratory settings is frequently distorted. People tend to jump to conclusions, biasing their judgments and their memories on the basis of their "implicit personality theories" (Schneider, 1973) or "scripts" (Abelson, 1976; Schank & Abelson, 1977). Studies of these attributional errors clearly demonstrate that people have biased expectations and that they routinely go beyond the information they are given.

However, for two reasons such studies do not establish that personality resides solely in the eye of the beholder. First, some of the errors are more a product of the unusual experimental situation than of a fundamentally biased cognitive process (cf. Block, Weiss, & Thorne, 1979; Trope, Bassok, & Alon, 1984). More important, the existence of judgmental biases does not necessarily imply the existence of mistakes. The expectations and biases demonstrated in laboratory tasks are, in principle, liable to lead to correct judgments in the real world (Funder, 1987). Many demonstrations of this principle can be found in the field of visual perception, where a useful rule of thumb underlies every "optical illusion" (Gregory, 1971). The "Ponzo" or "railroad lines" illusion, for example, produces errors in the lab but correct judgments when applied to three-dimensional reality. In the field of

social perception, even the "fundamental attribution error" will lead to correct judgments to the extent that real people actually are somewhat consistent in their behavior. In short, demonstrations of laboratory errors are not informative, one way or the other, as to whether the associated judgmental biases lead mostly to mistakes or correct judgments in real life (see also McArthur & Baron, 1983).

A different line of support for the "eye of the beholder" hypothesis has been the belief that people generally do not agree with each other in their judgments of the same personality. For example, Dornbusch, Hastorf, Richardson, Muzzy, and Vreeland (1965) found that the constructs children in a summer camp used to describe personality were more a function of the person doing the ratings than they were of the person being rated. Such studies do show that people have individually preferred constructs for thinking about others. But these judgmental idiosyncrasies must be interpreted in the light of frequent findings that (a) when raters and ratees get a chance to know one another, their ratings come to agree with each other more (Funder & Colvin, 1987; Norman & Goldberg, 1966), and (b) when common rating categories are imposed on raters, their judgments will show substantial agreement in orderings of individual targets (e.g., Amelang & Borkenau, 1986; Bem & Allen, 1974; Cheek, 1982; Funder, 1987; Funder & Dobroth, 1987; Kenrick & Braver, 1982; Koretzky, Kohn, & Jeger, 1978; McCrae, 1982; Mischel & Peake, 1982).

Table 2 demonstrates some fairly typical findings in the area. In each of these studies, adult targets rated their own personalities and were also rated by more than one person who knew them well (parents, spouses, housemates, or friends). Correlations represent agreement about the same person by different raters who filled out the scales independently. Studies on the left side of the table used single-item scales (Funder & Dobroth, 1987; Kenrick & Stringfield, 1980); Dantchik (1985) and Cheek (1982) used 5-item and 3-item scales, respectively; and the studies to the right used lengthier scales with better established psychometric

TABLE 2

INTERRATER CORRELATIONS FROM RECENT TRAIT STUDIES

| Trait | Kenrick & Stringfield (1980) | | Funder & Dobroth (1987) | Dantchik (1985) | | Cheek (1982) | | McCrae (1982) | Paunonen & Jackson (1985) | Mischel & Peake (1982) |
	(n = 71)	Obs[a] (n = 34)	(n = 69)	(n = 92)	Obs[a] (n = 36)	1/2/3[b] (n = 81)	Obs[a] (n = 40)	(n = 139)	(n = 90)	(n = 63)
Intellectance	.17	.04	.36	.40	.52		.36	.50	.53	
Likability	.35	.52	.41	.14	.14	.22/.33/.39	.49	.47	.57	
Self-control	.26	.26	.25	.19	.47	.27/.40/.47	.64	.48	.67	.52
Sociability	.40	.55	.34	.46	.53	.43/.53/.59	.46	.53	.74	
Adjustment	.23	.43	.23	.38	.40	.22/.25/.27		.58	.48	
Dominance	.35	.41	.40	.58	.61			.52	.60	
M	.29	.37	.34	.37	.45	.29/.38/.44	.50	.51	.59	.52
	(.53)[c]	(.67)		(.51)	(.64)					

Note. The trait labels used here are based on Hogan's (1982) terminology, and we have used roughly equivalent scales from studies that did not use those exact terms (denoting the major "factors" usually found in trait rating studies).
[a] Data from subjects who rated their behaviors on a given dimension as publicly observable (Obs).
[b] Data based on 1, 2, and 3 judges, respectively.
[c] Figures in parentheses are corrected for attenuation.

properties. It is clear that the use of reliable rating scales leads to high agreement regarding a target's personality, but even single-item scales can produce consistently positive (and statistically significant) levels of agreement.[1] * * *

A consideration of this first hypothesis has taught us something about when the eyes of different beholders will behold different characteristics in the persons at whom they are looking. For instance, when rating strangers, observers will be quite happy to make attributions about what the strangers are like but will show little consensus (Funder & Colvin, 1987; Monson, Keel, Stephens, & Genung, 1982; Passini & Norman, 1966). So, although strangers' ratings provide an excellent domain for the study of bias (Fiske & Taylor, 1984),

it is probably futile to expect them to manifest much validity. However, when observers are well acquainted with the person they are judging, they nevertheless do manage to see something on which they can agree. The findings of consensus (such as those in Table 2) are sufficient to rule out the radical hypothesis that personality resides solely in the eye of the beholder.

* * *

HYPOTHESIS 2: AGREEMENT IS DUE TO SEMANTIC GENERALIZATION The first hypothesis, in its radical form, considered traits to be idiosyncratic constructions of the individual perceiver. The second hypothesis concedes that there is consensus in the use of trait terms but views that agreement as due simply to shared delusions based on common linguistic usage. According to the semantic generalization hypothesis, as soon as one judgment about another person is made, many other judgments follow based on nothing more than implicit expectations about which words "go together." Anyone judged as "friendly" may also be judged as "empathic," "altruistic," and "sincere" because the

---

[1]Most rating scales consist of a total score computed across the ratings of several or more individual items. The more the ratings of these different items within a scale tend to agree with each other, the more reliable the total scale is. More-reliable scales tend to yield larger correlations with other variables. Single-item scales, by contrast, usually produce lower correlations.

concepts are semantically linked, even though the component behaviors themselves may not be so linked. For instance, "helping others in distress" and "contributing to charities" (behavioral components of "altruism") may not be correlated with "smiling a lot" and "talking to strangers" (behavioral components of "friendliness"), but judges who see evidence of "smiling a lot" might still infer "altruism," at least sometimes incorrectly. Shweder (1975) argued that shared preconceptions about "what goes with what" affected judgments so pervasively as to raise the question "How relevant is an individual differences theory of personality?" (See also D'Andrade, 1974.) Bourne (1977) went even further, suggesting that trait ratings might not reflect "anything more than raters' conceptual expectancies about which traits go together" (p. 863).

* * *

It is crucial to realize, as Block, Weiss, and Thorne (1979) pointed out, that semantic generalization cannot explain how different judges agree on attributing a *single* trait to a target person (as research such as that in Table 2 shows they do). To take a well-known example, the Passini and Norman (1966) study has been cited as evidence that trait ratings are based on "nothing more" than semantic similarity judgments. Indeed, Passini and Norman's data yielded a similar factor structure for ratings of friends and for ratings of strangers (who had been observed only briefly).[2] Because the strangers had very little time to observe one another, it is clear that an implicit personality theory guided their judgments. However, this issue of the relationships between trait words is completely orthogonal to the question of accuracy in application of any one of those words. Passini and Norman's subjects not only reached significant agreement about which trait applied to which per-

son but they also agreed more about friends' ratings than about strangers' (see also Funder & Colvin, 1987; Norman & Goldberg, 1966).

In light of such arguments, Shweder and D'Andrade (1979) seem to have reversed their earlier claim that semantic generalization negates the importance of judgments of individual differences. Although semantic structure might tell us to expect "friendly" to go with "altruistic" and not with "aggressive," it does not tell us whether we should apply the term more strongly to Walter or Seymour or Daryl. We must seek further for an adequate explanation of findings like those in Table 2.

HYPOTHESIS 3: AGREEMENT IS DUE TO BASE-RATE ACCURACY According to this hypothesis, interrater agreement is an artifact of the highly stable base rates that many traits have in the population at large. For example, the trait "needs to be with other people" characterizes most of us, whereas "has murderous tendencies" characterizes few. If one is trying to describe someone one does not know, therefore, one can achieve a certain degree of "accuracy" just by rating the first trait higher than the second. The base-rate hypothesis, like the semantic structure hypothesis, allows for consensus between observers but regards their judgments as indiscriminate. "Accuracy" of this sort might reflect knowledge about what people in general are like, what Cronbach (1955) called "stereotype accuracy," but does not necessarily reflect any knowledge specific to the person being described.

The base-rate accuracy problem helps us understand phenomena such as the "Barnum effect" (Ulrich, Stachnik, & Stainton, 1963), reflected in widespread acceptance of generalized descriptions such as, "You have a strong need for other people to like you and for them to admire you."[3] Questions

---

[2]This reference to "factor structure" means that the different traits on which raters judged others tended to be correlated with each other in a similar manner whether the targets of judgment were close acquaintances or strangers. For example, people rated high on "talkativeness" also tend to be rated high on "friendliness," whether these people are well known to the rater or not.

[3]The "Barnum effect" was named for the circus promoter P. T. Barnum, who is said to have claimed "there's a sucker born every minute." In demonstrations of this effect a group of people are all given descriptions of their personalities that include phrases such as "you have a strong need for other people to like you." People often report that the descriptions are remarkably accurate, but in reality they were all given the same description!

of when and for whom base-rate accuracy becomes an issue are interesting ones. For example, a recent study by Miller, McFarland, and Turnbull (1985) found that Barnum statements are more likely to be accepted by subjects when the statements refer to attributes that are publicly observable and flattering. However, to argue that base-rate accuracy is a basis for doubting whether we "can . . . describe an individual's personality" (Bourne, 1977) takes things too far. The base-rate accuracy hypothesis, like the semantic similarity hypothesis, can explain how judges reach consensus but not how they distinguish *between* the targets they judge. To take a simple case, imagine that a group of sorority sisters rates one another on a dichotomous item (as either "friendly" or "unfriendly"). If "friendly" is chosen over "unfriendly" 9 out of 10 times, there could be a very high percentage of "agreement," in terms of overlapping judgments, even if there were absolutely no agreement about who the 10th, unfriendly person is. But if there is truly no agreement about individual targets, correlations calculated between judges will show no relationship at all. So base-rate accuracy cannot explain the results of inter-rater studies such as those in Table 2 either (cf. Funder, 1980a; Funder & Colvin, 1987; Funder & Dobroth, 1987).

Summarizing thus far, we may say that whatever role solipsism and glittering generality play as noise in personality assessment, a signal of consensus and discrimination comes through. Can that signal be explained without acceding to the existence of trait-like consistencies in behavior? The answer is still yes, and in at least three ways.

HYPOTHESIS 4: AGREEMENT IS DUE TO STEREOTYPES BASED ON OBVIOUS (BUT ERRONEOUS) CUES

None of the arguments considered so far can account for interjudge agreement about the differences between people. One hypothesis that does is this: Perhaps agreement about peers is due to shared (but incorrect) stereotypes based on one or another readily accessible (e.g., physical) cues. Many such stereotypes come to mind: physical types (athlete, fat person, dumb blonde), racial and ethnic stereotypes, and so forth. Judges might

share cultural stereotypes and so "agree" about burly, obese, or blond targets regardless of whether there were any corresponding consistencies in the targets' behavior.

Note that this hypothesis is very different from the sort of "stereotype accuracy" discussed under Hypothesis 3. That hypothesis referred to the possibility of indiscriminate responding based on raters' common preconceptions about what *everybody* is like. Hypothesis 4 refers to consensual agreement about traits that are *differentially* assigned to others. None of the first three hypotheses requires the observer to really "observe" anything distinctive about the person he or she is describing. This hypothesis, however, does require that the observer at least take a look at the target person—but assumes that the observer hardly looks much further than the end of his or her nose, just enough to assign the target person to a general category.

Such categorical stereotypes undoubtedly exist, but this does not mean we cannot become more accurate after getting to know someone beyond their "surface" categorization. Raters will try to make "reasonable" (i.e., stereotypic) guesses in the absence of real behavioral information. But as we mentioned earlier, their ratings increasingly converge as they actually observe the person's behavior (e.g., Funder & Colvin, 1987; Monson, Tanke, & Lund, 1980; Moskowitz & Schwarz, 1982; Norman & Goldberg, 1966; Passini & Norman, 1966).

The data that are most difficult for the stereotype hypothesis to explain are relationships between judgments and independent, objective behavioral measurements. For example, parents and teachers can provide general personality descriptions of children that not only agree with each other but also predict the children's "delay of gratification" behavior, measured in minutes and seconds, in a lab situation that none of the raters have ever seen (Bem & Funder, 1978; Funder, Block, & Block, 1983; Mischel, 1984). Other examples include Funder's studies of personality correlates of attributional style (1980b), attitude change (1982), and social acuity (Funder & Harris, 1986b); Gormly and Edelberg's (1974) work on aggression;

Moskowitz and Schwarz's (1982) work on dominance; and Alker and Owen's (1977) research on reactions to stressful events. This sort of predictive capability must arise from something beyond the use of invalid stereotypes.

Although the existence of stereotypes does not negate the existence of traits, it is useful to consider how stereotypes and personality traits interact. For example, physical attractiveness may actually lead one to become more friendly, via self-fulfilling prophecies (Goldman & Lewis, 1977; Snyder, Tanke, & Berscheid, 1977). Likewise, burly males really are more aggressive (Glueck & Glueck, 1956), probably because aggressiveness has a higher payoff for a muscular youth than it does for a skinny or flabby one.

In sum, although stereotypes may be informative about the genesis of some traits, and may account for judgments of strangers, the findings that observers agree more with one another after they have gotten to know the target and the correlations between ratings and independent assessments of behavior rule out the possibility that inter-rater agreement is due solely to the use of shared stereotypes based on superficial cues.

HYPOTHESIS 5: AGREEMENT IS DUE TO DISCUSSION BETWEEN OBSERVERS

We just considered evidence that observers agree with each other better when they know the target person well. Is this because acquaintances have had more time to observe the relevant behaviors and hence are more truly accurate than strangers? Perhaps not. It could be argued that observers ignore the truly relevant nonverbal behaviors of a target person but are attentive to the target's verbalizations about himself or herself and come to regard the target as the target does for that reason (cf. Funder, 1980a; Funder & Colvin, 1987). Alternatively, observers might get together and discuss the target (McClelland, 1972), agree on his or her reputation, and then inform the target about how to regard himself or herself (as in the classical "looking glass self" formulations of C. H. Cooley, 1902).

The research cited earlier, showing how ratings of personality traits can predict behavior in unique settings, strongly suggests that such explicit "negotiation" is not all that underlies interjudge agreement. Moreover, several researchers have found that agreement between parents "back home" and peers at college is about as good as that among peers or among parents (Bem & Allen, 1974; Kenrick & Stringfield, 1980). Likewise, Koretzky et al. (1978) found respectable agreement between judges from different settings. In that study, the various settings were all within the same (mental) institution, but the Kenrick and Stringfield (1980) study was conducted in an isolated college town in Montana and used parents who often lived several hundred miles away from campus and were unlikely to have met the peers (whose home towns may have been hundreds of miles in the opposite direction), much less to have had intimate discussions with them about their children's traits.

Findings of higher agreement on traits that relate to observable behaviors (such as "friendliness" as opposed to "emotionality") are also relevant here. Kenrick and Stringfield (1980) found that "observable" traits are reported with better agreement than "unobservable" ones. * * * Related findings are reported by Amelang and Borkenau (1986), Cheek (1982), Funder and Colvin (1987), Funder and Dobroth (1987), and McCrae (1982) and in two unpublished studies, one by Dantchik (1985) and one by McCall, Linder, West, and Kenrick (1985). If judges simply manufacture a reputation for a subject, it seems that it would be just as easy to agree about terms relating to emotionality as it would be to agree about terms relating to extraversion. Higher agreement about publicly observable traits thus suggests that behavior is in fact being observed and accurately reported.

A tenacious adherent could still rescue this hypothesis by adding one more assumption. Perhaps we talk more about the so-called observable traits like extraversion than about "unobservable" traits. However, other findings further undermine the "discussion" hypothesis. Several studies have shown that when subjects' self-reports contradict their nonverbal behaviors, observers pay more attention to what is done than to what is said

(Amabile & Kabat, 1982; Bryan & Walbek, 1970). In the Amabile and Kabat study, subjects viewed a target who described herself as either "introverted" or "extraverted," and they also watched her behave in a way that was either consistent with, or inconsistent with, her self-description. Observers' subsequent judgments were much more strongly influenced by her actual behaviors than by the way she had described herself. It seems, then, that observers give more credence to trait-relevant behaviors than to self-descriptions.

Summarizing our arguments thus far, there is good evidence that trait ratings are more than solipsistic fantasies. Observers can agree in their trait ratings and can use them differently for different people. For those we know well, at least, trait ratings involve more than just stereotypes based on easily observable categories, and they are based more on behavioral observation than on unfounded gossip. Are we therefore now compelled to allow some veracity to the trait construct? Alas, the answer is still no, not necessarily.

HYPOTHESIS 6: AGREEMENT IS DUE TO SEEING OTHERS IN THE SAME SETTING

It is possible to allow for consensus and discrimination in the use of trait terms, and even to allow that observers are really and truly observing behavioral consistencies, without allowing that those behavioral consistencies stem from factors that are "internal" to the target person. As William James (1890), noted,

> Many a youth who is demure enough before his parents and teachers, swears and swaggers like a pirate among his "tough" young friends. We do not show ourselves to our children as to our club-companions, to our customers as to the laborers we employ, to our masters and employers as to our intimate friends. (p. 294)

Fellow club-companions may all agree that a particular merchant is consistently rather "wild," whereas his customers agree that he is quite "conventional." Because club-companions and customers live in "separate worlds," their different mutual delusions about the merchant's traits can be maintained. If behavior is mostly due to the sit-uation, then the people who inhabit a given situation with a target will agree about that person's behavioral attributes, even if they are not actually general attributes of the individual's personality.

A good deal of the evidence we have already discussed poses difficulties for this hypothesis as a final explanation of rater agreement. Much of the research that uses trait ratings is based on studies of students who are rated by fellow fraternity members or college roommates (e.g., Bem & Allen, 1974; Cheek, 1982; Funder, 1980a; Funder & Dobroth, 1987; Kenrick & Stringfield, 1980). These individuals see each other across many settings, yet agree well. Recall also that studies such as those done by Bem and Allen (1974) and Kenrick and Stringfield (1980) found agreement across peer and parent groups—who see the targets in very different situations. In the Kenrick and Stringfield (1980) study, for instance, peers knew the target as a college student (and perhaps fellow beer drinker), whereas parents knew the target as a child (and perhaps a ranch hand). Restriction of range of environmental experience could even constrain correlations. For example, perhaps the college dorm is a setting that constrains one to be "friendly." If so, it will be a difficult and subtle task for raters who know two targets only in that setting to agree about which one is the more "dispositionally" friendly.

Finally, a good deal of the research just discussed shows how personality ratings made by parents, teachers, and friends often correlate well with behavior measured in settings that are very different from the contexts from which their judgments were derived. From observing their children at home, for example, parents can provide personality descriptions that predict behavior measured in a unique experimental setting (Bem & Funder, 1978)—even when a dozen or more years separate the personality judgments from the behavior (Mischel, 1984). Such predictability has to be based on the parents' detection of true "cross-situational consistency."

Although the "situational" hypothesis is often viewed as an alternative to the trait position, they need not be at odds with one another. Researchers have begun to uncover useful information about how persons and situations "interact" (e.g., Bem & Funder, 1978; Kenrick & Dantchik, 1983; Magnusson & Endler, 1977; Snyder & Ickes, 1985):

1. Traits influence behavior only in relevant situations (Allport, 1966; Bem & Funder, 1978). Anxiety, for example, shows up only in situations that the person finds threatening.

2. A person's traits can change a situation (Rausch, 1977). For instance, an aggressive child can bring out the hostility in a previously peaceful playground.

3. People with different traits will choose different settings (Snyder & Ickes, 1985). Highly sex-typed males, for example, seek out sexually stimulating situations; highly sex-typed females avoid them (Kenrick, Stringfield, Wagenhals, Dahl, & Ransdell, 1980).

4. Traits can change with chronic exposure to certain situations. For instance, Newcomb's students became less conservative during their Bennington college experience and stayed that way for decades (Newcomb, Koenig, Flacks, & Warwick, 1967).

5. Traits are more easily expressed in some situations than others. They have more influence when situations are low in constraint—for example, a picnic as opposed to a funeral (Monson et al., 1982; Price & Bouffard, 1974; Schutte, Kenrick, & Sadalla, 1985). Traits are also more likely to be influential in settings that are highly prototypical or exemplary (Schutte et al., 1985). For instance, the postinterview cocktail party for an academic job applicant is more difficult to categorize than the in-office interview or the office Christmas party and would probably allow for the operation of greater individual differences. Note that laboratory situations, where psychologists often look for evidence of individual differences, will constrain the operation of traits precisely because they are rigidly controlled, are imposed arbitrarily on subjects, and are usually not reactive to anything the subject does (Monson & Snyder, 1977; Wachtel, 1973).

The data we have discussed thus far require us to concede that some degree of consensus, discrimination, and internality exists in the trait domain. Is it time, therefore, to give the store back to the "trait" position? Even with the distance we have come, the answer is still no. It is possible to argue that although some true cross-situational consistencies in behavior may exist, they are too small to worry about.

HYPOTHESIS 7: THE RELATIONSHIPS BETWEEN TRAITS AND BEHAVIOR ARE "TOO SMALL" TO BE IMPORTANT

Just how small is "too small"? Mischel's (1968) review concluded that correlations between trait scores and behaviors and between different behaviors are seldom larger than about .30. This conclusion hit the field of personality with devastating force because of two separable assumptions: (a) The coefficient .30 is not simply an artifact of poorly developed research tools but is the true upper limit for the predictability of behavior from personality, and (b) this upper limit is a small upper limit. Acceptance of both of these assumptions was necessary for Mischel's critique to have had a major impact, and many initially did accept them.

Several personologists (e.g., Block, 1977; Hogan, DeSoto, & Solano, 1977) have challenged the first assumption, arguing that Mischel's review did not give a fair hearing to the better studies in the personality literature. More than the several studies cited in earlier sections of this article have used direct behavioral observations and found larger correlations with behavior (see also Block, Buss, Block, & Gjerde, 1981; Block, von der Lippe, & Block, 1973; McGowen & Gormly, 1976; Moskowitz, 1982). Epstein (1979, 1983) reported that such correlations can be especially high when aggregates of behavior[4] rather than single instances are used.

Indeed, in everyday life, what we usually wish

---

[4]An "aggregate" is an average of several variables or observations. Aggregates tend to be more reliable and therefore more predictable than single observations. For example, the average of your friendliness on 10 different occasions over the next 3 weeks would be easier to predict than how friendly you will be tomorrow at 3 P.M.

to predict on the basis of our personality judgments are not single acts, but aggregate trends: Will this person make an agreeable friend, a reliable employee, an affectionate spouse? Given such broad criteria, the Spearman-Brown formula shows how even "small" single-act correlations compound into extremely high predictive validities. For example, Mischel and Peake (1982) found that interitem correlations between behavior measures are relatively low (.14 to .21) for single, unaggregated observations but that coefficient alpha for their total behavioral aggregate is .74. That is, a similar aggregate of behaviors would correlate .74 with that one. Along the same lines, Epstein and O'Brien (1985) reanalyzed several classical studies in the field of personality. In all of these studies behavior was situation specific at the single-item level (in line with Mischel's point) but cross-situationally general at the level of behavioral aggregates. Protagonists on both sides of the controversy now seem ready to allow that the ".30 ceiling" applies only to behavior in unaggregated form (Epstein, 1983; Mischel, 1983).

Even if one were to allow that it is difficult to surpass correlations of .30 to .40 (e.g., in the case of unaggregated measures), it may be a mistake to assume that such correlations are "small." In fact, correlations in this range characterize the strength of some of the most interesting and important situational effects found by experimental social psychology (Funder & Ozer, 1983; Sarason, Smith, & Diener, 1975) and even some of Mischel's own work on situational determinants of delay of gratification behavior (Funder & Harris, 1986a). These observations echo Hogan et al.'s (1977) warning that a correlation of .30 does not necessarily mean that the "remaining 91% of the variance" can be assigned, by subtraction, to the situation.

Moreover, a correlation of .30 may not be as small as many psychologists seem to believe. Common practice, as exemplified in the above warning, is to square such a correlation and report that it "accounts for 9% of the variance." However, Ozer (1985) claimed that, contrary to common belief and practice, the unsquared correlation coefficient is directly interpretable as the percentage of the variance accounted for. For example, $r = .30$ accounts for 30%, not 9%, of the relevant variance. Another way of clarifying the size of an effect in this range is Rosenthal and Rubin's (1979, 1982) binomial effect size display, which reveals that a predictor that correlates .30 with a dichotomous criterion will yield correct discriminations 65% of the time.[5] Abelson (1985) made the point in a vivid way with an application of the "percentage of variance" approach to batting performances in major league baseball players. Noting that most are in the .200s to .300s, he calculates that the percentage of variance explained in a single batting performance is less than 1%. Yet, with aggregation over seasons, these minuscule differences compound to result in discriminations important enough to determine hundreds of thousands of dollars in salary differentials. Thus, the .30 statistic that had such a devastating effect on the enterprise of personality assessment may have been badly misunderstood.

The hypothesis that personality coefficients are "too small" has been quite useful in elucidating some important limitations on what can be measured and how it should be measured. Minute and unaggregated behavioral indexes, no matter what their face validity, are not necessarily good criterion measures (Golding, 1978; West, 1983). They may be full of various sorts of error, lack temporal stability, or measure something other than what they seem to measure (Bem & Funder, 1978; Moskowitz & Schwarz, 1982; Romer & Revelle, 1984). Even if it is true, as Fiske (1979) pointed out, that judges can agree quite well about the occurrence of a given facial twitch, the twitch may be meaningless unless its context is understood (Block et al., 1979; Dahlstrom, 1972; Hogan, DeSoto, & Solano, 1977). These problems may account for the repeated finding that when objective behavioral measures are compared with observers' ratings, the results do not support the superiority of behavioral measures (e.g., Eaton & Enns, 1986; Moskowitz & Schwarz, 1982).

---

[5]See the selection by Rosenthal and Rubin in Part I, which is what is being referred to here.

What Have We Learned?

As with most controversies, the truth finally appears to lie not in the vivid black or white of either extreme, but somewhere in the less striking gray area. It would be a mistake, however, to claim that the interchange served only to bring out a number of "straw man" positions that no one ever took seriously anyway, that the repetitive cycle of argument and reply produced no more than fatigue and déjà vu, or that we are no closer to understanding personality traits than we were two decades ago. Radical versions of each of these hypotheses were suggested, not just for rhetorical purposes, and were passed uncritically onward to a generation of students in psychology courses. We were trained as experimental social psychologists during the heat of the debate, and the shade of gray we see now seemed much closer to a gloomy black back then. Indeed, for a time, and in some places, it was not unusual for the very idea of personality traits to be dismissed out of hand and even ridiculed.

On the other hand, one of us also underwent clinical training during that era and came across a viewpoint much closer to the "pure trait" position than is remotely tenable on the basis of the data available now. Ten years ago, there were, and probably still are (Mischel, 1983; Wade & Baker, 1977), clinical professionals overconfidently making grand predictions from minute samples of behavior of highly questionable reliability and validity. We can eliminate the radical forms of each of the seven critical hypotheses, but that does not imply that the so-called "pure trait" position has regained the day. Systematic sources of judgmental bias, systematic effects of situations, and systematic interactions between persons and situations must be explicitly dealt with before we can predict from trait measures.

So although there may be enough signal amidst the noise in this research area to make it worthwhile to turn on the radio, the device must still be carefully tuned. Instead of simply viewing each of the seven critical hypotheses as being resolved in favor of the trait position, it is better to view each as a clue about one ever-present source of noise to be tuned out. Kenny and La Voie (1984) showed how factors such as idiosyncratic rater bias (the problem of Hypothesis 1) can even, under the proper circumstances, be turned to statistical advantage in estimating a person's "true" trait score.

Other practical lessons have emerged from this controversy. The research now indicates quite clearly that anyone who seeks predictive validity from trait ratings will do better to use (a) raters who are thoroughly familiar with the person being rated; (b) multiple behavioral observations; (c) multiple observers; (d) dimensions that are publicly observable; and (e) behaviors that are relevant to the dimension in question.

On the other hand, one should *not* expect great accuracy when predicting (a) behavior in "powerful" and clearly normatively scripted situations from trait ratings and (b) a single behavioral instance from another single behavioral instance.

Those who would respond to this list by claiming that they "knew it all along" may or may not be guilty of hindsight bias (Fischoff, 1975). But they should at least acknowledge that many of us did not know these principles all along and needed the light generated by controversy to open our eyes. For instance, the apparently "obvious" insight that we should not rely on ratings made by strangers can help us understand why some of the data on clinical assessment (e.g., Goldberg & Werts, 1966; Golden, 1964; Soskin, 1959) have been so disappointing, and the awareness that traits will not show up in overpowering situations has led to a dramatic reassessment of failures to find "consistency" in brief laboratory observations. Likewise, if these issues and that of the unreliability of single behavioral instances were so obvious, one is left to wonder why the field responded so strongly to Mischel's (1968) critique. "Déjà vu" may be an accurate description of our current situation after all, because the term actually refers to the *illusion* that one has previously experienced something that is really new.

One side effect of the person-situation debate has been an intensification of the antagonism between personality and social psychology. Social psychologists have historically focused on situational determinants of behavior and were therefore quite willing to join with behavioral clinicians in the situationist attack on personality (Hogan & Emler, 1978; Kenrick & Dantchik, 1983). Personologists share a very different set of assumptions, and the two subdisciplines have sometimes seemed intent on defining each other out of existence (Kenrick, 1986). To continue such separation between the two fields would be a mistake. Many exciting developments are beginning to emerge at the interface of social and personality psychology. For instance, research that combines personality with biology suggests a vast array of questions about the connection between personality traits and social interaction (Kenrick, 1987; Kenrick & Trost, 1987; Sadalla, Kenrick, & Vershure, 1987). And research on the accuracy of interpersonal judgment draws equally on both personality and social psychology (Funder, 1987; Funder & Colvin, 1987; Funder & Dobroth, 1987).

Houts, Cook, and Shadish (1986) made a strong case that science best progresses through multiple and mutually critical attempts to understand the same problem. When camps with strongly opposing sets of biases manage to come to some level of agreement, we may be more confident of the validity of the conclusions that are agreed upon. Viewed in this light, the controversy stimulated by the situationist attack on personality may be seen more as a life-giving transfusion than as a needless bloodletting.

References

Abelson, R. P. (1976). A script theory of understanding, attitude, and behavior. In J. Carroll & J. Payne (Eds.), *Cognition and social behavior* (pp. 33–45). Hillsdale, NJ: Erlbaum.

Abelson, R. P. (1985). A variance explanation paradox: When a little is a lot. *Psychological Bulletin, 97*, 129–133.

Alker, H. A. (1972). Is personality situationally specific or intrapsychically consistent? *Journal of Personality, 40*, 1–16.

Alker, H. A., & Owen, D. W. (1977). Biographical, trait, and behavioral-sampling predictions of performance in a stressful life setting. *Journal of Personality and Social Psychology, 35*, 717–723.

Allport, G. W. (1931). What is a trait of personality? *Journal of Abnormal and Social Psychology, 25*, 368–372.

Allport, G. W. (1966). Traits revisited. *American Psychologist, 21*, 1–10.

Alston, W. P. (1975). Traits, consistency, and conceptual alternatives for personality theory. *Journal for the Theory of Social Behavior, 5*, 17–48.

Amabile, T. M., & Kabat, L. G. (1982). When self-description contradicts behavior: Actions do speak louder than words. *Social Cognition, 1*, 311–335.

Amelang, M., & Borkenau, P. (1986). The trait concept: Current theoretical considerations, empirical facts, and implications for personality inventory construction. In A. Angleitner & J. S. Wiggins (Eds.), *Personality assessment via questionnaire* (pp. 7–24). Berlin: Springer-Verlag.

Argyle, M., & Little, B. R. (1972). Do personality traits apply to social behavior? *Journal for the Theory of Social Behavior, 2*, 1–35.

Bem, D. J. (1972). Constructing cross-situational consistencies in behavior: Some thoughts on Alker's critique of Mischel. *Journal of Personality, 40*, 17–26.

Bem, D. J. (1983). Further *déjà vu* in the search for cross situational consistency: A reply to Mischel and Peake. *Psychological Review, 90*, 390–393.

Bem, D. J., & Allen, A. (1974). On predicting some of the people some of the time: The search for cross-situational consistencies in behavior. *Psychological Review, 81*, 506–520.

Bem, D. J., & Funder, D. C. (1978). Predicting more of the people more of the time: Assessing the personality of situations. *Psychological Review, 85*, 485–501.

Block, J. (1968). Some reasons for the apparent inconsistency of personality. *Psychological Bulletin, 70*, 210–212.

Block, J. (1977). Advancing the science of personality: Paradigmatic shift or improving the quality of research? In D. Magnusson & N. S. Endler (Eds.), *Personality at the crossroads: Current issues in interactional psychology* (pp. 37–63). Hillsdale, NJ: Erlbaum.

Block, J., Buss, D. M., Block, J. M., & Gjerde, P. F. (1981). The cognitive style of breadth of categorization: The longitudinal consistency of personality correlates. *Journal of Personality and Social Psychology, 40*, 770–779.

Block, J., von der Lippe, A., & Block, J. H. (1973). Sex-role and socialization patterns: Some personality concomitants and environmental antecedents. *Journal of Consulting and Clinical Psychology, 41*, 321–341.

Block, J., Weiss, D. S., & Thorne, A. (1979). How relevant is a semantic similarity interpretation of personality ratings? *Journal of Personality and Social Psychology, 37*, 1055–1074.

Bourne, E. (1977). Can we describe an individual's personality? Agreement on stereotype versus individual attributes. *Journal of Personality and Social Psychology, 35*, 863–872.

Bowers, K. S. (1973). Situationism in psychology: An analysis and critique. *Psychological Review, 80*, 307–336.

Bryan, J., & Walbek, N. (1970). Impact of words and deeds concerning altruism upon children. *Child Development, 41*, 747–757.

Carlson, R. (1984). What's social about social psychology? Where's the person in personality research? *Journal of Personality and Social Psychology, 35*, 1055–1074.

Cheek, J. M. (1982). Aggregation, moderator variables, and the validity of personality tests: A peer-rating study. *Journal of Personality and Social Psychology, 43*, 1254–1269.

Cooley, C. H. (1902). *Human nature and the social order.* New York: Scribner's.

Cronbach, L. J. (1955). Processes affecting scores on "understanding of others" and "assumed similarity." *Psychological Bulletin, 52*, 177–193.

Dahlstrom, W. G. (1972). *Personality systematics and the problem of types*. Morristown, NJ: General Learning Press.

D'Andrade, R. G. (1974). Memory and the assessment of behavior. In H. M. Blalock (Ed.), *Measurement in the social sciences* (pp. 159–186). Chicago: Aldine-Atherton.

Dantchik, A. (1985). *Idiographic approaches to personality assessment*. Unpublished master's thesis, Arizona State University, Tempe.

Dornbusch, S. M., Hastorf, A. H., Richardson, S. A., Muzzy, R. E., & Vreeland, R. S. (1965). The perceiver and perceived: Their relative influence on categories of interpersonal perception. *Journal of Personality and Social Psychology, 1,* 434–440.

Eaton, W. D., & Enns, L. R. (1986). Sex differences in human activity level. *Psychological Bulletin, 100,* 19–28.

Endler, N. S. (1973). The person vs. situation: A pseudo issue? *Journal of Personality, 41,* 287–303.

Epstein, S. (1977). Traits are alive and well. In D. Magnusson & N. S. Endler (Eds.), *Personality at the crossroads: Current issues in interactional psychology* (pp. 83–98). Hillsdale, NJ: Erlbaum.

Epstein, S. (1979). The stability of behavior: I. On predicting most of the people much of the time. *Journal of Personality and Social Psychology, 37,* 1097–1126.

Epstein, S. (1980). The stability of behavior: II. Implications for psychological research. *American Psychologist, 35,* 790–806.

Epstein, S. (1983). The stability of confusion: A reply to Mischel and Peake. *Psychological Review, 90,* 390–393.

Epstein, S., & O'Brien, E. J. (1985). The person-situation debate in historical and current perspective. *Psychological Bulletin, 98,* 513–537.

Farber, I. E. (1964). A framework for the study of personality as a behavioral science. In P. Worchel & D. Bryne (Eds.), *Personality change* (pp. 3–37). New York: Wiley.

Fischoff, B. (1975). Hindsight does not equal foresight: The effect of outcome knowledge on judgment under uncertainty. *Journal of Experimental Psychology: Human Perception and Performance, 1,* 288–299.

Fiske, D. W. (1974). The limits for the conventional science of personality. *Journal of Personality, 42,* 1–11.

Fiske, D. W. (1979). Two worlds of psychological phenomena. *American Psychologist, 34,* 733–739.

Fiske, S., & Taylor, S. (1984). *Social cognition*. New York: Random House.

Funder, D. C. (1980a). On seeing ourselves as others see us: Self-other agreement and discrepancy in personality ratings. *Journal of Personality, 48,* 473–493.

Funder, D. C. (1980b). The "trait" of ascribing traits: Individual differences in the tendency to trait ascription. *Journal of Research in Personality, 14,* 376–385.

Funder, D. C. (1982). On assessing social psychological theories through the study of individual differences: Template matching and forced compliance. *Journal of Personality and Social Psychology, 43,* 100–110.

Funder, D. C. (1983). Three issues in predicting more of the people: A reply to Mischel and Peake. *Psychological Review, 90,* 283–289.

Funder, D. C. (1987). Errors and mistakes: Evaluating the accuracy of social judgment. *Psychological Bulletin, 101,* 75–90.

Funder, D. C., Block, J., & Block, J. H. (1983). Delay of gratifica-

tion: Some longitudinal personality correlates. *Journal of Personality and Social Psychology, 44,* 1198–1213.

Funder, D. C., & Colvin, C. R. (1987). *Friends and strangers: Acquaintanceship, agreement, and the accuracy of personality judgment*. Manuscript submitted for publication.

Funder, D. C., & Dobroth, J. M. (1987). Differences between traits: Properties associated with interjudge agreement. *Journal of Personality and Social Psychology, 52,* 409–418.

Funder, D. C., & Harris, M. J. (1986a). Experimental effects and person effects in delay of gratification. *American Psychologist, 41,* 476–477.

Funder, D. C., & Harris, M. J. (1986b). On the several facets of personality assessment: The case of social acuity. *Journal of Personality, 54,* 528–550.

Funder, D. C., & Ozer, D. J. (1983). Behavior as a function of the situation. *Journal of Personality and Social Psychology, 44,* 107–112.

Gergen, K. J. (1968). Personal consistency and the presentation of self. In C. Gordon & K. J. Gergen (Eds.), *The self in social interaction* (pp. 299–308). New York: Wiley.

Glueck, S., & Glueck, E. (1956). *Physique and delinquency*. New York: Harper & Row.

Goldberg, L. R., & Werts, C. E. (1966). The reliability of clinician's judgments: A multitrait-multimethod approach. *Journal of Consulting Psychology, 30,* 199–206.

Golden, M. (1964). Some effects of combining psychological tests on clinical inferences. *Journal of Consulting Psychology, 28,* 440–446.

Golding, S. L. (1978). Toward a more adequate theory of personality: Psychological organizing principles. In H. London (Ed.), *Personality: A new look at metatheories* (pp. 69–96). New York: Wiley.

Goldman, W., & Lewis, P. (1977). Beautiful is good: Evidence that the physically attractive are more socially skilled. *Journal of Experimental Social Psychology, 13,* 125–130.

Gormly, J., & Edelberg, W. (1974). Validity in personality trait attributions. *American Psychologist, 29,* 189–193.

Gregory, R. L. (1971). Visual illusions. In R. C. Atkinson (Ed.), *Contemporary psychology* (pp. 167–177). San Francisco: W. H. Freeman.

Hogan, R. (1982). A socioanalytic theory of personality. In R. A. Dienstbier & M. M. Page (Eds.), *Nebraska symposium on motivation* (Vol. 30, pp. 55–89). Lincoln: University of Nebraska Press.

Hogan, R., DeSoto, C. B., and Solano, C. (1977). Traits, tests, and personality research. *American Psychologist, 32,* 255–264.

Hogan, R. T., & Emler, N. P. (1978). The biases in contemporary social psychology. *Social Research, 45,* 478–534.

Houts, A. C., Cook, T. D., & Shadish, W. R. (1986). The person-situation debate: A critical multiplist perspective. *Journal of Personality, 54,* 52–105.

Hunt, J. McV. (1965). Traditional personality theory in the light of recent evidence. *American Scientist, 53,* 80–96.

Ichheisser, G. (1943). Misinterpretations of personality in everyday life and the psychologist's frame of reference. *Character and Personality, 12,* 145–160.

Jackson, D. N. (1983). Some preconditions for valid person perception. In M. P. Zanna, E. T. Higgins, & C. P. Herman (Eds.), *Consistency in social behavior: The Ontario Symposium* (pp. 251–279). Hillsdale, NJ: Erlbaum.

James, W. (1890). *Principles of psychology* (Vol. 1). London: Macmillan.

Kenny, D. A., & La Voie, L. (1984). The social relations model. In L. Berkowitz (Ed.), *Advances in experimental social psychology* (Vol. 18, pp. 141–182). Orlando, FL: Academic Press.

Kenrick, D. T. (1986). How strong is the case against contemporary social and personality psychology? A response to Carlson. *Journal of Personality and Social Psychology, 50,* 839–844.

Kenrick, D. T. (1987). Gender, genes, and the social environment. In P. C. Shaver & C. Hendrick (Eds.), *Review of personality and social psychology: Vol. 7. Sex and gender* (pp. 14–43). Beverly Hills, CA: Sage.

Kenrick, D. T., & Braver, S. L. (1982). Personality: Idiographic and nomothetic! A rejoinder. *Psychological Review, 89,* 182–186.

Kenrick, D. T., & Dantchik, A. (1983). Interactionism, idiographics, and the social psychological invasion of personality. *Journal of Personality, 51,* 286–307.

Kenrick, D. T., & Stringfield, D. O. (1980). Personality traits and the eye of the beholder: Crossing some traditional philosophical boundaries in the search for consistency in all of the people. *Psychological Review, 87,* 88–104.

Kenrick, D. T., Stringfield, D. O., Wagenhals, W. L., Dahl, R. H., & Ransdell, H. J. (1980). Sex differences, androgyny, and approach responses to erotica: A new variation on the old volunteer problem. *Journal of Personality and Social Psychology, 40,* 1039–1056.

Kenrick, D. T., & Trost, M. R. (1987). A biosocial theory of heterosexual relationships. In K. Kelley (Ed.), *Males, females, and sexuality: Theory and research* (pp. 59–100). Albany: State University of New York Press.

Koretzky, M. B., Kohn, M., & Jeger, A. M. (1978). Cross-situational consistency among problem adolescents: An application of the two-factor model. *Journal of Personality and Social Psychology, 36,* 1054–1059.

Magnusson, D., & Endler, N. S. (Eds.). (1977). *Personality at the crossroads: Current issues in interactional psychology.* Hillsdale, NJ: Erlbaum.

McArthur, L. Z., & Baron, R. M. (1983). Toward an ecological theory of social perception. *Psychological Review, 90,* 215–235.

McCall, M., Linder, D. E., West, S. G., & Kenrick, D. T. (1985). *Some cautions on the template-matching approach to assessing person/environment interactions.* Unpublished manuscript, Arizona State University, Tempe.

McClelland, D. C. (1972). Opinions reflect opinions: So what else is new? *Journal of Consulting and Clinical Psychology, 38,* 325–326.

McCrae, R. R. (1982). Consensual validation of personality traits: Evidence from self-reports and ratings. *Journal of Personality and Social Psychology, 43,* 293–303.

McGowen, J., & Gormly, J. (1976). Validation of personality traits: A multicriteria approach. *Journal of Personality and Social Psychology, 34,* 791–795.

Miller, D. T., McFarland, C., & Turnbull, W. (1985). *Pluralistic ignorance: Its causes and consequences.* Paper presented at the annual meeting of the Eastern Psychological Association, Boston.

Mischel, W. (1968). *Personality and assessment.* New York: Wiley.

Mischel, W. (1983). Alternatives in the pursuit of the predictability and consistency of persons: Stable data that yield unstable interpretations. *Journal of Personality, 51,* 578–604.

Mischel, W. (1984). Convergences and challenges in the search for consistency. *American Psychologist, 39,* 351–364.

Mischel, W., & Peake, P. K. (1982). Beyond *déjà vu* in the search for cross-situational consistency. *Psychological Review, 89,* 730–755.

Mischel, W., & Peake, P. K. (1983). Some facets of consistency: Replies to Epstein, Funder, and Bem. *Psychological Review, 90,* 394–402.

Monson, T. C., Keel, R., Stephens, D., & Genung, V. (1982). Trait attributions: Relative validity, covariation with behavior, and prospect of future interaction. *Journal of Personality and Social Psychology, 42,* 1014–1024.

Monson, T. C., Tanke, E. D., & Lund, J. (1980). Determinants of social perception in a naturalistic setting. *Journal of Research in Personality, 14,* 104–120.

Monson, T. C., & Snyder, M. (1977). Actors, observers, and the attribution process: Toward a reconceptualization. *Journal of Experimental Social Psychology, 13,* 89–111.

Moskowitz, D. S. (1982). Coherence and cross-situational generality in personality: A new analysis of old problems. *Journal of Personality and Social Psychology, 43,* 754–768.

Moskowitz, D. S., & Schwarz, J. C. (1982). Validity comparison of behavior counts and ratings by knowledgeable informants. *Journal of Personality and Social Psychology, 42,* 518–528.

Newcomb, T. M., Koenig, K. E., Flacks, R., & Warwick, D. P. (1967). *Persistence and change: Bennington College and its students after twenty-five years.* New York: Wiley.

Nisbett, R. E., & Ross, L. D. (1980). *Human inference: Strategies and shortcomings of social judgment.* New York: Prentice-Hall.

Norman, W. T., & Goldberg, L. R. (1966). Raters, ratees, and randomness in personality structure. *Journal of Personality and Social Psychology, 4,* 681–691.

Ozer, D. J. (1985). Correlation and the coefficient of determination. *Psychological Bulletin, 97,* 307–315.

Passini, F. T., & Norman, W. T. (1966). A universal conception of personality structure? *Journal of Personality and Social Psychology, 4,* 44–49.

Paunonen, S. V., & Jackson, D. N. (1985). Idiographic measurement strategies for personality and prediction: Some unredeemed promissory notes. *Psychological Review, 92,* 486–511.

Platt, J. R. (1964). Strong inference. *Science, 146,* 347–353.

Popper, K. (1959). *The logic of scientific discovery.* New York: Basic Books.

Price, R. H., & Bouffard, D. L. (1974). Behavioral appropriateness and situational constraint as dimensions of social behavior. *Journal of Personality and Social Psychology, 30,* 579–586.

Rausch, M. L. (1977). Paradox, levels, and junctures in person-situation systems. In D. Magnusson & N. S. Endler (Eds.), *Personality at the crossroads* (pp. 287–304). Hillsdale, NJ: Erlbaum.

Romer, D., & Revelle, W. (1984). Personality traits: Fact or fiction? A critique of the Shweder and D'Andrade systematic distortion hypothesis. *Journal of Personality and Social Psychology, 47,* 1028–1042.

Rosenthal, R., & Rubin, D. B. (1979). A note on percent variance explained as a measure of the importance of effects. *Journal of Applied Social Psychology, 9,* 385–396.

Rosenthal, R., & Rubin, D. B. (1982). A simple, general purpose display of magnitude of experimental effect. *Journal of Educational Psychology, 74,* 166–169.

Ross, L. (1977). The intuitive psychologist and his shortcomings: Distortions in the attribution process. In L. Berkowitz (Ed.), *Advances in experimental social psychology* (Vol. 10, pp. 174–221). New York: Academic Press.

Sadalla, E. K., Kenrick, D. T., & Vershure, B. (1987). Dominance and heterosexual attraction. *Journal of Personality and Social Psychology, 52*, 730–738.

Sarason, I. G., Smith, R. E., & Diener, E. (1975). Personality research: Components of variance attributable to the person and the situation. *Journal of Personality and Social Psychology, 32*, 199–204.

Schank, R. C., & Abelson, R. P. (1977). *Scripts, plans, goals, and understanding.* Hillsdale, NJ: Erlbaum.

Schneider, D. (1973). Implicit personality theory: A review. *Psychological Bulletin, 79*, 294–309.

Schutte, N. A., Kenrick, D. T., & Sadalla, E. K. (1985). The search for predictable settings: Situational prototypes, constraint, and behavioral variation. *Journal of Personality and Social Psychology, 49*, 121–128.

Shweder, R. A. (1975). How relevant is an individual-difference theory of personality? *Journal of Personality, 43*, 455–485.

Shweder, R. A., & D'Andrade, R. G. (1979). Accurate reflection or systematic distortion: A reply to Block, Weiss, and Thorne. *Journal of Personality and Social Psychology, 37*, 1075–1084.

Snyder, M., & Ickes, W. (1985). Personality and social behavior. In G. Lindzey & E. Aronson (Eds.), *Handbook of social psychology* (3rd ed., Vol. 2, pp. 883–948). Reading, MA: Addison-Wesley.

Snyder, M., Tanke, E. D., & Berscheid, E. (1977). Social perception and interpersonal behavior: On the self-fulfilling nature of social stereotypes. *Journal of Personality and Social Psychology, 35*, 656–666.

Soskin, W. F. (1959). Influence of four types of data on diagnostic conceptualization in psychological testing. *Journal of Abnormal and Social Psychology, 58*, 69–78.

Trope, Y., Bassok, M., & Alon, E. (1984). The questions lay interviewers ask. *Journal of Personality, 52*, 90–106.

Ulrich, R. E., Stachnik, T. J., & Stainton, N. R. (1963). Student acceptance of generalized personality interpretations. *Psychological Reports, 13*, 831–834.

Wachtel, P. (1973). Psychodynamics, behavior therapy, and the implacable experimenter: An inquiry into the consistency of personality. *Journal of Abnormal Psychology, 82*, 324–334.

Wade, T. C., & Baker, T. B. (1977). Opinions and use of psychological tests: A survey of clinical psychologists. *American Psychologist, 32*, 874–882.

West, S. G. (1983). Personality and prediction: An introduction. *Journal of Personality, 51*, 275–285.

Wiggins, J. S. (1973). *Personality and prediction: Principles of personality assessment.* Reading, MA: Addison-Wesley.

Zuroff, D. C. (1986). Was Gordon Allport a trait theorist? *Journal of Personality and Social Psychology, 51*, 993–1000.

A FIVE-FACTOR THEORY OF PERSONALITY

Robert R. McCrae and Paul T. Costa Jr.

More than 60 years ago, Gordon Allport and one of his students counted the trait words in an unabridged dictionary and came up with 17,953 (Allport & Odbert, 1936)! Personality psychologists have not made up tests to measure all of these, but it is safe to estimate that at least a couple of thousand different personality traits have been investigated by one researcher or another. It is reasonable to wonder whether all these different trait distinctions are strictly necessary. Can we reduce the vast number of trait terms in the language and the research literature down to an essential few? If so, this would be an important accomplishment, for it would vastly simplify the task of personality assessment and go a long way toward making it possible to compare the research of different psychologists.

In recent years, the personality psychologists Robert McCrae and Paul Costa Jr. have argued that the "Big Five" traits of personality are the truly essential ones. They call these traits extraversion, neuroticism, openness to experience, agreeableness, *and* conscientiousness. *Not everybody believes these traits are important (see Block, 1995, for one vigorous dissent), but many psychologists find the Big Five to be a useful—if not all-encompassing—common framework for the conceptualization of individual differences in personality. As Ozer and Reise (1994) stated, the Big Five can serve a useful purpose as the "latitude and longitude" along which the thousands of other possible personality traits can be located.*

In this article, McCrae and Costa present the latest wrinkle in their thinking about the Big Five, which is that these traits are useful not only for describing personality but also for explaining it. They present a theory of personality that presents the Big Five traits as the "basic tendencies" that underlie all of personality, and include a figure that shows how these tendencies interact with culture, situations, the self-concept, and behavior.

The research and theorizing relevant to the Big Five—pro and con— continue to be lively, and the final chapter on this topic has not yet been written. In the meantime, it is worth pondering two questions. First, how much of human personality can be encompassed by five basic traits—is anything important left out? And second, are these traits simply descriptions *of personality, or are* *they the actual* causes?

From *Handbook of Personality: Theory and Research* (2nd ed.), edited by L. A. Pervin and O. P. John (New York: Guilford, 1999), pp. 139–153.

Empirical and Conceptual Bases of a New Theory

In a narrow sense, the Five-Factor Model (FFM) of personality is an empirical generalization about the covariation of personality traits. As Digman and Inouye (1986) put it, "If a large number of rating scales is used and if the scope of the scales is very broad, the domain of personality descriptors is almost completely accounted for by five robust factors" (p. 116). The five factors, frequently labeled Neuroticism (N), Extraversion (E), Openness (O), Agreeableness (A), and Conscientiousness (C), have been found not only in the peer rating scales in which they were originally discovered (Tupes & Christal, 1961/1992) but also in self-reports on trait descriptive adjectives (Saucier, 1997), in questionnaire measures of needs and motives (Costa & McCrae, 1988), in expert ratings on the California Q-Set (Lanning, 1994), and in personality disorder symptom clusters (Clark & Livesley, 1994). Much of what psychologists mean by the term *personality* is summarized by the FFM, and the model has been of great utility to the field by integrating and systematizing diverse conceptions and measures.

In a broader sense, the FFM refers to the entire body of research that it has inspired, amounting to a reinvigoration of trait psychology itself. Research associated with the FFM has included studies of diverse populations (McCrae, Costa, del Pilar, Rolland, & Parker, 1998), often followed over decades of the lifespan (Costa & McCrae, 1992b); employed multiple methods of assessment (Funder, Kolar, & Blackman, 1995); and even featured case studies (Costa & McCrae, 1998b; McCrae, 1993–94). * * * After decades of floundering, personality psychology has begun to make steady progress, accumulating a store of replicable findings about the origins,

development, and functioning of personality traits (McCrae, 1992).

But neither the model itself nor the body of research findings with which it is associated constitutes a theory of personality. A theory organizes findings to tell a coherent story, to bring into focus those issues and phenomena that can and should be explained. * * * Five-Factor Theory (FFT; McCrae & Costa, 1996) represents an effort to construct such a theory that is consistent with current knowledge about personality. In this chapter we summarize and elaborate it.

* * *

ASSUMPTIONS ABOUT HUMAN NATURE The trait perspective, like every psychological theory, is based on a set of assumptions about what people are like and what a theory of personality ought to do. Most of these assumptions—for example, that explanations for behavior are to be sought in the circumstances of this life, not karma from a previous one—are implicit. FFT explicitly acknowledges four assumptions about human nature (cf. Hjelle & Siegler, 1976)—*knowability, rationality, variability,* and *proactivity*; all of these appear to be implicit in the standard enterprise of trait research.

Knowability is the assumption that personality is a proper object of scientific study. In contrast to some humanistic and existential theories that celebrate human freedom and the irreducible uniqueness of the individual, FFT assumes that there is much to be gained from the scientific study of personality in individuals and groups.

* * *

Rationality is the assumption that, despite errors and biases (e.g., Robins & John, 1997), people are in general capable of understanding themselves and others (Funder, 1995). In this respect, psychology is an unusual science. Physicians would not ask their patients to estimate their own white blood cell count, because patients could not be expected to possess such information. But trait psychologists routinely—and properly—ask people how sociable or competitive or irritable they are and interpret the answers (suitably aggregated and normed) as meaning what they say. Psychologists are able to do this because with respect to personality traits, laypersons are extraordinarily sophisticated judges who employ a trait language evolved over centuries to express important social judgments (cf. Saucier & Goldberg, 1996).

* * *

Variability asserts that people differ from each other in psychologically significant ways—an obvious premise for differential psychology. Note, however, that this position sets trait theories apart from all those views of human nature, philosophical and psychological, that seek a single answer to what human nature is really like. Are people basically selfish or altruistic? Creative or conventional? Purposeful or lazy? Within FFT, those are all meaningless questions; *creative* and *conventional* define opposite poles of a dimension along which people vary.

Proactivity refers to the assumption that the locus of causation of human action is to be sought in the person. It goes without saying that people are not absolute masters of their destinies, and that (consistent with the premise of variability) people differ in the extent to which they control their lives. But trait theory holds that it is worthwhile to seek the origins of behavior in characteristics of the person. People are neither passive victims of their life circumstances nor empty organisms programmed by histories of reinforcements. Personality is actively involved in shaping people's lives.

* * *

A Universal Personality System

Personality traits are individual difference variables; to understand them and how they operate, it is necessary to describe personality itself, the dynamic psychological organization that coordinates experience and action. * * *

COMPONENTS OF THE PERSONALITY SYSTEM   The personality system [shown in Figure 1] consists of components that correspond to the definitions of FFT and dynamic processes that indicate how these components are interrelated—the basic postulates of FFT. The definitions would probably seem reasonable to personologists from many different theoretical backgrounds; the postulates distinguish FFT from most other theories of personality and reflect interpretations of empirical data.

The core components of the personality system, indicated in rectangles, are designated as *basic tendencies, characteristic adaptations*, and the *self-concept* (actually a subcomponent of characteristic adaptations, but one of sufficient interest to warrant its own box). The elliptical peripheral components, which represent the interfaces of personality with adjoining systems, are labeled *biological bases, external influences*, and the *objective biography*. Figure 1 can be interpreted cross-sectionally as a diagram of how personality operates at any given time; in that case the external influences constitute the situation, and the objective biography is a specific instance of behavior, the output of the system. Figure 1 can also be interpreted longitudinally to indicate personality development (in basic tendencies and characteristic adaptations) and the unfolding of the life course (objective biography).

It may be helpful to consider some of the substance of personality to flesh out the abstractions in Figure 1. Table 1 presents some examples. For each of the five factors, an illustrative trait is identified in the first column of the table. The intrapsychic and interpersonal adaptations that develop over time as expressions of these facet traits are illustrated in the second column, and the third column mentions an instance of behavior from an individual characterized by the high or low pole of the facet.

At present, FFT has relatively little to say about the peripheral components of the personality system. Biological bases certainly include genes and brain structures, but the precise mechanisms—developmental, neuroanatomical, or psychophysiological—are not yet specified. Similarly, FFT does not detail types of external influences or aspects of

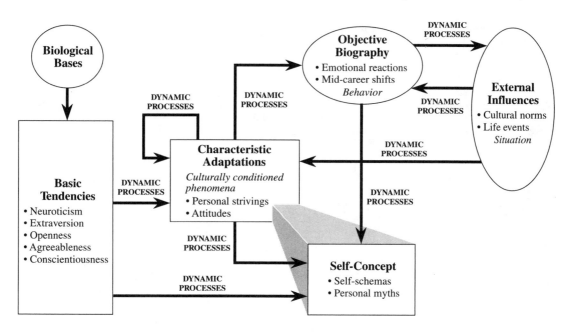

Figure 1. A representation of the five-factor theory personality system. Core components are in rectangles; interfacing components are in ellipses. Adapted from McCrae and Costa (1996).

the objective biography. Like most theories of personality, FFT presumes that "situation" and "behavior" are more or less self-evident.

What FFT does focus attention on is the distinction between basic tendencies (abstract psychological potentials) and characteristic adaptations (their concrete manifestations). Somewhat similar distinctions have been made by others—for example, in the familiar contrast of genotypic and phenotypic traits (Wiggins, 1973/1997) and in McAdams's (1996) distinction between Level 1 and Level 2 personality variables. FFT, however, insists on a distinction that other theories usually make only in passing, and it assigns traits exclusively to the category of basic tendencies. In FFT, traits are not patterns of behavior (Buss & Craik, 1983), nor are they the plans, skills, and desires that lead to patterns of behavior (Johnson, 1997). They are directly accessible neither to public observation nor to private introspection. Instead, they are deeper psychological entities that can only be *inferred* from behavior and experience. Self-reports

of personality traits are based on such inferences, just as observer ratings are.

Although it smacks of obfuscation, there are good reasons to uncouple personality traits from the more observable components of personality. Characteristic adaptations—habits, attitudes, skills, roles, relationships—are influenced both by basic tendencies and by external influences. They are *characteristic* because they reflect the enduring psychological core of the individual, and they are *adaptations* because they help the individual fit into the ever-changing social environment. Characteristic adaptations and their configurations inevitably vary tremendously across cultures, families, and portions of the lifespan. *But personality traits do not:* The same five factors are found in all cultures studied so far (McCrae & Costa, 1997); parent–child relations have little lasting effect on personality traits (Rowe, 1994; see also Fraley, 1998, on the precipitous drop in the continuity of attachment); and traits are generally stable across the adult lifespan (McCrae & Costa, 1990). These

TABLE 1

SOME EXAMPLES OF FFT PERSONALITY SYSTEM COMPONENTS

Basic tendencies	Characteristic adaptations	Objective biography
Neuroticism N3: Depression (a tendency to experience dysphoric effect—sadness, hopelessness, guilt)	Low self-esteem, irrational perfectionistic beliefs, pessimistic attitudes	"Betty" (very high N3) feels guilty about her low-prestige job (Bruehl, 1994).
Extraversion E2: Gregariousness (a preference for companionship and social stimulation)	Social skills, numerous friendships, enterprising vocational interests, participation in sports, club memberships	J.-J. Rousseau (very low E2) leaves Paris for the countryside (McCrae, 1996).
Openness to Experience O4: Actions (a need for variety, novelty, and change)	Interest in travel, many different hobbies, knowledge of foreign cuisine, diverse vocational interests, friends who share tastes	Diane Ackerman (high O4) cruises the Antarctic (McCrae, 1993–1994).
Agreeableness A4: Compliance (a willingness to defer to others during interpersonal conflict)	Forgiving attitudes, belief in cooperation, inoffensive language, reputation as a pushover	Case 3 (very low A4) throws things at her husband during a fight (Costa & McCrae, 1992b).
Conscientiousness C4: Achievement Striving (strong sense of purpose and high aspiration levels)	Leadership skills, long-term plans, organized support network, technical expertise	Richard Nixon (very high C4) runs for President (Costa & McCrae, 2000).

well-replicated empirical generalizations make sense only if personality traits are insulated from the direct effects of the environment. Human nature is proactive because personality traits are endogenous basic tendencies (McCrae, Costa, Ostendorf, et al., 1998).

OPERATION OF THE SYSTEM The welter of arrows in Figure 1 indicate some of the most important paths by which personality components interact. The plural *processes* is used because many quite distinct processes may be involved in each pathway. For example, the arrow from objective biography to self-concept implies that we learn who we are in part from observing what we do. But interpreting what we have done may involve social comparison, selective attention, defensive denial, implicit learning, or any number of other cognitive-affective processes. * * *

One implication is that personality theories that posit a small handful of key dynamic processes (repression, learning, self-actualization, getting ahead and getting along) are unlikely to prove adequate. Another is that psychologists who prefer to study processes instead of traits—"doing" instead of "having" (Cantor, 1990)—face the challenging prospect of identifying the most important of these many processes to study. There is as yet nothing like an adequate taxonomy of processes, and although evolutionary theory points to certain adaptive functions for which mechanisms must presumably have evolved, the evolutionary significance of much of human behavior is not clear (Buss, Haselton, Shackelford, Bleske, & Wakefield, 1998). FFT acknowledges the issue of multiple dynamic processes and specifies important categories of processes that share a common function in the organization of the personality system. It does not, however, detail the specifics. A complete theory of personality will ultimately include sub-theories that elaborate on such specific topics (cf. Mayer, 1998).

Table 2 lists the 16 postulates originally proposed to specify how the personality system operates (McCrae & Costa, 1996). They are intended to be empirically testable, and in fact most of them are based on a body of empirical literature. Although it may generate novel predictions, FFT was designed primarily to make understandable what was already known.

The most radical of these postulates is 1b, *Origin*, which flatly declares that traits are endogenous basic tendencies. This postulate is based chiefly on results from studies of behavior genetics, which consistently point to a large role played by genetic factors and little or no role for common environmental factors (Riemann, Angleitner, & Strelau, 1997). Future research may well force some modification of this postulate; culture (McCrae, Yik, Trapnell, Bond, & Paulhus, 1998) or birth order (Sulloway, 1996) may be shown to affect trait levels. But as stated, Postulate 1b parsimoniously summarizes most of what is now known and offers a clear alternative to most older theories of personality, which emphasize the importance of culture and early life experience in forming personality. Today, even clinicians have begun to recognize that the standard environmental theories of personality are inadequate (Bowman, 1997).

Postulates 1b and 1d recently inspired a novel twin study (Jang, McCrae, Angleitner, Riemann, & Livesley, 1998). FFT clearly implies that N, E, O, A, and C are heritable, a claim long since supported in the cases of N and E, and more recently with respect to O, A, and C (Loehlin, McCrae, Costa, & John, 1998; Riemann, Angleitner, & Strelau, 1997). But are the specific facet traits that define the five factors also specifically heritable; or are they better interpreted as characteristic adaptations, the environmentally molded forms in which the heritable factors are manifested? One could easily suppose that people inherit only a global tendency to be Open to Experience and become open to Aesthetics, or to Ideas, or to Values as a result of individual learning experiences. But behavior genetic analyses of specific facet scores (from which the variance accounted for by the five factors had been partialled) showed that in almost all cases, specific variance was significantly heritable. It appears that the genetic blueprint for personality includes detailed specifications of dozens, perhaps hundreds, of traits.

Postulate 1c is also ripe for minor revision. At the time it was proposed, there was little convincing evidence of systematic personality change after age 30. Newer analyses, especially cross-cultural analyses (McCrae, Costa, Lima, et al., 1999), suggest that cross-sectional decreases in N, E, and O and increases in A and C continue at a very modest pace throughout adulthood. Strikingly similar results from cross-cultural studies of adult age differences in personality do, however, strongly support the basic idea that change in the level of personality traits is part of an intrinsic, endogenous maturational process that belongs in the category of basic tendencies.

* * *

Postulate 2a states the obvious claim that traits affect the way one adapts to the world. A recent example is found in analyses of the need for closure (Kruglanski & Webster, 1996). This tendency to "seize" the first credible answer and to "freeze" on one's initial decisions was shown to be strongly inversely related to Openness to Experience. It is easy to imagine the paths by which such habits of thought might develop:

> Lacking a need for change and uncertainty, closed people come to prefer a simple, structured, familiar world. Through experience they discover that tradition, conventionality, and stereotypes offer tried-and-true answers that they can adopt without much thought. They begin to think of themselves as conservative, down-to-earth people, and they seek out like-minded friends and spouses who will not challenge their beliefs. Thus, basic tendencies of closedness develop into preferences, ideologies, self-construals, and social roles; these characteristic adaptations habitualize, legitimatize, and socially support a way of thinking that expresses a high need for closure. (Costa & McCrae, 1998a, p. 117)

TABLE 2

FIVE-FACTOR THEORY POSTULATES

1. Basic tendencies

   1a. *Individuality.* All adults can be characterized by their differential standing on a series of personality traits that influence patterns of thoughts, feelings, and actions.

   1b. *Origin.* Personality traits are endogenous basic tendencies.

   1c. *Development.* Traits develop through childhood and reach mature form in adulthood; thereafter they are stable in cognitively intact individuals.

   1d. *Structure.* Traits are organized hierarchically from narrow and specific to broad and general dispositions; Neuroticism, Extraversion, Openness to Experience, Agreeableness, and Conscientiousness constitute the highest level of the hierarchy.

2. Characteristic adaptations

   2a. *Adaptation.* Over time, individuals react to their environments by evolving patterns of thoughts, feelings, and behaviors that are consistent with their personality traits and earlier adaptations.

   2b. *Maladjustment.* At any one time, adaptations may not be optimal with respect to cultural values or personal goals.

   2c. *Plasticity.* Characteristic adaptations change over time in response to biological maturation, changes in the environment, or deliberate interventions.

3. Objective biography

   3a. *Multiple determination.* Action and experience at any given moment are complex functions of all those characteristic adaptations that are evoked by the situation.

   3b. *Life course.* Individuals have plans, schedules, and goals that allow action to be organized over long time intervals in ways that are consistent with their personality traits.

4. Self-concept

   4a. *Self-schema.* Individuals maintain a cognitive–affective view of themselves that is accessible to consciousness.

   4b. *Selective perception.* Information is selectively represented in the self-concept in ways that (i) are consistent with personality traits; and (ii) give a sense of coherence to the individual.

5. External influences

   5a. *Interaction.* The social and physical environment interacts with personality dispositions to shape characteristic adaptations and with characteristic adaptations to regulate the flow of behavior.

   5b. *Apperception.* Individuals attend to and construe the environment in ways that are consistent with their personality traits.

   5c. *Reciprocity.* Individuals selectively influence the environment to which they respond.

6. Dynamic processes

   6a. *Universal dynamics.* The ongoing functioning of the individual in creating adaptations and expressing them in thoughts, feelings, and behaviors is regulated in part by universal cognitive, affective, and volitional mechanisms.

   6b. *Differential dynamics.* Some dynamic processes are differentially affected by basic tendencies of the individual, including personality traits.

Note. Adapted from McCrae & Costa (1996).

According to FFT, the personality system represented in Figure 1 is a universal of human nature. All people have basic tendencies, characteristic adaptations, and a self-concept, and they are related to biology and to society in the same basic ways. FFT adopts this system as a framework for explaining the operation of personality; it does not explain why the system exists. Various hypotheses might be offered, most probably based on Darwinian evolution (Buss, 1991); rudimentary forms of this system might be seen in animals (Gosling & John, in press). More formally, the FFT personality system includes the two features that characterize many dynamic systems: a distinctive core that is preserved, and mechanisms for adapting to a changing environment. Species that did not reproduce or adapt to their environments are now extinct; personality traits that did not endure over time and transcend situational influences would never have been recognized in lay lexicons or psychological theories.

Individual Differences in Personality

Consider as a thought experiment the possibility of a utopian community—call it Walden Three—based on the findings of trait psychology. Because individual differences can lead to misunderstanding and conflict (McCrae, 1996), its founders decide to people their society with clones from a single individual; to ensure happiness, they choose an adjusted extravert (Costa & McCrae, 1980). We will let medical ethicists and social philosophers debate the wisdom of this plan and turn our attention to the consequences for personality psychology.

In one respect nothing will have changed. The personality system is universal, and the denizens of Walden Three would still have needs, plans, skills, habits, relationships; they would still interact with the world in ways that external observers would recognize as reflecting their sociability and emotional stability—they would be happy people.

But personality psychologists who attempted to study them by the usual methods would reach startling conclusions. Except for error of measurement, everyone would score the same on every personality scale, and with no variance there could be no covariance. Traits would appear to have no longitudinal stability, no heritability, no five-factor structure. Indigenous psychologists might conclude that traits were a myth, and if asked, residents of Walden Three would probably attribute their behavior solely to situational causes ("Why did you go to that party?" "I was invited!").

What this thought experiment demonstrates is the curious relation of trait psychology to individual differences. On the one hand, it might be argued that personality psychology is not about individual differences; it is about how basic tendencies of a certain class affect thoughts, feelings, and actions. Employers seek conscientious employees not because they differ from lazy and careless employees, but because they work hard and well (Barrick & Mount, 1991). On the other hand, it is only the existence of individual differences in personality that reveals that hard work and carefulness are in part the result of heritable and enduring dispositions. Variation in personality traits across individuals is the ultimate natural experiment that illuminates the workings of personality.

* * *

Five-Factor Theory and the Individual

Although it is doubtless true that every person is in some respects like no other person (Kluckhohn & Murray, 1953), FFT (like most personality theories) has nothing to say about this aspect of the person. It is, from a scientific perspective, error variance. This most emphatically does not mean that personality is irrelevant to understanding the individual.

In the typical application in clinical or personnel psychology, the individual case is understood by inferring personality traits from one set of indicators and using the resulting personality profile to interpret a life history or predict future adjustment.

This is not circular reasoning, because if valid personality measures are used, the traits identified carry surplus meaning that allows the interpreter to go beyond the information given (McCrae & Costa, 1995b). If respondents tell us that they are cheerful and high-spirited, we detect Extraversion and can guess with better-than-chance accuracy that they will be interested in managerial and sales positions. However, it would be much harder to predict their current occupation: Just as the theory of evolution is better at explaining how existing species function than it is at predicting which species will evolve, so personality profiles are more useful in understanding a life than in making specific predictions about what a person will do. This is not a limitation of FFT; it is an intrinsic feature of complex and chaotic systems.

Postulate 3a, *Multiple determination*, points out that there is rarely a one-to-one correspondence between characteristic adaptations and behaviors; the same is of course equally true for the traits that underlie characteristic adaptations. Consequently, interpreting individual behaviors even when the personality profile is well known is a somewhat speculative art. Consider the case of Horatio, Lord Nelson (Costa & McCrae, 1998b; Southey, 1813/1922). In the course of his campaigns against Napoleon's France, he spent many months defending the woefully corrupt court of Naples against a democratic insurrection that had been encouraged by the French. Why would so heroic a figure take on so shabby a task?

We know from a lifetime of instances that Nelson was a paragon of dutifulness, and we might suspect that he was simply following orders—certainly he would have rationalized his conduct as devotion to the war against France. But we also know that Nelson was fiercely independent in his views of what constituted his duty: "I always act as I feel right, without regard to custom" (Southey, 1813/1922, p. 94). He might equally well have supported the insurrection and won its allegiance to the English cause.

We should also consider another trait Nelson possessed: He was excessively low in modesty. Great as his naval achievements were, he never failed to remind people of them. His sympathies were thus with the aristocracy, and he was flattered by the court of Naples, which ultimately named him Duke Di Bronte.

Together, diligence (C), independence (O), and vanity (low A) go far to explain this episode of behavior.

To be sure, there are other factors, including Nelson's relationship to the English ambassador's wife, Lady Hamilton (Simpson, 1983). That notorious affair itself reflects Nelson's independence and vanity, but seems strikingly incongruent with his dutifulness. At the level of the individual, the operations of personality traits are complex and often inconsistent (a phenomenon Mischel and Shoda, 1995, have recently tried to explain).

THE SUBJECTIVE EXPERIENCE OF PERSONALITY   A number of writers (e.g., Hogan, 1996) have suggested that the FFM does not accurately represent personality as it is subjectively experienced by the individual. Daniel Levinson dismissed the whole enterprise of trait psychology as a concern for trivial and peripheral aspects of the person (Rubin, 1981). McAdams (1996) has referred to it as the "psychology of the stranger," because standing on the five factors is the sort of thing one would want to know about a stranger to whom one has just been introduced. Ozer (1996) claims that traits are personality as seen from the standpoint of the other, not the self.

We believe this last position represents a slight confusion. Individuals, who have access to private thoughts, feelings, and desires, and who generally have a more extensive knowledge of their own history of behavior, have a quite different perspective on their own traits than do external observers. What they nonetheless share with others is the need to infer the nature of their own traits and to express their inference in the comparative language of traits. We have no direct intuition of our trait profile; we can only guess at it from its manifestations in our actions and experience. (One possible reason for the increasing stability of personality as assessed by self-reports from age 20 to age 30—see Siegler et al., 1990—is that we continue to learn about ourselves in this time period.)

The fact that traits must be inferred does not, however, mean that they are or seem foreign. When adults were asked to give 20 different answers to the question "Who am I?," about a quarter of the responses were personality traits, and many others combined trait and role characteristics (e.g., "a loving mother"). Traits seem to form an important component of the spontaneous self-concept (McCrae & Costa, 1988); even children use trait terms to describe themselves (Donahue, 1994).

Sheldon, Ryan, Rawsthorne, and Ilardi (1997) brought a humanistic perspective to this issue by assessing sense of authenticity in individuals as they occupied different social roles. They also asked for context-specific self-reports of personality (e.g., how extraverted respondents were as students and as romantic partners). They found that individuals who described themselves most consistently across roles also claimed the highest feelings of authenticity. They concluded that "more often than not, one's true self and one's trait self are one and the same" (p. 1392).

Conclusion

* * *

Historically, personality psychology has been characterized by elaborate and ambitious theories with only the most tenuous links to empirical findings, and theorists have often been considered profound to the extent that their visions of human nature departed from commonsense. Freud's glorification of the taboo, Jung's obscure mysticism, Skinner's denial of that most basic experience of having a mind—such esoteric ideas set personality theorists apart from normal human beings and suggested they were privy to secret knowledge. By contrast, FFT is closely tied to the empirical findings it summarizes, and its vision of human nature, at least at the phenotypic level, is not far removed from folk psychology. If that makes it a rather pro-

saic Grand Theory, so be it. What matters is how far it takes us in understanding that endlessly fascinating phenomenon, personality.

References

Barrick, M. R., & Mount, M. K. (1991). The Big Five personality dimensions and job performance: A meta-analysis. *Personnel Psychology, 44*, 1–26.

Bowman, M. (1997). *Individual differences in posttraumatic response: Problems with the adversity–distress connection.* Mahwah, NJ: Erlbaum.

Bruehl, S. (1994). A case of borderline personality disorder. In P. T. Costa, Jr., & T. A. Widiger (Eds.), *Personality disorders and the five-factor model of personality* (pp. 189–197). Washington, DC: American Psychological Association.

Buss, D. M. (1991). Evolutionary personality psychology. *Annual Review of Psychology, 42*, 459–491.

Buss, D. M., & Craik, K. H. (1983). The act frequency approach to personality. *Psychological Review, 90*, 105–126.

Buss, D. M., Haselton, M. G., Shackelford, T. K., Bleske, A. L. & Wakefield, J. C. (1998). Adaptations, exaptations, and spandrels. *American Psychologist, 53*, 533–548.

Cantor, N. (1990). From thought to behavior: "Having" and "doing" in the study of personality and cognition. *American Psychologist, 45*, 735–750.

Clark, L. A., & Livesley, W. J. (1994). Two approaches to identifying dimensions of personality disorder: Convergence on the five-factor model. In P. T. Costa Jr. & T. A. Widiger (Eds.), *Personality disorders and the five-factor model of personality* (pp. 261–278). Washington, DC: American Psychological Association.

Costa, P. T., Jr., & McCrae, R. R. (1980). Influence of extraversion and neuroticism on subjective well-being: Happy and unhappy people. *Journal of Personality and Social Psychology, 38*, 668–678.

Costa, P. T., Jr., & McCrae, R. R. (1988). From catalog to classification: Murray's needs and the five-factor model. *Journal of Personality and Social Psychology, 55*, 258–265.

Costa, P. T., Jr., & McCrae, R. R. (1992a). *Revised NEO Personality Inventory (NEO-PI-R) and NEO Five-Factor Inventory (NEO-FFI) professional manual.* Odessa, FL: Psychological Assessment Resources.

Costa, P. T., Jr., & McCrae, R. R. (1992b). Trait psychology comes of age. In T. B. Sonderegger (Ed.), *Nebraska Symposium on Motivation: Psychology and aging* (pp. 169–204). Lincoln: University of Nebraska Press.

Costa, P. T., & McCrae, R. R. (1998a). Trait theories of personality. In D. F. Barone, M. Hersen, & V. B. V. Hasselt (Eds.), *Advanced personality* (pp. 103–121). New York: Plenum Press.

Costa, P. T., Jr., & McCrae, R. R. (1998b). Six approaches to the explication of facet-level traits: Examples from conscientiousness. *European Journal of Personality, 12*, 117–134.

Costa, P. T., Jr., & McCrae, R. R. (2000). Theories of personality and psychopathology: Approaches derived from philosophy and psychology. In H. I. Kaplan & B. J. Saddock (Eds.), *Kaplan & Saddock's Comprehensive textbook of psychiatry* (7th ed.) Philadelphia: Lippincott, Williams & Wilkins.

Digman, J. M., & Inouye, J. (1986). Further specification of the five robust factors of personality. *Journal of Personality and Social Psychology, 50*, 116–123.

Donahue, E. M. (1994). Do children use the Big Five, too? Content and structural form in personality description. *Journal of Personality, 62*, 45–66.

Fraley, R. C. (1998). *Attachment continuity from infancy to adulthood: Meta-analysis and dynamic modeling of developmental mechanisms.* Unpublished manuscript, University of California, Davis.

Funder, D. C. (1995). On the accuracy of personality judgment: A realistic approach. *Psychological Review, 102*, 652–670.

Funder, D. C., Kolar, D. C., & Blackman, M. C. (1995). Agreement among judges of personality: Interpersonal relations, similarity, and acquaintanceship. *Journal of Personality and Social Psychology, 69*, 656–672.

Gosling, S. D., & John, O. P. (in press). Personality dimensions in non-human animals: A cross-species review. *Current Directions in Psychological Science.*

Hjelle, L. A., & Siegler, D. J. (1976). *Personality: Theories, basic assumptions, research and applications.* New York: McGraw-Hill.

Hogan, R. (1996). A socioanalytic perspective on the five-factor model. In J. S. Wiggins (Ed.), *The five-factor model of personality: Theoretical perspectives* (pp. 163–179). New York: Guilford Press.

Jang, K. L., McCrae, R. R., Angleitner, A., Riemann, R., & Livesley, W. J. (1998). Heritability of facet-level traits in a cross-cultural twin study: Support for a hierarchical model of personality. *Journal of Personality and Social Psychology, 74*, 1556–1565.

Johnson, J. A. (1997). Units of analysis for the description and explanation of personality. In R. Hogan, J. A. Johnson, & S. R. Briggs (Eds.), *Handbook of personality psychology* (pp. 73–93). New York: Academic Press.

Kluckhohn, C., & Murray, H. A. (1953). Personality formation: The determinants. In C. Kluckhohn, H. A. Murray, & D. M. Schneider (Eds.), *Personality in nature, society, and culture* (pp. 53–67). New York: Knopf.

Kruglanski, A. W., & Webster, D. M. (1996). Motivated closing of the mind: "Seizing" and "freezing." *Psychological Review, 103*, 263–283.

Lanning, K. (1994). Dimensionality of observer ratings on the California Adult Q-Set. *Journal of Personality and Social Psychology, 67*, 151–160.

Loehlin, J. C., McCrae, R. R., Costa, P. T., Jr., & John, O. P. (1998). Heritabilities of common and measure-specific components of the Big Five personality factors. *Journal of Research in Personality, 32*, 431–453.

Mayer, J. D. (1998). A systems framework for the field of personality. *Psychological Inquiry, 9*, 118–144.

McAdams, D. P. (1996). Personality, modernity, and the storied self: A contemporary framework for studying persons. *Psychological Inquiry, 7*, 295–321.

McCrae, R. R. (1992). The five-factor model: Issues and applications [Special issue]. *Journal of Personality, 60*(2).

McCrae, R. R. (1993–1994). Openness to Experience as a basic dimension of personality. *Imagination, Cognition and Personality, 13*, 39–55.

McCrae, R. R. (1996). Social consequences of experiential openness. *Psychological Bulletin, 120*, 323–337.

McCrae, R. R., & Costa, P. T., Jr. (1988). Age, personality, and the spontaneous self-concept. *Journal of Gerontology: Social Sciences, 43*, S177–S185.

McCrae, R. R., & Costa, P. T., Jr. (1990). *Personality in adulthood.* New York: Guilford Press.

McCrae, R. R., & Costa, P. T., Jr. (1995b). Trait explanations in personality psychology. *European Journal of Personality, 9*, 231–252.

McCrae, R. R., & Costa, P. T., Jr. (1996). Toward a new generation of personality theories: Theoretical contexts for the five-factor model. In J. S. Wiggins (Ed.), *The five-factor model of personality: Theoretical perspectives* (pp. 51–87), New York: Guilford Press.

McCrae, R. R., & Costa, P. T., Jr. (1997). Personality trait structure as a human universal. *American Psychologist, 52*, 509–516.

McCrae, R. R., Costa, P. T., Jr., del Pilar, G. H., Rolland, J. P., & Parker, W. D. (1998). Cross-cultural assessment of the five-factor model: The Revised NEO Personality Inventory. *Journal of Cross-Cultural Psychology, 29*, 171–188.

McCrae, R. R., Costa, P. T., Jr., Lima, M. P., Simóes, A., Ostendorf, F., Angleitner, A., Marusic, I., Bratko, D., Caprara, G. V., Barbaranelli, C., Chae, J. H., & Piedmont, R. L. (1999). Age differences in personality across the adult lifespan: Parallels in five cultures. *Development Psychology 35*, 466–477.

McCrae, R. R., Costa, P. T., Jr., Ostendorf, F., Angleitner, A., Hrebickova, M., Avia, M. D., Sanz, J., Sánchez-Bernardos, M. L., Kusdil, M. E., Wood-field, R., Saunders, P. R., & Smith, P. B. (1998). *Nature over nurture: Temperament, personality, and lifespan development.* Unpublished manuscript. Gerontology Research Center.

McCrae, R. R., Yik, M. S. M., Trapnell, P. D., Bond, M. H., & Paulhus, D. L. (1998). Interpreting personality profiles across cultures: Bilingual, acculturation, and peer rating studies of Chinese undergraduates. *Journal of Personality and Social Psychology 74*, 1041–1058.

Mischel, W., & Shoda, Y. (1995). A cognitive–affective system theory of personality: Reconceptualizing situations, dispositions, dynamics, and invariance in personality structure. *Psychological Review, 102*, 246–268.

Ozer, D. J. (1996). The units we should employ. *Psychological Inquiry, 7*, 360–363.

Riemann, R., Angleitner, A., & Strelau, J. (1997). Genetic and environmental influences on personality: A study of twins reared together using the self-and-peer report NEO-FFI scales. *Journal of Personality, 65*, 449–475.

Robins, R. W., & John, O. P. (1997). Effects of visual perspective and narcissism on self-perceptions: Is seeing believing? *Psychological Science, 8*, 37–42.

Rowe, D. C. (1994). *The limits of family influence: Genes, experience, and behavior.* New York: Guilford Press.

Rubin, Z. (1981). Does personality really change after 20? *Psychology Today, 15*, 18–27.

Saucier, G. (1997). Effects of variable selection on the factor structure of person descriptors. *Journal of Personality and Social Psychology, 73*, 1296–1312.

Saucier, G., & Goldberg, L. R. (1996). The language of personality: Lexical perspectives on the five-factor model. In J. S. Wiggins (Ed.), *The five-factor model of personality: Theoretical perspectives* (pp. 21–50). New York: Guilford Press.

Sheldon, K. M., Ryan, R. M., Rawsthorne, L. J., & Ilardi, B.

(1997). Trait self and true self: Cross-role variation in the Big-Five personality traits and its relations with psychological authenticity and subjective well-being. *Journal of Personality and Social Psychology, 73,* 1380–1393.

Siegler, I. C., Zonderman, A. B., Barefoot, J. C., Williams, R. B., Jr., Costa, P. T., Jr., & McCrae, R. R. (1990). Predicting personality in adulthood from college MMPI scores: Implications for follow-up studies in psychosomatic medicine. *Psychosomatic Medicine, 52,* 644–652.

Simpson, C. (1983). *Emma: The life of Lady Hamilton.* London: The Bodley Head.

Southey, R. (1922). *Life of Nelson.* New York: Dutton. (Original work published 1813)

Sulloway, F. J. (1996). *Born to rebel: Birth order, family dynamics, and creative lives.* New York: Pantheon Books.

Tupes, E. C., & Christal, R. E. (1992). Recurrent personality factors based on trait ratings. *Journal of Personality, 60,* 225–251. (Original work published 1961)

Wiggins, J. S. (1997). In defense of traits. In R. Hogan, J. A. Johnson, & S. R. Briggs (Eds.), *Handbook of personality psychology* (pp. 97–115). San Diego: Academic Press. (Original work presented 1973)

Personality and the Prediction of Consequential Outcomes

Daniel J. Ozer and Verónica Benet-Martínez

Why does personality matter? Clearly, the answer to this question is found in what it affects. This essay by Daniel Ozer (one of the editors of this book) and Verónica Benet-Martínez, summarizes a wide range of outcomes that ample research has shown to be predictable from personality variables. The personality variables are organized around the "big five" traits described in the previous selection by McCrae and Costa, which are Extraversion, Neuroticism, Agreeableness, Conscientiousness, and Openness to Experience. Without trying to quantify the exact sizes of the relationships, Ozer and Benet-Martínez provide a list of a large number of major life outcomes that are associated with personality. These findings are summarized in the table reproduced on page 101.

Can you think of important life outcomes that are not listed in the table? Do you think they are reflected by personality? For example, while marriage is in the table, the number of children one has is not. Is there a personality difference between people who have a lot of children as opposed to few or none? As participants in current, ongoing longitudinal research studies grow older, and as new longitudinal studies are started, it should become possible for psychological research to answer this question and many others like it.

From *Annual Review of Psychology, 57,* 401–421, 2006.

What makes a personality characteristic important? . . . The ultimate test of any individual difference personality characteristic is its implicative meaning. Does the construct help us understand what people want, say, do, feel, or believe? Although personality characteristics have the capacity to predict individual differences in behavior within circumscribed laboratory contexts, such results are largely of theoretical interest unless the specific situation is one of compelling importance. But certain life outcomes and events are widely recognized as important—important for individuals and important for the society in which they live. Successful prediction of such consequential outcomes is a demonstration of the practical importance of personality that demands attention, and any successful theory of personality must account for those personality differences that have consequential implications.

Recent emphases in personality research have included personality structure, personality process, and personality stability and change (see, for example Caspi, Roberts, Shiner, 2005; Cervone, 2005). Each of these topics has been a core concern of personality psychology throughout its history. But these topics do not directly address what we understand to be the source of abiding interest in individual differences in character and temperament since antiquity. Personality matters, not just in ways that interest the differential psychologist or those attached to a "romantic" conception of human nature (Hofstee & Ten Berge, 2004),[1] but also in ways that matter to most people and policy makers.

There is not and probably never will be some final list of important life outcomes. There will always be disagreement about what makes an outcome consequential or important, and such disagreement will not be resolved by new data or advances in theory. Beliefs about what are important life outcomes are not simply value-laden, but are constitutive of values. So we make no claim that all of the outcomes we examine will be regarded as universally important, or that we have included all of the important outcomes that might be nominated. Rather, we suggest that most of our readers will find most of the outcomes we discuss to be of consequence in their own lives. We assert, without providing evidence, that most people care about their own health and well being, care about their marital relationships, and care about success and satisfaction in their career. These may not be outcomes understood as universally important across time and culture, but neither are they concerns unique to our own venue of southern California at the start of the twenty-first century.

What personality characteristics might be used to forecast consequential life outcomes, and what characteristics might best serve to enable a useful summary of the current literature? Personality psychology is now in the fortunate position to offer the same answer to both questions: The broad superordinate dimensions (extraversion, agreeableness, conscientiousness, neuroticism, and openness or intellect) of the Five-Factor Model of Personality (John & Srivastava, 1999) are now widely used in the personality and prediction literature, and studies that utilize different dimensions often reference these dimensions of the Big Five model.[2] Of the many different kinds of units used in personality psychology (Hooker & McAdams, 2003), trait dimensions, by virtue of their context independence and noncontingent nature,[3] should be most useful for predicting the multiply determined outcomes that arise from the natural aggregation of acts and events as they occur through time and across situations. More contingent and context-specific units may well be required to understand the mechanisms by which traits and outcomes are related; but that is not the present task. Alternatively, there is much to be said for the use of narrow traits and more focused predictor variables (Paunonen et al., 2003). From the perspective of maximizing accuracy in prediction, using multiple, narrow trait measures is likely to be more effective than using fewer broader measures. But there is no consensus about what might constitute even the beginning of a comprehensive list of narrow traits. Ideally, prediction would utilize a consistent set of broad superordinate dimensions (like the Big Five) plus whatever narrow predictors provided incremental validity for specific outcomes. Identifying narrow predictors for specific outcomes with incremental validity above the Big Five as a criterion is a research endeavor only now really getting underway. There is yet another reason to focus on the prediction of outcomes from the Big Five: Further

---

[1]The two critics cited here argue that individual differences in personality traits have no practical importance, because people are largely the same, but that their study might have literary or "romantic" interest.

[2]See the previous selection by McCrae and Costa for a prominent theory of why and how the "Big Five" are important.

[3]That is, trait constructs, by design, ignore specific context and describe how persons behave *in general,* averaged across all the specific situations of life.

refinement of these factors might best be pursued by attending to the structure of the external correlates of the factors (as Gangestad & Snyder [2000] show for the case of self-monitoring) rather than solely on the structure of the factor indicators.

In our review of the literature, we characterize three different types of outcomes: Individual, interpersonal, and social/institutional. By individual outcomes, we mean those outcomes that can be manifested by an individual outside of a social context, in contrast to interpersonal outcomes that inherently involve other individuals. Moreover, this involvement is personal in a sense: It generally matters who the other is. By social/institutional outcomes, we mean more impersonal, organizational, and sometimes, societal-level processes involving interactions with more generalized others. These distinctions are as much a convenience for organizing a vast literature as they are a claim about the structure of consequential life outcomes.

Individual Outcomes

By individual outcomes, we mean those that do not inherently depend upon a social process in order to define or give meaning to the outcome variable. Physical health and psychopathology are routinely understood as individual outcomes, while the inclusion here of happiness, spirituality, and virtue reflects the growing influence of positive psychology. Although these variables might be understood as features of personality rather than outcomes influenced by personality, we would argue that conscientiousness (to choose the most difficult trait for our view) as a virtue and conscientiousness as a trait are not quite the same things, though they clearly are related. Someone might be conscientious (in the trait sense) for purely instrumental purposes, and this would not constitute a virtue under at least some conceptions of that term.

Identity and self-concept, understood as outcomes, provide the greatest challenge to this kind of organizational scheme. The role of the individual, important others, and the larger social environment most certainly play a part in the development of self and identity; but ultimately, we believe that individuals experience aspects of their identity as a part of themselves, and so we include identity as an individual outcome.

HAPPINESS AND SUBJECTIVE WELL-BEING Few topics have attracted as much recent attention in personality psychology as the study of subjective well-being (SWB), persons' evaluations of their own lives (Diener, Suh, Lucas, Smith, 1999). SWB includes both a cognitive component, such as a judgment of one's life satisfaction (Diener, Emmons, Larsen, Griffin, 1985), and an affective component that includes the experience of positive and absence of negative emotions (Larsen, 2000). Two robust conclusions from studies in this area are that personality dispositions are strong predictors of most components of SWB (see Diener & Lucas [1999] for a review), and demographic and contextual factors, including age, sex, marital status, employment, social class, and culture, are only weakly to moderately related to SWB (Diener et al., 1999; Ryan & Deci, 2001).

Studies trying to unpack the link between personality dispositions and SWB mainly point to the relations between certain largely genetic, affective/cognitive traits related to neuroticism and extraversion (e.g., positive and negative affect, optimism, self-esteem) and the way individuals appraise and react to environmental rewards and punishments (DeNeve & Cooper, 1998). Specifically, individuals high in extraversion and low in neuroticism tend to see events and situations in a more positive light, are less responsive to negative feedback, and tend to discount opportunities that are not available to them. Individual differences in conscientiousness, agreeableness, and openness to experience are less strongly and consistently associated with SWB, mostly because these traits sources reside in "rewards in the environment" (Diener & Lucas, 1999). In summary, SWB is strongly predicted by personality traits that are largely a function of temperament (i.e., extraversion and neuroticism) and moderately predicted by personality dispositions significantly driven by environmental influences (conscientiousness, agreeableness, and openness to experience).

Recent cross-cultural studies of SWB (Benet-Martínez & Karakitapoglu-Aygün, 2003; Kwan, Bond, and Singelis, 1997; Schimmack, Radhakrishnon, Oishi, Dzokoto, Ahadi, 2002) shed light on some possible moderator and mediator variables in the relation between personality factors and SWB. First, the links between both extraversion and neuroticism and SWB are moderated by culture. In individualist societies like the United States, where pleasure and positive mood are highly emphasized and valued, hedonic balance (i.e., the ratio of positive to negative affect) is a particularly strong predictor of SWB (Schimmack et al., 2002). Secondly, across cultures, the links between the Big Five and SWB are largely mediated by intra- and interpersonal esteem evaluations. Specifically, self-esteem appears to be a powerful mediator of the influence of extraversion, neuroticism, and conscientiousness on SWB, whereas relational esteem (i.e., satisfaction with relationships with family and friends) mediates the influence of agreeableness and extraversion on SWB (Benet-Martínez & Karakitapoglu-Aygün, 2003; Kwan et al., 1997). Although the relative weights of self-esteem and relationship harmony in predicting SWB vary across cultures (e.g., self-esteem is a uniquely important predictor in Western cultures), the weights of each of the Big Five dimensions on self-esteem and relationship harmony seem to be cross-culturally equivalent (Benet-Martínez & Karakitapoglu-Aygün, 2003; Kwan et al., 1997).

SPIRITUALITY AND VIRTUES There is very little research directly investigating the relation between personality dispositions and variables referring to religious or spiritual concerns. This lack of attention to spiritual matters in personality psychology is puzzling for two reasons, as described by Emmons (1999): First, personality psychologists such as Allport and Murphy were among the first to study religion and spirituality from a psychological perspective. Despite this early interest in spirituality, the topic fell out of favor in the 1960s and 1970s, as various controversies flourished. Second, personality psychology's neglect of spirituality has occurred in the context of a discipline centrally concerned with understanding the whole person, a concern that undoubtedly involves understanding what is meaningful to the person and how this meaning is experienced as bringing growth and transcendence to one's life. Emmons (1999) argues that spiritual and religious goals and practices are not only a distinctive element of a person's beliefs and behaviors; for many, religious beliefs and practices may be a central theme of their identity.

Piedmont (1999, 2004) developed a measure of spiritual transcendence, with universality, connectedness, and prayer fulfillment subscales, that is unrelated to the traits of the Five-Factor Model and has incremental validity in predicting post-treatment symptoms and coping resources in an outpatient substance abuse sample. MacDonald (2000) also explored the links between basic personality traits and spiritual concerns and behaviors. Five distinct components are identified and described by MacDonald: cognitive orientation (perceptions and attitudes regarding spirituality), experiential/phenomenological (mystical, transcendental, and transpersonal experiences), existential well-being (a sense of meaning, purpose, and resilience regarding one's existence), paranormal beliefs (including ESP and other paranormal phenomena), and religiousness (religious practices). These five components are differentially related to the Big Five personality constructs but are not subsumed by them. In particular, the religiousness and cognitive orientation components were most notably predicted by agreeableness and conscientiousness. Not surprisingly, the experiential/phenomenological and paranormal components were predicted by openness, while existential well-being was strongly predicted by extraversion and low neuroticism.

Recent theoretical work on the classification and delineation of core character strengths and virtues—which can be grouped in terms of their relevance to wisdom, courage, humanity, justice, temperance, and transcendence (Peterson &

Seligman, 2002)—convincingly relates most of these attributes to different sets of personality dispositions. Clearly, certain traits facilitate or impede the development of specific strengths and virtues (e.g., agreeableness facilitates compassion, conscientiousness facilitates perseverance, openness fosters creativity), while at the same time the cultivation of these virtues consolidates the very same personality dispositions from which these virtues sprang. Although most of the aforementioned personality–virtue links have yet to be examined empirically, the following virtues have been shown to have clear associations with personality: gratitude (extraversion and agreeableness; McCullough, Emmons, Tsang, 2002), forgiveness (agreeableness and openness; Thompson, Snyder, Hoffman, Michael, Rasmussen et al., 2005), inspiration (extraversion and openness; Thrash & Elliot, 2004), and humor (low neuroticism and agreeableness; Cann & Calhoun, 2001).

PHYSICAL HEALTH AND LONGEVITY Personality traits have a stable and cumulative effect on both the health and length of individuals' lives (Caspi et al., 2005). With regard to longevity, studies show that positive emotionality (extraversion) and conscientiousness predict longer lives (Danner, Snowdon, Friesen, 2001; Friedman, Tucker, Schwartz, Tomlinson-Keasey, Martin et al., 1995), and hostility (low agreeableness) predicts poorer physical health (e.g., cardiovascular illness) and earlier mortality (Miller, Smith, Turner, Guijarro, Hallet, 1996). The relation between neuroticism and health and longevity is more complex, given that some studies support an association between neuroticism and increased risk of actual disease, whereas others show links with illness behavior only (Smith & Spiro, 2002). The link between personality and health may reflect three different though overlapping processes (Contrada, Cather, O'Leary, 1999). First, personality traits are associated with factors that cause disease. The hostility component of low agreeableness (i.e., anger, cynicism, and mistrust) is associated with sympathetic nervous system activation that is in turn associated with coronary artery disease (Smith & Spiro, 2002). Whether personality

has a causal role or whether the association is spurious remains unclear (Caspi et al., 2005).[4] Second, personality may lead to behaviors that protect or diminish health. Extraversion is associated with more numerous social relationships and greater social support, both of which are positively correlated with health outcomes (Berkman, Glass, Brissette, Seeman, 2000). Various unhealthy habits and behaviors including smoking, improper diet, and lack of exercise are negatively correlated to conscientiousness (Bogg & Roberts 2004, Hampson, Andrews, Barckley, Lichtenstein, Lee, 2000). Last, personality traits are related to the successful implementation of health-related coping behaviors (David & Suls, 1999, Scheier & Carver, 1993) and adherence to treatment regimens (Kenford, Smith, Wetter, Jorenby, Fiore, Baker, 2002). The increasing evidence for these three personality-health processes is clarifying the particular health outcomes associated with particular traits (Caspi et al., 2005): Agreeableness (e.g., hostility) seems to be most directly associated with the disease processes, conscientiousness (e.g., low impulse control) is clearly implicated in health-risk behaviors, and neuroticism (e.g., vulnerability and rumination) seems to contribute to disease by shaping reactions to illness.

Finally, in contrast with the more traditional medical approach to personality and health, which tends to focus on "negative" traits such as anxiety, hostility, and impulsivity, positive psychology research informs us about personality traits that define resiliency (e.g., optimism, self-esteem, creativity), predict health, and represent important resources for the individual and society (Seligman & Csikszentmihalyi, 2000). There is growing evidence that the positive emotions and dispositions subsumed by the extraversion dimension lead to improved coping and the development of psychological skills and resources (Fredrickson & Joiner, 2002).

---

[4]The association might be "spurious" in the sense that both hostility and coronary disease might be associated with other, "third" variables that are the real reason they are correlated.

PSYCHOPATHOLOGY The previously described links between personality and SWB are not sufficient for understanding the relation between personality and psychopathology (e.g., personality disorders, clinical depression, and schizophrenia). This is so because SWB is not synonymous with mental or psychological health (Diener et al., 1999). Some delusional individuals may feel happy and satisfied with their lives, and yet we would not say that they possess mental health.

Recent research demonstrates strong links between the personality dispositions and both Axis I and II psychological disorders.[5] Specifically, substance abuse disorders are largely predicted by higher openness and lower conscientiousness (Trull & Sher, 1994). Anxiety disorders are primarily predicted by higher neuroticism, and depression is mostly linked to neuroticism and low extraversion (Trull & Sher, 1994). Associations between personality traits and Axis II disorders are even more evident given the growing prevalence of dimensional conceptualizations of personality disorders. Dimensional models of personality disorders suggest that they may be understood as extreme expressions of personality traits (Trull & Durrett, 2005). It is apparent that personality disorders have substantial associations with the five factors; neuroticism has the strongest relationship with personality disorders, whereas openness to experience has only a modest relationship.

SELF-CONCEPT AND IDENTITY While many psychologists would understand self-concept and identity to be an integral part of personality, how one characterizes oneself, the groups one belongs to, and the goals and values one possesses may be understood as outcomes as well. The structure of social and personal identifications, goals, and priorities that constitute self and identity (Marcia,

1980) may be understood not only as a function of life experience and cultural context, but also as a domain where personality dispositions play a part. How do personality traits influence self-concept and identity? Work in this area shows that personality traits affect the formation of identity, while at the same time identity both directs and becomes a part of personality through exploration and commitment processes in identity development (Helson & Srivastava, 2001). Clancy & Dollinger (1993) have shown robust relations between personality traits and Marcia's (1980) four categories of identity development (achieved, moratorium, diffuse, and foreclosed). Specifically, foreclosure is predicted by low levels of openness to experience; identity achievement is predicted by low neuroticism, conscientiousness, and extraversion. Both moratorium and diffusion stages involve neuroticism. Additionally, diffusion is inversely related to agreeableness. Openness to experience may be the most important personality trait in terms of impact on identity development (Duriez, Soenens, Beyers, 2004; Helson & Srivastava, 2001).

Furthering this typological approach to identity, recent longitudinal studies have explored the interactive roles of personality and identity over the life span, while focusing on more complex identity constructs such as identity consolidation (development of a coherent, grounded, and positive identity; Pals, 1999) and identity integration (Helson & Srivastava, 2001). This work shows that identity consolidation is predicted by an early configuration of personality traits related to openness to experience (desire for exploration and stimulation), low neuroticism (low rumination), and conscientiousness (ambition). This pattern of personality traits leads to an organized and committed yet flexible exploration of identity, which in turn predicts well-being. These identity choices lead to particular personal and professional choices that consolidate earlier personality traits (Helson & Srivastava, 2001; Pals, 1999). The influence of personality traits is seen both at the level of narrower, cognitive, identity-relevant processes such as identity language (Pennebaker & King, 1999), autobiographical memories (Thorne & Klohnen, 1993),

---

[5]In the widely used *Diagnostic and Statistical Manual* of the American Psychiatric Association, disorders listed under Axis I are severe psychopathologies (such as depression or schizophrenia) and Axis II disorders are less severe but more chronic personality disorders (such as narcissism or antisocial disorder).

and self-concept clarity (Campbell, Trapnell, Heine, Katz, Lavallee, Lehman, 1996), as well as at the broad level of life story narratives (McAdams, 2001).

Personality dispositions also influence more contextualized types of identities, such as cultural identity. For example, among immigrants, ethnic cultural identity is mainly predicted by conscientiousness and agreeableness (i.e., warmth and commitment towards one's culture of origin), whereas identification with the dominant host culture is largely predicted by openness and extraversion (Benet-Martínez & Haritatos, 2005; Ryder, Alden, Paulhus, 2000). Further, supporting other studies on identity consolidation, openness to experience and low neuroticism predict the degree to which an individual's ethnic and mainstream identities are well integrated within a coherent sense of self (Benet-Martínez & Haritatos, 2005).

Interpersonal Outcomes

One of the most important tasks faced by individuals is the establishment and maintenance of successful relationships with friends and peers, family members, and romantic partners. Relationships do have emergent properties, but the nature and quality of the relationship nonetheless is partially shaped by the dispositions and skills of the individuals involved. The length and quality of most relationships is predicted by socioemotional competence (or socioemotional intelligence), a broad cognitive, affective, and behavioral construct typically operationalized in terms of social skills (e.g., ability to engage and effectively maintain social interaction), emotional skills (expression, empathy, regulation), popularity, and relationship satisfaction (Bost, Vaughn, Washington, Cielinski, Bradbard, 1998; Cantor & Kilstrom, 1987).

Although socioemotional competence involves personality characteristics related to all the Big Five domains (Sjöberg, 2001; van der Zee, Thijs, Schakel, 2002; Vollrath, Krahé, Hampson, 2004), the strongest personality links are shown for the components of empathy, which seems to be primarily a combination of extraversion and agreeable-

ness, and emotional regulation, which is best predicted by low neuroticism. The above personality–social behavior links are robust and interesting but too broad for an adequate understanding of the role played by personality in more specific types of relationships, including family, peer, and romantic relationships, as we describe below.

PEER AND FAMILY RELATIONSHIPS Much of the research examining personality and its role in friendships and peer relations has been conducted with children and adolescents. Given how much time children spend at school and playing with friends, understanding how children and adolescents successfully establish and maintain friendships is important for its own sake (i.e., to predict personal and school adjustment) and also because social adjustment in childhood has been shown to be a very strong predictor of the quality of relationships in adulthood (Parker & Asher, 1987).

Of all of the Big Five dimensions, agreeableness and extraversion are the best predictors of processes and outcomes related to peer relations in children, such as peer acceptance and friendship (Jensen-Campbell, Adams, Perry, Workman, Furdella, Egan, 2002). Specifically, low agreeableness (hostility) and low extraversion (being withdrawn) are associated with rejected peer status (Newcomb, Bukowski, Pattee, 1993). These findings are not surprising given that both agreeableness and extraversion are related to motives and skills necessary to build and maintain satisfying relations with peers. Longitudinal studies of peer relations in children show that the benefits of agreeableness accumulate over time by protecting children from victimization (Jensen-Campbell et al., 2002).

Personality also affects the quality of the relationship young adults have with their parents. These intergenerational relationships are negatively affected by young adults' neuroticism, low conscientiousness, and low extraversion (Belsky, Jaffee, Caspi, Moffett, Silva, 2003). These findings support the notion that the very same life events and experiences that affect intergenerational relationships in young adulthood (e.g., timing of parenthood, when the young adult leaves home, or length of unemployment) could be a function of earlier and concurrent personality traits (Caspi et al., 2005).

Surprisingly few studies have examined the personality predictors of popularity, status, and peer acceptance in adulthood. This is unfortunate since these social outcomes (i.e., amount of respect, influence, and prominence a person enjoys in the eyes of others) presumably influence professional and personal social networks and support. Most of the available evidence points to extraversion (but not agreeableness) as the most important predictor of popularity and status among adults. Paunonen (2003), for instance, finds evidence that extraversion is related to popularity, dating variety, and self-reported attractiveness. The Anderson, John, Keltner, and Kring (2001) study of the links between personality and status also supports extraversion as the main predictor of social acceptance, concurrently and over time, and for both sexes. This study is also informative regarding the role (or lack thereof) played by the other Big Five dimensions in adult peer relations: Neuroticism appears to be a (negative) predictor of status among men only, supporting the traditional gender role expectation that men who feel anxious and vulnerable are less deserving of status and respect (Anderson et al., 2001). Agreeableness does not predict status for either women or men, which supports the socioanalytic notion that status (or "getting ahead") may be inimical to "getting along" (Hogan, 1983). Status is unrelated to either conscientiousness or openness in informal groups; however, as noted by Anderson et al. (2001), conscientiousness may play a role in more formal organizations and professional groups, where task performance and achievement play a central role.

ROMANTIC RELATIONSHIPS Some of the richest evidence for the consequentiality of personality dispositions with regard to interpersonal relations stems from longitudinal studies exploring the links between adult personality and romantic relationships. Attaining and maintaining a satisfying romantic relationship is a central feature of most adult lives, and such relationships play a key role in fostering emotional well-being and physical health (Berscheid, 1999). Do personality dispositions explain why some individuals are involved in satisfying romantic relationships, whereas others are involved in less satisfying and more distressed relationships?

Neuroticism and low agreeableness consistently emerge as predictors of negative relationship outcomes such as relationship dissatisfaction, conflict, abuse, and ultimately dissolution (Karney & Bradbury, 1995). Naturally, the predisposition to easily experience anger and frustration, distress, and anxiety is potentially destructive for relationships (although see Gottman (1994) for a discussion of how interpersonal conflict may not always be detrimental in intimate relationships). Relationship quality is directly affected by neuroticism (Donnellan, Larsen-Rife, Conger, 2005); this relation between neuroticism and relationship dissatisfaction involves a reciprocal process such that negative emotions increase relationship distress, which in turn accentuates negative emotionality (Robins, Caspi, Moffitt, 2002). These effects seem to be consistent across relationships, as neuroticism and low agreeableness predict dissatisfaction across relationships with different partners (Robins et al., 2002). Longitudinal evidence shows that personality traits predict not only concurrent relationship outcomes, but also future ones (Donnellan et al., 2005).

Recent multimethod research with dyads shows that the link between personality and relationship status and quality is more than an artifact of shared method variance arising from self-report measurement procedures (Donnellan, Conger, Bryant, 2004; Watson, Klohnen, Casillas, Nus Simms, Haig, Berry, 2000). Watson et al. (2000) used both self-ratings and partner ratings of personality in both dating and married samples. Positive and negative affect were related to relationship satisfaction in the predicted direction in both samples. Conscientiousness and agreeableness predicted satisfaction in dating couples, whereas extraversion predicted satisfaction in the married couples.

In general, there appears to be modest to moderate assortative marriage across a wide range of psychological characteristics (e.g., intellectual abilities, values, political attitudes, and religious beliefs) and sociodemographic variables (e.g., age, education). But recent studies of personality and assortment indicate low levels of partner similarity in personality (Gattis, Berns, Simpson, Christensen, 2004; Luo & Klohnen, 2005, Watson et al. 2004). It is not clear whether spouse similarity and relationship satisfaction are related, with some studies suggesting a positive relation (e.g., Luo & Klohnen, 2005), whereas others (Gattis et al., 2004) report that personality similarity does not independently predict relationship satisfaction.

Finally, it is important to note that personality dispositions, besides predicting romantic relationship outcomes such as quality, satisfaction, and length, also influence relationship-relevant cognitive-motivational mechanisms such as attitudes, goals, and emotional scripts that people bring to their romantic relationships. Traits from all the Big Five domains have been related to attachment styles (Shaver & Brennan, 1992), dating attitudes and behavior (Schmitt, 2002), and love styles (Heaven, DaSilva, Carey, Holen, 2004).

Social/Institutional Outcomes

In this section, we examine three outcomes in the world of work and occupation: vocational interests, work satisfaction, and job performance. These three outcomes subsume the basic components of work of interest to psychology: What kind of work is preferred, how well is it performed, and how much satisfaction is attained? There has been a surge of recent interest in the relation between personality and political attitudes and ideology, giving proof to the longevity and fruitfulness of the construct of authoritarianism. Criminality and community involvement are also discussed below, representing the extremes of antisocial and prosocial societal outcomes.

OCCUPATIONAL CHOICE AND PERFORMANCE Organizations and institutions require individuals to fill specific roles that require different skills and bestow different rewards. Individuals seek, to varying degrees, roles that provide personal satisfaction and reward. This is most clearly true in the context of individuals' work, occupation, and relation with an employer, but is also true in their relations with their community, though here arrangements may be much less formal.

Two recently completed meta-analyses (Barrick, Mount, Gupta, 2003; Larson, Rottinghaus, Borgen, 2002) examining the relation between personality traits and occupational types concurred in finding that extraversion was related to social and enterprising occupational interests, agreeableness to social interests, and openness to investigative and artistic interests. Neuroticism was not related to any occupational interest. Barrick et al. (2003) (but not Larson et al., 2002) reported conscientiousness to be related to conventional interests. Personality traits appear to broadly influence occupational interests and choices.

The meta-analytic finding that conscientiousness predicts job performance reported by Barrick & Mount (1991) was broadly influential. Research examining job and occupational variables began to include personality and especially Big Five measures, and personality researchers began to examine the consequential meaning of the five factors. Barrick, Mount, and Judge (2001) performed a meta-analysis of the meta-analytic studies of the relation between job performance and Big Five personality traits. Conscientiousness predicts performance, assessed in various ways, in all included occupations. Smaller, though nearly as broad, effects were found for extraversion and emotional stability—which seem important for some, though not all, occupational groups—while only weak and narrow effects for agreeableness and openness were identified. So, for example, agreeableness relates to job performance when a teamwork criterion is used. Perhaps the most well known occupation-specific measure of job performance is grade point average for students, and it can hardly be a surprise to find a positive relation between GPA and conscientiousness (Paunonen, 2003). Another educational outcome, the number of years of education, is related to intellect, or openness (Goldberg, Sweeney, Merenda, Hughes, 1998).

Although job performance is inarguably an important outcome from the standpoint of the employer, the employees may be more concerned with their feelings about work and their perceptions of the workplace. The meta-analysis[6] of Thoresen, Kaplan, Barsky, Warren, and deChermont (2003) examined work attitudes and job perceptions and their relation to positive and negative affect.... The results of Thoresen et al. (2003) show that extraversion and emotional stability are associated with job satisfaction and organizational commitment, and are negatively related to a wish to change jobs and with outcomes associated with burnout. Conscientiousness may best predict how well one does at work, but extraversion and emotional stability are more important for understanding how one feels about work.

Career success may be understood as having both extrinsic (e.g., salary and authority) and intrinsic (satisfaction) components. In longitudinal data, both extrinsic and intrinsic career success were predicted by childhood conscientiousness, openness, and emotional stability. When controlling for other personality variables, agreeableness was negatively related to extrinsic success (Judge, Higgins, Thoresen, Barrick, 1999).

Roberts, Caspi, and Moffitt (2003) report that personality assessed in late adolescence affects various workplace experiences and outcomes in early adulthood. Emotional stability (negative emotionality) is most strongly related to financial security; agreeableness (positive emotionality-communion) is related to occupational attainment. Resource power and work involvement are predicted by extraversion (positive emotionality-agency).

POLITICAL ATTITUDES AND VALUES Although political attitudes may be most frequently understood as predictor rather than outcome variables, the political attitudes and beliefs of individuals in a democratic society may affect social policies in diverse and consequential ways. Certainly, candidates for public office and those who financially support these candidates appear to believe that political attitudes are important. Since the publication of *The Authoritarian Personality* (Adorno,

Frenkel-Brunswik, Levinson, and Sanford, 1950), linkages between personality and political beliefs have been of considerable interest. Saucier's (2000) analysis of the broad domain of social and political attitudes ("isms") suggests that openness is related to the content of social attitudes, with political conservativism and right-wing authoritarianism being negatively related to this personality characteristic. Heaven & Bucci (2001) also report this negative association between openness and right-wing authoritarianism. Van Hiel, Mervielde, and DeFruyt (2004) report this same negative correlation between openness and conservative political beliefs, as well as smaller relations between these same beliefs and low agreeableness and conscientiousness.

Jost, Glaser, Kruglanski, and Sulloway (2003a) integrate personality characteristics within a motivated social cognition approach to understanding political conservativism, and their meta-analysis suggests that death anxiety, dogmatism–intolerance of ambiguity, and the needs for order, structure, and closure are positive correlates of conservativism, whereas negative correlates include openness to experience, uncertainty tolerance, and integrative complexity. These traits, individually and as a set, suggest a susceptibility to a fear of uncertainty that may be assuaged by political conservativism. Greenberg & Jonas (2003) object to the Jost et al. (2003a) claims, posing an alternative conception of conservativism and suggesting that other political points of view may also serve the same psychological function. In their view, the rigidity or fixedness of one's political point of view is independent of the left-versus-right content of political belief. Jost, Glaser, Kruglanski, and Sulloway (2003b) respond both by considering the temporal context of political movements and by directly pitting a "rigidity-of-the-right" hypothesis against the alternative "ideological extremity" hypothesis. The evidence reviewed by Jost et al. (2003a,b) is more consistent with associating conservativism rather than extremity of belief with psychological rigidity, though some studies do suggest that both processes may be involved. One of the next challenges would appear to be to examine extreme liberalism to determine when rigidity does, and does not, come into play.

---

[6]A meta-analysis is a review of research literature that uses statistical techniques to combine the results of diverse studies into powerful, broadly based conclusions.

One might also ask whether specific substantive features of conservative ideology are associated with particular person attributes. Van Hiel & Mervielde (2004) found political conservativism to be negatively related to openness, and their data suggest that this relationship is apparently more a function of cultural than of economic conservative beliefs.

When it comes to candidates and elections, Caprara & Zimbardo (2004) describe a model of the political process that depends directly and considerably on the personalities of voters and their perceptions of candidates' personalities. They report that those supporting more liberal candidates describe themselves and the candidates they prefer as higher on openness and agreeableness, whereas those who support more conservative candidates describe themselves and the candidates they support as more extraverted and conscientious. This congruency involving the perceived personality of the politician, the personality of the voter, and the ideological preferences of the politician and the voter suggests a deep involvement of personality in the political process.

VOLUNTEERISM AND COMMUNITY INVOLVEMENT

Among the more socially important kinds of outcomes that might be imagined are prosocial behavior and volunteerism. Clearly, there are important differences among people in their willingness to get involved in helping others, both in formal contexts of volunteering and social service as well as in less planned, everyday acts of helping. Penner, Fritzsche, Craiger, and Freifeld (1995) have developed a measure of prosocial behavior that includes an other-oriented empathy scale that correlates strongly with agreeableness. Helpfulness, a second factor on Penner's measure, appears more related to extraversion. These interpersonal traits are related to a wide variety of prosocial behaviors and volunteerism (Penner, 2002). The link between volunteerism and the interpersonal traits of extraversion and agreeableness was also found in a large college student sample (Carlo, Okun, Knight, de-Guzman, 2005), where there is some evidence that the trait-behavior link was mediated by prosocial motivation.

Extraversion and agreeableness not only predict community involvement, but these same traits also seem to predict who assumes a leadership role. The interpersonal traits of extraversion and agreeableness are positively associated with a transformational leadership style among community leaders (Judge & Bono, 2000).

CRIMINALITY Criminal activity lies at the opposite end of the spectrum of community involvement, but it is not simply the opposite or lack of altruism. Krueger, Hicks, and McGue (2001) found that antisocial behavior and altruism are distinct, with different origins and correlates. In contrast to the involvement of extraversion in prosocial behavior, antisocial behavior was associated with low constraint and negative emotionality (low conscientiousness and neuroticism).

Low conscientiousness seems to be consistently associated with various aspects of criminal and antisocial actions: It is related to behavior problems in adolescent boys (Ge & Conger, 1999), antisocial behavior (Shiner, Masten, Tellegen, 2002), deviance and suicide attempts (Verona, Patrick, Joiner, 2001), and along with low agreeableness, low conscientiousness is associated with substance abuse (Walton & Roberts, 2004). Wiebe (2004) reports that low agreeableness and low conscientiousness predict criminal acts in college student and in prison samples. But Wiebe (2004) also warns that self-deception and/or other deception may importantly attenuate the ability to predict criminal acts from self-reported personality traits.

Conclusion

In discussing the relation between personality characteristics and consequential outcomes, we have not attempted to evaluate effect size.[7] The

---

[7]That is, this review noted the direction in which traits were associated with outcomes (positively or negatively) rather than attempting to provide a quantitative estimate of the strength of the association (such as the correlational r discussed in the earlier selection by Rosenthal and Rubin).

TABLE 1

SUMMARY OF THE RELATION BETWEEN PERSONALITY TRAITS AND CONSEQUENTIAL OUTCOMES

	Individual outcomes	Interpersonal outcomes	Social institutional outcomes
Extraversion	Happiness: subjective well-being Spirituality & virtues: existential well-being, gratitude, inspiration Health: longevity, coping, resilience Psychopathology: (−) depression, (−/+) personality disorders Identity: majority culture identification (for minorities)	Peer & family relations: peers' acceptance and friendship (children and adults); dating variety, attractiveness, status (adults) Romantic relations: satisfaction	Occupational choice & performance: social and enterprising interests, satisfaction, commitment, involvement Community involvement: volunteerism, leadership
Agreeableness	Spirituality & virtues: religious beliefs and behavior, gratitude, forgiveness, humor Health: longevity, (−) heart disease Psychopathology: (−/+) personality disorders Identity: ethnic culture identification (for minorities)	Peer & family relations: peers' acceptance and friendship (children) Romantic relations: satisfaction (dating couples only)	Occupational choice & performance: social interests, job attainment, (−) extrinsic success Community involvement: volunteerism, leadership Criminality: (−) criminal behavior
Conscientiousness	Spirituality & virtues: religious beliefs and behavior Health: longevity, (−) risky behavior Psychopathology: (−) substance abuse, (−/+) personality disorders Identity: achievement, ethnic culture identification (for minorities)	Peer & family relations: family satisfaction Romantic relations: satisfaction (dating couples only)	Occupational choice & performance: performance, success Political attitudes & values: conservatism Criminality: (−) antisocial and criminal behavior
Neuroticism	Happiness: (−) subjective well-being Spirituality & virtues: (−) existential well-being, (−) humor Health: (−) coping Psychopathology: anxiety, depression, (+/−) personality disorders Identity: (−) identity integration/consolidation	Peer & family relations: (−) family satisfaction, (−) status (males only) Romantic relations: dissatisfaction, conflict, abuse, dissolution	Occupational choice & performance: (−) satisfaction, (−) commitment, (−) financial security, (−) success Criminality: antisocial behavior
Openness	Spirituality & virtues: existential/phenomenological concerns, forgiveness, inspiration Psychopathology: substance abuse Identity: (−) foreclosure, identity integration/consolidation, majority culture identification (for minorities)		Occupational choice & performance: investigative and artistic interests, success Political attitudes & values: (−) right-wing authoritarianism, liberalism

Note: (−) indicates a negative relation between the trait and outcome.

various meta-analyses cited here provide such estimates, and in not noting the specific results, we do not wish to suggest that such quantitative indicators are unimportant. However, making fine distinctions about the relative sizes of particular effects may be largely premature, and we wish to emphasize a rather different consideration. Any nonzero effect of a personality characteristic on most of the outcome measures we describe would be a large effect in practical terms. In parallel to the argument of Abelson (1985), it should be clear that even if the relation between agreeableness and volunteerism is small, then even a small change in mean agreeableness scores might increase by thousands the number of volunteers serving community needs in AIDS clinics and elsewhere. Our claim is not that personality effects are "large" at a completely disaggregated level of analysis (i.e., the prediction of what one person will do on a particular occasion), but rather that personality effects are ubiquitous, influencing each of us all the time, and when aggregated to the population level such effects are routinely consequential.

Our account of specific outcomes associated with personality factors is summarized in Table 1. At first glance, it is apparent from the table that each of the five superordinate traits is broadly implicative. It would be impossible, simply from the summary of the evidence as presented in Table 1, to claim that any of the five traits has a narrow and circumscribed set of correlates. There is, in fact, but one empty cell in the table: Openness as yet has no well-documented effects in the interpersonal domain that we were able to locate. Any nominee for a sixth factor should possess the same kind of breadth in its external correlates as shown by the present five. This is not to say that additional variables outside of the five-factor structure are not useful in prediction. But the expectation, at present, is that such a variable will have a narrower band of consequential outcomes. Nor should Table 1 be taken as an endorsement of the claim that the five superordinate traits are those that should be used in applied prediction contexts. As noted earlier, there is both good reason and some evidence to expect that larger effects would be obtained by using multiple narrow predictor variables (Paunonen et al., 2003). Although such an approach would maximize predictive accuracy, it would do so at the price of cumulative knowledge of the kind depicted in Table 1. When the mechanism that relates personality process to consequential outcome is identified, then the time to utilize specific measures of that process will have arrived.

Arguments about whether personality is consistent over time and context, arguments about the proper units of personality, and arguments about the utility of different types of measures have all had one common and unfortunate effect: They have obscured the reasons why proponents of different positions cared about personality in the first place, and first and foremost among these reasons is that personality matters.

References

Abelson R. (1985). A variance explanation paradox: when a little is a lot. *Psychol. Bull., 97,* 129–33.

Adorno TW, Frenkel-Brunswik E, Levinson DJ, & Sanford RN. (1950) *The Authoritarian Personality.* New York: Harper.

Anderson C, John OP, Keltner D, & Kring AM. (2001). Who attains social status? Effects of personality and physical attractiveness in social groups. *J. Personal. Soc. Psychol., 81,* 116–32.

Barrick MR, & Mount MK. (1991). The Big Five personality dimensions and job performance: a meta analysis. *Personal. Psychol., 44,* 1–26.

Barrick MR, Mount MK, & Gupta R. (2003). Meta-analysis of the relationship between the Five Factor model of personality and Hol-land's occupational types. *Personal. Psychol., 56,* 45–74.

Barrick MR, Mount MK, & Judge TA. (2001). Personality and performance at the beginning of the new millennium: What do we know and where do we go next? *Int. J. Sel. Assess., 9,* 9–30.

Belsky J, Jaffee SR, Caspi A, Moffitt T, & Silva PA. (2003). Intergenerational relationships in young adulthood and their life course, mental health, and personality correlates. *J. Fam. Psychol., 17,* 460–71.

Benet-Martínez V, & Haritatos J. (2005). Bicultural Identity Integration (BII): components and socio-personality antecedents. *J. Personal., 73,* 1015–50.

Benet-Martínez V, & Karakitapoglu-Aygün Z. (2003). The interplay of cultural values and personality in predicting life-satisfaction: comparing Asian- and European- Americans. *J. Cross-Cult. Psychol., 34,* 38–61.

Berkman LF, Glass T, Brissette I, & Seeman TE. (2000). From social integration to health. *Soc. Sci. Med., 51,* 843–57.

Berscheid E. (1999). The greening of relationship science. *Am. Psychol., 54,* 260–66.

Bogg T, & Roberts BW. (2004). Conscientiousness and health behaviors: a meta-analysis. *Psychol. Bull., 130:* 887–919.

Bost KK, Vaughn BE, Washington WN, Cielinski KL, & Bradbard MR. (1998). Social competence, social support, and attachment: demarcation of construct domains, measurement, and paths of influence for preschool children attending Head Start. *Child Dev., 69,* 192–218.

Campbell JD, Trapnell PD, Heine SJ, Katz IM, Lavallee LF, & Lehman DR. (1996). Self-concept clarity: measurement, personality correlates, and cultural boundaries. *J. Personal. Soc. Psychol., 70,* 141–56.

Cann A, & Calhoun LG. (2001). Perceived personality associations with differences in sense of humor: stereotypes of hypothetical others with high or low senses of humor. *Humor: Int. J. Humor Res., 14,* 117–30.

Cantor N, & Kihlstrom JF. (1987). *Personality and Social Intelligence.* Englewood Cliffs, NJ: Prentice-Hall.

Caprara GV, & Zimbardo PG. (2004). Personalizing politics: a congruency model of political preference. *Am. Psychol., 59,* 581–94.

Carlo G, Okun MA, Knight GP, & de Guzman MRT. (2005). The interplay of traits and motives on volunteering: agreeableness, extraversion, and prosocial value motivation. *Personal. Individ. Differ., 38,* 1293–305.

Caspi A, Roberts BW, & Shiner RL. (2005). Personality development: stability and change. *Annu. Rev. Psychol., 56,* 453–84.

Cervone D. (2005). Personality architecture: within-person structures and processes. *Annu. Rev. Psychol., 56,* 423–52.

Clancy SM, & Dollinger SJ. (1993). Identity, self, and personality: I. Identity status and the Five Factor model of personality. *J. Res. Adolesc., 3,* 227–45.

Contrada RJ, Cather C, & O'Leary A. (1999). Personality and health: dispositions and processes in disease susceptibility and adaptation to illness. In *Handbook of Personality*, ed. LA Pervin, OP John, pp. 576–604. New York: Guilford.

Danner DD, Snowdon DA, & Friesen WV. (2001). Positive emotions in early life and longevity: findings from the nun study. *J. Personal. Soc. Psychol., 80,* 804–13.

David J, & Suls J. (1999). Coping efforts in daily life: role of Big Five traits and problem appraisal. *J. Personal., 67,* 119–40.

DeNeve KM, & Cooper H. (1998). The happy personality: a meta-analysis of 137 personality traits and subjective well-being. *Psychol. Bull., 124,* 197–229.

Diener E, Emmons RA, Larsen RJ, & Griffin S. (1985). The Satisfaction with Life Scale. *J. Personal. Assess., 49,* 71–75.

Diener E, & Lucas RE. (1999). Personality and subjective well-being. In *Well-Being: The Foundations of Hedonic Psychology*, ed. D Kahneman, E Diener, & N Schwarz, pp. 213–29. New York: Russell Sage Found.

Diener E, Suh EM, Lucas RE, & Smith HL. (1999). Subjective well-being: three decades of progress. *Psychol. Bull. 125,* 276–302.

Donnellan MB, Conger RD, & Bryant CM. (2004). The Big Five and enduring marriages. *J. Res. Personal., 38,* 481–504.

Donnellan MB, Larsen-Rife D, & Conger RD. (2005). Personality, family history, and competence in early adult romantic relationships. *J. Personal. Soc. Psychol., 88,* 562–76.

Duriez B, Soenens B, & Beyers W. (2004). Personality, identity styles, and religiosity: an integrative study among late adolescents in Flanders (Belgium). *J. Personal., 72,* 877–908.

Emmons RA. (1999). Religion in the psychology of personality: an introduction. *J. Personal., 67,* 873–88.

Fredrickson BL, & Joiner T. (2002). Positive emotions trigger upward spirals toward emotional well-being. *Psychol. Sci., 13,* 172–75.

Friedman HS, Tucker JS, Schwartz JE, Tomlinson-Keasey C, & Martin LR, et al. (1995). Psychosocial and behavioral predictors of longevity. *Am. Psychol., 50,* 69–78.

Gangestad SW, & Snyder M. (2000). Self-monitoring: appraisal and reappraisal. *Psychol. Bull., 126,* 530–55.

Gattis KS, Berns S, Simpson LE, & Christensen A. (2004). Birds of a feather or strange birds? Ties among personality dimensions, similarity, and marital quality. *J. Fam. Psychol., 8,* 564–74.

Ge X, & Conger RD. (1999). Adjustment problems and emerging personality characteristics from early to late adolescence. *Am. J. Community Psychol., 27,* 429–59.

Goldberg LR, Sweeney D, Merenda PF, & Hughes JE. (1998). Demographic variables and personality: the effects of gender, age, education, and ethnic/racial status on self-descriptions of personality attributes. *Personal. Individ. Differ., 24,* 393–403.

Gottman JM. (1994). *What Predicts Divorce? The Relationship Between Marital Processes and Marital Outcomes.* Hillsdale, NJ: Erlbaum.

Greenberg J, & Jonas E. (2003). Psychological motives and political orientation—the left, the right, and the rigid: comment on Jost et al. (2003). *Psychol. Bull., 129,* 376–82.

Hampson SE, Andrews JA, Barckley M, Lichtenstein E, & Lee ME. (2000). Conscientiousness, perceived risk, and risk-reduction behaviors: a preliminary study. *Health Psychol., 19,* 247–52.

Heaven PC, & Bucci S. (2001). Right-wing authoritarianism, social dominance orientation and personality: an analysis using the IPIP measure. *Eur. J. Personal., 15,* 49–56.

Heaven PC, DaSilva T, Carey C, & Holen J. (2004). Loving styles: relationships with personality and attachment atyles. *Eur. J. Personal., 18,* 103–13.

Helson R, & Srivastava S. (2001). Three paths of adult development: conservers, seekers, and achievers. *J. Personal. Soc. Psychol., 80,* 995–1010.

Hofstee WKB, & Ten Berge JMF. (2004). Personality in proportion: a bipolar proportional scale for personality assessments and its consequences for trait structure. *J. Personal. Assess., 83,* 120–27.

Hogan R. (1983). A socioanalytic theory of personality. In: MM Page ed. *Nebraska Symposium on Motivation 1982*, Lincoln: Univ. Nebraska Press, pp. 55–89.

Hooker K, & McAdams DP. (2003). Personality reconsidered: a new agenda for aging research. *J. Gerontol. B Psychol. Sci. Soc. Sci., 58,* 296–304.

Jensen-Campbell LA, Adams R, Perry DG, Workman KA, Furdella JQ, & Egan SK. (2002). Agreeableness, extraversion, and peer relations in early adolescence: winning friends and deflecting aggression. *J. Res. Personal., 36,* 224–51.

John OP, & Srivastava S. (1999). The Big Five Trait taxonomy: history, measurement, and theoretical perspectives. In *Handbook of Personality: Theory and Research* ed. LA Pervin, OP John, pp. 102–38. New York: Guilford.

Jost JT, Glaser J, Kruglanski AW, & Sulloway FJ. (2003a). Political conservatism as motivated social cognition. *Psychol. Bull., 129,* 339–75.

Jost JT, Glaser J, Kruglanski AW, & Sulloway FJ. (2003b). Exceptions that prove the rule—using a theory of motivated social cognition to account for ideological incongruities and political anomalies: reply to Greenberg and Jonas 2003. *Psychol. Bull., 129,* 383–93.

Judge TA, & Bono JE. (2000). Five Factor model of personality and transformational leadership. *J. Appl. Psychol., 85,* 751–65.

Judge TA, Higgins CA, Thoresen CJ, & Barrick MR. (1999). The Big Five personality traits, general mental ability, and career success across the lifespan. *Personnel Psychol., 52,* 621–52.

Karney BR, & Bradbury TN. (1995). The longitudinal course of marital quality and stability: a review of theory, method, and research. *Psychol. Bull., 118,* 3–34.

Kenford SL, Smith SS, Wetter DW, Jorenby DE, Fiore MC, & Baker TB. (2002). Predicting relapse back to smoking: contrasting affective and physical models of dependence. *J. Consult. Clin. Psychol., 70,* 216–27.

Krueger RF, Hicks BM, & McGue M. (2001). Altruism and antisocial behavior: independent tendencies, unique personality correlates, distinct etiologies. *Psychol. Sci., 12,* 397–402.

Kwan VS, Bond MH, & Singelis TM. (1997). Pancultural explanations for life-satisfaction: adding relationship harmony to self-esteem. *J. Personal. Soc. Psychol., 73,* 1038–51.

Larsen RJ. (2000). Toward a science of mood regulation. *Psychol. Inq., 11,* 129–41.

Larson LM, Rottinghaus PJ, & Borgen FH. (2002). Meta-analyses of Big Six interests and Big Five personality factors. *J. Voc. Behav., 61,* 217–39.

Luo S, & Klohnen EC. (2005). Assortative mating and marital quality in newlyweds: a couple-centered approach. *J. Personal. Soc. Psychol., 88,* 304–26.

MacDonald DA. (2000). Spirituality: description, measurement, and relation to the Five Factor model of personality. *J. Personal., 68,* 153–97.

Marcia JE. (1980). Identity in adolescence. In *Handbook of Adolescent Psychology*, ed. J Adelson. New York: Wiley, pp. 159–87.

McAdams DP. (2001). The psychology of life stories. *Rev. Gen. Psychol., 5,* 100–22.

McCullough ME, Emmons RA, & Tsang J. (2002). The grateful disposition: a conceptual and empirical topography. *J. Personal. Soc. Psychol., 82,* 112–27.

Miller TQ, Smith TW, Turner CW, Guijarro ML, & Hallet AJ. (1996). A meta-analytic review of research on hostility and physical health. *Psychol. Bull., 119,* 322–48.

Newcomb AF, Bukowski WM, & Pattee L. (1993). Children's peer relations: a meta-analytic review of popular, rejected, neglected, controversial, and average sociometric status. *Psychol. Bull., 113,* 99–128.

Pals J. (1999). Identity consolidation in early adulthood: relations with ego-resiliency, the context of marriage, and personality change. *J. Personal. Soc. Psychol., 67,* 295–329.

Parker JG, & Asher SR. (1987). Peer relations and later personal adjustment: Are low-accepted children at risk? *Psychol. Bull., 102,* 357–89.

Paunonen SV. (2003). Big Five factors of personality and replicated predictions of behavior. *J. Personal. Soc. Psychol., 84,* 411–22.

Paunonen SV, Haddock G, Forsterling F, & Keinonen M. (2003). Broad versus narrow personality measures and the prediction of behaviour across cultures. *Eur. J. Personal., 17,* 413–33.

Pennebaker JW, & King LA. (1999). Linguistic styles: language use as an individual difference. *J. Personal. Soc. Psychol., 77,* 1296–312.

Penner LA. (2002). Dispositional and organizational influences on sustained volunteerism: an interactionist perspective. *J. Soc. Issues 58,* 447–67.

Penner LA, Fritzsche BA, Craiger JP, & Freifeld TR. (1995). Measuring the prosocial personality. In *Advances in Personality Assessment*, ed. J Butcher, CD Spielberger, 10, 147–63. Hillsdale, NJ: Erlbaum.

Peterson C, & Seligman M. (2002). *The VIA Taxonomy of Human Strengths and Virtues.* Washington, DC: Am. Psychol. Assoc.

Piedmont RL. (1999). Does spirituality represent the sixth factor of personality? Spiritual transcendence and the Five Factor Model. *J. Personal., 67,* 985–1013.

Piedmont RL. (2004). Spiritual transcendence as a predictor of psychosocial outcome from an outpatient substance abuse program. *Psychol. Addict. Behav., 18,* 213–22.

Roberts BW, Caspi A, & Moffitt TE. (2003). Work experiences and personality development in young adulthood. *J. Personal. Soc. Psychol., 84,* 582–93.

Robins RW, Caspi A, & Moffitt TE. (2002). It's not just who you're with, it's who you are: personality and relationship experiences across multiple relationships. *J. Personal., 70,* 925–64.

Ryan RM, & Deci EL. (2001). On happiness and human potentials: a review of research on hedonic and eudaimonic well-being. *Annu. Rev. Psychol., 52,* 141–66.

Ryder AG, Alden LE, & Paulhus DL. (2000). Is acculturation unidimensional or bidimensional? A head-to-head comparison in the prediction of personality, self-identity, and adjustment. *J. Personal. Soc. Psychol., 79,* 49–65.

Saucier G. (2000). Isms and the structure of social attitudes. *J. Personal. Soc. Psychol., 78,* 366–85.

Scheier MF, & Carver CS. (1993). On the power of positive thinking. *Curr. Dir. Psychol. Sci., 2,* 26–30.

Schimmack U, Radhakrishnan P, Oishi S, Dzokoto V, & Ahadi S. (2002). Culture, personality, and subjective well-being: integrating process models of life-satisfaction. *J. Personal. Soc. Psychol., 82,* 582–93.

Schmitt D. (2002). Personality, attachment, and sexuality related to dating relationship outcomes: contrasting three perspectives on personal attribute interaction. *Br. J. Soc. Psychol., 41,* 589–610.

Seligman M, & Csikszentmihalyi M. (2000). Positive psychology: an introduction. *Am. Psychol., 55,* 5–14.

Shaver PR, & Brennan K. (1992). Attachment styles and the "Big Five" personality traits: their connections with each other and with romantic relationship outcomes. *Personal. Soc. Psychol. Bull., 18,* 536–45.

Shiner R, Masten AS, & Tellegen A. (2002). A developmental perspective on personality in emerging adulthood: childhood antecedents and concurrent adaptation. *J. Personal. Soc. Psychol., 83,* 1165–77.

Sjöberg L. (2001). Emotional intelligence: a psychometric analysis. *Eur. Psychol., 6,* 79–95.

Smith TW, & Spiro A. (2002). Personality, health, and aging: prolegomenon for the next generation. *J. Res. Personal., 36,* 363–94.

Thompson L, Snyder CR, Hoffman L, Michael ST, & Rasmussen HN, et al. (2005). Dispositional forgiveness of self, others, and situations. *J. Personal., 73,* 313–59.

Thoresen CJ, Kaplan SA, Barsky AP, Warren CR, & de Chermont K. (2003). The affective underpinnings of job perceptions and attitudes: a meta-analytic review and integration. *Psychol. Bull.*, *129*, 914–45.

Thorne A, Klohnen E. (1993). Interpersonal memories as maps for personality consistency. In *Studying Lives Through Time: Personality and Development*, ed. DC Funder, RD Parke, C Tomlinson-Keasey, & K Widaman, pp. 223–54. Washington, DC: Am. Psychol. Assoc.

Thrash TM, & Elliot AJ. (2004). Inspiration: core characteristics, component processes, antecedents, and function? *J. Personal. Soc. Psychol.*, *87*, 957–73.

Trull TJ, & Durrett CA. (2005). Categorical and dimensional models of personality disorder. *Annu. Rev. Clin. Psychol.*, *1*, 355–80.

Trull TJ, & Sher KJ. (1994). Relationship between the Five Factor model of personality and Axis I disorders in a nonclinical sample. *J. Ab-norm. Psychol.*, *103*, 350–60.

van der Zee K, Thijs M, & Schakel L. (2002). The relationship of emotional intelligence with academic intelligence and the Big Five. *Eur. J. Personal.*, *16*, 103–25.

Van Hiel A, & Mervielde I. (2004). Openness to experience and boundaries in the mind: relationships with cultural and economic conservative beliefs. *J. Personal.*, *72*, 659–86.

Van Hiel A, Mervielde I, & DeFruyt F. (2004). The relationship between maladaptive personality and right wing ideology. *Personal. Individ. Differ.*, *36*, 405–17.

Verona E, Patrick CJ, Joiner TE. (2001). Psychopathy, antisocial personality, and suicide risk. *J. Abnorm. Psychol.* 110, 462–70.

Vollrath M, Krahé B, & Hampson S. (2004). Editorial: personality and social relations. *Eur. J. Personal.*, *18*, 239.

Walton KE, & Roberts BW. (2004). On the relationship between substance use and personality traits: abstainers are not maladjusted. *J. Res. Personal.*, *38*, 515–35.

Watson D, Hubbard B, & Wiese D. (2000). General traits of personality and affectivity as predictors of satisfaction in intimate relationships. evidence from self-and partner-ratings. *J. Personal.*, *68*, 413–49.

Watson D, Klohnen EC, Casillas A, Nus Simms E, Haig J, & Berry DS. (2004). Match makers and deal breakers: analyses of assortative mating in newlywed couples. *J. Personal.*, *72*, 1029–68.

Wiebe RP. (2004). Delinquent behavior and the Five Factor model: hiding in the adaptive landscape? *Individ. Differ. Res.*, *2*, 38–62.

PART III

Biological Approaches to Personality

The field of biology has made remarkable progress over the past century, and particularly in the past few decades. It was only natural, therefore, for personality psychologists to begin to use biology to help them understand the roots of important human behaviors. A biological psychology of personality has developed that is based upon four different areas of biology and that therefore comprises four rather different approaches.

One approach relates the anatomy of the brain to personality. Perhaps the oldest field of biological psychology, work in this area began by cataloging the ways in which accidental brain damage affected behavior, and it has proceeded in recent years to the use of sophisticated techniques such as fMRI (functional magnetic resonance imaging). A second approach, very active today, relates the physiology of the nervous system to personality. This approach can be traced back to the ancient Greeks, who proposed that "humors" or bodily fluids influenced personality. Modern research addresses the complex interactions still being discovered between neurotransmitters, hormones, and behavior. A third approach, called "behavioral genetics," studies the way individual differences in personality are inherited from one's parents and shared among family members. Finally, a fourth approach applies Darwin's theory of evolution—the foundation of modern biology—to understand the behavioral propensities of the human species.

The readings in this section sample all of these approaches. The section begins with an article by James Dabbs and his colleagues that describes research on the association between a "humor" of modern interest—testosterone—and aggressive or, as they call it, "rambunctious" behavior by members of college fraternities. Research on testosterone can be traced back to ancient humoral theories of personality. The next selection, by Turhan Canli, could be said to have its ultimate roots in phrenology. His paper describes very recent research using fMRI technology to ascertain the precise location in the brain of neural processes associated with extraversion and neuroticism.

Behavioral genetics is introduced in the next selection, by Peter Borkenau and his colleagues working on the large and impressive German Observational Study of Adult Twins (GOSAT). Their research, based on direct behavioral observations of a large number of monozygotic and dizygotic twins, challenges the widely advertised finding of behavioral genetics that the shared family environment has only a small influence on personality development; it also demonstrates the state of the art for research in quantitative behavioral genetics. Recently, using very different methods, the study of behavioral genetics has made progress in understanding the workings of genes at the molecular level. One of the most important of these advances is reported in the next selection, by Avshalom Caspi and his colleagues. This article, originally published in Science, describes the first measured genotype–environment interaction found in the behavioral domain. Individuals with a particular form of the 5-HTT gene were prone to depression, but only if they had experienced stressful life events.

The next two articles address the application of evolutionary theory to personality psychology. David Buss and his co-workers describe research that measures gender differences in jealousy through self-report and physiological indicators, and provide an evolution-based account of their results. The evolutionary approach to psychology comes under fire in the next selection, by Alice Eagly and Wendy Wood, which argues that sex differences in behavior are better viewed as stemming from social structure than from biological mechanisms.

The final selection, by Martha Farah, describes some of the vexing philosophical and ethical issues that arise in trying to account for human psychology in biological terms. These include issues of privacy, the ethics of enhancing brain performance through drugs, the meaning of personal responsibility as we learn how brain damage can make one susceptible to antisocial behavior, and even the relations between science and the soul!

Testosterone Differences Among College Fraternities: Well-Behaved vs. Rambunctious

James M. Dabbs Jr., Marian F. Hargrove, and Colleen Heusel

Of all the substances in the body that might affect behavior, the male sex hormone testosterone probably has received the most attention. Although both males and females have testosterone in their bodies, males have much more and, it is commonly observed, are more aggressive. These observations have led directly to the hypothesis that testosterone might be a cause of aggressive or "rambunctious" behavior.

This hypothesis is tested in the next selection, by the personality psychologist James Dabbs Jr. and his collaborators. Dabbs spent much of his career in pursuit of the relationship between testosterone, behavior, and personality. His usual technique was to have subjects spit in a cup and to measure the testosterone level in their saliva. He then gathered some measure of his subjects' personality or behavior and correlated the two measurements.

For the research reported in the next selection, Dabbs and his colleagues addressed a phenomenon that is familiar to any college student: some fraternities are always getting themselves into trouble by their habitually rambunctious behavior, while others are more sedate. Dabbs speculated that such an average difference in behavior between groups might be explained, in part, by average differences in testosterone level of the groups' members. So he sent assistants to both kinds of fraternities at two universities, convinced their members to donate some of their saliva, and obtained ratings of the fraternities' behavior. The results showed that fraternities with higher average testosterone levels tended to be the more rambunctious ones.

Of course, these are correlational data. That means the direction of causality cannot be assumed to be one-way. Perhaps testosterone causes rambunctious behavior, but perhaps, too, living in a house full of rambunctious "brothers" tends to raise one's testosterone level. Probably both happen. High-testosterone students are drawn to certain fraternities, and certain environments (such as fraternity houses) make testosterone levels higher.

Finally, notice how the research on the behavioral correlates of testosterone is squarely in the tradition of theorizing about bodily "humors" and temperament. Here, the humor is testosterone and the behavior is aggressiveness. The technology is modern and the data much better, but the basic idea—substances in the body explain why people behave as they do—is ancient.

From *Personality and Individual Differences, 20,* 157–161, 1996.

Introduction

The character of groups arises from their circumstances and history. It also arises from the nature of the people who belong to the groups. People are social and biological creatures, and among the qualities that affect their behavior in groups is the hormone testosterone.

Testosterone in animals is related to aggression, dominance, and sexual activity (Archer, 1988; Lesher, 1978). In people it is related to dominance (Gladue, Boechler, & McCaul, 1989), aggression (Archer, 1991), libido (Booth & Dabbs, 1993; Morris, Udry, Kahn-Dawood, & Dawood, 1987; Sherwin, Gelfand, & Brender, 1985), sensation seeking (Daitzman & Zuckerman, 1980), drug abuse (Dabbs & Morris, 1990), low educational achievement (Dabbs, 1992; Kirkpatrick, Campbell, Wharry, & Robinson, 1993), and marital discord and divorce (Booth & Dabbs, 1993). The picture is one of excess and delinquency, although Dabbs and Ruback (1988) found high testosterone college students engaging and likeable.

Testosterone can be regarded as a characteristic of groups as well as of individuals. Mean testosterone levels differ across occupations (Dabbs, 1992; Dabbs, de La Rue, & Williams, 1990a; Schindler, 1979). Because people affiliate with others similar to themselves (Buss, 1985), we might expect them to have testosterone levels like those of their friends and associates. When individuals join together into groups, their shared conversations and social activities should intensify their preexisting characteristics. Testosterone is important in the lives of young men, and it is plausibly related to the kind of groups to which they belong. Relationships between testosterone and group behavior could be studied in friendship groups, civic clubs, or college fraternities.

The present study dealt with college fraternities. Fraternities are allowed a large latitude of behavior on most campuses, and there is room for individual members to shape the overall tone of the fraternity. The present study was initiated by Hargrove's (1991) observation that Ss[1] from a fraternity known for good behavior and high grades appeared somewhat low in testosterone, although she had no comparative data from other fraternities. Hargrove hypothesized that, consistent with findings about other occupations including the ministry (Dabbs et al., 1990a), low testosterone fraternities would be more intellectually oriented and socially responsible than high testosterone fraternities. Based on this hypothesis and the studies cited above, we expected higher testosterone groups to be wilder and more rambunctious and lower testosterone groups to be more docile and well-behaved. The present study addresses two specific questions: Do fraternities differ among themselves in mean testosterone level? If they do, what best describes the behavior associated with these differences?

---

[1]Following the format of the journal in which this article originally appeared, *Ss* stands for subjects, or research participants.

Method

We examined five fraternities at the one university and seven fraternities at another. At the first university there were 26 fraternities, and interfraternity council members helped us identify those most similar to and those most different from the one studied by Hargrove (1991). This resulted in two sets of fraternities, containing two and three fraternities each. We labeled the first set, which included Hargrove's original fraternity, "responsible," and we labeled the second set "rambunctious." At the second university there were 31 fraternities. We were unable to group these clearly, but a university official helped us identify a diverse set of seven that represented a range of popularity, social skill, academic achievement, and university rule violations.

A female researcher visited each fraternity in the hour before noon on a weekday. She contacted a fraternity officer and offered $75 for a set of saliva samples from approx. 20 members. The officer recruited Ss, each of whom chewed a stick of sugar-free gum and deposited 3 ml saliva into a 20-ml polyethylene vial. The samples were stored frozen until assayed. While Ss collected saliva samples, the officer completed a questionnaire that asked about the fraternity's current grade point average; its number of parties and community service projects during the past year; and its number of academic awards, sports awards, interfraternity council awards, and national fraternity awards during the past two years.

Photographs of Ss and the researcher's notes provided other information. At the first university three judges, blind as to testosterone scores, examined the photographs of all members of the five fraternities appearing in the university yearbook. Each judge scored each picture as smiling or not, with a smile defined as "an apparent smile with teeth showing." The task was not difficult, and all judges agreed on 99% of the photographs. Each fraternity was assigned a score representing the proportion of its members the judges agreed were smiling. At the second university, the yearbook did not contain individual student photographs, and smiling was scored differently. Two judges counted smiles in fraternity group pictures that appeared in the yearbook, and two judges visited the fraternity houses and counted smiles in composite membership photographs hanging there. There was 100% agreement between the judges. Each fraternity was assigned a mean score combining the proportion smiling in the yearbook and the proportion smiling in the house photograph. All smile proportion scores, including the separate yearbook and house scores at the second university, were transformed from proportions to arcsin values prior to any statistical treatment.

Salivary testosterone levels were determined using an in-house radioimmunoassay procedure with ^{125}I-testosterone tracer and charcoal separation (Dabbs, 1990). Testosterone concentrations in saliva and serum are highly correlated, and the day-to-day reliability of salivary testosterone measurements is about $r = 0.64$ (Dabbs, 1990), approximately the same as the reliability of serum measurements (Gutai, Dai, La Porte, & Kuller, 1988). * * *

Results

UNIVERSITY ONE   We analyzed testosterone scores from the first university using a two factor (Fraternity and Set) analysis of variance, with 98 Ss in five Fraternities nested in two Sets. Mean testosterone level was significantly higher in the rambunctious than the responsible set (14.3 vs. 12.3 ng/dL), $F(1, 93) = 6.59$, $P < 0.05$. Differences in testosterone among fraternities within the sets was not significant, $F < 1.0$.

Questionnaire responses and yearbook smile scores were analyzed using t-tests, with the fraternities treated as five Ss in two groups. Rambunctious fraternities had more parties (33.0 vs. 10.5 each), $t(3) = 3.68$, $P < 0.05$, lower grade point averages (2.5 vs. 2.9), $t(3) = 5.03$, $P < 0.05$, fewer academic awards (0.0 vs. 2.5), $t(3) = 6.71$, $P < 0.01$, fewer community service projects (0.3 vs. 3.0), $t(3) = 6.20$, $P < 0.01$, and fewer members smiling in yearbook photographs (34 vs. 62%), $t(3) = 3.61$, $P < 0.05$, than responsible fraternities.[2]

The researcher's notes indicated the fraternities differed in other ways. Fraternities in the rambunctious set more often ignored letters of inquiry or failed to return telephone calls. When the researcher arrived at their houses, all they needed to comply was an offer of money. One fraternity officer listened to her request and translated it for his brothers: "Hey guys, want to spit for a keg?" Two of the three houses were decorated in spartan fashion, with furniture in disrepair, as with a sofa supported by three legs and a brick. The third house, according to the housemother, was "only standing because it was constructed of steel and concrete." (Note: As of the time of publication, two of the three rambunctious fraternities had been banned from campus for misbehavior.)

Fraternities in the responsible set were more deliberate and considerate. One postponed participating to discuss the researcher's request at a chapter meeting, and the other telephoned her advisor long distance to make sure the request was legitimate. The responsible fraternities were polite when she visited. They invited her to have a seat and offered her something to eat or drink. Rambunctious fraternities were slower to respond to her arrival, letting her stand unattended, unfed, and apparently unwanted.

UNIVERSITY TWO At the second university we had no clear basis for clustering fraternities into sets, and we analyzed the data using one-way analysis of variance, which 142 *Ss* nested in seven fraternities. The fraternities differed significantly among themselves in testosterone, $F(6, 135) = 2.64$, $P < 0.05$. Their mean scores, ordered from low to high, were 10.3, 10.5, 11.2, 11.5, 11.6, 12.1 and 14.0 ng/dL. In comparisons among specific fraternities,

Neuman–Keuls tests indicated that the highest fraternity was significantly different from the two lowest fraternities.

Contrary to the difference between two sets of fraternities at the first university, questionnaires completed by fraternity officers did not differentiate significantly among the seven fraternities at the second university. However, as at the first university, more smiling was associated with lower levels of testosterone. The correlation between proportion of members smiling and mean testosterone level across the seven fraternities was $r = -0.78$, 5 d.f.,[3] $P < 0.05$. The proportion smiling ranged from 55% in the fraternity with the lowest testosterone level to 35% in the fraternity with the highest level.

The researcher's notes revealed behavioral differences between fraternities that the Neuman–Keuls tests found significantly different in testosterone, the highest one and the two lowest ones. The highest fraternity was rough to a degree beyond rambunctiousness. The notes, stated, "I felt as if I'd been thrown to the lions. Very good looking, pumped up. No manners. They'd walk around without shirts, belch. 'Macho meatheads' is very fitting." The two lowest fraternities shared a common friendliness, though they differed in social skill. The notes on one of the two stated, "They talked a lot about computers and calculus. Very mild-mannered. They were nice, and we all sat around and talked while waiting for more people. Not great socially or good looking. Discussed their difficulty finding girls." The notes on the other stated, "These guys were nice and cooperative. Their house was well kept, and everyone was neatly dressed (preppy). One guy went upstairs and recruited other members of the fraternity to come spit."

Discussion

At both universities there were significant mean differences in testosterone among fraternities. At both universities there was less smiling in higher

---

[2]The *t*'s and *F*'s reported in this article are derived from *t*-tests and the analysis of variance, respectively, both of which yield *P*-values, which are estimates of the probability that between-group differences of the magnitude found would appear, by chance, if no such differences existed.

---

[3]The abbreviation "d.f." represents degrees of freedom, which is related to *N* or the number of participants.

testosterone fraternities. At the first university, fraternities with higher testosterone levels were lower in academic achievement and community service and less friendly, as revealed by questionnaire measures and reactions to the researcher. Although they smiled less they had more parties, reminiscent of Barratt's (1993) description of impulsive aggressive individuals, high in gregariousness but low in warmth. At the second university, members of the highest testosterone fraternity were boisterous and macho, and members of the lowest testosterone fraternities were attentive and helpful. Testosterone was not related to academic achievement or community service at the second university.

Inconsistencies between the universities in the relationship of testosterone to academic achievement and community service present a puzzle. We spent more time identifying extreme fraternities at the first university, which may account for our finding of differences in socially responsible behavior there. However, we did examine a diverse set of fraternities at the second university, and we think that different cultures at the two universities may have led to different correlates of testosterone. The second university placed more emphasis on engineering and less on service and altruistic activities. To obtain descriptions of the two universities, we examined *The Insider's Guide to Colleges* (Yale Daily News, 1991). According to this source, the second university had half as many students as the first. It accepted fewer applicants (69 vs. 79%), and its students had higher mean SAT scores (1190 vs. 1080). It had fewer degree-granting programs (4 vs. 12), and its academic pressure was more intense. It was located near the heart of a city, and more of its students came from urban backgrounds.

At the larger and more heterogenous first university, there was more room for students of varied abilities and more time for students to express values of community, altruism, and responsibility. The university was in a small town in a rural setting. The community depended upon help from students to get things done, while the urban community around the other university was relatively independent of student participation.

We would expect the more diverse academic and civic activities at the first university to allow more room for the play of individual differences. Low testosterone Ss were friendly at both universities, but only at the first was their friendliness translated into what we called more socially responsible behavior. We suspect that university differences moderated the positive effects of low testosterone, analogous to the way in which social control forces can moderate violent and antisocial aspects of high testosterone (Dabbs & Morris, 1990; Udry, 1990). We think that while high testosterone fraternities are rambunctious, low-testosterone fraternities are not necessarily responsible. "Well-behaved vs rambunctious" may be better than "responsible vs. rambunctious" to describe the underlying dimension that characterized the differences between fraternities.

We have several caveats regarding the present findings. There was undoubtedly some error in the information provided by fraternity officers. We cannot know that testosterone caused the behavioral differences we found, although we are unaware of studies showing causation in the opposite direction, in which behavioral differences like those we observed cause differences in testosterone. And finally, smiles may be something other than a measure of friendliness. There is literature on the enjoyment reflected in smiles (Ekman, Davidson, & Friesen, 1990) and on emotional feeling vs. social context as determinants of smiles (Hess, Banse, & Kappas, 1995), but there is little information on whether people who smile are more friendly in other ways. People smile for many reasons, including a desire to ingratiate themselves to others (DePaulo, 1992). In the present findings we have taken smiling to indicate friendliness, and we suggest that friendliness provides a link between smiling and low testosterone. Consistent with this notion about friendliness, Hargrove (1991) found low testosterone Ss more generous than high testosterone Ss in judging their peers. At the other end of the friendliness continuum, there is considerable evidence linking high testosterone to hostile and antisocial behavior (Booth & Dabbs, 1993; Dabbs, Carr, Frady, & Riad, 1995; Dabbs &

Morris, 1990) and thus, one might expect, to lower levels of smiling.

It is somewhat surprising to find differences in testosterone among fraternities, given the paucity of other testosterone findings with college students. Questionnaire studies have seldom found personality measures related to testosterone (Dabbs, Hopper, & Jurkovic, 1990b), though Harris and Rushton (1993) found testosterone in college students related to high aggression and low pro-social behavior, when they treated aggression and pro-social behavior as latent variables defined by several indicators. The present findings suggest mean testosterone level can be regarded as a significant characteristic of a fraternity. It is possible that testosterone has more effect in groups than in individuals, as small individual tendencies accumulate into large group tendencies. Observing groups rather than individuals may be a way of making more visible the effects of testosterone.

Findings with fraternities may extend beyond the college campus. Many groups are central to modern life, and groups can have distinct and lasting natures. An acquaintance explained to one of the present authors when she moved to a new city, "Marian, this town is just like any other. The Rotarians own it, the Kiwanians raise money for it, and the Lions just enjoy it." These stereotypes fitted with her own knowledge of stuffy Rotary balls and luncheons where Lions threw rolls at their speakers. Fraternity members are like young Rotarians, Kiwanians, or Lions in training, waiting to take their place in the grown-up clubs when they leave the university. The hormones of individuals may shape the culture of groups.

References

Archer, J. (1988). *The behavioral biology of aggression*. Cambridge: Cambridge University Press.

Archer, J. (1991). The influence of testosterone on human aggression. *British Journal of Psychology, 82*, 1–28.

Barratt, E. S. (1993). Defining impulsive aggression. Unpublished manuscript, University of Texas Medical Branch at Galveston.

Booth, A., & Dabbs, J. M., Jr. (1993). Testosterone and men's marriages. *Social Forces, 72*, 463–477.

Buss, D. M. (1985). Human mate selection. *American Scientist, 73*, 47–51.

Dabbs, J. M., Jr. (1990). Salivary testosterone measurements: Reliability across hours, days, and weeks. *Physiology and Behavior, 48*, 83–86.

Dabbs, J. M., Jr. (1992). Testosterone and occupational achievement. *Social Forces, 70*, 813–824.

Dabbs, J. M., Jr. Carr, T. S., Frady, R. L., & Riad, J. K. (1995). Testosterone, crime, and misbehavior among 692 male prison inmates. *Personality and Individual Differences, 18*, 627–633.

Dabbs, J. M., Jr., de La Rue, D., & Williams, P. M. (1990a). Testosterone and occupational choice: Actors, ministers, and other men. *Journal of Personality and Social Psychology, 59*, 1261–1265.

Dabbs, J. M., Jr., Hopper, C. H., & Jurkovic, G. J. (1990b). Testosterone and personality among college students and military veterans. *Personality and Individual Differences, 11*, 1263–1269.

Dabbs, J. M., Jr., & Morris, R. (1990). Testosterone, social class, and antisocial behavior in a sample of 4,462 men. *Psychological Science, 1*, 209–211.

Dabbs, J. M., Jr., & Ruback, R. B. (1988). Saliva testosterone and personality of male college students. *Bulletin of the Psychonomic Society, 26*, 244–247.

Daitzman, R., & Zuckerman, M. (1980). Disinhibitory sensation seeking, personality and gonadal hormones. *Personality and Individual Differences, 1*, 103–110.

DePaulo, B. M. (1992). Nonverbal behavior and self-presentation. *Psychological Bulletin, 111*, 203–243.

Ekman, P., Davidson, R., & Friesen, W. V. (1990). Emotional expression and brain physiology II: The Duchenne smile. *Journal of Personality and Social Psychology, 58*, 342–353.

Gladue, B. A., Boechler, M., & McCaul, K. D. (1989). Hormonal response to competition in human males. *Aggressive Behavior, 15*, 409–422.

Gutai, J. P., Dai, W. S., LaPorte, R. E., & Kuller, L. H. (1988). The reliability of sex hormone measurements in men for epidemiologic research. Unpublished manuscript, University of Pittsburgh.

Hargrove, M. F. (1991). An investigation of personality correlates of testosterone using peer perceptions. Unpublished Master's Thesis, Georgia State University.

Harris, J. A., & Rushton, J. P. (1993). Salivary testosterone and aggression and altruism. Unpublished manuscript, University of Western Ontario.

Hess, U., Banse, R., & Kappas, A. (1995). Implicit audience and solitary smiling revisited. *Journal of Personality and Social Psychology, 69*, 280–288.

Kirkpatrick, S. W., Campbell, P. S., Wharry, R. E., & Robinson, S. L. (1993). Saliva testosterone in children with and without learning disabilities. *Physiology and Behavior, 53*, 583–586.

Lesher, A. I. (1978). *An introduction to behavioral endocrinology*. New York: Oxford.

Morris, N. M., Udry, J. R., Kahn-Dawood, F., & Dawood, M. Y. (1987). Marital sex frequency and midcycle female testosterone. *Archives of Sexual Behavior, 16*, 27–37.

Schindler, G. L. (1979). Testosterone concentration, personality patterns, and occupational choice in women. *Dissertation Abstracts International, 40*, 1411A (University Microfilms No. 79–19, 403).

Sherwin, B. B., Gelfand, M. M., & Brender, W. (1985). Androgen enhances sexual motivation in females: A prospective, crossover study of sex steroid administration in the surgical menopause. *Psychosomatic Medicine, 47*, 339–351.

Udry, J. R. (1990). Biosocial models of adolescent behavior problems. *Social Biology, 37*, 1–10.

Yale Daily News (1991). *The insider's guide to the colleges, 1991* (17th ed.). New Haven: Yale Daily News.

Functional Brain Mapping of Extraversion and Neuroticism: Learning from Individual Differences in Emotion Processing

Turhan Canli

Way back when personality psychology was just getting started, the pioneering theorist Gordon Allport defined personality as "the dynamic organization within the individual of those psychophysical systems that determine his unique adjustments to his environment" (Allport, 1937, p. 48). For the next seventy years Allport's reference to "psychophysical systems" served more as a promissory note for what he hoped research would someday show than as a description of anything actually realized. This article, by the biological psychologist Turhan Canli, shows how modern technology is, at long last, beginning to cash in on this promise. The technique Canli uses, fMRI (functional magnetic resonance imagery), provides vivid images of the activity of living brains. He uses fMRI to locate in the brain patterns of activity associated with the personality traits of extraversion and neuroticism, the two traits (of the Big Five) that have the longest history of speculation about a biological foundation. While much of the presentation in this article is highly technical, we believe it is important to see firsthand the kinds of methods and analyses that are currently being used to illuminate brain processes that might be relevant to personality. Canli's research—published in 2004—is groundbreaking. We can expect to see much more like it, and increasingly interesting and well-founded conclusions concerning the relationship between personality and the brain, in the next few years.

From *Journal of Personality, 72,* 1105–1132, 2004.

Investigations of the biological basis of personality have led to the development of several influential models of personality. * * * Studies have been conducted with respect to the heritability of traits, the role of neurotransmitters, and the identification of neural structures that mediate trait-typical behaviors. Recent advances in noninvasive brain imaging and molecular genetics have now opened the gates for novel and interdisciplinary approaches to the neuroscience of personality, which will be reviewed here.

Specifically, I will focus on imaging studies of extraversion (E) and neuroticism (N). The association between these traits, emotion, and health is intriguing, but the biological mechanisms underlying these associations are still poorly understood. One approach is to identify brain systems that are associated with E, N, and the processing of emotional stimuli. I will discuss recent work that has used functional magnetic resonance imaging (fMRI)[1] to correlate individual differences in participants' E and N scores with brain activation differences during the processing of emotional stimuli. This will lead to the question by what mechanism individual differences in participants' E and N scores affect brain activation levels. I will discuss one exciting new line of research that combines functional neuroimaging with molecular genetics in human participants in order to develop molecular models of individual brain activation differences. * * *

Extraversion, Neuroticism, and Emotion

Extraverted and neurotic individuals are characterized by positive and negative affect, respectively. In an analysis of multiple samples (the total sample size was 4457), Watson and colleagues (Watson, Wiese, Vaidya, & Tellegen, 1999) reported a correlation of 0.58 between N and the Negative Affect scale of the PANAS (Watson, Clark, & Tellegen, 1988) and a correlation of 0.51 between E and the Positive Affect scale. Costa and McCrae (1980)

---

[1]Functional magnetic resonance imaging (fMRI) provides a dynamic picture of the brain such that portions of the image "light up" to depict regions with increased blood flow. An fMRI scan during some psychological or physical task allows one to see which areas of the brain have increased activity.

reported that participants who scored high in E reported more positive affect in their daily life than more introverted individuals and that participants who scored high in N reported more negative daily affect than those who score low. Indeed, measures of E and N predicted positive and negative affect in everyday life for periods of up to 10 years. Larsen and Ketelaar (1991) found that E and N were associated with greater responsiveness to the effects of positive and negative mood induction procedures, respectively.

Could the association between these two dimensions of personality and two dimensions of affect simply reflect a tautology, perhaps due to the use of similar terms in measurement instruments? Gross, Sutton, and Ketalaar (1998) caution of this possibility but also provide data that suggest some independence of the two constructs. They measured self-reported positive and negative affect prior to, during, and after a set of mood-induction film clips were shown and correlated these state levels of affect with E and N, as well as dispositional Positive and Negative Affect. They found that acute affective state, especially in response to the film clips, was more strongly associated with E and N than with dispositional affect.

Another line of research has shown differences between E, N, and positive and negative affectivity using a longitudinal design. Vaidya and colleagues in Watson's laboratory (Vaidya, Gray, Haig, & Watson, 2002) studied the temporal stability of the Big Five personality traits and positive and negative trait affect. They reported that affective traits were less stable than personality traits: over a 2.5-year period, the median stability coefficient for affective trait scales was 0.49, whereas the stability coefficients for E and N were 0.72 and 0.61, respectively. Life experiences played a moderating effect but were stronger for affective traits than for E and N. This finding, along with the study by Gross, Sutton, and Ketelaar (1998), suggests that personality and affect are dissociable constructs.

* * *

A Brain Imaging Approach to Individual Differences in Emotion Processing

BRAIN IMAGING OF E AND N

Passive viewing of emotional scenes. Given that E is associated with reactivity to positive emotional stimuli and N with reactivity to negative emotional stimuli, we (Canli et al., 2001) hypothesized that a similar relationship should exist at the brain systems level of analysis. Using fMRI, we predicted that greater E scores across participants should correlate with greater brain activation to positive images in regions known to play a role in affective processing. We made a similar prediction for participants with higher N scores and brain activation to negative stimuli.

Fourteen women completed a self-report measure of the Big Five personality traits (Costa & McCrae, 1992) and participated in an fMRI study in which blocked presentations of emotionally negative and positive images were presented in the scanner. These images were taken from a library of normed affective stimuli, the International Affective Picture Series (IAPS) (Lang & Greenwald, 1993). Participants were scanned as they passively viewed images that were presented for 6 seconds each. After the scan, a manipulation check was conducted to verify that the stimuli produced the intended emotional response in each subject.

Brain activation to positive and negative images across participants was correlated with their respective E and N scores. The resultant correlation map revealed regions where greater activation to emotional images was significantly correlated with higher scores in either E or N. Figure 1 shows a scatter plot from one region, the right amygdala. It illustrates that greater activation to positive, relative to negative, pictures was associated with higher scores in E across subjects. Similar correlations were seen in other subcortical and cortical regions, but the example of the amygdala is of particular interest because this structure is prima-

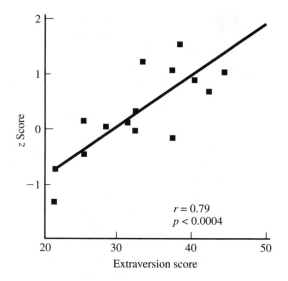

Figure 1 Brain response to positive stimuli correlates with participants' E scores. Scatter plot from the left amygdala, showing correlation between E and brain activatin to valenced stimuli. Positive z scores denote significance level of greater activation to positive, relative to negative, pictures. Negative z scores denote significance level of greater activation to negative, relative to positive pictures.

rily associated with the processing of negative affect. This was the first demonstration that individual differences in amygdala activation to positive stimuli vary as a function of E.

Several features of this correlation map were noteworthy. First, the correlations were very robust, especially given the relatively small sample size, compared to behavioral studies. Second, the correlations were in the expected direction, such that greater activation to positive stimuli was associated with E (but not N) and greater activation to negative stimuli was associated with N (but not E). Third, both cortical and subcortical regions exhibited these correlations, suggesting that neural systems associated with personality are not confined to higher-level executive brain regions, but rather represented at all levels of neural processing.

The interpretation of these findings is constrained by several limitations, some of which are inherent to fMRI in general. First, the correlation between the recorded signal (blood oxygenation) and underlying neural activity remains a matter of debate: although it is commonly assumed that it represents excitatory neural activity, there is disagreement about whether it cannot also represent inhibitory neural activity (Heeger, Boynton, Demb, Seidemann, & Newsome, 1999; Waldvogel et al., 2000). Second, the determination of significant signal change is based on the relative comparison between two conditions, rather than some absolute measure. Therefore, an increase in activation during one condition is equivalent to a decrease during the other condition. In our study, what was interpreted as an increase in activation to positive pictures could instead have represented a decrease in activation to negative pictures.

* * *

Another limitation was that scores were collected for the broad dimensions of E and N, but not for specific facets. It is therefore possible that some regions that were associated with E reflect different facets of this personality trait. Indeed, one could speculate that brain regions associated with aggression may relate to the facet of "assertiveness," but brain regions associated with attachment would be related to the facet of "warmth." Future studies should, therefore, measure facets of E and N and include different conditions designed to capture distinguishing features of these facets.

A final concern was the nature of the task and its relation to the observed brain regions. Because the task was unconstrained, any number of mental processes may have been engaged. Although it is likely that the observed brain activations represent emotional experience (since subjects reported emotional responses to the images), it is unclear how this experience was generated, whether participants attempted to regulate it, and whether additional processes, such as retrieval of autobiographical memories, were activated during the viewing.

Perception of emotional faces. Our second study focused on emotion perception, rather then emotional experience, and used a highly constrained task design that targeted one a priori region of interest. The study focused on the processing of emotional faces and activation in the amygdala. Studies of brain-damaged patients and functional neuroimaging studies of healthy participants have consistently reported amygdala involvement in the processing of facial expressions of fear (Adolphs, Tranel, Damasio, & Damasio, 1994; Adolphs, Tranel, Damasio, & Damasio, 1995; Broks et al., 1998; Calder et al., 1996; Dolan, Morris, & de Gelder, 2001; Killgore & Yurgelun-Todd, 2001; Morris, deBonis, & Dolan, 2002; Morris et al., 1996; Whalen, Rauch et al., 1998). The response of the amygdala to facial expressions of other emotions, however, was found to be less consistent. For instance, Breiter and colleagues (1996) reported increases in amygdala activation to happy versus neutral faces, whereas Morris et al. (1996) and Whalen and colleagues (Whalen, Rauch et al., 1998) found decreases in amygdala activation when comparing happy versus fearful faces. Did this inconsistency reflect random variation or the presence of a previously uncontrolled determinant of individual differences?

Based on our previous study, we predicted that E would turn out to be a critical variable in amygdala activation. Specifically, we expected that amygdala activation to happy (but not fearful) faces would vary as a function of E. Participants answered a self-report assessment of personality characteristics (Costa & McCrae, 1992) and were then scanned while viewing blocks of photographs of emotional facial expressions (angry, fearful, happy, and sad, along with neutral faces).

The analysis of the fMRI data confirmed our expectations. Analyzing data in the traditional way (i.e., grouped activations, not taking individual personality scores into account), we found significant amygdala activation to fearful (relative to neutral) faces, but not to any other facial emotion. This finding was consistent with prior reports of amygdala sensitivity towards facial expressions of fear. The critical test of our hypothesis was whether there would be a significant correlation between participants' E scores and amygdala activation to

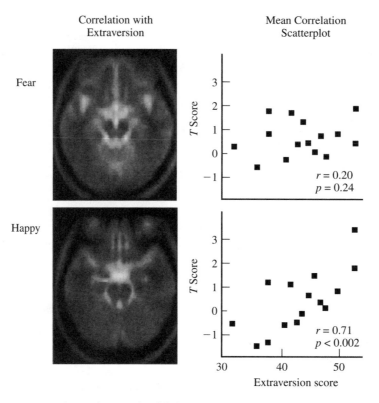

Figure 2 Amygdala response to happy, but not fearful, faces correlates with E. Amygdala response to happy and fearful faces as a function of E. A significant correlation was seen only in response to happy-neutral, but not fearful-neutral, faces (left column). Scatterplots in the right column show significance of amygdala activation for each of the fifteen participants as a function of their E scores.

happy faces. Figure 2 shows that this was indeed the case. Furthermore, additional analyses revealed that this correlation was specific to happy faces and E; none of the other facial emotions were correlated with E, nor were any of the remaining Big Five personality traits correlated significantly with greater amygdala activation to any of the emotional faces.

One clear limitation of this study is its focus on one brain structure. It is, therefore, not clear how activation in the amygdala relates to other regions. For example, it is possible that amygdala activation was due to modulatory influences from other, perhaps cortical, regions. Evidence for such modulatory influences comes from a study by Hariri and colleagues (Hariri, Bookheimer, & Mazziotta, 2000). These investigators presented

emotional face pictures (target faces) and asked participants to select a matching face stimulus (a perceptual task) or word label (a linguistic task) from two given choices. Robust amygdala activation to angry or fearful target faces was observed when participants engaged in a perceptual matching task, but was diminished when they engaged in a linguistic matching task. The decrease in amygdala activation was correlated with an increase in the right prefrontal cortex. This study suggests that activation in higher cortical areas can inhibit amygdala response to stimuli that would otherwise drive it.

* * *

Attention to emotional stimuli. We conducted two studies of attentional processes, one based on the emotional Stroop task[2] (Canli et al., 2003) and one based on the dot-probe target detection task (Amin et al., in press). Similar to the study on face processing, these experiments focused on a priori regions of interest associated with attentional processes.

During the emotional Stroop task, participants were scanned while viewing words on a screen that are displayed in different colors. Their task was to indicate, as quickly and accurately as possible, the color in which each word was printed by pressing a corresponding key on a button box. Although the semantic meaning of the word was irrelevant to the task, the valence of the word did not seem to go unnoticed by the brain. A prior imaging study showed that participants exhibit greater activation to negative than neutral words in the anterior cingulate (Whalen, Bush et al., 1998), a brain region associated with emotional experience and awareness (Canli et al., 2002; Lane, Fink, Chau, & Dolan, 1997; Lane et al., 1998). Activation in this region to positive, relative to negative, pictures was also found to correlate with E (Canli et al., 2001). We, therefore, predicted that during the emotional Stroop task, greater activation to positive stimuli should correlate with E in the anterior cingulate. This was found to be the case. Additional analyses are currently underway to investigate the interaction of the anterior cingulate with other brain regions that play a role in attention and/or emotional processing.

Subjects in the dot-probe task were asked to respond to a probe stimulus that was initially hidden from view behind one of two stimuli, but revealed when both stimuli disappeared. In behavioral studies, a fast reaction time (RT) implies that the participant's attention is directed at the stimulus that obscures the probe, whereas a slow reaction time suggests that attention is drawn away

[2]The traditional Stroop Test requires participants to name the color of the ink used to print stimulus words. For example the word "red" might be printed in blue ink. The response to the easier task (read the word) must be inhibited to quickly respond by naming the color. The emotional version of the Stroop task is described in the following paragraph.

from the stimulus that obscures the probe. In this imaging study, we focused on a priori regions of interest to ask the question whether activation in these regions to positive and negative stimuli would correlate with E and N, respectively. Based on imaging studies of emotion and attention, we focused on the amygdala, anterior cingulate cortex, parietal regions, and fusiform gyrus (Davis & Whalen, 2001; Donner et al., 2000; Whalen, Bush et al., 1998).

Stimuli were presented in pairs of pictures that were negative and neutral (neg/neut), positive and neutral (pos/neut), or neutral and neutral (neut/neut). The probe was placed behind either item of the pair (both the placement of the probe and the placement of valenced and neutral items were counterbalanced across trials) so that, for any given trial, the probe was either behind a positive, negative, or neutral item. The analyses were based on contrasts where only the location of the probe differed between the two conditions. For example, one analysis identified brain regions that were significantly more activated when the probe was behind the positive item of a pos/neut pair, relative to when it was behind the neutral item. It needs to be stressed how subtle the difference between these two conditions was: both showed pairs of positive and neutral pictures, both showed a probe; both presented all stimuli for exactly the same amount of time; both required the same response; in both cases, the subject had no knowledge where the probe would appear.

We found that for pos/neut stimulus presentations, there was significantly greater activation, as a function of E, in the right fusiform gyrus when the probe was obscured by the neutral stimulus than when it was obscured by the positive stimulus (see Figure 3). For neg/neut stimulus presentations, there was significantly greater activation, as a function of E, in the right fusiform gyrus when the probe was obscured by the negative stimulus than when it was obscured by the neutral stimulus.

Activation in the right fusiform gyrus has previously been associated with visual search (Donner et al., 2000). We therefore speculated that greater activation in extraverted subjects in this region

Activation to Positive/Neutral Pairs:
Probe Behind Neutral

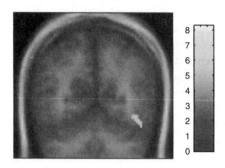

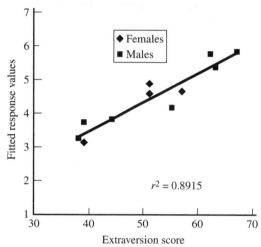

$r^2 = 0.8915$

Figure 3 Correlations between E and brain activation in the right fusiform gyrus as a function of probe placement for pos/neut stimulus presentations.

represented greater effort to search for the probe. This would be a reasonable interpretation if it were shown that highly extraverted subjects were less likely to look at the negative item of a neg/neut pair or the neutral item of a pos/neut pair than less extraverted subjects. Indeed, analysis of RT data showed that E was correlated with significantly faster RTs when the probe was placed behind the neutral than the negative stimulus, suggesting that highly extraverted participants avoided attending to the negative item of neg/neut pairs.

Yet a clear limitation of this study is the lack of independent verification of gaze direction. Future work should combine functional imaging with eye tracking to determine which item of a stimulus pair was attended to.

Furthermore, the fusiform gyrus is involved in a wide range of behaviors, so that alternative interpretations need to be ruled out. For example, activation in the right fusiform gyrus is also associated with autonomic arousal (Critchley, Elliott, Mathias, & Dolan, 2000). It is therefore possible that the correlations observed in this study reflect increased arousal associated with the regulation of affect, rather than greater effort in visual search. Concurrent measures of brain activation with autonomic arousal could address this possibility.

Some comments on localizing the neural basis of E and N. The mapping of psychological processes onto specific brain regions has been likened by Uttal as a form of "new phrenology"[3] (Uttal, 2001). Such skepticism is buoyed by presentations that imply that complex psychological processes are represented by a single brain region, such as "fear is processed by the amygdala." Under the constraints of limited journal space, and with few a priori regions of interest, it is not uncommon to limit the discussion to a small number of regions. Yet one striking aspect of our first study (Canli et al., 2001) was the number of regions that exhibited a significant correlation; we listed 15 clusters where greater activation to positive, relative to negative, pictures correlated with E. This illustrates how distributed the neural representation of personality traits is likely to be.

Indeed, it has been suggested that the role that one region plays in the neural representation of a psychological function depends on the activity in other regions at that same time, a concept that has been named "neural context" (McIntosh, 1998). A related idea is that of "functional connectivity" (Friston et al., 1997) or "effective connectivity" (Friston, Harrison, & Penny, 2003). These terms

[3]Phrenology was an approach popular in the nineteenth century (but now discredited) that claimed to be able to locate and measure various traits and abilities in the brain by feeling bumps on the head.

refer to the idea that the activation in one brain region is the result of an interaction between another brain region and some other (e.g., psychological or experimenter-controlled) factor. Examples include brain-imaging studies demonstrating that the connectivity between different brain regions can vary as a function of attention (Friston & Buchel, 2000) or learning (Buchel, Coull, & Friston, 1999). To give a specific example, Buchel, Coull, and Friston (1999) used fMRI to show that associative learning of visual objects and their locations was associated with an increase in effective connectivity between brain regions involved in spatial and object processing. Subjects who performed best also showed the highest degree of effective connectivity, suggesting that the ability to make associations depended on functional interactions between these brain areas.

Could personality serve as a factor that modulates effective connectivity between brain regions? To the extent that personality traits are viewed as stable within individuals, the answer should be "no." Effective connectivity is capricious. Its temporal dynamics can change rapidly, as the subject enters a different mind state or focuses on different inputs. Presumably, traits like E and N don't exhibit these kinds of rapid fluctuations within subjects. On the other hand, I speculate that, between individuals, effective connectivity may very well be associated with personality. For example, it is possible that positive mood induction can dramatically change effective connectivity between two brain regions in individuals who are highly extraverted, but not in individuals who are introverted. As this speculation illustrates, current thinking in function imaging on topics like effective connectivity can inspire much new work in personality neuroscience.

BRAIN IMAGING OF GENOTYPED INDIVIDUALS

Genetic contributions to personality have long been recognized (Bouchard, 1994; Ebstein, Benjamin, & Belmaker, 2000; Heath, Cloninger, & Martin, 1994; Plomin et al., 1994; Reif & Lesch, 2003; Zuckerman, 1991). This section will focus on functional brain imaging studies in which allelic variation in genes is associated with individual differences in brain activation. This approach has been called "imaging genomics" (Hariri & Weinberger, 2003).

The gene that has received the most attention so far, at least with respect to personality, is the serotonin (5-HT) transporter gene (referred to as 5HTT or SERT). Lesch and colleagues (Lesch et al., 1996) reported an association between individual differences in the structure of this gene (polymorphism) and participants' neuroticism scores. The 5HTT comes in two variants, which are physically longer (l) or shorter (s), due to the inclusion or deletion of a number of base pairs in the promotor region of the gene. The s variant is functional, but produces less of the transporter molecule that is responsible for removing serotonin from the synaptic cleft between two neurons (Lesch et al., 1996). Because participants carry two copies (alleles) of each gene, one from each parent, they can be homozygous for s (s/s), homozygous for l (l/l), or heterozygous (s/l). It was found that participants who carry at least one copy of the s-allele had significantly higher Harm Avoidance and N scores (Lesch et al., 1996) and significantly lower Agreeableness scores (Greenberg et al., 2000) than participants who were homozygous for the l-allele.

These molecular studies of gene-personality relations, however, have been hampered by replication concerns. As discussed by Reif and Lesch (2003), more than 20 studies have investigated the relation between personality and the 5-HTT polymorphism. Only about half of them replicated the original finding. How can one explain such inconsistency?

Reif and Lesch (2003) identified several critical variables that may have contributed to null results in failed replication studies. First, they noted that only two replication attempts studied large samples (N4400) as did the original study (Lesch et al., 1996) (N 5 505). Second, several non-replication studies examined unusual populations (e.g., alcoholic violent offenders, participants with substance dependence or personality disorders). Third, different studies used different measures to quantify personality traits. In that context, of particular interest is the assertion by Reif and Lesch that the contribution of the 5-HTT polymorphism to neuroticism is greatest in the central range of the distribution and least robust at the extremes (Sirota, Greenberg, Murphy, & Hamer, 1999), which may explain why two studies that selected extreme high-and low-scoring participants failed to replicate the original study. A fourth reason for poor replication across studies was that ethnic differences in study populations may also have been a factor. Two nonreplication studies of Japanese individuals reported a population frequency of the l/l allele of only 6% (compared to 32% in Caucasians, Lesch et al., 1996), yielding low statistical power to detect genotype-related differences.

Finally, and perhaps most importantly, molecular geneticists readily acknowledge that the contributions of individual genes to personality will likely be very modest. Based on twin studies, genetic factors contribute about 40%–60% of the variance in N and other personality traits (Bergeman, Plomin, McClearn, Pedersen, & Friberg, 1988; Bouchard, 1994; Heath et al., 1994; Lander & Schork, 1994; Loehlin, 1989; Loehlin, McCrae, Costa, & John, 1998; Pedersen, Plomin, McClearn, & Friberg, 1988; Plomin et al., 1994). The 5-HTT polymorphism was found to account for 3%–4% of the total variance and 7%–9% of the genetic variance (Lesch et al., 1996). Assuming that other genes make similar contributions to the observed variance, one would expect about 10–15 genes to be associated with personality measures (Lesch et al., 1996; Lesch & Mossner, 1998).

By combining molecular genetic approaches with functional imaging, the modest contributions of specific genes may be better isolated. In "Rethinking Behavior Genetics," Hamer (2002) made the point that a genetic explanation of human behavior is oversimplified if it relies on a direct linear relationship between genes and behavior. Rather, he suggested, one needs to incorporate the brain, the environment, and gene expression networks in future models. He pointed to a study by Hariri and colleagues (Hariri et al., 2002) to illustrate the power of combining the genotyping and functional neuroimaging approaches: using

fMRI data, genotype accounted for 20% of the total variance, or about five to seven times the effect size of Lesch's original study using behavioral measures.

The study referred to by Hamer (2002) was conducted by Hariri and colleagues (Hariri et al., 2002) and asked the question, "If the 5HTT polymorphism is indeed associated with N or anxiety-related behavior, could it be associated with individual differences in brain activation to fear-related stimuli?" If this is so, then amygdala activation to these stimuli should be greater in participants who carry at least one copy of the s-form than participants who are instead homozygous for the l-form. This was indeed found to be the case. Remarkably, this finding was established with two independent samples of only a total of 28 participants, whereas behavioral genetic studies typically require hundreds of participants to attain statistical significance. Importantly, this study has been replicated by two independent groups in Germany and Italy (Hariri, personal communication), as well as by Hariri and colleagues in a third and larger sample (Hariri et al., 2003). Together, these studies argue strongly that the 5HTT polymorphism is a determinant of amygdala reactivity to fear-related stimuli.

This focus on genetic contributions to brain activation and behavior does in no way imply that environmental factors are not equally important. Indeed, recent work by Caspi and colleagues firmly makes the point that it is the interaction between environmental and genetic factors that shapes behavioral outcomes (Caspi et al., 2002; Caspi et al., 2003). For example, Caspi and colleagues (Caspi et al., 2003) conducted a longitudinal (23-year) study of a large cohort (N 5 1037 at time one, 96% retention over 23 years) to assess the interaction of life stress and the serotonin transporter polymorphism. They found that a significantly greater proportion of carriers of the s-allele responded to stressful life events with depressive symptoms or diagnosed depression than homozygous l-allele carriers. For example, among participants who had encountered four or more stressful life events, 33% who carried at least one copy of the s-allele became depressed, versus 17% of homozygous l-allele carriers. Importantly, there were no significant differences in the number of stressful life events across groups, and the alternative hypothesis that exposure to life events is influenced by the 5HTT gene polymorphism was tested and could be rejected. Based on these observations and additional analyses, the authors concluded that the 5HTT polymorphism moderates individuals' response to stressful life events.

What is exciting about this work is that it begins to offer molecular hypotheses about the biological basis of personality traits. Whereas prior work noted an association between genetic variation (in the 5HTT gene) and a complex behavioral trait (N), imaging genomics relates these variations to specific brain structures that are associated with the processing of stimuli that are relevant to the trait (e.g., fear-related stimuli in the amygdala). Future work will then need to address the mechanisms by which individual differences in genotype scale up to individual differences in brain activations.

* * *

References

Adolphs, R., Tranel, D., Damasio, H., & Damasio, A. (1994). Impaired recognition of emotion in facial expressions following bilateral damage to the human amygdala. *Nature, 372,* 669–672.

Adolphs, R., Tranel, D., Damasio, H., & Damasio, A. R. (1995). Fear and the human amygdala. *The Journal of Neuroscience, 15,* 5879–5891.

Amin, Z., Constable, R. T., & Canli, T. (in press). Attentional bias for valenced stimuli as a function of personality in the dot-probe task. *Journal of Research in Personality.*

Bergeman, C. S., Plomin, R., McClearn, G. E., Pedersen, N. L., & Friberg, L. T. (1988). Genotype-environment interaction in personality development: Identical twins reared apart. *Psychological Aging, 3* (4), 399–406.

Bouchard, T. J. Jr. (1994). Genes, environment, and personality. *Science, 264* (5166), 1700–1701.

Breiter, H. C., Etcoff, N. L., Whalen, P. J., Kennedy, W. A., Rauch, S. L., & Buckner, R. L., et al. (1996). Response and habituation of the human amygdala during visual processing of facial expression. *Neuron, 17,* 875–887.

Broks, P., Young, A. W., Maratos, E. J., Coffey, P. J., Calder, A. J., & Isaac, C. L., et al. (1998). Face processing impairments after encephalitis: Amygdala damage and recognition of fear. *Neuropsychologia, 36,* 59–70.

Buchel, C., Coull, J. T., & Friston, K. J. (1999). The predictive value of changes in effective connectivity for human learning. *Science, 283* (5407), 1538–1541.

Calder, A. J., Young, A. W., Rowland, D., Perrett, D. I., Hodges, J. R., & Etcoff, N. L. (1996). Facial emotion recognition after bilateral amygdala damage: Differentially severe impairment of fear. *Cognitive Neuropsychology, 13,* 699–745.

Canli, T., Desmond, J. E., Zhao, Z., & Gabrieli, J. D. E. (2002). Sex differences in the neural basis of emotional memories. *Proceedings of the National Academy of Sciences, 99* (16), 10789–10794.

Canli, T., Haas, B., Amin, Z., & Constable, R. T. (2003). An fMRI study of personality traits during performance of the emotional Stroop task. *Society for Neuroscience Abstracts, 33,* 725–727.

Canli, T., Zhao, Z., Desmond, J. E., Kang, E., Gross, J., & Gabrieli, J. D. E. (2001). An fMRI study of personality influences on brain reactivity to emotional stimuli. *Behavioral Neuroscience, 115* (1), 33–42.

Caspi, A., McClay, J., Moffitt, T. E., Mill, J., Martin, J., & Craig, I. W., et al. (2002). Role of genotype in the cycle of violence in maltreated children. *Science, 297* (5582), 851–854.

Caspi, A., Sugden, K., Moffitt, T. E., Taylor, A., Craig, I. W., & Harrington, H. J., et al. (2003). Influence of life stress on depression: Moderation by a polymorphism in the 5-HTT gene. *Science, 301* (18 Jul 2003), 386–389.

Costa, P. T. Jr, & McCrae, R. R. (1980). Influence of extraversion and neuroticism on subjective well-being: Happy and unhappy people. *Journal of Personality and Social Psychology, 38,* 668–678.

Costa, P. T., & McCrae, R. R. (1992). *Professional manual of the revised NEO personality inventory and NEO five-factor inventory.* Odessa, FL: PAR Inc.

Critchley, H. D., Elliott, R., Mathias, C. J., & Dolan, R. J. (2000). Neural activity relating to generation and representation of galvanic skin conductance responses: A functional magnetic resonance imaging study. *Journal of Neuroscience, 20* (8), 3033–3040.

Davis, M., & Whalen, P. J. (2001). The amygdala: vigilance and emotion. *Molecular Psychiatry, 6* (1), 13–34.

Dolan, R. J., Morris, J. S., & deGelder, B. (2001). Crossmodal binding of fear in voice and face. *Proc Natl Acad Sci USA, 98* (17), 10006–10010.

Donner, T., Kettermann, A., Diesch, E., Ostendorf, F., Villringer, A., & Brandt, S. A. (2000). Involvement of the human frontal eye field and multiple parietal areas in covert visual selection during conjunctive search. *European Journal of Neuroscience, 12,* 3407–3414.

Ebstein, R. P., Benjamin, J., & Belmaker, R. H. (2000). Personality and polymorphisms of genes involved in aminergic neurotransmission. *European Journal Pharmacology, 410* (2–3), 205–214.

Friston, K. J., & Buchel, C. (2000). Attentional modulation of effective connectivity from V2 to V5/MT in humans. *Proc Natl Acad Sci USA, 97* (13), 7591–7596.

Friston, K. J., Buechel, C., Fink, G. R., Morris, J., Rolls, E., & Dolan, R. J. (1997). Psychophysiological and modulatory interactions in neuroimaging. *Neuroimage, 6* (3), 218–229.

Friston, K. J., Harrison, L., & Penny, W. (2003). Dynamic causal modelling. *Neuroimage, 19* (4), 1273–1302.

Greenberg, B. D., Li, Q., Lucas, F. R., Hu, S., Sirota, L. A., & Benjamin, J., et al. (2000). Association between the serotonin transporter promoter polymorphism and personality traits in a primarily female population sample. *American Journal Medical Genetics, 96* (2), 202–216.

Gross, J. J., Sutton, S. K., & Ketelaar, T. V. (1998). Relations between affect and personality: Support for the affect-level and affective-reactivity views. *Personality and Social Psychology Bulletin, 24*, 279–288.

Hamer, D. (2002). Genetics. Rethinking behavior genetics. *Science, 298* (5591), 71–72.

Hariri, A. R., Bookheimer, S. Y., & Mazziotta, J. C. (2000). Modulating emotional responses: effects of a neocortical network on the limbic system. *Neuroreport, 11* (1), 43–48.

Hariri, A. R., Mattay, V. S., Tessitore, A., Kolachana, B., Fera, F., & Goldman, D. et al. (2002). Serotonin transporter genetic variation and the response of the human amygdala. *Science, 297* (5580), 400–403.

Hariri, A. R., Munoz, K. E., Kolachana, B. S., Goldsmith, D. R., Mattay, V. S., & Goldberg, T., et al. (2003). Genetically driven variation in serotenergic neurotransmission alters amygdala reactivity associated with fearful temperament. *Society for Neuroscience Abstracts, 662.*

Hariri, A. R., & Weinberger, D. R. (2003). Imaging genomics. *British Medical Bulletin, 65*, 259–270.

Heath, A. C., Cloninger, C. R., & Martin, N. G. (1994). Testing a model for the genetic structure of personality: a comparison of the personality systems of Cloninger and Eysenck. *Journal of Personal and Social Psychology, 66* (4), 762–775.

Heeger, D. J., Boynton, G. M., Demb, J. B., Seidemann, E., & Newsome, W. T. (1999). Motion opponency in visual cortex. *Journal of Neuroscience, 19* (16), 7162–7174.

Killgore, W. D., & Yurgelun-Todd, D. A. (2001). Sex differences in amygdala activation during the perception of facial affect. *Neuroreport, 12* (11), 2543–2547.

Lander, E. S., & Schork, N. J. (1994). Genetic dissection of complex traits. *Science, 265* (5181), 2037–2048.

Lane, R. D., Fink, G. R., Chau, P. M., & Dolan, R. J. (1997). Neural activation during selective attention to subjective emotional responses. *Neuroreport, 8* (18), 3969–3972.

Lane, R. D., Reiman, E. M., Axelrod, B., Yun, L. S., Holmes, A., & Schwartz, G. E. (1998). Neural correlates of levels of emotional awareness: Evidence of an interaction between emotion and attention in the anterior cingulate cortex. *Journal of Cognitive Neuroscience, 10* (4), 525–535.

Lang, P. J., & Greenwald, M. K. (1993). *International affective picture system standardization procedure and results for affective judgments: Technical reports 1A-1C.* University of Florida Center for Research in Psychophysiology.

Larsen, R. J., & Ketelaar, T. (1991). Personality and susceptibility to positive and negative emotional states. *Journal of Personality and Social Psychology, 61*, 132–140.

Lesch, K.-P., Bengel, D., Heils, A., Sabol, S. Z., Greenberg, B. D., & Petri, S. et al. (1996). Association of anxiety-related traits with a polymorphism in the serotonin transporter gene regulatory region. *Science, 274*, 1527–1531.

Lesch, K. P., & Mossner, R. (1998). Genetically driven variation in serotonin uptake: Is there a link to affective spectrum, neurodevelopmental, and neurodegenerative disorders? *Biological Psychiatry, 44* (3), 179–192.

Loehlin, J. C. (1989). Partitioning environmental and genetic contributions to behavioral development. *American Psychology, 44* (10), 1285–1292.

Loehlin, J. C., McCrae, R. R., Costa, P. T., & John, O. P. (1998). Heritability of common and measure-specific components of the Big Five personality factors. *Journal of Research in Personality, 32*, 431–453.

McIntosh, A. R. (1998). Understanding neural interactions in learning and memory using functional neuroimaging. *Ann N Y Acad Sci, 855*, 556–571.

Morris, J. S., deBonis, M., & Dolan, R. J. (2002). Human amygdala responses to fearful eyes. *Neuroimage, 17* (1), 214–222.

Morris, J. S., Frith, C. D., Perrett, D. I., Rowland, D., Young, A. W., Calder, A. J., & Dolan, R. J. (1996). A differential neural response in the human amygdala to fearful and happy facial expressions. *Nature, 383*, 812–815.

Pedersen, N. L., Plomin, R., McClearn, G. E., & Friberg, L. (1988). Neuroticism, extraversion, and related traits in adult twins reared apart and reared together. *Journal of Personality and Social Psychology, 55* (6), 950–957.

Plomin, R., Owen, M. J., & McGuffin, P. (1994). The genetic basis of complex human behaviors. *Science, 264* (5166), 1733–1739.

Reif, A., & Lesch, K. P. (2003). Toward a molecular architecture of personality. *Behavioral Brain Research, 139* (1–2), 1–20.

Sirota, L. A., Greenberg, B. D., Murphy, D. L., & Hamer, D. H. (1999). Nonlinear association between the serotonin transporter promoter polymorphism and neuroticism: a caution against using extreme samples to identify quantitative trait loci. *Psychiatry and Genetics, 9* (1), 35–38.

Uttal, W. R. (2001). *The new phrenology: The limits of localizing cognitive processes in the brain.* Cambridge, MA: The MIT Press.

Vaidya, J. G., Gray, E. K., Haig, J., & Watson, D. (2002). On the temporal stability of personality: Evidence for differential stability and the role of life experiences. *Journal of Personality and Social Psychology, 83* (6), 1469–1484.

Waldvogel, D., van Gelderen, P., Muellbacher, W., Ziemann, U., Immisch, I., & Hallett, M. (2000). The relative metabolic demand of inhibition and excitation. *Nature, 406* (6799), 995–998.

Watson, D., Clark, L. A., & Tellegen, A. (1988). Development and validation of brief measures of positive and negative affect: The PANAS scales. *Journal of Personality and Social Psychology, 54*, 1063–1070.

Watson, D., Wiese, D., Vaidya, J., & Tellegen, A. (1999). The two general activation systems of affect: Structural findings, evolutionary considerations, and psychobiological evidence. *Journal of Personality and Social Psychology, 76*, 820–838.

Whalen, P. J., Bush, G., McNally, R. J., Wilhelm, S., McInerney, S. C., & Jenike, M. A., et al. (1998). The emotional counting Stroop paradigm: a functional magnetic resonance imaging probe of the anterior cingulate affective division. *Biological Psychiatry, 44* (12), 1219–1228.

Whalen, P. J., Rauch, S. L., Etcoff, N. L., McInerney, S. C., Lee, M. B., & Jenike,

M. A. (1998). Masked presentations of emotional facial expressions modulate amygdala activity without explicit knowledge. *Journal of Neuroscience, 18*, 411–418.

Zuckerman, M. (1991). *Psychobiology of personality.* Cambridge: Cambridge University Press.

Genetic and Environmental Influences on Observed Personality: Evidence from the German Observational Study of Adult Twins

Peter Borkenau, Rainer Riemann, Alois Angleitner, and Frank M. Spinath

Behavioral genetics is a field of research that seeks the bases of individual differences in personality and ability by estimating the degree to which they can be accounted for by variation in genes, as opposed to variation in the environment. The usual method for doing this is the twin study. While analytic methods are complex, the basic idea is simple: If monozygotic (MZ, genetically identical) twins resemble each other on a trait more closely than do dizygotic twins (DZ, who share only 50% of their variable genes), then variation in the trait can be attributed, to some degree, to variation in genes. The past three decades of research have established conclusively that many attributes of personality and ability, and maybe all of them, are in fact influenced to some degree by genes.

Beyond this fact, one of the best-known and most controversial conclusions to emerge so far from research on behavioral genetics is that very little if any variation in personality can be attributed to the "shared family environment," usually interpreted as the aspects of the childhood environment that are the same for all children in a family. This would include variables such as family income, neighborhood, father's presence in the home, and so on. A large number of behavioral genetic studies have found that siblings raised together actually resemble each other to a surprisingly small degree, and various more complex analyses have shared the conclusion that, for all intents and purposes, the family doesn't matter (e.g., Harris, 1995).

The present article notes that almost all of the research leading to this conclusion has been based upon self-report measures of personality, such as standard personality inventories. Despite what the term might seem to imply, "behavioral genetics" research has rarely included direct measures of behavior. The purpose of the ambitious German Observational Study of Adult Twins (GOSAT) is to remedy this deficiency. The study brings together a large number of MZ and DZ twins and observes their behavior in a variety of experimental situations, ranging from simply introducing oneself to "rigging a high and stable paper tower." Behaviors are rated from videotapes of these situations and combined into observationally based personality estimates, which can then be put through the usual behavioral genetic analyses.

The conclusion of this study is important and, given the pre-existing literature, surprising. It turns out that behaviorally based estimates of personality appear to be influenced much more by the shared family environment than have been previously obtained self-report-based estimates. This conclusion has two implications. First, it implies that behavioral geneticists were a bit too quick to conclude that the shared family environment is not an important influence on the development of personality. Second, it points out the danger of basing sweeping conclusions on limited methods. Multimethod studies are not only highly desirable, as the authors state near the end of this article, but they are also probably necessary before we can have much confidence in the conclusions from research.

From *Journal of Personality and Social Psychology, 80,* 655–668, 2001.

Numerous behavior-genetic studies suggest that individual differences in adult personality are almost exclusively accounted for by genetic and nonshared environmental influences. In a meta-analysis[1] of behavior-genetic studies on personality, Loehlin (1992) concluded that additive effects of genes accounted for 22–46% of the phenotypic variance, that nonshared environment accounted for another 44–55%, and that shared environmental influences were weak, accounting for 0–11% of individual differences in personality. More recently, Plomin, DeFries, McClearn, and Rutter (1997) suggested that genes accounted for about 40% of the variance in personality, that nonshared environment accounted for the other 60%, and that there were no effects of the shared environment.

Whereas it is now generally accepted that genes have a substantial influence on individual differ-

ences in personality, it is still a puzzle why almost all environmental influences on personality seem to be of the nonshared variety. *Shared environment* is defined as environmental factors that contribute to twin and sibling similarity, whereas *nonshared environment* is defined as environmental factors that do not contribute to sibling similarity. * * *

Lack of importance of the shared environment is inferred from three findings. First, the correlations between adoptive siblings and those between adoptees and their adoptive parents tend to be small, usually about .05[2] (Loehlin, Willerman, & Horn, 1987; Plomin, Corley, Caspi, Fulker, & DeFries, 1998; Scarr, Webber, Weinberg, & Wittig, 1981). Second, twins reared together are not systematically more similar in personality than are twins reared apart (Loehlin, 1992). Finally, the correlations between monozygotic (MZ) twins tend to be twice or even more than twice as high as are the correlations between dizygotic (DZ) twins

---

[1]Meta-analysis is a technique for reviewing large research literatures that yields quantitative estimates of the effects of variables, based on many participants in a large number of studies.

[2]For background on how to interpret a correlation coefficient, see the selection by Rosenthal and Rubin in Part I.

(Loehlin, 1989, 1992; Plomin, DeFries, McClearn, & Rutter, 1997), which suggests genetic and non-shared environmental but no shared environmental influence.

Psychology has reacted to these findings in several ways. Some authors (Rowe, 1994; Harris, 1995, 1998) have suggested theories of peer socialization to explain why children in the same family are so different from one another. Other authors have set out to demonstrate that there are shared environmental influences on at least some traits, such as religious orthodoxy (Beer, Arnold, & Loehlin, 1998). Finally, theorists have suggested that the importance of the shared environment may be systematically underestimated in adoption studies, because of range restriction (Stoolmiller, 1999), as well as in studies that rely on self-reports or ratings by knowledgeable informants, because of contrast effects (Miles & Carey, 1997; Rose, 1995; Saudino & Eaton, 1991). The present article focuses on the latter hypothesis.

* * *

Peer Report Studies on Adult Twins

Peer reports by at least two independent judges per target allow one to separate reliable target variance from perceiver effects and thus overcome a drawback of self-reports. Despite that advantage, however, there are only two peer-report studies on adult personality in twins (Heath et al., 1992; Riemann, Angleitner, & Strelau, 1997). In the study by Heath et al. (1992), 460 pairs of MZ and 366 pairs of same-gender DZ twins described their own and their twin's extraversion and neuroticism. Genes accounted for 63% of the reliable variance in Neuroticism and for 73% of the reliable variance in Extraversion, the remaining variance being accounted for by nonshared environment. Riemann, Angleitner, and Strelau (1997) administered the German self-report version (Borkenau & Ostendorf, 1993) of Costa and McCrae's (1992) NEO Five-Factor Inventory (NEO-FFI) to 660 pairs of MZ and 200 pairs of same-gender DZ twins and collected ad-ditional peer reports by two acquaintances per twin, using the peer report ver-

sion of the NEO-FFI. In their analyses, the broad-sense heritabilities of the true scores ranged from 57% to 81% for the five trait domains measured by the NEO-FFI, the remaining variance being accounted for by nonshared environment. Thus, these two peer report studies suggest that genes account for about two thirds and nonshared environment accounts for the other third of the reliable variance in peer reports of adult personality. This is quite different from the 40% genetic and 60% nonshared environmental variance that are usually estimated from self-report studies (Plomin, DeFries, et al., 1997).

Contrast Effects

However, self-reports and peer reports share the problem that they may be subject to contrast effects. Two kinds of contrast effects have to be distinguished in behavior-genetic research on personality.

1. Relatives in general and twins in particular may mutually influence each other in ways that make their actual personalities different from one another. An example might be different roles taken by twins or siblings to emphasize their unique identities.

2. Apart from the relatives' actual behavioral similarity, contrast effects may affect the similarity of their personality descriptions, because they may be compared (and may compare themselves) with each other instead of with the population mean. This kind of rater bias would inflate the differences within and reduce the differences between pairs, resulting in lower correlations between relatives. Such a process is quite plausible, as persons tend to compare the targets of personality descriptions with particular other persons who come to their minds (Schwarz, 1999), and for twins, a particularly accessible other person may be their cotwin. Consider, for example, the questionnaire item "Do you enjoy going to parties?" that is a marker of Extraversion. Twins may endorse this item if they enjoy parties more than their cotwin does, and they may deny it if the cotwin enjoys parties more. This would reduce the correlations between

cotwins and result in underestimates of the importance of the shared environment, no matter whether it operated in MZ and DZ twins alike or whether the effect was stronger in DZ twins.

Both kinds of contrast effects may yield negative correlations between relatives, a phenomenon that is inconsistent with the standard behavior-genetic models that imply positive (or at least zero) correlations between all kinds of relatives. But even for DZ twins who share half their genes in addition to their family environment, negative correlations have repeatedly been found (Heath et al., 1992), particularly if young twins were described by their parents (Neale & Stevenson, 1989; Spinath & Angleitner, 1998). Such negative correlations indicate one or the other sort of contrast effect.

Whereas negative correlations between relatives clearly indicate contrast effects, positive correlations are no proof of the lack of contrast effects. This is because contrast effects may attenuate the usually positive correlations between relatives without turning them negative. If contrast effects affect the actual behavior of relatives only, the influence of shared environment will actually be reduced and the parameter estimates will not be biased. However, if rater bias is involved, the importance of the shared environment may be underestimated. This makes it desirable to use personality measures in twin research that may not be subject to that kind of rater bias. That requires observational studies. * * *

Observational Twin and Adoption Studies

We identified about a dozen observational studies on twins and adoptees and reviewed them in another article (Borkenau, Riemann, Spinath, & Angleitner, 2000). In none of these studies were the observed target persons adults. Generally, lack of shared environmental influence is not as clearly suggested by these observational studies as it is by studies that rely on self-reports and ratings by knowledgeable informants. However, most of the observational studies used small samples, and in many of these studies, short-term external influences shared by cotwins or adoptees may have contributed to the similarity of their behavior.

Miles and Carey (1997) published a meta-analysis on genetic and environmental influences on human aggression and concluded that shared environmental effects seemed to be stronger for observational than for rating measures. However, their meta-analysis included only two observational studies on aggression in children. Moreover, they did not find the behavioral measures of aggression convincing, arguing that "perhaps one or both of the studies capitalized on state-specific, reciprocal influences of twin or adoptive dyads when they were tested at the same time" (p. 213).

Thus, the answer to the question of whether there is shared environmental influence on children's behavior is still open. However, even if observational studies on children conveyed a clear message, any straightforward inference from these studies to adult personality would be questionable: Behavior-genetic evidence suggests that genetic and environmental influences on human behavior change across the life span and that shared environmental influence decreases with age (McCartney, Harris, & Bernieri, 1990; Plomin, DeFries, et al., 1997). Thus, observational behavior-genetic studies on adult personality are highly desirable. This was the prime reason that we started the German Observational Study of Adult Twins (GOSAT).

Method

A comprehensive description of the procedure and the data that were collected in GOSAT has been published elsewhere (Spinath et al., 1999). Therefore, we describe only those measures here for which results are reported below.

Participants Three hundred pairs of adult twins (168 MZ and 132 DZ) who had been recruited from all over Germany by reports in German media participated in GOSAT. They were invited for a 1-day testing session that took place at

the University of Bielefeld in Germany. * * *
Women (234 pairs) participated more frequently
than men did (66 pairs), with gender not significantly associated with zygosity, $\chi^2(1, N = 300) =$
2.00, $p = .16$.[3] The twins' age varied between 18
and 70 years, with a mean of 34.28 ($SD = 12.99$)
and a median of 30.5 years. An analysis of variance
(ANOVA) showed that neither gender nor zygosity
nor their interaction was significantly related to the
participants' age, all $Fs \leq 1$.[4]

* * *

MEASURES

Self-reports and peer reports. Most of the GOSAT
twin pairs had previously participated in the peer
rating study reported by Reimann et al. (1997), in
which they had been administered, among others,
the German version of Costa and McCrae's (1992)
NEO-FFI. The NEO-FFI measures the personality
domains Neuroticism, Extraversion, Openness to
Experience, Agreeableness, and Conscientiousness
with 12 items each. Moreover, each twin had
been described by two acquaintances who differed
between cotwins, using the peer-report version of
the NEO-FFI, in which the items are worded in
the third person instead of the first person singular.
A few twin pairs had not participated in the peer
rating study, but for most of these pairs, self-reports
and peer reports could be collected in GOSAT.

Videotaped behavior sequences. A main goal of
GOSAT was to obtain reliable and valid personality
measures of twins that could not be subject to rater
bias. We achieved this by (a) videotaping the twins

in 15 settings in which they had to complete different tasks, (b) presenting these videotapes to judges
who never met the twins they described, and
(c) never letting a judge of 1 twin observe the
cotwin as well.

Because it was desirable to collect personality
descriptions by strangers that were highly informative of the targets' actual personality, we wanted to
have the twins complete tasks in which personality
differences were likely to become observable. * * *
Specifically, our tasks included the following (with
average duration in parentheses):

1. Introduce oneself (1.25 min).
2. Arrange three photographs in a meaningful order and tell an interesting story
   that the three pictures might illustrate
   (4.50 min).
3. Tell dramatic stories about three cards
   from Murray's (1943) Thematic Apperception Test (6.00 min).
4. Tell a joke to an experimental confederate
   (1.50 min).
5. Persuade an "obstinate neighbor" (actually
   a confederate) on the phone to reduce
   the volume of her stereo after 11 PM
   (2.25 min).
6. Refuse a request for help by "a friend"
   (actually a confederate) who says that she
   has just had a car accident (2.00 min).
7. Introduce oneself to a stranger (an experimental confederate) and tell her about
   one's hobbies after the confederate has
   introduced herself (12.00 min).
8. Recall objects that one has just seen in a
   waiting room (3.00 min).
9. Solve a complex logical problem as fast as
   possible. Another "participant" (actually
   the confederate) received the same problem and ostensibly "solved" it at an enormous speed (4.50 min).
10. Introduce the stranger from Setting 4 to
    the experimenter (2.50 min).
11. Invent a "definition" for a neologism and
    provide arguments for why that definition
    would be appropriate (6.25 min).

---

[3]The "chi-square" test is a statistical technique for estimating the probability that the distribution of outcomes across categories can be attributed solely to
chance. The "1" refers to the degrees of freedom in the
test. N is the number of participants, and p is the probability of this result as a chance outcome.

[4]SD means "standard deviation." The F statistic, derived
from an analysis of variance, when combined with the
degrees of freedom in the design, yields an estimate of
the probability that observed mean differences occurred
solely by chance. F's less than 1 are very small and are
generally interpreted as reflecting chance variation.

12. Rig up a high and stable paper tower within 5 min, using scissors, paper, and glue only (5.25 min).
13. Read 14 newspaper headlines and their subtitles aloud (3.00 min).
14. Describe multiple uses of a brick, using pantomime only (2.75 min).
15. Sing a song of one's choice (1.00 min).

Approximately 60 min of videotapes per participant, or about 600 hrs of videotapes altogether, were collected this way.

Video-based personality ratings. Numerous judges provided trait ratings of the twins, relying solely on these videotapes. To increase the reliability of the trait ratings, each twin was observed in each setting by four independent judges. Moreover, the behavior in different settings was rated by different panels of four judges to secure independence of ratings for different settings. Finally, different panels of judges were employed for twins from the same pair to prevent contrast effects in twin perception. Thus, 4 (parallel judgments) × 15 (number of settings) × 2 (cotwins) = 120 judges were employed, each of them providing ratings of 300 persons. All judges were students either of the University of Bielefeld or of the University of Halle and were paid for their participation.

The judges provided by a computer their ratings on bipolar 5-point ratings scales. Each of Goldberg's (1990) Big Five factors (i.e., Extraversion, Agreeableness, Conscientiousness, Emotional Stability, and Intellect) was represented by 4 scales, and 4 additional scales were included to measure Openness to Experience (McCrae & Costa, 1987). * * * Moreover, ratings of the targets' attractiveness and likeability were included, mainly to control for the higher expected similarity of MZ twins in physical attractiveness. * * *

The judges' work stations were equipped with a video recorder, a video monitor, and a computer. The judges were instructed to watch a video sequence for 1 twin and then provide the trait ratings for that twin using the computer keyboard, then restart the video recorder to watch 1 twin

from another pair, and so forth, until they had provided ratings of 300 persons, 1 twin of each pair. The computer had been programmed (a) to present the adjective scales in a random order that differed between video sequences and (b) to store the judges' responses. * * *

Ratings by experimenters and confederates. The twins were also described by the experimenter and the confederate, using the peer-rating version of the NEO-FFI. The (always female) confederate was involved in six observational settings (Setting 4–Setting 9), and she provided her descriptions when she had interacted with the target for about 1 hr. The experimenter described the target at the end of the observation day after about 6 hrs of interaction and observation. Whereas the experimenter saw both cotwins of a pair (although 1 much longer than the other), the confederate met only 1 twin sibling.

* * *

Results

* * *

BEHAVIOR-GENETIC ANALYSES OF THE VIDEO-BASED PERSONALITY RATINGS

Twin correlations. * * * Table 1 reports the interrater reliabilities and the ICCs between MZ and DZ twins separately for the 7 odd settings, the 8 even settings, and all 15 settings.[5] * * * The interrater reliabilities predict the ICC of the averaged rating by 28 (odd settings), 32 (even settings), or 60 (all settings) judges with averaged ratings by the same number of hypothetical judges who observed the same targets. This is a useful standard of comparison for the correlations between cotwins who were observed by different panels of judges: The

---

[5]ICC means "intraclass correlation," which is a type of correlation coefficient calculated when assessing covariation of twin pairs. Although the formula for its computation is different, it can be interpreted in the same way as the standard *r* correlation discussed by Rosenthal and Rubin in Part I.

TABLE 1

RELIABILITIES (r_k) AND TWIN CORRELATIONS FOR THE RESIDUALIZED VIDEO-BASED RATINGS AVERAGED ACROSS ODD SETTINGS, ACROSS EVEN SETTINGS, AND ACROSS ALL SETTINGS

Adjective and domain	Odd settings			Even settings			All settings		
	r_{28}	MZ	DZ	r_{32}	MZ	DZ	r_{60}	MZ	DZ
Frank	.89	.54	.24	.89	.49	.26	.94	.55	.30
Active	.86	.50	.18	.87	.47	.25	.93	.55	.25
Talkative	.90	.51	.20	.92	.55	.23	.95	.61	.25
Gregarious	.90	.54	.20	.92	.59	.24	.95	.61	.25
Extraversion	.92	.55	.21	.93	.55	.25	.96	.59	.23
Assertive	.89	.60	.35	.87	.51	.33	.93	.62	.40
Calm	.84	.49	.33	.82	.40	.31	.90	.54	.39
Self-confident	.88	.57	.36	.86	.51	.31	.93	.59	.37
Even-tempered	.75	.29	.19	.80	.35	.38	.87	.42	.34
Emotional Stability	.90	.59	.37	.88	.51	.33	.94	.61	.38
Kind	.86	.52	.39	.86	.54	.32	.92	.62	.38
Polite	.84	.48	.32	.83	.47	.24	.91	.57	.31
Agreeable	.83	.58	.33	.82	.50	.32	.90	.63	.39
Pleasant	.73	.32	.29	.80	.47	.31	.85	.49	.35
Agreeableness	.89	.54	.38	.88	.55	.32	.93	.61	.38
Thorough	.80	.44	.38	.82	.47	.34	.89	.53	.38
Neat	.79	.45	.19	.79	.36	.32	.88	.48	.32
Conscientious	.81	.45	.34	.84	.48	.33	.90	.51	.37
Systematic	.77	.44	.20	.78	.31	.41	.87	.49	.40
Conscientiousness	.86	.51	.31	.86	.44	.39	.92	.52	.39
Inventive	.83	.44	.29	.85	.56	.45	.91	.59	.42
Imaginative	.81	.43	.29	.84	.46	.38	.90	.53	.40
Original	.84	.40	.23	.84	.49	.23	.91	.52	.26
Creative	.81	.43	.25	.83	.51	.40	.90	.56	.39
Openness to Experience	.87	.47	.28	.88	.54	.40	.93	.56	.38
Refined	.85	.48	.41	.85	.46	.36	.91	.55	.44
Intelligent	.89	.63	.38	.89	.59	.52	.94	.66	.52
Sophisticated	.84	.56	.38	.85	.56	.46	.91	.62	.50
Flexible	.80	.42	.34	.79	.38	.27	.88	.56	.34
Intellect	.91	.62	.43	.90	.57	.50	.95	.64	.51
Median single adjectives	.84	.48	.31	.84	.49	.32	.91	.56	.38
Median domain scores	.90	.55	.32	.88	.55	.36	.94	.60	.38

Note. Domain names are in italics. MZ = monozygotic; DZ = dizygotic.

differences between the reliability coefficients and the MZ correlations estimate the contribution of the nonshared environment apart from error of measurement. As the reliabilities of the video-based personality ratings were about .35 higher than the MZ correlations, nonshared environmental influence turned out to be substantial even when measurement error was controlled.

Another notable feature in Table 1 is that although the MZ correlations were higher than the DZ correlations, suggesting genetic influence, the DZ correlations exceeded half the MZ correlations for all personality domains except Extraversion, thus suggesting shared environmental influence.

* * *

Thus, there was strong evidence for genetic influence on the twins' personality as assessed by the video-based personality ratings.

The support for shared environmental influence on the video-based personality ratings was weaker, because although the estimates of c^2 from the video-based personality ratings had a mean of .23 and a median of .29, in only 5 of the 30 (16.7%) relevant comparisons the ACE model fit significantly better than the AE model did.

* * *

ESTIMATES FROM SELF-REPORTS AND PEER REPORTS Whereas the estimates of genetic contributions were by and large consistent with previous findings (Plomin, DeFries, et al., 1997), the partitioning of environmental influences between the shared and the nonshared variety was different. These different estimates might reflect differences between the methods of personality assessment (e.g., methods allowing or not allowing for contrast effects) or differences between samples: Twins who have the time and who are willing to travel large distances to spend an entire day at a university under extensive observation may differ from twins who merely complete self-report or peer report instruments at home. Thus, a within-sample comparison was desirable. We therefore analyzed the MZ and DZ correlations for the NEO-FFI self-report and peer report data that had been collected for the GOSAT twin sample. Complete self-reports were available for 277 (159 MZ and 118 DZ) of the 300 GOSAT pairs, and complete peer reports were available for 278 (159 MZ and 119 DZ) of these pairs. These data overlap with those that were published by Riemann et al. (1997) for a larger sample.

Twin correlations and univariate models. * * * Table 2 reports the twin ICCs for MZ and DZ twins and the tests of univariate models for the self-report and averaged peer report data. Table 2 does not suggest that the GOSAT sample differs systematically from previous twin samples. Rather, the finding of approximately 40% genetic and 60% nonshared environmental influence is consistent

with the results of previous studies. A significant c^2 parameter was obtained for self-reported Extraversion but did not replicate for peer-reported Extraversion. Thus, the significant c^2 for self-reported Extraversion may be a chance finding. For Openness to Experience, substantial shared environmental influence was found according to self-reports as well as peer reports. We come back to that point in the Discussion.

* * *

Discussion

The main finding of the present study is that video-based personality ratings yield estimates of shared environmental influence of about .15 higher than suggested by self-reports and peer reports; the main source of these higher c^2 estimates is the relatively high DZ correlations. At the level of the trait domains, the median twin correlations were .60 (MZ) and .38 (DZ) for the video-based personality ratings, .45 (MZ) and .26 (DZ) for the twins' self-reports, and .42 (MZ) and .13 (DZ) for the averaged peer reports. If these correlations are corrected for lack of interrater reliability (which is not possible for self-reports for obvious reasons), they become, approximately, .64 (MZ) and .44 (DZ) for video-based ratings and .72 (MZ) and .21 (DZ) for peer ratings. These findings support the assumption of a contrast effect in descriptions of DZ twins by parents and peers (Health et al., 1992; Neale & Stevenson, 1989; Saudino & Eaton, 1991; Spinath & Angleitner, 1998), whereas they do not point to a contrast effect in descriptions of MZ twins or in self-reports of twins in general. This is consistent with findings by Saudino and Eaton (1991), who also reported a contrast effect in ratings of DZ but not of MZ twins.

* * *

DIFFERENCES BETWEEN PERSONALITY DOMAINS Generally, the video-based personality ratings suggest more shared environmental influence than do the self-reports and peer reports. But there are also differences between personality domains. Thus, we did not find any shared environmental influence

TABLE 2

RESULTS FROM THE UNIVARIATE MODEL FIT ANALYSES OF SELF- AND AVERAGED PEER RATINGS
ON THE NEO FIVE FACTOR INVENTORY (NEO-FFI) IN THE GOSAT SAMPLE

NEO-FFI scale	Twin correlations		Parameter estimates			Fit of the ACE model		Comparisons	
								AE vs. ACE	CE vs. ACE
	MZ	DZ	a^2	c^2	e^2	χ^2	$p\ (df = 3)$		
Self-reports									
Extraversion	.45	.41	.06	.38	.56	1.67	.64	*	
Agreeableness	.42	.04	.36	.00	.64	16.38	.00		**
Conscientiousness	.50	.24	.48	.00	.52	0.30	.96		**
Neuroticism	.40	.26	.27	.12	.61	1.78	.62		
Openness to Experience	.60	.38	.44	.16	.41	7.12	.07		**
Averaged peer reports									
Extraversion	.42	.13	.41	.00	.59	1.94	.58		**
Agreeableness	.37	.11	.35	.00	.65	1.25	.74		*
Conscientiousness	.45	.20	.44	.00	.56	3.04	.39		*
Neuroticism	.38	.02	.33	.00	.67	4.18	.24		**
Openness to Experience	.47	.28	.40	.07	.52	1.93	.59		*

Note. For chi-squares, $N = 277$ for self-reports and 278 for averaged peer reports. Asterisks in the two right-most columns indicate that the full model fit significantly better than the reduced model did. ACE is a model that combines the additive effects of genes (A), the effects of the shared environment (C), and the effects of the nonshared environment (E). a, c, and e are parameter estimates of the additive effects of genes, the effects of the shared environment, and the effects of the nonshared environment, respectively. GOSAT = German Observational Study of Adult Twins; MZ = monozygotic; DZ = dizygotic.
$*p < .05. **p < .01.$

on Extraversion. This is consistent with the results of Loehlins's (1989, 1992) meta-analyses, which identified Extraversion as the domain that was least influenced by the shared environment. Moreover, the lack of shared environmental influence on Extraversion in our study shows that there is no general bias that inflated the DZ-twin correlations.

The trait domain that was most strongly influenced by shared environment was Intellect, which raises the issue of whether substantial shared environmental influence on Intellect is also found if it is measured by intelligence tests. In his model-fitting meta-analysis of studies on family resemblance in IQ, Loehlin (1989) concluded that environments shared by twins account for 39% of their individual differences in IQ. Admittedly, there is some consensus now that this estimate relies

largely on studies of intelligence in children and should not be generalized to adults, as the importance of shared environment for IQ tends to decrease with age (McCartney et al., 1990; Plomin, Fulker, Corley, & DeFries, 1997; Wilson, 1983). Thus, it is useful to look at the intelligence test data that were collected for the GOSAT sample.

In a behavior-genetic analysis of these data that is reported in detail by Neubauer et al. (2000), no shared environmental influence on Raven's APM was found. It is important to note, however, that the APM was less strongly related to the video-based ratings of Intellect than was the LPS. Thus, the behavior-genetic findings for the LPS are of greater interest here. Shared environment accounted for 24% of the variance in the LPS scores (Neubauer et al., 2000), thus supporting the assumption that the video-based ratings of Intellect reflect actual shared environmental influence on this trait.

LIMITATIONS OF THE TWIN DESIGN It is widely known that the twin design has several limitations, as it relies on three assumptions that can only be tested with additional data: (a) the equal environments assumption, (b) the assumption of random mating, and (c) the assumption that there are no interactive effects of genes. If the equal environments assumption does not hold, environmental effects are misinterpreted as genetic effects, resulting in underestimates of the importance of the shared environment. Similarly, interactive effects of genes are detected by twin studies only if they overrule all possible effects of the shared environment and result in MZ correlations that exceed twice the DZ correlations. Otherwise, interactive effects of genes result in overestimates of additive genetic influence and underestimates of shared environmental influence. Consequently, our estimates of shared environment would be too low if there were unequal environments for MZ and DZ twins or interactive effects of genes.

Assortative mating has opposite effects, in that it increases the DZ but not the MZ correlation and thus inflates the estimates of shared environmental influence (Jensen, 1978). Assortative mating for personality traits like Extraversion, Agreeableness, Conscientiousness, and Emotional Stability is low, but it is substantial for intelligence and social attitudes (Beer et al., 1998; Buss 1985) that may be related to Openness to Experience. * * *

NEED OF AWARENESS OF MEASUREMENT ISSUES A more general conclusion from our study is that behavior-genetic research needs a widened awareness of assessment issues. * * * Genetic research has its roots mainly in biology and in medicine, where measurement issues cause less problems than in psychology. However, when it comes to the genetics of personality, where the data are self-reports and observer ratings, awareness of psychometric principles and of social–psychological evidence on person perception are indispensable, and multi-method studies that incorporate such considerations become highly desirable.

References

Beer, J. M., Arnold, R. D., & Loehlin, J. C. (1998). Genetic and environmental influences on MMPI factor scales: Joint model fitting to twin and adoption data. *Journal of Personality and Social Psychology, 74*, 818–827.

Borkenau, P., & Ostendorf, F. (1993). *NEO-Fuenf-Faktoren-Inventar (NEO-FFI) nach Costa und McCrae* [NEO Five-Factor Inventory by Costa & McCrae]. Goettingen, Germany: Hogrefe.

Borkenau, P., Riemann, R., Spinath, F. M., & Angleitner, A. (2000). Behavior-genetics of personality: The case of observational studies. In I. Mervielde (Series Ed.) & S. E. Hampson (Vol. Ed.), *Advances in personality psychology* (Vol. 1, pp. 107–137). Philadelphia: Taylor & Francis.

Buss, D. M. (1985). Human mate selection. *American Scientist, 73*, 47–51.

Costa, P. T., & McCrae, R. R. (1992). *Revised NEO Personality Inventory (NEO-PI-R) and NEO Five-Factor Inventory (NEO-FFI) professional manual.* Odessa, FL: Psychological Assessment Resources.

Goldberg, L. R. (1990). An alternative "description of personality": The big-five factor structure. *Journal of Personality and Social Psychology, 59*, 1216–1229.

Harris, J. R. (1995). Where is the child's environment? A group socialization theory of development. *Psychological Review, 102*, 458–489.

Harris, J. R. (1998). *The nurture assumption: Why children turn out the way they do.* New York: The Free Press.

Heath, A. C., Neale, M. C., Kessler, R. C., Eaves, L. J., & Kendler, K. S. (1992). Evidence for genetic influences on personality from self-reports and informant ratings. *Journal of Personality and Social Psychology, 63*, 85–96.

Jensen, A. R. (1978). Genetic and behavioral effects of nonrandom mating. In R. T. Osborne, C. E. Noble, & N. Weyl (Eds.), *Human variation: The biopsychology of age, race, and sex* (pp. 51–105). New York: Academic Press.

Loehlin, J. C. (1989). Partitioning environmental and genetic contributions to behavioral development. *American Psychologists, 44*, 1285–1292.

Loehlin, J. C. (1992). *Genes and environment in personality development.* Newbury Park, CA: Sage.

Loehlin, J. C. Willerman, L., & Horn, J. M. (1987). Personality resemblance in adoptive families: A 10-year-following-up. *Journal of Personality and Social Psychology, 53*, 961–969.

McCartney, K., Harris, M. J., & Bernieri, F. (1990). Growing up and growing apart: A developmental meta-analysis of twin studies. *Psychological Bulletin, 107*, 226–237.

McCrae, R. R., & Costa, P. T. (1987). Validation of the five factor model of personality across instruments and observers. *Journal of Personality and Social Psychology, 52*, 81–90.

Miles, D. R., & Carey, G. (1997). Genetic and environmental architecture of human aggression. *Journal of Personality and Social Psychology, 72*, 207–217.

Neale, M. C., & Stevenson, J. (1989). Rater bias in the EASI temperament scales: A twin study. *Journal of Personality and Social Psychology, 56,* 446–455.

Neubauer, A. C., Spinath, F. M., Riemann, R., Borkenau, P., Angleitner, A. (2000). Genetic and environmental influences on two measures of speed of information processing and their relation to psychometric intelligence. *Intelligence, 26,* 267–289.

Plomin, R., Corley, R., Caspi, A., Fulker, D. W., & DeFries, J. C. (1998). Adoption results for self-reported personality: Evidence for nonadditive effects? *Journal of Personality and Social Psychology, 75,* 211–218.

Plomin, R., DeFries, J. C., McClearn, G. E., & Rutter, M. (1997). *Behavioral genetics.* New York: Freeman.

Plomin, R., Fulker, D. W., Corley, R., & DeFries, J. C. (1997). Nature, nurture, and cognitive development from 1 to 16 years: A parent–offspring adoption study. *Psychological Science, 8,* 442–447.

Riemann, R., Angleitner, A., & Strelau, J. (1997). Genetic and environmental influences on personality: A study of twins reared together using the self- and peer report NEO-FFI scales. *Journal of Personality, 65,* 449–475.

Rose, R. (1995). Genes and human behavior. *Annual Review of Psychology, 46,* 625–654.

Rowe, D. C. (1994). *The limits of family influence: Genes, experience, and behavior.* New York: Guilford Press.

Saudino, K. J., & Eaton, W. O. (1991). Infant temperament and genetics: An objective twin study of motor activity level. *Child Development, 62,* 1167–1174.

Scarr, S., Webber, P. L., Weinberg, R. A., & Wittig, M. A. (1981). Personality resemblance among adolescents and their parents in biologically related and adoptive families. *Journal of Personality and Social Psychology, 40,* 885–898.

Schwarz, N. (1999). Self-reports: How the questions shape the answers. *American Psychologist, 54,* 93–105.

Spinath, F. M., & Angleitner, A. (1998). Contrast effects in Buss and Plomin's EAS questionnaire: A behavioral genetic study on early developing personality traits assessed through parental ratings. *Personality and Individual Differences, 25,* 947–963.

Stoolmiller, M. (1999). Implications of the restricted range of family environments for estimates of heritability and nonshared environment in behavior-genetic adoption studies. *Psychological Bulletin, 125,* 392–409.

Wilson, R. S. (1983). The Louisville Twin Study: Developmental synchronies in behavior. *Child Development, 54,* 298–316.

INFLUENCE OF LIFE STRESS ON DEPRESSION: MODERATION BY A POLYMORPHISM IN THE 5-HTT GENE

Avshalom Caspi, Karen Sugden, Terrie E. Moffitt, Alan Taylor, Ian W. Craig, HonaLee Harrington, Joseph McClay, Jonathan Mill, Judy Martin, Antony Braithwaite, and Richie Poulton

Psychologists have been saying for many years that personality is the product of an interaction between the individual's genes and the environment in which he or she grew up. However, historically we have not seen much progress toward specifying what aspects of the environment interact with which genes. This paper, by Avshalom Caspi and his colleagues, reports the first demonstration of an interaction between a measured aspect of the environment and an identified, measured gene that affects an important aspect of adult personality. Specifically the paper shows how childhood stress interacts with a polymorphism in the 5-HTT gene to affect the development of depression in adulthood.

While the previous paper by Borkenau and his colleagues demonstrated the achievements of state-of-the-art research in quantitative behavioral genetics, Caspi's article shows the tremendous promise of moving the study of behavioral genetics to the molecular level. While this study, published in 2003, is the first to concretely show this kind of interaction, now that Caspi has opened the door we can expect a rush of new research demonstrating measured genotype–environment interactions in the near future.

From *Science, 301*, 386–389.

Depression is among the top five leading causes of disability and disease burden throughout the world (Tang & Lopez, 1997). Across the life span, stressful life events that involve threat, loss, humiliation, or defeat influence the onset and course of depression (Brown, 1998; Kendler, Karkowski, & Prescott, 1999; Kessler, 1997; Pine et al., 2002). However, not all people who encounter a stressful life experience succumb to its depressogenic effect. Diathesis-stress theories of depression predict that individuals' sensitivity to stressful events depends on their genetic makeup (Costello et al., 2002; Monroe & Simons, 1991). Behavioral genetics research supports this prediction, documenting that the risk of depression after a stressful event is elevated among people who are at high genetic risk and diminished among those at low genetic risk (Kendler et al., 1995). However, whether specific genes exacerbate or buffer the effect of stressful life events on depression is unknown. In this study, a functional polymorphism in the promoter region of the serotonin transporter gene (*SLC6A4*) was used to characterize genetic vulnerability to depression and to test whether 5-HTT gene variation moderates the influence of life stress on depression.

The serotonin system provides a logical source of candidate genes for depression because this system is the target of selective serotonin reuptake–inhibitor drugs that are effective in treating depression (Tamminga et al., 2002). The serotonin transporter has received particular attention because it is involved in the reuptake of serotonin at brain synapses (Lesch et al., 2002). The promoter activity of the 5-HTT gene, located on 17q11.2, is modified by sequence elements within the proximal 5′ regulatory region, designated the 5-HTT gene-linked polymorphic region (5-HTTLPR). The short ("s") allele in the 5-HTTLPR is associated with lower transcriptional efficiency of the promoter compared with the long ("l") allele (Lesch et al., 1996).[1]

Evidence for an association between the short promoter variant and depression is inconclusive (Lesch, 2003). Although the 5-HTT gene may not be directly associated with depression, it could moderate the serotonergic response to stress. Three lines of experimental research suggest this hypothesis of a gene-by-environment (G × E) interaction. First, in mice with disrupted 5-HTT, homozygous and heterozygous (5-HTT −/− and +/−) strains exhibited more fearful behavior and greater increases in the stress hormone (plasma) adrenocorticortropin in response to stress compared to homozygous (5-HTT +/+) controls, but in the absence of stress no differences related to genotype

were observed (Murphy et al., 2001). Second, in rhesus macaques, whose length variation of the 5-HTTLPR is analogous to that of humans, the short allele is associated with decreased serotonergic function [lower cerebrospinal fluid (CSF) 5-hydroxyindoleacetic acid concentrations] among monkeys reared in stressful conditions but not among normally reared monkeys (Bennett et al., 2002). Third, human neuroimaging research suggests that the stress response is mediated by variations in the 5-HTTLPR. Humans with one or two copies of the s allele exhibit greater amygdala neuronal activity to fearful stimuli compared to individuals homozygous for the l allele (Hariri et al., 2002). Taken together, these finding suggest the hypothesis that variations in the 5-HTT gene moderated psychopathological reactions to stressful experiences.

We tested this G × E hypothesis among members of the Dunedin Multidisciplinary Health and Development Study. This representative birth cohort of 1037 children (52% male) has been assessed at ages 3, 5, 7, 9, 11, 13, 15, 18, and 21 and was virtually intact (96%) at the age of 26 years. A total of 847 Caucasian non-Maori study members, without stratification confounds, were divided into three groups on the basis of their 5-HTTLPR genotype (Lesch et al., 1996): those with two copies of the s allele (s/s homozygotes; $n = 147$; 17%), those with one copy of the s allele (s/l heterozygotes; $n = 435$; 51%), and those with two copies of the l allele (l/l homozygotes; $n = 265$; 31%). There was no difference in genotype frequencies between the sexes [$\chi^2(2) = 0.02$, $P = 0.99$]. Stressful life events occurring after the 21st birthday and before the 26th birthday were assessed with the aid of a life-history calendar (Caspi et al., 1996), a highly reliable method for ascertaining life-event histories (Bell, Shay, and Stafford, 2001). The 14 events included employment, financial, housing, health, and relationship stressors. Thirty percent of the study members experienced no stressful life events; 25% experienced one event; 20%, two events; 11% three events; and 15%, four or more events. There were no significant differences between the three genotype groups in the number of life events they

---

[1]These technical specifications, meaningful to molecular geneticists, describe the exact location in the human genome where the gene addressed by the present study can be found.

experienced, $F(2,846) = 0.56$, $P = 0.59$, suggesting that 5-HTTLPR genotype did not influence exposure to stressful life events.[2]

Study members were assessed for past-year depression at age 26 with the use of the Diagnostic Interview Schedule (Robins et al., 1995), which yields a quantitative measure of depressive symptoms and a categorical diagnosis of a major depressive episode according to *Diagnostic and Statistical Manual of Mental Disorders* (DSM-IV) criteria (APA, 1994). 17% of study members (58% female versus 42% male; odds ratio = 1.6; 95% confidence interval from 1.1 to 2.2) met criteria for a past-year major depressive episode, which is comparable to age and sex prevalence rates observed in U.S. epidemiological studies (Kessler et al., 1993). In addition, 3% of the study members reported past-year suicide attempts or recurrent thoughts about suicide in the context of a depressive episode. We also collected informant reports about symptoms of depression for 96% of study members at age 26 by mailing a brief questionnaire to persons nominated by each study member as "someone who knows you well."

We used a moderated regression framework (Aiken et al., 1991), with sex as a covariate, to test the association between depression and (i) 5-HTTLPR genotype, (ii) stressful life events, and (iii) their interaction.[3] The interaction between 5-HTTLPR and life events showed that the effect of life events on self-reports of depression symptoms at age 26 was significantly stronger ($P = 0.02$)[4] among individuals carrying an s allele than among l/l homozygotes (Fig. 1A). We further tested whether life events could predict within-individual increases in depression symptoms over time among individuals

with an s allele by statistically controlling for the baseline number of depressive symptoms they had before the life events occurred. The significant interaction ($P = 0.05$) showed that individuals carrying an s allele whose life events occurred after their 21st birthday experienced increases in depressive symptoms from the age of 21 to 26 years ($b = 1.55$, SE = 0.66, $t = 2.35$, $P = 0.02$ among s/s homozygotes and $b = 1.25$, SE = 0.34, $t = 3.66$, $P < 0.001$ among s/l heterozygotes) whereas l/l homozygotes did not ($b = 0.17$, SE = 0.41, $t = 0.41$, $P = 0.68$).[5]

The G × E interaction also showed that stressful life events predicted a diagnosis of major depression among carriers of an s allele but not among l/l homozygotes ($P = 0.056$, Fig. 1B). We further tested whether life events could predict the onset of new diagnosed depression among carriers of an s allele. We excluded from analysis study members who were diagnosed with depression before age 21. The significant interaction ($P = 0.02$) showed that life events occurring after their 21st birthdays predicted depression at age 26 among carriers of an s allele who did not have a prior history of depression ($b = 0.79$, SE = 0.25, $z = 3.16$, $P = 0.002$ among s/s homozygotes and $b = 0.41$, SE = 0.12, $z = 3.29$, $P = 0.001$ among s/l heterozygotes) but did not predict onset of new depression among l/l homozygotes ($b = 0.08$, SE = 0.20, $z = 0.42$, $P = 0.67$). Further analyses showed that stressful life events predicted suicide ideation or attempt among individuals carrying an s allele but not among l/l homozygotes ($P = 0.05$, Fig. 1C). The hypothesized G × E interaction was also significant when we predicted informant reports of age-26 depression ($P < 0.01$), an analysis that ruled out the possibility of self-report bias (Fig. 1D). The interaction showed that the effect of life events on informant reports of depression was stronger among individuals carrying an s allele than among l/l homozygotes. These analyses attest that the

---

[2]That is, the differences among the three genotypes were so small that they could easily have occurred by chance.

[3]Moderated regression allows a test as to whether correlations between two variables are affected by one or more other variables. In this case, the question is whether the correlation between the gene's presence and depression is affected by stressful life events.

[4]The probability is only 2/100 that this degree of difference between correlations would be found if the comparison groups varied only by chance.

---

[5]*b* refers to regression coefficient or effect size; SE is the standard error, *t* is a commonly used statistic used to compare means, and *P* is the probability that the result in question would have occurred by chance if no real effect were present.

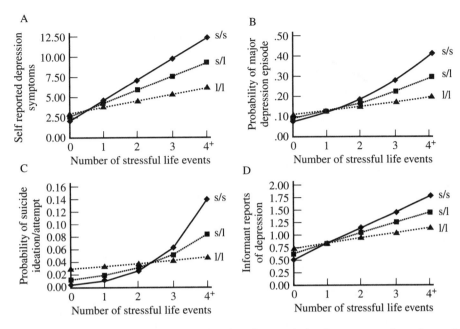

Figure 1 Results of multiple regression analyses estimating the association between number of stressful life events (between ages 21 and 26 years) and depression outcomes at age 26 as a function of 5-HTT genotype.

5-HTT gene interacts with life events to predict depression symptoms, an increase in symptoms, depression diagnoses, new-onset diagnoses, suicidality, and an informant's report of depressed behavior.

This evidence that 5-HTTLPR variation moderates the effect of life events on depression does not constitute unambiguous evidence of a G × E interaction, because exposure to life events may be influenced by genetic factors; if individuals have a heritable tendency to enter situations where they encounter stressful life events, these events may simply be a genetically saturated marker (Kendler et al., 1997; Plomin et al., 1991). Thus, what we have identified as a gene × environment interaction predicting depression could actually reflect a gene × "gene" interaction between the 5-HTTLPR and other genes we did not measure. We reasoned that, if our measure of life events represents merely genetic risk, then life events would interact with 5-HTTLPR even if they occurred after the depression episode. However, if our measure of life events

represents environmental stress, then the timing of life events relative to depression must follow cause-effect order and life events that occur after depression should not interact with 5-HTTLPR to postdict depression. We tested this hypothesis by substituting the age-26 measure of depression with depression assessed in this longitudinal study when study members were 21 and 18 years old, before the occurrence of the measured life events between the ages of 21 and 26 years. Whereas the 5-HTTLPR × life events interaction predicted depression at the age of 26 years, this same interaction did not postdict depression reported at age 21 nor at the age of 18 years, indicating our finding is a true G × E interaction.

If 5-HTT genotype moderates the depressogenic influence of stressful life events, it should moderate the effect of life events that occurred not just in adulthood but also of stressful experience that occurred in earlier developmental periods. Based on this hypothesis, we tested whether adult depression was predicted by the interaction

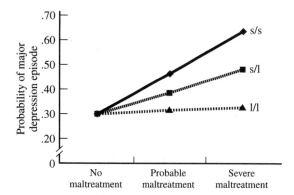

Figure 2 Results of regression analysis estimating the association between childhood maltreatment (between the ages of 3 and 11 years) and adult depression (ages 18 to 26), as a function of 5-HTT genotype.

between 5-HTTLPR and childhood maltreatment that occurred during the first decade of life (Caspi et al., 2002). Consistent with the G × E hypothesis, the longitudinal prediction from childhood maltreatment to adult depression was significantly moderated by 5-HTTLPR. The interaction showed ($P = 0.05$) that childhood maltreatment predicted adult depression only among individuals carrying an s allele but not among l/l homozygotes (Fig. 2).

We previously showed that variations in the gene encoding the neurotransmitter-metabolizing enzyme monoamine oxidase A (MAOA) moderate children's sensitivity to maltreatment (Caspi et al., 2002). MAOA has high affinity to 5-HTT, raising the possibility that the protective effect of the l/l

allele on psychiatric morbidity is further augmented by the presence of a genotype conferring high MAOA activity (Murphy et al., 2001; Salichon et al., 2001). However, we found that the moderations of life stress on depression was specific to a polymorphism in the 5-HTT gene, because this effect was observed regardless of the individual's MAOA gene status.

Until this study's findings are replicated, speculation about clinical implications is premature. Nonetheless, although carriers of an s 5-HTTLPR allele who experienced four or more life events constituted only 10% of the birth cohort, they accounted for almost one-quarter (23%) of the 133 cases of diagnosed depression. Moreover, among cohort members suffering four or more stressful life events, 33% of individuals with an s allele became depressed, whereas only 17% of the l/l homozygotes developed depression (Fig. 3). Thus, the G × E's attributable risk and predictive sensitivity indicate that more knowledge about the functional properties of the 5-HTT gene may lead to better pharmacological treatments for those already depressed. Although the short 5-HTTLPR variant is too prevalent for discriminatory screening (over half of the Caucasian population has an s allele), a microarray of genes might eventually identify those needing prophylaxis against life's stressful events (Evans and Relling, 1999).

Evidence of a direct relation between the 5-HTTLPR and depression has been inconsistent (Lesch, 2003), perhaps because prior studies have

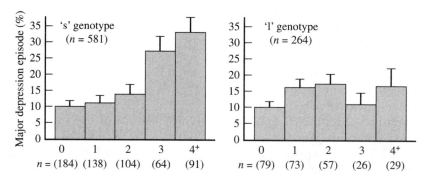

Figure 3 The percentage of individuals meeting diagnostic criteria for depression at age 26, as a function of 5-HTT genotype and number of stressful life events between the ages of 21 and 26.

not considered participants' stress histories. In this study, no direct association between the 5-HTT gene and depression was observed. Previous experimental paradigms, including 5-HTT knockout mice (Murphy et al., 2001), stress-reared rhesus macaques (Bennett et al., 2002), and human functional neuroimaging (Hariri et al., 2002), have shown that the 5-HTT gene can interact with environmental conditions, although these experiments did not address depression. Our study demonstrates that this G × E interaction extends to the natural development of depression in a representative sample of humans. However, we could not test hypotheses about brain endophenotypes (Gottesman and Gould, 2003) intermediate between the 5-HTT gene and depression because of the difficulty of taking CSF or functional magnetic resonance imaging measurements in an epidemiological cohort.

Much genetic research has been guided by the assumption that genes cause diseases, but the expectation that direct paths will be found from gene to disease has not proven fruitful for complex psychiatric disorders (Harner, 2002). Our findings of G × E interaction for the 5-HTT gene and another candidate gene, MAOA (Caspi et al., 2002), point to a different, evolutionary model. This model assumes that genetic variants maintained at high prevalence in the population probably act to promote organisms' resistance to environmental pathogens (Hill, 1999). We extend the concept of environmental pathogens to include traumatic, stressful life experiences and propose that the effects of genes may be uncovered when such pathogens are measured (in naturalistic studies) or manipulated (in experimental studies). To date, few linkage studies detect genes, many candidate gene studies fail consistent replication, and genes that replicate account for little variation in the phenotype (Hamer, 2002). If replicated, our G × E findings will have implications for improving research in psychiatric genetics. Incomplete gene penetrance, a major source of error in linkage pedigrees, can be explained if a gene's effects are expressed only among family members exposed to environmental risk. If risk exposure differs between samples, candidate genes may fail replication. If risk exposure differs among participants within a sample, genes may account for little variation in the phenotype. We speculate that some multifactorial disorders, instead of resulting from variations in many genes of small effect, may result from variations in fewer genes whose effects are conditional on exposure to environmental risks.

References

Aiken, L. S., & West, S. G. (1991). *Multiple Regression: Testing and Interpreting Interactions*. Thousand Oaks, CA: Sage.

APA (1994). *Diagnostic and Statistical Manual of Mental Disorders*. Washington, D.C.: APA, ed 4.

Belli, R. F., Shay, W. L., & Stafford, F. P.(2001). *Public Opin Q, 65*, 45.

Bennett, A. J. et al. (2002). *Mol Psychiatry, 7*, 188.

Brown, G. W. (1998). *Soc Psychiatry Psychiatr Epidemiol, 33*, 363.

Caspi, A. et al. (1996). *Int J Methods Psychiatr Res, 6*, 101.

Caspi, A. et al. (2002). *Science, 297*, 851.

Costello, E. J., et al. (2002). *Biol Psychiatr, 52*, 529.

Evans, W. E., & Relling, M. V. (1999). *Science, 286*, 487.

Gottesman, I. I., & Gould, T. D. (2003). *Am J Psychiatry, 160*, 636.

Hamer, D. (2002). *Science, 298*, 71.

Hariri, A. R. et al. (2002). *Science, 297*, 400.

Hill, A. V. S. (1999). *Br Med Bull, 55*, 401.

Kendler, K. S. et al. (1995). *Am J Psychiatr, 152*, 833.

Kendler, K. S., & Karkowski-Shurman, L. (1997). *Psychol Med, 27*, 539.

Kendler, K. S., Karkowski, L. M., & Prescott, C. A. (1999). *Am J Psychiatry, 156*, 837.

Kessler, R. C. (1997). *Annu Rev Psychol, 48*, 191.

Kessler, R. C., McGonagle, K. A., Swartz, M., Blazer, D. G., & Nelson, C. B. (1993). *J Affect Disorders, 29*, 85.

Lesch, K. P. (2003). In *Behavioral Genetics in the Postgenomics Era*, R. Plomin, J. C. DeFries, I. W. Craig, & P. McGuffin, eds. Washington, D.C.: American Psychiatric Association (APA). Pp. 389–424.

Lesch, K. P. et al. (1996). *Science, 274*, 1527.

Lesch, K. P., Greenberg, M. D., Higley, J. D., Bennett, A., & Murphy, D. L. (2002). In *Molecular Genetics and the Human Personality*, J. Benjamin, R. P. Ebstein, R. H. Belmaker, eds. Washington, D.C.: American Psychiatric Association (APA), pp. 109–136.

Monroe, S. M. & Simons, A. D. (1991). *Psycol Bull, 110*, 406.

Murphy, D. L. et al. (2001). *Brain Res Bull, 56*, 487.

Pine, D. S., Cohen, P., Johnson, J. G., & Brock, J. A. (2002). *J Affect Disorders, 68*, 49.

Plomin, R., & Bergeman, C. S. (1991). *Behav Brain Sci, 14*, 373.

Robins, L. N., Cottler, L. Bucholtz, K., & Compton, W. (1995). *Diagnostic Interview Schedule for DSM-IV*. St. Louis, MO: Washington University.

Salichon, N. et al. (2001). *J Neurosci, 21*, 884.

Tamminga, C. A. et al., (2002). *Biol Psychiatry, 52*, 589.

Tang, C.J., & Lopez, A. D. (1997). *Lancet, 349*, 1498.

Neuroethics: The Practical and the Philosophical

Martha J. Farah

Is personality reducible to biology? What would it mean if this were so? Thinking of humans—and oneself—as just another animal has some potentially disconcerting implications. For example, if behavior can be affected by genes, brain structures, and biochemical processes, does this mean that people are not really responsible for their deeds? Even more perplexing, if a drug could make you a better person, would you take it? Should you take it? Should you be required to take it?

This paper by Martha Farah, a pioneer in the emerging field of neuroethics, begins to address the implications of modern brain science on longstanding moral and ethical questions. You will notice that she does not provide final answers to any of these questions, but if Farah is right about the trajectory of the science, all of us need to begin to develop our own answers, soon.

From *Trends in Cognitive Sciences, 9,* 34–40, 2005.

Introduction

Almost three decades ago, in the picturesque coastal retreat of Asilomar, California, a group of molecular biologists gathered to discuss the safety of the newly developed recombinant DNA technology. In the years since, concern about the risks of genetic engineering have remained prominent in the public consciousness, as well as commanding the attention of academic bioethicists, government regulators, and biologists themselves. At the start of the 21st century, neuroscience has developed to a point where it, too, may have profound effects on society, extending far beyond the research laboratory or medical clinic.

Like the field of genetics, neuroscience concerns the biological foundations of who we are, of our essence. The relation of self to brain is, if anything, more direct than that of self to genome. Perhaps more important, neural interventions are generally more easily accomplished than genetic interventions. Yet until recently there has been little awareness of the ethical issues arising from neuroscience. Beginning in 2002, neuroscientists began to address these issues in the scientific literature (e.g. [1–5]) and the field gained a name: Neuroethics [6].

Neuroethics encompasses a large and varied set of issues, and initial discussions focused on various different subsets of those issues. Some neuroethical issues concern the practical implications of neurotechnology for individuals and society. Technological progress is making it possible to monitor and manipulate the human mind with ever more precision through a variety of neuroimaging methods and interventions. For the first time it may be possible to breach the privacy of the human mind, and judge people not only by their actions, but also by their thoughts and predilections. The alteration of brain function in normal humans, with the goal of enhancing psychological function, is increasingly feasible and indeed increasingly practiced. At the same time, progress in basic neuroscience is illuminating the relation between mind and brain, a topic of great philosophical importance. Our understanding of why people behave as they do is closely bound up with the content of our laws, social mores, and religious beliefs. Neuroscience is providing us with increasingly comprehensive explanations of human behavior in purely material terms. Although the field of neuroethics is young and still evolving rapidly, the time seems ripe for a review in which the key issues of neuroethics, both practical and philosophical, are surveyed and placed in relation to one another.

Brain Imaging and Brain Privacy

Among the neuroscience technologies that present new ethical challenges of a practical nature is functional brain imaging. This includes the familiar false-color images of positron emission tomography (PET) and functional magnetic resonance imaging (fMRI), as well as the electroencephalography-derived methods of event-related potentials (ERPs) and magnetoencephalography (MEG) and optical imaging methods such as near infrared spectroscopy (NIRS). These methods vary in their invasiveness and portability, which constrain the uses to which they can be put, although any one of them can be used to obtain personal information surreptitiously, in a study ostensibly designed for a different purpose. In principle, and increasingly in practice, imaging can be used to infer people's psychological states and traits [1, 3, 7].

For example, in "neuromarketing" brain imaging is used to measure limbic system response to a product that may indicate consumers' desire for it. In one recent demonstration, brain activity related to soft drink preference was sensitive to both the taste of the drink and to the brand name, with Coke™ evoking more activity than Pepsi™ only when subjects knew which brand they were tasting [8]. To the extent that neuroimaging can measure unconscious motivation to buy, it provides a valuable new kind of information for marketers.

Another potential use for functional imaging of brain states is lie detection. Although fMRI-based lie detection is far from feasible in real-world situations, researchers have found correlates of deception in the laboratory [9]. ERPs come closer to providing actual brain-based lie detection. They have been used to identify "guilty knowledge" by distinguishing responses to items that are generally known to be associated with a crime and items that only the perpetrator would know are associated [10].

* * *

Psychological traits also have physical correlates that are measurable with current brain imaging technology. Like genotyping, "brainotyping" may be able to reveal mental health vulnerabilities [11, 12] and predilection for violent crime [13]. Unconscious racial attitudes are manifest in brain activation [14]. Sexual attraction and even the attempt to suppress feelings of attraction have neuroimaging correlates [15]. A growing body of literature has investigated the neural correlates of personality using brain imaging, including extraversion and neuroticism, risk-aversion, pessimism, persistence and empathy (e.g. [16–22]).

Of course, none of these characteristics can be accurately inferred by imaging (or for that matter, by genotyping) at present. Brain imaging is at best a rough measure of personality, but this is not to say it is uninformative even in its current state of development. The work of Canli and colleagues [16, 17] on extraversion illustrates this. In their initial experiment, they found that extraversion was correlated with amygdala response to pleasant stimuli, using photographs of puppies, ice cream, sunsets and so on [16].

* * *

NEUROETHICAL ISSUES: PRIVACY AND PUBLIC UNDERSTANDING An important practical problem that brain imaging shares with genetics is privacy. It might not be in an individual's best interest to have certain personal information available to others. Another parallel is that with brain imaging, as with tissue sampling for DNA analysis, an individual need not know whether or what kind of personal information will be obtained. The experimental paradigm used by Canli and colleagues to correlate amygdala activation with personality simply required subjects to view pictures and could be administered in the guise of a picture perception study.

Another practical problem raised by progress in neuroimaging is that the public tends to view brain scans as more accurate and objective than in fact they are [23]. Statements like "the brain does not lie" crop up in popular writing on neuromarking and brain-based lie detection, reflecting a failure to appreciate the many layers of signal processing and statistical analysis that intervene between actual brain function and resulting image or waveform, as well as the complex set of assumptions required to interpret the psychological significance of such images or waveforms.

Brain-based measures do, in principle, have an advantage as indices of psychological states and traits over more familiar behavioral or autonomic measures, being one causal step closer to these states and traits than responses on personality questionnaires or polygraph tracings. For this reason imaging may eventually provide more sensitive and specific measures of psychological processes than are now available. At present, however, such uses must be approached carefully and with a healthy dose of skepticism.

Enhancement: Better Brains through Chemistry

The past two decades have seen the introduction of new antidepressant and antianxiety drugs with fewer side effects [24]. The greater tolerability of these medications, along with increased public awareness of mental illness and aggressive marketing of psychiatric medications to physicians and patients [25] has led to the widespread use of psychopharmacology by people who would not have been considered ill twenty years ago.

There is a substantial literature (which in fact includes literary genres such as essays and memoirs) [26–28] on the ways in which Prozac and other selective serotonin reuptake inhibitors (SSRIs) have become a part of life for many. However, there is surprisingly little scientific research on the effects of SSRIs on people who are not depressed. It seems clear that they are not happy pills, shifting depressed people to normalcy and normal people to bliss. Rather, for most people they seem to leave positive affect unchanged but attenuate negative affect [29, 30], for example reducing the subjectively experienced "hassle" factor of life [30]. They also have subtle effects on social behavior [29, 31].

* * *

The treatment of cognitive disorders has also begun to shade into cognitive enhancement for healthy people. Two main cognitive systems have been targeted for enhancement, executive function and memory [4, 36]. Stimulant medication, which has been shown to improve the executive function of individuals with ADHD, also enhances normal performance on a variety of executive function measures [37, 38]. This is not surprising because ADHD probably represents the lower tail of the whole population distribution of executive function rather than a qualitatively different state of functioning, discontinuous with the normal population (NIH Consensus Statement, 1998). Although methylphenidate (Ritalin) and amphetamine (Adderall) are ostensibly prescribed mainly for the treatment of ADHD, sales figures suggest that they are not uncommonly used for enhancement. Methylphenidate is currently widely used by high school and college students. Surveys have estimated that as many as 10% of high school students and 20% of college students have used prescription stimulants such as Ritalin illegally (see D. A. Kapner: www.edc.org/hec/pubs/factsheets/ritalin.html). * * *

The most commonly used method of memory enhancement involves manipulation not of memory circuits *per se* but of cerebrovascular function. Herbal supplements such as Gingko biloba affect memory mainly by increasing blood flow within the brain [39]. However, a huge research effort is now being directed to the development of memory-boosting drugs [4, 40, 41]. The candidate drugs target various stages in the molecular cascade that underlies memory formation, including the initial induction of long-term potentiation and the later stages of memory consolidation. Although this research is aimed at finding treatments for dementia, there is reason to believe that some of the products under development would enhance normal memory as well, particularly in middle and old age when a degree of increased forgetfulness is normal. * * * Finally, the ability to weaken or prevent the consolidation of unwanted memories constitutes another kind of enhancement that is also under development [42].

Nonpharmaceutical methods for altering brain function have also evolved rapidly over the past decade and in the future may offer complementary approaches to enhancement. Transcranial magnetic stimulation (TMS) has moved from laboratory to clinic as a means of treating depression [43] and is being explored with healthy subjects as a means to alter mood [44] and cognitive style [45]. More invasive methods such as surgery, brain and vagus nerve stimulation, and brain-machine interfaces may eventually expand our conception of brain enhancement yet further—and possibly our conception of human nature as well [46].

NEUROETHICAL ISSUES: RISKS TO THE INDIVIDUAL AND SOCIETY The ethical issues surrounding brain enhancement can be grouped into three general categories. In the first category are health issues: safety, side effects, and unintended consequences. Of course, these are a concern with all medications and procedures, but our tolerance for risk is lower for enhancement than for therapy. Furthermore, in comparison with other comparably elective treatments such as cosmetic surgery, brain-based enhancement involves intervening in a complex and poorly understood system, and the

likelihod of unanticipated problems is consequently higher.

The second category of ethical issue concerns the social effects of brain enhancement: How will it affect the lives of all of us, including those who may prefer not to enhance our brains? For example, the freedom to remain unenhanced may be difficult to maintain in a society where one's competition is using enhancement. American courts have already heard cases brought by parents who were coerced by schools to medicate their children for attentinal dysfunction [47]. Indirect coercion is already likely to be at work in schools where 30% or more of the boys take Ritalin [48]. The military has long used drugs such as amphetamine to enhance the attention of pilots and other personnel on long missions, and the U.S. defense department is a major funder of research on brain–machine interfaces [49]. This raises a concern about a very direct form of coercion, by which troops are ordered to undergo brain enhancement.

Conversely, barriers such as cost will prevent some who would like to enhance from doing so. This would exacerbate the disadvantages already faced by people of low socioeconomic status in education and employment.

NEUROETHICAL ISSUES: UNDERMINING PERSONHOOD Whereas the effects of enhancement on health and society are important practical issues, enhancement also raises what could be called philosophical issues. This third category includes the many ways in which brain enhancement challenges our understanding of personal effort and accomplishment, autonomy, and the value of people as opposed to things. Have we "cheated" if we study better with Ritalin, or can we take credit for our improved work? If we fall in love with someone who is on Prozac and then find she is difficult and temperamental off the drug, do we conclude we don't love her after all? Then who was it we loved? Are we treating people (including ourselves) as objects if we chemically upgrade their cognition, temperament or sexual performance? People vary in how troubling they find these scenarios, but at least some see a fundamental metaphysical distinction eroding, the distinction between things (even complex biophysical things), and persons.

Responsibility, Brain and Blame

As cognitive neuroscience expanded from the study of one-trial learning and color vision to decision-making and motivated behavior, its relevance to understanding real-world behavior, and misbehavior, grew. Starting from clinical observations of personality change in patients with ventromedial prefrontal damage, Bechara and others [50] developed experimental tasks in which the ability to make prudent, responsible choices could be quantified and went on to demonstrate that this ability is diminished after ventromedial damage. Subsequent research has enlarged the set of brain regions that play a role in decision making to include other prefrontal and limbic areas [51–53].

Another ability that is essential for prosocial behavior is the ability to take another's viewpoint, and this too has been linked with specific brain systems. Brain imaging has shown that when subjects understand stories or cartoon pictures whose plot or punch line depends on the thoughts or viewpoint of a character, some of the same cortical and limbic brain regions are more active than during similar tasks in which mental states are not relevant [54]. Damage to these areas impairs the ability to understand behavior in terms of the mental states of others [55, 56]. A network encompassing many of the same areas is active in experiments that evoke empathy [20, 57] or a sense of moral violation [58].

How do these scientific advances affect our understanding of moral and legal responsibility? We do not blame people for acts committed reflexively (e.g. as the result of a literal knee-jerk), in states of diminished awareness or control (e.g. while sleep-walking or under hypnosis) or under duress (e.g. with a gun held to the head), because in these cases we perceive the acts as not resulting from the exercise of free will [59]. The problem with neuroscience accounts of behavior is that everything we do is like a knee-jerk in the following important way: it results from a chain of purely physical events that are as impossible to resist as the laws of physics.

Furthermore, our intuitions about responsibility and blame are more influenced by knowledge of a specific physical mechanism than by the abstract principle that some physical mechanism must be at work. For this reason, we are not inclined to blame Phineas Gage for his bad behavior after an inch-wide, 3-foot-long iron bar was blown through his head, damaging his ventromedial prefrontal cortex [60] and transforming his personality from responsible and polite to slothful and ill-tempered. The challenge arises when we try to draw a principled line between the causes of bad behavior by someone like Gage and bad behavior that lacks *obvious* neurological causes.

Recent neuroscience research has begun to illuminate the more subtle and gradual ways in which the brain can be damaged, beyond the obvious lesions caused by flying iron bars. Most illicit drugs affect these areas and prolonged use has been linked to impaired prefrontal function [61, 62]. Even childhood abuse or severe neglect, which involve neither a direct mechanical insult to the brain nor a foreign substance crossing the blood-brain barrier, damages these systems [63]. There are also genetic factors that influence the function of these systems. For example, psychopathic personality disorder, which is characterized by an absence of empathy or remorse for victims and underlies some of the most abhorrent crimes, is moderately heritable [64] and is accompanied by abnormalities in some of the same prefrontal and limbic systems mentioned earlier in connection with normal social cognition [65]. The physical and mental health of criminal offenders is below that of their non-criminal peers, especially with respect to neuropsychiatric health [66].

NEUROETHICAL ISSUES: RETHINKING MORAL AND LEGAL RESPONSIBILITY Society is gradually responding to the emerging neuroscientific view of human behavior. This is evident in our treatment of criminals within the legal system, and also in our social mores and attitudes toward "bad" but noncriminal behavior such as compulsive drinking, gambling or sex. Within the legal system, evidence of neurological dysfunction is frequently introduced in the penalty phases of criminal trials. We naturally perceive this as relevant to the defendant's responsibility for his or her behavior, and it seems reasonable to punish a person less harshly if they are less responsible. This puts us on a slippery slope, however, once we recognize that all behavior is 100% determined by brain function, which is in turn determined by the interplay of genes and experience.

As ethicists and legal theorists have grappled with neuroscientific accounts of bad behavior, they have increasingly turned to alternative interpretations of responsibility that do not depend on free will [67, 68], and to so-called "forward thinking" penal codes, designed not to mete out punishments for previous behavior but to encourage good behavior and protect the public [69]. The "disease model" of substance addiction, and the extension of the medicalized notion of addiction to other compulsive behaviors such as compulsive gambling and compulsive sex, is another way in which brain-based explanations of behavior have impacted society. The disease model emphasizes the deterministic and physiological nature of the behaviors and thereby reduces their moral stigma.

Science and the Soul

Most people believe that mind and body are fundamentally different kinds of things [70]. Yet as neuroscience advances, more and more of human thought, feeling and action is being explained in terms of the functioning of the brain, a physical organ of the body. The reduction of mental to physical processes occurred first in the realms of perception and motor control, where mechanistic models of these processes have been under development for decades. Nevertheless, such models do not seriously threaten our intuitively "dualist" view of mind and brain. You can still believe in what Arthur Koestler called "the ghost in the machine" and simply conclude that vision and movement are features of the machine rather than the ghost.

However, as neuroscience begins to reveal the mechanisms of personality, this interpretation becomes strained. The brain imaging work reviewed earlier indicates that important aspects of our individuality, including some of the psychological traits that matter most to us as people, have physical correlates in brain function. Pharmacological influences on these traits also remind us of the physical bases of human personality. If an SSRI can help us take everyday problems in stride, and if a stimulant can help us meet our deadlines and keep our commitments at work, then must not unflappable temperaments and conscientious characters also be features of people's bodies? And if so, is there anything about people that is not a feature of their bodies?

A dualist might answer this question with consciousness or sense of spirituality. Yet neuroscience is making inroads with these mental phenomena too. Neuroscience research on consciousness began with the study of neurological patients who retained perceptual and memory abilities while professing no conscious awareness of perceiving or remembering [71]. From these early observations, research on consciousness has expanded to include brain imaging [72] and animal research [73], all aimed at understanding the neural correlates of conscious awareness. Although this work has not attempted to account for the private, subjective aspects of consciousness sometimes known as "qualia" [74], it has made progress in accounting for the observable differences between conscious and unconscious cognition. The relation between religious experience and the brain was first noted in the study of patients with temporal lobe epilepsy, whose seizures were sometimes accompanied by intense religious feelings. Recent neuroimaging research has shown a characteristic pattern of brain activation associated with states of religious transcendence, which is common to Buddhist meditation and Christian prayer [75].

NEUROETHICAL ISSUES: EDGING OUT THE SPIRIT
The idea that there is somehow more to a person than their physical instantiation runs deep in the human psyche and is a central element in virtually

all the world's religions. Neuroscience has begun to challenge this view by showing that not only perception and motor control, but also character, consciousness and sense of spirituality may all be features of the machine. If they are, then why think there's a ghost in there at all?

* * *

Neuroethics: Something Old and Something New

I have argued that interest in neuroethics is timely, much as interest in the ethics of molecular biology was timely in the latter decades of the 20th century. Cognitive neuroscience has already illuminated many aspects of human thought, feeling and behavior, and the technological and theoretical progress reviewed here will undoubtedly be surpassed in coming decades.

Although neuroscience has delivered some genuinely new methods and ideas and will continue to do so, nothing is ever entirely without precedent. In the case of neuroethics, we can draw on our experience with other areas of science and technology, and even our experiences in everyday life, to guide us. For example, as already mentioned, the practical issue of brain privacy has much in common with the privacy concerns that arise in genetics.

* * *

On the philosophical side, the challenges posed by neuroscience are not so much unprecedented as more difficult to ignore and blatant than previous challenges. Are we the same person on Prozac as off? This is a good question, but so is: are we the same person after a glass of wine as before—or even during a vacation as before? Similarly, the impulse to excuse bad behavior may be more powerful when we can see the specific physical mechanisms that caused it, but traditional psychological explanations of behavior also affect our moral judgments.

With brain images adorning Web sites and magazine articles on everything from children's

learning to compulsive gambling, neuroscience is gradually being incorporated into people's understanding of human behavior. The technological fruits of neuroscience are also being gradually incorporated into people's lives. The question is therefore not whether, but rather when and how, neuroscience will shape our future.

References

1. Canli, T. and Amin, Z. (2002). Neuroimaging of emotion and personality: Scientific evidence and ethical considerations. *Brain Cogn., 50*, 414–431.
2. Farah, M. (2002). Emerging ethical issues in neuroscience. *Nat. Neurosci., 5*, 1123–1129.
3. Illes, J. (2003). Neuroethics in a new era of neuroimaging. *AJNR Am. J. Neuroradiol., 24*, 1739–1741.
4. Rose, S.P.R. (2002). 'Smart drugs': Do they work? Are they ethical? Will they be legal? *Nat. Rev. Neurosci., 3*, 975–979.
5. Roskies, A. (2002). Neuroethics for the new millennium. *Neuron, 35*, 21–23.
6. Marcus, D. ed (2002). *Neuroethics: Mapping the Field*, Proceedings of the Dana Foundation Conference, University of Chicago Press.
7. Farah, M.J. and Wolpe, P.R. (2004). Monitoring and manipulating brain function: New neuroscience technologies and their ethical implications. *Hastings Cent. Rep., 34*, 35–45.
8. McClure, S.M. et al. (2004). Neural correlates of behavioral preference for culturally familiar drinks. *Neuron, 44*, 379–387.
9. Langleben, D.D. et al. (2002). Brain activity during simulated deception: an event-related functional magnetic resonance study. *Neuroimage, 15*, 727–732.
10. Farwell, L.A. and Smith, S.S. (2001). Using brain MERMER testing to detect concealed knowledge despite efforts to conceal. *J. Forensic Sci., 46*, 1–9.
11. Botteron, K.N. et al. (2002). Volumetric reduction in left subgenual prefrontal cortex in early onset depression. *Biol. Psychiatry, 51*, 342–344.
12. Ho, B.C. et al. (2003). Progressive structural brain abnormalities and their relationship to clinical outcome: a longitudinal magnetic resonance imaging study early in schizophrenia. *Arch. Gen. Psychiatry, 60*, 585–594.
13. Raine, A. et al. (1998). Reduced prefrontal and increased subcortical brain functioning assessed using positron emission tomography in predatory and affective murderers. *Behav. Sci. Law, 16*, 319–332.
14. Phelps, E.A. et al. (2000). Performance on indirect measures of race evaluation predicts amygdala activity. *J. Cogn. Neurosci., 12*, 1–10.
15. Beauregard, M. et al. (2001). Neural correlates of conscious self-regulation of emotion. *J. Neurosci., 21*, RC165.
16. Canli, T. et al. (2001). An fMRI study of personality influences on brain reactivity to emotional stimuli. *Behav. Neurosci., 115*, 33–42.
17. Canli, T. et al. (2002). Amygdala response to happy faces as a function of extraversion. *Science, 296*, 2191.

18. Fischer, H. et al. (2001). Dispositional pessimism and amygdala activity: A PET study in healthy volunteers. *Neuroreport, 12*, 1635–1638.

19. Johnson, D.L. et al. (2001). Cerebral blood flow and personality: A positron emission tomography study. *A. J. Psychiatry, 156*, 252–257.

20. Singer, T. et al. (2004). Empathy for pain involves the affective but not sensory components of pain. *Science, 303*, 1157–1162.

21. Sugiura, M. et al. (2000). Correlation between human personality and neural activity in cerebral cortex. *Neuroimage, 11*, 541–546.

22. Youn, T. et al. (2002). Relationship between personality trait and regional cerebral glucose metabolism assessed with positron emission tomography. *Biol. Psychol., 60*, 109–110.

23. Dumit, J. (2004). *Picturing Personhood: Brain Scans and Biomedical Identity*, Princeton University Press.

24. Barondes, S.H. (2003). *Better than Prozac: Creating the Next Generation of Psychiatric Drugs*, Oxford University Press.

25. Healy, D. (2004). *Let Them Eat Prozac: The Unhealthy Relationship Between the Pharmaceutical Industry and Depression*, New York University Press.

26. Kramer, P.D. (1993). *Listening to Prozac*, Penguin.

27. Slater, L. (1998). *Prozac Diary*, Random House.

28. Wurtzel, E. (1997). *Prozac Nation: Young and Depressed in America*, Riverhead Books.

29. Knutson, B. et al. (1998). Selective alteration of personality and social behavior by serotonergic intervention. *Am. J. Psychiatry, 155*, 373–379.

30. Furlan, P.M. et al. (2004). SSRIs do not cause affective blunting in healthy elderly volunteers. *Am. J. Geriatr. Psychiatry, 12*, 323–330.

31. Tse, W.S. and Bond, A.J. (2002). Serotonergic intervention affects both social dominance and affiliative behaviour. *Psychopharmacology, (Berl.) 161*, 324–330.

32. Teitelman, E. (2001). Off-label uses of modafinil. *Am. J. Psychiatry, 158*, 1341.

33. Vastag, B. (2004). Poised to challenge need for sleep, "wakefulness enhancer" rouses concerns. *JAMA, 291*, 167–170.

34. Wangsness, M. (2000). Pharmacological treatment of obesity: Past, present, and future. *Minn. Med., 83*, 21–26.

35. Flower, R. (2004). Lifestyle drugs: pharmacology and the social agenda. *Trends Pharmacol. Sci., 25*, 182–185.

36. Farah, M.J. et al. (2004). Neurocognitive enhancement: What can we do? What should we do? *Nat. Rev. Neurosci., 5*, 421–425.

37. Elliott, R. et al. (1997). Effects of methylphenidate on spatial working memory and planning in healthy young adults. *Psychopharmacology, (Berl.) 131*, 196–206.

38. Mehta, M.A. et al. (2000). Methylphenidate enhances working memory by modulating discrete frontal and parietal lobe regions in the human brain. *J. Neurosci., 20*, RC65.

39. Gold, P.E. et al. (2002). Ginkgo Biloba: a cognitive enhancer? *Psychol. Sci. Public Interest, 3*, 2–11.

40. Hall, S.S. (2003). The quest for a smart pill. *Sci. Am., 289*, 54–57, 60–65.

41. Lynch, G. (2002). Memory enhancement: the search for mechanism-based drugs. *Nat. Neurosci., 5*, 1035–1038.

42. Pittman, R.K. et al. (2002). Pilot study of secondary prevention of posttraumatic stress disorder with propranolol. *Biol. Psychiatry, 51*, 189–192.

43. George, M. (1996). Transcranial magnetic stimulation: A neuropsychiatric tool for the 21st century. *J. Neuropsychiatry Clin. Neurosci., 8*, 373–382.

44. Mosimann, U.P. et al. (2000). Mood effects of repetitive transcranial magnetic stimulation of left prefrontal cortex in healthy volunteers. *Psychiatry Res., 94*, 251–256.

45. Snyder, A.W. et al. (2003). Savant-like skills exposed in normal people by suppressing the left fronto-temporal lobe. *J. Integr. Neurosci., 2*, 149–158.

46. Clark, A. (2003). *Natural-Born Cyborgs*, Oxford University Press.

47. O'Leary, J.C. (1993). An analysis of the legal issue surrounding the forced use of Ritalin: protecting a child's right to "just say no". *New Engl. Law Rev., 27*, 1173–1209.

48. Diller, L.H. (1996). The run on Ritalin: Attention deficit disorder and stimulant treatment in the 1990s. *Hastings Cent. Rep., 26*, 12–14.

49. Hoag, H. (2003). Neuroengineering: Remote control. *Nature, 423*, 796–798.

50. Bechara, A. et al. (1994). Insensitivity to future consequences following damage to human prefrontal cortex. *Cognition, 50*, 7–15.

51. Bechara, A. et al. (1999). Different contributions of the human amygdala and ventromedial prefrontal cortex to decision making. *J. Neurosci., 19*, 5473–5481.

52. Fellows, L.K. and Farah, M.J. (2004). Different underlying impairments in decision making following ventromedial and dorsolateral frontal lobe damage in humans. *Cereb. Cortex* DOI: 10.1093/cercor/bhh108 (http://cercor.oupjournals.org/current.dtl).

53. Manes, F. et al. (2002). Decision-making processes following damage to the prefrontal cortex. *Brain, 125*, 624–639.

54. Siegal, M. and Varley, R. (2002). Neural systems involved in "theory of mind". *Nat. Rev. Neurosci., 3*, 463–471.

55. Heberlein, A.S. and Adolphs, R. (2004). Impaired spontaneous anthropomorphizing despite intact perception and social knowledge. *Proc. Nat. Acad. Sci., 101*, 7487–7491.

56. Stone, V.E. et al. (1998). Frontal lobe contributions to theory of mind. *J. Cogn. Neurosci., 10*, 640–656.

57. Decety, J. and Chaminade, T. (2003). When the self represents the other: a new cognitive neuroscience view on psychological identification. *Conscious. Cogn., 12*, 577–596.

58. Greene, J.D. et al. (2001). An fMRI investigation of emotional engagement in moral judgement. *Science, 293*, 2105–2108.

59. Denno, D. (2003). A mind to blame: new views on involuntariness. *Behav. Sci. Law, 21*, 601–618.

60. Damasio, H. et al. (1994). The return of Phineas Gage: clues about the brain from the skull of a famous patient. *Science, 264*, 1102–1105.

61. Bechara, A. et al. (2001). Decision-making deficits, linked to a dysfunctional ventromedial prefrontal cortex, revealed in alcohol and stimulant abusers. *Neuropsychologia, 39*, 376–389.

62. Rogers, R.D. and Robbins, T. (2001). Investigating the neurocognitive deficits associated with chronic drug misuse. *Curr. Opin. Neurobiol., 11*, 250–257.

63. Teicher, M.H. et al. (2003). The neurobiological consequences of early stress and childhood maltreatment. *Neurosci. Biobehav. Rev., 27*, 33–44.

64. Slutske, W. (2001). The genetics of antisocial behavior. *Curr. Psychiatry Rep., 3*, 158–162.

65. Blair, R.J. (2004). The roles of orbital frontal cortex in the modulation of antisocial behavior. *Brain Cogn., 55,* 198–208.

66. Frierson, R.L. and Finkenbine, R.D. (2004). Psychiatric and neurological characteristics of murder defendants. *J. Forensic Sci., 49,* 604–609.

67. Greene, J.D. and Cohen, J.D. (2004). For the law, neuroscience changes nothing and everything. In S. Zeki & O. Goodenough (eds.). *Law and the Brain,* pp. 207–226, Oxford University Press.

68. Morse, S.J. (1998). Excusing and the new excuse defenses: a legal and conceptual review. In *Crime and Justice* (Tonry, M. ed.), University of Chicago Press.

69. Denno, D. (2003). A mind to blame: New views on involuntary acts. *Behav. Sci. Law, 21,* 601–618.

70. Bloom, P. (2004). *Descartes' Baby,* Basic Books.

71. Farah, M.J. (1994). Visual perception and visual awareness after brain damage: A tutorial review. In *Conscious and Unconscious Information Processing: Attention and Performance XV* (Moscovitch, M. and Umilta, C. eds), pp. 37–76, MIT Press.

72. Rees, G. (2001). Neuroimaging of visual awareness in patients and normal subjects. *Curr. Opin. Neurobiol., 11,* 150–156.

73. Stoerig, P. (2001). The neuroanatomy of phenomenal vision: a psychological perspective. *Ann. N. Y. Acad. Sci., 929,* 176–194.

74. Dennett, D. (1992). *Consciousness Explained,* Back Bay Books/Penguin.

75. Newberg, A. and D'Aquili, E. (2002). *Why God Won't Go Away: Brain Science and the Biology of Belief,* Ballantine Books.

SEX DIFFERENCES IN JEALOUSY: EVOLUTION, PHYSIOLOGY, AND PSYCHOLOGY

David M. Buss, Randy J. Larsen, Drew Westen, and Jennifer Semmelroth

The essence of Darwin's theory of evolution is that those traits that are associated with successful reproduction will be increasingly represented in succeeding generations. For this reason, the obvious place to look for an evolutionarily based influence on behavior is in the area of sex. It is unsurprising, therefore, that as the evolutionary biology of personality has grown into an active research area in its own right, sex has come in for special attention.

The following article is a collaboration of several personality psychologists led by David Buss, one of the leaders in the application of evolutionary theory to personality. It derives hypotheses about the different approaches to mating that evolutionary theory would expect to be manifest by women and by men. In a nutshell, evolutionary considerations would lead one to expect men to be particularly worried that "their" children might have been fathered by other men, and therefore to be prone to sexual jealousy. Women, however, are not doubtful about their maternity but rather about the possibility that their mates might not continue to provide resources and protection for their children. They would, therefore, be more prone to emotional jealousy.

The next step taken by Buss and his co-workers was to test this hypothesis in a sample of undergraduates, presenting each with scenarios designed to trigger emotional and sexual jealousy. Not only were the expected sex differences found, but also physiological indices of emotional arousal, such as heart rate, yielded results that were consistent with the feelings that the subjects reported.

The final paragraphs of this article acknowledge that these findings might be the result of cultural conditioning, not a process biologically built in through evolution. Nonetheless, Buss et al. point out that their results were predicted by their evolutionary theorizing, not merely explained after they were obtained. This fact does not prove their theory, but does give it added plausibility.

From *Psychological Science*, 3, 251–255, 1992.

* * *

In species with internal female fertilization and gestation, features of reproductive biology characteristic of all 4,000 species of mammals, including humans, males face an adaptive problem not confronted by females—uncertainty in their paternity of offspring. Maternity probability in mammals rarely or never deviates from 100%. Compromises in paternity probability come at substantial reproductive cost to the male—the loss of mating effort expended, including time, energy, risk, nuptial gifts, and mating opportunity costs. A cuckolded male also loses the female's parental effort, which becomes channeled to a competitor's gametes. The adaptive problem of paternity uncertainty is exacerbated in species in which males engage in some postzygotic parental investment (Trivers, 1972). Males risk investing resources in putative offspring that are genetically unrelated.

These multiple and severe reproductive costs should have imposed strong selection pressure on males to defend against cuckoldry. Indeed, the literature is replete with examples of evolved anti-cuckoldry mechanisms in lions (Bertram, 1975), bluebirds (Power, 1975), doves (Erickson & Zenone, 1976), numerous insect species (Thornhill & Alcock, 1983), and nonhuman primates (Hrdy, 1979). Since humans arguably show more paternal investment than any other of the 200 species of primates (Alexander & Noonan, 1979), this selection pressure should have operated especially intensely on human males. Symons (1979); Daly, Wilson, and Weghorst (1982); and Wilson and Daly (1992) have hypothesized that male sexual jealousy evolved as a solution to this adaptive problem (but see Hupka, 1991, for an alternative view). Men who were indifferent to sexual contact between their mates and other men presumably experienced lower paternity certainty, greater investment in competitors' gametes, and lower reproductive success than did men who were motivated to attend to cues of infidelity and to act on those cues to increase paternity probability.

Although females do not risk maternity uncertainty, in species with biparental care they do risk the potential loss of time, resources, and commitment from a male if he deserts or channels investment to alternative mates (Buss, 1988; Thornhill & Alcock, 1983; Trivers, 1972). The redirection of a mate's investment to another female and her offspring is reproductively costly for a female, especially in environments where offspring suffer in survival and reproductive currencies without investment from both parents.

In human evolutionary history, there were likely to have been at least two situations in which a woman risked losing a man's investment. First, in a monogamous marriage, a woman risked having her mate invest in an alternative woman with whom he was having an affair (partial loss of investment) or risked his departure for an alternative woman (large or total loss of investment). Second, in polygynous marriages, a woman was at risk of having her mate invest to a larger degree in other wives and their offspring at the expense of his investment in her and her offspring. Following Buss (1988) and Mellon (1981), we hypothesize that cues to the development of a deep emotional attachment have been reliable leading indicators to women of potential reduction or loss of their mate's investment.

Jealousy is defined as an emotional "state that is aroused by a perceived threat to a valued relationship or position and motivates behavior aimed at countering the threat. Jealousy is 'sexual' if the valued relationship is sexual" (Daly et al., 1982, p. 11; see also Salovey, 1991; White & Mullen, 1989). It is reasonable to hypothesize that jealousy involves physiological reactions (autonomic arousal) to perceived threat and motivated action to reduce the threat, although this hypothesis has not been examined. Following Symons (1979) and Daly et al. (1982), our central hypothesis is that the events that activate jealousy physiologically and psychologically differ for men and women because of the different adaptive problems they have faced over human evolutionary history in mating contexts. Both sexes are hypothesized to be distressed over both sexual and emotional infidelity, and previous findings bear this out (Buss, 1989). However, these two kinds of infidelity should be weighted differently by men and women. Despite the importance of these hypothesized sex differences, no systematic scientific work has been directed toward verifying or falsifying their existence (but for suggestive data, see Francis, 1977; Teismann & Mosher, 1978; White & Mullen, 1989).

Study 1: Subjective Distress over a Partner's External Involvement

This study was designed to test the hypothesis that men and women differ in which form of infidelity—sexual versus emotional—triggers more upset and subjective distress, following the adaptive logic just described.

METHOD After reporting age and sex, subjects (N = 202 undergraduate students) were presented with the following dilemma:

> Please think of a serious committed romantic relationship that you have had in the past, that you currently have, or that you would like to have. Imagine that you discover that the person with whom you've been seriously involved became interested in someone else. What would distress or upset you more (*please circle only one*):
>
> (A) Imagining your partner forming a deep emotional attachment to that person.
> (B) Imagining your partner enjoying passionate sexual intercourse with that other person.
>
> Subjects completed additional questions, and then encountered the next dilemma, with the same instructional set, but followed by a different, but parallel, choice:
> (A) Imagining your partner trying different sexual positions with that other person.
> (B) Imagining your partner falling in love with that other person.

RESULTS Shown in Figure 1 are the percentages of men and women reporting more distress in response to sexual infidelity than emotional infidelity. The first empirical probe, contrasting distress over a partner's sexual involvement with distress over a partner's deep emotional attachment, yielded a large and highly significant sex dif-

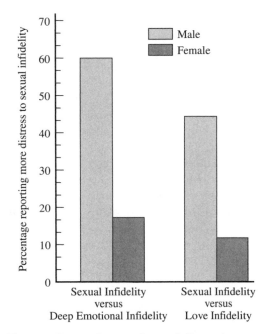

Figure 1 Reported comparisons of distress in response to imagining a partner's sexual or emotional infidelity. The panel shows the percentage of subjects reporting more distress to the sexual infidelity scenario than to the emotional infidelity (left) and the love infidelity (right) scenarios.

ference ($\chi^2 = 47.56$, $df = 3$, $p < .001$).[1] Fully 60% of the male sample reported greater distress over their partner's potential sexual infidelity; in contrast, only 17% of the female sample chose that option, with 83% reporting that they would experience greater distress over a partner's emotional attachment to a rival.

This pattern was replicated with the contrast between sex and love. The magnitude of the sex difference was large, with 32% more men than women reporting greater distress over a partner's sexual involvement with someone else, and the majority of women reporting greater distress over a partner's falling in love with a rival ($\chi^2 = 59.20$, $df = 3$, $p < .001$).

---

[1]This "chi-square" statistic is a test for the randomness of arrangement of outcomes into categories, *df* refers to the degrees of freedom in the design, and the *p* is the "significance," or probability that a χ^2 this large would have been produced by chance if the population value were 0.

Study 2: Physiological Responses to a Partner's External Involvement

Given the strong confirmation of jealousy sex linkage from Study 1, we sought next to test the hypotheses using physiological measures. Our central measures of autonomic arousal were electrodermal activity (EDA), assessed via skin conductance, and pulse rate (PR). Electrodermal activity and pulse rate are indicators of autonomic nervous system activation (Levenson, 1988). Because distress is an unpleasant subjective state, we also included a measure of muscle activity in the brow region of the face—electromyographic (EMG) activity of the *corrugator supercilii* muscle. This muscle is responsible for the furrowing of the brow often seen in facial displays of unpleasant emotion or affect (Fridlund, Ekman, & Oster, 1987). Subjects were asked to imagine two scenarios in which a partner became involved with someone else—one sexual intercourse scenario and one emotional attachment scenario. Physiological responses were re-corded during the imagery trials.

SUBJECTS Subjects were 55 undergraduate students, 32 males and 23 females, each completing a 2-hr laboratory session.

PHYSIOLOGICAL MEASURES Physiological activity was monitored on the running strip chart of a Grass Model 7D polygraph and digitized on a laboratory computer at a 10-Hz rate, following principles recommended in Cacioppo and Tassinary (1990).

Electrodermal activity. Standard Beckman Ag/AgCl surface electrodes, filled with a .05 molar NaCl solution in a Unibase paste, were placed over the middle segments of the first and third fingers of the right hand. A Wheatstone bridge applied a 0.5-V voltage to one electrode.

Pulse rate. A photoplethysmograph was attached to the subject's right thumb to monitor the pulse wave. The signal from this pulse transducer was fed into a Grass Model 7P4 cardiotachometer to detect the rising slope of each pulse wave, with the internal circuitry of the Schmitt trigger individually adjusted for each subject to output PR in beats per minute.

Electromyographic activity. Bipolar EMG recordings were obtained over the *corrugator supercilii* muscle. The EMG signal was relayed to a wideband AC-preamplifier (Grass Model 7P3), where it was band-pass filtered, full-wave rectified, and integrated with a time constant of 0.2 s.[2]

PROCEDURE After electrode attachment, the subject was made comfortable in a reclining chair and asked to relax. After a 5-min waiting period, the experiment began. The subject was alone in the room during the imagery session, with an intercom on for verbal communication. The instructions for the imagery task were written on a form which the subject was requested to read and follow.

Each subject was instructed to engage in three separate images. The first image was designed to be emotionally neutral: "Imagine a time when you were walking to class, feeling neither good nor bad, just neutral." The subject was instructed to press a button when he or she had the image clearly in mind, and to sustain the image until the experimenter said to stop. The button triggered the computer to begin collecting physiological data for 20 s, after which the experimenter instructed the subject to "stop and relax."

The next two images were infidelity images, one sexual and one emotional. The order of presentation of these two images was counterbalanced. The instructions for sexual jealousy imagery were as follows: "Please think of a serious romantic relationship that you have had in the past, that you currently have, or that you would like to have. Now imagine that the person with whom you're seriously involved becomes interested in someone else. *Imagine you find out that your partner is having sex-*

---

[2]The preceding paragraphs are a detailed technical description of state-of-the-art techniques for measuring autonomic arousal, for the use of researchers who might want to replicate these results.

ual intercourse with this other person. Try to feel the feelings you would have if this happened to you."

The instructions for emotional infidelity imagery were identical to the above, except the italicized sentence was replaced with "*Imagine that your partner is falling in love and forming an emotional attachment to that person.*" Physiological data were collected for 20 s following the subject's button press indicating that he or she had achieved the image. Subjects were told to "stop and relax" for 30 s between imagery trials.

RESULTS

Physiological scores. The following scores were obtained: (a) the amplitude of the largest EDA response occurring during each 20-s trial; (b) PR in beats per minute averaged over each 20-s trial; and (c) amplitude of EMG activity over the *corrugator supercilii* averaged over each 20-s trial. Difference scores were computed between the neutral imagery trial and the jealousy induction trials. Within-sex *t* tests revealed no effects for order of presentation of the sexual jealousy image, so data were collapsed over this factor.

Jealousy induction effects. Table 1 shows the mean scores for the physiological measures for men and women in each of the two imagery conditions. Differences in physiological responses to the two jealousy images were examined using paired-comparison *t* tests for each sex separately for EDA, PR, and EMG. The men showed significant increases in EDA during the sexual imagery compared with the emotional imagery ($t = 2.00$, $df = 29$, $p < .05$).[3] Women showed significantly greater EDA to the emotional infidelity image than to the sexual infidelity image ($t = 2.42$, $df = 19$, $p < .05$). A similar pattern was observed with PR. Men showed a substantial increase in PR to both images, but significantly more so in response to the

---

[3]The *t* statistic here indicates that given the number of subjects (related to *df*) in this sample, the data obtained would have occurred less than 5% of the time if there were no sex differences.

TABLE 1

MEANS AND STANDARD DEVIATIONS ON PHYSIOLOGICAL MEASURES DURING TWO IMAGERY CONDITIONS

Measure	Imagery type	Mean	SD
	Males		
EDA	Sexual	1.30	3.64
	Emotional	−0.11	0.76
Pulse rate	Sexual	4.76	7.80
	Emotional	3.00	5.24
Brow EMG	Sexual	6.75	32.96
	Emotional	1.16	6.60
	Females		
EDA	Sexual	−0.07	0.49
	Emotional	0.21	0.78
Pulse rate	Sexual	2.25	4.68
	Emotional	2.57	4.37
Brow EMG	Sexual	3.03	8.38
	Emotional	8.12	25.60

Note. Measures are expressed as changes from the neutral image condition. EDA is in microsiemen units, pulse rate is in beats per minute, and EMG is in microvolt units.

---

sexual infidelity image ($t = 2.29$, $df = 31$, $p < .05$). Women showed elevated PR to both images, but not differentially so. The results of the *corrugator* EMG were similar, although less strong. Men showed greater brow contraction to the sexual infidelity image, and women showed the opposite pattern, although results with this nonautonomic measure did not reach significance ($t = 1.12$, $df = 30$, $p < .14$, for males; $t = −1.24$, $df = 22$, $p < .12$, for females). The elevated EMG contractions for both jealousy induction trials in both sexes support the hypothesis that the effect experienced is negative.

* * *

Discussion

The results of the empirical studies support the hypothesized sex linkages in the activators of jealousy. Study 1 found large sex differences in reports of the subjective distress individuals would experience upon exposure to a partner's sexual infidelity versus emotional infidelity. Study 2 found a sex linkage in autonomic arousal to imagined sexual infidelity versus emotional infidelity; the results were particularly strong for the EDA and PR. * * *

These studies are limited in ways that call for additional research. First, they pertain to a single age group and culture. Future studies could explore the degree to which these sex differences transcend different cultures and age groups. Two clear evolutionary psychological predictions are (a) that male sexual jealousy and female commitment jealousy will be greater in cultures where males invest heavily in children, and (b) that male sexual jealousy will diminish as the age of the male's mate increases because her reproductive value decreases. Second, future studies could test the alternative hypotheses that the current findings reflect (a) domain-specific psychological adaptations to cuckoldry versus potential investment loss or (b) a more domain-general mechanism such that any thoughts of sex are more interesting, arousing, and perhaps disturbing to men whereas any thoughts of love are more interesting, arousing, and perhaps disturbing to women, and hence that such responses are not specific to jealousy or infidelity. Third, emotional and sexual infidelity are clearly correlated, albeit imperfectly, and a sizable percentage of men in Study 1 reported greater distress to a partner's emotional infidelity. Emotional infidelity may signal sexual infidelity and vice versa, and hence both sexes should become distressed at both forms (see Buss, 1989). Future research could profitably explore in greater detail the correlation of these forms of infidelity as well as the sources of within-sex variation.

Within the constraints of the current studies, we can conclude that the sex differences found here generalize across both psychological and physiological methods—demonstrating an empirical robustness in the observed effect. The degree to which these sex-linked elicitors correspond to the hypothesized sex-linked adaptive problems lends support to the evolutionary psychological framework from which they were derived. Alternative theoretical frameworks, including those that invoke culture, social construction, deconstruc-

tion, arbitrary parental socialization, and structural powerlessness, undoubtedly could be molded post hoc to fit the findings—something perhaps true of any set of findings. None but the Symons (1979) and Daly et al. (1982) evolutionary psychological frameworks, however, generated the sex-differentiated predictions in advance and on the basis of sound evolutionary reasoning. The recent finding that male sexual jealousy is the leading cause of spouse battering and homicide across cultures worldwide (Daly & Wilson, 1988a, 1988b) offers suggestive evidence that these sex differences have large social import and may be species-wide.

References

Alexander, R. D., & Noonan, K. M. (1979). Concealment of ovulation, parental care, and human social evolution. In N. Chagnon & W. Irons (Eds.), *Evolutionary biology and human social behavior* (pp. 436–453). North Scituate, MA: Duxbury.

Bertram, B. C. R. (1975). Social factors influencing reproduction in wild lions. *Journal of Zoology, 177*, 463–482.

Buss, D. M. (1988). From vigilance to violence: Tactics of mate retention. *Ethology and Sociobiology, 9*, 291–317.

Buss, D. M. (1989). Conflict between the sexes: Strategic interference and the evocation of anger and upset. *Journal of Personality and Social Psychology, 56*, 735–747.

Cacioppo, J. T., & Tassinary, L. G. (Eds.). (1990). *Principles of psychophysiology: Physical, social, and inferential elements.* Cambridge, England: Cambridge University Press.

Daly, M., & Wilson, M. (1988a). Evolutionary social psychology and family violence. *Science, 242*, 519–524.

Daly, M., & Wilson, M. (1988b). *Homicide.* Hawthorne, NY: Aldine.

Daly, M., Wilson, M., & Weghorst, S. J. (1982). Male sexual jealousy. *Ethology and Sociobiology, 3*, 11–27.

Erickson, C. J., & Zenone, P. G. (1976). Courtship differences in male ring doves: Avoidance of cuckoldry? *Science, 192*, 1353–1354.

Francis, J. L. (1977). Toward the management of heterosexual jealousy. *Journal of Marriage and Family Counseling, 10*, 61–69.

Fridlund, A., Ekman, P., & Oster, J. (1987). Facial expressions of emotion. In A. Siegman & S. Feldstein (Eds.), *Nonverbal behavior and communication* (pp. 143–224). Hillsdale, NJ: Erlbaum.

Hrdy, S. B. G. (1979). Infanticide among animals: A review, classification, and examination of the implications for the reproductive strategies of females. *Ethology and Sociobiology, 1*, 14–40.

Hupka, R. B. (1991). The motive for the arousal of romantic jealousy: Its cultural origin. In P. Salovey (Ed.), *The psychology of jealousy and envy* (pp. 252–270). New York: Guilford Press.

Levenson, R. W. (1988). Emotion and the autonomic nervous system: A prospectus for research on autonomic specificity.

In H. Wagner (Ed.), *Social psychophysiology: Theory and clinical applications* (pp. 17–42). London: Wiley.

Mellon, L. W. (1981). *The evolution of love*. San Francisco: W. H. Freeman.

Power, H. W. (1975). Mountain bluebirds: Experimental evidence against altruism. *Science, 189*, 142–143.

Salovey, P. (Ed.). (1991). *The psychology of jealousy and envy*. New York: Guilford Press.

Symons, D. (1979). *The evolution of human sexuality*. New York: Oxford University Press.

Teismann, M. W., & Mosher, D. L. (1978). Jealous conflict in dating couples. *Psychological Reports, 42*, 1211–1216.

Thornhill, R., & Alcock, J. (1983). *The evolution of insect mating systems*. Cambridge, MA: Harvard University Press.

Trivers, R. (1972). Parental investment and sexual selection. In B. Campbell (Ed.), *Sexual selection and the descent of man, 1871–1971* (pp. 136–179). Chicago: Aldine.

White, G. L., & Mullen, P. E. (1989). *Jealousy: Theory, research, and clinical strategies*. New York: Guilford Press.

Wilson, M., & Daly, M. (1992). The man who mistook his wife for a chattel. In J. Barkow, L. Cosmides, & J. Tooby (Eds.), *The adapted mind: Evolutionary psychology and the generation of culture*. New York: Oxford University Press.

The Origins of Sex Differences in Human Behavior: Evolved Dispositions vs. Social Roles

Alice H. Eagly and Wendy Wood

The increasing fame and popularity of evolutionary explanations of behavior such as seen in the previous selection have been accompanied by an increasing amount of criticism. Not all critics offer alternative explanations of their own, however. Alice Eagly and Wendy Wood, to their credit, do have an explanation of widespread sex differences in behavior that is different from the evolutionary account. Their alternative, which they call "social structural theory," is that it is the structure of society rather than biological evolution that determines differences between what men and women desire and view as important. So the next selection offers both a critique of some evolutionary reasoning and an alternative framework for understanding some important data.

Although Eagly and Wood believe that evolutionary theorizing about personality is mostly wrong, to some degree the evolutionary and structural approaches address different data, rather than necessarily being incompatible. Evolutionary theorists such as Buss and Haselton explain the components of sex differences that seem to be universal across cultures, whereas social structural theory addresses the components that vary. Thus, in the data that are reinterpreted in this article, Buss (who gathered the data) focused on how the direction of the sex difference was the same in all cultures, whereas Eagly and Wood address how the degree of difference differs across cultures. Both components are clearly important and perhaps deserve to be examined together in an integrated approach.

Eagly and Wood's article can be read as an argument for social change. If, as they maintain, sex differences in behavior are a function of social structure, then if society can be changed, behavioral change will soon follow. The evolutionary account of these differences can be taken to imply that things will not be so simple, because any changes in social structure will interact with and perhaps in some cases be resisted by innate biological preferences, propensities, and mechanisms.

From *American Psychologist*, 54, 408–423, 1999.

As more research psychologists have become willing to acknowledge that some aspects of social behavior, personality, and abilities differ between women and men (e.g., Eagly, 1995; Halpern, 1997), their attention has begun to focus on the causes of these differences. Debates about causes center, at least in part, on determining what can be considered the basic or ultimate causes of sex differences. Theories of sex differences that address causes at this level are termed in this article *origin theories* (Archer, 1996). In such theories, causation flows from a basic cause to sex-differentiated behavior, and biological, psychological, and social processes mediate the relation between the basic cause and behavior. In this article, we consider two types of origin theories: One of these implicates evolved psychological dispositions, and the other implicates social structure. Evolutionary psychology, as illustrated in the work of Buss (1995a), Kenrick and Keefe (1992), and Tooby and Cosmides (1992), thus represents the first type of origin theory, and social psychological theories that emphasize social structure represent the second type of origin theory (e.g., Eagly, 1987; Eagly, Wood, & Diekman, in press; Lorenzi-Cioldi, 1998; Ridgeway, 1991; West & Zimmerman, 1987; Wiley, 1995).

In the origin theory proposed by evolutionary psychologists, the critical causal arrow points from evolutionary adaptations to psychological sex differences. Because women and men possess sex-specific evolved mechanisms, they differ psychologically and tend to occupy different social roles. In contrast, in the social structural origin theory, the critical causal arrow points from social structure to psychological sex differences. Because men and women tend to occupy different social roles, they become psychologically different in ways that adjust them to these roles.

One important feature is shared by these two origin theories: Both offer a functional analysis of behavior that emphasizes adjustment to environ-

Author's note. Thanks are extended to David Buss for making available for reanalysis data from his 37-culture study (Buss, 1989b; Buss et al., 1990).

mental conditions. However, the two schools of thought differ radically in their analysis of the nature and timing of the adjustments that are most important to sex-differentiated behavior. Evolutionary psychologists believe that females and males faced different pressures in primeval environments and that the sexes' differing reproductive status was the key feature of ancestral life that framed sex-typed adaptive problems. The resolutions of these problems produced sex-specific evolved mechanisms that humans carry with them as a species and that are held to be the root cause of sex-differentiated behavior. Although evolutionary psychologists readily acknowledge the abstract principle that environmental conditions can influence the development and expression of evolved dispositions, they have given limited attention to variation of sex differences in response to individual, situational, and cultural conditions (e.g., Archer, 1996; Buss, 1995b; Buss & Kenrick, 1998). For example, Buss (1998, p. 421) emphasized "universal or near-universal sex differences" in preferences for long-term mates.

Social structuralists maintain that the situations faced by women and men are quite variable across societies and historical periods as social organization changes in response to technological, ecological, and other transformations. From a social structural perspective, a society's division of labor between the sexes is the engine of sex-differentiated behavior, because it summarizes the social constraints under which men and women carry out their lives. Sex differences are viewed as accommodations to the differing restrictions and opportunities that a society maintains for its men and women, and sex-differentiated behavior is held to be contingent on a range of individual, situational, and cultural conditions (see Deaux & LaFrance, 1998). Despite this emphasis on the social environment, social structuralists typically acknowledge the importance of some genetically mediated sex differences. Physical differences between the sexes, particularly men's greater size and strength and women's childbearing and lactation, are very important because they interact with shared cultural beliefs, social organization, and the demands of the economy to influence the role assignments that constitute the sexual division of labor within a society and produce psychological sex differences (Eagly, 1987; Wood & Eagly, 1999).

These thumbnail sketches of these two origin theories should make it clear that this debate about the origins of sex differences cannot be reduced to a simple nature-versus-nurture dichotomy. Both evolutionary psychology and social structural theory are interactionist in the sense that they take both biological and environmental factors into account, but they treat these factors quite differently. Evolutionary psychology views sex-specific evolved dispositions as psychological tendencies that were built in through genetically mediated adaptation to primeval conditions; the theory treats contemporary environmental factors as cues that interact with adaptations to yield sex-typed responses. Social structural theory views sex-differentiated tendencies as built in through accommodation to the contemporaneous sexual division of labor; in this approach, physical differences between the sexes serve as one influence on role assignment.

* * *

To illustrate the contrasting approaches of evolutionary psychology and social structural theory, we first present and discuss each theory. Then we examine their predictions concerning the criteria men and women use in selecting mates. This domain of behavior has been central to evolutionary theorizing about human sex differences (e.g., Buss & Schmitt, 1993; Kenrick & Keefe, 1992), and the cross-cultural findings available in this area provide an opportunity to examine empirically some of the predictions of evolutionary and social structural analyses.

Evolutionary Psychology as an Origin Theory of Sex Differences

From the perspective of evolutionary psychology, human sex differences reflect adaptations to the pressures of the differing physical and social environments that impinged on females and males during primeval times (Buss, 1995a; Tooby & Cosmides, 1992). Evolutionary psychologists thus label the environment that produced a species' evolved tendencies as its environment of evolutionary adaptedness (EEA; Cosmides, Tooby, & Barkow, 1992; Symons, 1979, 1992; Tooby & Cosmides, 1990b). They loosely identify the Pleistocene era as the human EEA and generally assume that it was populated by hunter–gatherer groups. To the extent that males and females faced different adaptive problems as they evolved, the two sexes developed different strategies to ensure their survival and to maximize their reproductive success. The resolutions to these problems produced evolved psychological mechanisms that are specific to each problem domain and that differ between women and men.

Although humans' evolved mechanisms developed in response to the types of problems consistently encountered by their ancestors and thus are presumed to be universal attributes of humans, environmental input affects how these mechanisms develop in individuals and how they are expressed in behavior (e.g., Buss & Kenrick, 1998). Because culture influences developmental experiences and patterns current situational input, culture is in principle important to the expression of adaptive mechanisms (Tooby & Cosmides, 1992). However, evolutionary psychologists have devoted relatively little attention to the interaction between such broader attributes of the social and cultural environment and the evolved mechanisms that may underlie sex differences. The contextual factors that have interested them generally relate directly to these hypothesized mechanisms. For example, Buss and Schmitt (1993) maintained that the characteristics that people seek in mates depend, not only on their sex, but also on whether they are engaging in short-term or long-term mating. Because of a relative neglect of broader social context, evolutionary psychologists have generated little understanding of how variation in sex-differentiated behavior arises from developmental factors and features of social structure and culture (for an exception, see Draper & Harpending, 1982).

The aspect of evolutionary theory that has been applied most extensively to sex differences is the theory of sexual selection initially proposed by

Darwin (1871) and further developed by Trivers (1972). In the evolutionary psychologists' rendition of these views, sex-typed features of human behavior evolved through male competition and female choice of mates. Because women constituted the sex that devoted greater effort to parental investment, they were a limited reproductive resource for men, who were the less investing sex. Women were restricted in the number of children they could propagate during their life span because of their investment through gestating, bearing, and nursing their children; men did not have these restrictions. Men therefore competed for access to women, and women chose their mates from among the available men. As the more investing sex, women were selected for their wisdom in choosing mates who could provide resources to support their parenting efforts. Women's preferences for such men, in turn, produced sexual selection pressures on men to satisfy these criteria.

Proponents of sexual selection theory argue that sex differences in parental investment favored different strategies for reproductive success for men and women and consequently established different adaptive mechanisms governing mating behavior (Buss, 1996; Kenrick, Trost, & Sheets, 1996). It was to men's advantage in terms of fitness outcomes to "devote a larger proportion of their total mating effort to short-term mating than do women" (Buss & Schmitt, 1993, p. 205)—that is, to be relatively promiscuous. Women, in contrast, benefited from devoting a smaller proportion of their effort to short-term mating and a larger proportion to long-term mating. Also, because of women's concealed fertilization, men were unable to determine easily which children could proffer the fitness gains that follow from genetic relatedness. Men ostensibly adapted to this problem of paternity uncertainty by exerting sexual control over women and developing sexual jealousy and a motive to control women's sexuality (Daly & Wilson, 1998).

According to evolutionary psychologists (e.g., Buss, 1995b; Buss & Kenrick, 1998), sex differences in numerous psychological dispositions arose from differing fitness-related goals of women and men

that followed from their contrasting sexual strategies. Because men competed with other men for sexual access to women, men's evolved dispositions favor violence, competition, and risk taking. Women in turn developed a proclivity to nurture and a preference for long-term mates who could support a family. As a result, men strived to acquire more resources than other men in order to attract women, and women developed preferences for successful, ambitious men who could provide resources.

Critical to some of evolutionary psychologists' claims about sex differences is the assumption that ancestral humans living in the EEA had a hunter–gatherer socioeconomic system (e.g., Buss, 1995b; Cosmides et al., 1992; DeKay & Buss, 1992). The idea of a division of labor in which men hunted while women gathered suggests sex-differentiated pressures linked to survival and reproduction. Such an ancestral division of labor might have favored men who were psychologically specialized for hunting and women who were specialized for gathering. For example, cognitive abilities could have been affected, with men acquiring the superior spatial skills that followed from ancestral hunting, and women acquiring the superior spatial location memory that followed from ancestral gathering (e.g., Geary, 1995; Silverman & Phillips, 1998).

Various mediating processes are implied in evolutionary psychology models of behavioral sex differences. The first and most important involves some means of retaining effective adaptations in human design and perpetuating them over time. Thus, sex-differentiated psychological mechanisms and developmental programs, like other adaptations, are "genetic, hereditary, or inherited in the sense that . . . their structured design has its characteristic form because of the information in our DNA" (Tooby & Cosmides, 1990a, p. 37; see also Buss, Haselton, Shackelford, Bleske, & Wakefield, 1998; Crawford, 1998). Some evolutionary accounts also emphasize that genetic factors trigger biochemical processes that mediate psychological sex differences, especially by means of sex differences in hormone production (e.g., Daly & Wilson,

1983; Geary, 1995, 1996). In addition, sex-typed evolved mechanisms are translated into behavioral sex differences by various cognitive and affective processes. Establishing these links requires theoretical understanding and empirical documentation of the range of processes by which the genetic factors implicated in innate dispositions might affect human behavior (e.g., Collear & Hines, 1995).

Buss and Kenrick (1998) described evolutionary psychology's approach to understanding sex differences as a "metatheory" and summarized it as follows: "Men and women differ in domains where they faced different adaptive problems over human evolutionary history" (p. 994). These theorists thus derive sex differences from heritable adaptations built into the human species. Because these differences are assumed to follow from evolutionary adaptations, they are predicted to occur as central tendencies of male versus female behavior. Human behavior would thus be characterized by a deep structure of sex-differentiated dispositions, producing similar, albeit not identical, behavioral sex differences in all human societies.

CRITIQUE OF THE EVOLUTIONARY ORIGIN THEORY

A number of questions can be raised about evolutionary psychology's account of the origins of sex differences. One consideration is that evolutionary analyses have generally identified adaptations by relying on "informal arguments as to whether a presumed function is served with sufficient precision, economy, efficiency, etc. to rule out pure chance as an adequate explanation" (Williams, 1966, p. 10). Explanations that reflect this approach consist of an analysis of the functional relations served by a particular psychological mechanism, along with the construction of a convincing story about how the adaptation might have made an efficient contribution to genetic survival or to some other goal contributing to reproduction in the EEA. These explanations serve as hypotheses that require additional validation and thus can be useful for initiating scientific research.

In developing these analyses of the possible functions of behaviors, evolutionary scientists face special challenges in distinguishing adaptations from other possible products of evolution—for example, features that were random or that had utility for one function but were subsequently coopted to fulfill a new function (see Buss et al., 1998; Gould, 1991; Williams, 1966). Moreover, the products of evolution must be distinguished from the products of cultural change. Behaviors that provide effective solutions to problems of reproduction and survival can arise from inventive trial-and-error among individuals who are genetically indistinguishable from other members of their living groups; such beneficial behaviors are then imitated and transmitted culturally.

An understanding of humans' primeval environment might help validate evolutionary hypotheses because adaptations evolved as solutions to past environmental challenges. Various bodies of science have some relevance, including observational studies of other primates, the fossil record, and ethnographic studies. However, models of human nature constructed from the behavior of nonhuman primates do not yield a uniform picture that reflects key features of sex differences in modern human societies (see Fedigan, 1986: Strier, 1994; Travis & Yeager, 1991). Similarly ambiguous concerning sex differences are the models of early human social conditions that paleontologists and paleoanthropologists have developed from fossil evidence. Anthropologists continue to debate fundamental points—for example, whether hunting of dangerous prey might have emerged during the period that is usually identified as the human EEA (e.g., Potts, 1984; Rose & Marshall, 1996). As a consequence, assumptions that certain traits were adaptive and consequently are under genetic control cannot be firmly supported from analyzing attributes of the EEA. Moreover, early human societies likely took a wide variety of forms during the period when the species was evolving toward its modern anatomical form (Foley, 1996). Variability in social organization is consistent with observations of more contemporary hunter–gatherer societies, which show great diversity in their social organization (Kelly, 1995). For example, studies of power relations between the sexes across diverse cultures show variability in the extent to which men control women's sexuality (Whyte, 1978), although evolutionary psychologists have assumed that this control is a defining feature of male–female relations. Therefore, because the EEA likely encompassed a variety of conditions, tracing humans' evolution requires understanding of the timing, social organization, and ecological circumstances of multiple periods of adaptation (Foley, 1996). The ambiguity and complexity of the relevant scientific findings leave room for evolutionary psychologists to inadvertently transport relatively modern social conditions to humans' remote past by inappropriately assuming that the distinctive characteristics of contemporary relations between the sexes were also typical of the EEA.

Given the difficulty of knowing the functions of behaviors and the attributes of the EEA, other types of scientific evidence become especially important to validating the claims of evolutionary psychologists. The most convincing evidence that a behavioral pattern reflects an adaptation would be that individuals who possessed the adaptation enjoyed a higher rate of survival and reproduction than individuals who did not possess it. However, such evidence is difficult, if not impossible, to produce. Because humans' evolved mechanisms emerged in relation to past selection pressures, present reproductive advantage does not necessarily reflect past advantage, and evolutionary psychologists have warned against relying on measures of current reproductive success to validate hypothesized adaptations (Buss, 1995a; Tooby & Cosmides, 1992). In the absence of evidence pertaining to reproductive success, scientists might document the genetic inheritance of postulated mechanisms and the processes by which genetic factors result in sex differences in behavior. However, for the psychological dispositions considered in this article, such evidence has not been produced. Instead, the scientific case for these sex-differentiated evolved dispositions rests on tests of evolutionary psychologists' predictions concerning the behavior of men and women in contemporary societies (e.g., Buss & Schmitt, 1993; Kenrick & Keefe, 1992). We evaluate some of these predictions in this article.

Social Structural Theory as an Origin Theory of Sex Differences

A respected tradition in the social sciences locates the origins of sex differences, not in evolved psychological dispositions that are built into the human psyche, but in the contrasting social positions of women and men. In contemporary American society, as in many world societies, women have less power and status than men and control fewer resources. This feature of social structure is often labeled gender hierarchy, or in feminist writing it may be called patriarchy. In addition, as the division of labor is realized in the United States and many other nations, women perform more domestic work than men and spend fewer hours in paid employment (Shelton, 1992). Although most women in the United States are employed in the paid workforce, they have lower wages than men, are concentrated in different occupations, and are thinly represented at the highest levels of organizational hierarchies (Jacobs, 1989; Reskin & Padavic, 1994; Tomaskovic-Devey, 1995). From a social structural perspective, the underlying cause of sex-differentiated behavior is this concentration of men and women in differing roles.

The determinants of the distribution of men and women into social roles are many and include the biological endowment of women and men. The sex-differentiated physical attributes that influence role occupancy include men's greater size and strength, which gives them priority in jobs demanding certain types of strenuous activity, especially activities involving upper body strength. These physical attributes of men are less important in societies in which few occupational roles require these attributes, such as postindustrial societies. Also important in relation to role distributions are women's childbearing and in many societies their activity of suckling infants for long periods of time; these obligations give them priority in roles involving the care of very young children and cause conflict with roles requiring extended absence from home and uninterrupted activity. These reproductive activities of women are less important in societies with low birthrates, less reliance on lactation for feeding infants, and greater reliance on nonmaternal care of young children.

In general, physical sex differences, in interaction with social and ecological conditions, influence the roles held by men and women because certain activities are more efficiently accomplished by one sex. The benefits of this greater efficiency can be realized when women and men are allied in cooperative relationships and establish a division of labor. The particular character of the activities that each sex performs then determines its placement in the social structure (see Wood & Eagly, 1999). As historians and anthropologists have argued (e.g., Ehrenberg, 1989; Harris, 1993; Lerner, 1986; Sanday, 1981), men typically specialized in activities (e.g., warfare, herding) that yielded greater status, wealth, and power, especially as societies became more complex. Thus, when sex differences in status emerged, they tended to favor men.

The differing distributions of men and women into social roles form the basis for a social structural metatheory of sex differences, just as evolutionary theory provides a metatheory. The major portion of this social structural theory follows from the typical features of the roles of men and women. Thus, the first metatheoretical principle derives from the greater power and status that tends to be associated with male-dominated roles and can be succinctly stated as follows: Men's accommodation to roles with greater power and status produces more dominant behavior, and women's accommodation to roles with lesser power and status produces more subordinate behavior (Ridgeway & Diekema, 1992). Dominant behavior is controlling, assertive, relatively directive and autocratic, and may involve sexual control. Subordinate behavior is more compliant to social influence, less overtly aggressive, more cooperative and conciliatory, and may involve a lack of sexual autonomy.

The second metatheoretical principle follows from the differing balance of activities associated with the typical roles of each sex. Women and men seek to accommodate sex-typical roles by acquiring the specific skills and resources linked to successful role performance and by adapting their social behavior to role requirements. A variety of sex-specific skills and beliefs arise from the typical family and economic roles of men and women, which in many societies can be described as resource provider and homemaker. Women and men seek to accommodate to these roles by acquiring role-related skills, for example, women learning domestic skills such as cooking and men learning skills that are marketable in the paid economy. The psychological attributes and social behaviors associated with these roles have been characterized in terms of the distinction between communal and agentic characteristics (Bakan, 1966; Eagly, 1987). Thus, women's accommodation to the domestic role and to female-dominated occupations favors a pattern of interpersonally facilitative and friendly behaviors that can be termed communal. In particular, the assignment of the majority of child rearing to women encourages nurturant behaviors that facilitate care for children and other individuals. The importance of close relationships to women's nurturing role favors the acquisition of superior interpersonal skills and the ability to communicate nonverbally. In contrast, men's accommodation to the employment role, especially to male-dominated occupations, favors a pattern of assertive and independent behaviors that can be termed agentic (Eagly & Steffen, 1984). This argument is not to deny that paid occupations show wide variation in the extent to which they favor more masculine or feminine qualities. In support of the idea that sex-differentiated behaviors are shaped by paid occupations are demonstrations that to the extent that occupations are male dominated, they are thought to require agentic personal qualities. In contrast, to the extent that occupations are female dominated, they are thought to require communal personal qualities (Cejka & Eagly, 1999; Glick, 1991).

In social structural theories, differential role occupancy affects behavior through a variety of mediating processes. In social role theory (Eagly, 1987; Eagly et al., in press), an important mediating process is the formation of gender roles by which people of each sex are expected to have characteristics that equip them for the tasks that they typically carry out. These expectations encompass the preferred or desirable attributes of men and women as well as their typical attributes. Gender roles are emergents from the productive work of the sexes; the characteristics that are required to perform sex-typical tasks become stereotypic of women or men. To the extent that women more than men occupy roles that demand communal behaviors, domestic behaviors, or subordinate behaviors for successful role performance, such tendencies become stereotypic of women and are incorporated into a female gender role. To the extent that men more than women occupy roles that demand agentic behaviors, resource acquisition behaviors, or dominant behaviors for successful role performance, such tendencies become stereotypic of men and are incorporated into a male gender role. Gender roles facilitate the activities typically carried out by people of each sex. For example, the expectation that women be other-oriented and compassionate facilitates their nurturing activities within the family as well as their work in many female-dominated occupations (e.g., teacher, nurse, social worker).

People communicate gender-stereotypic expectations in social interaction and can directly induce the targets of these expectations to engage in behavior that confirms them (e.g., Skrypnek & Snyder, 1982; Wood & Karten, 1986). Such effects of gender roles are congruent with theory and research on the behavioral confirmation of stereotypes and other expectancies (see Olson, Roese, & Zanna, 1996). Gender-stereotypic expectations can also affect behavior by becoming internalized as part of individuals' self-concepts and personalities (Feingold, 1994). Under such circumstances, gender roles affect behavior through self-regulatory processes (Wood, Christensen, Hebl, & Rothgerber, 1997). The individual psychology that underlies these processes is assumed to be the maximization of utilities. People perceive these utilities from the rewards and costs that emerge in social interaction, which takes place within the constraints of organizational and societal arrangements.

* * *

In summary, in social structural accounts, women and men are differently distributed into social roles, and these differing role assignments can be broadly described in terms of a sexual division of labor and a gender hierarchy. This division of labor and the patriarchal hierarchy that sometimes accompanies it provide the engine of sex-differentiated behavior because they trigger social and psychological processes by which men and women seek somewhat different experiences to maximize their outcomes within the constraints that societies establish for people of their sex. Sex differences in behavior thus reflect contemporaneous social conditions.

* * *

Sex Differences in Mate Selection Criteria Predicted From Evolutionary Psychology and Social Structural Theory

One reasonable area for comparing the predictive power of the evolutionary and the social structural origin theories of sex differences is human mating behavior, especially the criteria that people use for selecting mates. Evolutionary predictions have been articulated especially clearly for mating activities, and these behaviors can also be used to test a social structural perspective. Furthermore, empirical findings concerning mate selection preferences have been well-established for many years in the literature on the sociology of the family (e.g., Coombs & Kenkel, 1966). Powers's (1971) summary of 30 years of research concluded that at least in the United States, women generally prefer mates with good earning potential, whereas men prefer mates who are physically attractive and possess good domestic skills. Furthermore, women typically prefer a mate who is older than them, whereas men prefer a mate who is younger. Feingold's (1990, 1991, 1992a) meta-analyses of studies drawn from various research paradigms established that the sex differences in valuing potential mates' earning potential and physical attractiveness are robust, despite sex similarity on most criteria for selecting mates. Subsequent research based on a national probability sample of single adults provided further confirmation of the sex differences in age preferences as well as in valuing earning potential and physical attractiveness (Sprecher, Sullivan, & Hatfield, 1994).

Evolutionary psychologists have adopted mate preferences as signature findings of their analysis. Women's valuing of mates' resources and men's valuing of mates' youth and physical attractiveness are thought to arise from the different parental investment of the sexes that was outlined in Trivers's (1972) sexual selection theory. It is commonly argued that women, as the more investing sex, seek mates with attributes that can support their parenting efforts. However, human mate selection does not follow a strict version of Trivers's males-compete-and-females-choose model, because among humans, selection is a product of the behavior of both sexes, a process Darwin (1871) called "dual selection." In Buss's (1989a) account, male choice derives from women's time-limited reproductive capacity and the tendency for men to seek mates with attributes that suggest such capacity. In Kenrick and Keefe's (1992) account, men and women are both selective about potential mates and both invest heavily in offspring but with different kinds of resources. In particular, "males invest relatively more indirect resources (food, money, protection, and security), and females invest relatively more direct physiological resources (contributing their own bodily nutrients to the fetus and nursing child)" (Kenrick & Keefe, 1992, p. 78). As a result, women prefer mates who can provide indirect resources, and men prefer healthy mates with reproductive potential.

In contrast, from a social structural perspective, the psychology of mate selection reflects people's effort to maximize their utilities with respect to mating choices in an environment in which these utilities are constrained by societal gender roles as well as by the more specific expectations associated with marital roles. Consistent with these ideas, Becker's (1976) economic analysis of mating decisions characterized marriage as occurring between utility-maximizing men and women who can reach an equilibrium with a variety of types of exchanges, including, for example, an exchange between men's wages and women's household production and other attributes such as education and beauty. This cost–benefit analysis of mating appears even on occasion in the writings of evolutionary scientists. For example, Tattersall (1998) maintained that behavioral regularities, such as sex differences in mate selection criteria, are as likely to be due to rational economic decisions as to inherited predispositions, and Hrdy (1997) wrote that "a woman's preference for a wealthy man can be explained by the simple reality that . . . males monopolize ownership of productive resources" (p. 29).

The outcomes that are perceived to follow from mating decisions depend on marital and family arrangements. To the extent that women and men occupy marital and family roles that entail different responsibilities and obligations, they should select mates according to criteria that reflect these divergent responsibilities and obligations. Consider, for example, the family system based on a male provider and a female domestic worker. This system became especially pronounced in industrial economies and is still prevalent in many world societies. To the extent that societies have this division of labor, women maximize their outcomes by seeking a mate who is likely to be successful in the economic, wage-earning role. In turn, men maximize their outcomes by seeking a mate who is likely to be successful in the domestic role.

The sex differences in the preferred age of mates also can be understood as part of the general tendency of men and women to seek partners likely to provide a good fit to their society's sexual division of labor and marital roles. Specifically, the marital system based on a male breadwinner and a female homemaker favors the age gap in marriage. Marriageable women who are younger than their potential mates tend to have lesser wages, social status, and education and knowledge than women who are the same age as potential mates. With the combination of a younger, less experienced woman and an older, more experienced man, it would be easier to establish the power differential favoring men that is normative for marital roles defined by a male breadwinner and a female domestic worker (Lips, 1991; Steil, 1997). Moreover, compared with somewhat older women, young women lack independent resources and therefore are more likely to perceive that their utilities are maximized in the domestic worker role. In complementary fashion, older men are more likely to have acquired the economic resources that make them good candidates for the provider role. The older man and younger woman thus fit more easily than same-age partners into the culturally expected pattern of breadwinner and homemaker.

CROSS-CULTURAL EVIDENCE FOR SEX DIFFERENCES IN MATE PREFERENCES Evolutionary psychologists' predictions that women select for resources and older age and men for attractiveness and younger age have been examined cross-culturally. Buss's (1989a; Buss et al., 1990) impressive study in 37 cultures of the characteristics that people desire in mates suggested that consistent with evolutionary psychology, these sex differences in mate preferences emerged cross-culturally. Similarly, Kenrick and Keefe (1992) examined the preferred ages of mates in five countries and across various time periods in the 20th century and concluded that all provided evidence of sex differences in these preferences. Specifically, for dating and marriage, women preferred older men and men preferred younger women, although men's preferences were moderated by their age, with teenage boys preferring girls of similar age.

On the basis of these investigations, evolutionary accounts have emphasized the cross-cultural commonality in women's preference for resources and older age and men's preference for attractiveness and younger age. According to Buss (1989a) and Tooby and Cosmides (1989), uniformity across diverse cultures and social circumstances suggests powerful sex-differentiated evolved mechanisms that reflect an innate, universal human nature. Kenrick and Keefe (1992) also argued that "invariance across cultures is evidence that supports a species-specific, rather than a culture-specific, explanation" (p. 76).

Despite evidence for cross-cultural commonality in sex differences in mate selection criteria, these investigations also yielded evidence for cultural variation. For example, Kenrick and Keefe (1992) found that the preference for younger wives was evident among Philippine men of all ages, but only among older men (i.e., age 30 or over) in the United States. However, the simple existence of uniformity or variability does not provide a definitive test of either the evolutionary or the social structural origin theory. Although evolutionary psychologists emphasize uniformity and social structural theorists emphasize variability, both perspectives have some power to explain both of these cross-cultural patterns. To account for uniformity, social structuralists can point to similarities in the sexual division of labor in the studied societies and can argue that these similarities produce these relatively invariant sex differences. As Buss (1989a) noted, his 37 cultures, which were drawn from 33 nations, were biased toward urbanized cash-economy cultures, with 54% from Europe and North America. Furthermore, respondents selected from each society tended to be young, comparatively well-educated, and of relatively high socio-economic status. To the extent that these societies similarly defined the roles of women and men and that the respondents were similarly placed in these societies' social structures, commonality in the sex differences that follow from social structure should characterize these societies.

To account for cross-cultural variability, both evolutionary and social structural origin theories recognize that developmental processes and social factors that are unique to each society direct behavior in ways that can yield variability in sex differences across cultures. Beyond this insight that some evidence of cross-cultural variability would not surprise theorists in either camp, the particular pattern of cross-cultural variation provides an informative test of the mechanisms underlying sex differences. Specifically, the social structural argument that a society's sexual division of labor and associated gender hierarchy are responsible for sex differences in social behavior yields predictions concerning cross-cultural variability in mate preferences.

In the nations included in Buss et al.'s (1990) cross-cultural sample, whose economies ranged from agrarian to postindustrial, some cultures were still strongly marked by this division of labor between the provider and domestic worker, whereas other cultures had departed from it. In advanced economies like the United States, women have entered the paid labor force and spend a smaller proportion of their time in domestic labor (Haas, 1995; Shelton, 1992). Although the tendency for men to increase their hours of domestic work is much more modest, the lives of men and women become more similar with greater gender equality. Therefore, people of both sexes should lessen their emphasis on choosing mates whose value is defined by their fit to the division between domestic work and wage labor. Even in postindustrial economies such as the United States, however, the sex-typed division of labor remains in modified form, with men devoting longer hours than women to wage labor and women devoting longer hours to domestic work (e.g., Ferree, 1991; Presser, 1994; Shelton, 1992). Therefore, the social structural prediction is that the sex differences in mate selection criteria that follow from the male-female division of labor should be substantially weakened in societies characterized by greater gender equality, albeit they should still be present to the extent that complete equality has not been achieved.

REANALYSIS OF BUSS ET AL.'S (1990) 37 CULTURES DATA To evaluate whether the division of labor within a society could explain the mate preferences of men and women, we reanalyzed Buss et al.'s (1990) 37 cultures data. Our efforts focused on men's tendencies to select wives for domestic skill and younger age and women's tendencies to select husbands for earning capacity and older age. To test the hypothesis that a higher level of gender equality lessens these sex differences, we represented societies' gender equality in terms of archival data available from the United Nations (United Nations Development Programme, 1995).

Buss et al. (1990) derived the data on criteria for selecting mates from questionnaire measures of preferences for a wide range of characteristics that might be desired in a mate: (a) One instrument obtained rankings of a set of 13 characteristics according to "their desirability in someone you might marry" (p. 11); (b) the other instrument obtained ratings on a 4-point scale of each of 18 characteristics on "how important or desirable it would be in choosing a mate" (p. 11). Buss et al. represented each culture by the male and female respondents' mean ranking of each of the 13 male selection criteria and by their mean rating of each of the 18 criteria. A separate question inquired about preferences for a spouse's age. The data that we reanalyzed consisted of mean preferences for each culture.

Our reanalysis confirmed Buss et al.'s (1990) conclusion that women placed more value than men on a mate's wage-earning ability. Furthermore, consistent with the greater domestic responsibility of women than men in most cultures, men valued *good cook and housekeeper* more than women did, a sex difference that has received little attention from evolutionary psychologists. When the sex differences in the mean preference ratings were averaged across the cultures, this difference was of comparable magnitude to those obtained on the attributes most strongly emphasized by evolutionary psychologists. Specifically, in both the rating and ranking data, the criteria of *good earning capacity, good housekeeper and cook*, and *physically attractive* produced the largest sex differences. The appropriateness of focusing on the criteria pertaining to earning ability and domestic skill within Buss et al.'s data was also supported by the good agreement across the ranking and rating data sets for sex differences in the valuation of the qualities of financial prospect, $r(33) = .76$, $p < .001$, and domestic skill, $r(33) = .68$, $p < .001$, whereas the agreement in the valuation of physical attractiveness was poorer, $r(33) = .34$, $p < .05$.[1] In addition, as Buss et al. reported, the sex difference in the preferred age of mates was fully intact in the 37 cultures data.

---

[1] r is the correlation coefficient, the number in parentheses is the degrees of the freedom (in this case the number of participants minus 2), and p is the significance, or probability that an r this large would have been found by chance alone if the population value were in fact 0.

Additional evidence for the social structural predictions emerged when we evaluated the pattern of sex differences in preferences across societies. Consistent with the division of labor principle, a substantial relation emerged between the sex difference in valuing a spouse's domestic skills and the sex difference in valuing a spouse's capacity to provide a good income. Specifically, on the basis of the ranking measure, the sex differences in the good earning capacity criterion and the good housekeeper criterion were correlated across the cultures, $r(33) = .67$, $p < .001$. On the basis of the rating measure, the sex differences in the financial prospect criterion and the housekeeper–cook criterion were also correlated, $r(35) = .38$, $p < .05$. These positive correlations indicate that to the extent that women more than men reported seeking a mate who is a good breadwinner, men more than women reported seeking a mate who is a good homemaker. In addition, the sex difference in the preferred age of one's spouse bore a positive relation to the sex difference in preference for a good earner, $r(33) = .34$, $p < .05$ for the ranking data, and $r(35) = .32$, $p < .06$ for the rating data. Similarly, the sex difference in preferred age bore a positive relation to the sex difference in preference for a good housekeeper and cook, $r(33) = .58$, $p < .001$ for the ranking data, and $r(35) = .60$, $p < .001$ for the rating data. These relationships show that to the extent that the sex difference in the preferred age of spouses was large, women more than men preferred mates who were good providers and men more than women preferred mates who were good domestic workers. The division of labor provides the logic of all of these relationships: Women who serve in the domestic role are the complement of men who serve as breadwinners, and the combination of older husbands and younger wives facilitates this form of marriage.

Analysis of gender equality. To test our hypothesis that sex differences in mate preferences erode to the extent that women and men are similarly placed in the social structure, we sought cross-national indicators of gender equality. Among the many such indicators compiled by United Nations researchers, the most direct indicator of gender equality is the aggregate Gender Empowerment Measure, which represents the extent to which women participate equally with men in economic, political, and decision-making roles (United Nations Development Programme, 1995). This index increases as (a) women's percentage share of administrative and managerial jobs and professional and technical jobs increases, (b) women's percentage share of parliamentary seats rises, and (c) women's proportional share of earned income approaches parity with men's.

The Gender-Related Development Index is another useful indicator of societal-level gender equality provided by United Nations researchers. It increases with a society's basic capabilities to provide health (i.e., greater life expectancy), educational attainment and literacy, and wealth, but imposes a penalty for gender inequality in these capabilities (United Nations Development Programme, 1995). Whereas this measure reflects equality in basic access to health care, education and knowledge, and income, the Gender Empowerment Measure is a purer indicator of equal participation in economic and political life.

In the set of 37 cultures, the Gender Empowerment Measure and the Gender-Related Development Index were correlated, $r(33) = .74$, $p < .001$, and both of these indexes were moderately correlated with general indexes of human development and economic development. One limitation of the indexes of gender equality is that they are based on data from the early 1990s. Because Buss et al.'s (1990) data were collected in the mid-1980s, these indexes are from a slightly later time period, but the relative positions of the cultures should remain approximately the same.

To examine the relation between societal gender equality and mate preferences, we calculated the correlations of these indexes with the sex differences in valuing a mate as a breadwinner and as a domestic worker—the two criteria most relevant to the traditional division of labor. These correlations for the ranking and the rating data, which appear in Table 1, are generally supportive of the

TABLE 1

CORRELATIONS OF MEAN RANKINGS AND RATINGS OF MATE SELECTION CRITERIA WITH UNITED
NATIONS INDEXES OF GENDER EQUALITY FOR BUSS ET AL.'S (1990) 37 CULTURES SAMPLE

| | Ranked criteria | | Rated criteria | |
| | Gender Empowerment Measure ($n = 33$) | Gender-Related Development Index ($n = 34$) | Gender Empowermnt Measure ($n = 35$) | Gender-Related Devevlopment Index ($n = 36$) |
Mate selection criterion and rater				
Good earning capacity (financial prospect)				
Sex difference	−.43*	−.33†	−.29†	−.23
Women	−.29	−.18	−.49**	−.42**
Men	.24	.27	−.40*	−.36*
Good housekeeper (and cook)				
Sex difference	−.62***	−.54**	−.61***	−.54**
Women	.04	−.01	.11	−.07
Men	−.46**	−.42*	−.60***	−.61***
Physically attractive (good looks)				
Sex difference	.13	−.12	.20	.18
Women	.14	.34†	−.45**	−.25
Men	.20	.28	−.33†	−.14

Note. The criteria were described slightly differently in the ranking and the rating tasks: The ranking term is given first, with the rating term following in parentheses. Higher values on the gender equality indexes indicate greater equality. For the preferences of women or men, higher values of the mean rankings and ratings of mate selection criteria indicate greater desirability in a mate; therefore, a positive correlation indicates an increase in the desirability of a criterion as gender equality increased, and a negative correlation indicates a decrease. Sex differences in these preferences were calculated as female minus male means for good earning capacity and male minus female means for good housekeeper and physically attractive. A positive correlation thus indicates an increase in the sex difference as gender equality increased, and a negative correlation indicates a decrease in the sex difference.

†$p < .10$. *$p < .05$. **$p < .01$. ***$p < .001$.

social structural predictions. As the Gender Empowerment Measure increased in value, the tendency decreased for women to place greater emphasis than men on a potential spouse's earning capacity, although the correlation with the rated criterion was relatively weak. Also, as the Gender Empowerment Measure increased, the tendency decreased for men to place greater emphasis than women on a potential spouse's domestic skills. As expected in terms of the Gender-Related Development Index's less direct representation of the similarity of the roles of women and men, its correlations with these sex differences were somewhat weaker.

The preference data for each sex reported in Table 1 provide insight into these sex-difference findings. For good housekeeper and cook, the correlations for both the rating data and the ranking data indicated that as gender equality increased, men decreased their interest in choosing mates for their skill as domestic workers, and women showed no change in this preference. In contrast, for good earning capacity, as gender equality increased, women decreased their emphasis on mates' earning potential in the rating data (although nonsignificantly in the ranking data). However, men's preferences for good earning capacity are more difficult to interpret because their relations to gender equality were inconsistent across the ranking and rating measures. Inconsistencies between the two measures may reflect that rankings are judgments of the relative importance of the criteria in relation to

TABLE 2

CORRELATIONS OF MEAN PREFERRED AGE DIFFERENCE BETWEEN
SELF AND SPOUSE WITH UNITED NATIONS INDEXES OF GENDER
EQUALITY FOR BUSS ET AL.'S (1990) 37 CULTURES SAMPLE

Rater	Gender Empowerment Measure ($n = 35$)	Gender-Related Development Index ($n = 36$)
Sex difference	−.73***	−.70***
Women	−.64***	−.57***
Men	.70***	.70***

Note. Higher values on the gender equality indexes indicate greater equality. Positive ages indicate preference for an older spouse, and negative ages indicate preference for a younger spouse. Therefore, for the preferences of women, a negative correlation indicates a decrease in the tendency to prefer an older spouse as gender equality increased, whereas for the preferences of men, a positive correlation indicates a decrease in the tendency to prefer a younger spouse. Because the sex difference in preferred age was calculated as female minus male mean preferred spouse age in relation to self, a negative correlation indicates a decrease in the sex difference in preferred age as gender equality increased.

***$p < .001$.

the others in the list, whereas ratings are judgments of the absolute importance of the different criteria.

As shown in Table 2, examination of preferences for a spouse's age showed that as gender equality increased, women expressed less preference for older men, men expressed less preference for younger women, and consequently the sex difference in the preferred age of mates became smaller. These relations suggest that sex differences in age preferences reflect a sex-differentiated division of labor.

* * *

Preference for physical attractiveness. As also shown in Table 1, correlations between the sex difference in valuing potential mates' physical attractiveness and the United Nations indexes of gender equality were low and nonsignificant. These findings are not surprising, because this mate selection criterion does not mirror the division between wage labor and domestic labor in the manner that earning potential, domestic skill, and age do. Nevertheless, under some circumstances, physical

attractiveness may be part of what people exchange for partners' earning capacity and other attributes.

Assuming that attractiveness is sometimes exchanged for other gains, the social structural perspective offers possibilities for understanding its value. Research on the physical attractiveness stereotype has shown that attractiveness in both sexes conveys several kinds of meaning—especially social competence, including social skills, sociability, and popularity (Eagly, Ashmore, Makhijani, & Longo, 1991; Feingold, 1992b). Therefore, men's greater valuing of attractiveness might follow from the greater importance of this competence in women's family and occupational roles, including women's paid occupations in postindustrial societies (Cejka & Eagly, 1999; Lippa, 1998), and the consequent inclusion of this competence in the female gender role. If women's roles demand greater interpersonal competence in societies with greater and lesser gender equality, the tendency for men to place greater value on mates' attractiveness would not covary with indexes that assess equality.

Another possibility is that the value of attractiveness stems from its perceived association with the ability to provide sexual pleasure. This idea receives support from research showing that attractiveness conveys information about sexual warmth (Feingold, 1992b). If so, men might seek sexiness in a mate in all societies, in addition to attributes such as domestic skill, whose importance varies with the society's level of gender equality. Given that the female gender role often includes sexual restraint and lack of sexual autonomy, women may place less emphasis on sexiness in mates than men do.

It is less certain that physical attractiveness conveys information about women's fertility, as should be the case if men's preference for attractiveness in mates developed because attractiveness was a cue to fertility (Buss, 1989a; Jones, 1995; Singh, 1993). It seems reasonable that perceptions of attractiveness and potential fertility would covary even in contemporary data, but these relations have proven to be inconsistent (e.g., Cunningham, 1986; Tassinary & Hansen, 1998). Moreover, Singh's (1993) research on judgments of female figures that varied in weight and waist-to-hip ratio suggested three somewhat independent groupings of attributes: health, attractiveness, and sexiness; capacity and desire for children; and youth.

Although little is known about the relation between women's attractiveness and their actual fecundity, Kalick, Zebrowitz, Langlois, and Johnson (1998) found that facial attractiveness in early adulthood was unrelated to number of children produced or to health across the life span. Although the few participants in their sample who did not marry were less attractive than those who did marry, once the nonmarried were excluded, physical attractiveness was unrelated to the number of children produced by male or female participants. Kalick et al. (1998) concluded that "any relation between attractiveness and fecundity was due to mate-selection chances rather than biological fertility" (p. 10). Of course, as we noted in our critique of evolutionary psychology in this article, proponents of the theory do not predict that hypothesized evolved dispositions, such as men's preference for physically attractive partners, would necessarily be related to current reproductive success. Evolutionary psychologists argue instead that

actual fertility in modern societies may bear little relation to the factors indicative of reproductive success in the EEA.

In summary, several aspects of the findings from Buss et al.'s (1990) 37 cultures study are compatible with the social structural origin theory of sex differences. The idea that the extremity of the division between male providers and female homemakers is a major determinant of the criteria that people seek in mates fits with the observed covariation between men placing more emphasis than women on younger age and domestic skill and women placing more emphasis than men on older age and earning potential. The lessening of these sex differences with increasing gender equality, as represented by the United Nations indexes, is consistent with our claim that these sex differences are by-products of a social and family structure in which the man acts as a provider and the woman acts as a homemaker. More ambiguous are the sex differences in valuing mates' physical attractiveness. Without evidence that men's greater valuing of attractiveness follows from one or more specific mechanisms, the simple absence of a relation between gender equality and sex differences in valuing attractiveness in our reanalysis does not advance the claims of evolutionary psychology or the social structural theory. Convincing evidence for either interpretation has yet to be generated. However, with respect to the other sex differences emphasized by evolutionary psychologists, their cross-cultural patterning suggests that they arise from a particular economic and social system.

* * *

Conclusion

Considered at the level of a general metatheory of sex differences, social structural theories provide alternative explanations of the great majority of the general predictions about sex-differentiated social behavior that have been featured in evolutionary psychology. Because the central tendencies of sex differences (see Eagly, 1995; Halpern, 1997; Hyde, 1996) are readily encompassed by both of these perspectives, neither the evolutionary metatheory nor the social structural metatheory is convincingly substantiated by a mere noting of the differences established in the research literature. It is far too easy to make up sensible stories about how these differences might be products of sex-differentiated evolved tendencies or the differing placement of women and men in the social structure. This overlap in general main-effect predictions calls for more refined testing of the two theoretical perspectives, and each perspective is associated with numerous more detailed predictions and empirical tests.

Certainly there are many possibilities for distinguishing between the two approaches with appropriate research designs (see Jackson, 1992). Evolutionary psychologists have been especially resourceful in obtaining cross-cultural data intended to support their claims of invariance across cultures in sex-differentiated behavior. To be maximally informative about social structural factors, cross-cultural research should be systematically designed to represent cultures with differing forms of social organization and levels of gender equality. In addition, a variety of other research methods, including experiments and field studies, can yield tests of predictions that emerge from evolutionary and social structural perspectives.

Although this article contrasts social structural explanations of sex differences with those based on evolutionary psychology, social structural analyses may be generally compatible with some evolutionary perspectives, as we noted in the introductory section of this article. Our argument that sex differences in behavior emerge primarily from physical sex differences in conjunction with influences of the economy, social structure, ecology, and cultural beliefs is potentially reconcilable with theories of coevolution by genetic and cultural processes (Janicki & Krebs, 1998). Our position is also sympathetic to the interest that some evolutionary biologists and behavioral ecologists have shown in the maintenance of behavioral patterns from generation to generation through nongenetic, cultural processes (e.g., Sork, 1997). However, despite our acknowledgement of the importance of some evolved genetic influences on the behavior of women and men, an implicit assumption of our approach is that social change emerges, not from individuals' tendencies to maximize their inclusive fitness, but instead from their efforts to maximize their personal benefits and minimize their personal costs in their social and ecological settings.

One test of the evolutionary psychology and social structural origin theories of sex differences lies in the future—that is, in the emerging postindustrial societies in which the division between men's wage labor and women's domestic labor is breaking down. Notable is the increase in women's paid employment, education, and access to many formerly male-dominated occupations. Accompanying these changes is a marked attitudinal shift toward greater endorsement of equal opportunity for women in the workplace and role-sharing in the home (e.g., Simon & Landis, 1989; Spence & Hahn, 1997; Twenge, 1997). Nonetheless, occupational sex segregation is still prevalent with women concentrated in occupations that are thought to require feminine qualities and with men in occupations thought to require masculine qualities (Cejka & Eagly, 1999; Glick, 1991). Given that occupational distributions currently take this form and that the homemaker–provider division of labor remains weakly in place, social structuralists would not predict that sex differences in behavior should have already disappeared. Instead, to the extent that the traditional sexual division between wage labor and domestic labor disappears and women and men become similarly distributed into paid occupations, men and women should converge in their psychological attributes.

References

Archer, J. (1996). Sex differences in social behavior: Are the social role and evolutionary explanations compatible? *American Psychologist, 51,* 909–917.

Bakan, D. (1966). *The duality of human existence: An essay on psychology and religion.* Chicago: Rand McNally.

Becker, G. S. (1976). *The economic approach to human behavior.* Chicago: University of Chicago Press.

Buss, D. M. (1989a). Sex differences in human mate preferences: Evolutionary hypotheses tested in 37 cultures. *Behavioral and Brain Sciences, 12,* 1–14.

Buss, D. M. (1989b). Toward an evolutionary psychology of human mating. *Behavioral and Brain Sciences, 12,* 39–49.

Buss, D. M. (1995a). Evolutionary psychology: A new paradigm for psychological science. *Psychological Inquiry, 6*, 1–30.

Buss, D. M. (1995b). Psychological sex differences: Origins through sexual selection. *American Psychologist, 50*, 164–168.

Buss, D. M. (1996). The evolutionary psychology of human social strategies. In E. T. Higgins & A. W. Kruglanski (Eds.), *Social psychology: Handbook of basic principles* (pp. 3–38). New York: Guilford Press.

Buss, D. M. (1998). The psychology of human mate selection: Exploring the complexity of the strategic repertoire. In C. Crawford & D. L. Krebs (Eds.), *Handbook of evolutionary psychology: Ideas, issues, and applications* (pp. 405–429). Mahwah, NJ: Erlbaum.

Buss, D. M., et al. (1990). International preferences in selecting mates: A study of 37 cultures. *Journal of Cross-Cultural Psychology, 21*, 5–47.

Buss, D. M., Haselton. M. G., Shackelford, T. K., Bleske, A. L., & Wakefield, J. C. (1998). Adaptations, exaptations, and spandrels. *American Psychologist, 53*, 533–548.

Buss, D. M., & Kenrick, D. T. (1998). Evolutionary social psychology. In D. T. Gilbert, S. T. Fiske, & G. Lindzey (Eds.). *The handbook of social psychology* (4th ed., Vol. 2, pp. 982–1026). Boston: McGraw-Hill.

Buss, D. M., & Schmitt, D. P. (1993). Sexual strategies theory: An evolutionary perspective on human mating. *Psychological Review, 100*, 204–232.

Cejka, M. A., & Eagly, A. H. (1999). Gender-stereotypic images of occupations correspond to the sex segregation of employment. *Personality and Social Psychology Bulletin, 25*, 413–423.

Collear, M. L., & Hines, M. (1995). Human behavioral sex differences: A role for gonadal hormones during early development? *Psychological Bulletin, 118*, 55–107.

Coombs, R. H., & Kenkel, W. F. (1966). Sex differences in dating aspiration and satisfaction with computer-selected partners. *Journal of Marriage and the Family, 28*, 62–66.

Cosmides, L., Tooby, J., & Barkow, J. H. (1992). Introduction: Evolutionary psychology and conceptual integration. In J. H. Barkow, L. Cosmides, & J. Tooby (Eds.). *The adapted mind: Evolutionary psychology and the generation of culture* (pp. 3–15). New York: Oxford University Press.

Crawford, C. (1998). The theory of evolution in the study of human behavior: An introduction and overview. In C. Crawford & D. L. Krebs (Eds.), *Handbook of evolutionary psychology: Ideas, issues, and applications* (pp. 3–41). Mahwah, NJ: Erlbaum.

Cunningham, M. R. (1986). Measuring the physical in physical attractiveness: Quasi-experiments on the sociobiology of female facial beauty. *Journal of Personality and Social Psychology, 50*, 925–935.

Daly, M., & Wilson, M. (1983). *Sex, evolution, and behavior* (2nd ed.). Boston: Grant Press.

Daly, M., & Wilson, M. (1998). The evolutionary social psychology of family violence. In C. Crawford & D. L. Krebs (Eds.), *Handbook of evolutionary psychology: Ideas, issues, and applications* (pp. 431–456). Mahwah, NJ: Erlbaum.

Darwin, C. (1871). *The descent of man and selection in relation to sex.* London: Murray.

Deaux, K., & LaFrance, M. (1998). Gender. In D. T. Gilbert, S. T. Fiske, & G. Lindzey (Eds.), *The handbook of social psychology* (4th ed., Vol. 1, pp. 788–827). Boston: McGraw-Hill.

DeKay, W. T., & Buss. D. M. (1992). Human nature, individual differences, and the importance of context: Perspectives from evolutionary psychology. *Current Directions in Psychological Science, figure 1*, 184–189.

Draper, P., & Harpending, H. (1982). Father absence and reproductive strategy: An evolutionary perspective. *Journal of Anthropological Research, 38*, 255–273.

Eagly, A. H. (1987). *Sex differences in social behavior: A social-role interpretation.* Hillsdale, NJ: Erlbaum.

Eagly, A. H. (1995). The science and politics of comparing women and men. *American Psychologist, 50*, 145–158.

Eagly, A. H., Ashmore, R. D., Makhijani, M. G., & Longo, L. C. (1991). What is beautiful is good, but . . . : A meta-analytic review of research on the physical attractiveness stereotype. *Psychological Bulletin, 110*, 109–128.

Eagly, A. H., & Steffen, V. J. (1984). Gender stereotypes stem from the distribution of women and men into social roles. *Journal of Personality and Social Psychology, 46*, 735–754.

Eagly, A. H., Wood, W., & Diekman, A. (in press). Social role theory of sex differences and similarities: A current appraisal. In T. Eckes & H. M. Trautner (Eds.), *The developmental social psychology of gender.* Mahwah, NJ: Erlbaum.

Ehrenberg, M. (1989). *Women in prehistory.* London: British Museum Publications.

Fedigan, L. M. (1986). The changing role of women in models of human evolution. *Annual Review of Anthropology, 15*, 25–66.

Feingold, A. (1990). Gender differences in effects of physical attractiveness on romantic attraction: A comparison across five research paradigms. *Journal of Personality and Social Psychology, 59*, 981–993.

Feingold, A. (1991). Sex differences in the effects of similarity and physical attractiveness on opposite-sex attraction. *Basic and Applied Social Psychology, 12*, 357–367.

Feingold, A. (1992a). Gender differences in mate selection preferences: A test of the parental investment model. *Psychological Bulletin, 112*, 125–139.

Feingold, A. (1992b). Good-looking people are not what we think. *Psychological Bulletin, 111*, 304–341.

Feingold, A. (1994). Gender differences in personality: A meta-analysis. *Psychological Bulletin, 116*, 429–456.

Ferree, M. M. (1991). The gender division of labor in two-earner marriages: Dimensions of variability and change. *Journal of Family Issues, 12*, 158–180.

Foley, R. (1996). The adaptive legacy of human evolution: A search for the environment of evolutionary adaptedness. *Evolutionary Anthropology, 4*, 194–203.

Geary, D. C. (1995). Sexual selection and sex differences in spatial cognition. *Learning and Individual Differences, 7*, 289–301.

Geary, D. C. (1996). Sexual selection and sex differences in mathematical abilities. *Behavioral and Brain Sciences, 19*, 229–284.

Glick, P. (1991). Trait-based and sex-based discrimination in occupational prestige, occupational salary, and hiring. *Sex Roles, 25*, 351–378.

Gould, S. J. (1991). Exaptation: A crucial tool for an evolutionary psychology. *Journal of Social Issues, 47*, 43–65.

Haas, L. L. (1995). Household division of labor in industrial societies. In B. B. Ingoldsby & S. Smith (Eds.), *Families in multicultural perspective: Perspectives on marriage and the family* (pp. 268–296). New York: Guilford Press.

Halpern, D. F. (1997). Sex differences in intelligence: Implications for education. *American Psychologist, 52,* 1091–1102.

Harris, M. (1993). The evolution of human gender hierarchies: A trial formulation. In B. D. Miller (Ed.), *Sex and gender hierarchies* (pp. 57–79). New York: Cambridge University Press.

Hrdy, S. B. (1997). Raising Darwin's consciousness: Female sexuality and the prehominid origins of patriarchy. *Human Nature, 8,* 1–49.

Hyde, J. S. (1996). Where are the gender differences? Where are the gender similarities? In D. M. Buss & N. M. Malamuth (Eds.), *Sex, power, conflict: Evolutionary and feminist perspectives.* New York: Oxford University Press.

Jackson, L. A. (1992). *Physical appearance and gender: Sociobiological and sociocultural perspectives.* Albany: State University of New York Press.

Jacobs, J. A. (1989). *Revolving doors: Sex segregation and women's careers.* Stanford, CA: Stanford University Press.

Janicki, M. G., & Krebs, D. L. (1998). Evolutionary approaches to culture. In C. Crawford & D. L. Krebs (Eds.), *Handbook of evolutionary psychology: Ideas, issues, and applications* (pp. 163–207), Mahwah, NJ: Erlbaum.

Jones, D. (1995). Sexual selection, physical attractiveness, and facial neoteny: Cross-cultural evidence and implications. *Current Anthropology, 36,* 723–748.

Kalick, S. M., Zebrowitz, L. A., Langlois, J. H., & Johnson, R. M. (1998). Does human facial attractiveness honestly advertise health? Longitudinal data on an evolutionary question. *Psychological Science, 9,* 8–13.

Kelly, R. L. (1995). *The foraging spectrum: Diversity in hunter–gatherer lifeways.* Washington, DC: Smithsonian Institution Press.

Kenrick, D. T., & Keefe, R. C. (1992). Age preferences in mates reflect sex differences in human reproductive strategies. *Behavioral and Brain Sciences, 15,* 75–91.

Kenrick, D. T., Trost, M. R., & Sheets, V. L. (1996). Power, harassment, and trophy mates: The feminist advantages of an evolutionary perspective. In D. M. Buss & N. M. Malamuth (Eds.), *Sex, power, and conflict: Evolutionary and feminist perspectives* (pp. 29–53). New York: Oxford University Press.

Lerner, G. (1986). *The creation of patriarchy.* New York: Oxford University Press.

Lippa, R. (1998). Gender-related individual differences and the structure of vocational interests: The importance of the "people-things" dimension. *Journal of Personality and Social Psychology, 74,* 996–1009.

Lips, H. M. (1991). *Women, men, and power.* Mountain View, CA: Mayfield.

Lorenzi-Cioldi, F. (1998). Group status and perceptions of homogeneity. In W. Stroebe & M. Hewstone (Eds.), *European review of social psychology* (Vol. 9, pp. 31–75). Chichester, England: Wiley.

Olson, J. M., Roese, N. J., & Zanna, M. P. (1996). Expectancies. In E. T. Higgins & A. W. Kruglanski (Eds.), *Social psychology: Handbook of basic principles* (pp. 211–238). New York: Guilford.

Potts, R. (1984). Home bases and early hominids. *American Scientist, 72,* 338–347.

Powers, E. A. (1971). Thirty years of research on ideal mate characteristics: What do we know? *International Journal of Sociology of the Family, 1,* 207–215.

Presser, H. B. (1994). Employment schedules among dual-earner spouses and the division of household labor by gender. *American Sociological Review, 59,* 348–364.

Reskin, B. F., & Padavic, I. (1994). *Women and men at work.* Thousand Oaks, CA: Pine Forge Press.

Ridgeway, C. L. (1991). The social construction of status value: Gender and other nominal characteristics. *Social Forces, 70,* 367–386.

Ridgeway, C. L., & Diekema, D. (1992). Are gender differences status differences? In C. L. Ridgeway (Ed.), *Gender, interaction, and inequality* (pp. 157–180). New York: Springer-Verlag.

Rose, L., & Marshall, F. (1996). Meat eating, hominid sociality, and home bases revisited. *Current Anthropology, 37,* 307–338.

Sanday, P. R. (1981). *Female power and male dominance: On the origins of sexual inequality.* New York: Cambridge University Press.

Shelton, B. A. (1992). *Women, men and time: Gender differences in paid work, housework, and leisure.* New York: Greenwood Press.

Silverman, I., & Phillips, K. (1998). The evolutionary psychology of spatial sex differences. In C. Crawford & D. L. Krebs (Eds.), *Handbook of evolutionary psychology: Ideas, issues, and applications* (pp. 595–612). Mahwah, NJ: Erlbaum.

Simon, R. J., & Landis, J. M. (1989). The polls—A report: Women's and men's attitudes about a woman's place and role. *Public Opinion Quarterly, 53,* 265–276.

Singh, D. (1993). Adaptive significance of female physical attractiveness: Role of waist-to-hip ratio. *Journal of Personality and Social Psychology, 65,* 293–307.

Skrypnek, B. J., & Snyder, M. (1982). On the self-perpetuating nature of stereotypes about women and men. *Journal of Experimental Social Psychology, 18,* 277–291.

Sork, V. L. (1997). Quantitative genetics, feminism, and evolutionary theories of gender differences. In P. A. Gowaty (Ed.), *Feminism and evolutionary biology: Boundaries, intersections, and frontiers* (pp. 86–115). New York: Chapman & Hall.

Spence, J. T., & Hahn, E. D. (1997). The Attitudes Toward Women: Scale and attitude change in college students. *Psychology of Women Quarterly, 21,* 17–34.

Sprecher, S., Sullivan, Q., & Hatfield, E. (1994). Mate selection preferences: Gender differences examined in a national sample. *Journal of Personality and Social Psychology, 66,* 1074–1080.

Steil, J. M. (1997). *Marital equality: Its relationship to the well-being of husbands and wives.* Thousand Oaks, CA: Sage.

Strier, K. B. (1994). Myth of the typical primate. *Yearbook of Physical Anthropology, 37,* 233–271.

Symons, D. (1979). *The evolution of human sexuality.* New York: Oxford University Press.

Symons, D. (1992). On the use and misuse of Darwinism in the study of human behavior. In J. H. Barkow, L. Cosmides, & J. Tooby (Eds.), *The adapted mind: Evolutionary psychology and the generation of culture* (pp. 137–159). New York: Oxford University Press.

Tassinary, L. G., & Hansen, K. A. (1998). A critical test of the waist-to-hip-ratio hypothesis of female physical attractiveness. *Psychological Science, 9,* 150–155.

Tattersall, I. (1998). *Becoming human: Evolution and human uniqueness.* New York: Harcourt Brace.

Tomaskovic-Devey, D. (1995). Sex composition and gendered earnings inequality: A comparison of job and occupational models. In J. A. Jacobs (Ed.), *Gender inequality at work* (pp. 23–56). Thousand Oaks, CA: Sage.

Tooby, J., & Cosmides, L. (1989). The innate versus the manifest: How universal does universal have to be? *Behavioral and Brain Sciences, 12,* 36–37.

Tooby, J., & Cosmides, L. (1990a). On the universality of human nature and the uniqueness of the individual: The role of genetics and adaptation. *Journal of Personality, 58,* 17–67.

Tooby, J., & Cosmides, L. (1990b). The past explains the present: Emotional adaptations and the structure of ancestral environments. *Ethology and Sociobiology, 11,* 375–424.

Tooby, J., & Cosmides, L. (1992). The psychological foundations of culture. In J. H. Barkow, L. Cosmides, & J. Tooby (Eds.), *The adapted mind: Evolutionary psychology and the generation of culture* (pp. 19–136). New York: Oxford University Press.

Travis, C. B., & Yeager, C. P. (1991). Sexual selection, parental investment, and sexism. *Journal of Social Issues, 47*(3), 117–129.

Trivers, R. (1972). Parental investment and sexual selection. In B. Campbell (Ed.), *Sexual selection and the descent of man: 1871–1971* (pp. 136–179). Chicago: Aldine.

Twenge, J. M. (1997). Attitudes toward women, 1970–1995: A meta-analysis. *Psychology of Women Quarterly, 21,* 35–51.

United Nations Development Programme. (1995). *Human development report 1995.* New York: Oxford University Press.

West, C., & Zimmerman, D. H. (1987). Doing gender. *Gender & Society, 1,* 125–151.

Whyte, M. K. (1978). *The status of women in preindustrial societies.* Princeton, NJ: Princeton University Press.

Wiley, M. G. (1995). Sex category and gender in social psychology. In K. S. Cook, G. A. Fine, & J. S. House (Eds.). *Sociological perspectives on social psychology* (pp. 362–386). Boston: Allyn & Bacon.

Williams, G. C. (1966). *Adaptation and natural selection: A critique of some current evolutionary thought.* Princeton, NJ: Princeton University Press.

Wood, W., Christensen, P. N., Hebl, M. R., & Rothgerber, H. (1997). Conformity to sex-typed norms, affect, and the self-concept. *Journal of Personality and Social Psychology, 73,* 523–535.

Wood, W., & Eagly, A. H. (1999). *Social structure and the origins of sex differences in social behavior.* Manuscript in preparation.

Wood, W., & Karten, S. J. (1986). Sex differences in interaction style as a product of perceived sex differences in competence. *Journal of Personality and Social Psychology, 50,* 341–347.

PART IV

The Psychoanalytic Approach to Personality

About a century ago, the brilliant Viennese psychiatrist Sigmund Freud began to present his psychoanalytic theory of personality to the world. Freud continued to publish prolifically and to develop his theory right up to the time of his death in 1939. The result of all this labor was not only a long-lasting and pervasive influence on the field of psychology, but also a fundamental influence on the way members of Western culture think about people. The "Freudian slip" is the commonplace idea most obviously identified with Freud, but his writings also continue to affect the way we talk about child-rearing, psychological conflict, sexuality, aggression, and emotion.

Freud's own contributions were impressive enough, but he also attracted a remarkable group of followers, several of whom eventually broke away from his influence. These include some of the major intellectual figures of the early twentieth century, including Carl Jung, Karen Horney, and Erik Erikson. Freud's theory continues to influence modern psychological research both directly and indirectly. The readings in this section sample from the writings of Freud himself, several other important figures in psychoanalysis, and other writers who have attempted to evaluate psychoanalysis on empirical or theoretical grounds.

The lecture that begins this section concerns the basic structure of the mind. The next three selections are from the writings of other major psychoanalysts. Carl Jung describes the nature of extraversion and introversion, Karen Horney explains the "distrust" between the sexes, and Erik Erikson outlines the eight stages of psychological development that occur over an individual's entire life span.

The next paper, by Roy Baumeister, Karen Dale, and Kristin Sommer, is a recent survey of modern research particularly relevant to the psychoanalytic concept of the defense mechanism. The final selection in this chapter is a scathing but also humorous critique of psychoanalytic theory, written by the feminist Gloria Steinem. Vehemently attacking psychoanalysis at perhaps its weakest point—its obvious sexism—Steinem describes how the theory might have looked if Freud were a woman, living in a matriarchy.

Perhaps no theory in psychology has been as admired, and as reviled, as psychoanalysis. As you will see in the following articles, there are good reasons for both kinds of reaction.

LECTURE XXXI: THE DISSECTION OF THE PSYCHICAL PERSONALITY

Sigmund Freud

In this first selection the founder of psychoanalysis, Sigmund Freud himself, describes the core of the theory. Freud describes how the mind is divided into three parts, the now-famous id, ego, and super-ego. These roughly map onto the animalistic part, the logical part, and the moral part of the mind.

One of your editors remembers years ago having seen a Donald Duck cartoon in which the unfortunate duck was tormented by an angel who rode on one shoulder and a devil who rode on the other. The angel was always scolding him, and the devil was always egging him on to do things he knew he shouldn't do. Donald himself, in the middle, was confused and prone to obey first one of his tormentors, then the other.

Disney's animators seem to have known their Freud. The situation described near the end of this selection is nearly identical. When Freud has the poor ego cry, "Life is not easy!" he is describing the torment of having to resolve the three-way conflict between what one believes one should do, what one wants to do, and what is really possible.

This selection was written late in Freud's career and originally published in 1933, six years before his death. Freud had 15 years earlier delivered a famous set of introductory lectures on psychoanalysis, and he hit upon the idea of writing a new set of lectures to update and expand upon the earlier ones. But by this time Freud, an old man, had undergone repeated surgeries for cancer of the palate and could not speak in public. So although this and several other articles were written in the form of lectures, they were never meant to be delivered. In Freud's own words (from his preface),

> If, therefore, I once more take my place in the lecture room during the remarks that follow, it is only by an artifice of the imagination; it may help me not to forget to bear the reader in mind as I enter more deeply into my subject. . . . [this lecture is] addressed to the multitude of educated people to whom we

may perhaps attribute a benevolent, even though cautious, interest in the characteristics and discoveries of the young science. (Freud, 1965/1933, p, 5).

From *New Introductory Lectures on Psycho-analysis*, by Sigmund Freud, in *The Standard Edition of the Complete Psychological Works of Sigmund Freud*, edited and translated by James Strachey (New York: Norton, 1966), pp. 51–71.

* * *

The situation in which we find ourselves at the beginning of our enquiry may be expected itself to point the way for us. We wish to make the ego the matter of our enquiry, our very own ego.[1] But is that possible? After all, the ego is in its very essence a subject; how can it be made into an object? Well, there is no doubt that it can be. The ego can take itself as an object, can treat itself like other objects, can observe itself, criticize itself, and do Heaven knows what with itself. In this, one part of the ego is setting itself over against the rest. So the ego can be split; it splits itself during a number of its functions—temporarily at least. Its parts can come together again afterwards. That is not exactly a novelty, though it may perhaps be putting an unusual emphasis on what is generally known. On the other hand, we are familiar with the notion that pathology, by making things larger and coarser, can draw our attention to normal conditions which would otherwise have escaped us. Where it points to a breach or a rent, there may normally be an articulation present. If we throw a crystal to the floor, it breaks; but not into haphazard pieces. It comes apart along its lines of cleavage into fragments whose boundaries, though they were invisible, were predetermined by the crystal's structure. Mental patients are split and broken structures of this same kind. Even we cannot withhold from them something of the reverential awe which peoples of the past felt for the insane. They have turned away from external reality, but for that very reason they know more about internal, psychical reality and can reveal a number of things to us that would otherwise be inaccessible to us.

We describe one group of these patients as suffering from delusions of being observed. They complain to us that perpetually, and down to their most intimate actions, they are being molested by the observation of unknown powers—presumably persons—and that in hallucinations they hear these persons reporting the outcome of their observation: "now he's going to say this, now he's dressing to go out," and so on. Observation of this sort is not yet the same thing as persecution, but it is not far from it; it presupposes that people distrust them, and expect to catch them carrying out forbidden actions for which they would be punished. How would it be if these insane people were right, if in each of us there is present in his ego an agency like this which observes and threatens to punish, and which in them has merely become sharply divided from their ego and mistakenly displaced into external reality?

I cannot tell whether the same thing will happen to you as to me. Ever since, under the powerful impression of this clinical picture, I formed the idea that the separation of the observing agency from the rest of the ego might be a regular feature of the ego's structure, that idea has never left me, and I was driven to investigate the further characteristics and connections of the agency which was thus separated off. The next step is quickly taken. The content of the delusions of being observed already suggests that the observing is only a preparation for judging and punishing, and we accordingly guess that another function of this agency must be what we call our conscience. There is scarcely anything else in us that we so regularly separate from our ego and so easily set over against

---

[1] "Ego" has also been translated as "the I." Freud is referring to the self as it experiences itself—a paradoxical but common situation that leads Freud to conclude that dividing up the self is not so odd as it might seem.

it as precisely our conscience. I feel an inclination to do something that I think will give me pleasure, but I abandon it on the ground that my conscience does not allow it. Or I have let myself be persuaded by too great an expectation of pleasure into doing something to which the voice of conscience has objected and after the deed my conscience punishes me with distressing reproaches and causes me to feel remorse for the deed. I might simply say that the special agency which I am beginning to distinguish in the ego is conscience. But it is more prudent to keep the agency as something independent and to suppose that conscience is one of its functions and that self-observation, which is an essential preliminary to the judging activity of conscience, is another of them. And since when we recognize that something has a separate existence we give it a name of its own, from this time forward I will describe this agency in the ego as the "*super-ego.*"

*   *   *

Hardly have we familiarized ourselves with the idea of a super-ego like this which enjoys a certain degree of autonomy, follows its own intentions and is independent of the ego for its supply of energy, than a clinical picture forces itself on our notice which throws a striking light on the severity of this agency and indeed its cruelty, and on its changing relations to the ego. I am thinking of the condition of melancholia,[2] or, more precisely, of melancholic attacks, which you too will have heard plenty about, even if you are not psychiatrists. The most striking feature of this illness, of whose causation and mechanism we know much too little, is the way in which the super-ego—"conscience," you may call it, quietly—treats the ego. While a melancholic can, like other people, show a greater or lesser degree of severity to himself in his healthy periods, during a melancholic attack his super-ego becomes over-severe, abuses the poor ego, humiliates it and ill-treats it, threatens it with the direst punishments, reproaches it for actions in the

remotest past which had been taken lightly at the time—as though it had spent the whole interval in collecting accusations and had only been waiting for its present access of strength in order to bring them up and make a condemnatory judgement on their basis. The super-ego applies the strictest moral standard to the helpless ego which is at its mercy; in general it represents the claims of morality, and we realize all at once that our moral sense of guilt is the expression of the tension between the ego and the super-ego. It is a most remarkable experience to see morality, which is supposed to have been given us by God and thus deeply implanted in us, functioning [in these patients] as a periodic phenomenon. For after a certain number of months the whole moral fuss is over, the criticism of the super-ego is silent, the ego is rehabilitated and again enjoys all the rights of man till the next attack. In some forms of the disease, indeed, something of a contrary sort occurs in the intervals; the ego finds itself in a blissful state of intoxication, it celebrates a triumph, as though the super-ego had lost all its strength or had melted into the ego; and this liberated, manic ego permits itself a truly uninhibited satisfaction of all its appetites. Here are happenings rich in unsolved riddles!

No doubt you will expect me to give you more than a mere illustration when I inform you that we have found out all kinds of things about the formation of the super-ego—that is to say, about the origin of conscience. Following a well-known pronouncement of Kant's which couples the conscience within us with the starry Heavens, a pious man might well be tempted to honor these two things as the masterpieces of creation. The stars are indeed magnificent, but as regards conscience God has done an uneven and careless piece of work, for a large majority of men have brought along with them only a modest amount of it or scarcely enough to be worth mentioning. We are far from overlooking the portion of psychological truth that is contained in the assertion that conscience is of divine origin; but the thesis needs interpretation. Even if conscience is something "within us," yet it is not so from the first. In this it is a real contrast to

---

[2] "Modern terminology would probably speak of 'depression.' "—Translator

sexual life, which is in fact there from the beginning of life and not only a later addition. But, as is well known, young children are amoral and possess no internal inhibitions against their impulses striving for pleasure. The part which is later taken on by the super-ego is played to begin with by an external power, by parental authority. Parental influence governs the child by offering proofs of love and by threatening punishments which are signs to the child of loss of love and are bound to be feared on their own account. This realistic anxiety is the precursor of the later moral anxiety. So long as it is dominant there is no need to talk of a super-ego and of a conscience. It is only subsequently that the secondary situation develops (which we are all too ready to regard as the normal one), where the external restraint is internalized and the super-ego takes the place of the parental agency and observes, directs and threatens the ego in exactly the same way as earlier the parents did with the child.

The super-ego, which thus takes over the power, function and even the methods of the parental agency, is however not merely its successor but actually the legitimate heir of its body. It proceeds directly out of it, we shall learn presently by what process. First, however, we must dwell upon a discrepancy between the two. The super-ego seems to have made a one-sided choice and to have picked out only the parents' strictness and severity, their prohibiting and punitive function, whereas their loving care seems not to have been taken over and maintained. If the parents have really enforced their authority with severity we can easily understand the child's in turn developing a severe super-ego. But, contrary to our expectation, experience shows that the super-ego can acquire the same characteristic of relentless severity even if the upbringing had been mild and kindly and had so far as possible avoided threats and punishments. * * *

* * *

The basis of the process is what is called an "identification"—that is to say, the assimilation of

one ego to another one,[3] as a result of which the first ego behaves like the second in certain respects, imitates it and in a sense takes it up into itself. Identification has been not unsuitably compared with the oral, cannibalistic incorporation of the other person. It is a very important form of attachment to someone else, probably the very first, and not the same thing as the choice of an object. The difference between the two can be expressed in some such way as this. If a boy identifies himself with his father, he wants to *be like* his father; if he makes him the object of his choice, he wants to *have* him, to possess him. In the first case his ego is altered on the model of his father; in the second case that is not necessary. Identification and object-choice are to a large extent independent of each other; it is however possible to identify oneself with someone whom, for instance, one has taken as a sexual object, and to alter one's ego on his model. It is said that the influencing of the ego by the sexual object occurs particularly often with women and is characteristic of femininity. I must already have spoken to you in my earlier lectures of what is by far the most instructive relation between identification and object-choice. It can be observed equally easily in children and adults, in normal as in sick people. If one has lost an object or has been obliged to give it up, one often compensates oneself by identifying oneself with it and by setting it up once more in one's ego, so that here object-choice regresses, as it were, to identification.

I myself am far from satisfied with these remarks on identification; but it will be enough if you can grant me that the installation of the super-ego can be described as a successful instance of identification with the parental agency. The fact that speaks decisively for this view is that this new creation of a superior agency within the ego is most intimately linked with the destiny of the Oedipus complex[4] so that the super-ego appears as

---

[3]"I.e., one ego coming to resemble another one." —Translator

[4]The "Oedipus complex" is the result of a complex process in which, according to Freud, a young boy falls in love with his mother, fears his father's jealous retaliation, and as a defense against that fear comes to identify with his father.

the heir of that emotional attachment which is of such importance for childhood. With his abandonment of the Oedipus complex a child must, as we can see, renounce the intense object-cathexes[5] which he has deposited with his parents, and it is as a compensation for this loss of objects that there is such a strong intensification of the identifications with his parents which have probably long been present in his ego. Identifications of this kind as precipitates of object-cathexes that have been given up will be repeated often enough later in the child's life; but it is entirely in accordance with the emotional importance of this first instance of such a transformation that a special place in the ego should be found for its outcome. Close investigation has shown us, too, that the super-ego is stunted in its strength and growth if the surmounting of the Oedipus complex is only incompletely successful. In the course of development the super-ego also takes on the influences of those who have stepped into the place of parents—educators, teachers, people chosen as ideal models. Normally it departs more and more from the original parental figures; it becomes, so to say, more impersonal. Nor must it be forgotten that a child has a different estimate of its parents at different periods of its life. At the time at which the Oedipus complex gives place to the super-ego they are something quite magnificent; but later they lose much of this. Identifications then come about with these later parents as well, and indeed they regularly make important contributions to the formation of character; but in that case they only affect the ego, they no longer influence the super-ego, which has been determined by the earliest parental imagos.

* * *

* * * In face of the doubt whether the ego and super-ego are themselves unconscious or merely produce unconscious effects, we have, for good reasons, decided in favour of the former possibility. And it is indeed the case that large portions of the ego and super-ego can remain unconscious and are normally unconscious. That is to say, the

individual knows nothing of their contents and it requires an expenditure of effort to make them conscious. It is a fact that ego and conscious, repressed and unconscious do not coincide. We feel a need to make a fundamental revision of our attitude to the problem of conscious-unconscious. At first we are inclined greatly to reduce the value of the criterion of being conscious since it has shown itself so untrustworthy. But we should be doing it an injustice. As may be said of our life, it is not worth much, but it is all we have. Without the illumination thrown by the quality of consciousness, we should be lost in the obscurity of depth-psychology; but we must attempt to find our bearings afresh.

There is no need to discuss what is to be called conscious: it is removed from all doubt. The oldest and best meaning of the word "unconscious" is the descriptive one; we call a psychical process unconscious whose existence we are obliged to assume— for some such reason as that we infer it from its effects—but of which we know nothing. In that case we have the same relation to it as we have to a psychical process in another person, except that it is in fact one of our own. If we want to be still more correct, we shall modify our assertion by saying that we call a process unconscious if we are obliged to assume that it is being activated *at the moment*, though *at the moment* we know nothing about it. This qualification makes us reflect that the majority of conscious processes are conscious only for a short time; very soon they become *latent*, but can easily become conscious again. We might also say that they had become unconscious, if it were at all certain that in the condition of latency they are still something psychical. So far we should have learnt nothing new; nor should we have acquired the right to introduce the concept of an unconscious into psychology. [But] in order to explain a slip of the tongue, for instance, we find ourselves obliged to assume that the intention to make a particular remark was present in the subject. We infer it with certainty from the interference with his remark which has occurred; but the intention did not put itself through and was thus unconscious. If, when we subsequently put it before the speaker,

---

[5]An "object-cathexis" is an investment of emotional energy in an important "object," usually a person.

he recognizes it as one familiar to him, then it was only temporarily unconscious to him; but if he repudiates it as something foreign to him, then it was permanently unconscious. From this experience we retrospectively obtain the right also to pronounce as something unconscious what had been described as latent. A consideration of these dynamic relations permits us now to distinguish two kinds of unconscious—one which is easily, under frequently occurring circumstances, transformed into something conscious, and another with which this transformation is difficult and takes place only subject to a considerable expenditure of effort or possibly never at all. In order to escape the ambiguity as to whether we mean the one or the other unconscious, whether we are using the word in the descriptive or in the dynamic sense, we make use of a permissible and simple way out. We call the unconscious which is only latent, and thus easily becomes conscious, the "preconscious" and retain the term "unconscious" for the other. We now have three terms, "conscious," "preconscious," and "unconscious," with which we can get along in our description of mental phenomena. Once again: the preconscious is also unconscious in the purely descriptive sense, but we do not give it that name, except in talking loosely or when we have to make a defence of the existence in mental life of unconscious processes in general.

You will admit, I hope, that so far that is not too bad and allows of convenient handling. Yes, but unluckily the work of psychoanalysis has found itself compelled to use the word "unconscious" in yet another, third, sense, and this may, to be sure, have led to confusion. Under the new and powerful impression of there being an extensive and important field of mental life which is normally withdrawn from the ego's knowledge so that the processes occurring in it have to be regarded as unconscious in the truly dynamic sense, we have come to understand the term "unconscious" in a topographical or systematic sense as well; we have come to speak of a "system" of the preconscious and a "system" of the unconscious, of a conflict between the ego and the system Ucs. [unconscious], and have used the word more and more to denote a mental province rather than a quality of what is mental. The discovery, actually an inconvenient one, that portions of the ego and super-ego as well are unconscious in the dynamic sense, operates at this point as a relief—it makes possible the removal of a complication. We perceive that we have no right to name the mental region that is foreign to the ego "the system Ucs.," since the characteristic of being unconscious is not restricted to it. Very well; we will no longer use the term "unconscious" in the systematic sense and we will give what we have hitherto so described a better name and one no longer open to misunderstanding. Following a verbal usage of Nietzsche's and taking up a suggestion by Georg Groddeck [1923],[6] we will in future call it the "id".[7] This impersonal pronoun seems particularly well suited for expressing the main characteristic of this province of the mind—the fact of its being alien to the ego. The super-ego, the ego and the id—these, then, are the three realms, regions, provinces, into which we divide an individual's mental apparatus, and with the mutual relations of which we shall be concerned in what follows.

* * *

You will not expect me to have much to tell you that is new about the id apart from its new name. It is the dark, inaccessible part of our personality; what little we know of it we have learnt from our study of the dream-work and of the construction of neurotic symptoms, and most of that is of a negative character and can be described only as a contrast to the ego. We approach the id with analogies: we call it a chaos, a cauldron full of seething excitations. We picture it as being open at its end to somatic influences, and as there taking up into itself instinctual needs which find their psychical expression in it, but we cannot say in what substratum. It is filled with energy reaching it from the instincts, but it has no organization, produces no collective will, but only a striving to bring

---

[6]"A German physician by whose unconventional ideas Freud was much attracted."—Translator

[7]"In German, Es, the ordinary word for 'it.'"—Translator

about the satisfaction of the instinctual needs subject to the observance of the pleasure principle. The logical laws of thought do not apply in the id, and this is true above all of the law of contradiction. Contrary impulses exist side by side, without cancelling each other out or diminishing each other: at the most they may converge to form compromises under the dominating economic pressure towards the discharge of energy. There is nothing in the id that could be compared with negation; and we perceive with surprise an exception to the philosophical theorem that space and time are necessary forms of our mental acts. There is nothing in the id that corresponds to the idea of time; there is no recognition of the passage of time, and—a thing that is most remarkable and awaits consideration in philosophical thought—no alteration in its mental processes is produced by the passage of time. Wishful impulses which have never passed beyond the id, but impressions, too, which have been sunk into the id by repression, are virtually immortal; after the passage of decades they behave as though they had just occurred. They can only be recognized as belonging to the past, can only lose their importance and be deprived of their cathexis of energy, when they have been made conscious by the work of analysis, and it is on this that the therapeutic effect of analytic treatment rests to no small extent.

Again and again I have had the impression that we have made too little theoretical use of this fact, established beyond any doubt, of the unalterability by time of the repressed. This seems to offer an approach to the most profound discoveries. Nor, unfortunately, have I myself made any progress here.

The id of course knows no judgements of value: no good and evil, no morality. The economic or, if you prefer, the quantitative factor, which is intimately linked to the pleasure principle, dominates all its processes. Instinctual cathexes seeking discharge—that, in our view, is all there is in the id.[8] It even seems that the energy of these instinctual impulses is in a state different from that in the other regions of the mind, far more mobile and capable of discharge; otherwise the displacements and condensations would not occur which are characteristic of the id and which so completely disregard the *quality* of what is cathected—what in the ego we should call an idea. We would give much to understand more about these things! You can see, incidentally, that we are in a position to attribute to the id characteristics other than that of its being unconscious, and you can recognize the possibility of portions of the ego and super-ego being unconscious without possessing the same primitive and irrational characteristics.

* * *

* * * We need scarcely look for a justification of the view that the ego is that portion of the id which was modified by the proximity and influence of the external world, which is adapted for the reception of stimuli and as a protective shield against stimuli, comparable to the cortical layer by which a small piece of living substance is surrounded. The relation to the external world has become the decisive factor for the ego; it has taken on the task of representing the external world to the id—fortunately for the id, which could not escape destruction if, in its blind efforts for the satisfaction of its instincts, it disregarded that supreme external power. In accomplishing this function, the ego must observe the external world, must lay down an accurate picture of it in the memory-traces of its perceptions, and by its exercise of the function of "reality-testing" must put aside whatever in this picture of the external world is an addition derived from internal sources of excitation. The ego controls the approaches to motility under the id's orders; but between a need and an action it has interposed a postponement in the form of the activity of thought, during which it makes use of the mnemic residues of experience. In that way it has dethroned the pleasure principle which dominates the course of events in the id without any restriction, and has replaced it by the reality principle, which promises more certainty and greater success.

---

[8]In other words, the id seeks immediately to satisfy all "instinctual"—physical—desires.

* * *

* * * To adopt a popular mode of speaking, we might say that the ego stands for reason and good sense while the id stands for the untamed passions.

So far we have allowed ourselves to be impressed by the merits and capabilities of the ego; it is now time to consider the other side as well. The ego is after all only a portion of the id, a portion that has been expediently modified by the proximity of the external world with its threat of danger. From a dynamic point of view it is weak, it has borrowed its energies from the id, and we are not entirely without insight into the methods—we might call them dodges—by which it extracts further amounts of energy from the id. One such method, for instance, is by identifying itself with actual or abandoned objects. The object-cathexes spring from the instinctual demands of the id. The ego has in the first instance to take note of them. But by identifying itself with the object it recommends itself to the id in place of the object and seeks to divert the id's libido on to itself. * * * The ego must on the whole carry out the id's intentions, it fulfils its task by finding out the circumstances in which those intentions can best be achieved. The ego's relation to the id might be compared with that of a rider to his horse. The horse supplies the locomotive energy, while the rider has the privilege of deciding on the goal and of guiding the powerful animal's movement. But only too often there arises between the ego and the id the not precisely ideal situation of the rider being obliged to guide the horse along the path by which it itself wants to go.

* * *

We are warned by a proverb against serving two masters at the same time. The poor ego has things even worse: it serves three severe masters and does what it can to bring their claims and demands into harmony with one another. These claims are always divergent and often seem incompatible. No wonder that the ego so often fails in its task. Its three tyrannical masters are the external world, the super-ego and the id. When we follow the ego's efforts to satisfy them simultaneously—or rather, to obey them simultaneously—we cannot feel any regret at having personified this ego and having set it up as a separate organism. It feels hemmed in on three sides, threatened by three kinds of danger, to which, if it is hard pressed, it reacts by generating anxiety. Owing to its origin from the experiences of the perceptual system, it is earmarked for representing the demands of the external world, but it strives too to be a loyal servant of the id, to remain on good terms with it, to recommend itself to it as an object and to attract its libido to itself. In its attempts to mediate between the id and reality, it is often obliged to cloak the *Ucs.* commands of the id with its own *Pcs.* [preconscious] rationalizations, to conceal the id's conflicts with reality, to profess, with diplomatic disingenuousness, to be taking notice of reality even when the id has remained rigid and unyielding. On the other hand it is observed at every step it takes by the strict super-ego, which lays down definite standards for its conduct, without taking any account of its difficulties from the direction of the id and the external world, and which, if those standards are not obeyed, punishes it with tense feelings of inferiority and of guilt. Thus the ego, driven by the id, confined by the super-ego, repulsed by reality, struggles to master its economic task of bringing about harmony among the forces and influences working in and upon it; and we can understand how it is that so often we cannot suppress a cry: "Life is not easy!" If the ego is obliged to admit its weakness, it breaks out in anxiety—realistic anxiety regarding the external world, moral anxiety regarding the super-ego and neurotic anxiety regarding the strength of the passions in the id.

I should like to portray the structural relations of the mental personality, as I have described them to you, in the unassuming sketch which I now present you with:[9]

---

[9] The "perceptual conscious" (*pcpt.-cs*) is Freud's name for the system and processes that create our sense of consciousness and the immediate contents of our awareness.

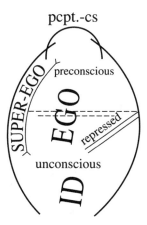

Figure 1 Freud's
diagram of the
structure of personality.

As you see here, the super-ego merges into the id; indeed, as heir to the Oedipus complex it has intimate relations with the id; it is more remote than the ego from the perceptual system. The id has intercourse with the external world only through the ego—at least, according to this diagram. It is certainly hard to say today how far the drawing is correct. In one respect it is undoubtedly not. The space occupied by the unconscious id ought to have been incomparably greater than that of the ego or the preconscious. I must ask you to correct it in your thoughts.

And here is another warning, to conclude these remarks, which have certainly been exacting and not, perhaps, very illuminating. In thinking of this division of the personality into an ego, a super-ego and an id, you will not, of course, have pic-tured sharp frontiers like the artificial ones drawn in political geography. We cannot do justice to the characteristics of the mind by linear outlines like those in a drawing or in primitive painting, but rather by areas of colour melting into one another as they are presented by modern artists. After making the separation we must allow what we have separated to merge together once more. You must not judge too harshly a first attempt at giving a pictorial representation of something so intangible as psychical processes. It is highly probable that the development of these divisions is subject to great variations in different individuals; it is possible that in the course of actual functioning they may change and go through a temporary phase of involution. Particularly in the case of what is phylogenetically the last and most delicate of these divisions—the differentiation between the ego and the super-ego—something of the sort seems to be true. There is no question but that the same thing results from psychical illness. It is easy to imagine, too, that certain mystical practices may succeed in upsetting the normal relations between the different regions of the mind, so that, for instance, perception may be able to grasp happenings in the depths of the ego and in the id which were otherwise inaccessible to it. It may safely be doubted, however, whether this road will lead us to the ultimate truths from which salvation is to be expected. Nevertheless it may be admitted that the therapeutic efforts of psychoanalysis have chosen a similar line of approach. Its intention is, indeed, to strengthen the ego, to make it more independent of the super-ego, to widen its field of perception and enlarge its organization, so that it can appropriate fresh portions of the id. Where id was, there ego shall be. It is a work of culture—not unlike the draining of the Zuider Zee.[10]

---

[10] The Zuider Zee was a landlocked arm of the North Sea in the Netherlands. Its draining was a major land-reclamation project completed in 1932, about the time this essay was written.

PSYCHOLOGICAL TYPES

Carl Jung

One mark of Freud's stature in intellectual history is the number of his adherents—and former adherents—who became major figures in their own right. Perhaps the best known of these is Carl Jung. Jung began his career in psychoanalysis as Freud's anointed "crown prince." Freud intended that Jung succeed him as president of the International Psychoanalytic Association. The two carried on an intense correspondence for years and also traveled to the United States together in 1909.

When it came, the split between Freud and Jung was bitter. Jung felt that Freud overemphasized the role of sexuality and underemphasized the constructive role of the unconscious. But the conflict may have been deeper than that; Jung chafed under Freud's dominating role as his intellectual father figure and felt a need to achieve more independence. For his part, Freud regarded major departures from his theory simply as error, and was particularly alarmed by a turn Jung took in midlife toward a mystical view of the human psyche. Jung formulated ideas, still famous today, about a "collective unconscious" full of mysterious images and ideas shared by all members of the human race, and an "oceanic feeling" of being at one with the universe. Such ideas were anathema to the atheistic and hardheaded Freud.

In the following selection Jung explains one of the more down-to-earth of his theoretical ideas, his conception of introversion and extraversion and four related styles of thinking. These ideas have had an obvious and lasting influence. Recall, for example, that extraversion is one of the Big Five factors of personality identified in the second section of this reader by Costa and McCrae. But Jung's conception is somewhat different from the behavioral styles labeled as extraversion and introversion today. Jung's introvert is someone who in a fundamental way has turned into himself or herself and away from the world; his extravert is wholly dependent on others for his or her intellectual and emotional life.

A widely used personality test, the Myers–Briggs Type Indicator (Myers & McCaulley, 1985), was designed to classify people as to their style of thinking, in Jungian terms. You might be classified as dominated by sensation, thinking, feeling, or intuition. This test is often used for vocational guidance. For example, the sensation style might be appropriate for an athlete, the thinking style for a lawyer, the feeling style for a poet, and the intuitive style for a clinical psychologist.

The following selection is an excerpt from a lecture Jung delivered in Territet, Switzerland, in 1923. By this time Jung had split thoroughly from Freud and was well known for his own work.

3 groups of people
~~Above~~ external - extrave
internal - introvete
in middle

From *Psychological Types*, translated by R. Hull and H. Baynes (Princeton, NJ: Princeton University Press, 1971), pp. 510–523.

* * *

We shall discover, after a time, that in spite of the great variety of conscious motives and tendencies, certain groups of individuals can be distinguished who are characterized by a striking conformity of motivation. For example, we shall come upon individuals who in all their judgments, perceptions, feelings, affects, and actions feel external factors to be the predominant motivating force, or who at least give weight to them no matter whether causal or final motives are in question. I will give some examples of what I mean. St. Augustine: "I would not believe the Gospel if the authority of the Catholic Church did not compel it." A dutiful daughter: "I could not allow myself to think anything that would be displeasing to my father." One man finds a piece of modern music beautiful because everybody else pretends it is beautiful. Another marries in order to please his parents but very much against his own interests. There are people who contrive to make themselves ridiculous in order to amuse others; they even prefer to make butts of themselves rather than remain unnoticed. There are not a few who in everything they do or don't do have but one motive in mind: what will others think of them? "One need not be ashamed of a thing if nobody knows about it." There are some who can find happiness only when it excites the envy of others; some who make trouble for themselves in order to enjoy the sympathy of their friends.

Such examples could be multiplied indefinitely. They point to a psychological peculiarity that can be sharply distinguished from another attitude which, by contrast, is motivated chiefly by internal or subjective factors. A person of this type might say: "I know I could give my father the great-

est pleasure if I did so and so, but I don't happen to think that way." Or: "I see that the weather has turned out bad, but in spite of it I shall carry out my plan." This type does not travel for pleasure but to execute a preconceived idea. Or: "My book is probably incomprehensible, but it is perfectly clear to me." Or, going to the other extreme: "Everybody thinks I could do something, but I know perfectly well I can do nothing." Such a man can be so ashamed of himself that he literally dares not meet people. There are some who feel happy only when they are quite sure nobody knows about it, and to them a thing is disagreeable just because it is pleasing to everyone else. They seek the good where no one would think of finding it. At every step the sanction of the subject must be obtained, and without it nothing can be undertaken or carried out. Such a person would have replied to St. Augustine: "I would believe the Gospel if the authority of the Catholic Church did *not* compel it." Always he has to prove that everything he does rests on his own decisions and convictions, and never because he is influenced by anyone, or desires to please or conciliate some person or opinion.

This attitude characterizes a group of individuals whose motivations are derived chiefly from the subject, from inner necessity. There is, finally, a third group, and here it is hard to say whether the motivation comes chiefly from within or without. This group is the most numerous and includes the less differentiated normal man, who is considered normal either because he allows himself no excesses or because he has no need of them. The normal man is, by definition, influenced as much from within as from without. He constitutes the extensive middle group, on one side of which are those whose motivations are determined mainly by the external object, and, on the other, those whose motivations are determined from within. I call the first group *extraverted*, and the second group *introverted*. The terms scarcely require elucidation as they explain themselves from what has already been said.

Although there are doubtless individuals whose type can be recognized at first glance, this is by no means always the case. As a rule, only careful observation and weighing of the evidence permit a sure classification. However simple and clear the fundamental principle of the two opposing attitudes may be, in actual reality they are complicated and hard to make out, because every individual is an exception to the rule. Hence one can never give a description of a type, no matter how complete, that would apply to more than one individual, despite the fact that in some ways it aptly characterizes thousands of others. Conformity is one side of a man, uniqueness is the other. Classification does not explain the individual psyche. Nevertheless, an understanding of psychological types opens the way to a better understanding of human psychology in general.

Type differentiation often begins very early, so early that in some cases one must speak of it as innate. The earliest sign of extraversion in a child is his quick adaptation to the environment, and the extraordinary attention he gives to objects and especially to the effect he has on them. Fear of objects is minimal; he lives and moves among them with confidence. His apprehension is quick but imprecise. He appears to develop more rapidly than the introverted child, since he is less reflective and usually without fear. He feels no barrier between himself and objects, and can therefore play with them freely and learn through them. He likes to carry his enterprises to the extreme and exposes himself to risks. Everything unknown is alluring.

To reverse the picture, one of the earliest signs of introversion in a child is a reflective, thoughtful manner, marked shyness and even fear of unknown objects. Very early there appears a tendency to assert himself over familiar objects, and attempts are made to master them. Everything unknown is regarded with mistrust; outside influences are usually met with violent resistance. The child wants his own way, and under no circumstances will he submit to an alien rule he cannot understand. When he asks questions, it is not from curiosity or a desire to create a sensation, but because he wants names, meanings, explanations to give him subjective protection against the object. I have seen an introverted child who made his first attempts to walk only after he had learned the names of all the objects in the room he might touch. Thus very early in an introverted child the characteristic defensive attitude can be noted which the adult introvert displays towards the object; just as in an extraverted child one can very early observe a marked assurance and initiative, a happy trustfulness in his dealings with objects. This is indeed the basic feature of the extraverted attitude: psychic life is, as it were, enacted outside the individual in objects and objective relationships. In extreme cases there is even a sort of blindness for his own individuality. The introvert, on the contrary, always acts as though the object possessed a superior power over him against which he has to defend himself. His real world is the inner one.

Sad though it is, the two types are inclined to speak very badly of one another. This fact will immediately strike anyone who investigates the problem. And the reason is that the psychic values have a diametrically opposite localization for the two types. The introvert sees everything that is in any way valuable for him in the subject; the extravert sees it in the object. This dependence on the object seems to the introvert a mark of the greatest inferiority, while to the extravert the preoccupation with the subject seems nothing but infantile autoeroticism. So it is not surprising that the two types often come into conflict. This does not, however, prevent most men from marrying women of the opposite type. Such marriages are very valuable as psychological symbioses so long as the partners do not attempt a mutual "psychological" understanding. But this phase of understanding belongs to the normal development of every marriage provided the partners have the necessary leisure or the necessary urge to development—though even if both these are present real courage is needed to risk a rupture of the marital peace. In favourable circumstances this phase enters automatically into the lives of both types, for the reason that each type is an example of one-sided development. The one develops only external relations and neglects the inner; the other develops inwardly but remains outwardly at a standstill. In time the need arises for the individual to develop what has been neglected. The development takes the form of a differentiation of certain functions, to which I must now turn in view of their importance for the type problem.

The conscious psyche is an apparatus for adaptation and orientation, and consists of a number of different psychic functions. Among these we can distinguish four basic ones: *sensation, thinking, feeling, intuition.* Under sensation I include all perceptions by means of the sense organs; by thinking I mean the function of intellectual cognition and the forming of logical conclusions; feeling is a function of subjective valuation; intuition I take as perception by way of the unconscious, or perception of unconscious contents.

So far as my experience goes, these four basic functions seem to me sufficient to express and represent the various modes of conscious orientation. For complete orientation all four functions should contribute equally: thinking should facilitate cognition and judgment, feeling should tell us how and to what extent a thing is important or unimportant for us, sensation should convey concrete reality to us through seeing, hearing, tasting, etc., and intuition should enable us to divine the hidden possibilities in the background, since these too belong to the complete picture of a given situation.

In reality, however, these basic functions are seldom or never uniformly differentiated and equally at our disposal. As a rule one or the other function occupies the foreground, while the rest remain undifferentiated in the background. Thus there are many people who restrict themselves to the simple perception of concrete reality, without thinking about it or taking feeling values into account. They bother just as little about the possi-

bilities hidden in a situation. I describe such people as *sensation types.* Others are exclusively oriented by what they think, and simply cannot adapt to a situation which they are unable to understand intellectually. I call such people *thinking types.* Others, again, are guided in everything entirely by feeling. They merely ask themselves whether a thing is pleasant or unpleasant, and orient themselves by their feeling impressions. These are the *feeling types.* Finally, the *intuitives* concern themselves neither with ideas nor with feeling reactions, nor yet with the reality of things, but surrender themselves wholly to the lure of possibilities, and abandon every situation in which no further possibilities can be scented.

Each of these types represents a different kind of one-sidedness, but one which is linked up with and complicated in a peculiar way by the introverted or extraverted attitude. It was because of this complication that I had to mention these function-types, and this brings us back to the question of the one-sidedness of the introverted and extraverted attitudes. This one-sidedness would lead to a complete loss of psychic balance if it were not compensated by an unconscious counterposition. Investigation of the unconscious has shown, for example, that alongside or behind the introvert's conscious attitude there is an unconscious extraverted attitude which automatically compensates his conscious one-sidedness. *Ying & Yang*

* * *

The alteration of the conscious attitude is no light matter, because any habitual attitude is essentially a more or less conscious ideal, sanctified by custom and historical tradition, and founded on the bedrock of one's innate temperament. The conscious attitude is always in the nature of a *Weltanschauung*, if it is not explicitly a religion. It is this that makes the type problem so important. The opposition between the types is not merely an external conflict between men, it is the source of endless inner conflicts; the cause not only of external disputes and dislikes, but of nervous ills and psychic suffering. It is this fact, too, that obliges us physicians constantly to widen our medical horizon and to include within it not only general

Sensation Types — go on what perceive / what is obvious — do not think about it on deeper plane.

Thinking type — if cannot understand it intellectually — about accept / like it

Precursor to Multiple intelligences

psychological standpoints but also questions concerning one's views of life and the world.

* * *

Recapitulating, I would like to stress that each of the two general attitudes, introversion and extraversion, manifests itself in a special way in an individual through the predominance of one of the four basic functions. Strictly speaking, there are no introverts and extraverts pure and simple, but only introverted and extraverted function-types, such as thinking types, sensation types, etc. There are thus at least eight clearly distinguishable types. Obviously one could increase this number at will if each of the functions were split into three subgroups, which would not be impossible empirically. One could, for example, easily divide thinking into its three well-known forms: intuitive and speculative, logical and mathematical, empirical and positivist, the last being mainly dependent on sense perception. Similar subgroups could be made of the other functions, as in the case of intuition, which has an intellectual as well as an emotional and sensory aspect. In this way a large number of types could be established, each new division becoming increasingly subtle.

For the sake of completeness, I must add that I do not regard the classification of types according to introversion and extraversion and the four basic functions as the only possible one. Any other psychological criterion could serve just as well as a classifier, although, in my view, no other possesses so great a practical significance.

8 types
Introverted thinking
Extraverted thinking
Introverted feeling
Extraverted feeling
etc...

THE DISTRUST BETWEEN THE SEXES

Karen Horney

*Like Jung, Karen Horney began her psychoanalytic career as a follower and
defender of Freud. But Horney was too much of an independent thinker to remain
anyone's disciple for long. First practicing in Germany and then in America for
most of her career, Horney invented a distinctly feminist form of psychoanalysis.
The combination of a psychoanalytic style of thinking with ideas of the sort that it
is difficult to imagine a male analyst propounding is well illustrated in the following selection.*

*The selection comes from a paper Horney delivered before the German
Women's Medical Association in 1930. Horney was ahead of her time, and
her gentle critique of and subtle revisions to conventional psychoanalytic theory
anticipated feminist objections that would be expressed over the following
decades.*

From *Feminine Psychology* (New York: Norton, 1967), pp. 104–116.

* * *

The relationship between men and women is
quite similar to that between children and
parents, in that we prefer to focus on the
positive aspects of these relationships. We prefer
to assume that love is the fundamentally given factor and that hostility is an accidental and avoid-
able occurrence. Although we are familiar with
slogans such as "the battle of the sexes" and "hostility between the sexes," we must admit that they
do not mean a great deal. They make us overfocus
on sexual relations between men and women,
which can very easily lead us to a too one-sided
view. Actually, from our recollection of numerous
case histories, we may conclude that love relationships are quite easily destroyed by overt or covert
hostility. On the other hand we are only too ready
to blame such difficulties on individual misfortune, on incompatibility of the partners, and on
social or economic causes.

The individual factors, which we find causing
poor relations between men and women, may be
the pertinent ones. However, because of the great
frequency, or better, the regular occurrence of disturbances in love relations, we have to ask ourselves whether the disturbances in the individual
cases might not arise from a common background;
whether there are common denominators for this
easily and frequently arising suspiciousness
between the sexes?

* * *

I would like to start with something very commonplace—namely, that a good deal of this atmosphere of suspiciousness is understandable and even justifiable. It apparently has nothing to do with the individual partner, but rather with the intensity of the affects and with the difficulty of taming them.

We know or may dimly sense that these affects can lead to ecstasy, to being beside oneself, to surrendering oneself, which means a leap into the unlimited and the boundless. This is perhaps why real passion is so rare. For like a good businessman, we are loath to put all our eggs in one basket. We are inclined to be reserved and ever ready to retreat. Be that as it may, because of our instinct for self-preservation, we all have a natural fear of losing ourselves in another person. That is why what happens to love, happens to education and psychoanalysis; everybody thinks he knows all about them, but few do. One is inclined to overlook how little one gives of oneself, but one feels all the more this same deficiency in the partner, the feeling of "You never really loved me." A wife who harbors suicidal thoughts because her husband does not give her all his love, time, and interest will not notice how much of her own hostility, hidden vindictiveness, and aggression are expressed through her attitude. She will feel only despair because of her abundant "love," while at the same time she will feel most intensely and see most clearly the lack of love in her partner. * * *

Here we are not dealing with pathological phenomena at all. In pathological cases we merely see a distortion and exaggeration of a general and normal occurrence. Anybody, to a certain extent, will be inclined to overlook his own hostile impulses, but under pressure of his own guilty conscience, may project them onto the partner. This process must, of necessity, cause some overt or covert distrust of the partner's love, fidelity, sincerity, or kindness. This is the reason why I prefer to speak of distrust between the sexes and not of hatred; for in keeping with our own experience we are more familiar with the feeling of distrust.

A further, almost unavoidable, source of disappointment and distrust in our normal love life derives from the fact that the very intensity of our feelings of love stirs up all of our secret expectations and longings for happiness, which slumber deep inside us. All our unconscious wishes, contradictory in their nature and expanding boundlessly on all sides, are waiting here for their fulfillment. The partner is supposed to be strong, and at the same time helpless, to dominate us and be dominated by us, to be ascetic and to be sensuous. He should rape us and be tender, have time for us exclusively and also be intensely involved in creative work. As long as we assume that he could actually fulfill all these expectations, we invest him with the glitter of sexual overestimation. We take the magnitude of such overvaluation for the measure of our love, while in reality it merely expresses the magnitude of our expectations. The very nature of our claims makes their fulfillment impossible. Herein lies the origin of the disappointments with which we may cope in a more or less effective way. Under favorable circumstances we do not even have to become aware of the great number of our disappointments, just as we have not been aware of the extent of our secret expectations. Yet there remain traces of distrust in us, as in a child who discovers that his father cannot get him the stars from the sky after all.

Thus far, our reflections certainly have been neither new nor specifically analytical and have often been better formulated in the past. The analytical approach begins with the question: What special factors in human development lead to the discrepancy between expectations and fulfillment and what causes them to be of special significance in particular cases? Let us start with a general consideration. There is a basic difference between human and animal development—namely, the long period of the infant's helplessness and dependency. The paradise of childhood is most often an illusion with which adults like to deceive themselves. For the child, however, this paradise is inhabited by too many dangerous monsters. Unpleasant experiences with the opposite sex seem to be unavoidable. We need only recall the capacity that children possess, even in their very early years, for passionate and instinctive sexual desires similar to those of adults and yet different from them. Children are different in the aims of their drives, but above all, in the pristine integrity of their demands. They find it hard to express their desires directly, and where they do, they are not taken seriously. Their seriousness sometimes is looked upon as being cute, or it may be overlooked or rejected. In short, children will undergo painful and humiliating experiences of being rebuffed, being betrayed, and being told lies. They also may have to take second place to a parent or sibling, and they are threatened and intimidated when they seek, in playing with their own bodies, those pleasures that are denied them by adults. The child is relatively powerless in the face of all this. He is not able to ventilate his fury at all, or only to a minor degree, nor can he come to grips with the experience by means of intellectual comprehension. Thus, anger and aggression are pent up within him in the form of extravagant fantasies, which hardly reach the daylight of awareness, fantasies that are criminal when viewed from the standpoint of the adult, fantasies that range from taking by force and stealing, to those about killing, burning, cutting to pieces, and choking. Since the child is vaguely aware of these destructive forces within him, he feels, according to the talion law,[1] equally threatened by the adults. Here is the origin of those infantile anxieties of which no child remains entirely free. This already enables us to understand better the fear of love of which I have spoken before. Just here, in this most irrational of all areas, the old childhood fears of a threatening father or mother are reawakened, putting us instinctively on the defensive. In other words, the fear of love will always be mixed with the fear of what we might do to the other person, or what the other person might do to us. A lover in the Aru Islands, for example, will never make a gift of a lock of hair to his beloved, because should an argument arise, the beloved might burn it, thus causing the partner to get sick.

I would like to sketch briefly how childhood conflicts may affect the relationship to the opposite

sex in later life. Let us take as an example a typical situation: The little girl who was badly hurt through some great disappointment by her father will transform her innate instinctual wish to receive from the man into a vindictive one of taking from him by force. Thus the foundation is laid for a direct line of development to a later attitude, according to which she will not only deny her maternal instincts, but will have only one drive, i.e., to harm the male, to exploit him, and to suck him dry. She has become a vampire. Let us assume that there is a similar transformation from the wish to receive to the wish to take away. Let us further assume that the latter wish was repressed due to anxiety from a guilty conscience; then we have here the fundamental constellation for the formation of a certain type of woman who is unable to relate to the male because she fears that every male will suspect her of wanting something from him. This really means that she is afraid that he might guess her repressed desires. Or by completely projecting onto him her repressed wishes, she will imagine that every male merely intends to exploit her, that he wants from her only sexual satisfaction, after which he will discard her. Or let us assume that a reaction formation of excessive modesty will mask the repressed drive for power. We then have the type of woman who shies away from demanding or accepting anything from her husband. Such a woman, however, due to the return of the repressed, will react with depression to the nonfulfillment of her unexpressed, and often unformulated, wishes. She thus unwittingly jumps from the frying pan into the fire, as does her partner, because a depression will hit him much harder than direct aggression. Quite often the repression of aggression against the male drains all her vital energy. The woman then feels helpless to meet life. She will shift the entire responsibility for her helplessness onto the man, robbing him of the very breath of life. Here you have the type of woman who, under the guise of being helpless and childlike, dominates her man.

These are examples that demonstrate how the fundamental attitude of women toward men can be disturbed by childhood conflicts. In an attempt

---

[1]The law of retaliative justice, sometimes called "an eye for an eye."

to simplify matters, I have stressed only one point, which, however, seems crucial to me—the disturbance in the development of motherhood.

I shall now proceed to trace certain traits of male psychology. I do not wish to follow individual lines of development, though it might be very instructive to observe analytically how, for instance, even men who consciously have a very positive relationship with women and hold them in high esteem as human beings, harbor deep within themselves a secret distrust of them; and how this distrust relates back to feelings toward their mothers, which they experienced in their formative years. I shall focus rather on certain typical attitudes of men toward women and how they have appeared during various eras of history and in different cultures, not only as regards sexual relationships with women, but also, and often more so, in nonsexual situations, such as in their general evaluation of women.

I shall select some random examples, starting with Adam and Eve.[2] Jewish culture, as recorded in the Old Testament, is outspokenly patriarchal. This fact reflects itself in their religion, which has no maternal goddesses; in their morals and customs, which allow the husband the right to dissolve the marital bond simply by dismissing his wife. Only by being aware of this background can we recognize the male bias in two incidents of Adam's and Eve's history. First of all, woman's capacity to give birth is partly denied and partly devaluated: Eve was made of Adam's rib and a curse was put on her to bear children in sorrow. In the second place, by interpreting her tempting Adam to eat of the tree of knowledge as a sexual temptation, woman appears as the sexual temptress, who plunges man into misery. I believe that these two elements, one born out of resentment, the other out of anxiety, have damaged the relationship between the sexes from the earliest times to the present. Let us follow this up briefly. Man's fear of woman is deeply rooted in sex, as is shown by the simple fact that it

is only the sexually attractive woman of whom he is afraid and who, although he strongly desires her, has to be kept in bondage. Old women, on the other hand, are held in high esteem, even by cultures in which the young woman is dreaded and therefore suppressed. In some primitive cultures the old woman may have the decisive voice in the affairs of the tribe; among Asian nations also she enjoys great power and prestige. On the other hand, in primitive tribes woman is surrounded by taboos during the entire period of her sexual maturity. Women of the Arunta tribe are able to magically influence the male genitals. If they sing to a blade of grass and then point it at a man or throw it at him, he becomes ill or loses his genitals altogether. Women lure him to his doom. In a certain East African tribe, husband and wife do not sleep together, because her breath might weaken him. If a woman of a South African tribe climbs over the leg of a sleeping man, he will be unable to run; hence the general rule of sexual abstinence two to five days prior to hunting, warfare, or fishing. Even greater is the fear of menstruation, pregnancy, and childbirth. Menstruating women are surrounded by extensive taboos—a man who touches a menstruating woman will die. There is one basic thought at the bottom of all this: Woman is a mysterious being who communicates with spirits and thus has magic powers that she can use to hurt the male. He must therefore protect himself against her powers by keeping her subjugated. Thus the Miri in Bengal do not permit their women to eat the flesh of the tiger, lest they become too strong. The Watawela of East Africa keep the art of making fire a secret from their women, lest women become their rulers. The Indians of California have ceremonies to keep their women in submission; a man is disguised as a devil to intimidate the women. The Arabs of Mecca exclude women from religious festivities to prevent familiarity between women and their overlords. We find similar customs during the Middle Ages—the Cult of the Virgin side by side with the burning of witches; the adoration of "pure" motherliness, completely divested of sexuality, next to the cruel destruction of the sexually seductive woman. Here

---

[2]The long paragraph that follows provides a good illustration of Horney's distinctly feminist style of psychoanalytic thinking.

again is the implication of underlying anxiety, for the witch is in communication with the devil. Nowadays, with our more humane forms of aggression, we burn women only figuratively, sometimes with undisguised hatred, sometimes with apparent friendliness. * * * In friendly and secret autos-da-fé, many nice things are said about women, but it is just unfortunate that in her God-given natural state, she is not the equal of the male. Moebius pointed out that the female brain weighs less than the male one, but the point need not be made in so crude a way. On the contrary, it can be stressed that woman is not at all inferior, only different, but that unfortunately she has fewer or none of those human or cultural qualities that man holds in such high esteem. She is said to be deeply rooted in the personal and emotional spheres, which is wonderful; but unfortunately, this makes her incapable of exercising justice and objectivity, therefore disqualifying her for positions in law and government and in the spiritual community. She is said to be at home only in the realm of eros. Spiritual matters are alien to her innermost being, and she is at odds with cultural trends. She therefore is, as Asians frankly state, a second-rate being. Woman may be industrious and useful but is, alas, incapable of productive and independent work. She is, indeed, prevented from real accomplishment by the deplorable, bloody tragedies of menstruation and childbirth. And so every man silently thanks his God, just as the pious Jew does in his prayers, that he was not created a woman.

Man's attitude toward motherhood is a large and complicated chapter. One is generally inclined to see no problem in this area. Even the misogynist is obviously willing to respect woman as a mother and to venerate her motherliness under certain conditions, as mentioned above regarding the Cult of the Virgin. In order to obtain a clearer picture, we have to distinguish between two attitudes: men's attitudes toward motherliness, as represented in its purest form in the Cult of the Virgin, and their attitude toward motherhood as such, as we encounter it in the symbolism of the ancient mother goddesses. Males will always be in favor of motherliness, as expressed in certain spiritual qualities of women, i.e., the nurturing, selfless, self-sacrificing mother; for she is the ideal embodiment of the woman who could fulfill all his expectations and longings. In the ancient mother goddesses, man did not venerate motherliness in the spiritual sense, but rather motherhood in its most elemental meaning. Mother goddesses are earthy goddesses, fertile like the soil. They bring forth new life and they nurture it. It was this life-creating power of woman, an elemental force, that filled man with admiration. And this is exactly the point where problems arise. For it is contrary to human nature to sustain appreciation without resentment toward capabilities that one does not possess. Thus, a man's minute share in creating new life became, for him, an immense incitement to create something new on his part.[3] He has created values of which he might well be proud. State, religion, art, and science are essentially his creations, and our entire culture bears the masculine imprint.

However, as happens elsewhere, so it does here; even the greatest satisfactions or achievements, if born out of sublimation,[4] cannot fully make up for something for which we are not endowed by nature. Thus there has remained an obvious residue of general resentment of men against women. This resentment expresses itself, also in our times, in men's distrustful defensive maneuvers against the threat of women's invasion of their domains; hence their tendency to devalue pregnancy and childbirth and to overemphasize male genitality. This attitude does not express itself in scientific theories alone, but is also of far-reaching consequence for the entire relationship between the sexes, and for sexual morality in general. Motherhood, especially illegitimate motherhood, is very insufficiently protected by law. * * * Conversely, there is ample opportunity for the fulfillment of the male's sexual needs. Emphasis on

---

[3]Famously, Freud thought women suffered from "penis envy." In this passage, Horney seems to claim that men suffer from womb envy.

[4]"Sublimation" is the psychoanalytic mechanism by which a motivation to do one thing is turned to another purpose.

irresponsible sexual indulgence, and devaluation of women to an object of purely physical needs, are further consequences of this masculine attitude.

* * *

I do not want to be misunderstood as having implied that all disaster results from male supremacy and that relations between the sexes would improve if women were given the ascendency. However, we must ask ourselves why there should have to be any power struggle at all between the sexes. At any given time, the more powerful side will create an ideology suitable to help maintain its position and to make this position acceptable to the weaker one. In this ideology the differentness of the weaker one will be interpreted as inferiority, and it will be proven that these differences are unchangeable, basic, or God's will.[5] It is the function of such an ideology to deny or conceal the existence of a struggle. Here is one of the answers to the question raised initially as to why we have so little awareness of the fact that there is a struggle between the sexes. It is in the interest of men to obscure this fact; and the emphasis they place on their ideologies has caused women, also, to adopt these theories. Our attempt at resolving these rationalizations and at examining these ideologies as to their fundamental driving forces, is merely a step on the road taken by Freud.

* * *

That many-faceted thing called love succeeds in building bridges from the loneliness on this shore to the loneliness on the other one. These bridges can be of great beauty, but they are rarely built for eternity and frequently they cannot tolerate too heavy a burden without collapsing. Here is the other answer to the question posed initially of why we see love between the sexes more distinctly than we see hate—because the union of the sexes offers us the greatest possibilities for happiness. We therefore are naturally inclined to overlook how powerful are the destructive forces that continually work to destroy our chances for happiness.

We might ask in conclusion, how can analytical insights contribute to diminish the distrust between the sexes? There is no uniform answer to this problem. The fear of the power of the affects and the difficulty in controlling them in a love relationship, the resulting conflict between surrender and self-preservation, between the I and the Thou, is an entirely comprehensible, unmitigatable, and as it were, normal phenomenon. The same thing applies in essence to our readiness for distrust, which stems from unresolved childhood conflicts. These childhood conflicts, however, can vary greatly in intensity, and will leave behind traces of variable depth. Analysis not only can help in individual cases to improve the relationship with the opposite sex, but it can also attempt to improve the psychological conditions of childhood and forestall excessive conflicts. This, of course, is our hope for the future. In the momentous struggle for power, analysis can fulfill an important function by uncovering the real motives of this struggle. This uncovering will not eliminate the motives, but it may help to create a better chance for fighting the struggle on its own ground instead of relegating it to peripheral issues.

---

[5]Some modern, feminist critiques of evolutionary personality theory (see Part III) are suspicious of its account of sex differences on exactly these grounds.

EIGHT STAGES OF MAN

Erik Erikson

The last of the classic neo-Freudians to be included in these readings, Erik Erikson, was not really a contemporary of Freud. His career took place across the years following Freud's death in 1939, until Erikson's own death in 1994. But Erikson became the major figure among the neo-Freudians who never broke with the master. He considered himself a loyal disciple to the end, as many passages in the following selection demonstrate.

Despite his loyalty, Erikson's theory goes into territory far outside anything Freud ever seriously considered. The theoretical development for which he is best known, described in this selection, goes beyond Freud in a specific way. Freud viewed psychosexual development as a process that occurred in infancy and early childhood, and was essentially finished shortly after the attainment of puberty. For many years developmental psychology followed the same basic presumption.

But Erikson changed all that. Of his "eight stages of man," four take place during and after the final stage of development from a traditional Freudian perspective. Erikson viewed psychological development as something that occurs throughout life, as challenges, opportunities, and obligations change. At the very last stage, one comes to terms with one's impending death and the meaning of one's life past. The outcome of this stage is crucial for the next generation. In one of his most thought-provoking comments, Erikson writes "healthy children will not fear life if their parents have integrity enough not to fear death." So the last stage of one's own development intersects with the earlier stages in one's children, and the cycle begins again.

The entire field of developmental psychology—not just the part within psychoanalysis—was changed in a profound way as Erikson's framework became widely influential. Without ever using the term, Erikson invented what is today called "life-span developmental psychology," a psychology that studies the way people develop every step of the way from the first day of their life to the last. Erikson's most lasting contribution is the reminder that development is not aimed at an end point, but is a continuing process.

From *Childhood and Society* (New York: Norton, 1950), pp. 219–234.

1. Trust vs. Basic Mistrust

The first demonstration of social trust in the baby is the ease of his feeding, the depth of his sleep, the relaxation of his bowels. The experience of a mutual regulation of his increasingly receptive capacities with the maternal techniques of provision gradually helps him to balance the discomfort caused by the immaturity of homeostasis with which he was born. In his gradually increasing waking hours he finds that more and more adventures of the senses arouse a feeling of familiarity, of having coincided with a feeling of inner goodness. Forms of comfort, and people associated with them, become as familiar as the gnawing discomfort of the bowels. The infant's first social achievement, then, is his willingness to let the mother out of sight without undue anxiety or rage, because she has become an inner certainty as well as an outer predictability. Such consistency, continuity, and sameness of experience provide a rudimentary sense of ego identity which depends, I think, on the recognition that there is an inner population of remembered and anticipated sensations and images which are firmly correlated with the outer population of familiar and predictable things and people. Smiling crowns this development.

The constant tasting and testing of the relationship between inside and outside meets its crucial test during the rages of the biting stage, when the teeth cause pain from within and when outer friends either prove of no avail or withdraw from the only action which promises relief: biting. I would assume that this experience of an urge turning upon the self has much to do with the masochistic tendency of finding cruel and cold comfort in hurting oneself whenever an object has eluded one's grasp.

Out of this, therefore, comes that primary sense of badness, that original sense of evil and malevolence which signifies the potential loss of all that is good because we could not help destroying it inside, thus driving it away outside. This feeling persists in a universal homesickness, a nostalgia for familiar images undamaged by change. Tribes dealing with one segment of nature develop a collective magic which seems to treat the Supernatural Providers of food and fortune as if they were angry and must be appeased by prayer and self-torture. Primitive religions, the most primitive layer in all religions, and the religious layer in each individual, abound with efforts at atonement which try to make up for vague deeds against a maternal matrix and try to restore faith in the goodness of one's strivings and in the kindness of the powers of the universe.

* * * The general state of trust implies not only that one has learned to rely on the sameness and continuity of the outer providers, but also that one may trust oneself and the capacity of one's own organs to cope with urges; and that one is able to consider oneself trustworthy enough so that the providers will not need to be on guard lest they be nipped.

In psychopathology the absence of basic trust can best be studied in infantile schizophrenia, while weakness of such trust is apparent in adult personalities of schizoid and depressive character. The reestablishment of a state of trust has been found to be the basic requirement for therapy in these cases. For no matter what conditions may have caused a psychotic break, the bizarreness and withdrawal in the behavior of many very sick individuals hides an attempt to reconquer social mutuality by a testing of the borderlines between senses and physical reality, between words and social meanings.

Psychoanalysis assumes the early process of differentiation between inside and outside to be the origin of the mechanisms of projection and introjection which remain some of our deepest and most dangerous defense mechanisms. In introjection we feel and act as if an outer goodness had become an inner certainty. In projection, we experience an inner harm as an outer one: we endow significant people with the evil which actually is in us. These two mechanisms, then, projection and introjection, are assumed to be modeled after whatever goes on in infants when they would like to externalize pain and internalize pleasure, an intent which must yield to the testimony of the maturing senses and ultimately of reason.

These mechanisms are, more or less normally, reinstated in acute crises of love, trust, and faith in the adult. Where they persist, they mark the "psychotic character."

The firm establishment of enduring patterns for the solution of the nuclear conflict of basic trust versus basic mistrust in mere existence is the first task of the ego, and thus first of all a task for maternal care. But let it be said here that the amount of trust derived from earliest infantile experience does not seem to depend on absolute quantities of food or demonstrations of love, but rather on the quality of the maternal relationship. Mothers, I think, create a sense of trust in their children by that kind of administration which in its quality combines sensitive care of the baby's individual needs and a firm sense of personal trustworthiness within the trusted framework of their culture's life style. This forms the basis in the child for a sense of identity which will later combine a sense of being "all right," of being oneself, and of becoming what other people trust one will become. * * *

2. Autonomy vs. Shame and Doubt

Anal-muscular maturation sets the stage for experimentation with two simultaneous sets of social modalities: holding on and letting go. As is the case with all of these modalities, their basic conflicts can lead in the end to either hostile or benign expectations and attitudes. Thus, to hold can become a destructive and cruel retaining or restraining, and it can become a pattern of care: to have and to hold. To let go, too, can turn into an inimical letting loose of destructive forces, or it can become a relaxed "to let pass" and "to let be." Culturally speaking, these attitudes are neither good nor bad; their value depends on whether their hostile implications are turned against enemy, or fellow man—or the self.

The latter danger is the one best known to us. For if denied the gradual and well-guided experience of the autonomy of free choice (or if, indeed, weakened by an initial loss of trust) the child will turn against himself all his urge to discriminate and to manipulate. He will overmanipulate himself, he will develop a precocious conscience. Instead of taking possession of things in order to test them by purposeful repetition, he will become obsessed by his own repetitiveness. By such obsessiveness, of course, he then learns to repossess the environment and to gain power by stubborn and minute control, where he could not find large-scale mutual regulation. Such hollow victory is the infantile model for a compulsion neurosis. It is also the infantile source of later attempts in adult life to govern by the letter, rather than by the spirit.

Outer control at this stage, therefore, must be firmly reassuring. The infant must come to feel that the basic faith in existence, which is the lasting treasure saved from the rages of the oral stage, will not be jeopardized by this about-face of his, this sudden violent wish to have a choice, to appropriate demandingly, and to eliminate stubbornly. Firmness must protect him against the potential anarchy of his as yet untrained sense of discrimination, his inability to hold on and to let go with discretion. As his environment encourages him to "stand on his own feet," it must protect him against meaningless and arbitrary experiences of shame and of early doubt.

Shame is an emotion insufficiently studied, because in our civilization it is so early and easily absorbed by guilt. Shame supposes that one is completely exposed and conscious of being looked at: in one word, self-conscious. One is visible and not ready to be visible; which is why we dream of shame as a situation in which we are stared at in a condition of incomplete dress, in night attire, "with one's pants down." Shame is early expressed in an impulse to bury one's face, or to sink, right then and there, into the ground. But this, I think, is essentially rage turned against the self. He who is ashamed would like to force the world not to look at him, not to notice his exposure. He would like to destroy the eyes of the world. Instead he must wish for his own invisibility. This potentiality is abundantly used in the educational method of "shaming" used so exclusively by some primitive peoples; its destructiveness is balanced in some civilizations by devices for "saving face." Visual shame precedes auditory guilt, which is a sense of badness to be had all by oneself when nobody watches and when everything is quiet—except the voice of the superego. Such shaming exploits an increasing sense of being small, which can develop only as the child stands up and as his awareness permits him to note the relative measures of size and power. * * *

Doubt is the brother of shame. Where shame is dependent on the consciousness of being upright and exposed, doubt, so clinical observation leads me to believe, has much to do with a consciousness of having a front and a back—and especially a "behind." For this reverse area of the body, with its aggressive and libidinal focus in the sphincters and in the buttocks, cannot be seen by the child, and yet it can be dominated by the will of others. The "behind" is thus the individual's dark continent, an area of the body which can be magically dominated and effectively invaded by those who would attack one's power of autonomy and who would designate as evil those products of the bowels which were felt to be all right when they were being passed. This basic sense of doubt in whatever one has left behind forms a substratum for later and more verbal forms of compulsive doubting; this finds its adult expression in paranoiac fears concerning hidden persecutors and secret persecutions threatening from behind and from within the behind.

3. Initiative vs. Guilt

The ambulatory stage and that of infantile genitality add to the inventory of basic social modalities that of "making," first in the sense of "being on the make." There is no simpler, stronger word to match the social modalities previously enumerated. The word suggests pleasure in attack and conquest. In the boy, the emphasis remains on phallic-intrusive modes; in the girl it turns to modes of "catching" in more aggressive forms of snatching and "bitchy" possessiveness, or in the milder form of making oneself attractive and endearing.

The danger of this stage is a sense of guilt over the goals contemplated and the acts initiated in one's exuberant enjoyment of new locomotor and mental power: acts of aggressive manipulation and coercion which go far beyond the executive capacity of organism and mind and therefore call for an energetic halt on one's contemplated initiative. While autonomy concentrates on keeping potential rivals out, and is therefore more an expression of jealous rage most often directed against encroachments by younger siblings, initiative brings with it anticipatory rivalry with those who have been there first and may, therefore, occupy with their superior equipment the field toward which one's initiative is directed. Jealousy and rivalry, those often embittered and yet essentially futile attempts at demarcating a sphere of unquestioned privilege, now come to a climax in a final contest for a favored position with the mother; the inevitable failure leads to resignation, guilt, and anxiety. The child indulges in fantasies of being a giant and a tiger, but in his dreams he runs in terror for dear life. This, then, is the stage of the "castration complex," the fear of losing the (now energetically eroticized) genitals as a punishment for the fantasies attached to their excitements.

Infantile sexuality and incest taboo, castration complex and superego all unite here to bring about that specifically human crisis during which the child must turn from an exclusive, pregenital attachment to his parents to the slow process of becoming a parent, a carrier of tradition. Here the most fateful split and transformation in the emotional powerhouse occurs, a split between potential human glory and potential total destruction. For here the child becomes forever divided in himself. The instinct fragments which before had enhanced the growth of his infantile body and mind now become divided into an infantile set which perpetuates the exuberance of growth potentials, and a parental set which supports and increases self-observation, self-guidance, and self-punishment.

Naturally, the parental set is at first infantile in nature: the fact that human conscience remains partially infantile throughout life is the core of human tragedy. For the superego of the child can be primitive, cruel, and uncompromising, as may be observed in instances where children overcontrol and overconstrict themselves to the point of self-obliteration; where they develop an over-obedience more literal than the one the parent has wished to exact; or where they develop deep regressions and lasting resentments because the parents themselves do not seem to live up to the new conscience which they have installed in the child. One of the deepest conflicts in life is the hate for a parent who served as the model and the executor of the superego, but who (in some form) was found trying to get away with the very transgressions which the child can no longer tolerate in himself. The suspiciousness and evasiveness which is thus mixed in with the all-or-nothing quality of the superego, this organ of tradition, makes moral (in the sense of moralistic) man a great potential danger to his own ego—and to that of his fellow men.

The problem, again, is one of mutual regulation. Where the child, now so ready to overmanipulate himself, can gradually develop a sense of paternal responsibility, where he can gain some insight into the institutions, functions, and roles which will permit his responsible participation, he will find pleasurable accomplishment in wielding tools and weapons, in manipulating meaningful toys—and in caring for younger children.

* * *

4. Industry vs. Inferiority

Before the child, psychologically already a rudimentary parent, can become a biological parent, he must begin to be a worker and potential provider. With the oncoming latency period,[1] the normally advanced child forgets, or rather sublimates, the necessity to "make" people by direct attack or to become papa and mama in a hurry: he now learns to win recognition by producing things. He has mastered the ambulatory field and the organ modes. He has experienced a sense of finality

regarding the fact that there is no workable future within the womb of his family, and thus becomes ready to apply himself to given skills and tasks, which go far beyond the mere playful expression of his organ modes or the pleasure in the function of his limbs. He develops industry—i.e., he adjusts himself to the inorganic laws of the tool world. He can become an eager and absorbed unit of a productive situation. To bring a productive situation to completion is an aim which gradually supersedes the whims and wishes of his autonomous organism. His ego boundaries include his tools and skills: the work principle teaches him the pleasure of work completion by steady attention and persevering diligence.

His danger, at this stage, lies in a sense of inadequacy and inferiority. If he despairs of his tools and skills or of his status among his tool partners, his ego boundaries suffer, and he abandons hope for the ability to identify early with others who apply themselves to the same general section of the tool world. To lose the hope of such "industrial" association leads back to the more isolated, less tool-conscious "anatomical" rivalry of the Oedipal time.[2] The child despairs of his equipment in the tool world and in anatomy, and considers himself doomed to mediocrity or mutilation. It is at this point that wider society becomes significant in its ways of admitting the child to an understanding of meaningful roles in its total economy. Many a child's development is disrupted when family life may not have prepared him for school life, or when school life may fail to sustain the promises of earlier stages.

5. Identity vs. Role Diffusion

With the establishment of a good relationship to the world of skills and tools, and with the advent of sexual maturity, childhood proper comes to an end. Youth begins. But in puberty and adolescence

---

[1]At the end of the phallic period, around age 7, Freud described children as entering a "latency period" until the beginning of puberty a few years later. During this period issues of sexual development are temporarily set aside while the child learns important skills for later life.

[2]Part of the story of the Oedipal crisis told by Freud consists of the young boy comparing the size of his genitals with that of his father's, and feeling thoroughly inferior as a result.

all samenesses and continuities relied on earlier are questioned again, because of a rapidity of body growth which equals that of early childhood and because of the entirely new addition of physical genital maturity. The growing and developing youths, faced with this physiological revolution within them, are now primarily concerned with what they appear to be in the eyes of others as compared with what they feel they are, and with the question of how to connect the roles and skills cultivated earlier with the occupational prototypes of the day. In their search for a new sense of continuity and sameness, adolescents have to refight many of the battles of earlier years, even though to do so they must artificially appoint perfectly well-meaning people to play the roles of enemies; and they are ever ready to install lasting idols and ideals as guardians of a final identity: here puberty rites "confirm" the inner design for life.

The integration now taking place in the form of ego identity is more than the sum of the childhood identifications. It is the accrued experience of the ego's ability to integrate these identifications with the vicissitudes of the libido, with the aptitudes developed out of endowment, and with the opportunities offered in social roles. The sense of ego identity, then, is the accrued confidence that the inner sameness and continuity are matched by the sameness and continuity of one's meaning for others, as evidenced in the tangible promise of a "career."

The danger of this stage is role diffusion. Where this is based on a strong previous doubt as to one's sexual identity, delinquent and outright psychotic incidents are not uncommon. If diagnosed and treated correctly, these incidents do not have the same fatal significance which they have at other ages. It is primarily the inability to settle on an occupational identity which disturbs young people. To keep themselves together they temporarily overidentify, to the point of apparent complete loss of identity, with the heroes of cliques and crowds. This initiates the stage of "falling in love," which is by no means entirely, or even primarily, a sexual matter—except where the mores demand it. To a considerable extent adolescent love is an attempt to arrive at a definition of one's identity by projecting one's diffused ego images on one another and by seeing them thus reflected and gradually clarified. This is why many a youth would rather converse, and settle matters of mutual identification, than embrace.

Puberty rites and confirmations help to integrate and to affirm the new identity. * * *

6. Intimacy vs. Isolation

It is only as young people emerge from their identity struggles that their egos can master the sixth stage, that of intimacy. What we have said about genitality now gradually comes into play. Body and ego must now be masters of the organ modes and of the nuclear conflicts, in order to be able to face the fear of ego loss in situations which call for self-abandon: in orgasms and sexual unions, in close friendships and in physical combat, in experiences of inspiration by teachers and of intuition from the recesses of the self. The avoidance of such experiences because of a fear of ego loss may lead to a deep sense of isolation and consequent self-absorption.

This, then, may be the place to complete our discussion of genitality.

For a basic orientation in the matter I shall quote what has come to me as Freud's shortest saying. It has often been claimed, and bad habits of conversation seem to sustain the claim, that psychoanalysis as a treatment attempts to convince the patient that before God and man he has only one obligation: to have good orgasms, with a fitting "object," and that regularly. This, of course, is not true. Freud was once asked what he thought a normal person should be able to do well. The questioner probably expected a complicated answer. But Freud, in the curt way of his old days, is reported to have said: "Lieben und arbeiten" (to love and to work). It pays to ponder on this simple formula; it gets deeper as you think about it. For when Freud said "love" he meant *genital* love, and genital *love*; when he said love *and* work, he meant a general work-productiveness which would not preoccupy the individual to the extent that he loses his right or capacity to be a genital and a loving being. Thus we may ponder, but we cannot improve on the formula which includes the doctor's prescription for human dignity—and for democratic living.

Genitality, then, consists in the unobstructed capacity to develop an orgastic potency so free of pregenital interferences that genital libido (not just the sex products discharged in Kinsey's "outlets"[3]) is expressed in heterosexual mutuality, with full sensitivity of both penis and vagina, and with a convulsion-like discharge of tension from the whole body. This is a rather concrete way of saying something about a process which we really do not understand. To put it more situationally: the total fact of finding, via the climactic turmoil of the orgasm, a supreme experience of the mutual regulation of two beings in some way breaks the point off the hostilities and potential rages caused by the oppositeness of male and female, of fact and fancy, of love and hate. Satisfactory sex relations thus make sex less obsessive, overcompensation less necessary, sadistic controls superfluous.

* * * The kind of mutuality in orgasm which psychoanalysis has in mind[4] is apparently easily obtained in classes and cultures which happen to make a leisurely institution of it. In more complex societies this mutuality is interfered with by so many factors of health, of tradition, of opportunity, and of temperament, that the proper formulation of sexual health would be rather this: A human being should be potentially able to accomplish mutuality of genital orgasm, but he should also be so constituted as to bear frustration in the matter without undue regression wherever considerations of reality and loyalty call for it.

* * * In order to be of lasting social significance, the utopia of genitality should include:

1. mutuality of orgasm
2. with a loved partner
3. of the other sex[5]
4. with whom one is able and willing to share a mutual trust
5. and with whom one is able and willing to regulate the cycles of
   a. work
   b. procreation
   c. recreation
6. so as to secure to the offspring, too, a satisfactory development.

It is apparent that such utopian accomplishment on a large scale cannot be an individual or, indeed, a therapeutic task. Nor is it a purely sexual matter by any means.

7. Generativity vs. Stagnation

The discussion of intimacy versus isolation has already included a further nuclear conflict which, therefore, requires only a short explicit formulation: I mean generativity versus stagnation. I apologize for creating a new and not even pleasant term. Yet neither creativity nor productivity nor any other fashionable term seems to me to convey what must be conveyed—namely, that the ability to lose oneself in the meeting of bodies and minds leads to a gradual expansion of ego interests and of libidinal cathexis over that which has been thus generated and accepted as a responsibility. Generativity is primarily the interest in establishing and guiding the next generation or whatever in a given case may become the absorbing object of a parental kind of responsibility. Where this enrichment fails, a regression from generativity to an obsessive need for pseudo intimacy, punctuated by moments of mutual repulsion, takes place, often with a pervading sense (and objective evidence) of individual stagnation and interpersonal impoverishment.

---

[3]The reference here is to Alfred Kinsey, one of the first modern sex researchers. Kinsey focused closely on the nature and meaning of literal sex acts and "outlets," a term and approach Erikson obviously found limited and even distasteful.

[4]As the ideal outcome of a sexual relationship.

---

[5]Although Erikson obviously here expresses a different view, current psychology generally does not regard homosexuality as a neurosis or psychological failure.

8. Ego Integrity vs. Despair

Only he who in some way has taken care of things and people and has adapted himself to the triumphs and disappointments adherent to being, by necessity, the originator of others and the generator of things and ideas—only he may gradually grow the fruit of these seven stages. I know no better word for it than ego integrity. Lacking a clear definition, I shall point to a few constituents of this state of mind. It is the ego's accrued assurance of its proclivity for order and meaning. It is a post-narcissistic love of the human ego—not of the self—as an experience which conveys some world order and spiritual sense, no matter how dearly paid for. It is the acceptance of one's one and only life cycle as something that had to be and that, by necessity, permitted of no substitutions; it thus means a new, a different love of one's parents. It is a comradeship with the ordering ways of distant times and different pursuits, as expressed in the simple products and sayings of such times and pursuits. Although aware of the relativity of all the various lifestyles which have given meaning to human striving, the possessor of integrity is ready to defend the dignity of his own life style against all physical and economic threats. For he knows that an individual life is the accidental coincidence of but one life cycle with but one segment of history; and that for him all human integrity stands or falls with the one style of integrity of which he partakes. The style of integrity developed by his culture or civilization thus becomes the "patrimony of his soul," the seal of his moral paternity of himself.[6] * * * Before this final solution, death loses its sting.

The lack or loss of this accrued ego integration is signified by fear of death: the one and only life cycle is not accepted as the ultimate of life. Despair expresses the feeling that the time is short, too short for the attempt to start another life and to try out alternate roads to integrity. Disgust hides despair.

Each individual, to become a mature adult, must to a sufficient degree develop all the ego qualities mentioned, so that a wise Indian, a true gentleman, and a mature peasant share and recognize in one another the final stage of integrity. But each cultural entity, to develop the particular style of integrity suggested by its historical place, utilizes a particular combination of these conflicts, along with specific provocations and prohibitions of infantile sexuality. Infantile conflicts become creative only if sustained by the firm support of cultural institutions and of the special leader classes representing them. In order to approach or experience integrity, the individual must know how to be a follower of image bearers in religion and in politics, in the economic order and in technology, in aristocratic living and in the arts and sciences. Ego integrity, therefore, implies an emotional integration which permits participation by followership as well as acceptance of the responsibility of leadership.

Webster's dictionary is kind enough to help us complete this outline in a circular fashion. Trust (the first of our ego values) is here defined as "the assured reliance on another's integrity," the last of our values. I suspect that Webster had business in mind rather than babies, credit rather than faith. But the formulation stands. And it seems possible to further paraphrase the relation of adult integrity and infantile trust by saying that healthy children will not fear life if their parents have integrity enough not to fear death.

* * * In order to indicate the whole conceptual area which is awaiting systematic treatment, I shall conclude this chapter with a diagram.[7] In this, as in the diagram of pregenital zones and modes, the diagonal represents the sequence of enduring solutions, each of which is based on the integration of the earlier ones. At any given stage of the life cycle the solution of one more nuclear conflict adds a new ego quality, a new criterion of increas-

---

[6]Erikson seemed to take this advice to heart. He never knew his father and in midlife abandoned his stepfather's name and took instead the name Erikson, as a way of claiming his own moral paternity of himself.

[7]The meaning of this diagram, reproduced in many textbooks, is not made entirely clear by Erikson. But Franz and White (1985) "fill in" the rows and columns associated with identity and intimacy, showing the heuristic power of Erikson's theory even as they seek to offer their own revision of it.

Oral Sensory	Trust vs. Mistrust						
Muscular-Anal		Autonomy vs. Shame, Doubt					
Locomotor-Genital			Initiative vs. Guilt				
Latency				Industry vs. Inferiority			
Puberty and Adolescence					Identity vs. Role Diffusion		
Young Adulthood						Intimacy vs. Isolation	
Adulthood							Generativity vs. Stagnation	
Maturity								Integrity vs. Disgust, Despair

Figure 1

ing strength. The criteria proposed in this chart are to be treated in analogy to the criteria for health and illness in general—i.e., by ascertaining whether or not there is "a pervading subjective sense of" the criterion in question, and whether or not "objective evidence of the dominance of" the criterion can be established by indirect examination (by means of depth psychology). Above the diagonal there is space for a future elaboration of the precursors of each of these solutions, all of which begin with the beginning; below the diagonal there is space for the designation of the derivatives of these solutions in the maturing and the mature personality.

Freudian Defense Mechanisms and Empirical Findings in Modern Social Psychology: Reaction Formation, Projection, Displacement, Undoing, Isolation, Sublimation, and Denial

Roy F. Baumeister, Karen Dale, and Kristin L. Sommer

In the following selection, Roy Baumeister, Karen Dale, and Kristin Sommer manage to recruit a surprising amount of contemporary research to the task of evaluating Freudian ideas. They do this by making a crucial reinterpretation of the psychoanalytic idea of the defense mechanism. Freud originally said that defense mechanisms existed to protect the ego. Baumeister and colleagues interpret the purpose of these mechanisms as the defense of self-esteem. This narrows the focus of the defense mechanisms because a psychoanalyst would surely believe that their purpose is to defend against anxiety, and a threat to self-esteem is just one among many things that might cause a person anxiety. However, this narrowing of focus makes a huge amount of literature suddenly relevant; nearly everything published on the self—thousands of studies—is pertinent to psychological defense.

From *Journal of Personality*, 66, 1081–1124, 1998.

Nearly all adults hold preferred views of themselves. In most cases, these are favorable views of self—indeed, somewhat more favorable than the objective facts would entirely warrant, as nearly all writers on the self have observed. A recurrent problem of human functioning, therefore, is how to sustain these favorable views of self. Patterns of self-deception can help create these inflated self-perceptions (for reviews, see Baumeister, 1998; Gilovich, 1991; Taylor, 1989). Yet a particular crisis in self-perception may arise when an internal or external event occurs that clearly violates the preferred view of self. In such cases, it is necessary for the self to have some mechanism or process to defend itself against the threatening implications of this event. Such processes are commonly called *defense mechanisms* (e.g., Cramer, 1991; A. Freud, 1936).

Sigmund Freud proposed a set of defense mechanisms, in a body of work that has long been influential (e.g., S. Freud, 1915/1961a, 1923/1961b, 1926/1961c). His work focused on how the ego defended itself against internal events, specifically, impulses that were regarded by the ego as unacceptable. He emphasized sexual or aggressive desires that would violate the ego's internalized standards, such as if those desires were directed toward one's parents. In his view, the efforts by the self to avoid recognizing its own sexual and aggressive desires were systematically important in shaping the personality.

Modern personality and social psychology has not generally accepted the view that personality is heavily based on efforts to disguise one's sexual and aggressive impulses. Nonetheless, the need for defense mechanisms remains quite strong. A revisionist idea, proposed by Fenichel (1945), is that defense mechanisms are actually designed to protect self-esteem. This reformulation is far more in keeping with current work in social and personality psychology than Freud's original view was. One can search long and hard through today's research journals without finding much evidence about how human behavior reflects attempts to ward off sexual and violent feelings, but evidence about efforts to protect self-esteem is abundant.

Ultimately, the view that defense mechanisms are oriented toward protecting self-esteem may not contradict Freud's views so much as it merely changes his emphasis. Acknowledging that one possessed socially unacceptable impulses of sex or violence may have constituted a self-esteem threat for the Victorian middle-class adults he studied. Today's adults are presumably less afraid of having sexual or violent feelings, and indeed the absence of sexual interest may constitute an esteem threat to some modern citizens—in which case their defense mechanisms would ironically try to increase the self-perceived frequency or power of sexual impulses, contrary to the Freudian pattern.

Most researchers in personality and social psychology today would readily acknowledge that people defend their self-concepts against esteem threats. Yet relatively few researchers have made explicit efforts to relate their findings about defensive processes to the general theory of defense mechanisms. The purpose of the present article is to review research findings from personality and social psychology that can be interpreted as reflecting the major defense mechanisms that Freud proposed. In a sense, then, this review will ask how Freud's list of insights stacks up against today's experimental work.

How much should one expect? Obviously, any accuracy at all would be impressive. Few researchers today would feel confident about having dozens of their theoretical hypotheses tested many decades into the future by empirical techniques that they today could not even imagine.

To anticipate the conclusion, we found substantial support for many (but not all) of the processes of defense Freud outlined. There are also some aspects to the causal process that Freud does not appear to have anticipated, as one would naturally expect. We shall describe a series of the major defense mechanisms and conclude that some of his ideas were correct, some require minor or major revision, and others have found little support. All in all, this amounts to a rather impressive positive testimony to Freud's seminal theorizing.

Plan and Task

* * *

We have chosen to emphasize defenses that are arguably most relevant to normal (as opposed to clinical) human functioning. The list is as follows: reaction formation, projection, displacement, * * * and denial.[1]

With each defense mechanism, we shall first ask whether research evidence shows that it actually occurs. The strength and generality of this evidence must also be considered. If the defense mechanism is supported in some sense, then we must ask what the cognitive, affective, and behavioral processes are. A related question is whether there is evidence of defensive motivation, as opposed to evidence of some merely cognitive error or bias. To qualify as a full-fledged defense, it must do more than merely make people feel better: It must actually ward off some threat to the self.

---

[1]The original article also addressed three other defense mechanisms: undoing, isolation, and sublimation.

Purely conscious maneuvers are not generally considered full-fledged defense mechanisms. Like self-deception generally, defense mechanisms must involve some motivated strategy that is not consciously recognized, resulting in a desirable conclusion or favorable view of self that is conscious.

Review of Findings

In this section, we shall examine * * * major defense mechanisms in turn. The review will try to ascertain how well each defense mechanism is supported in modern research in personality and social psychology and what theoretical adjustments may be required to make the theory fit modern findings.

* * *

REACTION FORMATION

Concept. The concept of reaction formation involves converting a socially unacceptable impulse into its opposite. To apply this notion to esteem protection, one may propose the following: People respond to the implication that they have some unacceptable trait by behaving in a way that would show them to have the opposite trait. Insinuations of hostility or intolerance might, for example, be countered with exaggerated efforts to prove oneself a peace-loving or tolerant person.

Evidence. The original ideas about reaction formation pertained to aggressive and sexual impulses, and these are still plausible places for finding defenses, provided that acknowledging those impulses or feelings would damage self-esteem. With sex, there are undoubtedly still cases in which people regard their own potential sexual responses as unacceptable.

One such finding was provided by Morokoff (1985), who exposed female subjects to erotic stimuli after assessing sex guilt. Women high in sex guilt would presumably regard erotica as unacceptable, and consistent with this attitude they reported lower levels of arousal in response to those stimuli. Physiological measures suggested,

however, that these women actually had higher sexual arousal than other participants. The contradiction between the genital response and the self-report findings suggests that these women subjectively repudiated their physical sexual arousal and insisted that they were not aroused.

A comparable finding with male subjects was recently reported by Adams, Wright, and Lohr (1996). They assessed homophobia and then exposed participants to videotapes depicting homosexual intercourse. Homophobic men reported low levels of sexual arousal, but physiological measures indicated higher levels of sexual response than were found among other participants. Thus, again, the subjective response reported by these participants was the opposite of what their bodies actually indicated. This finding also fits the view that homophobia may itself be a reaction formation against homosexual tendencies, insofar as the men who were most aroused by homosexuality were the ones who expressed the most negative attitudes toward it.

Prejudice would provide the most relevant form of unacceptable aggressive impulse, because American society has widely endorsed strong norms condemning prejudice. If people are led to believe that they may hold unacceptably prejudiced beliefs (or even that others perceive them as being prejudiced), they may respond with exaggerated displays of not being prejudiced.

An early and convincing demonstration of reaction formation (although it was not called that) against prejudice was provided by Dutton and Lake (1973; see also Dutton, 1976). Nonprejudiced, egalitarian, White individuals were provided with false physiological feedback allegedly indicating that they held racist prejudices against Blacks. In one study, for example, they were shown slides of interracial couples, and the experimenter commented that the subject's skin response indicated severe intolerance of interracial romance, which was tantamount to racism. After the procedure was ostensibly completed, the participant left the building and was accosted by either a Black or a White panhandler. People who had been implicitly accused of racism gave significantly more money to the Black panhandler than people who had not been threatened in that way. Donations to the White panhandler were unaffected by the racism feedback. The implication was that people became generous toward the Black individual as a way of counteracting the insinuation that they were prejudiced against Blacks.

* * *

There is a related set of findings in which White subjects show preferential favorability toward Black stimulus persons without any threat. One might argue that White people often feel threatened by the possibility of seeming racist when interacting with Black people. Rogers and Prentice-Dunn (1981) found that White subjects playing the role of teacher administered fewer shocks to a Black than to a White confederate in the role of learner, although the effect was reversed if the learner had previously insulted them. Johnson, Whitestone, Jackson, and Gatto (1995) showed that White subjects as simulated jurors gave lighter sentences to Black than to White defendants, although this effect was reversed when a more severe sentence to the Black man could be defended on nonracial grounds. Shaffer and Case (1982) found that heterosexual simulated jurors gave lighter sentences to a homosexual defendant than to a heterosexual one, although this effect was found only among people who scored low in dogmatism.

Whether these effects constitute reaction formation is not entirely clear. Biernat, Manis, and Nelson (1991) provided evidence that people may use different standards when judging minority targets as opposed to judging members of the majority category. For example, a Black candidate for law school might be judged more favorably than a White candidate with identical credentials if the judges use more lenient criteria for Blacks. (Then again, the use of more lenient criteria might itself qualify as a reaction formation, insofar as it is a strategy to defend against one's own prejudice.)

* * *

Reaction formation may also be involved when self-appraisals paradoxically rise in response to negative feedback. McFarlin and Blascovich (1981) showed that people with high self-esteem made more optimistic predictions for future performance following initial failure than following initial success. Baumeister, Heatherton, and Tice (1993) showed this confidence to be irrational and unwarranted, and also showed it to be sufficiently powerful to motivate costly monetary bets. These responses do appear defensive and irrational, for there is no obvious reason that confidence should be increased by an initial failure experience.

Last, some evidence suggests a loose pattern of increasing favorable self-ratings in response to receiving bad (instead of good) personality feedback. Baumeister and Jones (1978) found enhanced self-ratings in response to bad feedback that was seen by other people, although the increased favorability was found only on items unrelated to the content of the feedback, indicating a compensatory mechanism rather than a pure reaction formation. Baumeister (1982b) provided evidence that people with high self-esteem were mainly responsible for the effect. Greenberg and Pyszczynski (1985) showed that this inflation of self-ratings occurred even on private ratings, although again mainly in response to public feedback. They pointed out that public bad feedback constitutes a stronger threat than private feedback. * * *

Conclusion. Plenty of research findings conform to the broad pattern of reaction formation, defined loosely as a means of defending against esteem threat by exhibiting an exaggerated or extreme reaction in the opposite direction. Although the mechanism underlying reaction formation may not conform precisely to Freud's model, the human phenomena he characterized with that term do appear to be real. In particular, when people are publicly or implicitly accused of having socially undesirable sexual feelings, prejudiced attitudes, or failures of competence, some respond by asserting the opposite (and attempting to prove it) to an exceptionally high degree.

The consistency of these results across seemingly quite different spheres of esteem threat suggests that reaction formation deserves acceptance in social and personality psychology. Apparently it is one of the more prominent and common responses to esteem threat.

Still, the causal process underlying reaction formation remains to be elaborated. Many of the findings may be merely self-presentational strategies designed to correct another person's misperception rather than a genuinely intrapsychic defense mechanism. Moreover, if reaction formation can be firmly established as an intrapsychic response, it would be desirable to know how it operates. How, for example, does someone manage to feel sexually turned off when his or her body is exhibiting a strong positive arousal? How do people come to convince themselves that the money they give to a Black panhandler reflects a genuine attitude of racial tolerance rather than a response to the specific accusation of racism they recently received—especially when, as the researchers can show, those people would not have given nearly as much money to the same panhandler if they had not been accused of racism?

PROJECTION

Concept. Projection is a popular concept in everyday discourse as well as in psychological thought. In its simplest form, it refers to seeing one's own traits in other people. A more rigorous understanding involves perceiving others as having traits that one inaccurately believes oneself not to have. As a broad form of influence of self-concept on person perception, projection may be regarded as more a cognitive bias than a defense mechanism. Nonetheless, projection *can* be seen as defensive if perceiving the threatening trait in others helps the individual in some way to avoid recognizing it in himself or herself, and indeed this is how Freud (e.g., 1915/1961a) conceptualized projection. Thus, there are multiple ways of understanding projection, and they vary mainly along the dimension of how effectively the undesirable trait or motive is repudiated as part of the self.

Evidence. The simpler, more loosely defined version of projection is fairly well documented. The *false consensus effect*, first described by Ross,

Greene, and House (1977), is probably the best-known form of this, insofar as it is a broad tendency to assume that others are similar to oneself. The false consensus effect is defined as overestimating the percentage of other people who share one's traits, opinions, preferences, or motivations. This effect has both cognitive and motivational influences (Krueger & Clement, 1994; Marks, Graham, & Hansen, 1992; Sherman, Presson, & Chassin, 1984); is found if anything more with positive, desirable traits than with bad traits (Davis, Conklin, Smith, & Luce 1996; Halpern & Goldschmitt, 1976; Lambert & Wedell, 1991; Paulhus & Reynolds, 1995); has been especially shown with competitiveness (Kelley & Stahelski, 1970a, 1970b) and jealousy (Pines & Aronson, 1983); and is linked to higher self-esteem and lower depression (Campbell, 1986; Crocker, Alloy, & Kayne, 1988). Some contrary patterns have been found, especially insofar as people wish to regard their good traits and abilities as unusual (Dunning & Cohen, 1992; Suls & Wan, 1987). In general, these findings show that people like to see themselves as similar to others, but the evidence does not show this to be a defense mechanism that helps people avoid recognizing their own bad traits.

It could be argued that the false consensus effect achieves a kind of defensive success insofar as it reduces the distinctiveness of one's bad traits. To be the only person who cheats on taxes or breaks the speed limit would imply that one is uniquely immoral, even evil—but if everyone else is likewise breaking those laws, one's own actions can hardly be condemned with great force. Consistent with this, Sherwood (1981) concluded that attributing one's undesirable traits to targets who are perceived favorably can reduce stress. This explanation could also fit Bramel's (1962, 1963) demonstration that males who were told they had homosexual tendencies were later more likely to interpret other males' behavior as having similar tendencies. Likewise, it may explain the findings of Agostinelli, Sherman, Presson, and Chassin (1992): Receiving bogus failure feedback on a problem-solving task made people (except depressed people) more likely to predict that others would fail too.

None of these findings links seeing the trait in others to denying it in oneself, and so they fall short of the more rigorous definition of projection. Given the failure to show that projective responses can function to conceal one's own bad traits, Holmes (1968, 1978, 1981) concluded that defensive projection should be regarded as a myth. In retrospect, it was never clear how seeing another person as dishonest (for example) would enable the individual to avoid recognizing his or her own dishonesty. The notion that projection would effectively mask one's own bad traits was perhaps incoherent.

Recognizing the implausibility in the classical concept of projection, Newman, Duff, and Baumeister (1997) proposed a new model of defensive projection. In this view, people try to suppress thoughts of their undesirable traits, and these efforts make those trait categories highly accessible—so that they are then used all the more often when forming impressions of others (see Wegner, 1994; Wegner & Erber, 1992). In a series of studies, Newman et al. showed that repressors (as defined by Weinberger, Schwartz, & Davidson, 1979) were more likely than others to deny having certain bad traits, even though their acquaintances said they did have those bad traits. Repressors were then also more likely to interpret the ambiguous behaviors of others as reflecting those bad traits. Thus, they both denied their own faults and overinterpreted other people as having those faults.

The view that suppressing thoughts about one's undesirable traits leads to projection was then tested experimentally by Newman et al. (1997). Participants were given bogus feedback based on a personality test, to the effect that they had both good and bad traits. They were then instructed to avoid thinking about one dimension on which they had received (bad) feedback. Next, they observed a videotape of a stimulus person and rated that person on all the dimensions on which they had received feedback. Participants rated the stimulus person about the same on all dimensions, except that they rated her higher on the trait for which they had received bad feedback and been instructed to suppress. They did not rate the stim-

ulus person higher on traits for which they had received bad feedback without trying to suppress it. Thus, projection results from trying to suppress thoughts about some bad trait in oneself.

Conclusion. Considerable evidence indicates that people's conceptions of themselves shape their perceptions of other people. The tendency to see others as having one's own traits has limitations and is found with good traits along with bad ones. The view that people defensively project specific bad traits of their own onto others as a means of denying that they have them is not well supported. The concept of projection thus needs to be revised in order to fit modern research findings.

The view of projection as a defense mechanism is best supported by the findings of Newman et al. (1997), but even these deviate from the classic psychodynamic theory of projection. Newman et al. found that efforts to suppress thoughts about a particular bad trait made this trait into a highly accessible category that thereafter shaped the perception of others. In this view, the projecting of the trait onto other people is a by-product of the defense, rather than being central to the defensive strategy. To put this another way: In the original Freudian view, seeing the bad trait in another person is the essential means of avoiding seeing it in oneself. In Newman et al.'s view, however, the defense is simply a matter of trying not to recognize one's bad trait, and the success of that effort is not related to whether a suitable target for projection presents himself or herself.

This mechanism could well account for the observations that might have led Freud to postulate the defense mechanism of projection in the first place. After all, the person does refuse at some level to accept some fault in himself or herself and does, as a result, end up seeing other people as having that same fault. The Freudian view implied the transfer of the schema from one's self-concept directly into the impression of the other person. It may, however, be more accurate to see the effect on impression formation as simply a consequence of heightened accessibility resulting from efforts at suppression.

DISPLACEMENT

Concept. Displacement refers to altering the target of an impulse. For example, an unacceptable violent impulse toward one's father might be transformed into a hostile attitude toward policemen or other authority figures. The targets of the actual aggression would be related by meaningful associations to the target of the original, inhibited impulse.

Evidence. Several studies have directly examined displacement of aggression. In a study by Hokanson, Burgess, and Cohen (1963), subjects were frustrated (or not) by the experimenter and then given an opportunity to aggress against the experimenter, the experimenter's assistant, a psychology student, or no one. The experiment yielded a marginal main effect for frustration, insofar as frustrated subjects were more aggressive than others, but the target made no difference. Measurements of systolic blood pressure did, however, suggest that tension levels among frustrated subjects dropped most when they aggressed against the experimenter, followed by the assistant, followed by the psychology major. Thus, the level of aggression remained the same whether it was aimed at the original target, at a relevant displaced target, or at an irrelevant target, but there was some physiological evidence suggesting that aggressing against the original target (or a closely linked one) was most satisfying.

The possibility of displaced aggression was also investigated by Fenigstein and Buss (1974). In this study, the instigator was not the experimenter, thereby removing alternative explanations based on the experimenter–subject relationship. Angered and nonangered subjects were given an opportunity to aggress either toward the instigator directly or toward a friend of his. As in the Hokanson et al. (1963) study, anger produced a main effect on aggression, but there were no differences in aggressive behavior as a function of target.

These findings can be interpreted in various ways. One might point to them as evidence for the high efficacy of displacement, given that people are equally aggressive toward other people as toward the person who has provoked them—suggesting, in other words, that the full amount of aggression can be displaced readily.

On the other hand, they could be interpreted as mere mood or arousal effects: People who are angry are more aggressive in general. Indeed, Miller (1948) showed similar effects with rats (e.g., attacking a dummy doll when the original enemy, another rat, is absent), and it is difficult to assert that rats have defense mechanisms. Meanwhile, there is ample evidence that arousal can carry over from one situation to another. Research by Zillman and his colleagues has shown *excitation transfer* effects, in which arousal from one situation can carry over into another and influence aggressive behavior. Riding a stationary bicycle boosts arousal while not being either especially pleasant or unpleasant, but people who ride a bicycle are then subsequently more aggressive in response to a provocation than people who have not just exercised (Zillman, Katcher, & Milavsky, 1972), and indeed highly aroused subjects will ignore mitigating circumstances when someone provokes them, unlike moderately aroused people who will tone down their aggressive responses when they learn of the same mitigating facts (Zillman, Bryant, Cantor, & Day, 1975). Arousal that is caused by watching exciting films can likewise increase aggressive responses to provocation, even though the arousal itself has no relation to the provocation (Cantor, Zillmann, & Einsiedel, 1978; Ramirez, Bryant, & Zillman, 1982; Zillman, 1971).

To complicate matters further, recent work has not confirmed displacement. Bushman and Baumeister (1998) studied aggressive responses to an ego threat as a function of narcissism. Narcissists became more aggressive toward someone who had insulted them, but neither narcissists nor nonnarcissists showed any increased aggression toward a third person. This study was specifically designed to examine displaced aggression and failed to find any sign of it.

Scapegoating has been regarded as one instance of displaced aggression. In this view, people may become angry or hostile toward one target but are required for whatever reasons to avoid aggressing, and so they redirect their aggression toward a safer target. A classic paper by Hovland and Sears (1940) showed that the frequency of lynchings in the American South was negatively correlated with cotton prices. When prices dropped, according to the scapegoat interpretation, farmers suffered material deprivation, frustration, and hostility, and they redirected their hostility toward relatively safe targets in the form of Black men accused of crimes. Hepworth and West (1988) reexamined those data with more modern statistical techniques and confirmed the relationship.

Such evidence of scapegoating does not, however, embody a pure instance of displacement. The original hostility may not have had a specific target; rather, the cotton farmers may have been generally distraught. Recent work by Esses and Zanna (1995) offered an alternative explanation in terms of mood-congruent stereotypes. They showed that bad moods induced by musical stimuli (hence having no esteem threat) caused negative stereotypes to become more accessible. This accessibility might explain the southern farmers' willingness to react violently to alleged misdeeds by Black citizens, without postulating that the violence was borrowed from another source or impulse.

In principle, unacceptable sexual or other impulses should also be amenable to displacement. Mann, Berkowitz, Sidman, Starr, and West (1974) exposed long-married couples to pornographic movies and found that this exposure led to an increased likelihood of marital intercourse on that same evening. This could be interpreted as displacement of sexual desire from the inaccessible movie star onto the socially acceptable target of one's mate. Unfortunately, however, this effect is likewise amenable to alternative explanations based simply on a generalized arousal response.

Conclusion. Despite the intuitive appeal of the concept of displacement, research has not provided much in the way of clear evidence for it. The handful of findings that do suggest displacement are susceptible to alternative explanations such as general tendencies for arousal or bad moods to facilitate aggression.

Some might contend that the arousal or mood effects should not be considered alternative explanations but rather can be subsumed under a looser conception of displacement. If Harry gets angry at his boss for criticizing him, and because of this anger Harry later gets into a fight with a stranger whom he normally might have ignored, should this qualify as displacement? It is, however, in no sense the same impulse that is displaced onto a new target. Whether he had inhibited his anger against his boss or expressed it might make no difference. Given that artificial mood or arousal inductions, even including the arousal from riding a bicycle, can produce the same readiness to respond aggressively to a new provocation, it seems misleading to speak of such an effect as displacement.

More to the point, there is no evidence that such arousal or mood effects serve a defensive function. Displacement would only qualify as a defense mechanism if the original, unacceptable impulse were prevented from causing some damage to self-esteem (or having some similar effect, such as stimulating anxiety). There is no evidence of any such effect.

The concept of displacement seems to be based on the now largely discredited catharsis model, according to which people have a well-defined quantity of aggressive impulses that require expression in one sphere or another. If aggression (or sexual desire, for that matter) cannot be expressed toward its original target, it must be redirected toward another, in this view. Meanwhile, of course, if it could be expressed toward the original target, there would be no displacement. Both effects seem highly implausible in light of what is now known about aggression. More likely, a person who is aggressive in one situation would be more, not less, aggressive in a subsequent one.

* * *

DENIAL

Concept. Freudian conceptions of denial embrace everything from a rare, almost psychotic refusal to perceive the physical facts of the immediate environment, to the common reluctance to accept the implications of some event (e.g., Laplanche & Pontalis, 1973). The distinction between denial and repression is sometimes blurred and difficult to articulate in a meaningful fashion (Cramer, 1991). For the present, it is sufficient to consider denial as the simple refusal to face certain facts. Insofar as these facts are highly upsetting or represent potential damage to self-esteem, denial can in principle be a very useful defense mechanism.

Denial can be understood very narrowly or quite broadly. Broad definitions encompass an assortment of other defenses. Cramer (1991) subsumes perceptual defenses, constructing personal fantasies, negation, minimizing, maximizing, ridicule, and reversal as forms of denial. Paulhus, Fridhandler, and Hayes (1997) suggested that previous theoretical works were sufficient to distinguish at least seven different kinds of denial. If such a broad view proves correct, it may be more appropriate to regard denial as a category of defense mechanisms than as a single defense.

Evidence. Personality and social psychologists have not provided much evidence that people systematically refuse to accept the physical reality of actual events, especially when confronted with palpable proof. (They are of course willing to be skeptical of rumors or other reports that lack credibility and that attest to disagreeable events.) On the other hand, there is abundant evidence that people will reject implications and interpretations that they find threatening.

Probably the most common form of denial involves dismissive responses to failure or other bad feedback. When people receive negative evaluations, they often reject the implications rather than incorporating them into their self-concepts. Making external attributions for failure, such as by pointing to bad luck or task difficulty, is one common and well-documented pattern of denying the implications of failure, because it insists that the failure does not reflect any lack of ability or of other good traits on the part of the self. Zuckerman (1979) reviewed 38 studies to confirm a general pattern that people make more external attributions for failure than for success.

A variation on the response of external attribution is to find faults or flaws in whatever method of evaluation led to one's bad feedback. Several studies have shown that students believe a test to be invalid or unfair when they perform poorly on it, whereas the same test will be regarded more favorably if their feedback is positive (Pyszczynski, Greenberg, & Holt, 1985; Schlenker, Weigold, & Hallam, 1990; Wyer & Frey, 1983; see also Kunda, 1990). Kernis, Cornell, Sun, Berry, and Harlow (1993) found this to be especially common among people with unstable high self-esteem, suggesting that it is an appealing mode of defense to people who especially need to shore up a fragile sense of personal superiority.

Another variation is to dismiss bad feedback as motivated by prejudice. Crocker, Voelkl, Testa, and Major (1991) measured self-esteem among African American subjects who had received negative feedback from a White evaluator. Self-esteem decreased in response to the criticism if the subject believed the evaluator to be unaware of his race. But if the subject thought the evaluator did know his race, then the evaluation had no effect on self-esteem. In the latter case, subjects attributed the bad evaluation to racist prejudice and therefore denied its validity, so it did not affect their self-esteem.

Researchers in health psychology have provided some findings that parallel the ones about threats to self-esteem. The notion that people use denial in response to health-related threats can be traced back at least to Kübler-Ross's (1969) listing of denial as one "stage" or type of response to learning that one's illness will be fatal. Recent work has demonstrated some mechanisms of denial with less extreme threats. Croyle and Hunt (1991) showed that people minimize risks, specifically reducing their level of personal concern over a threatening test result if a confederate made a minimizing comment ("It doesn't seem like a big deal to me"; p. 384). Ditto and Lopez (1992) showed that people selectively questioned the validity of a test when it produced an unfavorable result. Liberman and Chaiken (1992) showed that caffeine users tended to criticize (selectively) and dismiss evidence of a link between caffeine consumption and fibrocystic disease, whereas nonusers showed no such bias.

A quite different sphere in which to find evidence of denial is people's projections about their personal futures. Weinstein (1980) demonstrated that people tend to be unrealistically optimistic, and subsequent work has confirmed that pattern repeatedly (see Taylor & Brown, 1988, for a review). That is, on average people think they are less likely than the average person to suffer various misfortunes, such as career failure, debilitating illness, or accidental crippling. Perloff and Fetzer (1986) coined the term "the illusion of unique invulnerability" to refer to the average person's sense that bad things will not happen to him or her. By definition, the average person cannot be below average in the likelihood of experiencing such misfortunes, so the subjective perceptions must be based in some sense on a denial of the actual likelihood of such events.

The illusion of unique invulnerability does not remain an abstract or vague surmise. Burger and Burns (1988) linked it to sexual risk-taking, as in unprotected promiscuous sexual intercourse. It is well established that sexually transmitted diseases can be serious and even fatal and that they can be prevented by condom use, but people's sense of personal invulnerability leads them to neglect such precautions. In such cases, denying risks makes people take more extreme ones.

Potentially maladaptive consequences of denial were also shown by Carver and Scheier (1994). In a longitudinal study, they measured stress and coping responses before an exam, right after the exam, and later when grades were posted. Various forms of denial were evident at all times, but none was effective overall at reducing negative emotions. Dispositional denial, evident particularly among people who used denial prior to the exam, led to greater feelings of threat and harm. Carver et al. (1993) found that denial predicted greater distress among breast cancer patients. A review by Suls and Fletcher (1985) concluded that avoidance responses such as denial promote positive outcomes in the short run but are inferior to other coping strategies in the long run.

Although denial may undermine some potentially adaptive responses, it may be quite adaptive in other circumstances. We have already noted that denial of personal responsibility for failure tends to be associated with high self-esteem. Indeed, much of the impact of works by Alloy and Abramson (1979) and Taylor and Brown (1988) came from their conclusion that mental health and high self-esteem were associated with biased processing patterns that denied personal responsibility for bad outcomes while taking credit for good outcomes. Low self-esteem and depression were associated with the more even-handed approach of accepting responsibility equally for both positive and negative outcomes.

Such links are essentially correlational, but they could possibly mean that denial contributes (presumably as a successful defense mechanism) to mental health and high self-esteem. Recent work by Forgas (1994) suggests the opposite causal direction, however. Forgas induced sad and happy moods experimentally, by having people read passages with a strong affective tone, and then he investigated their attributions for relationship conflicts. Sad people blamed themselves more than happy people, who attributed conflict to the situation or to the partner. Apparently happy moods foster denial while sad moods undermine it. An optimal defense mechanism would presumably show the opposite pattern.

Janoff-Bulman (1992) suggested that denial may be especially adaptive following trauma, because it allows the reinterpretation process to proceed piecemeal. After suffering a serious personal trauma such as an accident or victimization, there is often little that the person can do, and so denial does not prevent adaptive responses. Meanwhile, the task of coping with the trauma involves restoring one's positive conceptions of self and world. In Janoff-Bulman's view, one starts by denying the trauma in general, and then the denial drops away piece by piece, allowing the person to begin the task of rebuilding those positive conceptions, as opposed to having to find some new interpretations all at once.

Although we have emphasized the more elaborate forms of denial, such as discrediting sources of criticism, there is some evidence for the more elementary forms as well. Lipp, Kolstoe, James, and Randall (1968) defined perceptual defense operationally in terms of the difference in minimal recognition time for nonthreatening pictures as opposed to threatening ones. The threatening ones in their study were pictures of people who were disabled. Subjects in the study included disabled and nondisabled people. The researchers found that disabled people showed greater perceptual defense: that is, they took relatively longer to recognize tachistoscopically presented slides of disabled people. The authors interpreted this as evidence of denial. To be sure, it was hardly a successful defense mechanism in this case, because all it accomplished was delaying the recognition by a fraction of a second. Still, it suggests that some people do have defenses that work to minimize the recognition of threatening stimuli.

Perceptual denial may be difficult, but memory may be far more amenable to denial. Crary (1966) showed that people protected their self-esteem by not remembering failures. Kuiper and Derry (1982) showed that nondepressed people recalled favorable adjectives pertaining to self better than unfavorable ones. Mischel, Ebbesen, and Zeiss (1976) found that people recalled feedback about their good traits better than feedback about their faults and shortcomings. Whether these effects reflect biased encoding, biased recall, or both is unclear. Baumeister and Cairns (1992) showed that repressors tend to minimize the encoding of bad feedback, but it is plausible that additional biases operate on recall processes. In any case, the memory processes seem quite up to the task of selectively denying disagreeable information.

The heterogeneity of findings on denial suggests that a more differentiated conceptual framework may be useful. Baumeister and Newman (1994) reviewed the ways in which people try to alter and direct their cognitive processes, and in particular they distinguished between regulating the collection of evidence versus regulating the interpretive meaning assigned to the evidence. Most of what we have reviewed here pertains to the latter (interpretation) stage, such as denying the pos-sible implications. More evidence is needed about whether (and how) people prevent disagreeable evidence from entering into the conscious decision process.

Conclusion. The concept of denial encompasses a variety of possible defenses, and it may eventually become desirable on theoretical grounds for the concept to be replaced by several more specific and particular mechanisms. This may be particularly desirable insofar as the various mechanisms are not all equally well documented. Still, for the present, it is fair to say that denial is a genuine and efficacious defense mechanism.

The most stringent definition of denial involves the failure of sensory perception to recognize physical stimuli associated with threat. Restricted to this definition, denial is not a common or successful defense mechanism. There is some evidence of perceptual defense, but it seems to involve slight delays rather than an effective misperception of threat. It is possible that such processes occur among the mentally ill, but researchers in personality and social psychology have found little evidence of perceptual denial in the normal population.

There is, however, ample evidence of other forms of denial. People dispute or minimize information that threatens their self-esteem, and they reject its implications. They discount bad feedback about their health. They dismiss various risks and dangers and sometimes act as if they were personally invulnerable. They selectively forget material that is disagreeable or esteem-threatening. Some patterns have been linked to high self-esteem, adjustment, and happiness, which is consistent with the view that denial can be an effective defense, although some questions remain about how denial actually operates and whether it actually functions to defend self-esteem.

General Discussion

* * *

REVISING DEFENSE MECHANISM THEORY The present review has identified several key challenges for the theory of the defense mechanisms. One concerns the extremity of the response. We noted for several defense mechanisms (* * * [e.g.], denial) that pure, severe forms of the defense had not been documented in the normal population whereas weaker versions were well supported. It is plausible that the extreme forms (e.g., being physically unable to see a person who represents a threat) would occur among the mentally ill.

* * *

Another key issue is whether defense mechanisms involve intrapsychic maneuvers or interpersonal, self-presentational strategies. Freud's theories pertained mainly to the former, but many research findings used explicitly interpersonal settings. In our view, it would be justified to speak of defense mechanisms in both cases, because the logic would be similar. For example, donating money to someone of a different race may counter the accusation of racism regardless of whether the origin of that accusation is internal or external. Furthermore, it is well established that there are important links between public self and private self, so that convincing others of one's good traits may be an important step toward convincing oneself (e.g., Baumeister, 1982a, 1986; Haight, 1980; Schlenker, 1980; Tice, 1992; Wicklund & Gollwitzer, 1982). In any case, further work would benefit from attending to evidence of any systematic differences between defense mechanisms that operate at the interpersonal level and those that operate intrapsychically.

Meanwhile, the change from an energy model to a cognitive model as the basic framework for defense mechanism theory appears to be underway. It is probably no accident that the * * * least well-supported defense mechanism in our survey (displacement * * *) * * * [was] also the one most tied to a model based on instinctual energy—while the more cognitive defenses, such as denial, * * * and projection, fared much better. Clearly, shifting the emphasis from unacceptable impulses to self-esteem threats has implications beyond the nature of the threat: Self-esteem threats are more easily rendered in cognitive terms, while the transformation of unacceptable impulses is inherently more closely tied to energy models. Modern theories about the self tend to be heavily cognitive and not at all energy-based, and defense mechanism theory may have to adjust similarly. Thus, the thrust of our review suggests that defense mechanism theory may need to shift its emphasis from impulse transformation to cognitive and behavioral rejection.

The nature of threat is perhaps the undesirable image of self rather than the impulse itself. The nature of defense is therefore to refute or otherwise reject an undesirable view of self. Such a characterization fits the defenses that fared best in this review (reaction formation, * * * denial). It also encompasses other defenses that were not necessarily on Freud's list. It is far beyond the scope of this article to suggest what further defense mechanisms might exist, but while doing this review we did certainly find plenty of evidence of various self-esteem maintenance strategies that did not correspond directly to our list of Freudian defense mechanisms. Future work may make a valuable contribution by listing, taxonomizing, and providing a conceptual framework for all these defenses.

CONCLUDING REMARKS It is impressive to consider how well modern findings in social psychology, mostly obtained in systematic laboratory experiments with well-adjusted American university students, have confirmed the wisdom of Freud's theories, which were mostly based on informal observations of mentally afflicted Europeans nearly a century ago. Not only were several of the defense mechanisms well supported, but in other cases the basic behavioral observations appear to have been sound and only the underlying causal process needs revision.

To be sure, social psychologists have not always given Freud full credit for his insights. Many of the findings covered in this literature review made no reference to defense mechanism theory or to Freud's work. The phenomena Freud described have in some cases been relabeled or rediscovered under the aegis of social cognition or other current theoretical frameworks. Some of these cases may be attributable to career pressures to come up with novel ideas, but others may reflect the fact that researchers working with new ideas and problems are led back to defensive patterns resembling what Freud discussed. The latter cases suggest the pervasive and fundamental importance of defense mechanisms, insofar as Freudian observations and modern socially psychological experimentation converge in producing evidence for the same phenomena.

Our review has suggested that some specific psychoanalytic concepts of defense should be tentatively discarded and some other views need serious revision. More generally, we have suggested that defense mechanism theory may need to downplay its original focus on impulse transformations and instead focus more directly on how possible images of self are protected and rejected. Regardless of these changes, our review provides a solid endorsement of the fundamental insight that human life in civilized society powerfully motivates people to cultivate a set of cognitive and behavioral strategies in order to defend their preferred views of self against threatening events.

References

Adams, H. E., Wright, L. W., & Lohr, B. A. (1996). Is homophobia associated with homosexual arousal? *Journal of Abnormal Psychology, 105,* 440–445.

Agostinelli, G., Sherman, S. J., Presson, C. C., & Chassin, L. (1992). Self-protection and self-enhancement biases in estimates of population prevalence. *Personality and Social Psychology Bulletin, 18,* 631–642.

Alloy, L. B., & Abramson, L. Y. (1979). Judgment of contingency in depressed and nondepressed students: Sadder but wiser? *Journal of Experimental Psychology: General, 108,* 441–485.

Baumeister, R. F. (1982a). A self-presentational view of social phenomena. *Psychological Bulletin, 91,* 3–26.

Baumeister, R. F. (1982b). Self-esteem, self-presentation, and future interaction: A dilemma of reputation. *Journal of Personality, 50,* 29–45.

Baumeister, R. F. (Ed.). (1986). *Public self and private self.* New York: Springer-Verlag.

Baumeister, R. F. (1998). The self. In D. T. Gilbert, S. T. Fiske, & G. Lindzey (Eds.), *Handbook of social psychology* (4th ed., pp. 680–740). New York: McGraw-Hill.

Baumeister, R. F., & Cairns, K. J. (1992). Repression and self-presentation: When audiences interfere with self-deceptive strategies. *Journal of Personality and Social Psychology, 62,* 851–862.

Baumeister, R. F., Heatherton, T. F., & Tice, D. M. (1993). When ego threats lead to self-regulation failure: The negative consequences of high self-esteem. *Journal of Personality and Social Psychology, 64,* 141–156.

Baumeister, R. F., & Jones, E. E. (1978). When self-presentation is constrained by the target's knowledge: Consistency and compensation. *Journal of Personality and Social Psychology, 36,* 608–618.

Baumeister, R. F., & Newman, L. S. (1994). Self-regulation of cognitive inference and decision processes. *Personality and Social Psychology Bulletin, 20,* 3–19.

Biernat, M., Manis, M., & Nelson, T. E. (1991). Stereotypes and standards of judgment. *Journal of Personality and Social Psychology, 60,* 485–499.

Bramel, D. (1962). A dissonance theory approach to defensive projection. *Journal of Abnormal and Social Psychology, 64,* 121–129.

Bramel, D. (1963). Selection of a target for defensive projection. *Journal of Abnormal and Social Psychology, 66,* 318–324.

Burger, J. M., & Burns, L. (1988). The illusion of unique invulnerability and the use of effective contraception. *Personality and Social Psychology Bulletin, 14,* 264–270.

Bushman, B., & Baumeister, R. F. (1998). Threatened egotism, narcissism, self-esteem, and direct and displaced aggression: Does self-love or self-hate lead to violence? *Journal of Personality and Social Psychology, 75,* 219–229.

Campbell, J. D. (1986). Similarity and uniqueness: The effects of attribute type, relevance, and individual differences in self-esteem and depression. *Journal of Personality and Social Psychology, 50,* 281–294.

Cantor, J. R., Zillman, D., & Einsiedel, E. G. (1978). Female responses to provocation after exposure to aggressive and erotic films. *Communication Research, 5,* 395–411.

Carver, C. S., Pozo, C., Harris, S. D., Noriega, V., Scheier, M. F., Robinson, D. S., Ketcham, A. S., Moffat, F. L., Jr., & Clark, K. C. (1993). How coping mediates the effect of optimism on distress: A study of women with early stage breast cancer. *Journal of Personality and Social Psychology, 65,* 375–390.

Carver, C. S., & Scheier, M. F. (1994). Situational coping and coping dispositions in a stressful transaction. *Journal of Personality and Social Psychology, 66,* 184–195.

Cramer, P. (1991). *The development of defense mechanisms.* New York: Springer-Verlag.

Crary, W. G. (1966). Reactions to incongruent self-experiences. *Journal of Consulting Psychology, 30,* 246–252.

Crocker, J., Alloy, L. B., & Kayne, N. T. (1988). Attributional style, depression, and perceptions of consensus for events. *Journal of Personality and Social Psychology, 54,* 840–846.

Crocker, J., Voelkl, K., Testa, M., & Major, B. (1991). Social stigma: The affective consequences of attributional ambiguity. *Journal of Personality and Social Psychology, 60,* 218–228.

Croyle, R. T., & Hunt, J. R. (1991). Coping with health threat: Social influence processes in reactions to medical test results. *Journal of Personality and Social Psychology, 60,* 382–389.

Davis, M. H., Conklin, L., Smith, A., & Luce, C. (1996). Effects of perspective taking on the cognitive representation of persons: A merging of self and other. *Journal of Personality and Social Psychology, 70,* 713–726.

Ditto, P. H., & Lopez, D. F. (1992). Motivated skepticism: Use of differential decision criteria for preferred and nonpreferred conclusions. *Journal of Personality and Social Psychology, 63,* 568–584.

Dunning, D., & Cohen, G. L. (1992). Egocentric definitions of traits and abilities in social judgment. *Journal of Personality and Social Psychology, 63,* 341–355.

Dutton, D. G. (1976). Tokenism, reverse discrimination, and egalitarianism in interracial behavior. *Journal of Social Issues, 32,* 93–107.

Dutton, D. G., & Lake, R. A. (1973). Threat of own prejudice and reverse discrimination in interracial situations. *Journal of Personality and Social Psychology, 28,* 94–100.

Esses, V. M., & Zanna, M. P. (1995). Mood and the expression of ethnic stereotypes. *Journal of Personality and Social Psychology, 69*, 1052–1068.

Fenichel, O. (1945). *The psychoanalytic theory of neurosis.* New York: Norton.

Fenigstein, A., & Buss, A. H. (1974). Association and affect as determinants of displaced aggression. *Journal of Research in Personality, 7*, 306–313.

Forgas, P. (1994). Sad and guilty? Affective influences on the explanation of conflict in close relationships. *Journal of Personality and Social Psychology, 66*, 56–68.

Freud, A. (1936). *The ego and the mechanisms of defense.* New York: Hogarth Press.

Freud, S. (1961a). Instincts and their vicissitudes. In J. Strachey (Ed. and Trans.), *The standard edition of the complete works of Sigmund Freud* (Vol. 14, pp. 111–142). London: Hogarth Press. (Original work published in 1915.)

Freud, S. (1961b). The ego and the id. In J. Strachey (Ed. and Trans.), *The standard edition of the complete works of Sigmund Freud* (Vol. 19, pp. 12–66). London: Hogarth Press. (Original work published in 1923.)

Freud, S. (1961c). Inhibitions, symptoms, and anxiety. In J. Strachey (Ed. and Trans.), *The standard edition of the complete works of Sigmund Freud* (Vol. 20, pp. 77–178). London: Hogarth Press. (Original work published in 1926.)

Gilovich, T. (1991). *How we know what isn't so: The fallibility of human reason in everyday life.* New York: Free Press.

Greenberg, J., & Pyszczynski, J. (1985). Compensatory self-inflation: A response to the threat to self-regard of public failure. *Journal of Personality and Social Psychology, 49*, 273–280.

Haight, M. R. (1980). *A study of self-deception.* Atlantic Highlands, NJ: Humanities Press.

Halpern, J., & Goldschmitt, M. (1976). Attributive projection: Test of defensive hypotheses. *Perceptual and Motor Skills, 42*, 707–711.

Hepworth, J. T., & West, S. G. (1988). Lynchings and the economy: A time-series reanalysis of Hofland and Sears (1940). *Journal of Personality and Social Psychology, 55*, 239–247.

Hokanson, J. E., Burgess, M., & Cohen, M. F. (1963). Effects of displaced aggression on systolic blood pressure. *Journal of Abnormal and Social Psychology, 67*, 214–218.

Holmes, D. S. (1968). Dimensions of projection. *Psychological Bulletin, 69*, 248–268.

Holmes, D. S. (1978). Projection as a defense mechanism. *Psychological Bulletin, 85*, 677–688.

Holmes, D. S. (1981). Existence of classical projection and the stress-reducing function of attributive projection: A reply to Sherwood. *Psychological Bulletin, 90*, 460–466.

Hovland, C. I., & Sears, R. (1940). Minor studies of aggression: Correlation of lynchings with economic indices. *Journal of Psychology, 9*, 301–310.

Janoff-Bulman, R. (1992). *Shattered assumptions: Towards a new psychology of trauma.* New York: Free Press.

Johnson, J. D., Whitestone, E., Jackson, L. A., & Gatto, L. (1995). Justice is still not colorblind: Differential racial effects of exposure to inadmissible evidence. *Personality and Social Psychology Bulletin, 21*, 893–898.

Kelley, H. H., & Stahelski, A. J. (1970a). Errors in perception of intentions in a mixed motive game. *Journal of Experimental Social Psychology, 6*, 379–400.

Kelley, H. H., & Stahelski, A. J. (1970b). Social interaction basis

of cooperators and competitors' beliefs about others. *Journal of Personality and Social Psychology, 16*, 66–91.

Kernis, M. H., Cornell, D. P., Sun, C-R., Berry, A., & Harlow, T. (1993). There's more to self-esteem whether it's high or low: The importance of stability of self-esteem. *Journal of Personality and Social Psychology, 65*, 1190–1204.

Krueger, J., & Clement, R. W. (1994). The truly false consensus effect: An ineradicable and egocentric bias in social perception. *Journal of Personality and Social Psychology, 67*, 596–610.

Kübler-Ross, E. (1969). *On death and dying.* New York: Macmillan.

Kuiper, N. A., & Derry, P. A. (1982). Depressed and nondepressed content self-reference in mild depression. *Journal of Personality, 50*, 67–79.

Kunda, Z. (1990). The case for motivated reasoning. *Psychological Bulletin, 108*, 480–498.

Lambert, A. J., & Weddell, D. H. (1991). The self and social judgment: Effects of affective reaction and "own position" on judgments of unambiguous and ambiguous information about others. *Journal of Personality and Social Psychology, 61*, 884–897.

Laplanche, J., & Pontalis, J.-B. (1973). *The language of psychoanalysis* (D. Nicholson-Smith, Trans.). New York: Norton.

Liberman, A., & Chaiken, S. (1992). Defensive processing of personally relevant health messages. *Personality and Social Psychology Bulletin, 18*, 669–679.

Lipp, L., Kolstoe, R., James, W., & Randall, H. (1968). Denial of disability and internal control of reinforcement: A study using a perceptual defense paradigm. *Journal of Consulting and Clinical Psychology, 32*, 72–75.

Mann, J., Berkowitz, L., Sidman, J., Starr, S., & West, S. (1974). Satiation of the transient stimulating effect of erotic films. *Journal of Personality and Social Psychology, 30*, 729–735.

Marks, G., Graham, J. W., & Hansen, W. B. (1992). Social projection and social conformity in adolescent alcohol use: A longitudinal analysis. *Personality and Social Psychology Bulletin, 18*, 96–107.

McFarlin, D. B., & Blascovich, J. (1981). Effects of self-esteem and performance feedback on future affective preferences and cognitive expectations. *Journal of Personality and Social Psychology, 40*, 521–531.

Miller, N. E. (1948). Theory and experiment relating psychoanalytic displacement to stimulus-response generalization. *Journal of Abnormal and Social Psychology, 43*, 155–178.

Mischel, W., Ebbesen, E. B., & Zeiss, A. R. (1976). Determinants of selective memory about the self. *Journal of Consulting and Clinical Psychology, 44*, 92–103.

Morokoff, P. J. (1985). Effects of sex guilt, repression, sexual "arousability," and sexual experience on female sexual arousal during erotica and fantasy. *Journal of Personality and Social Psychology, 49*, 177–187.

Newman, L. S., Duff, K., & Baumeister, R. F. (1997). A new look at defensive projection: Suppression, accessibility, and biased person perception. *Journal of Personality and Social Psychology, 72*, 980–1001.

Paulhus, D. L., Fridhandler, B., & Hayes, S. (1997). Psychological defense: Contemporary theory and research. In R. Hogan & J. Johnson (Eds.), *Handbook of personality psychology* (pp. 543–579). San Diego, CA: Academic Press.

Paulhus, D. L., & Reynolds, S. (1995). Enhancing target variance in personality impressions: Highlighting the person in person perception. *Journal of Personality and Social Psychology, 69,* 1233–1242.

Perloff, L. S., & Fetzer, B. K. (1986). Self-other judgments and perceived vulnerability to victimization. *Journal of Personality and Social Psychology, 50,* 502–510.

Pines, M., & Aronson, E. (1983). Antecedents, correlates, and consequences of sexual jealousy. *Journal of Personality, 51,* 108–135.

Pyszczynski, T., Greenberg, J., & Holt, K. (1985). Maintaining consistency between self-serving beliefs and available data: A bias in information processing. *Personality and Social Psychology Bulletin, 11,* 179–190.

Ramirez, J., Bryant, J., & Zillman, D. (1982). Effects of erotica on retaliatory behavior as a function of level of prior provocation. *Journal of Personality and Social Psychology, 43,* 971–978.

Rogers, R. W., & Prentice-Dunn, S. (1981). Deindividuation and anger-mediated interracial aggression: Unmasking regressive racism. *Journal of Personality and Social Psychology, 41,* 63–73.

Ross, L., Greene, D., & House, P. (1977). The "false consensus effect": An egocentric bias in social perception and attribution processes. *Journal of Experimental Social Psychology, 13,* 279–301.

Schlenker, B. R. (1980). *Impression management: The self-concept, social identity, and interpersonal relations.* Monterey, CA: Brooks/Cole.

Schlenker, B. R., Weigold, M. F., & Hallam, J. R. (1990). Self-serving attributions in social context: Effects of self-esteem and social pressure. *Journal of Personality and Social Psychology, 58,* 855–863.

Shaffer, D. R., & Case, T. (1982). On the decision to testify in one's own behalf: Effects of withheld evidence, defendant's sexual preferences, and juror dogmatism on juridic decisions. *Journal of Personality and Social Psychology, 42,* 335–346.

Sherman, S. J., Presson, C. C., & Chassin, L. (1984). Mechanisms underlying the false consensus effect: The special role of threats to the self. *Personality and Social Psychology Bulletin, 10,* 127–138.

Sherwood, G. G. (1981). Self-serving biases in person perception: A reexamination of projection as a mechanism of defense. *Psychological Bulletin, 90,* 445–459.

Suls, J., & Fletcher, B. (1985). The relative efficacy of avoidant and nonavoidant coping strategies: A meta-analysis. *Health Psychology, 4,* 249–288.

Suls, J., & Wan, C. K. (1987). In search of the false-uniqueness phenomenon: Fear and estimates of social consensus. *Journal of Personality and Social Psychology, 52,* 211–217.

Taylor, S. E. (1989). *Positive illusions: Creative self-deception and the healthy mind.* New York: Basic Books.

Taylor, S. E., & Brown, J. D. (1988). Illusion and well-being: A social psychological perspective on mental health. *Psychological Bulletin, 103,* 193–210.

Tice, D. M. (1992). Self-presentation and self-concept change: The looking glass self as magnifying glass. *Journal of Personality and Social Psychology, 63,* 435–451.

Wegner, D. M. (1994). Ironic processes of mental control. *Psychological Review, 101,* 34–52.

Wegner, D. M., & Erber, R. (1992). The hyperaccessibility of supressed thoughts. *Journal of Personality and Social Psychology, 63,* 903–912.

Weinberger, D. A., Schwartz, G. E., & Davidson, R. J. (1979). Low-anxious, high-anxious, and repressive coping styles: Psychometric patterns and behavioral and physiological responses to stress. *Journal of Abnormal Psychology, 88,* 369–380.

Weinstein, N. D. (1980). Unrealistic optimism about future life events. *Journal of Personality and Social Psychology, 39,* 806–820.

Wicklund, R. A., & Gollwitzer, P. M. (1982). *Symbolic self-completion.* Hillsdale, NJ: Erlbaum.

Wyer, R. S., & Frey, D. (1983). The effects of feedback about self and others on the recall and judgments of feedback-relevant information. *Journal of Experimental Social Psychology, 19,* 540–559.

Zillmann, D. (1971). Excitation transfer in communication-mediated aggressive behavior. *Journal of Experimental Social Psychology, 7,* 419–434.

Zillmann, D., Bryant, J., Cantor, J. R., & Day, K. D. (1975). Irrelevance of mitigating circumstances in retaliatory behavior at high levels of excitation. *Journal of Research in Personality, 9,* 286–306.

Zillman, D., Katcher, A. H., & Milavsky, B. (1972). Excitation transfer from physical exercise to subsequent aggressive behavior. *Journal of Experimental Social Psychology, 8,* 247–259.

Zuckerman, M. (1979). Attribution of success and failure revisited; or, The motivational bias is alive and well in attribution theory. *Journal of Personality, 47,* 245–287.

WOMB ENVY, TESTYRIA, AND BREAST CASTRATION ANXIETY: WHAT IF FREUD WERE FEMALE?

Gloria Steinem

Over the century since its introduction, both psychoanalysis and Freud personally have been the subject of numerous criticisms. Freud has been pilloried for being a plagiarist, liar, and sexist. His theory has been denounced as immoral, dirty, unscientific, and politically incorrect. During his lifetime Freud complained about the criticism he received, but also seemed to revel in it somewhat (Gay, 1988). He expected his theory to upset people. In fact, Freud believed that because psychoanalysis exposes essential but uncomfortable truths, it should upset people.

It is astonishing to see how often modern critics attack psychoanalysis by attacking Freud himself. The underlying assumption seems to be that if Freud was a scoundrel, then his theory must be wrong. (It is tempting to wonder if this very unscientific style of argument is at all related to modern trends in political reporting, where the desperate race to uncover "scandal" in politicians' lives increasingly pushes out analysis of the policies they pursue.)

Other, more legitimate criticisms of Freud have some degree of merit. For example, there is no question that the empirical base of psychoanalytic theory would not be considered even marginally sufficient for a new theory today. Freud based his theory on introspection and his experience with patients; he reported very little that would today be considered "data." Modern research, such as seen in the preceding selection, only begins to rectify this shortcoming. But other kinds of information besides controlled research—such as the degree to which therapists and people in general have found the theory useful over the years—may also be relevant.

The most difficult charge from which to defend Freud and psychoanalysis is that of sexism. Unlike so many other areas of his thought, Freud's view of women seems to have been influenced by the conventional attitudes of his time. As a result, some of his ideas appear strange by contemporary standards. Freud thought women experienced "penis envy," and in general seemed to describe men as normal humans, and women as damaged men.

In the final selection in this section, the prominent feminist writer Gloria Steinem (writing in Ms. *magazine) attacks without mercy Freud's most vulnerable point. She invents a fictitious psychoanalyst named Dr. Phyllis Freud. The Madame Doctor expounds a famous theory that takes everything psychoanalysis says about women, and says it about men instead. Steinem appends footnotes to this paper* documenting some astonishing statements about women uttered by psychoanalysts over the years. Steinem's article also demonstrates the continuing truth of an aspect of Freud's theory that he expected, and even seemed to relish, from the beginning—psychoanalysis makes people mad.*

Freud will perhaps always be a controversial figure, and psychoanalysis is a highly imperfect creation. It is a challenging task to balance what the theory has to offer with the things that are clearly wrong about it. Similarly, when reading pieces such as the one that follows, it is difficult to separate out serious criticisms from outspoken indignation. And it is worth pondering just what it is about psychoanalysis that makes it still worth attacking, again and again, more than half a century after its founder's death.

From "Womb Envy, Testyria, and Breast Castration Anxiety: What If Freud Were Female?" by G. Steinem (1994). In *Ms.*, 49–56. Adapted with permission.

To sense the difference between *what is* and *what could be*, we may badly need the "Aha!" that comes from exchanging subject for object; the flash of recognition that starts with a smile. I've grown to have a lot of faith in this technique of reversal. It not only produces empathy, but it's a great detector of bias, in ourselves as well as in others. In fact, the deeper the bias, the more helpful it is to make a similar statement about the other gender—or a different race, class, sexuality, physical ability, whatever—and see how it sounds.

* * *

In pursuit of the reasons why Sigmund Freud is still with us, and, most important, how it feels to be on the wrong side of his ubiquitous presence, I propose that male human beings in general, as well as everyone in the psychological trade, male or female, imagine themselves on the receiving end of a profession—indeed, a popular culture—suffused with the work and worship of one of the most enduring, influential, and fiercely defended thinkers in Western civilization: Dr. Phyllis Freud.

You will come to know her here through the words of her biographer, a scholar who is a little defensive because of criticisms of Freud, but still starstruck, and very sure of being right—in other words, a typical Freudian. Every detail of Phyllis' biography springs from Sigmund's, with only first names, pronouns, and anything else related to gender changed in order to create a gender-reversed world.

As in so much of life, the fun is in the text, but the truth is in the footnotes. Read both.

> It's important to understand that when little Phyllis was growing up in Vienna in the mid-1800s, women were considered superior because of their ability to give birth. This belief in female superiority was so easily mistaken for an immutable fact of life that conditions like *womb envy* had become endemic among males.[1]

---

*All footnotes are by the author (Gloria Steinem) and appeared in the original.

[1] Modern Freudians *still* won't give up on penis envy. In 1981, *Freud and Women*, by Lucy Freeman and Dr. Herbert S. Strean (Continuum), contained this typical de-

Indeed, the belief in women's natural right to dominate was the very foundation of matriarchal Western civilization. At the drop of a hat, wise women would explain that, while men might dabble in the arts, they could never become truly *great* painters, sculptors, musicians, poets, or anything else that demanded creativity, for they lacked the womb, which was the very source of creativity. Similarly, since men had only odd, castrated breasts that created no sustenance, they might become adequate family cooks, but certainly they could never become great chefs, vintners, herbalists, nutritionists, or anything else that required a flair for food, a knowledge of nutrition, or a natural instinct for gustatory nuance. And because childbirth caused women to use the health care system more than men did, making childbirth its natural focus,[2] there was little point in encouraging young men to become physicians, surgeons, researchers, or anything other than low-paid health care helpers.

Even designing their own clothes was left to men only at the risk of unfortunate results. When allowed to dress themselves, they could never get beyond the envy of wombs and female genitals that condemned them to an endless repetition of female sexual symbolism. Thus, the open button-to-neck "V" of men's jackets was a recapitulation of the "V" of female genitalia; the knot in men's ties replicated the clitoris while the long ends of the tie took the shape of labia; and men's bow ties were

the clitoris *erecta* in all its glory. They were, to use Phyllis Freud's technical term, "representations."[3]

In addition, men's lack of firsthand experience with birth and nonbirth—with choosing between conception and contraception, existence and nonexistence, as women did so wisely for all their fertile years—also reduced any sense of justice and ethics they might develop.[4] This tended to disqualify them as philosophers, whose very purview was the question of existence versus nonexistence plus all the calibrations in between. Certainly, it also lessened men's ability to make life-and-death judgments, which explained—and perhaps still does—their absence from decision-making positions in the law, law enforcement, the military, or other such professions.

After life-giving wombs and sustenance-giving breasts, women's ability to menstruate was the most obvious proof of their superiority. Only women could bleed without injury or death; only they rose from the gore each month like a phoenix; only their bodies were in tune with the ululations of the universe and the timing of the tides. Without this innate lunar cycle, how could men have a sense of time, tides, space, seasons, the movement of the universe, or the ability to measure anything at all? How could men mistress that skills of measurement for mathematics, engineering, architecture, surveying—and many other fields? In Christian churches, how could males serve the Daughter of the Goddess with no monthly evidence of Her

---

fense: "Contemporary psychoanalysts . . . agree penis envy is a universal fantasy of little girls at the age of four, [but . . .] if a little girl's emotional needs are understood by a loving mother and protective father, the normal fantasies of penis envy that occur during her phallic stage of sexual development will be accepted, then suppressed . . . and she will be able to love a man not for the physical attribute which, as a little girl, she envied and unconsciously wished to possess, but out of her feelings for him as a total person. She will want him not as a possessor of the desired phallus, but as mate and father of her child. In Freud's words, her original wish for a penis has changed into the wish for a baby."—Author

[2]Actually, this is true—women do use the health care system about 30 percent more than men do—but you'd never know it from who's in charge. Logic is in the eye of the logician.—Author

[3]Here are Freeman and Strean: "In her unconscious envy of the penis, many a woman adorns herself with feathers, sequins, furs, glistening silver and gold ornaments that 'hang down'—what psychoanalysts call 'representations' of the penis." I rest my case.—Author

[4]At the age of 76, with all the wisdom of his career to guide him, Freud wrote: "We also regard women as weaker in their social interests and as having less capacity for sublimating their instincts than men." His assumption that women were incapable of reaching the highest stage of ethical development—which was, in masculinist thought, the subordination of the individual to an abstract principle—became the foundation of the field of ethics. For an antidote, see Carol Gilligan's *In a Different Voice* (Harvard University Press). —Author

death and resurrection? In Judaism, how could they honor the Matriarchal God without the symbol of Her sacrifices recorded in the Old Ovariment? Thus insensible to the movements of the planets and the turning of the universe, how could men become astronomers, naturalists, scientists—or much of anything at all?[5]

It was simply accepted for males to be homemakers, ornaments, devoted sons, and sexual companions (providing they were well trained, of course, for, though abortion was well accepted, it was painful and to be avoided, and a careless impregnation could be punished by imprisonment).[6]

Once Phyllis Freud got into brilliant theorizing that went far beyond her training as a nineteenth-century neurologist, however, her greatest impact was to come not from phrases like *womb envy* and *anatomy is destiny*. No, those truths were already part of the culture. It was her interest in and treatment of *testyria*, a disease marked by uncontrollable fits of emotion and mysterious physical symptoms so peculiar to males that most experts assumed the condition to be related to the testicles. Though testyrical males were often thought to be

perverse, pretending, or otherwise untreatable, some treatments had been devised. They ranged from simple water cures, bed rest, mild electric shock, or, for the well-to-do, trips to a spa, to circumcision, the removal of the testicles, cauterization of the penis, and other remedies that may seem draconisn now, but were sometimes successful in subduing testyrical fits, and, in any case, were a product of their times.[7] In Paris, Phyllis Freud had also been among the hundreds of women who assembled in lecture halls to see demonstrations of hypnosis—a new technique for treating these mysterious symptoms by reaching into the unconscious—on male testyrics brought in for the purpose.

In fact, that sight had coalesced in Freud's mind with a case of testyria she had heard about in Vienna. A neurologist colleague, Dr. Josephine Breuer, had discussed her progress in relieving testyrical symptoms by encouraging a patient to explore the memories of earlier painful experiences with which the symptoms seemed associated—first with the aid of hypnosis, later by just talking them out through free association. Actually, this method had been improvised and named the "talking cure" by the young patient in question, Bert Pappenheim.

When Freud began her practice in the study of her Vienna apartment, hypnosis and Pappenheim's "talking cure" combined in her courageous focus on testyria. The symptoms she saw included depression, hallucinations, and a whole array of ailments, from paralysis, incapacitating headaches, chronic vomiting and coughing, and difficulty in swallowing, to full-scale testyrical fits, imitative pregnancies, and self-injury that included "couvade," or slitting the skin of the penis—an extreme

---

[5]As another antidote to antimenstruation bias, try this argument: Since in women's "difficult" days before the onset of the menstrual period, the female hormone is at its lowest ebb, women are in those few days the most like what men are like *all month long.*—Author

[6]Yes, abortion was punishable by imprisonment at that time, and yes, the other reversals are also true. Descriptions of the era's sexism have been used to make Sigmund's attitude toward women seem understandable, even enlightened. Ignoring the many advances of his day flattens the ground around him to make him look taller. Here are a few other realities: George Sand was born a half century before Freud, and was one of many women who managed to live a life more free and unconventional than Freud could imagine even for himself. U.S. suffragists had issued the Declaration of Sentiments at Seneca Falls eight years before Freud was born. Throughout his formative years, Austrian suffragists, socialists, and reformers were working on every area of women's social and political rights—as were their counterparts in other countries. And there was an active movement in Austria for homosexual rights at the turn of the century.—Author

[7]For from-the-horse's-mouth documents of the period on the sadistic treatment of female patients—from electrical shocks to clitoridectomy and other sex-related surgeries—see Jeffrey Moussaieff Masson's *A Dark Science: Women, Sexuality, and Psychiatry in the Nineteenth Century* (Farrar, Straus & Giroux). For this tradition as adapted in the Freudian era, see Phyllis Chesler's *Women and Madness* (Harcourt Brace Jovanovich). —Author

form of womb and menstruation envy that was an imitation of female functions.[8]

Even as Freud worked first with hypnosis, then more and more with psychoanalysis (for she had honored Pappenheim's "talking cure" with that new and scientific name), she theorized about what might be the cause. Because testyria was particularly common among men in their teens and twenties, she surmised that homemaking, child-rearing, sexual service, sperm production, and other parts of men's natural sphere had not yet yielded their mature satisfactions. Since some young men were also indulging in the dangerous practice of masturbation, they were subject to severe neurosis and sexual dysfunction per se. Among older and more rebellious or intellectual men, there was also the problem of being too womb-envying to attract a mate. Finally, there were those husbands who were married to women who had no regard for their sexual satisfaction; who, for example, practiced coitus interruptus either as a form of contraception, or from simple disregard.[9]

Extreme gratitude from her patients was understandable. Not only was Phyllis Freud the rare woman who listened to men, but she took what they said seriously and made it the subject of her own brilliant theories, even of science. This advanced attitude joins other evidence in exposing the gratuitous hostility of masculinists who accuse Freud of androphobia.[10] As a young woman, Phyllis had even translated into German Harriet Taylor Mill's *The Emancipation of Men*, a tract on male equality that a less enlightened woman would never have read.[11] Later, she supported the idea that men could also become psychoanalysts—provided, of course, they subscribed to Freudian theory, just as any female analyst would do. (Certainly, Freud would not have approved of the current school of equality that demands "men's history" and other special treatment.)

I'm sure that if you read carefully each of Freud's case histories, you will see the true depth of her understanding for the opposite sex.[12]

Freud wisely screened all she heard from testyrical men through her understanding, well accepted to this day, that men are sexually passive, just as they are intellectually and ethically. The libido was intrinsically feminine, or, as she put it with her genius for laywoman's terms, "man possesses a weaker sexual instinct."

This was proved by man's mono-orgasmic nature. No serious authority disputed the fact that females, being multiorgasmic, were well adapted to pleasure, and thus were the natural sexual aggressors; in fact, "envelopment," the legal term for intercourse, was an expression of this active/passive understanding.[13] It was also acted out in microcosm in the act of conception itself. Think about

---

[8]I couldn't resist *couvade*, a pregnancy-imitating ritual among men in tribal cultures where pregnancy and birth are worshiped. Women are made out to be the "naturally" masochistic ones in patriarchal cultures, but doesn't slitting the penis sound pretty masochistic to you?

In the case of Freud and his colleagues, however, the self-cutting and other mutilations they were seeing in their practices were probably what has now been traced to real events of sexual and other sadistic abuse in childhood: females (and males when they are similarly abused) repeat what was done to them, punishing the body that "attracted" or "deserved" such abuse, and anesthetizing themselves against pain, just as they were forced to do in the past.—Author

[9]Interesting—this one works both ways. Since "coitus interruptus" could be defined as an "interruptus" by whichever half of the pair has finished coitus—if you see what I mean—it needs no reversal.—Author

[10]O.K., maybe it's not perfect, but you try making up a word for man-hating. Also try figuring out why there isn't one.—Author

[11]Freud picked up a little extra money by translating John Stuart Mill's *The Emancipation of Women* while doing peacetime military service. What this mostly proves is that he was exposed to ideas of equality early—and rejected them. As he wrote to his wife, Martha: "Am I to think of my delicate sweet girl as a competitor?. . . the position of woman cannot be other than what it is: to be an adored sweetheart in youth, and a beloved wife in maturity."—Author

[12]You bet.—Author

[13]Try replacing "penetration" with "envelopment" and see what happens to your head.—Author

it: the large ovum expends no energy, waits for the sperm to seek out its own destruction in typically masculine and masochistic fashion, and then simply envelops the infinitesimal sperm. As the sperm disappears into the ovum, it is literally eaten alive—much like the male spider eaten by his mate. Even the most quixotic male liberationist would have to agree that biology leaves no room for doubt about an intrinsic female dominance.[14]

What intrigued Freud was not these biological facts, however, but their psychological impact: for instance, the way males were rendered incurably narcissistic, anxious, and fragile by having their gentials so precariously perched and visibly exposed on the outside of their bodies. Men's womblessness and loss of all but vestigial breasts and useless nipples were the end of a long evolutionary journey toward the sole functions of sperm production, sperm carrying, and sperm delivery. Women were responsible for all the other processes of reproduction. Female behavior, health, and psychology governed gestation and birth. Since time immemorial, this disproportionate share in reproductive influence had unbalanced the sexes. (Freud realized the consequences for women as well, among them *breast castration anxiety*: a woman who looks at the flattened male chest with its odd extraneous nipples fears deep in her psyche that she will return to that breast-castrated state.)

Finally, there was the physiological fact of the penis. It confirmed the initial bisexuality of all humans.[15] After all, life begins as female, in the womb as elsewhere[16] (the explanation for men's residual nipples). Penile tissue has its origin in, and thus has retained a comparable number of nerve endings as, the clitoris.[17] But somewhere along the evolutionary line, the penis acquired a double function: excretion of urine and sperm delivery. (Indeed, during boys' feminine, masturbatory, clitoral stage of development—before they had seen female genitals and realized that their penises were endangered and grotesque compared to the compact, well-protected clitoris—the penis had a third, albeit immature, function of masturbatory pleasure.)[18] All this results in an organ suffering from functional overload. The most obvious, painful, diurnal, nocturnal (indeed, even multidiurnal and multinocturnal) outcome for this residual clitoral tissue was clear: *men were forced to urinate through their clitorises.*

No doubt, this was the evolutionary cause for the grotesque enlargement and exposure of the penis, and for its resulting insensitivity due to lack of protection. Though the nerve endings in the female's clitoris remained exquisitely sensitive and close to the surface—carefully carried, as they were, in delicate mucous membranes, which were protected by the labia—the exposed penile versions of the same nerve endings had gradually become encased in a protective, deadening epidermis; a fact that deprived men of the intense, radiating, wholebody pleasure that only the clitoris could provide.

---

[14]Let's face it. Biology can be used to prove anything. Phyllis describes fertilization in terms of female dominance. Sigmund's terms are better suited to rape: "The male sex cell is actively mobile and searches out the female one, and the latter, the ovum, is immobile and waits passively," he wrote in "Femininity." "This behavior of the elementary sexual organisms is indeed a model for the conduct of sexual individuals during intercourse. The male pursues the female for the purpose of sexual union, seizes hold of her, and penetrates into her." What feminism asks—and I hope science, too, will ask one day—is, why do we have to assume domination? How about cooperation?—Author

[15]Actually, S. F. did believe in bisexuality—especially in young children, for they hadn't yet figured out how precious the penis was.—Author

[16]True.—Author

[17]Also true. *Somebody* had equality in mind.—Author

[18]Here is Sigmund in "Some Psychological Consequences of the Anatomical Distinction Between the Sexes": There is "a momentous discovery which little girls are destined to make. They notice the penis of a brother or playmate, strikingly visible and of large proportions, at once recognize it as the superior counterpart of their own small and inconspicuous organ, and from that time forward fall a victim to envy for the penis. . . . She has seen it and knows that she is without it and wants to have it."—Author

Men's lesser sex drive and diminished capacity for orgasm followed, as day follows night.

As Phyllis Freud proved in clinical studies that would become both widely accepted and tremendously influential, male sexuality became mature only when pleasure was transferred from the penis to the mature and appropriate area: the fingers and tongue. Freud reasoned brilliantly that since insemination and pregnancy could not accompany every orgasm experienced by multiorgasmic females, it must also be the case for males that sexual maturity would be measured by their ability to reach climax in a nonprocreative way. Immature *penile* orgasms had to be replaced by *lingual* and *digital* ones. In "Masculinity" as elsewhere, Phyllis Freud was very clear: "In the clitoral phase of boys, the penis is the leading erotogenic zone. But it is not, of course, going to remain so. . . . The penis should . . . hand over its sensitivity, and at the same time its importance, to the lingual/digital areas."[19]

---

[19]In "Femininity," Sigmund explained: "In the phallic phase of girls the clitoris is the leading erotogenic zone. But it is not, of course, going to remain so. . . . The clitoris should . . . hand over its sensitivity, and at the same time, its importance, to the vagina."

Should we excuse him as a man of his time? Here's the conclusion of Lisa Appignanesi and John Forrester in *Freud's Women* (HarperCollins): "It is almost inconceivable that Freud was not aware of the orthodox views of contemporary anatomists and physiologists, who had, from well before the early nineteenth century, demonstrated that the clitoris was the specific site of female sexual pleasure, and who, in the medical writing of his time, had asserted that the vagina had virtually no erotic functions at all. Nineteenth-century medical encyclopedia writers closed the file on the vagina in the same way Alfred Kinsey [did] in the mid-20th century, with a flourish of definitively and chillingly rank-pulling medical rhetoric: virtually the entire vagina could be operated on without the need of an anesthetic."

Still think the digital/lingual reversal is too outrageous? Maybe—but it allows men a lot more nerve endings than Freud allowed us.—Author

PART V

Humanistic Approach to Personality

The humanistic approaches to personality emphasize what is uniquely human about psychology's object of study. Studying people is not the same as studying rocks, trees, or animals, because people are fundamentally different. The unique aspects on which humanistic approaches focus are experience, awareness, free will, dignity, and the meaning of life. None of these mean much to rocks, trees, or animals, but they are all crucial to the human condition.

Humanistic psychologists view free will as an opportunity, and happiness as the essential goal of life. In our first selection, Abraham Maslow presents his well-known theory of motivation, often referred to as the "hierarchy of needs." What is humanistic about this theory is that motivation begins rather than ends with the basic needs for survival and safety. After those are satisfied, Maslow proposes, uniquely human needs for understanding, beauty, and self-actualization become important for happiness.

The best-known of the humanistic psychologists surely was Carl Rogers. In the second selection, Rogers argues that the "unconditional positive regard" that a humanistic psychotherapist gives his or her clients allows a clear, undistorted picture of his or her personality to emerge. He then draws on some experiences in the therapeutic context to illustrate his theory of personality dynamics, particularly what he regards as every individual's ability to reorganize his or her own personality. The next selection is by the modern humanistic psychologist Mihalyi Csikszentmihalyi. Csikszentmihalyi addresses the classic humanistic question: What is positive experience (the "good life") and how does one attain it? He concludes that true happiness consists not of ecstasy but rather in choosing to enter a state of calm absorption he calls "flow."

In the past few years, humanistic psychology has revived under the new rubric of "positive psychology," which echoes Csikszentmihalyi's point that happiness is more a matter of how one thinks about events, than the events in one's life themselves. Sonja Lyubomirsky explains this point in detail, outlining the ways in which people can, to some extent, take control of the degree to which they experience happiness.

If there is more to the good life than happiness, then that missing piece might be virtue. In our final selection, Katherine Dahlsgaard and her colleagues seek the meaning of this term by exploring the attributes that nearly all cultures see as virtuous.

A THEORY OF HUMAN MOTIVATION

Abraham H. Maslow

Maslow's best-known contribution to psychology is his proposal that human motivation is organized by a hierarchy of needs. Lower, physiological and safety needs must be satisfied before higher needs can emerge. These include the need for esteem, the need for self-actualization, the need to know and understand, and aesthetic needs. None of these latter needs are directly tied to survival; they become potent only after the survival needs are taken care of.

Maslow's theory, described in the following selection, is humanistic in two ways. First, he explicitly states that the study of human motivation does not need to be based on findings from research with animals. "It is no more necessary to study animals before one can study man than it is to study mathematics before one can study geology or psychology or biology." Second and more important, Maslow's higher needs are uniquely human. The needs to experience beauty, to understand the world, and to fulfill one's potential all stem from the quest for authentic existence at the core of existential philosophy and humanistic psychology.

Maslow's theory leads him to write a couple of prescriptions for human development. First, he observes that a child satisfied in basic needs early in life becomes relatively tolerant of deprivation in later life, and better able to focus on higher goals. Therefore, children should be raised to feel satisfied and safe. Second, "a man who is thwarted in any of his basic needs may fairly be envisaged as a sick man." Maslow concludes that a society that thwarts the basic needs of individuals is therefore itself sick. On the other hand, "the good or healthy society would then be defined as one that permitted man's highest purposes to emerge by satisfying all his basic needs."

From *Motivation and Personality*, 3d ed., by A. H. Maslow, revised by R. Frager, J. Fadiman, C. McReynolds, and R. Cox (New York: Harper & Row, 1954), pp. 80–106.

* * *

The Basic Needs

THE PHYSIOLOGICAL NEEDS The needs that are usually taken as the starting point for motivation theory are the so-called physiological drives. Two recent lines of research make it necessary to revise our customary notions about these needs: first, the development of the concept of homeostasis, and second, the finding that appetites (preferential choices among foods) are a fairly efficient indication of actual needs or lacks in the body.

Homeostasis refers to the body's automatic efforts to maintain a constant, normal state of the blood stream. * * *

* * * If the body lacks some chemical, the individual will tend (in an imperfect way) to develop a specific appetite or partial hunger for that food element.

Thus it seems impossible as well as useless to make any list of fundamental physiological needs, for they can come to almost any number one might wish, depending on the degree of specificity of description. We cannot identify all physiological needs as homeostatic. That sexual desire, sleepiness, sheer activity, and maternal behavior in animals are homeostatic has not yet been demonstrated. Furthermore, this list would not include the various sensory pleasures (tastes, smells, tickling, stroking), which are probably physiological and which may become the goals of motivated behavior.

These physiological drives or needs are to be considered unusual rather than typical because they are isolable, and because they are localizable somatically. That is to say, they are relatively independent of each other, of other motivations, and of the organism as a whole, and second, in many cases, it is possible to demonstrate a localized, underlying somatic base for the drive. This is true less generally than has been thought (exceptions are fatigue, sleepiness, maternal responses) but it is still true in the classic instances of hunger, sex, and thirst.

It should be pointed out again that any of the physiological needs and the consummatory behavior involved with them serve as channels for all sorts of other needs as well. That is to say, the person who thinks he is hungry may actually be seeking more for comfort, or dependence, than for vitamins or proteins. Conversely, it is possible to satisfy the hunger need in part by other activities such as drinking water or smoking cigarettes. In other words, relatively isolable as these physiological needs are, they are not completely so.

Undoubtedly these physiological needs are the most prepotent of all needs. What this means specifically is that in the human being who is missing everything in life in an extreme fashion, it is most likely that the major motivation would be the physiological needs rather than any others. A person who is lacking food, safety, love, and esteem would most probably hunger for food more strongly than for anything else.

If all the needs are unsatisfied, and the organism is then dominated by the physiological needs, all other needs may become simply nonexistent or be pushed into the background. It is then fair to characterize the whole organism by saying simply that it is hungry, for consciousness is almost completely preëmpted by hunger. All capacities are put into the service of hunger-satisfaction, and the organization of these capacities is almost entirely determined by the one purpose of satisfying hunger. The receptors and effectors, the intelligence, memory, habits, all may now be defined simply as hunger-gratifying tools. Capacities that are not useful for this purpose lie dormant, or are pushed into the background. The urge to write poetry, the desire to acquire an automobile, the interest in American history, the desire for a new pair of shoes are, in the extreme case, forgotten or become of secondary importance. For the man who is extremely and dangerously hungry, no other interests exist but food. He dreams food, he remembers food, he thinks about food, he emotes only about food, he perceives only food, and he wants only food. The more subtle determinants that ordinarily fuse with the physiological drives in organizing even feeding, drinking, or sexual behavior, may now be so completely overwhelmed as to allow us to speak at this time (but *only* at this time) of pure hunger drive and behavior, with the one unqualified aim of relief.

Another peculiar characteristic of the human organism when it is dominated by a certain need is that the whole philosophy of the future tends also to change. For our chronically and extremely hungry man, Utopia can be defined simply as a place where there is plenty of food. He tends to think that, if only he is guaranteed food for the rest of his life, he will be perfectly happy and will never want anything more. Life itself tends to be defined in terms of eating. Anything else will be defined as unimportant. Freedom, love, community feeling, respect, philosophy, may all be waved aside as fripperies that are useless, since they fail to fill the stomach. Such a man may fairly be said to live by bread alone.

It cannot possibly be denied that such things are true, but their *generality* can be denied. Emergency conditions are, almost by definition, rare in the normally functioning peaceful society. That this truism can be forgotten is attributable mainly to two reasons. First, rats have few motivations other than physiological ones, and since so much of the research upon motivation has been made with these animals, it is easy to carry the rat picture over to the human being. Second, it is too often not realized that culture itself is an adaptive tool, one of whose main functions is to make the physiological emergencies come less and less often. In most of the known societies, chronic extreme hunger of the emergency type is rare, rather than common. In any case, this is still true in the United States. The average American citizen is experiencing appetite rather than hunger when he says, "I am hungry." He is apt to experience sheer life-and-death hunger only by accident and then only a few times through his entire life.

Obviously a good way to obscure the higher motivations, and to get a lopsided view of human capacities and human nature, is to make the organism extremely and chronically hungry or thirsty. Anyone who attempts to make an emergency picture into a typical one, and who will measure all of man's goals and desires by his behavior during extreme physiological deprivation is certainly being blind to many things. It is quite true that man lives by bread alone—when there is no bread. But what happens to man's desires when there *is* plenty of bread and when his belly is chronically filled?

At once other (and higher) needs emerge and these, rather than physiological hungers, dominate the organism. And when these in turn are satisfied, again new (and still higher) needs emerge, and so on. This is what we mean by saying that the basic human needs are organized into a hierarchy of relative prepotency.

One main implication of this phrasing is that gratification becomes as important a concept as deprivation in motivation theory, for it releases the organism from the domination of a relatively more physiological need, permitting thereby the emergence of other more social goals. The physiological needs, along with their partial goals, when chronically gratified cease to exist as active determinants or organizers of behavior. They now exist only in a potential fashion in the sense that they may emerge again to dominate the organism if they are thwarted. But a want that is satisfied is no longer a want. The organism is dominated and its behavior organized only by unsatisfied needs. If hunger is satisfied, it becomes unimportant in the current dynamics of the individual.

This statement is somewhat qualified by a hypothesis to be discussed more fully later, namely, that it is precisely those individuals in whom a certain need has always been satisfied who are best equipped to tolerate deprivation of that need in the future, and that furthermore, those who have been deprived in the past will react differently to current satisfactions than the one who has never been deprived.

THE SAFETY NEEDS   If the physiological needs are relatively well gratified, there then emerges a new set of needs, which we may categorize roughly as the safety needs. All that has been said of the physiological needs is equally true, although in less degree, of these desires. The organism may equally well be wholly dominated by them. They may serve as the almost exclusive organizers of behavior, recruiting all the capacities of the organism in their service, and we may then fairly describe the whole organism as a safety-seeking mechanism. Again we may say of the receptors, the effectors, of the intellect, and of the other capacities that they are primarily safety-seeking tools. Again, as in the hungry man, we find that the dominating goal is a strong determinant not only of his current world outlook and philosophy but also of his philosophy of the future. Practically everything looks less important than safety (even sometimes the physiological needs, which being satisfied are now underestimated). A man in this state, if it is extreme enough and chronic enough, may be characterized as living almost for safety alone.

Although in this chapter we are interested primarily in the needs of the adult, we can approach an understanding of his safety needs perhaps more efficiently by observation of infants and children, in whom these needs are much more simple and obvious. One reason for the clearer appearance of the threat or danger reaction in infants is that they do not inhibit this reaction at all, whereas adults in our society have been taught to inhibit it at all costs. Thus even when adults do feel their safety to be threatened, we may not be able to see this on the surface. Infants will react in a total fashion and as if they were endangered, if they are disturbed or dropped suddenly, startled by loud noises, flashing light, or other unusual sensory stimulation, by rough handling, by general loss of support in the mother's arms, or by inadequate support.

Another indication of the child's need for safety is his preference for some kind of undisrupted routine or rhythm. He seems to want a predictable, orderly world. For instance, injustice, unfairness, or inconsistency in the parents seems to make a child feel anxious and unsafe. This attitude may be not so much because of the injustice *per se* or any particular pains involved, but rather because this treatment threatens to make the world look unreliable, or unsafe, or unpredictable. Young children seem to thrive better under a system that has at least a skeletal outline of rigidity, in which there is a schedule of a kind, some sort of routine, something that can be counted upon, not only for the present but also far into the future. Child psychologists, teachers, and psychotherapists have found that permissiveness within limits, rather than unrestricted permissiveness is preferred as well as *needed* by children. Perhaps one could express this more accurately by saying that the child needs an organized world rather than an unorganized or unstructured one.

The central role of the parents and the normal family setup are indisputable. Quarreling, physical assault, separation, divorce, or death within the family may be particularly terrifying. Also parental outbursts of rage or threats of punishment directed to the child, calling him names, speaking to him harshly, handling him roughly, or actual physical punishment sometimes elicit such total panic and terror that we must assume more is involved than the physical pain alone. While it is true that in some children this terror may represent also a fear of loss of parental love, it can also occur in completely rejected children, who seem to cling to the hating parents more for sheer safety and protection than because of hope of love.

Confronting the average child with new, unfamiliar, strange, unmanageable stimuli or situations will too frequently elicit the danger or terror reaction, as for example, getting lost or even being separated from the parents for a short time, being confronted with new faces, new situations, or new tasks, the sight of strange, unfamiliar, or uncontrollable objects, illness, or death. Particularly at such times, the child's frantic clinging to his parents is eloquent testimony to their role as protectors (quite apart from their roles as food givers and love givers).

From these and similar observations, we may generalize and say that the average child in our society generally prefers a safe, orderly, predictable, organized world, which he can count on, and in which unexpected, unmanageable, or other dangerous things do not happen, and in which, in any case, he has all-powerful parents who protect and shield him from harm.

* * *

The healthy, normal, fortunate adult in our culture is largely satisfied in his safety needs. The peaceful, smoothly running, good society ordinarily makes its members feel safe enough from wild animals, extremes of temperature, criminal assault, murder, tyranny, etc. Therefore, in a very real sense, he no longer has any safety needs as active motivators. Just as a sated man no longer feels hungry, a safe man no longer feels endangered. If we wish to see these needs directly and clearly we must turn to neurotic or near-neurotic individuals, and to the economic and social underdogs. In between these extremes, we can perceive the expressions of safety needs only in such phenomena as, for instance, the common preference for a job with tenure and protection, the desire for a savings account and for insurance of various kinds (medical, dental, unemployment, disability, old age).

Other broader aspects of the attempt to seek safety and stability in the world are seen in the very common preference for familiar rather than unfamiliar things, or for the known rather than the unknown. The tendency to have some religion or world philosophy that organizes the universe and the men in it into some sort of satisfactorily coherent, meaningful whole is also in part motivated by safety seeking. Here too we may list science and philosophy in general as partially motivated by the safety needs (we shall see later that there are also other motivations to scientific, philosophical, or religious endeavor).

Otherwise the need for safety is seen as an active and dominant mobilizer of the organism's resources only in emergencies, e.g., war, disease, natural catastrophes, crime waves, societal disorganization, neurosis, brain injury, chronically bad situations.

Some neurotic adults in our society are, in many ways, like the unsafe child in their desire for safety, although in the former it takes on a somewhat special appearance. Their reaction is often to unknown, psychological dangers in a world that is perceived to be hostile, overwhelming, and threatening. Such a person behaves as if a great catastrophe were almost always impending, i.e., he is usually responding as if to an emergency. His safety needs often find specific expression in a search for a protector, or a stronger person on whom he may depend, perhaps a fuehrer.

* * *

The neurosis in which the search for safety takes its clearest form is in the compulsive obsessive neurosis. Compulsive-obsessives try frantically to order and stabilize the world so that no unmanageable, unexpected, or unfamiliar dangers will ever appear. They hedge themselves about with all sorts of ceremonials, rules, and formulas so that every possible contingency may be provided for and so that no new contingencies may appear. They are much like the brain-injured cases described by Goldstein,[1] who manage to maintain their equilibrium by avoiding everything unfamiliar and strange and by ordering their restricted world in such a neat, disciplined, orderly fashion that everything in the world can be counted on. They try to arrange the world so that anything unexpected (dangers) cannot possibly occur. If, through no fault of their own, something unexpected does occur, they go into a panic reaction as if this unexpected occurrence constituted a grave danger. What we can see only as a none-too-strong preference in the healthy person, e.g., preference for the familiar, becomes a life-and-death necessity in abnormal cases. The healthy taste for the novel and unknown is missing or at a minimum in the average neurotic.

THE BELONGINGNESS AND LOVE NEEDS If both the physiological and the safety needs are fairly well gratified, there will emerge the love and affection and belongingness needs, and the whole cycle already described will repeat itself with this new center. Now the person will feel keenly, as never before, the absence of friends, or a sweetheart, or a wife, or children. He will hunger for affectionate relations with people in general, namely, for a place in his group, and he will strive with great intensity to achieve this goal. He will want to attain such a place more than anything else in the world and may even forget that once, when he was hungry, he sneered at love as unreal or unnecessary or unimportant.

In our society the thwarting of these needs is the most commonly found core in cases of maladjustment and more severe psychopathology. Love and affection, as well as their possible expression in sexuality, are generally looked upon with

---

[1]Kurt Goldstein was a neurologist and psychiatrist who wrote on clinical psychology, human nature, and language.

ambivalence and are customarily hedged about with many restrictions and inhibitions. Practically all theorists of psychopathology have stressed thwarting of the love needs as basic in the picture of maladjustment. * * *

One thing that must be stressed at this point is that love is not synonymous with sex. Sex may be studied as a purely physiological need. Ordinarily sexual behavior is multidetermined, that is to say, determined not only by sexual but also by other needs, chief among which are the love and affection needs. Also not to be overlooked is the fact that the love needs involve both giving *and* receiving love.

THE ESTEEM NEEDS All people in our society (with a few pathological exceptions) have a need or desire for a stable, firmly based, usually high evaluation of themselves, for self-respect, or self-esteem, and for the esteem of others. These needs may therefore be classified into two subsidiary sets. These are, first, the desire for strength, for achievement, for adequacy, for mastery and competence, for confidence in the face of the world, and for independence and freedom.[2] Second, we have what we may call the desire for reputation or prestige (defining it as respect or esteem from other people), status, dominance, recognition, attention, importance, or appreciation. These needs have been relatively stressed by Alfred Adler and his followers, and have been relatively neglected by Freud. More and more today, however, there is appearing wide-spread appreciation of their central importance, among psychoanalysts as well as among clinical psychologists.

---

[2]Whether or not this particular desire is universal we do not know. The crucial question, especially important today, is, Will men who are enslaved and dominated inevitably feel dissatisfied and rebellious? We may assume on the basis of commonly known clinical data that a man who has known true freedom (not paid for by giving up safety and security but rather built on the basis of adequate safety and security) will not willingly or easily allow his freedom to be taken away from him. But we do not know that this is true for the person born into slavery.—Author

Satisfaction of the self-esteem need leads to feelings of self-confidence, worth, strength, capability, and adequacy, of being useful and necessary in the world. But thwarting of these needs produces feelings of inferiority, of weakness, and of helplessness. These feelings in turn give rise to either basic discouragement or else compensatory or neurotic trends. * * *

* * * We have been learning more and more of the dangers of basing self-esteem on the opinions of others rather than on real capacity, competence, and adequacy to the task. The most stable and therefore most healthy self-esteem is based on *deserved* respect from others rather than on external fame or celebrity and unwarranted adulation.

THE NEED FOR SELF-ACTUALIZATION Even if all these needs are satisfied, we may still often (if not always) expect that a new discontent and restlessness will soon develop, unless the individual is doing what he is fitted for. A musician must make music, an artist must paint, a poet must write, if he is to be ultimately at peace with himself. What a man *can* be, he *must* be. This need we may call self-actualization.

* * * [This term] refers to a man's desire for self-fulfillment, namely, to the tendency for him to become actualized in what he is potentially. This tendency might be phrased as the desire to become more and more what one is, to become everything that one is capable of becoming.

The specific form that these needs will take will of course vary greatly from person to person. In one individual it may take the form of the desire to be an ideal mother, in another it may be expressed athletically, and in still another it may be expressed in painting pictures or in inventions.

The clear emergence of these needs usually rests upon prior satisfaction of the physiological, safety, love, and esteem needs.

* * *

THE DESIRES TO KNOW AND TO UNDERSTAND The main reason we know little about the cognitive impulses, their dynamics, or their pathology, is that they are not important in the clinic, and certainly not in the clinic dominated by the medical-therapeutic tradition, i.e., getting rid of disease. The florid, exciting, and mysterious symptoms found in the classical neuroses are lacking here. Cognitive psychopathology is pale, subtle, and easily over-looked, or defined as normal. It does not cry for help. As a consequence we find nothing on the subject in the writings of the great inventors of psychotherapy and psychodynamics, Freud, Adler, Jung, etc. Nor has anyone yet made any systematic attempts at constructing cognitive psychotherapies.

*   *   *

* * * There are some reasonable grounds for postulating positive *per se* impulses to satisfy curiosity, to know, to explain, and to understand.

Support for of cognitive desires

1. Something like human curiosity can easily be observed in the higher animals. The monkey will pick things apart, will poke his finger into holes, will explore in all sorts of situations where it is improbable that hunger, fear, sex, comfort status, etc., are involved. Harlow's experiments (1950) have amply demonstrated this in an acceptably experimental way.

2. The history of mankind supplies us with a satisfactory number of instances in which man looked for facts and created explanations in the face of the greatest danger, even to life itself. There have been innumerable humbler Galileos.

3. Studies of psychologically healthy people indicate that they are, as a defining characteristic, attracted to the mysterious, to the unknown, to the chaotic, unorganized, and unexplained. This seems to be a *per se* attractiveness; these areas are in themselves and of their own right interesting. The contrasting reaction to the well known is one of boredom.

4. It may be found valid to extrapolate from the psychopathological. The compulsive-obsessive neurotic (and neurotic in general), Goldstein's brain-injured soldiers, Maier's fixated rats (1939), all show (at the clinical level of observation) a compulsive and anxious clinging to the familiar and a dread of the unfamiliar, the anarchic, the unexpected, the undomesticated. On the other hand, there are some phenomena that may turn out to nullify this possibility. Among these are forced unconventionality, a chronic rebellion against any authority whatsoever, Bohemianism, the desire to shock and to startle, all of which may be found in certain neurotic individuals, as well as in those in the process of deacculturation.

*   *   *

5. Probably there are true psychopathological effects when the cognitive needs are frustrated. For the moment, though, we have no really sound data available. The following clinical impressions are pertinent.

6. I have seen a few cases in which it seemed clear to me that the pathology (boredom, loss of zest in life, self-dislike, general depression of the bodily functions, steady deterioration of the intellectual life, of tastes, etc.) were produced in intelligent people leading stupid lives in stupid jobs. I have at least one case in which the appropriate cognitive therapy (resuming part-time studies, getting a position that was more intellectually demanding, insight) removed the symptoms.

I have seen *many* women, intelligent, prosperous, and unoccupied, slowly develop these same symptoms of intellectual inanition. Those who followed my recommendation to immerse themselves in something worthy of them showed improvement or cure often enough to impress me with the reality of the cognitive needs. In those countries in which access to the news, to information, and to the facts [was] cut off, and in those where official theories were profoundly contradicted by obvious facts, at least some people responded with generalized cynicism, mistrust of *all* values, suspicion even of the obvious, a profound disruption of ordinary interpersonal relationships, hopelessness, loss of morale, etc. Others seem to have responded in the more passive direction with dullness, submission, loss of capacity, coarctation, and loss of initiative.

7. The needs to know and to understand are seen in late infancy and childhood, perhaps even more strongly than in adulthood. Furthermore this seems to be a spontaneous product of maturation rather than of learning, however defined. Children

do not have to be taught to be curious. But they *may* be taught, as by institutionalization, *not* to be curious.

8. Finally, the gratification of the cognitive impulses is subjectively satisfying and yields end-experience. Though this aspect of insight and understanding has been neglected in favor of achieved results, learning, etc., it nevertheless remains true that insight is usually a bright, happy, emotional spot in any person's life, perhaps even a high spot in the life span.

The overcoming of obstacles, the occurrence of pathology upon thwarting, the widespread occurrence (cross-species, cross-cultural), the never-dying (though weak) insistent pressure, the need of gratification of this need as a prerequisite for the fullest development of human potentialities, the spontaneous appearance in the early history of the individual, all these point to a basic cognitive need.

This postulation, however, is not enough. Even after we know, we are impelled to know more and more minutely and microscopically on the one hand, and on the other, more and more extensively in the direction of a world philosophy, theology, etc. The facts that we acquire, if they are isolated or atomistic, inevitably get theorized about, and either analyzed or organized or both. This process has been phrased by some as the search for meaning. We shall then postulate a desire to understand, to systematize, to organize, to analyze, to look for relations and meanings, to construct a system of values.

Once these desires are accepted for discussion, we see that they too form themselves into a small hierarchy in which the desire to know is prepotent over the desire to understand. All the characteristics of a hierarchy of prepotency that we have described above seem to hold for this one as well.

We must guard ourselves against the too easy tendency to separate these desires from the basic needs we have discussed above, i.e., to make a sharp dichotomy between cognitive and conative needs. The desire to know and to understand are themselves conative, i.e., having a striving character, and are as much personality needs as the basic needs we have already discussed. Furthermore, as we have seen, the two hierarchies are interrelated rather than sharply separated; and as we shall see below, they are synergic rather than antagonistic.

THE AESTHETIC NEEDS   We know even less about these than about the others, and yet the testimony of history, of the humanities, and of aestheticians forbids us to bypass this uncomfortable (to the scientist) area. I have attempted to study this phenomenon on a clinical-personological basis with selected individuals, and have at least convinced myself that in *some* individuals there is a truly basic aesthetic need. They get sick (in special ways) from ugliness, and are cured by beautiful surroundings; they *crave* actively, and their cravings can be satisfied *only* by beauty. It is seen almost universally in healthy children. Some evidence of such an impulse is found in every culture and in every age as far back as the cavemen.

Much overlapping with conative and cognitive needs makes it impossible to separate them sharply. The needs for order, for symmetry, for closure, for completion of the act, for system, and for structure may be indiscriminately assigned to *either* cognitive, conative, or aesthetic, or even to neurotic needs. * * * What, for instance, does it mean when a man feels a strong conscious impulse to straighten the crookedly hung picture on the wall?

Further Characteristics of the Basic Needs

THE DEGREE OF FIXITY OF THE HIERARCHY OF BASIC NEEDS   We have spoken so far as if this hierarchy were a fixed order, but actually it is not nearly so rigid as we may have implied. It is true that most of the people with whom we have worked have seemed to have these basic needs in about the order that has been indicated. However, there have been a number of exceptions.

1. There are some people in whom, for instance, self-esteem seems to be more important than love. This most common reversal in the hierarchy is usually due to the development of the notion that the person who is most likely to be loved is a strong or powerful person, one who inspires respect or fear, and who is self-confident or aggressive. Therefore such people who lack love and seek it may try hard to put on a front of aggressive, confident behavior. But essentially they seek high self-esteem and its behavior expressions more as a means to an end than for its own sake; they seek self-assertion for the sake of love rather than for self-esteem itself.

2. There are other apparently innately creative people in whom the drive to creativeness seems to be more important than any other counterdeterminant. Their creativeness might appear not as self-actualization released by basic satisfaction, but in spite of lack of basic satisfaction.

3. In certain people the level of aspiration may be permanently deadened or lowered. That is to say, the less prepotent goals may simply be lost, and may disappear forever, so that the person who has experienced life at a very low level, e.g., chronic unemployment, may continue to be satisfied for the rest of his life if only he can get enough food.

4. The so-called psychopathic personality is another example of permanent loss of the love needs. These are people who, according to the best data available, have been starved for love in the earliest months of their lives and have simply lost forever the desire and the ability to give and to receive affection (as animals lose sucking or pecking reflexes that are not exercised soon enough after birth).

5. Another cause of reversal of the hierarchy is that when a need has been satisfied for a long time, this need may be underevaluated. People who have never experienced chronic hunger are apt to underestimate its effects and to look upon food as a rather unimportant thing. If they are dominated by a higher need, this higher need will seem to be the most important of all. It then becomes possible, and indeed does actually hap-

pen, that they may, for the sake of this higher need, put themselves into the position of being deprived in a more basic need. We may expect that after a longtime deprivation of the more basic need there will be a tendency to reevaluate both needs so that the more prepotent need will actually become consciously prepotent for the individual who may have given it up lightly. Thus a man who has given up his job rather than lose his self-respect, and who then starves for six months or so, may be willing to take his job back even at the price of losing his self-respect.

6. Another partial explanation of *apparent* reversals is seen in the fact that we have been talking about the hierarchy of prepotency in terms of consciously felt wants or desires rather than of behavior. Looking at behavior itself may give us the wrong impression. What we have claimed is that the person will *want* the more basic of two needs when deprived in both. There is no necessary implication here that he will act upon his desires. Let us stress again that there are many determinants of behavior other than the needs and desires.

7. Perhaps more important than all these exceptions are the ones that involve ideals, high social standards, high values, and the like. With such values people become martyrs; they will give up everything for the sake of a particular ideal, or value. These people may be understood, at least in part, by reference to one basic concept (or hypothesis), which may be called increased frustration-tolerance through early gratification. People who have been satisfied in their basic needs throughout their lives, particularly in their earlier years, seem to develop exceptional power to withstand present or future thwarting of these needs simply because they have strong, healthy character structure as a result of basic satisfaction. They are the strong people who can easily weather disagreement or opposition, who can swim against the stream of public opinion, and who can stand up for the truth at great personal cost. It is just the ones who have loved and been well loved, and who have had many deep friendships who can hold out against hatred, rejection, or persecution.

I say all this in spite of the fact that a certain amount of sheer habituation is also involved in any full discussion of frustration tolerance. For instance, it is likely that those persons who have been accustomed to relative starvation for a long time are partially enabled thereby to withstand food deprivation. What sort of balance must be made between these two tendencies, of habituation on the one hand, and of past satisfaction breeding present frustration tolerance on the other hand, remains to be worked out by further research. Meanwhile we may assume that both are operative, side by side, since they do not contradict each other. In respect to this phenomenon of increased frustration tolerance, it seems probable that the most important gratifications come in the first two years of life. That is to say, people who have been made secure and strong in the earliest years tend to remain secure and strong thereafter in the face of whatever threatens.

DEGREES OF RELATIVE SATISFACTION So far, our theoretical discussion may have given the impression that these five sets of needs are somehow in such terms as the following: If one need is satisfied, then another emerges. This statement might give the false impression that a need must be satisfied 100 percent before the next need emerges. In actual fact, most members of our society who are normal are partially satisfied in all their basic needs and partially unsatisfied in all their basic needs at the same time. A more realistic description of the hierarchy would be in terms of decreasing percentages of satisfaction as we go up the hierarchy of prepotency. For instance, if I may assign arbitrary figures for the sake of illustration, it is as if the average citizen is satisfied perhaps 85 percent in his physiological needs, 70 percent in his safety needs, 50 percent in his love needs, 40 percent in his self-esteem needs, and 10 percent in his self-actualization needs.

As for the concept of emergence of a new need after satisfaction of the prepotent need, this emergence is not a sudden, saltatory phenomenon, but rather a gradual emergence by slow degrees from nothingness. For instance, if prepotent need A is satisfied only 10 percent, then need B may not be visible at all. However, as this need A becomes satisfied 25 percent, need B may emerge 5 percent; as need A becomes satisfied 75 percent, need B may emerge 50 percent, and so on.

* * *

ANIMAL AND HUMAN CENTERING This theory starts with the human being rather than any lower and presumably simpler animal. Too many of the findings that have been made in animals have been proved to be true for animals but not for the human being. There is no reason whatsoever why we should start with animals in order to study human motivation. The logic or rather illogic behind this general fallacy of pseudosimplicity has been exposed often enough by philosophers and logicians as well as by scientists in each of the various fields. It is no more necessary to study animals before one can study man than it is to study mathematics *before* one can study geology or psychology or biology.

* * *

THE ROLE OF GRATIFIED NEEDS It has been pointed out above several times that our needs usually emerge only when more prepotent needs have been gratified. Thus gratification has an important role in motivation theory. Apart from this, however, needs cease to play an active determining or organizing role as soon as they are gratified.

What this means is that, e.g., a basically satisfied person no longer has the needs for esteem, love, safety, etc. The only sense in which he might be said to have them is in the almost metaphysical sense that a sated man has hunger, or a filled bottle has emptiness. If we are interested in what *actually* motivates us, and not in what has, will, or might motivate us, then a satisfied need is not a motivator. It must be considered for all practical purposes simply not to exist, to have disappeared. This point should be emphasized because it has been either overlooked or contradicted in every theory of motivation I know. The perfectly healthy, normal, fortunate man has no sex needs or hunger needs, or needs for safety, or for love, or for prestige, or self-esteem, except in stray moments of quickly passing threat. * * *

It is such considerations as these that suggest the bold postulation that a man who is thwarted in any of his basic needs may fairly be envisaged simply as a sick man. This is a fair parallel to our designation as sick of the man who lacks vitamins or minerals. Who will say that a lack of love is less important than a lack of vitamins? Since we know the pathogenic effects of love starvation, who is to say that we are invoking value questions in an unscientific or illegitimate way, any more than the physician does who diagnoses and treats pellagra or scurvy? If I were permitted this usage, I should then say simply that a healthy man is primarily motivated by his needs to develop and actualize his fullest potentialities and capacities. If a man has any other basic needs in any active, chronic sense, he is simply an unhealthy man. He is as surely sick as if he had suddenly developed a strong salt hunger or calcium hunger. If we were to use the word *sick* in this way, we should then also have to face squarely the relations of man to his society. One clear implication of our definition would be that (1) since a man is to be called sick who is basically thwarted, and (2) since such basic thwarting is made possible ultimately only by forces outside the individual, then (3) sickness in the individual must come ultimately from a sickness in the society. The good or healthy society would then be defined as one that permitted man's highest purposes to emerge by satisfying all his basic needs.

* * *

References

Harlow, H. F. (1950). Learning motivated by a manipulation drive. *Journal of Experimental Psychology, 40*, 228–234.

Maier, N. R. F. (1939). *Studies of abnormal behavior in the rat.* New York: Harper.

Some Observations on the Organization of Personality

Carl R. Rogers

This selection is an article by perhaps the best known of the classic humanistic psychologists, Carl Rogers. One of the most famous and important parts of Rogers's theory is that a therapist needs to give his or her client "unconditional positive regard." This frees the client to say whatever is on his or her mind, and eventually helps the client to develop unconditional self-regard. Unconditional self-regard, in turn, allows the client to see himself or herself without defenses or distortions and thereby to become a fully functioning person.

In this article, Rogers argues that the nonjudgmental attitude of the therapist allows a complete and undistorted picture of the client's personality to emerge. He draws on some clinical experiences to illustrate his point, and—perhaps not surprisingly—finds that what his clients say in therapy tends to support his theory of personality dynamics and self-organization.

After you read this article, you may wish to think back to the earlier selections by Freud and his critics, and to note that the free-wheeling use of clinical anecdotes in support of one's theoretical position is not a practice limited to psychoanalysis. Just as Freud repeatedly found "confirmation" for his theoretical ideas in his clinical cases—and was roundly criticized for the shortcomings of such evidence later— so too Rogers was able to interpret what his clients said in the light of his own preferred theory. However, Rogers has yet to receive the kind of criticism for his method that Freud receives continually, and it is interesting to ponder just why this may be.

From *American Psychologist, 2,* 358–368, 1947.

In various fields of science rapid strides have been made when direct observation of significant processes has become possible. In medicine, when circumstances have permitted the physician to peer directly into the stomach of his patient, understanding of digestive processes has increased and the influence of emotional tension upon all aspects of that process has been more accurately observed and understood. In our work with nondirective therapy we often feel that we are having a psychological opportunity comparable to this medical experience—an opportunity to observe directly a number of the effective processes of personality. Quite aside from any question regarding nondirective therapy as therapy, here is a precious vein of observational material of unusual value for the study of personality.

Characteristics of the Observational Material

There are several ways in which the raw clinical data to which we have had access is unique in its value for understanding personality. The fact that these verbal expressions of inner dynamics are preserved by electrical recording makes possible a detailed analysis of a sort not heretofore possible. Recording has given us a microscope by which we may examine at leisure, and in minute detail, almost every aspect of what was, in its occurrence, a fleeting moment impossible of accurate observation.

Another scientifically fortunate characteristic of this material is the fact that the verbal productions of the client are biased to a minimal degree by the therapist. Material from client-centered interviews probably comes closer to being a "pure" expression of attitudes than has yet been achieved through other means. One can read through a complete recorded case or listen to it, without finding more than a half-dozen instances in which the therapist's views on any point are evident. One would find it impossible to form an estimate as to the therapist's views about personality dynamics. One could not determine his diagnostic views, his standards of behavior, his social class. The one value or standard held by the therapist which would exhibit itself in his tone of voice, responses, and activity, is a deep respect for the personality and attitudes of the client as a separate person. It is difficult to see how this would bias the content of the interview, except to permit deeper expression than the client would ordinarily allow himself. This almost complete lack of any distorting attitude is felt, and sometimes expressed by the client. One woman says:

"It's almost impersonal. I like you—of course I don't know why I should like you or why I shouldn't like you. It's a peculiar thing. I've never had that relationship with anybody before and I've often thought about it. . . . A lot of times I walk out with a feeling of elation that you think highly of me, and of course at the same time I have the feeling that 'Gee, he must think I'm an awful jerk' or something like that. But it doesn't really—those feelings aren't so deep that I can form an opinion one way or the other about you."

Here it would seem that even though she would like to discover some type of evaluational attitude, she is unable to do so. Published studies and research as yet unpublished bear out this point that counselor responses which are in any way evaluational or distorting as to content are at a minimum, thus enhancing the worth of such interviews for personality study.

The counselor attitude of warmth and understanding, well described by Snyder (1946) and Rogers (1946), also helps to maximize the freedom of expression by the individual. The client experiences sufficient interest in him as a person, and sufficient acceptance, to enable him to talk openly, not only about surface attitudes, but increasingly about intimate attitudes and feelings hidden even from himself. Hence in these recorded interviews we have material of very considerable depth so far as personality dynamics is concerned, along with a freedom from distortion.

Finally the very nature of the interviews and the techniques by which they are handled give us a rare opportunity to see to some extent through the eyes of another person—to perceive the world as it appears to him, to achieve at least partially, the internal frame of reference of another person. We see his behavior through his eyes, and also the psychological meaning which it had for him. We see also changes in personality and behavior, and the meanings which those changes have for the individual. We are admitted freely into the backstage of the person's living where we can observe from within some of the dramas of internal change, which are often far more compelling and moving than the drama which is presented on the stage viewed by the public. Only a novelist or a poet could do justice to the deep struggles which we are permitted to observe from within the client's own world of reality.

This rare opportunity to observe so directly and so clearly the inner dynamics of personality is a learning experience of the deepest sort for the clinician. Most of clinical psychology and psychiatry involves judgements *about* the individual, judgements which must, of necessity, be based on some framework brought to the situation by the clinician. To try continually to see and think *with* the individual, as in client-centered therapy, is a mind-stretching experience in which learning goes on apace because the clinician brings to the interview no pre-determined yardstick by which to judge the material.

I wish in this paper to try to bring you some of the clinical observations which we have made as we have repeatedly peered through these psychological windows into personality, and to raise with you some of the questions about the organization of personality which these observations have forced upon us. I shall not attempt to present these observations in logical order, but rather in the order in which they impressed themselves upon our notice. What I shall offer is not a series of research findings, but only the first step in that process of gradual approximation which we call science, a description of some observed phenomena which appear to be significant, and some highly tentative explanations of these phenomena.

The Relation of the Organized Perceptual Field to Behavior

One simple observation, which is repeated over and over again in each successful therapeutic case, seems to have rather deep theoretical implications. It is that as changes occur in the perception of self and in the perception of reality, changes occur in behavior. In therapy, these perceptual changes are more often concerned with the self than with the external world. Hence we find in therapy that as the perception of self alters, behavior alters. Perhaps an illustration will indicate the type of observation upon which this statement is based.

A young woman, a graduate student whom we

shall call Miss Vib, came in for nine interviews. If we compare the first interview with the last, striking changes are evident. Perhaps some features of this change may be conveyed by taking from the first and last interviews all the major statements regarding self, and all the major statements regarding current behavior. In the first interview, for example, her perception of herself may be crudely indicated by taking all her own statements about herself, grouping those which seem similar, but otherwise doing a minimum of editing, and retaining so far as possible, her own words. We then come out with this as the conscious perception of self which was hers at the outset of counseling.

"I feel disorganized, muddled; I've lost all direction; my personal life has disintegrated.

"I sorta experience things from the forefront of my consciousness, but nothing sinks in very deep; things don't seem real to me; I feel nothing matters; I don't have any emotional response to situations; I'm worried about myself.

"I haven't been acting like myself; it doesn't seem like me; I'm a different person altogether from what I used to be in the past.

"I don't understand myself; I haven't known what was happening to me.

"I have withdrawn from everything, and feel all right only when I'm all alone and no one can expect me to do things.

"I don't care about my personal appearance.

"I don't know *anything* anymore.

"I feel guilty about the things I have left undone.

"I don't think I could ever assume responsibility for anything."

If we attempt to evaluate this picture of self from an external frame of reference various diagnostic labels may come to mind. Trying to perceive it solely from the client's frame of reference we observe that to the young woman herself she appears disorganized, and not herself. She is perplexed and almost unacquainted with what is going on in herself. She feels unable and unwilling to function in any responsible or social way. This is at least a sampling of the way she experiences or perceives her self.

Her behavior is entirely consistent with this picture of self. If we abstract all her statements describing her behavior, in the same fashion as we abstracted her statements about self, the following pattern emerges—a pattern which in this case was corroborated by outside observation.

"I couldn't get up nerve to come in before; I haven't availed myself of help.

"Everything I should do or want to do, I don't do.

"I haven't kept in touch with friends; I avoid making the effort to go with them; I stopped writing letters home; I don't answer letters or telephone calls; I avoid contacts that would be professionally helpful; I didn't go home though I said I would.

"I failed to hand in my work in a course though I had it all done; I didn't even buy clothing that I needed; I haven't even kept my nails manicured.

"I didn't listen to material we were studying; I waste hours reading the funny papers; I can spend the whole afternoon doing absolutely nothing."

The picture of behavior is very much in keeping with the picture of self, and is summed up in the statement that "Everything I should do or want to do, I don't do." The behavior goes on, in ways that seem to the individual beyond understanding and beyond control.

If we contrast this picture of self and behavior with the picture as it exists in the ninth interview, thirty-eight days later, we find both the perception of self and the ways of behaving deeply altered. Her statements about self are as follows:

"I'm feeling much better; I'm taking more interest in myself.

"I do have some individuality, some interests.

"I seem to be getting a newer understanding of myself. I can look at myself a little better.

"I realize I'm just one person, with so much ability, but I'm not worried about it; I can accept the fact that I'm not always right.

"I feel more motivation, have more of a desire to go ahead.

"I still occasionally regret the past, though I feel less unhappy about it; I still have a long ways to go; I don't know whether I can keep the picture of myself I'm beginning to evolve.

"I can go on learning—in school or out.

"I do feel more like a normal person now; I feel more I can handle my life myself; I think I'm at the point where I can go along on my own."

Outstanding in this perception of herself are three things—that she knows herself, that she can view with comfort her assets and liabilities, and finally that she has drive and control of that drive.

In this ninth interview the behavioral picture is again consistent with the perception of self. It may be abstracted in these terms.

"I've been making plans about school and about a job; I've been working hard on a term paper; I've been going to the library to trace down a topic of special interest and finding it exciting.

"I've cleaned out my closets; washed my clothes.

"I finally wrote my parents; I'm going home for the holidays.

"I'm getting out and mixing with people; I am reacting sensibly to a fellow who is interested in me—seeing both his good and bad points.

"I will work toward my degree; I'll start looking for a job this week."

Her behavior, in contrast to the first interview, is now organized, forward-moving, effective, realistic and planful. It is in accord with the realistic and organized view she has achieved of her self.

It is this type of observation, in case after case, that leads us to say with some assurance that as perceptions of self and reality change, behavior changes. Likewise, in cases we might term failures, there appears to be no appreciable change in perceptual organization or in behavior.

What type of explanation might account for these concomitant changes in the perceptual field and the behavioral pattern? Let us examine some of the logical possibilities.

In the first place, it is possible that factors unrelated to therapy may have brought about the altered perception and behavior. There may have been physiological processes occurring which produced the change. There may have been alterations in the family relationships, or in the social forces, or in the educational picture or in some other area of cultural influence, which might account for the rather drastic shift in the concept of self and in the behavior.

There are difficulties in this type of explanation. Not only were there no known gross changes in the physical or cultural situation as far as Miss Vib was concerned, but the explanation gradually becomes inadequate when one tries to apply it to the many cases in which such change occurs. To postulate that some external factor brings the change and that only by chance does this period of change coincide with the period of therapy, becomes an untenable hypothesis.

Let us then look at another explanation, namely that the therapist exerted, during the nine hours of contact, a peculiarly potent cultural influence which brought about the change. Here again we are faced with several problems. It seems that nine hours scattered over five and one-half weeks is a very minute portion of time in which to bring about alteration of patterns which have been building for thirty years. We would have to postulate an influence so potent as to be classed as traumatic. This theory is particularly difficult to maintain when we find, on examining the recorded interviews, that not once in the nine hours did the therapist express any evaluation, positive or negative, of the client's initial or final perception of self, or her initial or final mode of behavior. There was not only no evaluation, but no standards expressed by which evaluation might be inferred.

There was, on the part of the therapist, evidence of warm interest in the individual, and thoroughgoing acceptance of the self and of the behavior as they existed initially, in the intermediate stages, and at the conclusion of therapy. It appears reasonable to say that the therapist established certain definite conditions of interpersonal relations, but since the very essence of this relationship is respect for the person as he is at that moment, the therapist can hardly be regarded as a cultural force making for change.

We find ourselves forced to a third type of explanation, a type of explanation which is not new to psychology, but which has had only partial

acceptance. Briefly it may be put that the observed phenomena of change seem most adequately explained by the hypothesis that *given certain psychological conditions, the individual has the capacity to reorganize his field of perception, including the way he perceives himself, and that a concomitant or a resultant of this perceptual reorganization is an appropriate alteration of behavior.* This puts into formal and objective terminology a clinical hypothesis which experience forces upon the therapist using a client-centered approach. One is compelled through clinical observation to develop a high degree of respect for the ego-integrative forces residing within each individual. One comes to recognize that under proper conditions the self is a basic factor in the formation of personality and in the determination of behavior. Clinical experience would strongly suggest that the self is, to some extent, an architect of self, and the above hypothesis simply puts this observation into psychological terms.

In support of this hypothesis it is noted in some cases that one of the concomitants of success in therapy is the realization on the part of the client that the self has the capacity for reorganization. Thus a student says:

> "You know I spoke of the fact that a person's background retards one. Like the fact that my family life wasn't good for me, and my mother certainly didn't give me any of the kind of bringing up that I should have had. Well, I've been thinking that over. It's true up to a point. But when you get so that you can see the situation, then it's really up to you."

Following this statement of the relation of the self to experience many changes occurred in this young man's behavior. In this, as in other cases, it appears that when the person comes to see himself as the perceiving, organizing agent, then reorganization of perception and consequent change in patterns of reaction take place.

On the other side of the picture we have frequently observed that when the individual has been authoritatively told that he is governed by certain factors or conditions beyond his control, it makes therapy more difficult, and it is only when the individual discovers for himself that he can organize his perceptions that change is possible. In veterans who have been given their own psychiatric diagnosis, the effect is often that of making the individual feel that he is under an unalterable doom, that he is unable to control the organization of his life. When, however, the self sees itself as capable of reorganizing its own perceptual field, a marked change in basic confidence occurs. Miss Nam, a student, illustrates this phenomenon when she says, after having made progress in therapy:

"I think I do feel better about the future, too, because it's as if I won't be acting in darkness. It's sort of, well, knowing somewhat why I act the way I do
. . . and at least it isn't the feeling that you're simply out of your own control and the fates are driving you to act that way. If you realize it, I think you can do something more about it."

A veteran at the conclusion of counseling puts it more briefly and more positively: "My attitude toward myself is changed now to where I feel I *can* do something with my self and life." He has come to view himself as the instrument by which some reorganization can take place.

There is another clinical observation which may be cited in support of the general hypothesis that there is a close relationship between behavior and the way in which reality is viewed by the individual. It has been noted in many cases that behavior changes come about for the most part imperceptibly and almost automatically, once the perceptual reorganization has taken place. A young wife who has been reacting violently to her maid, and has been quite disorganized in her behavior as a result of this antipathy, says "After I . . . discovered it was nothing more than that she resembled my mother, she didn't bother me any more. Isn't that interesting? She's still the same." Here is a clear statement indicating that though the basic perceptions have not changed, they have been differently organized, have acquired a new meaning, and that behavior changes then occur. * * *

Thus we have observed that appropriate changes in behavior occur when the individual acquires a different view of his world of experience, including himself; that this changed perception does not need to be dependent upon a change in the "reality," but may be a product of internal reorganization; that in some instances the awareness of the capacity for reperceiving experience accompanies this process or reorganization; that the altered behavioral responses occur automatically and without conscious effort as soon as the perceptual reorganization has taken place, apparently as a result of this.

In view of these observations a second hypothesis may be stated, which is closely related to the first. It is that *behavior is not directly influenced or determined by organic or cultural factors, but primarily* (and perhaps only) *by the perception of these elements.* In other words the crucial element in the determination of behavior is the perceptual field of the individual. While this perceptual field is, to be sure, deeply influenced and largely shaped by cultural and physiological forces, it is nevertheless important that it appears to be only the field as it is *perceived*, which exercises a specific determining influence upon behavior. This is not a new idea in psychology, but its implications have not always been fully recognized.

It might mean, first of all, that if it is the perceptual field which determines behavior, then the primary object of study for psychologists would be the person and his world as *viewed by the person himself.* It could mean that the internal frame of reference of the person might well constitute the field of psychology. * * * It might mean that the laws which govern behavior would be discovered more deeply by turning our attention to the laws which govern perception.

Now if our speculations contain a measure of truth, if the *specific* determinant of behavior is the perceptual field, and if the self can reorganize that perceptual field, then what are the limits of this process? Is the reorganization of perception capricious, or does it follow certain laws? Are there limits to the degree of reorganization? If so, what are

what really happened is △ in perception of Self

even though on surface it seems we have solved prob.

they? In this connection we have observed with some care the perception of one portion of the field of experience, the portion we call the self.

The Relation of the Perception of the Self to Adjustment

Initially we were oriented by the background of both lay and psychological thinking to regard the outcome of successful therapy as the solution of problems. If a person had a marital problem, a vocational problem, a problem of educational adjustment, the obvious purpose of counseling or therapy was to solve that problem. But as we observe and study the recorded accounts of the conclusion of therapy, it is clear that the most characteristic outcome is not necessarily solution of problems, but a freedom from tension, a different feeling about, and perception of, self. Perhaps something of this outcome may be conveyed by some illustrations.

Several statements taken from the final interview with a twenty-year-old young woman, Miss Mir, give indications of the characteristic attitude toward self, and the sense of freedom which appears to accompany it.

> "I've always tried to be what the others thought I should be, but now I am wondering whether I shouldn't just see that I am what I am."

> "Well, I've just noticed such a difference. I find that when I feel things, even when I feel hate, I don't care. I don't mind. I feel more free somehow. I don't feel guilty about things."

> "You know it's suddenly as though a big cloud has been lifted off. I feel so much more content."

Note in these statements the willingness to perceive herself as she is, to accept herself "realistically," to perceive and accept her "bad" attitudes as well as "good" ones. This realism seems to be accompanied by a sense of freedom and contentment.

Miss Vib, whose attitudes were quoted earlier, wrote out her own feelings about counseling some six weeks after the interviews were over, and gave the statement to her counselor. She begins:

> "The happiest outcome of therapy has been a new feeling about myself. As I think of it, it might be the only outcome. Certainly it is basic to all the changes in my behavior that have resulted." In discussing her experience in therapy she states, "I was coming to see myself as a whole. I began to realize that I am *one* person. This was an important insight to me. I saw that the former good academic achievement, job success, ease in social situations, and the present withdrawal, dejection, apathy and failure were all adaptive behavior, performed by *me*. This meant that I had to reorganize my feelings about myself, no longer holding to the unrealistic notion that the very good adjustment was the expression of the real 'me' and this neurotic behavior was not. I came to feel that I am the same person, sometimes functioning maturely, and sometimes assuming a neurotic role in the face of what I had conceived as insurmountable problems. The acceptance of myself as one person gave me strength in the process of reorganization. Now I had a substratum, a core of unity on which to work." As she continues her discussion there are such statements as "I am getting more happiness in being myself." "I approve of myself more, and I have so much less anxiety."

As in the previous example, the outstanding aspects appear to be the realization that all of her behavior "belonged" to her, that she could accept both the good and bad features about herself and that doing so gave her a release from anxiety and a feeling of solid happiness. In both instances there is only incidental reference to the serious "problems" which had been initially discussed.

Since Miss Mir is undoubtedly above average intelligence and Miss Vib is a person with some psychological training, it may appear that such results are found only with the sophisticated individual. To counteract this opinion a quotation may be given from a statement written by a veteran of limited ability and education who had just completed counseling, and was asked to write whatever reactions he had to the experience. He says:

> "As for the consoleing I have had I can say this, It really makes a man strip his own mind bare, and when he does he knows then what he realy is and what he can do. Or at least thinks he knows himself party well. As for myself, I know that my ideas were a

little too big for what I realy am, but now I realize one must try start out at his own level.

"Now after four visits, I have a much clearer picture of myself and my future. It makes me feel a little depressed and disappointed, but on the other hand, it has taken me out of the dark, the load seems a lot lighter now, that is I can see my way now, I know what I want to do, I know about what I can do, so now that I can see my goal, I will be able to work a whole lot easier, at my own level."

Although the expression is much simpler one notes again the same two elements—the acceptance of self as it is, and the feeling of easiness, of lightened burden, which accompanies it.

As we examine many individual case records and case recordings, it appears to be possible to bring together the findings in regard to successful therapy by stating another hypothesis in regard to that portion of the perceptual field which we call the self. It would appear that *when all of the ways in which the individual perceives himself—all perceptions of the qualities, abilities, impulses, and attitudes of the person, and all perceptions of himself in relation to others—are accepted into the organized conscious concept of the self, then this achievement is accompanied by feelings of comfort and freedom from tension which are experienced as psychological adjustment.*

This hypothesis would seem to account for the observed fact that the comfortable perception of self which is achieved is sometimes more positive than before, sometimes more negative. When the individual permits all his perceptions of himself to be organized into one pattern, the picture is sometimes more flattering than he has held in the past, sometimes less flattering. It is always more comfortable.

It may be pointed out also that this tentative hypothesis supplies an operational type of definition, based on the client's internal frame of reference, for such hitherto vague terms as "adjustment," "integration," and "acceptance of self." They are defined in terms of perception, in a way which it should be possible to prove or disprove. When all of the organic perceptual experiences—the experiencing of attitudes, impulses, abilities and

disabilities, the experiencing of others and of "reality"—when all of these perceptions are freely assimilated into an organized and consistent system, available to consciousness, then psychological adjustment or integration might be said to exist. The definition of adjustment is thus made an internal affair, rather than dependent upon an external "reality."

Something of what is meant by this acceptance and assimilation of perceptions about the self may be illustrated from the case of Miss Nam, a student. Like many other clients she gives evidence of having experienced attitudes and feelings which are defensively denied because they are not consistent with the concept or picture she holds of herself. The way in which they are first fully admitted into consciousness, and then organized into a unified system may be shown by excerpts from the recorded interviews. She has spoken of the difficulty she has had in bringing herself to write papers for her university courses.

"I just thought of something else which perhaps hinders me, and that is that again it's two different feelings. When I have to sit down and do (a paper), though I have a lot of ideas, underneath I think I always have the feeling that I just can't do it. . . . I have this feeling of being terrifically confident that I can do something, without being willing to put the work into it. At other times I'm practically afraid of what I have to do. . . ."

Note that the conscious self has been organized as "having a lot of ideas," being "terrifically confident" but that "underneath," in other words not freely admitted into consciousness, has been the experience of feeling "I just can't do it." She continues:

"I'm trying to work through this funny relationship between this terrific confidence and then this almost fear of doing anything . . . and I think the kind of feeling that I can really do things is part of an illusion I have about myself of being, in my imagination, sure that it will be something good and very good and all that, but whenever I get down to the actual task of getting started, it's a terrible feeling of—well, incapacity, that I won't get it done either the way I want to do it, or even not being sure how I want to do it."

Again the picture of herself which is present in consciousness is that of a person who is "very good," but this picture is entirely out of line with the actual organic experience in the situation.

Later in the same interview she expresses very well the fact that her perceptions are not all organized into one consistent conscious self.

"I'm not sure about what kind of a person I am—well, I realize that all of these are a part of me, but I'm not quite sure of how to make all of these things fall in line."

In the next interview we have an excellent opportunity to observe the organization of both of these conflicting perceptions into one pattern, with the resultant sense of freedom from tension which has been described above.

"It's very funny, even as I sit here I realize that I have more confidence in myself, in the sense that when I used to approach new situations I would have two very funny things operating at the same time. I had a fantasy that I could do anything, which was a fantasy which covered over all these other feelings that I really couldn't do it, or couldn't do it as well as I wanted to, and it's as if now those two things have merged together, and it is more real, that a situation isn't either testing myself or proving something to myself or anyone else. It's just in terms of doing it. And I think I have done away both with that fantasy and that fear. . . . So I think I can go ahead and approach things—well, just sensibly."

No longer is it necessary for this client to "cover over" her real experiences. Instead the picture of herself as very able, and the experienced feeling of complete inability, have now been brought together into one integrated pattern of self as a person with real, but imperfect abilities. Once the self is thus accepted the inner energies making for self-actualization are released and she attacks her life problems more efficiently.

Observing this type of material frequently in counseling experience would lead to a tentative hypothesis of maladjustment, which like the other hypothesis suggested, focuses on the perception of self. It might be proposed that the tensions called psychological maladjustment exist when the organized concept of self (conscious or available to conscious awareness) is not in accord with the perceptions actually experienced.

This discrepancy between the concept of self and the actual perceptions seems to be explicable only in terms of the fact that the self concept resists assimilating into itself any percept which is inconsistent with its present organization. The feeling that she may not have the ability to do a paper is inconsistent with Miss Nam's conscious picture of herself as a very able and confident person, and hence, though fleetingly perceived, is denied organization as a part of her self, until this comes about in therapy.

The Conditions of Change of Self-Perception

If the way in which the self is perceived has as close and significant a relationship to behavior as has been suggested, then the manner in which this perception may be altered becomes a question of importance. If a reorganization of self-perceptions brings a change in behavior; if adjustment and maladjustment depend on the congruence between perceptions as experienced and the self as perceived, then the factors which permit a reorganization of the perception of self are significant.

Our observations of psychotherapeutic experience would seem to indicate that absence of any threat to the self-concept is an important item in the problem. Normally the self resists incorporating into itself those experiences which are inconsistent with the functioning of self. But a point overlooked by Lecky and others[1] is that when the self is free from any threat of attack or likelihood of attack, then it is possible for the self to consider these hitherto rejected perceptions, to make new

---

[1] That is, by Rogers's intellectual adversaries.

differentiations, and to reintegrate the self in such a way as to include them.

An illustration from the case of Miss Vib may serve to clarify this point. In her statement written six weeks after the conclusion of counseling, Miss Vib thus describes the way in which unacceptable percepts become incorporated into the self. She writes:

"In the earlier interviews I kept saying such things as, 'I am not acting like myself', 'I never acted this way before.' What I meant was that this withdrawn, untidy, and apathetic person was not myself. Then I began to realize that I was the same person, seriously withdrawn, etc. now, as I had been before. That did not happen until after I had talked out my self-rejection, shame, despair, and doubt, in the accepting situation of the interview. The counselor was not startled or shocked. I was telling him all these things about myself which did not fit into my picture of a graduate student, a teacher, a sound person. He responded with complete acceptance and warm interest without heavy emotional overtones. Here was a sane, intelligent person wholeheartedly accepting this behavior that seemed so shameful to me. I can remember an organic feeling of relaxation. I did not have to keep up the struggle to cover up and hide this shameful person."

Note how clearly one can see here the whole range of denied perceptions of self, and the fact that they could be considered as a part of self only in a social situation which involved no threat to the self, in which another person, the counselor, becomes almost an alternate self and looks with understanding and acceptance upon these same perceptions. She continues:

"Retrospectively, it seems to me that what I felt as 'warm acceptance without emotional overtones' was what I needed to work through my difficulties. . . . The counselor's impersonality with interest allowed me to talk out my feelings. The clarification in the interview situation presented the attitude to me as a 'ding an sich' which I could look at, manipulate, and put in place. In organizing my attitudes, I was beginning to organize me."

Here the nature of the exploration of experience, of seeing it as experience and not as a threat to self,

enables the client to reorganize her perceptions of self, which as she says was also "reorganizing me."

If we attempt to describe in more conventional psychological terms the nature of the process which culminates in an altered organization and integration of self in the process of therapy it might run as follows. The individual is continually endeavoring to meet his needs by reacting to the field of experience as he perceives it, and to do that more efficiently by differentiating elements of the field and reintegrating them into new patterns. Reorganization of the field may involve the reorganization of the self as well as of other parts of the field. The self, however, resists reorganization and change. In everyday life individual adjustment by means of reorganization of the field exclusive of the self is more common and is less threatening to the individual. Consequently, the individual's first mode of adjustment is the reorganization of that part of the field which does not include the self.

Client-centered therapy is different from other life situations inasmuch as the therapist tends to remove from the individual's immediate world all those aspects of the field which the individual can reorganize except the self. The therapist, by reacting to the client's feelings and attitudes rather than to the objects of his feelings and attitudes, assists the client in bringing from background into focus his own self, making it easier than ever before for the client to perceive and react to the self. By offering only understanding and no trace of evaluation, the therapist removes himself as an object of attitudes, becoming only an alternate expression of the client's self. The therapist, by providing a consistent atmosphere of permissiveness and understanding, removes whatever threat existed to prevent all perceptions of the self from emerging into figure. Hence in this situation all the ways in which the self has been experienced can be viewed openly, and organized into a complex unity.

It is then this complete absence of any factor which would attack the concept of self, and second, the assistance in focusing upon the perception of self, which seems to permit a more differentiated view of self and finally the reorganization of self.

He's proposing a whole new way" of doing" therapy.

If we created labels after "based upon internal perspectives. the labels would be really different

* * *

Implications

* * * We have discovered with some surprise that our clinical observations, and the tentative hypotheses which seem to grow out of them, raise disturbing questions which appear to cast doubt on the very foundations of many of our psychological endeavors, particularly in the fields of clinical psychology and personality study. To clarify what is meant, I should like to restate in more logical order the formulations I have given, and to leave with you certain questions and problems which each one seems to raise.

If we take first the tentative proposition that the specific determinant of behavior is the perceptual field of the individual, would this not lead, if regarded as a working hypothesis, to a radically different approach in clinical psychology and personality research? It would seem to mean that instead of elaborate case histories full of information about the person as an object, we would endeavor to develop ways of seeing his situation, his past, and himself, as these objects appear to him. We would try to see with him, rather than to evaluate him. It might mean the minimizing of the elaborate psychometric procedures by which we have endeavored to measure or value the individual from our own frame of reference. It might mean the minimizing or discarding of all the vast series of labels which we have painstakingly built up over the years. Paranoid, preschizophrenic, compulsive, constricted—terms such as these might become irrelevant because they are all based in thinking which takes an external frame of reference. They are not the ways in which the individual experiences himself. If we consistently studied each individual from the internal frame of reference of that individual, from within his own perceptual field, it seems probable that we should find generalizations which could be made, and principles which were operative, but we may be very sure that they would be of a different order from these externally based judgements *about* individuals.

Let us look at another of the suggested propositions. If we took seriously the hypothesis that integration and adjustment are internal conditions related to the degree of acceptance or nonacceptance of all perceptions, and the degree of organization of these perceptions into one consistent system, this would decidedly affect our clinical procedures. It would seem to imply the abandonment of the notion that adjustment is dependent upon the pleasantness or unpleasantness of the environment, and would demand concentration upon those processes which bring about self-integration within the person. It would mean a minimizing or an abandoning of those clinical procedures which utilize the alteration of environmental forces as a method of treatment. It would rely instead upon the fact that the person who is internally unified has the greatest likelihood of meeting environmental problems constructively, either as an individual or in cooperation with others.

If we take the remaining proposition that the self, under proper conditions, is capable of reorganizing, to some extent, its own perceptual field, and of thus altering behavior, this too seems to raise disturbing questions. Following the path of this hypothesis would appear to mean a shift in emphasis in psychology from focusing upon the fixity of personality attributes and psychological abilities, to the alterability of these same characteristics. It would concentrate attention upon process rather than upon fixed status. Whereas psychology has, in personality study, been concerned primarily with the measurement of the fixed qualities of the individual, and with his past in order to explain his present, the hypothesis here suggested would seem to concern itself much more with the personal world of the present in order to understand the future, and in predicting that future would be concerned with the principles by which personality and behavior are altered, as well as the extent to which they remain fixed.

Thus we find that a clinical approach, client-centered therapy, has led us to try to adopt the client's perceptual field as the basis for genuine understanding. In trying to enter this internal world of perception, not by introspection, but by observation and direct inference, we find ourselves in a new vantage point for understanding personality dynamics, a vantage point which opens up some disturbing vistas. We find that behavior seems to be better understood as a reaction to this reality-as-perceived. We discover that the way in which the person sees himself, and the perceptions he dares not take as belonging to himself, seem to have an important relationship to the inner peace which constitutes adjustment. We discover within the person, under certain conditions, a capacity for the restructuring and the reorganization of self,

and consequently the reorganization of behavior, which has profound social implications. We see these observations, and the theoretical formulations which they inspire, as a fruitful new approach for study and research in various fields of psychology.

References

Rogers, Carl R. (1946). Significant aspects of client-centered therapy. *American Psychologist, 1,* 415–422.

Snyder, W. U. (1946). 'Warmth' in nondirective counseling. *Journal of Abnormal and Social Psychology, 41,* 491–495.

IF WE ARE SO RICH, WHY AREN'T WE HAPPY?

Mihaly Csikszentmihalyi

What was classically called "humanistic psychology" has faded from view in recent years, but now a successor is stepping forward in its place. The "positive psychology movement" has become suddenly quite prominent and has taken up the humanistic mission of arguing that human nature is basically good and that the proper topic of psychology is human experience—especially positive human experience, also known as "the good life." The author of the next selection, Mihaly Csikszentmihalyi (pronounced chick-sent-me-high), *directly addresses the questions, what is positive experience and how does one attain it?*

Csikszentmihalyi argues that positive experience—happiness—is not a matter of material goods or entertainment but rather comes from matching one's capacities to one's activities. This produces a state he calls "flow," characterized by total focus, a loss of sense of time, and mildly pleasant emotion.

Notice how the modern humanist Csikszentmihalyi draws directly on the classic theorist Carl Rogers, when he refers to the way "human consciousness uses its self-organizing ability to achieve a positive internal state through its own efforts" (see footnote 1). This is just one indication that the positive psychology movement is the modern version of humanistic psychology.

From *American Psychologist*, 54, 821–827, 1999.

Psychology is the heir to those "sciences of man" envisioned by Enlightenment thinkers such as Gianbattista Vico, David Hume, and the Baron de Montesquieu. One of their fundamental conclusions was that the pursuit of happiness constituted the basis of both individual motivation and social well-being. This insight into the human condition was condensed by John Locke (1690/1975) in his famous statement, "That

we call Good which is apt to cause or increase pleasure, or diminish pain" (p. 2), whereas evil is the reverse—it is what causes or increases pain and diminishes pleasure.

The generation of utilitarian philosophers that followed Locke, including David Hartley, Joseph Priestley, and Jeremy Bentham, construed a good society as that which allows the greatest happiness for the greatest number (Bentham, 1789/1970, pp. 64–65). This focus on pleasure or happiness as the touchstone of private and public life is by no means a brainchild of post–Reformation Europe. It was already present in the writings of the Greeks—for instance, Aristotle noted that although humankind values a great many things, such as health, fame, and possessions, because we think that they will make us happy, we value happiness for itself. Thus, happiness is the only intrinsic goal that people seek for its own sake, the bottom line of all desire. The idea that furthering the pursuit of happiness should be one of the responsibilities of a just government was of course enshrined later in the Declaration of Independence of the United States.

Despite this recognition on the part of the human sciences that happiness is the fundamental goal of life, there has been slow progress in understanding what happiness itself consists of. Perhaps because the heyday of utilitarian philosophy coincided with the start of the enormous forward strides in public health and in the manufacturing and distribution of goods, the majority of those who thought about such things assumed that increases in pleasure and happiness would come from increased affluence, from greater control over the material environment. The great self-confidence of the Western technological nations, and especially of the United States, was in large part because of the belief that materialism—the prolongation of a healthy life, the acquisition of wealth, the ownership of consumer goods—would be the royal road to a happy life.

However, the virtual monopoly of materialism as the dominant ideology has come at the price of a trivialization that has robbed it of much of the truth it once contained. In current use, it amounts to little more than a thoughtless hedonism, a call to do one's thing regardless of consequences, a belief that whatever feels good at the moment must be worth doing.

This is a far cry from the original view of materialists, such as John Locke, who were aware of the futility of pursuing happiness without qualifications and who advocated the pursuit of happiness through prudence—making sure that

people do not mistake imaginary happiness for real happiness.

What does it mean to pursue happiness through prudence? Locke must have derived his inspiration from the Greek philosopher Epicurus, who 2,300 years ago already saw clearly that to enjoy a happy life, one must develop self-discipline. The materialism of Epicurus was solidly based on the ability to defer gratification. He claimed that although all pain was evil, this did not mean one should always avoid pain—for instance, it made sense to put up with pain now if one was sure to avoid thereby a greater pain later. He wrote to his friend Menoeceus

> The beginning and the greatest good . . . is prudence. For this reason prudence is more valuable even than philosophy: from it derive all the other virtues. Prudence teaches us how impossible it is to live pleasantly without living wisely, virtuously, and justly . . . take thought, then, for these and kindred matters day and night. . . . You shall be disturbed neither waking nor sleeping, and you shall live as a god among men. (Epicurus of Samos, trans. 1998, p. 48)

This is not the image of epicureanism held by most people. The popular view holds that pleasure and material comforts should be grasped wherever they can, and that these alone will improve the quality of one's life. As the fruits of technology have ripened and the life span has lengthened, the hope that increased material rewards would bring about a better life seemed for a while justified.

Now, at the end of the second millennium, it is becoming clear that the solution is not that simple. Inhabitants of the wealthiest industrialized Western nations are living in a period of unprecedented riches, in conditions that previous generations would have considered luxuriously comfortable, in relative peace and security, and they are living on the average close to twice as long as their great-grandparents did. Yet, despite all these improvements in material conditions, it does not seem that people are so much more satisfied with their lives than they were before.

The Ambiguous Relationship Between Material and Subjective Well-being

The indirect evidence that those of us living in the United States today are not happier than our ancestors were comes from national statistics of social pathology—the figures that show the doubling and tripling of violent crimes, family breakdown, and psychosomatic complaints since at least the halfway mark of the century. If material well-being leads to happiness, why is it that neither capitalist nor socialist solutions seem to work? Why is it that the crew on the flagship of capitalist affluence is becoming increasingly addicted to drugs for falling asleep, for waking up, for staying slim, for escaping boredom and depression? Why are suicides and loneliness such a problem in Sweden, which has applied the best of socialist principles to provide material security to its people?

Direct evidence about the ambiguous relationship of material and subjective well-being comes from studies of happiness that psychologists and other social scientists have finally started to pursue, after a long delay in which research on happiness was considered too soft for scientists to undertake. It is true that these surveys are based on self-reports and on verbal scales that might have different meanings depending on the culture and the language in which they are written. Thus, the results of culturally and methodologically circumscribed studies need to be taken with more than the usual grain of salt. Nevertheless, at this point they represent the state of the art—an art that will inevitably become more precise with time.

Although cross-national comparisons show a reasonable correlation between the wealth of a country as measured by its gross national product and the self-reported happiness of its inhabitants (Inglehart, 1990), the relationship is far from perfect. The inhabitants of Germany and Japan, for instance, nations with more than twice the gross national product of Ireland, report much lower levels of happiness.

Comparisons within countries show an even weaker relationship between material and subjective well-being. Diener, Horwitz, and Emmons (1985), in a study of some of the wealthiest individuals in the United States, found their levels of happiness to be barely above that of individuals with average incomes. After following a group of lottery winners, Brickman, Coates, and Janoff-Bulman (1978) concluded that despite their sudden increase in wealth, their happiness was no different from that of people struck by traumas, such as blindness or paraplegia. That having more money to spend does not necessarily bring about greater subjective well-being has also been documented on a national scale by David G. Myers (1993). His calculations show that although the adjusted value of after-tax personal income in the United States has more than doubled between 1960 and 1990, the percentage of people describing themselves as "very happy" has remained unchanged at 30% (Myers, 1993, pp. 41–42).

In the *American Psychologist*'s January 2000 special issue on positive psychology, David G. Myers (2000) and Ed Diener (2000) discuss in great detail the lack of relationship between material and subjective well-being, so I will not belabor the point here. Suffice it to say that in current longitudinal studies of a representative sample of almost 1,000 American adolescents conducted with the experience sampling method * * * , a consistently low negative relationship between material and subjective well-being has been found (Csikszentmihalyi & Schneider, in press). For instance, the reported happiness of teenagers (measured several times a day for a week in each of three years) shows a very significant inverse relationship to the social class of the community in which teens live, to their parents' level of education, and to their parents' occupational status. Children of the lowest socioeconomic strata generally report the highest happiness, and upper-middle-class children generally report the least happiness. Does this mean that more affluent children are in fact less happy, or does it mean that the norms of their social class prescribe that they should present themselves as less happy? At this point, we are unable to make this vital distinction.

Yet despite the evidence that the relationship

between material wealth and happiness is tenuous at best, most people still cling to the notion that their problems would be resolved if they only had more money. In a survey conducted at the University of Michigan, when people were asked what would improve the quality of their lives, the first and foremost answer was "more money" (Campbell, 1981).

Given these facts, it seems that one of the most important tasks psychologists face is to better understand the dynamics of happiness and to communicate these findings to the public at large. If the main justification of psychology is to help reduce psychic distress and support psychic well-being, then psychologists should try to prevent the disillusionment that comes when people find out that they have wasted their lives struggling to reach goals that cannot satisfy them. Psychologists should be able to provide alternatives that in the long run will lead to a more rewarding life.

Why Material Rewards Do Not Necessarily Make People Happy

To answer this question, I'll start by reflecting on why material rewards, which people regard so highly, do not necessarily provide the happiness expected from them. The first reason is the well-documented escalation of expectations. If people strive for a certain level of affluence thinking that it will make them happy, they find that on reaching it, they become very quickly habituated, and at that point they start hankering for the next level of income, property, or good health. In a 1987 poll conducted by the *Chicago Tribune*, people who earned less than $30,000 a year said that $50,000 would fulfill their dreams, whereas those with yearly incomes of over $100,000 said they would need $250,000 to be satisfied ("Pay Nags," 1987; "Rich Think Big," 1987; see also Myers, 1993, p. 57). Several studies have confirmed that goals keep getting pushed upward as soon as a lower level is reached. It is not the objective size of the reward but its difference from one's "adaptation level" that provides subjective value (e.g., Davis, 1959; Michalos, 1985; Parducci, 1995).

The second reason is related to the first. When resources are unevenly distributed, people evaluate their possessions not in terms of what they need to live in comfort, but in comparison with those who have the most. Thus, the relatively affluent feel poor in comparison with the very rich and are unhappy as a result. This phenomenon of "relative deprivation" (Martin, 1981; Williams, 1975) seems to be fairly universal and well-entrenched. In the United States, the disparity in incomes between the top percentage and the rest is getting wider; this does not bode well for the future happiness of the population.

The third reason is that even though being rich and famous might be rewarding, nobody has ever claimed that material rewards alone are sufficient to make us happy. Other conditions—such as a satisfying family life, having intimate friends, having time to reflect and pursue diverse interests—have been shown to be related to happiness (Myers, 1993; Myers & Diener, 1995; Voenhoven, 1988). There is no intrinsic reason why these two sets of rewards—the material and the socioemotional—should be mutually exclusive. In practice, however, it is very difficult to reconcile their conflicting demands. As many psychologists from William James (1890) to Herbert A. Simon (1969) have remarked, time is the ultimate scarce resource, and the allocation of time (or more precisely, of attention over time) presents difficult choices that eventually determine the content and quality of our lives. This is why professional and business persons find it so difficult to balance the demands of work and family, and why they so rarely feel that they have not shortchanged one of these vital aspects of their lives.

Material advantages do not readily translate into social and emotional benefits. In fact, to the extent that most of one's psychic energy becomes invested in material goals, it is typical for sensitivity to other rewards to atrophy. Friendship, art, literature, natural beauty, religion, and philosophy become less and less interesting. The Swedish economist Stephen Linder was the first to point out that as income and therefore the value of one's time increases, it becomes less and less "rational" to spend it on anything besides making money—or on spending it conspicuously (Linder, 1970). The opportunity costs of playing with one's child, reading poetry, or attending a family reunion become too high, and so one stops doing such irrational things. Eventually a person who only responds to material rewards becomes blind to any other kind and loses the ability to derive happiness from other sources (see also Benedikt, 1999; Scitovsky, 1975). As is true of addiction in general, material rewards at first enrich the quality of life. Because of this, we tend to conclude that more must be better. But life is rarely linear; in most cases, what is good in small quantities becomes commonplace and then harmful in larger doses.

Dependence on material goals is so difficult to avoid in part because our culture has progressively eliminated every alternative that in previous times used to give meaning and purpose to individual lives. Although hard comparative data are lacking, many historians (e.g., Polanyi, 1957) have claimed that past cultures provided a greater variety of attractive models for successful lives. A person could be valued and admired because he or she was a saint, a bon vivant, a wise person, a good craftsman, a brave patriot, or an upright citizen. Nowadays the logic of reducing everything to quantifiable measures has made the dollar the common metric by which to evaluate every aspect of human action. The worth of a person and of a person's accomplishments are determined by the price they fetch in the marketplace. It is useless to claim that a painting is good art unless it gets high bids at Sotheby's, nor can we claim that someone is wise unless he or she can charge five figures for a consultation. Given the hegemony of material rewards in our culture's restricted repertoire, it is not surprising that so many people feel that their only hope for a happy life is to amass all the earthly goods they can lay hands on.

To recapitulate, there are several reasons for the lack of a direct relationship between material well-being and happiness. Two of them are sociocultural: (a) The growing disparity in wealth makes even the reasonably affluent feel poor. (b) This relative deprivation is exacerbated by a cultural factor, namely, the lack of alternative values and a wide range of successful lifestyles that could compensate for a single, zero-sum hierarchy based on dollars and cents. Two of the reasons are more psychological: (a) When we evaluate success, our minds use a strategy of escalating expectations, so that few people are ever satisfied for long with what they possess or what they have achieved. (b) As more psychic energy is invested in material goals, less of it is left to pursue other goals that are also necessary for a life in which one aspires to happiness.

None of this is intended to suggest that the material rewards of wealth, health, comfort, and fame detract from happiness. Rather, after a certain minimum threshold—which is not stable but varies with the distribution of resources in the given society—they seem to be irrelevant. Of course, most people will still go on from cradle to grave believing that if they could only have had more money, or good looks, or lucky breaks, they would have achieved that elusive state.

Psychological Approaches to Happiness

If people are wrong about the relation between material conditions and how happy they are, then what *does* matter? The alternative to the materialist approach has always been something that used to be called a "spiritual" and nowadays we may call a "psychological" solution. This approach is based on the premise that if happiness is a mental state, people should be able to control it through cognitive means. Of course, it is also possible to control the mind pharmacologically. Every culture has developed drugs ranging from peyote to heroin to alcohol in an effort to improve the quality of experience by direct chemical means. In my opinion, however, chemically induced well-being lacks a vital ingredient of happiness: the knowledge that one is responsible for having achieved it. Happiness is not something that happens to people but something that they make happen.

In some cultures, drugs ingested in a ritual, ceremonial context appear to have lasting beneficial effects, but in such cases the benefits most likely result primarily from performing the ritual, rather than from the chemicals per se. Thus, in discussing psychological approaches to happiness, I focus exclusively on processes in which human consciousness uses its self-organizing ability to achieve a positive internal state through its own efforts[1] with minimal reliance on external manipulation of the nervous system.

There have been many very different ways to program the mind to increase happiness or at least to avoid being unhappy. Some religions have done it by promising an eternal life of happiness follows our earthly existence. Others, on realizing that most unhappiness is the result of frustrated goals and thwarted desires, teach people to give up desires altogether and thus avoid disappointment. Still others, such as Yoga and Zen, have developed complex techniques for controlling the stream of thoughts and feelings, thereby providing the means for shutting out negative content from consciousness. Some of the most radical and sophisticated disciplines for self-control of the mind were those developed in India, culminating in the Buddhist teachings 25 centuries ago. Regardless of its truth content, faith in a supernatural order seems to enhance subjective well-being: Surveys generally show a low but consistent correlation between religiosity and happiness (Csikszentmihalyi & Patton, 1997; Myers, 1993).

Contemporary psychology has developed several solutions that share some of the premises of these ancient traditions but differ drastically in content and detail. What is common to them is the assumption that cognitive techniques, attributions, attitudes, and perceptual styles can change the effects of material conditions on consciousness, help restructure an individual's goals, and consequently improve the quality of experience. Maslow's (1968, 1971) *self-actualization*, Block and Block's (1980) *ego-resiliency*, Diener's (1984, 2000) *positive emotionality*, Antonovsky's (1979) *salutogenic approach*, Seeman's (1996) *personality integration*, Deci and Ryan's (1985; Ryan & Deci, 2000) *auton-*

omy, Scheier and Carver's (1985) *dispositional optimism*, and Seligman's (1991) *learned optimism* are only a few of the theoretical concepts developed recently, many with their own preventive and therapeutic implications.

THE EXPERIENCE OF FLOW My own addition to this list is the concept of the *autotelic experience*, or *flow*, and of the autotelic personality. The concept describes a particular kind of experience that is so engrossing and enjoyable that it becomes autotelic, that is, worth doing for its own sake even though it may have no consequence outside itself. Creative activities, music, sports, games, and religious rituals are typical sources for this kind of experience. Autotelic persons are those who have such flow experiences relatively often, regardless of what they are doing.

Of course, we never do anything purely for its own sake. Our motives are always a mixture of intrinsic and extrinsic considerations. For instance, composers may write music because they hope to sell it and pay the bills, because they want to become famous, because their self-image depends on writing songs—all of these being extrinsic motives. But if the composers are motivated only by these extrinsic rewards, they are missing an essential ingredient. In addition to these rewards, they could also enjoy writing music for its own sake—in which case, the activity would become autotelic. My studies (e.g., Csikszentmihalyi, 1975, 1996, 1997) have suggested that happiness depends on whether a person is able to derive flow from whatever he or she does.

A brief selection from one of the more than 10,000 interviews collected from around the world might provide a sense of what the flow experience is like. Asked how it felt when writing music was going well, a composer responded.

> You are in an ecstatic state to such a point that you feel as though you almost don't exist. I have experienced this time and time again. My hand seems devoid of myself, and I have nothing to do with what is happening. I just sit there watching in a state of awe and wonderment. And the music just flows out by itself. (Csikszentmihalyi, 1975, p. 44)

---

[1]This "self-organizing" ability is a classic concern of humanistic psychologists such as Maslow and Rogers.

This response is quite typical of most descriptions of how people feel when they are thoroughly involved in something that is enjoyable and meaningful to the person. First of all, the experience is described as "ecstatic": in other words, as being somehow separate from the routines of everyday life. This sense of having stepped into a different reality can be induced by environmental cues, such as walking into a sport event, a religious ceremony, or a musical performance, or the feeling can be produced internally, by focusing attention on a set of stimuli with their own rules, such as the composition of music.

Next, the composer claims that "you feel as though you almost don't exist." This dimension of the experience refers to involvement in the activity being so demanding that no surplus attention is left to monitor any stimuli irrelevant to the task at hand. Thus, chess players might stand up after a game and realize that they have splitting headaches and must run to the bathroom, whereas for many hours during the game they had excluded all information about their bodily states from consciousness.

The composer also refers to the felt spontaneity of the experience: "My hand seems devoid of myself . . . I have nothing to do with what is happening." Of course, this sense of effortless performance is only possible because the skills and techniques have been learned and practiced so well that they have become automatic. This brings up one of the paradoxes of flow: One has to be in control of the activity to experience it, yet one should not try to consciously control what one is doing.

As the composer stated, when the conditions are right, action "just flows out by itself." It is because so many respondents used the analogy of spontaneous, effortless flow to describe how it felt when what they were doing was going well that I used the term *flow* to describe the autotelic experience. Here is what a well-known lyricist, a former poet laureate of the United States, said about his writing:

> You lose your sense of time, you're completely enraptured, you are completely caught up in what you're doing, and you are sort of swayed by the possibilities you see in this work. If that becomes too powerful, then you get up, because the excitement is too great. . . . The idea is to be so, so saturated with it that there's no future or past, it's just an extended present in which you are . . . making meaning. And dismantling meaning, and remaking it. (Csikszentmihalyi, 1996, p. 121)

This kind of intense experience is not limited to creative endeavors. It is reported by teenagers who love studying, by workers who like their jobs, by drivers who enjoy driving. Here is what one woman said about her sources of deepest enjoyment:

> [It happens when] I am working with my daughter, when she's discovered something new. A new cookie recipe that she has accomplished, that she has made herself, an artistic work that she's done and she is proud of. Her reading is something that she is really into, and we read together. She reads to me and I read to her, and that's a time when I sort of lose touch with the rest of the world. I am totally absorbed in what I am doing. (Allison & Duncan, 1988, p. 129)

This kind of experience has a number of common characteristics. First, people report knowing very clearly what they have to do moment by moment, either because the activity requires it (as when the score of a musical composition specifies what notes to play next), or because the person sets clear goals every step of the way (as when a rock climber decides which hold to try for next). Second, they are able to get immediate feedback on what they are doing. Again, this might be because the activity provides information about the performance (as when one is playing tennis and after each shot one knows whether the ball went where it was supposed to go), or it might be because the person has an internalized standard that makes it possible to know whether one's actions meet the standard (as when a poet reads the last word or the last sentence written and judges it to be right or in need of revision).

Another universal condition for the flow experience is that the person feels his or her abilities to act match the opportunities for action. If the challenges are too great for the person's skill, anxiety is likely to ensue; if the skills are greater than the challenges, one feels bored. When challenges are in balance with skills, one becomes lost in the activity and flow is likely to result (Csikszentmihalyi, 1975, 1997).

Even this greatly compressed summary of the flow experience should make it clear that it has little to do with the widespread cultural trope of "going with the flow." To go with the flow means to abandon oneself to a situation that feels good, natural, and spontaneous. The flow experience that I have been studying is something that requires skills, concentration, and perseverance. However, the evidence suggests that it is the second form of flow that leads to subjective well-being.

The relationship between flow and happiness is not entirely self-evident. Strictly speaking, during the experience people are not necessarily happy because they are too involved in the task to have the luxury to reflect on their subjective states. Being happy would be a distraction, an interruption of the flow. But afterward, when the experience is over, people report having been in as positive a state as it is possible to feel. Autotelic persons, those who are often in flow, tend also to report more positive states overall and to feel that their lives are more purposeful and meaningful (Adlai-Gail, 1994; Hektner, 1996).

The phenomenon of flow helps explain the contradictory and confusing causes of what we usually call happiness. It explains why it is possible to achieve states of subjective well-being by so many different routes: either by achieving wealth and power or by relinquishing them; by cherishing either solitude or close relationships; through ambition or through its opposite, contentment; through the pursuit of objective science or through religious practice. *People are happy not because of what they do, but because of how they do it.* If they can experience flow working on the assembly line, chances are they will be happy, whereas if they don't have flow while lounging at a luxury resort, they are not going to be happy. The same is true of the various psychological techniques for achieving positive mental health: If the process of becoming resilient or self-efficacious is felt to be boring or an external imposition, the technique is unlikely to lead to happiness, even if it is mastered to the letter. You have to enjoy mental health to benefit from it.

MAKING FLOW POSSIBLE The prerequisite for happiness is the ability to get fully involved in life. If the material conditions are abundant, so much the better, but lack of wealth or health need not prevent one from finding flow in whatever circumstances one finds at hand. In fact, our studies suggest that children from the most affluent families find it more difficult to be in flow—compared with less well-to-do teenagers, they tend to be more bored, less involved, less enthusiastic, less excited.

At the same time, it would be a mistake to think that each person should be left to find enjoyment wherever he or she can find it or to give up efforts for improving collective conditions. There is so much that could be done to introduce more flow in schools, in family life, in the planning of communities, in jobs, in the way we commute to work and eat our meals—in short, in almost every aspect of life. This is especially important with respect to young people. Our research suggests, for instance, that more affluent teenagers experience flow less often because, although they dispose of more material possessions, they spend less time with their parents, and they do fewer interesting things with them (Hunter, 1998). Creating conditions that make flow experiences possible is one aspect of that "pursuit of happiness" for which the social and political community should be responsible.

Nevertheless, flow alone does not guarantee a happy life. It is also necessary to find flow in activities that are complex, namely, activities that provide a potential for growth over an entire life span, allow for the emergence of new opportunities for action, and stimulate the development of new skills. A person who never learns to enjoy the company of others and who finds few opportunities within a meaningful social context is unlikely to achieve inner harmony (Csikszentmihalyi, 1993; Csikszentmihalyi & Rathunde, 1998; Inghilleri, 1999), but when flow comes from active physical, mental, or emotional involvement—from work, sports, hobbies, meditation, and interpersonal relationships—then the chances for a complex life that leads to happiness improve.

The Limits of Flow

There is at least one more important issue left to consider. In reviewing the history of materialism, I have discussed John Locke's warnings about the necessity of pursuing happiness with prudence and about the importance of distinguishing real from imaginary happiness. Are similar caveats applicable to flow? Indeed, flow is necessary to happiness, but it is not sufficient. This is because people can experience flow in activities that are enjoyable at the moment but will detract from enjoyment in the long run. For instance, when a person finds few meaningful opportunities for action in the environment, he or she will often resort to finding flow in activities that are destructive, addictive, or at the very least wasteful (Csikszentmihalyi & Larson, 1978; Sato, 1988). Juvenile crime is rarely a direct consequence of deprivation but rather is caused by boredom or the frustration teenagers experience when other opportunities for flow are blocked. Vandalism, gang fights, promiscuous sex, and experimenting with psychotropic drugs might provide flow at first, but such experiences are rarely enjoyable for long.

Another limitation of flow as a path to happiness is that a person might learn to enjoy an activity so much that everything else pales by comparison, and he or she then becomes dependent on a very narrow range of opportunities for action while neglecting to develop skills that would open up a much broader arena for enjoyment later. A chess master who can enjoy only the game and a workaholic who feels alive only while on the job are in danger of stunting their full development as persons and thus of forfeiting future opportunities for happiness.

In one respect, the negative impact on the social environment of an addiction to flow is less severe than that of an addiction to material rewards. Material rewards are zero–sum: To be rich means that others must be poor; to be famous means that others must be anonymous; to be powerful means that others must be helpless. If everyone strives for such self-limiting rewards, most people will necessarily remain frustrated, resulting in personal unhappiness and social instability. By contrast, the rewards of flow are open-ended and inexhaustible: If I get my joy from cooking Mediterranean food, or from surfing, or from coaching Little League, this will not decrease anyone else's happiness.

Unfortunately, too many institutions have a vested interest in making people believe that buying the right car, the right soft drink, the right watch, the right education will vastly improve their chances of being happy, even if doing so will mortgage their lives. In fact, societies are usually structured so that the majority is led to believe that their well-being depends on being passive and contented. Whether the leadership is in the hands of a priesthood, of a warrior caste, of merchants, or of financiers, their interest is to have the rest of the population depend on whatever rewards they have to offer—be it eternal life, security, or material comfort. But if one puts one's faith in being a passive consumer—of products, ideas, or mind-altering drugs—one is likely to be disappointed. However, materialist propaganda is clever and convincing. It is not so easy, especially for young people, to tell what is truly in their interest from what will only harm them in the long run. This is why John Locke cautioned people not to mistake imaginary happiness for real happiness and why 25 centuries ago Plato wrote that the most urgent task for educators is to teach young people to find pleasure in the right things. Now this task falls partly on our shoulders. The job description for psychologists should encompass discovering what promotes happiness, and the calling of psychologists should include bringing this knowledge to public awareness.

References

Adlai-Gail, W. (1994). *Exploring the autotelic personality.* Unpublished doctoral dissertation, University of Chicago.

Allison, M. T., & Duncan. M. C. (1988). Women, work, and flow. In M. Csikszentmihalyi & I. Csikszentmihalyi (Eds.).

Optimal experience: Psychological studies of flow in consciousness (pp. 118–137). New York: Cambridge University Press.

Antonovsky, A. (1979). *Health, stress, and coping.* San Francisco: Jossey-Bass.

Benedikt, M. (1999). *Values.* Austin: The University of Texas Press.

Bentham, J. (1970). *An introduction to the principles of morals and legislation.* Darien, CT: Hafner. (Original work published 1789)

Block, J. H., & Block, J. (1980). The role of ego-control and ego-resiliency in the organization of behavior. In W. A. Collins (Ed.). *The Minnesota Symposium on Child Psychology* (Vol. 13, pp. 39–101). Hillsdale, NJ: Erlbaum.

Brickman, P., Coates, D., & Janoff-Bulman, R. (1978). Lottery winners and accident victims: Is happiness relative? *Journal of Personality and Social Psychology, 36,* 917–927.

Campbell, A. (1981). *The sense of well-being in America.* New York: McGraw-Hill.

Csikszentmihalyi, M. (1975). *Beyond boredom and anxiety.* San Francisco: Jossey-Bass.

Csikszentmihalyi, M. (1993). *The evolving self.* New York: HarperCollins.

Csikszentmihalyi, M. (1996). *Creativity: Flow and the psychology of discovery and invention.* New York: HarperCollins.

Csikszentmihalyi, M. (1997). *Finding flow.* New York: Basic Books.

Csikszentmihalyi, M., & Larson, R. (1978). Intrinsic rewards in school crime. *Crime and Delinquency, 24,* 322–335.

Csikszentmihalyi, M., & Patton, J. D. (1997). *Le bonheur, l'experience optimale et les valeurs spirituelles: Une etude empirique aupres d'adolescents* [Happiness, the optimal experience, and spiritual values: An empirical study of adolescents]. *Revue Quebecoise de Psychologie, 18,* 167–190.

Csikszentmihalyi, M., & Rathunde, K. (1998). The development of the person: An experiential perspective on the ontogenesis of psychological complexity: In R. M. Lerner (Ed.). *Handbook of child psychology* (5th ed., Vol. 1). New York: Wiley.

Csikszentmihalyi, M., & Schneider, B. (2000). *Becoming adult: How teenagers prepare for the world of work.* New York: Basic Books.

Davis, J. A. (1959). A formal interpretation of the theory of relative deprivation. *Sociometry, 22,* 289–296.

Deci, E., & Ryan, M. (1985). *Intrinsic motivation and self-determination in human behavior.* New York: Plenum.

Diener, E. (1984). Subjective well-being. *Psychological Bulletin, 95,* 542–575.

Diener, E. (2000). Subjective well-being: The science of happiness, and a proposal for a national index. *American Psychologist, 55,* 34–43.

Diener, E., Horwitz, J., & Emmons, R. A. (1985). Happiness of the very wealthy. *Social Indicators, 16,* 263–274.

Epicurus of Samos (1998). Achieving the happy life. *Free Inquiry, 18,* 47–48.

Hektner, J. (1996). *Exploring optimal personality development: A longitudinal study of adolescents.* Unpublished doctoral dissertation, University of Chicago.

Hunter, J. (1998). The importance of engagement: A preliminary analysis. *North American Montessori Teacher's Association Journal, 23,* 58–75.

Inghilleri, P. (1999). *From subjective experience to cultural evolution.* New York: Cambridge-University Press.

Inglehart, R. (1990). *Culture shift in advanced industrial society.* Princeton, NJ: Princeton University Press.

James, W. (1890). *Principles of psychology* (Vol. 1). New York: Holt.

Linder, S. (1970). *The harried leisure class.* New York: Columbia University Press.

Locke, J. (1975). *Essay concerning human understanding.* Oxford, England: Clarendon Press. (Original work published 1690.)

Martin, J. (1981). Relative deprivation: A theory of distributive injustice for an era of shrinking resources. *Research in Organizational Behavior, 3,* 53–107.

Maslow, A. (1968). *Towards a psychology of being.* New York: Van Nostrand.

Maslow, A. (1971). *The farthest reaches of human nature.* New York: Viking.

Michalos, A. C. (1985). Multiple discrepancy theory (MDT). *Social Indicators Research, 16,* 347–413.

Myers, D. G. (1993). *The pursuit of happiness.* New York: Avon.

Myers, D. G. (2000). The funds, friends, and faith of happy people. *American Psychologist, 55,* 56–67.

Myers, D. G., & Diener, E. (1995). Who is happy? *Psychological Science, 6,* 10–19.

Parducci, A. (1995). *Happiness, pleasure, and judgment.* Mahwah, NJ: Erlbaum.

Pay nags at workers' job views. (1987, October 18). *Chicago Tribune,* 10B.

Polanyi, K. (1957). *The great transformation.* Boston: Beacon Press.

Rich think big about living well. (1987, September 24). *Chicago Tribune,* 3.

Ryan, R. M., & Deci, E. L. (2000). Self-determination theory and the facilitation of intrinsic motivation, social development, and well-being. *American Psychologist, 55,* 68–78.

Sato, I. (1988). Bozozoku: Flow in Japanese motorcycle gangs. In M. Csikszentmihalyi & I. Csikszentmihalyi (Eds.), *Optimal experience* (pp. 92–117). New York: Cambridge University Press.

Scheier, M. F., & Carver, C. S. (1985). Optimism, coping, and health: Assessment and implications of generalized outcome expectancies. *Health Psychology, 4,* 210–247.

Scitovsky, T. (1975). *The joyless economy.* New York: Random House.

Seeman, T. E. (1996). Social ties and health: The benefits of social integration. *Annals of Epidemiology, 6,* 442–451.

Seligman, M. E. P. (1991). *Learned optimism.* New York: Random House.

Simon, H. A. (1969). *Sciences of the artificial.* Boston: MIT Press.

Voenhoven, R. (1988). The utility of happiness. *Social Indicators Research, 20,* 333–354.

Williams, R. M., Jr. (1975). Relative deprivation. In L. A. Coser (Ed.). *The idea of social structure: Papers in honor of Robert K. Merton* (pp. 355–378). New York: Harcourt Brace Jovanovich.

PURSUING HAPPINESS: THE ARCHITECTURE OF SUSTAINABLE CHANGE

Sonja Lyubomirsky, Kennon M. Sheldon, and David Schkade

Happiness is a subjective experience, which means it is something that exists within the human mind. Accordingly, the previous article by Csikszentmihalyi offered a route toward happiness that involved directly controlling subjective experience by seeking to enter into and enjoy a state he calls "flow." In contrast, the present article by Sonja Lyubomirsky and her colleagues turns attention toward the tactics a person can use to affect his or her external environment so as to promote happiness, such as appreciating the positive qualities of important other persons, performing small but regular acts of kindness, and expressing gratitude. All of these behaviors can change the social world around a person into a more positive place and thereby serve to make him or her happier. Even though much of happiness is strongly influenced by built-in biological temperaments and associated "set points," Lyubomirksy and her colleagues point out—and demonstrate—that if you want to be happier there is much you can do.

From *Review of General Psychology, 9*, 111–131, 2005.

The pursuit of happiness holds an honored position in American society, beginning with the Declaration of Independence, where it is promised as a cherished right for all citizens. Today, the enduring U.S. obsession with how to be happy can be observed in the row upon row of popular psychology and self-help books in any major bookstore and in the millions of copies of these books that are sold. Indeed, many social contexts in the United States have the production of happiness and positive feelings as their primary purpose, and questions such as "Are you happy?" and "Are you having fun?" fit nearly every occasion (Markus & Kitayama, 1994). Not surprisingly, the majority of U.S. residents rate personal happiness as very important (Diener, Suh, Smith, & Shao, 1995; Triandis, Bontempo, Leung, & Hui, 1990) and report thinking about happiness at least once every day (Freedman, 1978). Furthermore, the pursuit of happiness is no longer just a North American obsession, but instead it is becoming ever more global as people seek to fulfill the promises of capitalism and political freedom (Diener et al., 1995; Freedman, 1978; Triandis et al., 1990). It seems that nearly all people believe, or would like to believe, that they can move in an "upward spiral" (Sheldon & Houser-Marko, 2001) toward ever greater personal well-being.

Is the pursuit of happiness merely a bourgeois concern, a symptom of Western comfort and self-centeredness, a factor that has no real impact on psychological adjustment and adaptation? The empirical evidence suggests that this is not the case. Indeed, a number of researchers and thinkers have argued that the ability to be happy and contented with life is a central criterion of adaptation and positive mental health (e.g., Diener, 1984; Jahoda, 1958; Taylor & Brown, 1988). Bolstering this notion, Lyubomirsky and her colleagues recently compiled evidence showing that happiness has numerous positive byproducts that appear to benefit individuals, families, and communities (Lyubomirsky, King, & Diener, 2004; see also Fredrickson, 2001). Furthermore, Lyubomirsky et al.'s analysis revealed that happy people gain tangible benefits in many different life domains from their positive state of mind, including larger social rewards (higher odds of marriage and lower odds of divorce, more friends, stronger social support, and richer social interactions; e.g., Harker & Keltner, 2001; Marks & Fleming, 1999; Okun, Stock, Haring, & Witter, 1984), superior work outcomes (greater creativity, increased productivity, higher quality of work, and higher income; e.g., Estrada, Isen, & Young, 1994; Staw, Sutton, & Pelled, 1995), and more activity, energy, and flow[1] (e.g., Csikszentmihalyi & Wong, 1991).

Further supporting the argument that subjective happiness may be integral to mental and physical health, happy people are more likely to evidence greater self-control and self-regulatory and coping abilities (e.g., Aspinwall, 1998; Fredrickson & Joiner, 2002; Keltner & Bonanno, 1997), to have a bolstered immune system (e.g., Dillon, Minchoff, & Baker, 1985; Stone et al., 1994), and even to live a longer life (e.g., Danner, Snowdon, & Friesen, 2001; Ostir, Markides, Black,

& Goodwin, 2000). Also, happy people are not just self-centered or selfish; the literature suggests that happy individuals instead tend to be relatively more cooperative, prosocial, charitable, and "other-centered" (e.g., Isen, 1970; Kasser & Ryan, 1996; Williams & Shiaw, 1999).

In summary, happy individuals appear more likely to be flourishing people, both inwardly and outwardly. Thus, we argue that enhancing people's happiness levels may indeed be a worthy scientific goal, especially after their basic physical and security needs are met. Unfortunately, however, relatively little scientific support exists for the idea that people's happiness levels can change for the better. For example, the happiness-boosting techniques proposed in the self-help literature generally have limited grounding in scientific theory and even less empirical confirmation of their effectiveness (Norcross et al., 2000). Consider a representative best seller, *You Can Be Happy No Matter What: Five Principles for Keeping Life in Perspective*, by Carlson (1997). Do the five principles work? Do some work better than others? Do the principles work better for some people than for others? Are any positive effects of the principles due, ultimately, to placebo effects? If the book actually helps people "get happier," does the happiness boost *last*? Although it is possible that some of the advice given in this and other similar books could well be appropriate and effective, the authors provide almost no empirical research in support of their claims.

One receives little more guidance from contemporary academic psychology. Of course, research psychologists have identified many predictors of people's happiness or subjective well-being. For example, well-being has been shown to be associated with a wide variety of factors, including demographic status (e.g., Argyle, 1999; Diener, Suh, Lucas, & Smith, 1999; Myers, 2000), personality traits and attitudes (e.g., Diener & Lucas, 1999), and goal characteristics (e.g., McGregor & Little, 1998). However, a limitation of previous research is that the vast majority of studies have been cross sectional and have reported between-subjects effects rather than investigating well-being longitudinally and examining within-subject effects. In

---

[1]"Flow" here refers to the pleasant state of mind described in the previous article in this book by Csikszentmihalyi.

addition, very few happiness intervention studies have been conducted. Thus, researchers still know surprisingly little about how to *change* well-being, that is, about the possibility of "becoming happier." Doubtless, part of the reason for this neglect is the difficulty of conducting longitudinal and intervention studies. The problem is further compounded by the tendency of applied mental health researchers to focus on pathology rather than on positive mental health (Seligman & Csikszentmihalyi, 2000) and by the thorny issues raised when theorists speculate on how people "should" live their lives to maximize their potential for happiness (Schwartz, 2000). However, we believe the principal reason for the neglect of this question is the considerable scientific pessimism over whether it is even *possible* to effect sustainable increases in happiness.

Historical Sources of Pessimism

Three considerations serve to illustrate the depth of this pessimism. First is the idea of a *genetically determined set point* (or *set range*) *for happiness*. Lykken and Tellegen (1996) have provided evidence, based on twin studies and adoption studies, that the heritability of well-being may be as high as 80%[2] (although a more widely accepted figure is 50%; Braungart, Plomin, DeFries, & Fulker, 1992; Tellegen et al., 1988; cf. Diener et al., 1999). Whatever the exact coefficient, its large magnitude suggests that for each person there is indeed a chronic or characteristic level of happiness. Consistent with this idea, Headey and Wearing (1989) found, in a four-wave panel study, that participants tended to keep returning to their own baselines over time (see also Suh, Diener, & Fujita, 1996). Thus, although there may be substantial variation around this baseline level in the short term, in the long term people perhaps cannot help but return to their set point, or to the middle of their set range: "What goes up must come down" (a more

detailed description of the happiness set point is provided later).

A second and closely related source of pessimism comes from the literature on personality traits. Traits are cognitive, affective, and behavioral complexes that are, by definition, consistent across situations and across the life span and therefore may account for part of the stability of the set point. In support of the latter assumption, McCrae and Costa (1990) have shown impressive long-term stability for the "Big Five" traits, including the two traits most closely related to well-being: neuroticism and extraversion.[3] Specifically, people tend to maintain the same rank ordering in their levels of worry, rumination, and guilt, as well as in their levels of social engagement, enthusiasm, and self-confidence. Because of the close relation between psychological well-being and these personality characteristics, McCrae and Costa argued that people also tend to maintain the same relative level of happiness over time (see also Costa, McCrae, & Zonderman, 1987; Diener & Lucas, 1999).

A third source of pessimism arises from the concept of the *hedonic treadmill* (Brickman & Campbell, 1971), which suggests that any gains in happiness are only temporary, because humans so quickly adapt to change (see also Kahneman, 1999; Tversky & Griffin, 1991). Thus, although new circumstances may temporarily cause people to become happier or sadder, they rapidly adjust, and the effect of these new circumstances on happiness then diminishes quickly or even disappears entirely. For example, Brickman, Coates, and Janoff-Bulman (1978) showed that, after 1 year, lottery winners were no happier than controls, and furthermore recent paralysis victims were not as unhappy as one would expect. Further evidence of hedonic adaptation comes from findings of remarkably small correlations between happiness and wealth (Diener & Lucas, 1999) and Myers's (2000) observation that while U.S. citizens' personal income has more than doubled in the past 50

---

[2]See the article by Borkenau and his colleagues, earlier in this book, for examples of how heritabilities can be calculated.

[3]The article by McCrae and Costa, earlier in this book, describes these traits in detail.

years, their happiness levels have remained the same. The notion of an individual fighting against the effects of adaptation brings to mind an image of a pedestrian walking up a descending escalator. Although the improving circumstances of her life may propel her upward toward ever greater happiness, the process of adaptation forces her back to her initial state.

Together, these concepts and findings suggest that trying to become happier may be as futile as trying to become taller (Lykken & Tellegen, 1996). Indeed, some have argued that pursuing happiness may backfire altogether, if the pursuit becomes a conscious "extrinsic" goal that distracts people from enjoying the moment (Schooler, Ariely, & Loewenstein, in press; see also Sheldon, 2004). Moreover, striving for happiness may inevitably result in deep disappointment for many people. From this perspective, rather than seeking an upward spiral, maybe people would be better off simply accepting their current personality and happiness levels (McCrae & Costa, 1994). In Zen terms, perhaps one should try to *transcend* the pursuit of happiness rather than trying to maximize it (Gaskins, 1999). Indeed, a number of philosophical traditions embrace the notion that happiness should not be increased beyond an ideal level, one akin to a "Golden Mean" (Aristotle, 1974) between agony and ecstasy. To be sure, most people would undoubtedly reject an unrestrained, ceaseless pursuit of well-being.

Present Sources of Optimism

Is the pursuit of happiness futile? We believe not. Despite the seemingly compelling reasons we have listed for pessimism regarding attempts to elevate levels of well-being, there are also compelling reasons for optimism. In the following, we briefly describe four sources of optimism, returning to consider some of them in greater detail later. First, some researchers have had success, albeit limited and short term, in using interventions to increase happiness (e.g., Fava, 1999; Fordyce, 1977, 1983, Lichter, Haye, & Kammann, 1980; Sheldon, Kasser, Smith, & Share, 2002). The potential of happiness-

enhancing interventions is further reflected in emerging research in the positive psychology tradition demonstrating that practicing certain *virtues*, such as gratitude (Emmons & McCullough, 2003), forgiveness (McCullough, Pargament, & Thoresen, 2000), and thoughtful self-reflection (King, 2001; Lyubomirsky, Sousa, & Dickerhoof, 2004), can bring about enhanced well-being. Furthermore, research documenting the long-term effectiveness of cognitive and behavioral strategies to combat negative affect and depression has encouraging implications for the possibility of elevating long-term happiness (e.g., Gloaguen, Cottraux, Cucherat, & Blackburn, 1998; Jacobson et al., 1996).

Second, many different *motivational* and *attitudinal* factors have been linked to well-being, factors that are presumably amenable to some volitional control. Examples of possible motivational factors include the successful pursuit of life goals that are intrinsic in content (e.g., Kasser & Ryan, 1996); concordant with a person's interests, motives, and values (Brunstein, Schultheiss, & Grassman, 1998; Sheldon & Elliot, 1999; Sheldon & Kasser, 1995); and internally consistent (e.g., Emmons & King, 1988; Sheldon & Kasser, 1995). Examples of potentially controllable attitudinal factors include the tendency to take an optimistic perspective on one's life situations (e.g., DeNeve & Cooper, 1998; McCrae & Costa, 1986), the inclination to avoid social comparisons and contingent self-evaluations (e.g., Lyubomirsky & Ross, 1997), and the tendency to feel a sense of optimism or efficacy regarding one's life (Bandura, 1997; Scheier & Carver, 1993; Seligman, 1991; Taylor & Brown, 1988).

A third reason for optimism is provided by recent findings that older people tend to be somewhat happier than younger people (Charles, Reynolds, & Gatz, 2001; Diener & Suh, 1998; Roberts & Chapman, 2000; Sheldon & Kasser, 2001). Specifically, both cross-sectional and longitudinal work has shown that older persons report higher life satisfaction and lower negative affect. Although these main effects do not always emerge, they are observed frequently enough to suggest that greater happiness can indeed be achieved over time, not just by a few people but perhaps by the majority of people. Indeed, Carstensen's (1995) socioemotional selectivity theory suggests that older people learn to structure their lives and pursue particular goals that maximize positive emotions, consistent with the proposal that people can learn to sustainably increase their well-being. Further supporting this notion are Sheldon and Kasser's (2001) results, which showed that age-related increases in well-being are in part mediated by volitional changes, including older people's ability to select more enjoyable and self-appropriate goals.

Yet another reason why genes are not necessarily destiny is that they appear to influence happiness indirectly, that is, by influencing the kinds of experiences and environments one has or seeks to have. Thus, unwanted effects of genes could be minimized by active efforts to steer oneself away from situations that detract from well-being or by avoiding being enticed toward maladaptive behaviors (Lykken, 2000; Lyubomirsky, 2001). In addition, it is worth noting that heritability coefficients describe covariations, not mean levels. Furthermore, even a high heritability coefficient for a particular trait (such as happiness) does not rule out the possibility that the mean level of that trait for a specific population can be raised. Under the right conditions, perhaps anyone can become happier, even if her or his rank ordering relative to others remains stable.

To summarize, it appears there is a paradox: Some theoretical perspectives and empirical data suggest that happiness can be increased, whereas other theories and data imply that it cannot. How can these conflicting perspectives on the possibility of happiness enhancement be resolved? Also, if enhanced happiness is indeed possible, what kinds of circumstances, activities, or habits of mind are most likely to bring gains, especially gains that can be maintained?

Model of Happiness

Accordingly, the primary question addressed in this article is the following: Through what mecha-

nisms, if any, can a chronic happiness level higher than the set point be achieved and sustained? To this end, we describe the *architecture of sustainable happiness*. The integrative model of happiness we present accommodates the role of both personality/genetic and circumstantial/demographic factors in happiness. However, it also goes beyond these cross-sectional or concurrent factors to incorporate dynamic, time-sensitive factors. This extension allows the question of within-subject change in well-being, and maintained change, to be addressed. Most important, the model incorporates the role of motivational and attitudinal factors, consistent with the assumption that happiness can be actively pursued. We attempt to show that certain types of intentional activities indeed offer ways to achieve sustainable changes in well-being, despite the counteracting effects of adaptation.

In the sections to follow, we first provide a working definition of chronic happiness. Then we define the three factors that affect it (genetic set point, circumstances, and activities) and argue that intentional activities offer the best potential route to higher and sustainable levels of happiness. Subsequently, we consider some more complex issues pertaining to the achievement of sustainable well-being via intentional activity, such as the role of person–activity fit, optimal timing and variety of activity, and the supportive role of sustained effort and positive habits. Then, in the final section of the article, we describe several preliminary efforts to increase happiness, based on our model, and discuss the nature of effective happiness interventions.

DEFINING HAPPINESS   Here we define happiness as it is most often defined in the literature, that is, in terms of frequent positive affect, high life satisfaction, and infrequent negative affect. These three constructs are the three primary components of subjective well-being, according to Diener and colleagues (for reviews, see Diener, 1984, 1994; Diener et al., 1999). Supporting the legitimacy of considering them as indicators of the same underlying construct, we find that the measures are highly correlated and typically yield a single factor after negative affect has been recoded[4] (Sheldon & Kasser, 1998, 2001; Sheldon & Lyubomirsky, 2004). To refer to this group of measures, we use the term *happiness* or *subjective well-being*, although we also discuss mood and life satisfaction at times according to the specific ideas and data being presented.

It is important to note as well that we use a subjectivist definition of happiness, one that commonly relies on people's self-reports. We believe this is appropriate and even necessary given our view that happiness must be defined from the perspective of the person. In other words, happiness is primarily a subjective phenomenon for which the final judge should be "whoever lives inside a person's skin" (Myers & Diener, 1995, p. 11; see also Diener, 1994). However, the fact that the judgment of happiness is necessarily subjective does not mean that influences on that judgment cannot be studied empirically; for example, researchers might investigate the effects of factors such as a person's recent experiences of positive emotion (Frijda, 1999), the frame in which the question is presented (Larsen & Fredrickson, 1999), the meaning that the person ascribes to the question (Schwarz & Strack, 1999), and the person's sense of making satisfactory progress toward life goals at the time of the judgment (Carver & Scheier, 1990). We consider some of these factors in greater detail in a later section. Finally, the fact that self-reported happiness is subjective does not mean that it is unrelated to relatively more "objective" variables. For example, research has shown significant convergence of self-reported well-being with peer and spouse reports of well-being (e.g., Lyubomirsky & Lepper, 1999; Sandvik, Diener, & Seidlitz, 1993), with recall of particular types of events (e.g., Seidlitz, Wyer, & Diener, 1997), with smiling behavior (e.g., Harker & Keltner, 2001), and with physiological responses (e.g., Lerner, Taylor, Gonzalez, & Stayn, 2002).

CHRONIC HAPPINESS LEVEL   Our primary focus in this article is on a person's characteristic level of

---

[4]That is, the statistical technique of factor analysis indicates that all these different measures tap into the same underlying construct.

happiness during a particular period in his or her life, which we term the *chronic happiness level*. We define happiness this way because we wish to identify a quantity that is more enduring than momentary or daily happiness but that is also somewhat malleable over time and, thus, amenable to meaningful pursuit. According to this definition, although it is possible to alter one's chronic happiness level, it is much more difficult to do so than to alter one's happiness level at a particular moment or on a particular day. Operationally, one might define a person's chronic happiness level in terms of his or her retrospective summary judgments regarding his or her mood and satisfaction during some recent period (such as the past 2, 6, or 12 months) or as the average of momentary judgments of mood and satisfaction made at several times during the selected period. It is worth adding, however, that people may vary in their "hedonic profiles," such that two individuals with similar chronic happiness levels might differ in their relative levels of contentment with life versus their relative frequency of experiencing positive and negative mood states.

DETERMINANTS OF THE CHRONIC HAPPINESS LEVEL   We focus on three primary types of factors that we believe causally affect the chronic happiness level, namely, the *set point, life circumstances,* and *intentional activity*. We focus on these three factors because they have historically received the majority of attention in the well-being literature, providing a substantial research base. We also focus on this three-factor distinction because it allows us to address several important issues and paradoxes, such as the question of whether it is even possible to "become happier" given strong genetic influences on happiness, the question of why past well-being research has revealed such weak associations between demographic/circumstantial variables and happiness, and the question of how a person might appropriately take action to "pursue" happiness.

Figure 1 provides an illustration of the approximate percentage of the variance that each of the three factors accounts for in cross-sectional

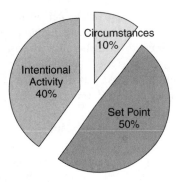

Figure 1 Three primary factors influencing the chronic happiness level.

well-being, as suggested by past research. As can be seen in the pie chart, existing evidence suggests that genetics account for approximately 50% of the population variation (Braungart et al., 1992; Lykken & Tellegen, 1996; Tellegen et al., 1988), and circumstances account for approximately 10% (Argyle, 1999; Diener et al., 1999). This leaves as much as 40% of the variance for intentional activity, supporting our proposal that volitional efforts offer a promising possible route to longitudinal increases in happiness. In other words, changing one's intentional activities may provide a happiness-boosting potential that is at least as large as, and probably much larger than, changing one's circumstances. In the following, we provide a definition of each factor, briefly consider whether and how changing that factor can lead to changes in people's chronic well-being, and discuss whether such changes may be sustainable over the long term, that is, whether the forces of hedonic adaptation can be counteracted by that factor.

HAPPINESS SET POINT   We assume that an individual's chronic happiness level is in part determined by her or his set point, which is defined as the central or expected value within the person's set range. The happiness set point is genetically determined and is assumed to be fixed, stable over time, and immune to influence or control. Consistent with this assumption, twin studies (Lykken & Tellegen, 1996; Tellegen et al., 1988), long-term

panel studies (Headey & Wearing, 1989), and studies of the effects of life events on well-being (Brickman et al., 1978) all indicate substantial long-term stability in happiness. For example, Lykken and Tellegen (1996) assessed well-being in twins at 20 years of age and then again at 30 years of age. The test–retest correlation was a considerable .50. Even more important, the cross-twin, cross-time correlation for the happiness of monozygotic twins was .40 (or 80% of the test–retest correlation), suggesting that the heritability of the "stable" component of happiness is approximately .80. In contrast, the cross-twin, cross-time correlation for dizygotic twins was close to zero (.07). Other studies, although differing in their estimates of heritability, have consistently shown that monozygotic twins exhibit considerably more similar patterns of happiness change than do dizygotic twins, providing converging support that the variance in adult happiness is in large part determined genetically.

The set point probably reflects relatively immutable intrapersonal, temperamental, and affective personality traits, such as extraversion, arousability, and negative affectivity, that are rooted in neurobiology (e.g., Ashby, Isen, & Turken, 1999; Davidson, 1999; Depue & Collins, 1999; Gray, 1990; Kagan, 2003; Robinson, Emde, & Corley, 2001), are highly heritable (Tellegen et al., 1988), and change little over the life span (McCrae & Costa, 1990). For example, Kagan has followed children from 4 months to 11 years of age and shown that sociability in 11-year olds can be traced to particular type of infant temperament (called "low reactive") that appears to involve a distinct neurochemical profile. Other writers, including Gray and Depue, have also compiled persuasive evidence for the neurobiological underpinnings of personality. This rapidly growing body of research supports the set point theory of personality and affect.

IMPLICATIONS OF THE SET POINT FOR SUSTAINABLE INCREASES IN CHRONIC HAPPINESS   The preceding analysis implies that one's chronic happiness during a particular life period can be increased, but not by changing one's set point, because by definition it is constant. In other words, although it is possible that future scientists will learn how to alter people's basic temperaments and dispositions, at present it appears that focusing on the set point is not a fruitful avenue for happiness increase. Again, however, one can posit that non-genetic factors also influence a person's chronic happiness level, helping to determine whether the person falls in the lower or upper portion of his or her potential range at a particular time. The remaining variables in the model are designed to represent these other factors.

CIRCUMSTANCES This category consists of happiness-relevant circumstantial factors, that is, the incidental but relatively stable facts of an individual's life. Happiness-relevant circumstances may include the national, geographical, and cultural region in which a person resides, as well as demographic factors such as age, gender, and ethnicity (see Diener et al., 1999, for a review). Circumstantial factors also include the individual's personal history, that is, life events that can affect his or her happiness, such as having experienced a childhood trauma, being involved in an automobile accident, or winning a prestigious award. Finally, circumstantial factors include life status variables such as marital status, occupational status, job security, income, health, and religious affiliation.

Again, previous cross-sectional research has linked all of the circumstantial factors just described to subjective well-being (Diener et al., 1999). For example, empirical evidence shows that people who are paid more are relatively happier (e.g., Diener, Sandvik, Seidlitz, & Diener, 1993) and that middle-class individuals are somewhat happier than working-class individuals (e.g., Warr & Payne, 1982). Married people are happier than those who are single, divorced, or widowed (e.g., Mastekaasa, 1994), even in cultures as diverse as those of Belarus and Spain (Diener, Gohm, Suh, & Oishi, 2000). Findings also reveal that religiously committed people are relatively more likely to rate themselves as "very happy" (Gallup, 1984) and that, not surprisingly, healthy people, especially older ones, declare themselves to be slightly happier than sick people (e.g., Okun et al., 1984).

However, as suggested earlier, all circumstances combined account for only 8% to 15% of the variance in happiness levels (Argyle, 1999; Diener et al., 1999). These relatively weak associations have been deemed surprising and paradoxical, given well-being researchers' initial expectations that circumstantial factors such as income and physical health would be strongly related to happiness (Diener et al., 1999). We believe that these counterintuitively small effects can be largely accounted for by hedonic adaptation and the fact that people adapt rapidly to new circumstances and life events. This appears to be the case because adaptation—whether it is sensory (e.g., to a foul odor or a heavy weight; Brown, 1953), physiological (e.g., to very hot or cold temperatures; Dar, Ariely, & Frank, 1995), or hedonic (e.g., to a salary raise; Brickman et al., 1978; Parducci, 1995)—occurs in response to stimuli that are constant or repeated. By definition, constancy is a feature of most circumstantial changes.

IMPLICATIONS OF CIRCUMSTANCES FOR SUSTAINABLE INCREASES IN CHRONIC HAPPINESS Of the different types of circumstances, life status variables in particular seem to offer some potential for increasing chronic happiness, in that individuals often have considerable control over them. For example, a college football player may sign a lucrative NFL contract, a middle-aged divorcee may remarry, or a retired couple may move to Florida to a condominium with a view, all becoming happier as a result. Will such new happiness last, however? Perhaps not, because, as mentioned earlier, hedonic adaptation tends to shuttle people back to their starting point following any positive circumstantial change. For example, Headey and Wearing (1989) found in their four-wave panel study that positive and negative events (e.g., "made lots of new friends," "got married," "experienced serious problems with children," or "became unemployed") influenced life satisfaction, positive affect, and negative affect as would be expected but that people kept returning to their original baselines.

And Schkade and Kahneman (1998) revealed that although "living in California" is a seductive notion for many, it does not actually make people any happier in the long run. Furthermore, Lucas, Clark, Georgellis, and Diener (2003) showed that, for most people, the life satisfaction benefits derived from getting married tended to fade over the years. Thus, although one may gain a temporary "boost" by moving to a new region, increasing one's income level, or changing one's appearance, such boosts will probably not last, because people tend to adapt to constant circumstances. Other reasons why circumstantial changes may prove ineffectual for permanently increasing happiness include the fact that circumstantial changes can be costly (e.g., in terms of money, resources, and time) and, in many cases, impractical or even impossible. Also, once a realistic "ceiling" of positive circumstances is reached, it may be difficult to improve matters further.

In short, the data suggest that changes in circumstances have limited potential for producing sustainable changes in chronic happiness. Although this strategy may work in the short term, it probably will not work in the long term. Of course, if people have not achieved basic subsistence and security, then it is logical for them to attend to these circumstances and basic needs first, before focusing on maximizing their happiness. However, we assume that, at best, satisfying basic needs can move people only up *to* their set point, not beyond.

INTENTIONAL ACTIVITY   Now we turn to the third and arguably most promising means of altering one's happiness level: intentional activity. This is a very broad category that includes the wide variety of things that people do and think in their daily lives. Obviously, humans are very active creatures, with innumerable behaviors, projects, and concerns to which they devote energy. By "intentional," we mean discrete actions or practices in which people can choose to engage (although the choice to initiate the activity may have become habitual, as discussed in a later section). We also assume that intentional activities require some

degree of *effort* to enact. That is, the person has to try to do the activity; it does not happen by itself. Indeed, this point touches on one of the critical distinctions between the category of activity and the category of life circumstances; that is, circumstances *happen* to people, and activities are ways that people *act* on their circumstances.

There is good reason to believe that intentional activity can influence well-being. For example, some types of *behavioral* activity, such as exercising regularly or trying to be kind to others, are associated with well-being (e.g., Keltner & Bonanno, 1997; Magen & Aharoni, 1991), as are some types of *cognitive* activity, such as reframing situations in a more positive light or pausing to count one's blessings (Emmons & McCullough, 2003; King, 2001; Seligman, 1991), and some kinds of *volitional* activity, such as striving for important personal goals (Sheldon & Houser-Marko, 2001) or devoting effort to meaningful causes (M. Snyder & Omoto, 2001). Notably, it is impossible to fully separate behavioral, cognitive, and volitional activity; still, we believe the distinction is useful, and we continue to use it throughout the article.

IMPLICATIONS OF INTENTIONAL ACTIVITY FOR SUSTAINABLE INCREASES IN CHRONIC HAPPINESS
Again, it appears that increasing one's set point and changing one's life circumstances are not fruitful avenues for sustainable increases in chronic happiness. What, if anything, can provide such an avenue? In the following, we argue that intentional behavioral, cognitive, or volitional activity offers the best potential route. Some work has already investigated the impact of adopting new *behaviors* on longitudinal well-being, showing, for example, that faithfully engaging in a new exercise program positively boosts people's mood and vitality and can even maintain the boosts for as long as 6 months (e.g., Ransford & Palisi, 1996; Stewart et al., 1997). Although little work has directly investigated the longitudinal effects of changing one's *cognitive* attitudes and practices on enhanced well-being, the general success of cognitive–behavioral therapy in reducing suffering (Gloaguen et al., 1998) and recent work indicating positive effects of

prompting people to practice positive psychological "virtues" such as gratitude (Emmons & McCullough, 2003), hope (C. R. Snyder, Ilardi, Michael, & Cheavens, 2000), and forgiveness (McCullough et al., 2000) suggest that cognitive activity offers many excellent possibilities for happiness interventions (Fordyce, 1983).

Turning to the third type of intentional activity, recent longitudinal studies have focused specifically on *volitional* activity as a producer of enhanced well-being (see Sheldon, 2002, for a review). In such studies, students are typically asked to pursue self-generated personal goals over the course of a semester. High levels of goal progress or attainment consistently predict increased well-being (i.e., higher positive affect and life satisfaction and lower negative mood) from the beginning to the end of the semester, whereas low levels of progress predict reduced well-being (Brunstein, 1993; Sheldon, 2002). Specifically, Sheldon's longitudinal research in this area (Sheldon & Elliot, 1998, 1999; Sheldon & Kasser, 1995, 1998) has shown that well-being increases are most likely when a person chooses and attains *self-concordant* goals, that is, goals that "fit" the person (as described subsequently). This work has also highlighted one potential mediator from successful volitional activity to enhanced well-being, namely, accumulations of positive daily experiences along the way. The question of what other proximal factors may mediate changes in chronic happiness is addressed in more detail in a later section.

Notably, these studies do not extend beyond a single span of time. Thus, they do not directly address the crucial question raised by the current article: whether gains in well-being last. Although Headey and Wearing's important (1989) work suggests that gains in happiness do *not* last, notably, their study focused only on life events ("circumstances," in our model) and did not take intentional activity into direct account.

Recently, Sheldon and Houser-Marko (2001) addressed the question of sustainability by examining the effects of goal attainment on emotional well-being over two consecutive semesters. Consistent with earlier studies, they found that students who attained their personal goals during the first semester of their freshman year experienced enhanced adjustment and emotional well-being at the end of that semester. More important, they found that students could *maintain* their enhanced level of well-being, but only if they continued to do well at their goals during the second semester. In contrast, students who did well in the first semester but not in the second semester tended to regress back to their original well-being levels. This study offers direct support for our assumption that happiness can be enhanced and then maintained at the new level, especially when volitional activity is effectively pursued over long periods of time. Further supporting this conclusion, Sheldon and Lyubomirsky (2004) recently resurveyed these participants 3 years after the original study and found that initially high-performing students had maintained their earlier gains in emotional well-being throughout their college career.

But what about adaptation? Is it not the case that even the most successful striver adapts to his or her happy situation eventually? More generally, is it not the case that people ultimately adapt to the positive effects of *any* activity in which they engage, whether it be behavioral, cognitive, or volitional, so that the activity loses its potency over time?

Although hedonic adaptation undoubtedly constrains the happiness-inducing effects of intentional activities, just as it does for circumstances, this adaptation effect appears to be weaker in the case of activity, as shown by recent data. For example, Sheldon and Lyubomirsky (2004) recently conducted several short-term longitudinal studies in which participants' well-being (positive affect, negative affect, and life satisfaction) was measured at Time 1, and positive circumstantial and activity-based life changes were measured at Time 2. Well-being was then measured twice more, at Times 3 and 4. These investigators found consistent support for a path model, displayed in Figure 2, in which both positive circumstantial change and positive activity change predicted enhanced life satisfaction and positive affect at Time 3, but only positive activity change predicted maintained happiness gains at Time 4, with positive circumstantial

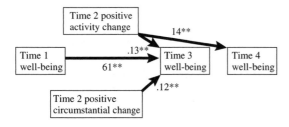

Figure 2 Longitudinal path model predicting maintained changes in well-being from positive circumstantial changes and positive activity changes. Asterisks indicate $p < .01$.

change dropping out of the model. In other words, consistent with the present model, only activity-based well-being change lasted; circumstance-based happiness change did not.

In a separate study, Sheldon and Lyubomirsky (2004) randomly assigned participants to report on either activity-based positive changes or circumstantially based positive changes in their lives. Relative to those in the circumstantial-change group, those in the activity-change group reported a weaker sense of "having gotten used to the change, such that it does not give the same boost as before," and more strongly endorsed the statement "the change is something that varies over time, that is, something that adds variety to my life." These findings further support the claim that activity changes are characterized by less hedonic adaptation than circumstantial changes. Parenthetically, Sheldon and Lyubomirsky's (2004) findings, taken as a whole, support the validity of our distinction between circumstantial changes and activity changes. Although the boundaries between these categories can be fuzzy, apparently they are clear enough to produce the predicted effects.

SPECIFIC ADVANTAGES OF INTENTIONAL ACTIVITY

What are the sources of the sustainable happiness gains afforded by intentional activity? We posit that activity-based change, unlike circumstance-based change, has several desirable features that may help to combat adaptation.

Intentional activity is episodic. One feature of activities is that they are, by definition, episodic and transient; after all, people cannot spend all of their time doing one thing. This in itself suggests that individuals may adapt less readily to new activities than to new circumstances. The episodic nature of activity also suggests that an additional way to maximize the impact of an activity is to attend to the *timing* of that activity. For example, a person might choose to "count her blessings" only after braving a difficult period, or only when she is especially needful of a boost. Suppose instead that she counts the same blessings every day, in a nonvarying routine. This person may become bored with the routine and cease to extract meaning from it. The *length* of time before one reengages in a happiness-boosting activity is an important part of its potency in the next application. By being mindful of the "refractory period" (Kalat, 2001) after which a recently performed activity regains its full happiness-inducing potential, individuals may maximize the benefits of the activity over time and avoid reducing or eliminating the activity's effectiveness through overuse. Thus, people should strive to discover the optimal timing for each activity, that is, a frequency of engagement that allows that activity to remain fresh, meaningful, and positive for a particular person.

Intentional activity can be varied. Another important parameter of behavioral, cognitive, and volitional activities is that people can continually *vary* them, both in their foci and in the ways they engage in them. This may help to reduce adaptation to the activity, allowing it to retain its potency (McAlister, 1982). Indeed, by definition, adaptation does not occur to stimuli that are variable or changeable but only to those that are constant or repeated (cf. Frederick & Loewenstein, 1999). For example, a scientist may regularly ask new questions and become involved in new projects. In the process, she often feels the joy of making fascinating new discoveries and thus may remain particularly happy (i.e., at the upper end of her potential range) over a long period of time. If the person counting her blessings varies the domains of life in which she counts them (i.e., in relationships, in work, in her health, or in her most recently successful domain), then the strategy may remain "fresh" and meaningful and work indefinitely. Supporting this notion, past research suggests that people tend to seek variety in their behavior (McAlister, 1982; Ratner, Kahn, & Kahneman, 1999), perhaps because change—in both thoughts and actions—is innately pleasurable and stimulating (Berlyne, 1970; Rolls et al., 1981).

Intentional activity can directly counteract adaptation. Yet another advantage of intentional activity is that it can directly tackle the problem presented by adaptation. For example, the cognitive practice of pausing to savor the good things in one's life can directly counteract the effects of hedonic adaptation to one's constant circumstances by drawing attention to the features that produced the initial happiness boost and helping to keep them from being taken for granted. As another example, practiced meditators frequently report renewed appreciation of the ordinary as a result of their intentional reencounters with the world.

The fact that intentional activity can directly counteract adaptation and the hedonic treadmill helps shed further light on the distinction between life circumstances and intentional activities. Obviously, many personal characteristics are both. For example, "being married" and "being a student" both denote demographic status, yet they also reflect particular sorts of activities. From our perspective, the crucial distinction with respect to well-being is whether one exerts intentional effort with respect to the circumstantial category, that is, whether one acts *upon* the circumstance (e.g., using intentional practices to keep the circumstance "fresh"). For example, an individual can engage in a number of intentional activities with respect to the circumstantial category "marriage": A husband can have the goal of making his marriage work (a volitional activity), he can make the effort to appreciate his wife's positive qualities (an attitudinal activity), and he can try to remember to bring her flowers (a behavioral activity). A person who performs these activities would probably best counteract adaptation to this particular circumstance and derive the most benefit from it. In contrast, consider a husband who is not intentionally engaged in his marriage; for him, this demographic circumstance would essentially become a background factor, to which adaptation is very likely.

For all of these reasons, intentional activity appears to offer the best prospects for increasing and sustaining happiness. Of course, following through on new intentions, such as the ubiquitous "New Year's resolutions," is not necessarily easy (Sheldon & Elliot, 1998). Indeed, we assume that happiness-increasing strategies can be initiated and effectively pursued only with concerted, consistent commitment and effort. Still, activity-based factors are, by definition, under greater potential control by the individual than are genetic, demographic, and most life status factors. In other words, if anything can do it, intentional activity can.

Implementing Happiness-Increasing Strategies

In this section, we briefly consider several important issues pertaining to how intentional activity might be used for increasing happiness. In other words, having established that activity can potentially sustainably elevate happiness, how might one put this potential to work? We discuss these strategic issues in roughly chronological order, proceeding from the question of how to *choose* a particular happiness-boosting activity to the question of how such activity may be *initiated* and the question of how the activity can be *maintained* over time to produce a sustained increase in the chronic level of happiness. In the process, we discuss the issue of person–strategy fit, the meaning and nature of effort, the definition and role of habits, and the impact of short-term versus long-term considerations.

CHOOSING AN ACTIVITY: THE ROLE OF PERSON–ACTIVITY FIT   Any one particular activity will not help every person become happier. People have enduring strengths, interests, values, and inclinations that undoubtedly predispose them to benefit more from some strategies than others. For example, extraverts may benefit most from activities that bring them into regular contact with other people, and people high in nurturance motivation may benefit most from activities that afford them opportunities to take care of others. This general "matching" hypothesis (Harackiewicz & Sansone, 1991) is supported by much recent work showing that the positive effects of goal attainment on well-being are moderated by goal–person fit (Brunstein et al., 1998; Diener & Fujita, 1995; Sheldon & Elliot, 1999; Sheldon & Kasser, 1998). It is also supported by past well-being intervention research. For example, in several studies that instructed participants to apply 14 different techniques to increase their personal happiness, the particular techniques considered most effective for raising happiness varied greatly from one individual to another and appeared to be determined by each participant's needs and areas of specific weakness (Fordyce, 1977, 1983).

The fit of an activity with a person might be conceptualized in a variety of ways, for example, with respect to individuals' motive dispositions, basic needs, core values, signature strengths, personal resources, hedonic profiles, or other individual-difference characteristics. There are also a variety of ways that fit might be operationalized, such as in terms of self-reported fit, in terms of consistency between implicit and explicit measures of activity-relevant motives, or in terms of informant-rated person—activity fit. Another approach is to assume that certain kinds of experiences are likely to be beneficial to *anyone*, because these experiences reflect universal psychological needs. From this point of view, any activity that provides certain experiences, such as those involving belongingness (Baumeister & Leary, 1995), self-efficacy (Bandura, 1997), or autonomy (Deci & Ryan, 2000), might be assumed to "fit" the person, a priori.

ROLE OF EFFORT

Initiating an activity. We assume that engaging in an activity requires at least two different kinds of effort: first, the effort required to *initiate* the activ-

ity and, second, the effort required to actually *carry out* and *maintain* the activity. This distinction is necessary because it is clear that many activities have definite positive effects *if* the person can only get started doing them. For example, exercising in the morning, making time to work on at least one important project during the day, or pausing to count one's blessings at the end of the day can have significant benefits, but only if the person can "get over the hurdle" of remembering to do them and overcoming any obstacles to initiating them. Obviously, those who do not implement their activity intentions stand a worse chance of benefiting from them than those who do! We assume that this kind of self-regulatory effort requires considerable self-discipline and willpower. Furthermore, such effort may constitute a limited resource, one that must be marshaled carefully; in Muraven and Baumeister's (2000) terms, self-regulatory will is like a "muscle" that has limited capacity in a given unit of time and must be used strategically to avoid fatigue.

If this analogy is accurate, then it seems logical that some people develop the muscle to a greater extent than others, thus attaining a greater ability to "get started" on their intentions and gaining greater happiness potential. Of course, some activities will appear intrinsically more appealing and will be easier to jumpstart; this is undoubtedly one advantage of selecting an activity that fits one's personality. For example, rather than running on a track, a fitness-seeking wilderness lover might instead choose to run on a trail through the woods, thereby feeling much less initial resistance to beginning the activity. As another example, rather than learning classical pieces, a jazz-loving piano student might instead choose to work on jazz standards, enhancing the intrinsic appeal of sitting down to practice.

Maintaining an activity. This brings us to the second type of effort. Obviously, if a particular activity is to yield sustained happiness change, the person must keep performing the activity over the long term. For many effective happiness-enhancing activities, this will not be difficult, because the task will probably be inherently interesting or rewarding and thus will be "autotelic" in nature (Deci & Ryan, 2000), that is, self-reinforcing and self-sustaining. This is especially true to the extent that the person continually varies what he or she does. If, for example, a person shifts attention among several projects at work, explores new trails in the state park, or seeks out interesting new piano pieces, his or her activities should remain intrinsically enjoyable and conducive to many rewarding "flow" experiences (Csikszentmihalyi, 1990).

What if the activity is not enjoyable and thus difficult to maintain? In this case, stopping the activity may not be problematic, because it probably is not working anyway. By emphasizing the importance of enjoying one's intentional activity, however, we do not mean to imply that people should seek out only "fun" activities. Sometimes choosing to endure boring or even aversive experiences in the short term can have considerable positive effects on chronic happiness in the long term; for example, studying for an important exam in a tedious but required class may well represent an excellent investment in one's future chronic happiness, even though it may detract from one's momentary happiness. As another example, a naval officer candidate is paying a short-term cost (boot camp) to receive a longer term benefit (a career as an officer).

Of note, self-determination theory (Deci & Ryan, 2000; Sheldon, Joiner, & Williams, 2003) posits that the crucial factor in such cases is whether the person has internalized the non-enjoyable activity, that is, whether he or she is able to find meaning and value expression in it, even if it is not pleasant to perform. From this perspective, the naval officer candidate would pay a smaller short-term cost if he could undergo boot camp thinking that "this is important and valuable" rather than thinking that "this is unnecessary and stupid." The question of when and how to sacrifice short-term happiness in exchange for longer term happiness is an important one, as is the question of how to promote internalization of important happiness-relevant activities that are not intrinsically enjoyable. These questions represent promising directions for future research.

ROLE OF HABITUAL ACTIVITY   If activities such as "looking on the bright side," "making time for the things that matter," and "working on an important life goal" make a difference for happiness, then it seems it would be a good idea to make a habit of doing them. However, on the surface, habits appear to present a conundrum for our model. Is it not the case that acquiring a habit means that one has turned a formerly conscious activity into an unconscious routine, practiced automatically and without variation? If so, is it not the case that one is especially likely to experience hedonic adaptation to that activity, such that it loses its happiness-boosting potential?

We think not. However, to illustrate, we must first distinguish between the habit of *regularly initiating* a potentially beneficial activity and the habit of *implementing it the same way every time* (the two types of effort mentioned earlier). We assume that hedonic adaptation occurs only with respect to particular experiences, and not with respect to the decisions that give rise to those experiences. Thus, making a habit out of deciding to initiate an activity is not problematic but may instead help people to keep getting "over the hump." For example, a woman might make running an automatic part of her daily routine, such that she does not even have to make the decision of whether or not to run each day, thus deriving considerable benefit. What *is* potentially problematic is when people make a habit out of *how* they implement the activity. When this happens, the flow of experiences produced by such a habit is likely to remain relatively constant, and thus, adaptation is likely to have the most pernicious effects. To overcome this, as suggested earlier, people should mindfully attend to optimal timing and variety in the ways they practice an activity. For example, the woman might want to vary the route, time of day, and speed of her running. This will help forestall the effects of adaptation.

Extensions and Further Questions

Now that we have presented our basic conceptual model of sustainable changes in happiness, we briefly consider a variety of additional issues that extend beyond this basic model. What are the key ingredients of particular activities that lead a person to a higher level of well-being? Although this question is somewhat peripheral to our model, it merits brief discussion. We assume that happiness increases come from at least two sources that are described, respectively, by bottom-up and top-down theories of well-being (Diener, 1994). Bottom-up theories postulate that people make global well-being judgments in part with reference to emotions associated with their recent experiences (Kahneman, 1999). If they can recall a large number of recent affectively positive experiences, then they report being very happy (see Sheldon & Elliot, 1999, for supporting data). Studies have produced support for this bottom-up perspective by showing that accumulations of need-satisfying daily experiences over time (such as competence, relatedness, and autonomy; Deci & Ryan, 2000) lead to enhanced global well-being at the end of that time (Reis, Sheldon, Ryan, Gable, & Roscoe, 2000; Sheldon, Ryan, & Reis, 1996). Furthermore, Sheldon and Lyubomirsky (2004) found, in their comparison of the sustained effects of circumstantial changes and activity changes on changes in well-being among students, that the more enduring activity-based effects on happiness were mediated by the greater feelings of competence and relatedness associated with activity changes during the semester.

But what about when people say they are happy despite having had recent *negative* emotional experiences? Although bottom-up theories cannot account for this, top-down theories can. According to such models, well-being judgments are in part determined by global attitudinal or meaning-based factors. Thus, a person who "suffers for a cause" might still feel very happy because her suffering demonstrates her commitment to, and also perhaps moves her closer to obtaining, an important life goal. As another example, a man who has a bad day at work might still report being very happy that night, because of a short but meaningful visit from his grandchildren that evening that helped him to reframe the day. Again,

we believe that intentional activity can lead to new well-being by both top-down and bottom-up routes, that is, both via accumulations of small positive experiences and via a sense of global meaning and purpose. * * *

What are the most general recommendations for increasing happiness suggested by our model? Simply, happiness seekers might be advised to find new activities to become engaged in, preferably activities that fit their values and interests. They should make a habit out of initiating the activity while at the same time varying their focus and timing in terms of the way they implement the activity. People might be advised to avoid basing their happiness on the acquisition of particular circumstances or objects (e.g., buying a luxury car or moving to California), because they will tend to habituate to such stable factors. Again, however, one can deter, or at least delay, such adaptation to positive circumstantial changes by engaging in intentional effort and activity with respect to them. That is, if one can remember to appreciate or actively engage with the object or circumstance (i.e., pause to savor the new Mercedes or take advantage of the California weather), then stable objects and circumstances may not be stable after all, from a phenomenological perspective. Thus, it remains the case that only life changes involving intentional activity can be expected to lead to sustainable changes in well-being.

Conclusion

If it is meaningful and important to pursue happiness, then it is crucial to find out how this can be accomplished. To what extent, and how, can people succeed in making themselves happier? In this article, we have attempted to integrate what is known about happiness change, especially longitudinal variations in well-being, into a single summary model. The model encompasses a wide variety of findings and suggests a number of new directions for research. More than two centuries have passed since the "pursuit of happiness" was proclaimed as a divinely ordained human right. We believe it is finally time for the issue of sustainable well-being to be given the scientific attention that it deserves.

References

Argyle, M. (1999). Causes and correlates of happiness. In D. Kahneman, E. Diener, & N. Schwarz (Eds.), *Well-being: The foundations of hedonic psychology* (pp. 353–373). New York: Russell Sage Foundation.

Aristotle. (1974). *The Nichomachean ethics* (J. A. K. Thomson, Trans.). New York: Penguin.

Ashby, F. G., Isen, A. M., & Turken, A. U. (1999). A neuropsychological theory of positive affect and its influence on cognition. *Psychological Review, 106*, 529–550.

Aspinwall, L. G. (1998). Rethinking the role of positive affect in self-regulation. *Motivation and Emotion, 22*, 1–32.

Bandura, A. (1997). *Self-efficacy: The exercise of control.* New York: Freeman. Baumeister, R. F., & Leary, M. R. (1995). The need to belong: Desire for interpersonal attachments as a fundamental human motivation. *Psychological Bulletin, 117*, 497–529.

Baumeister, R. F., & Leary, M. R. (1995). The need to belong: Desire for interpersonal attachments as a fundamental human motivation. *Psychological Bulletin, 117*, 497–529.

Berlyne, D. (1970). Novelty, complexity, and hedonic value. *Perception & Psychophysics, 8*, 279–286.

Braungart, J. M., Plomin, R., DeFries, J. C., & Fulker, D. W. (1992). Genetic influence on tester-rated infant temperament as assessed by Bayley's Infant Behavior Record: Nonadoptive and adoptive siblings and twins. *Developmental Psychology, 28*, 40–47.

Brickman, P., & Campbell, D. T. (1971). Hedonic relativism and planning the good society. In M. H. Appley (Ed.), *Adaptation-level theory* (pp. 287– 302). New York: Academic Press.

Brickman, P., Coates, D., & Janoff-Bulman, R. (1978). Lottery winners and accident victims: Is happiness relative? *Journal of Personality and Social Psychology, 36*, 917–927.

Brown, D. R. (1953). Stimulus similarity and the anchoring of subjective scales. *American Journal of Psychology, 66*, 199–214.

Brunstein, J. (1993). Personal goals and subjective well-being: A longitudinal study. *Journal of Personality and Social Psychology, 65*, 1061–1070.

Brunstein, J. C., Schultheiss, O. C., & Grassman, R. (1998). Personal goals and emotional well-being: The moderating role of motive dispositions. *Journal of Personality and Social Psychology, 75*, 494–508.

Carlson, R. (1997). *You can be happy no matter what: Five principles for keeping life in perspective.* Novato, CA: New World Library.

Carstensen, L. L. (1995). Evidence for a life-span theory of socioemotional selectivity. *Current Directions in Psychological Science, 4*, 151–156.

Carver, C. S., & Scheier, M. F. (1990). Origins and functions of positive and negative affect: A control-process view. *Psychological Review, 97*, 19–35.

Charles, S. T., Reynolds, C. A., & Gatz, M. (2001). Age-related differences and change in positive and negative affect over 23 years. *Journal of Personality and Social Psychology, 80*, 136–151.

Costa, P. T., McCrae, R. R., & Zonderman, A. B. (1987). Environmental and dispositional influences on well-being: Longi-

tudinal follow-up of an American national sample. *British Journal of Psychology, 78*, 299–306.

Csikszentmihalyi, M. (1990). *Flow: The psychology of optimal experience.* New York: Harper & Row.

Csikszentmihalyi, M., & Wong, M. M. (1991). The situational and personal correlates of happiness: A cross-national comparison. In F. Strack, M. Argyle, & N. Schwarz (Eds.), *Subjective well-being: An interdisciplinary perspective* (pp. 193–212). Elmsford, NY: Pergamon Press.

Danner, D. D., Snowdon, D. A., & Friesen, W. V. (2001). Positive emotions in early life and longevity: Findings from the nun study. *Journal of Personality and Social Psychology, 80*, 804–813.

Dar, R., Ariely, D., & Frank, H. (1995). The effect of past injury on pain threshold and tolerance. *Pain, 60*, 189–193.

Davidson, R. J. (1999). Neuropsychological perspectives on affective styles and their cognitive consequences. In T. Dalgleish & M. J. Power (Eds.), *Handbook of cognition and emotion* (pp. 103– 123). Chichester, England: Wiley.

Deci, E. L., & Ryan, R. M. (2000). The "what" and "why" of goal pursuits: Human needs and the self-determination of behavior. *Psychological Inquiry, 4*, 227–268.

DeNeve, K. M., & Cooper, H. (1998). The happy personality: A meta-analysis of 137 personality traits and subjective well-being. *Psychological Bulletin, 124*, 197–229.

Depue, R. A., & Collins, P. F. (1999). Neurobiology of the structure of personality: Dopamine, facilitation of incentive motivation, and extraversion. *Behavioral and Brain Sciences, 22*, 491–569.

Diener, E. (1984). Subjective well-being. *Psychological Bulletin, 95*, 542–575.

Diener, E. (1994). Assessing subjective well-being: Progress and opportunities. *Social Indicators Research, 31*, 103–157.

Diener, E., & Fujita, F. (1995). Resources, personal strivings, and subjective well-being: A nomothetic and idiographic approach. *Journal of Personality and Social Psychology, 68*, 926–935.

Diener, E., Gohm, C. L., Suh, E., & Oishi, S. (2000). Similarity of the relations between marital status and subjective well-being across cultures. *Journal of Cross-Cultural Psychology, 31*, 419–436.

Diener, E., & Lucas, R. E. (1999). Personality and subjective well-being. In D. Kahneman, E. Diener, & N. Schwartz (Eds.), *Well-being: The foundations of hedonic psychology* (pp. 213–229). New York: Russell Sage Foundation.

Diener, E., Sandvik, E., Seidlitz, L., & Diener, M. (1993). The relationship between income and subjective well-being: Relative or absolute? *Social Indicators Research, 28*, 195–223.

Diener, E., & Suh, E. M. (1998). Subjective wellbeing and age: An international analysis. In K. W. Schaie & M. P. Lawton (Eds.), *Annual review of gerontology and geriatrics: Focus on emotion and adult development* (Vol. 17, pp. 304–324). New York: Springer.

Diener, E., Suh, E. M., Lucas, R. E., & Smith, H. L. (1999). Subjective well-being: Three decades of progress. *Psychological Bulletin, 125*, 276–302.

Diener, E., Suh, E. M., Smith, H., & Shao, L. (1995). National differences in reported well-being: Why do they occur? *Social Indicators Research, 34*, 7–32.

Dillon, K. M., Minchoff, B., & Baker, K. H. (1985). Positive emotional states and enhancement of the immune system. *International Journal of Psychiatry in Medicine, 15*, 13–18.

Emmons, R. A., & King, L. A. (1988). Conflict among personal strivings: Immediate and long-term implications for psychological and physical well-being. *Journal of Personality and Social Psychology, 54,* 1040–1048.

Emmons, R. A., & McCullough, M. E. (2003). Counting blessings versus burdens: An experimental investigation of gratitude and subjective well-being in daily life. *Journal of Personality and Social Psychology, 84,* 377–389.

Estrada, C., Isen, A. M., & Young, M. J. (1994). Positive affect influences creative problem solving and reported source of practice satisfaction in physicians. *Motivation and Emotion, 18,* 285–299.

Fava, G. (1999). Well-being therapy: Conceptual and technical issues. *Psychotherapy and Psychosomatics, 68,* 171–179.

Fordyce, M. W. (1977). Development of a program to increase happiness. *Journal of Counseling Psychology, 24,* 511–521.

Fordyce, M. W. (1983). A program to increase happiness: Further studies. *Journal of Counseling Psychology, 30,* 483–498.

Frederick, S., & Loewenstein, G. (1999). Hedonic adaptation. In D. Kahneman, E. Diener, & N. Schwarz (Eds.), *Well-being: The foundations of hedonic psychology* (pp. 302–329). New York: Russell Sage Foundation.

Fredrickson, B. L. (2001). The role of positive emotions in positive psychology: The broaden-and-build theory of positive emotions. *American Psychologist, 56,* 218–226.

Fredrickson, B. L., & Joiner, T. (2002). Positive emotions trigger upward spirals toward emotional well-being. *Psychological Science, 13,* 172–175.

Freedman, J. (1978). *Happy people: What happiness is, who has it, and why.* New York: Harcourt Brace Jovanovich.

Frijda, N. H. (1999). Emotions and hedonic experience. In D. Kahneman, E. Diener, & N. Schwarz (Eds.), *Well-being: The foundations of hedonic psychology* (pp. 190–210). New York: Russell Sage Foundation.

Gallup, G. G., Jr. (1984, March). Commentary on the state of religion in the U. S. today. *Religion in America: The Gallup Report,* No. 222.

Gaskins, R. W. (1999). "Adding legs to a snake": A reanalysis of motivation and the pursuit of happiness from a Zen Buddhist perspective. *Journal of Educational Psychology, 91,* 204–215.

Gloaguen, V., Cottraux, J., Cucherat, M., & Blackburn, I. (1998). A meta-analysis of the effects of cognitive therapy in depressed patients. *Journal of Affective Disorders, 49,* 59–72.

Gray, J. A. (1990). Brain systems that mediate both emotion and cognition. *Cognition and Emotion, 4,* 269–288.

Harackiewicz, J. M., & Sansone, C. (1991). Goals and intrinsic motivation: You can get there from here. In M. L. Maehr & P. R. Pintrich (Eds.), *Advances in motivation and achievement* (Vol. 7, pp. 21–49). Greenwich, CT: JAI Press.

Harker, L., & Keltner, D. (2001). Expressions of positive emotions in women's college yearbook pictures and their relationship to personality and life outcomes across adulthood. *Journal of Personality and Social Psychology, 80,* 112–124.

Headey, B., & Wearing, A. (1989). Personality, life events, and subjective well-being: Toward a dynamic equilibrium model. *Journal of Personality and Social Psychology, 57,* 731–739.

Isen, A. M. (1970). Success, failure, attention and reaction to others: The warm glow of success. *Journal of Personality and Social Psychology, 15,* 294–301.

Jacobson, N. S., Dobson, K. S., Truax, P. A., Addis, M. E., Koerner, K., Gollan, J. K., et al. (1996). A component analysis of cognitive-behavioral treatment for depression. *Journal of Consulting and Clinical Psychology, 64,* 295–304.

Jahoda, M. (1958). *Current concepts of positive mental health.* New York: Basic Books.

Kagan, J. (2003). Biology, context and developmental inquiry. *Annual Review of Psychology, 54,* 1–23.

Kahneman, D. (1999). Objective happiness. In D. Kahneman, E. Diener, & N. Schwarz (Eds.), *Well-being: The foundations of hedonic psychology* (pp. 3–25). New York: Russell Sage Foundation.

Kalat, J. W. (2001). *Biological psychology* (7th ed.). Belmont, CA: Wadsworth.

Kasser, T., & Ryan, R. M. (1996). Further examining the American dream: Differential correlates of intrinsic and extrinsic goals. *Personality and Social Psychology Bulletin, 22,* 280–287.

Keltner, D., & Bonanno, G. A. (1997). A study of laughter and dissociation: Distinct correlates of laughter and smiling during bereavement. *Journal of Personality and Social Psychology, 73,* 687–702.

King, L. A. (2001). The health benefits of writing about life goals. *Personality and Social Psychology Bulletin, 27,* 798–807.

Larsen, R. J., & Fredrickson, B. L. (1999). Measurement issues in emotion research. In D. Kahneman, E. Diener, & N. Schwarz (Eds.), *Well-being: The foundations of hedonic psychology* (pp. 40–60). New York: Russell Sage Foundation.

Lerner, J. S., Taylor, S. E., Gonzalez, R. M., & Stayn, H. B. (2002). *Emotion, physiological reactivity, and visceral self-perception.* Manuscript submitted for publication.

Lichter, S., Haye, K., & Kammann, R. (1980). Increasing happiness through cognitive retraining. *New Zealand Psychologist, 9,* 57–64.

Lucas, R. E., Clark, A. E., Georgellis, Y., & Diener, E. (2003). Reexamining adaptation and the set point model of happiness: Reactions to changes in marital status. *Journal of Personality and Social Psychology, 84,* 527–539.

Lykken, D. (2000). *Happiness: The nature and nurture of joy and contentment.* New York: St. Martin's Press.

Lykken, D., & Tellegen, A. (1996). Happiness is a stochastic phenomenon. *Psychological Science, 7,* 186–189.

Lyubomirsky, S. (2001). Why are some people happier than others?: The role of cognitive and motivational processes in well-being. *American Psychologist, 56,* 239–249.

Lyubomirsky, S., King, L. A., & Diener, E. (2004). *Is happiness a strength?: An examination of the benefits and costs of frequent positive affect.* Manuscript submitted for publication.

Lyubomirsky, S., & Lepper, H. S. (1999). A measure of subjective happiness: Preliminary reliability and construct validation. *Social Indicators Research, 46,* 137–155.

Lyubomirsky, S., & Ross, L. (1997). Hedonic consequences of social comparison: A contrast of happy and unhappy people. *Journal of Personality and Social Psychology, 73,* 1141–1157.

Lyubomirsky, S., Sousa, L., & Dickerhoof, R. (2004). *The medium is the message: The costs and benefits of thinking, writing, and talking about life's triumphs and defeats.* Manuscript submitted for publication.

Lyubomirsky, S., Tkach, C., & Sheldon, K. M. (2004). [Pursuing sustained happiness through random acts of kindness and counting one's blessings: Tests of two six-week interventions]. Unpublished raw data.

Magen, Z., & Aharoni, R. (1991). Adolescents' contributing toward others: Relationship to positive experiences and transpersonal commitment. *Journal of Humanistic Psychology, 31*, 126–143.

Marks, G. N., & Fleming, N. (1999). Influences and consequences of well-being among Australian young people: 1980–1995. *Social Indicators Research, 46*, 301–323.

Markus, H. R., & Kitayama, S. (1994). The cultural shaping of emotion: A conceptual framework. In S. Kitayama & H. R. Markus (Eds.), *Emotion and culture: Empirical studies of mutual influences* (pp. 339–351). Washington, DC: American Psychological Association.

Mastekaasa, A. (1994). Marital status, distress, and well-being: An international comparison. *Journal of Comparative Family Studies, 25*, 183–205.

McAlister, L. (1982). A dynamic attribute satiation model of variety-seeking behavior. *Journal of Consumer Research, 9*, 141–150.

McCrae, R. R., & Costa, P. T. (1986). Personality, coping, and coping effectiveness in an adult sample. *Journal of Personality, 54*, 385–405.

McCrae, R. R., & Costa, P. T. (1990). *Personality in adulthood.* New York: Guilford Press.

McCrae, R. R., & Costa, P. T. (1994). The stability of personality: Observations and evaluations. *Current Directions in Psychological Science, 3*, 173–175.

McCullough, M. E., Pargament, K. I., & Thoresen, C. E. (Eds.). (2000). *Forgiveness: Theory, research, and practice.* New York: Guilford Press.

McGregor, I., & Little, B. R. (1998). Personal projects, happiness, and meaning: On doing well and being yourself. *Journal of Personality and Social Psychology, 74*, 494–512.

Muraven, M., & Baumeister, R. F. (2000). Self-regulation and depletion of limited resources: Does self-control resemble a muscle? *Psychological Bulletin, 126*, 247–259.

Myers, D. G. (2000). The funds, friends, and faith of happy people. *American Psychologist, 55*, 56–67.

Myers, D. G., & Diener, E. (1995). Who is happy? *Psychological Science, 6*, 10–19.

Norcross, J. C., Santrock, J. W., Campbell, L. F., Smith, T. P., Sommer, R., & Zuckerman, E. L. (2000). *Authoritative guide to self-help resources in mental health.* New York: Guilford Press.

Okun, M. A., Stock, W. A., Haring, M. J., & Witter, R. A. (1984). The social activity/subjective well-being relation: A quantitative synthesis. *Research on Aging, 6*, 45–65.

Ostir, G. V., Markides, K. S., Black, S. A., & Goodwin, J. S. (2000). Emotional well-being predicts subsequent functional independence and survival. *Journal of the American Geriatric Society, 48*, 473–478.

Parducci, A. (1995). *Happiness, pleasure, and judgment: The contextual theory and its applications.* Hove, England: Erlbaum.

Ransford, H. E., & Palisi, B. J. (1996). Aerobic exercise, subjective health and psychological well-being within age and gender subgroups. *Social Science and Medicine, 42*, 1555–1559.

Ratner, R. K., Kahn, B. E., & Kahneman, D. (1999). Choosing less-preferred experiences for the sake of variety. *Journal of Consumer Research, 26*, 1–15.

Reis, H. T., Sheldon, K. M., Ryan, R. M., Gable, S. L., & Roscoe, J. (2000). Daily well-being: The role of autonomy, competence, and relatedness. *Personality and Social Psychology Bulletin, 26*, 419–443.

Roberts, B. W., & Chapman, C. N. (2000). Change in dispositional well-being and its relation to role quality: A 30-year longitudinal study. *Journal of Research in Personality, 34*, 26–41.

Robinson, J. L., Emde, R. N., & Corley, R. P. (2001). Dispositional cheerfulness: Early genetic and environmental influences. In R. N. Emde & J. K. Hewitt (Eds.), *Infancy to early childhood: Genetic and environmental influences on developmental change* (pp. 163–177). London: Oxford University Press.

Rolls, B., Rowe, E., Rolls, E., Kingston, B., Megson, A., & Gunary, R. (1981). Variety in a meal enhances food intake in man. *Physiology and Behavior, 26*, 215–221.

Sandvik, E., Diener, E., & Seidlitz, L. (1993). Subjective well-being: The convergence and stability of self-report and non-self-report measures. *Journal of Personality, 61*, 317–342.

Scheier, M. F., & Carver, C. S. (1993). On the power of positive thinking: The benefits of being optimistic. *Current Directions in Psychological Science, 2*, 26–30.

Schkade, D. A., & Kahneman, D. (1998). Does living in California make people happy?: A focusing illusion in judgments of life satisfaction. *Psychological Science, 9*, 340–346.

Schooler, J. W., Ariely, D., & Loewenstein, G. (in press). The explicit pursuit and assessment of happiness can be self-defeating. In J. Carrillo & I. Brocas (Eds.), *Psychology and economics.* Oxford, England: Oxford University Press.

Schwartz, B. (2000). Pitfalls on the road to a positive psychology of hope. In J. E. Gillham & J. Templeton (Eds.), *The science of optimism and hope: Research essays in honor of Martin E. P. Seligman* (pp. 399–412). Philadelphia: Templeton Foundation Press.

Schwarz, N., & Strack, F. (1999). Reports of subjective well-being: Judgmental processes and their methodological implications. In D. Kahneman, E. Diener, & N. Schwarz (Eds.), *Well-being: The foundations of hedonic psychology* (pp. 61–84). New York: Russell Sage Foundation.

Seidlitz, L., Wyer, R. S., & Diener, E. (1997). Cognitive correlates of subjective well-being: The processing of valenced life events by happy and unhappy persons. *Journal of Research in Personality, 31*, 240–256.

Seligman, M. E. P. (1991). *Learned optimism.* New York: Alfred A. Knopf.

Seligman, M. E. P., & Csikszentmihalyi, M. (2000). Positive psychology: An introduction. *American Psychologist, 55*, 5–14.

Sheldon, K. M. (2002). The self-concordance model of healthy goal-striving: When personal goals correctly represent the person. In E. L. Deci & R. M. Ryan (Eds.), *Handbook of self-determination research* (pp. 65–86). Rochester, NY: University of Rochester Press.

Sheldon, K. M. (2004). The benefits of a "sidelong" approach to self-esteem need-satisfaction: Comment on Crocker and Park (2004). *Psychological Bulletin, 130*, 421–424.

Sheldon, K. M., & Elliot, A. J. (1998). Not all personal goals are personal: Comparing autonomous and controlled reasons for goals as predictors of effort and attainment. *Personality and Social Psychology Bulletin, 24*, 546–557.

Sheldon, K. M., & Elliot, A. J. (1999). Goal striving, need-satisfaction, and longitudinal well-being: The self-concordance model. *Journal of Personality and Social Psychology, 76*, 482–497.

Sheldon, K. M., & Houser-Marko, L. (2001). Self-concordance, goal-attainment, and the pursuit of happiness: Can there be an upward spiral? *Journal of Personality and Social Psychology, 80*, 152–165.

Sheldon, K. M., Joiner, T., & Williams, G. (2003). *Self-determination theory in the clinic: Motivating physical and mental health. New Haven, CT: Yale University Press.*

Sheldon, K. M., & Kasser, T. (1995). Coherence and congruence: Two aspects of personality integration. *Journal of Personality and Social Psychology, 68*, 531–543.

Sheldon, K. M., & Kasser, T. (1998). Pursuing personal goals: Skills enable progress but not all progress is beneficial. *Personality and Social Psychology Bulletin, 24*, 1319–1331.

Sheldon, K. M., & Kasser, T. (2001). Getting older, getting better?: Personal strivings and psychological maturity across the life span. *Developmental Psychology, 37*, 491–501.

Sheldon, K. M., Kasser, T., Smith, K., & Share, T. (2002). Personal goals and psychological growth: Testing an intervention to enhance goal-attainment and personality integration. *Journal of Personality, 70*, 5–31.

Sheldon, K. M., & Lyubomirsky, S. (2004). *Achieving sustainable gains in happiness: Change your actions, not your circumstances.* Manuscript submitted for publication.

Sheldon, K. M., Ryan, R. M., & Reis, H. T. (1996). What makes for a good day?: Competence and autonomy in the day and in the person. *Personality and Social Psychology Bulletin, 22*, 1270–1279.

Snyder, C. R., Ilardi, S., Michael, S. T., & Cheavens, J. (2000). Hope theory: Updating a common process for psychological change. In C. R. Snyder & R. E. Ingram (Eds.), *Handbook of psychological change: Psychotherapy processes and practices for the 21st century* (pp. 128–153). New York: Wiley.

Snyder, M., & Omoto, A. M. (2001). Basic research and practical problems: Volunteerism and the psychology of individual and collective action. In W. Wosinska, R. B. Cialdini, D. W. Barrett, & J. Reykowski (Eds.), *The practice of social influence in multiple cultures* (pp. 287–307). Mahwah, NJ: Erlbaum.

Staw, B. M., Sutton, R. I., & Pelled, L. H. (1995). Employee positive emotion and favorable outcomes at the workplace. *Organization Science, 5*, 51–71.

Stewart, A. L., Mills, K. M., Sepsis, P. G., King, A. C., McLellan, B. Y., Roitz, K., & Ritter, P. L. (1997). Evaluation of CHAMPS, a physical activity promotion program for older adults. *Annals of Behavioral Medicine, 19*, 353–361.

Stone, A. A., Neale, J. M., Cox, D. S., Napoli, A., Vadlimarsdottir, V., & Kennedy-Moore, E. (1994). Daily events are associated with a secretory immune response to an oral antigen in men. *Health Psychology, 13*, 440–446.

Suh, E. M., Diener, E., & Fujita, F. (1996). Events and subjective well-being: Only recent events matter. *Journal of Personality and Social Psychology, 70*, 1091–1102.

Taylor, S. E., & Brown, J. D. (1988). Illusion and well-being: A social psychological perspective on mental health. *Psychological Bulletin, 103*, 193–210.

Tellegen, A., Lykken, D. T., Bouchard, T. J., Wilcox, K. J., Segal, N. L., & Rich, S. (1988). Personality similarity in twins reared apart and together. *Journal of Personality and Social Psychology, 54*, 1031–1039.

Triandis, H. C., Bontempo, R., Leung, K., & Hui, C. H. (1990). A method for determining cultural, demographic, and personal constructs. *Journal of Cross-Cultural Psychology, 21*, 302–318.

Trivers, R. (1971). The evolution of reciprocal altruism. *Quarterly Review of Biology, 46*, 35–57.

Tversky, A., & Griffin, D. (1991). Endowment and contrast in judgments of well-being. In F. Strack, M. Argyle, & N. Schwarz (Eds.), *Subjective well-being: An interdisciplinary perspective* (pp. 101–118). Oxford, England: Pergamon Press.

Warr, P., & Payne, R. (1982). Experience of strain and pleasure among British adults. *Social Science and Medicine, 16*, 1691–1697.

Williams, S., & Shiaw, W. T. (1999). Mood and organizational citizenship behavior: The effects of positive affect on employee organizational citizenship behavior intentions. *Journal of Psychology, 133*, 656–668.

SHARED VIRTUE: THE CONVERGENCE OF VALUED HUMAN STRENGTHS ACROSS CULTURE AND HISTORY

Katherine Dahlsgaard, Christopher Peterson, and Martin E. P. Seligman

If there were not more to a good life than happiness, many people would pursue pleasure in ways that would rightfully be condemned as immoral. Thus, positive psychology has two major strands: the pursuit of happiness and the pursuit of virtue. Which raises the question: what is virtue? One pitfall in trying to answer this question is that the answer might be culture-bound, elevating what is valued in a particular place and time to the status of an absolute good. The present article by Katherine Dahlsgaard, Christopher Peterson and Martin Seligman attempts to get beyond that limitation by seeking attributes considered to be virtues in most or all of the world's major cultural traditions.

For any one of the ancient religious traditions surveyed in this article, the description of virtue provided here does little more than scratch the surface—important sources are obviously missing from the analysis. For example, a serious analysis of virtue within the Christian tradition would certainly encompass more than the writings of Thomas Aquinas. For a full understanding of the approaches to virtue summarized here, much broader reading will be necessary. For the time being, however, the present article makes clear the possibility that certain themes concerning what constitutes virtue may extend broadly across time and cultural traditions.

From *Review of General Psychology*, 9, 203–213, 2005.

In recent years, strides have been made in understanding, treating, and preventing psychological disorders. Critical to this progress are two widely accepted classification manuals—the American Psychiatric Association's *Diagnostic and Statistical Manual of Mental Disorders* (*DSM–IV*; 4th ed., 1994) and the World Health Organization's (1990) *International Classification of Diseases (ICD)*. Consensual classifications are important because they provide a common vocabulary for basic researchers and clinicians, allowing communication across professional groups as well as with the general public.

The *DSM–IV* and *ICD* describe much of what is wrong with people, but what about those things that are right? Psychology has long ignored human excellence, in part because we lack a crucial starting point: an empirically informed, consensual classification of human virtues. Nothing comparable to the *DSM–IV* or *ICD* exists for human strengths. When psychologists talk about mental health, wellness, or well-being, they mean little more than the absence of disease, distress, and disorder, as if falling short of diagnostic criteria should be the goal for which we all strive (cf. Jahoda, 1958).

We can either curse the darkness or light a candle. Our goal in this article is to extend what the *DSM–IV* and *ICD* have begun by proposing a foundation for the study of what is right about people, specifically the strengths of character that contribute to fulfillment and thereby enable the good life (Peterson & Seligman, 2004). We follow the example of the *DSM–IV* and *ICD* by proposing a classification scheme. The crucial difference is that our domain is not psychological illness but rather psychological strength.

The task of proposing an exhaustive list of virtues is so easy that it has been done hundreds of times. Moral philosophers, theologians, legislators, educators, and parents all have ideas about what character means, and few have resisted the temptation to articulate a definitive list of the virtues that constitute the well-lived life. The most frequent objection to previous classification schemes is that they fall short of being universal and are in fact idiosyncratic, culturally bound, and laden with tacit values. In short, goes the typical argument, there are no universals when it comes to virtue.

But perhaps there are some *ubiquitous* virtues and values that can be identified by looking for them at the appropriate level of abstraction. Perhaps some virtues exist that are so widely recognized that an anthropological veto ("The tribe I study does not have that one!") would be more interesting than damning. Accordingly, we undertook a historical survey with dual and complementary purposes. The first was a literature search and review of early and influential attempts to list virtues crucial to human thriving. The second aim was empirical: Would the virtue catalogs of early thinkers converge? Would certain virtues, regardless of tradition or culture, be widely valued?

Procedure

We limited the search to ancient traditions recognized for their enduring impact on human civilization. In his survey of world philosophies, Smart (1999) nominated China, South Asia, and the West as the most broadly influential traditions of thought in human history. We followed Smart's lead and focused specifically on Confucianism and Taoism in China, Buddhism and Hinduism in South Asia, and Athenian philosophy, Judaism, Christianity, and Islam in the West. We restricted our examinations to written texts from these traditions. With reluctance, we excluded other intellectually fertile cultures that lacked readily available texts.

Within the traditions included, we looked for expository discussions consensually recognized as the earliest, the most influential, or preferably both. We searched for those authors who deliberately developed a catalog, particularly one with a clear beginning and ending in the form of explicitly numbered virtues (e.g., the Ten Commandments, the Holy Eightfold Path).

If there were more than one possible entrant, we chose the one that reflected the most crucial aspects of the tradition under study. Thus, for example, we did not include Pantanjali's (1979) ideas on virtue as outlined in *The Yoga-Sutra*. Although this text is the basic one of the sixth orthodox school (yoga) of Hindu philosophy, the virtues outlined in *The Bhagavad Gita* (Thadani, 1990) are both more inclusive and more well known. Occasionally, no single text emerged as most representative, in which case we included more than one text per tradition.

If we could not find a deliberate or concise exposition on virtue within a tradition, we opted to study its best-known text, as well as respected secondary sources, and to extrapolate. For instance, nowhere in the *Analects* (1992) did Confucius reel off a discrete list of crucial virtues; rather, he referred to virtues throughout. But the text is so unanimously associated with the Confucian tradition that we focused our inquiries there.

Texts and their virtue catalogs were gathered in more or less chronological order. Nominated virtues were sometimes vaguely defined, in which case secondary sources and expert colleagues were consulted to determine the meaning of each entry within its cultural context. Analysis involved condensing each list by locating thematically similar virtues and classifying them under an obviously emerging *core virtue*. By that term, we mean an abstract ideal encompassing a number of other, more specific virtues that reliably converge to the recognizable higher order category. For instance, the core virtue justice is an abstract term representative of the ideals of more specific virtues captured by injunctions, laws, and procedural rules for fairness (Bok, 1995). To say that particular virtues, *within a tradition*, converged into a core virtue is not to argue that all of their features line up perfectly; rather, they exhibited a coherent resemblance to one another, sharing more features than not (Yearley, 1990). Individual virtues that could not, without pushing and squeezing, be classified within a core virtue category were considered distinct.

Furthermore, to say that certain virtues, *across traditions*, converged into a core virtue likewise does not mean that we found a one-to-one mapping of a virtue across cultures. Certainly, an abstraction such as justice means slightly different things—and is valued for somewhat different reasons—from one culture to another. Again, what we sought was coherent resemblance, that the higher order meaning behind a particular core virtue lined up better with its cross-cultural counterparts than with any other core virtue (e.g., examples of Confucian justice have more to do with those of Platonic justice than with those of Platonic wisdom). What we identified were instances in which the similarities across cultures outweighed the differences, and, again, when the

core virtue of a particular tradition did not have an obvious cross-cultural counterpart, it was considered as separate in the final analysis.

Convergence Across History and Culture

Our literature review revealed a surprising amount of similarity across cultures and strongly indicates a historical and cross-cultural convergence of six core virtues: courage, justice, humanity, temperance, wisdom, and transcendence (see Table 1); we remind readers that our goal was to discern broad family resemblances across traditions, not to argue for exact semantic and cultural equivalences. Let us turn to how each of these six core virtues is evident in the different traditions we surveyed.

CONFUCIAN VIRTUES   The teachings of Confucius (551–479 BCE) are the most influential in the history of Chinese thought and civilization. His moral and political philosophy, with its prescriptive focus on education and leadership, had become the official religion of China by the second century BCE and became compulsory study for 2,000 years beyond that (Smart, 1999).

His teachings were recorded mainly in the form of aphorisms, most reliably collected in the *Analects* (Confucius, 1992). His comments on virtue are scattered across the *Analects*, not presented as a formal catalog. There is, however, agreement among scholars that there are four or five central virtues espoused in the tenets of Confucianism: *jen* (translated variously as humanity, human heartedness, or benevolence), *yi* (duty, justice, or equity), *li* (etiquette or observance of the rites of ceremonious behavior), *zhi* (wisdom or perspicacity), and, possibly, *xin* (truthfulness, sincerity, or good faith; Cleary, 1992; Do-Dinh, 1969; Haberman, 1998a).

Humanity is the virtue most exalted by Confucius. Throughout the *Analects*, this core sentiment permeates all others. For instance, the Confucian ideal of duty (*yi*) is not one prescribing humble acquiescence of the many to the undeserving and powerful few; rather, it denotes the mutual respect

	TABLE 1
	CORE VIRTUES
Virtue	Description
Courage	Emotional strengths that involve the exercise of will to accomplish goals in the face of opposition, external or internal; examples include bravery, perseverance, and authenticity (honesty)
Justice	Civic strengths that underlie healthy community life; examples include fairness, leadership, and citizenship or teamwork
Humanity	Interpersonal strengths that involve "tending and befriending" others (Taylor et al., 2000); examples include love and kindness
Temperance	Strengths that protect against excess; examples include forgiveness, humility, prudence, and self-control
Wisdom	Cognitive strengths that entail the acquisition and use of knowledge; examples include creativity, curiosity, judgment, and perspective (providing counsel to others)
Transcendence	Strengths that forge connections to the larger universe and thereby provide meaning; examples include gratitude, hope, and spirituality

persons should have in relation to one another, beginning with the familial relationship and extending outward to the state (Huang, 1997).

The Confucian precept of good etiquette (*li*) is also best understood as a directive to treat others sensitively; Confucius (1992, p. 127) wrote, "to master oneself and return to courtesy is humaneness" (12:1). Thus, the cultivation of courtesy and deference in one's everyday behavior is the equivalent of the cultivation of humanity, because manners and deference are concerned more with consideration for another's feelings than they are with strict adherence to rules and empty ceremonial custom. Confucian wisdom (*zhi*) is best understood as the functional application of an informed intellect to humanity, justice, and etiquette, whereas truthfulness (*xin*) is that which is exemplified by fidelity to the ideals of the four preceding virtues (Cleary, 1992).

Confucius did not explicitly mention temperance, but its importance to the humane life is strongly implied. The importance placed on rites presumably involves a respect for propriety and self-control as much as for humanity. In both his personal affairs and the *Analects*, Confucius advocated modesty and self-control. In the *Analects*, he commended as virtuous those who lived simply (6:10), refrained from self-aggrandizing boasts (6:14) or extravagance (3: 4), and placed hard work before reward (6:22).

Another core virtue not explicitly named was transcendence. The Chinese did not believe in a divine lawgiver, and Confucius's philosophical focus was clearly on the secular and rational aspects of human functioning, not the cosmic or spiritual (5:13 and 11:12). This is not to say that Confucius completely ignored the transcendent or that he relegated it to insignificance (Hall & Ames, 1987). For instance, excellence in moral conduct was afforded the status of the transcendent: Confucius invoked heaven when discussing the origin of virtue (7:23) and urged reverence for sages whose perfect virtue was modeled after the divine (6:17 and 16:8; see also Haberman, 1998a).

TAOIST VIRTUES   The creator of Taoism, Lao Tzu (approximately 570 BCE–?), is thought to be a contemporary of Confucius, although there is some debate as to whether he was one sage or many and whether the primary work attributed to him, the

Tao Te Ching (Lao Tzu, 1963), came much later than he may have lived (Graham, 1998; Kohn, 1998; Lynn, 1999). The central tenet is one of transcendence: The *Tao*, or Way, that governs the heavens and earth is indescribable, unknowable, and even unnamable (Lao Tzu, 1963, chap. 1). It is also untranslatable: The Way (its Chinese character depicts a head in motion) refers simultaneously to direction, movement, method, and thought, and no single word can depict the profundity of its total meaning. Moreover, it is the creator of all things, including virtue (*Te*), but does not act: The Way is spontaneous and without effort (Cheng, 2000; Wong, 1997).

The text of the *Tao Te Ching* is often cryptic, and attempts, particularly Western ones, to interpret its verses can never be definitive (Clarke, 2000; LaFargue, 1998). Like Confucius, Lao Tzu attempted to use his philosophy to reform rulers and improve society, but the emphasis was not on virtue as social interaction (Cheng, 2000). Rather, what Lao Tzu believed in most was the virtue of "naturalness" or "spontaneity" (*tzu-jan*), or that quality of being without effort. Scholars tend to agree that naturalness is the cardinal virtue of Taoism, with nonaction (*wu-wei*) as the essential method to realize naturalness in social life (Cheng, 2000). The point is that Lao Tzu esteemed other virtues, but only if they arise from the higher one of spontaneity. Later in the *Tao Te Ching* he explicitly cited as important the virtues of humanity, justice, and propriety, but only after (or in the presence of) this higher one (chap. 38).

Likewise, wisdom is espoused in both rulers and commoners, but only if that knowledge is the true sort of the Way, not the superficial sort used for cunning: According to Lao Tzu (1963), a sage ruler is "a man of subtlety [but] with deep insight" (chap. 15); he does not "insist on his own views, thus he has a clear view," nor does he "justify himself, thus he sees the truth" (chap. 22; see also chaps. 3, 19, 33, and 49). And temperance, in terms of both humility and restraint from pursuing the false gods of material wealth and privilege, is advocated again and again: "He who becomes arrogant with wealth and power . . . sows the seeds of his own misfortune" (chap. 9); "he who boasts of his own achievements harms his credibility . . . he who is arrogant experiences no growth in wisdom" (chap. 24); "he who knows glory, but keeps to humility . . . is sufficient in the eternal virtue" (chap. 28).

BUDDHIST VIRTUES Buddhism is a philosophical–religious tradition of great variety and far reach; its tenets and practices today extend from its birthplace in South Asia to China, Tibet, Korea, Japan, Thailand, Indonesia, and beyond. The origins of all teachings, however, are traced to the Buddha (563?–483? BCE), or "Enlightened One," who lived at the same time as Confucius and six centuries before Jesus. Canonical texts describe his renunciation of his traditional and comfortable life to search for the end to the chronic suffering of life, death, and rebirth (*samsāra*). After years of travel, asceticism, and yogic meditation, the Buddha came upon the path to enlightenment, to *nirvana*: the ultimate destiny of existence, the state of bliss brought on by an effacement of the self and its desires (Bhatt, 2001). The Buddha believed that anyone, with the right sort of practice, could reach nirvana, and he spent the rest of his life teaching people the way to it (Dutt, 1983).

If there is a fundamental virtue catalog in classical Buddhism, it is the Holy Eightfold Path, a subset of the more inclusive doctrine of the Four Noble Truths (*ārya satyāni*), which the Buddha preached at his very first sermon. The Four Noble Truths are that (1) life is suffering; (2) the cause of this suffering is the "birth sin" of craving or desire; (3) suffering ceases only upon nirvana, the extinction of desire; and (4) nirvana may be achieved only by following the Holy Path (or Middle Way), an eight-pronged strategy to counteract the innate tendency toward desire. In turn, the Holy Eightfold Path invokes the notion of perfection or right in one's (1) understanding, (2) thinking, (3) speech, (4) action, (5) livelihood, (6) effort, (7) mindfulness, and (8) concentration (Fowler, 1999; see also Carter & Palihawadana, 2000).

A later Buddhist virtue catalog is suggested by what is known as the Five Virtues or Precepts (*pañca-śīla*). These are ritually chanted abstentions from (1) harming living things, (2) taking what is not given (theft or fraud), (3) misconduct concerning sense pleasures, (4) false speech (lying), and (5) unmindful states due to alcoholic drinks or drugs (Harvey, 1990). One can see notions of humanity and justice in the first, second, and fourth precepts and strong directives toward temperance or self-restraint in the third and fifth precepts.

Finally, there are the four Universal Virtues (*apramāna*; also known as "immeasurables") of Buddhism: benevolence (*maitrī*), compassion (*karunā*), joy (*muditā*), and equanimity (*upeksā*; see Nagao, 2000). These virtues are also mentioned in various canonical texts, concern the practical (as opposed to theoretical) aspects of Buddhism, and clearly advocate humanity.

Buddhism, with its emphasis on nonduality and enlightenment, is a forthrightly transcendent tradition. It is also—as a result of its fundamental tenet of the impermanence of all things, including the self—likely to frustrate Western hermeneutic endeavors. Armstrong (2001) warned against interpreting the action section of the Eightfold Path as some sort of collection of moral directives; to do so would be to blur Buddhist teaching (i.e., that voluntary adherence to these precepts helps remove hindrances to clarity and enlightenment) with Western notions of obeisance to a higher power. It is also important to note that Buddhist virtues are not metaphysically stable entities (because there are no stable entities in Buddhism) as they are in many traditions; rather, they are thought or behavior tendencies designed to end craving.

HINDU VIRTUES   The collection of sacred texts known as the *Upanishads* deals with spiritual and metaphysical aspects of Hinduism; the earliest of these texts appear to date to the sixth or seventh century BCE, marking their existence slightly before the rise of Buddhism. The oldest, the *Brihad Aranyaka Upanishad*, elucidated some of the central theological tenets of early and modern-day Hinduism: the unifying principle of *brahman*, the

sacred absolute power and the creator of the universe; the related notion of the interconnectedness of all things, as all ultimately extends back to *brahman*; and the cycle of rebirth, which comes from the blending of the self and *brahman* (Haberman, 1998b; Leaman, 1999). Hinduism and Buddhism diverge in the notion of the self: In the former tradition, the self is eternal, universal, and indistinguishable from *brahman*; in the latter, there is no permanent self and no ultimate creator (Harvey, 1990).

The emphasis in Hinduism is on personal virtues, such as self-denial and renunciation; these virtues promote self-improvement in the current life and a potential of salvation or attainment of a higher caste in the next. Hence, one catalog of Hindu virtues, as narrated in the sacred text of *The Bhagavad Gita* (Thadani, 1990), is intertwined with notions of caste. This text describes a stratified society consisting of the Brahmins (educated aristocrats), Kshatriyas (soldiers), Vaisyas (agricultural and lower trade laborers), and Sudras (menial laborers). Each of the four castes is distinguished by the characteristic virtues exhibited by its members. The spirituality of the Brahmin shows itself in penance, self-control, forbearance, purity, rectitude, knowledge, experience, and faith; the qualities ascribed to the soldier caste include those of valor, skill, glory, fortitude, and charity (generosity); and the lower castes are assigned the virtues of dutiful performance of labor: Little is expected in the way of spiritual and intellectual achievement for these people in their current lives (Thadani, 1990).

Hinduism, with its emphasis on personal improvement, echoes Buddhism but contrasts sharply with the Confucian (and later Athenian) belief in virtue as citizenship. And though their meanings have some cultural specificity, the core virtues are present thematically within the Hindu tradition. Consider wisdom: Although the Hindu (and Buddhist) ideal of attainment of transcendental knowledge of the self does not directly compare with the Confucian notion of the importance of wisdom gained through education and experience, the theme of coming to a higher knowledge is central to all traditions. Transcendence, as invoked by the concept of *brahman,* is diffused throughout *The Bhagavad Gita,* and examples of justice (rectitude), courage (valor), temperance (self-restraint), and humanity (charity) all make their appearance as virtues attributed to specific castes. Note also that the concept of justice is interwoven with the Hindu belief that actions in one life help to determine caste status in the next. That the text ascribes different virtues for different castes does not argue for nonubiquity within the culture; it is difficult to imagine that Hindu culture advocates bravery for soldiers and cowardice for everyone else.

ATHENIAN VIRTUES   The first major virtue catalog of the West was articulated by Plato (427–347 BCE) in the *Republic,* his magnum opus on the ideal human society. Here Plato, using Socrates as his mouthpiece, proposed wisdom (*sophia*), courage (*andreia*), self-restraint (*sôphrosune*), and justice (*dikaisunê*) as the four core virtues of the ideal city (1968, IV, 427e). He argued that these qualities compose a class-based hierarchy of civic virtues that has its anchor in the makeup of the individual soul (IV, 441c). That is, the desirable division of civic virtues—wisdom belongs to the ruling class, courage to the soldier class—is mirrored in an individual's healthily functioning psychology. The soul has its divisions, and to each belongs a virtue: Wisdom is exercised by reason, courage is exercised by the "spirited" part, and self-restraint is imposed on the appetite. In both the civic and individual cases, justice (moral action) will occur when each division properly carries out its assigned task (IV, 443d–e; see Johansen, 1991/1998). This Platonic vision of virtue is comparable to the Hindu notion already outlined: Virtues are categorized along professional and class lines.

In the *Nicomachean Ethics,* Plato's student Aristotle (384–322 BCE) continued the argument that virtuous behavior is a social practice exercised by a citizen of an ideal city (2000, V.I, 1129a). For Aristotle, virtue was an acquired skill learned through trial and error. Related to this is his characterization of virtue known as the doctrine of the mean: One encounters a situation and, relying on reason, experience, and context, selects a course of action from between two extremes of disposition, those of deficiency or excess. The mean between these two extremes *is* virtue (1107a). Generosity, for instance, is the mean between wastefulness and stinginess (1120a); courageousness is the mean between cowardliness and rashness (1116a).

Aristotle's list of the virtues included the original Platonic four (courage, justice, temperance, and wisdom), but to these he added others such as generosity, wit, friendliness, truthfulness, magnificence, and greatness of soul (Aristotle, 2000, IV). The latter two might sound strange to the modern reader: Magnificence has to do with spending lavishly, though in a tasteful way, on honorable items such as sacrifices or warships (IV.II); greatness of soul refers to thinking oneself worthy of great things, particularly honor (IV.III).

In neither Plato nor Aristotle's account is transcendence named as a virtue. But, as was the case with Confucius, the notion of transcendence as a crucial good suffuses their works. In the *Republic,* Plato described how the ideal city would be governed; philosophers, whose inner constitution of virtue is such that they are above selfish interests, should rule. But he admitted that this state is yet to be realized on Earth, and mortal man must look to the heavens to find its model (IX, 592a–b). Aristotle invoked the transcendent when he discussed the relationship between virtue and happiness (*eudaimonia*). For Aristotle (2000, p. 194), happiness was "activity in accordance with virtue" (X.VII, 1177a). He told us in the last book of the *Nicomachean Ethics* that, of all of the virtues, wisdom is the most perfect, and the exercise of it—contemplation—constitutes perfect happiness. "If intellect, then, is something divine compared with the human being, the life in accordance with it will also be divine compared with human life" (Aristotle, 2000, X.VII, 1177b, p. 194).

Likewise, humanity (kindness, love) was never specifically named as a virtue in either Athenian account. However, notions of shared humanity, of the importance of friendship, of generosity and charitable acts, of giving others pleasure and not pain, are scattered across both works.

CHRISTIAN VIRTUES The Seven Heavenly Virtues, the classic Christian enumeration of human strengths, are described in Aquinas's (1224–1274) *Summa Theologiae* (1273/1989). Because the work is celebrated as a successful interpretation of Aristotelian (pagan) philosophy in terms of Christian theology, we describe this text before Jewish ones.

In his virtue catalog, Aquinas deleted all of Aristotle's additions to Plato. He constructed his list by retaining the cardinal virtues of temperance, courage, justice, and wisdom and then adding the three theological virtues proposed by St. Paul: faith, hope, and charity (or love). Aquinas argued for a hierarchical organization of the virtues: Of the cardinal virtues, wisdom is the most important, but the transcendent virtues of faith and hope are more important than that, and of all the seven, charity (love) reigns supreme. Note that within the Seven Heavenly Virtues, Aquinas enumerated what we believe are the six core virtues: He presented the four cardinal virtues by name, invoked transcendence with the virtues of faith and hope, and invoked humanity with the virtue of charity.

JEWISH VIRTUES Within the Hebrew Bible, there are two sections particularly concerned with the virtues esteemed by Jewish culture: the account of the Ten Commandments received by Moses in Exodus and two books of Proverbs that provide specific instruction on the consequences of virtues and vices. The Ten Commandments is a list of "thou shalts" and "thou shalt nots" from which conclusions may be drawn about the virtues advocated in this tradition. The Commandments forbid polytheism, idolatry, taking God's name in vain, murder, adultery, theft, lying, and covetousness while commanding that the Sabbath be kept holy and parents honored (Exodus 20:1–17, Revised Standard Version). Justice is implied in prohibitions against murder, theft, and lying; temperance in those against adultery and covetousness; and transcendence generally within the divine origin of the commands.

Sage instructions to Jewish youth on moral and religious behavior are the main concerns of Proverbs. The opening lines of the first book of Proverbs are a call to edification and are quite clear in distinguishing those virtues that Judaism esteems, for example, wisdom, justice, and prudence. Books II and IV of Proverbs are attributed to Solomon and deal specifically with virtuous behavior (as well as admonitions against vice). Many of the maxims are still well known (e.g., "A man without self-control is like a city broken into and left without walls"). The verses of Proverbs are plentiful, and many virtues are advocated. They include integrity (courage); righteousness, just leadership, and trustworthiness (justice); love, graciousness, and kindness (humanity); diligence, prudence, humility, and restraint (temperance); hope and fear–love of God (transcendence); and understanding, knowledge, and respect for instruction (wisdom).

ISLAMIC VIRTUES Islam's core beliefs and practices took form during and shortly after the life of Muhammad (570–632 CE). Revelations communicated to him by the angel Gabriel, recorded in 114 chapters of scripture known as the *Koran* ("recitation"), founded Muhammad's claim to being the successor of Jesus and the last of the prophets. The revelations also established the foundation for his further teaching, which quickly developed into the organized Islamic faith (Leaman, 2002).

Although differing from Judaism and Christianity in crucial ways, Islam nonetheless was influenced by and includes some of the values of these other religions (Mahdi, 2001). The ideas presented in the Koran are thought to have germinated the tendency toward philosophic thought; in turn, the main influence on the development of Islamic philosophy is thought to be the Greeks, though with some Indian strains (Dunlop, 1971).

Islamic philosophy is distinguished by the central inclusion and importance of God (Leaman, 2002). Mahdi (2001) wrote that the "single attitude" that has historically characterized the Islamic community is "gratitude for the revelation and divine law" (p. 17), and so not surprisingly the transcendent plays a central and powerful role in most of the early philosophical texts, with the exception of the following.

Alfarabi (870–950 CE) is distinguished as the "first outstanding logician and metaphysician of Islam" (Fakhry, 1983, p. 107). He is also known for his numerous interpretative works of Platonic and Aristotelian philosophy, and his most concise virtue catalog, presented in *Fusul al-Madani* (*Aphorisms of the Statesman*; Alfarabi, 1961), is highly reminiscent of theirs. Alfarabi's discussion of virtue, though rare in its relative omission of the divine, is included here because he is generally regarded as the founder of Islamic philosophy.

Fusul al-Madani is composed of 96 aphorisms dealing broadly with the health of the soul. Specifically, Alfarabi (1961) described the government that best nourishes the individual soul in its quest for perfection. Again, this was a forthrightly political work: Alfarabi did not specifically invoke the prophet and mentioned revelation and philosophy only rarely; rather, his focus was on the city-state, and he constantly mentioned and described the activities of the ideal citizen and ruler (Butterworth, 2001).

Much of Alfarabi's (1961) catalog is familiar: Justice in the city-state is of central concern, and virtue is the middle way between two extremes, echoing Aristotle's doctrine of the mean (Aphorisms 61–67). Alfarabi also borrowed from the Athenians when he presented the notion of the divided soul: The soul is split into the Rational and the Appetitive, and the exercise of each part constitutes the corresponding Rational and Moral virtues (Aphorisms 8 and 9).

It appears that the virtues of the former category are the personal virtues of contemplation, whereas those in the second are the social virtues are invoked in dealings with others. Those included in the Rational category are "wisdom, intellect, cleverness, quick-wittedness, and excellent understanding"; those of the Ethical category are "moderation, courage, liberality (generosity), and justice" (Aphorism 8). Hence we see a repetition of the Platonic virtues, with a core humanity virtue (generosity) added and afforded equal standing. Despite his specific omission of the Prophet, transcendence is present in Alfarabi's (1961) account, given his contention that religion and philosophy can be harmonized and that the exercise of virtue is in itself a spiritual act (e.g., Aphorisms 68, 81, 86, 87, and 94).

Conclusion

The impetus for this project was our attempt to create a consensual classification of human strengths while avoiding the criticism that any specific list we proposed would be culturally or historically idiosyncratic (Peterson & Seligman, 2004). The primary lesson we learned from our historical exercise is that there is convergence across time, place, and intellectual tradition about certain core virtues. As one tradition bled into another, as one catalog infused and then gave way to the next, particular core virtues recurred with a sort of pleasant tenacity. Whereas others appeared on some lists and then were lost, certain virtues, either explicitly or thematically, had real staying power.

Putting aside the distinctions between virtues and values, these general traits agree with related efforts within philosophy and psychology to identify "universal" values (see Bok, 1995; Schwartz, 1994). They coincide as well with contemporary lists of traits that predispose individuals to the (psychological) good life, whether termed positive mental health, psychological well-being, psychosocial virtues, self-actualization, psychosocial maturity, or authentic happiness (Peterson & Seligman, 2004). They also agree with traits deemed most desirable in a romantic partner (Buss, 1989) or a friend (National Opinion Research Center, 2001), with individual differences identified as conducive to excellence in the contemporary workplace (Buckingham & Clifton, 2001), and with virtues celebrated in more recent centuries by Western philosophers (Comte-Sponville, 1995/2001).

Caveats are in order. First, it makes good sense to ask whether the six core virtues are equally ubiquitous. Probably not. Justice and humanity showed up the most reliably in that they made every tradition's list; they tended to be named explicitly, and we suspect, given their crucial importance to the survival of even the smallest society, that they are truly universal (Bok, 1995; de Waal, 2000; Ridley, 1996). Temperance and wisdom finished a close second: At least in our survey of the cultures with long literary traditions, they appeared reliably and usually explicitly. Transcendence seems the next most ubiquitous, finishing fifth only because it is the most implicit of the core six: Transcendence was not always nominated explicitly, but the notion that there is a higher meaning or purpose to life, be it religiously underpinned or not, infuses each tradition to the extent that even in some decidedly nonreligious lists (such as Confucianism or Athenian philosophy) the notion of virtue serving heaven or the gods seems taken for granted. Finally, courage is quite explicitly nominated (usually as physical valor) on most lists but is missing on others, notably those from the Confucian, Taoist, and Buddhist traditions. We doubt that this means bravery is not valued in these traditions, and more modern definitions of courage that extend its meaning beyond the battlefield to fortitude in other domains can readily be detected in their classic literatures (e.g., Yearley, 1990).

Second, we find variability across cultures in terms of what is most esteemed. Each tradition nominated some number of virtues as proper or necessary for the well-lived life, but no two lists were identical and, not surprisingly, many virtues we encountered fell by the wayside because they failed the test of ubiquity, even by expanded and fuzzy criteria. Among culture-bound (nonubiquitous) virtues, a number are familiar to those of us in the here-and-now, for example wit and glory. Other culture-bound virtues seem exotic from our vantage, for example magnificence and naturalness. These examples of nonubiquitous virtues are of course important and deserve serious attention by psychologists, but they were not the main concern of this endeavor. We hope that as our classification project develops, we can turn to these less ubiquitous, culture-bound virtues.

Third, all of the traditions we surveyed come from large, literate, and long-lived societies with cities, money, law, and division of labor. None of these cultures existed in total isolation from the others. Although we are quite interested in the matter, we do not pretend to know whether the six core virtues we have identified characterize small or short-lived or nonliterate or hunter-gatherer societies. However, contemporary field research conducted by Biswas-Diener and Diener (2003) has confirmed the core virtues identified here among the Maasai (in western Kenya) and the Inughuit (in northern Greenland).

To summarize, our survey of influential religious and philosophical traditions revealed six broad virtue classes to be ubiquitous. This conclusion has important implications for our attempt to classify positive traits. Most significant, we have a nonarbitrary basis for focusing on certain classes of virtues rather than others. Much of the ongoing societal discourse on "character" is tilted in one direction or another by less than universal political and personal values. Although our classification is decidedly about such values, it is descriptive of what is ubiquitous rather than prescriptive or idiosyncratic. * * *

Fourth, the ubiquity of these core virtues suggests the possibility of universality and a deep theory about moral excellence phrased in evolutionary terms (Wright, 1994). One possibility is that these virtues are purely cultural: acquired characteristics required by long-lived, moneyed, literate, citified societies with massive divisions of labor. Another possibility is that the core virtues are purely biological and define the "moral animal." And a third possibility, the one to which we lean, is that they are evolutionarily predisposed. These particular styles of behaving may have emerged and been sustained because each allows a crucial survival problem to be solved.

Philosophers often refer to virtues as corrective, meaning that they counteract some difficulty inherent in the human condition, some temptation that needs to be resisted, or some motivation that needs to be rechanneled into something good (Yearley, 1990, p. 16). We would not need to posit the virtue of courage if people were not (sometimes) swayed from doing the right thing by fear or the virtue of temperance if people were not (sometimes) reckless. Without the biologically predisposed mechanisms that allowed our ancestors to generate, recognize, and celebrate corrective virtues, their social groups would have died out quickly. The ubiquitous virtues, we believe, are what allow the human animal to struggle against and to triumph over what is darkest within us.

References

Alfarabi. (1961). *Aphorisms of the statesman* (D. M. Dunlop, Trans.). Cambridge, England: Cambridge University Press.

American Psychiatric Association. (1994). *Diagnostic and statistical manual of mental disorders* (4th ed.). Washington, DC: Author.

Aquinas, S. T. (1989). *Summa theologiae* (T. McDermott, Trans.). Westminster, MD: Christian Classics. (Original work published 1273)

Aristotle. (2000). *Nicomachean ethics* (R. Crisp, Trans.). Cambridge, England: Cambridge University Press.

Armstrong, K. (2001). *Buddha.* New York: Penguin Group.

Bhatt, S. R. (2001). The Buddhist doctrine of universal compassion and quality of life. In R. P. Singh & G. F. McLean (Eds.), *The Buddhist world view* (pp. 111–120). Faridabad, India: Om.

Biswas-Diener, R., & Diener, E. (2003). *From the equator to the north pole: A study of character strengths.* Unpublished manuscript.

Bok, S. (1995). *Common values.* Columbia: University of Missouri Press.

Buckingham, M., & Clifton, D. O. (2001). *Now, discover your strengths.* New York: Free Press.

Buss, D. M. (1989). Sex differences in human mate preferences: Evolutionary hypotheses tested in 37 cultures. *Behavioral and Brain Sciences, 12,* 1–14.

Butterworth, C. E. (2001). Introduction to selected aphorisms. In C. E. Butterworth (Trans.), *Alfarabi: The political writings* (pp. 3–10). Ithaca, NY: Cornell University Press.

Carter, J. R., & Palihawadana, M. (Trans.). (2000). *The dhammapada.* New York: Oxford University Press.

Cheng, D. H. (2000). *On Lao Tzu.* Belmont, CA: Wadsworth.

Clarke, J. J. (2000). *The Tao of the West: Western transformations of Taoist thought.* New York: Routledge.

Cleary, T. (1992). Introduction. In T. Cleary (Trans.), *The essential Confucius* (pp. 1–11). New York: HarperCollins.

Comte-Sponville, A. (2001). *A small treatise on the great virtues* (C. Temerson, Trans.). New York: Metropolitan Books. (Original work published 1995)

Confucius. (1992). *Analects* (D. Hinton, Trans.). Washington, DC: Counterpoint.

de Waal, F. (2000, July 28). Primates—A natural heritage of conflict resolution. *Science, 289,* 586–590.

Do-Dinh, P. (1969). *Confucius and Chinese humanism* (C. L. Markmann, Trans.). New York: Funk & Wagnalls.

Dunlop, D. M. (1971). *Arab civilization to A.D. 1500.* London: Longman.

Dutt, R. C. (1983). *Buddhism & Buddhist civilisation in India.* Delhi, India: Seema.

Fakhry, M. (1983). *A history of Islamic philosophy* (2nd ed.). New York: Columbia University Press.

Fowler, M. (1999). *Buddhism: Beliefs and practices.* Portland, OR: Sussex Academic Press.

Graham, A. C. (1998). The origins of the legend of Lao Tan. In L. Kohn & M. LaFargue (Eds.), *Laotzu and the Tao-te-ching* (pp. 23–40). Albany: State University of New York Press.

Haberman, D. L. (1998a). Confucianism: The way of the sages. In L. Stevenson & D. L. Haberman (Eds.), *Ten theories of human nature* (3rd ed., pp. 25–44). New York: Oxford University Press.

Haberman, D. L. (1998b). Upanishadic Hinduism: Quest for ultimate knowledge. In L. Stevenson & D. L. Haberman (Eds.), *Ten theories of human nature* (3rd ed., pp. 45–67). New York: Oxford University Press.

Hall, D. L., & Ames, R. T. (1987). *Thinking through Confucius.* Albany: State University of New York Press.

Harvey, P. (1990). *An introduction to Buddhism: Teaching, history and practices.* Cambridge, England: Cambridge University Press.

Huang, C. (1997). Terms. In C. Huang (Trans.), *The analects of Confucius* (pp. 14–35). New York: Oxford University Press.

Jahoda, M. (1958). *Current concepts of positive mental health.* New York: Basic Books.

Johansen, K. F. (1998). *A history of ancient philosophy: From the beginnings to Augustine* (H. Rosenmeier, Trans.). New York: Routledge. (Original work published 1991)

Kohn, L. (1998). The Lao-tzu myth. In L. Kohn & M. LaFargue (Eds.), *Lao-tzu and the Tao-te-ching* (pp. 41–62). Albany: State University of New York Press.

LaFargue, M. (1998). Recovering the Tao-te-ching's original meaning: Some remarks on historical hermeneutics. In L. Kohn & M. LaFargue (Eds.), *Lao-tzu and the Tao-te-ching* (pp. 255–276). Albany: State University of New York Press.

Lao Tzu. (1963). *Tao te ching* (D. C. Lau, Trans.). New York: Viking Penguin.

Leaman, O. (1999). *Key concepts in Eastern philosophy.* New York: Routledge.

Leaman, O. (2002). *An introduction to classical Islamic philosophy.* New York: Cambridge University Press.

Lynn, R. J. (1999). Introduction. In R. J. Lynn (Trans.), *The classic of the way and virtue: A new translation of the Tao-te-ching of Laozi as interpreted by Wang Bi* (pp. 3–29). New York: Columbia University Press.

Mahdi, M. S. (2001). *Alfarabi and the foundations of Islamic political philosophy.* Chicago: University of Chicago Press.

Nagao, G. M. (2000). The Bodhisattva's compassion described in *The mahāyāna-sūtrālamkāra.* In J. A. Silk (Ed.), *Wisdom, compassion, and the search for understanding: The Buddhist studies legacy of Gadjin M. Nagao* (pp. 1–38). Honolulu: University of Hawaii Press.

National Opinion Research Center. (2001). General Social Survey: 1972–1998 cumulative codebook. Retrieved December 25, 2003, from http://www .icpsr.umich.edu/GSS/

Pantanjali. (1979). *The yoga-sutra* (G. Feuerstein, Trans.). Folkstone, England: Dawson.

Peterson, C., & Seligman, M. E. P. (2004). *Character strengths and virtues: A handbook and classification.* Washington, DC: American Psychological Association.

Plato. (1968). *Republic* (A. Bloom, Trans.). New York: Basic Books.

Ridley, M. (1996). *The origins of virtue: Human instincts and the evolution of cooperation.* New York: Penguin Books.

Schwartz, S. H. (1994). Are there universal aspects in the structure and content of human values? *Journal of Social Issues, 50*(4), 19–45.

Smart, N. (1999). *World philosophies.* New York: Routledge.

Taylor, S. H., Klein, L. C., Lewis, B. P., Gruenewald, T., Gurung, R. A. R., & Updegraff, J. A. (2000). Biobehavioral responses to stress in females: Tend-and-befriend, not fight-or-flight. *Psychological Review, 107,* 411–429.

Thadani, N. V. (Trans.). (1990). *The Bhagavad Gita.* New Delhi, India: Munshiram Manoharlal.

Wong, E. (1997). *The Shambhala Guide to Taoism.* Boston: Shambhala.

World Health Organization. (1990). *International classification of diseases and related health problems* (10th rev.). Geneva, Switzerland: Author.

Wright, R. (1994). *The moral animal: The new science of evolutionary psychology.* New York: Random House.

Yearley, L. H. (1990). *Mencius and Aquinas: Theories of virtue and conceptions of courage.* Albany: State University of New York Press.

PART VI

Cross-Cultural Approaches to Personality

Migrations and technological advances have caused many cultures around the world to become both increasingly diverse and increasingly interconnected. This is perhaps nowhere more true than in America, where subcultures of European, African, Latin, and Asian origin coexist within the same borders. But elsewhere in the world as well, cultural diversity is becoming more the rule than the exception.

It is only natural, therefore, that psychologists have turned some of their attention to the way that psychological processes and personality might vary among cultures. After a long period of slow but steady progress, research activity on these topics has dramatically accelerated in the past few years. The articles in this section sample from some of this recent work.

The section begins with a classic summary of key research by one of the first prominent researchers in cross-cultural psychology, Harry Triandis. Triandis organizes his survey around several fundamental dimensions of cultural variation, which include the difference between what are called "collectivist" and "individualist" cultures. This is the dimension of variation that has received the most attention, by far, in subsequent research. The basic idea is that people in Eastern or Asian cultures, such as Japan, see themselves as an integral part of an overall "collective" comprising many different individuals and groups. People in Western cultures, especially America, are more prone to see themselves as "individuals," separate and apart.

In the next selection, Hazel Markus and Shinobu Kitayama argue that this cultural difference is so profound that some American psychologists are literally afraid to think about it. Collectivist cultures promote fundamentally different values, they argue, including a much greater emphasis on interpersonal relations and mutual support, and a lesser emphasis on individual achievement, competition, and dominance. Markus and Kitayama's article concerns a deep and impactful difference between what they describe as two basic types of culture. The following article, by Jeanne Tsai and Yulia Chentsova-Dutton, looks at differences among individuals who all reside within what is usually considered the same culture: that of the United States, and in particular the upper Midwest. Even there, they find, there are noticeable differences between the styles of emotional expression of Americans whose ancestors left Scandinavia, or Ireland, generations and many years ago.

The next article, by Robert McCrae, argues the unusual position that cultures might be different because different kinds of people live in them—rather than, as is usually assumed, the other way around. Taking the more widely accepted view that culture shapes personality, the final selection, by Shigehiro Oishi, describes how cultures can affect different individuals differently. Cultural differences are real, but within cultures it is always possible to find exceptional individuals who do not conform to or even oppose the cultural norm.

The Self and Social Behavior in Differing Cultural Contexts

Harry C. Triandis

The ultimate goal of cultural psychology should be to reconcile cultural variety with common humanity. Few psychologists have achieved this goal so well as Harry Triandis. Born in Greece, for the past several decades Triandis has had a steady influence on the development of cross-cultural psychology from his base at the University of Illinois. In his research Triandis has consistently tried to describe the ways in which cultures are both the same and different, and to formulate a set of dimensions along which all cultures can be characterized.

In the following selection, an excerpt from one of his major theoretical papers, Triandis proposes that cultures vary along three dimensions that are psychologically important. Some cultures are collectivist while others are relatively individualistic; this is the dimension that is discussed in detail in the next selection by Markus and Kitayama. In addition, cultures vary in the degree to which they do or do not tolerate deviations from social norms (a dimension called looseness vs. tightness) and in their complexity. Triandis describes the relations between these variables and the development of the self. For example, North American culture is individualist, loose, and complex, which may produce a uniquely American kind of personality. He also describes how these dimensions are related to aspects of the environment, child-rearing patterns, and social behavior.

Notice how Triandis manages to avoid the trap of being painted into one or another extreme corner on the question of whether human nature is universal or variable. He consistently expresses the view that all cultures have aspects they share with each other (called "etics") and aspects that are locally unique (called "emics"). Second, he never implies—as do other writers such as Markus and Kitayama—that some positions on the spectrum of cultural variation are better than others. It is neither good nor bad to be collectivist, individualist, tight, loose, complex or simple. It is always a matter of trade-offs; the disadvantages of one position are compensated for by advantages of the other. For example, members of collectivist cultures gain in group support what they lose in individual freedom; the reverse could be said about members of individualistic cultures.

In the end, what Triandis describes could be called a "Big Three" for cultures. The traits of collectivism-individualism, tightness-looseness, and complexity are a group of psychologically relevant attributes that, Triandis demonstrates, can provide a sort of personality profile for an entire culture.

From "The Self and Social Behavior in Differing Cultural Contexts," by H. C. Triandis. In *Psychological Review, 96*, 506–520.

The study of the self has a long tradition in psychology (e.g., Allport, 1943, 1955; Baumeister, 1987; Gordon & Gergen, 1968; James, 1890/1950; Murphy, 1947; Schlenker, 1985; Smith, 1980; Ziller, 1973), anthropology (e.g., Shweder & LeVine, 1984), and sociology (e.g., Cooley, 1902; Mead, 1934; Rosenberg, 1979). There is a recognition in most of these discussions that the self is shaped, in part, through interaction with groups. However, although there is evidence about variations of the self across cultures (Marsella, DeVos, & Hsu, 1985; Shweder & LeVine, 1984), the specification of the way the self determines aspects of social behavior in different cultures is undeveloped.

This article will examine first, aspects of the self; second, dimensions of variation of cultural contexts that have direct relevance to the way the self is defined; and third, the link between culture and self.

Definitions

THE SELF For purposes of this article, the self consists of all statements made by a person, overtly or covertly, that include the words "I," "me," "mine," and "myself" (Cooley, 1902). This broad definition indicates that all aspects of social motivation are linked to the self. Attitudes (e.g., *I* like X), beliefs (e.g., *I* think that X results in Y), intentions (e.g., *I* plan to do X), norms (e.g., in *my* group, people should act this way), roles (e.g., in *my* family, fathers act this way), and values (e.g., *I*

think equality is very important) are aspects of the self.

The statements that people make that constitute the self have implications for the way people sample information (sampling information that is self-relevant more frequently than information that is not self-relevant), the way they process information (sampling more quickly information that is self-relevant than information that is not self-relevant), and the way they assess information (assessing more positively information that supports their current self-structure than information that challenges their self-structure). Thus, for instance, a self-instruction such as "I must do X" is more likely to be evaluated positively, and therefore accepted, if it maintains the current self-structure than if it changes this structure. This has implications for behavior because such self-instructions are among the several processes that lead to behavior (Triandis, 1977, 1980).

In other words, the self is an active agent that promotes differential sampling, processing, and evaluation of information from the environment, and thus leads to differences in social behavior. Empirical evidence about the link of measures of the self to behavior is too abundant to review here. A sample will suffice: People whose self-concept was manipulated so that they thought of themselves (a) as "charitable" gave more to charity (Kraut, 1973), (b) as "neat and tidy" threw less garbage on the floor (Miller, Brickman, & Bolen, 1975), and (c) as "honest" were more likely to return a pencil (Shotland & Berger, 1970). Self-definition results in behaviors consistent with that definition (Wicklund & Gollwitzer, 1982). People who defined themselves as doers of a particular behavior were more likely to do that behavior (Greenwald, Carnot, Beach, & Young, 1987). Identity salience leads to behaviors consistent with that identity (Stryker & Serpe, 1982). Self-monitoring (Snyder, 1974) has been linked to numerous behaviors (e.g., Snyder, 1987; Snyder, Simpson, & Gangestad, 1986). The more an attitude (an aspect of the self) is accessible to memory, the more likely it is to determine behavior (Fazio & Williams, 1986). Those with high self-esteem were found to be more likely to behave independently of group norms (Ziller, 1973).

* * *

To the extent such aspects are *shared* by people who speak a common language and who are able to interact because they live in adjacent locations during the same historical period, we can refer to all of these elements as a cultural group's *subjective culture* (Triandis, 1972). This implies that people who speak different languages (e.g., English and Chinese) or live in nonadjacent locations (e.g., England and Australia) or who have lived in different time periods (e.g., 19th and 20th centuries) may have different subjective cultures.

Some aspects of the self may be universal. "I am hungry" may well be an element with much the same meaning worldwide and across time. Other elements are extremely culture-specific. For instance, they depend on the particular mythology-religion-worldview and language of a culture. "My soul will be reincarnated" is culture-specific. Some elements of the self imply action. For example, "I should be a high achiever" implies specific actions under conditions in which standards of excellence are present. Other elements do not imply action (e.g., I am tall).

* * *

One major distinction among aspects of the self is between the private, public, and collective self (Baumeister, 1986b; Greenwald & Pratkanis, 1984). Thus, we have the following: *the private self*—cognitions that involve traits, states, or behaviors of the person (e.g., "I am introverted," "I am honest," "I will buy X"); *the public self*—cognitions concerning the *generalized other*'s view of the self, such as "People think I am introverted" or "People think I will buy X"; and *the collective self*—cognitions concerning a view of the self that is found in some collective (e.g., family, coworkers, tribe, scientific society); for instance, "My family thinks I am introverted" or "My coworkers believe I travel too much."

The argument of this article is that people sample these three kinds of selves with different probabilities, in different cultures, and that has specific consequences for social behavior.

The private self is an assessment of the self by the self. The public self corresponds to an assessment of the self by the generalized other. The collective self corresponds to an assessment of the self by a specific reference group. Tajfel's (1978) notion of a *social identity*, "that part of the individual's self-concept which derives from his (or her) knowledge of his (her) membership in a social group (or groups) together with the values and emotional significance attached to that membership," (p. 63) is part of the collective self. Tajfel's theory is that people choose ingroups that maximize their positive social identity. However, that notion reflects an individualistic emphasis, because in many collectivist cultures people do not have a choice of ingroups. For instance, even though the Indian constitution has banned castes, caste is still an important aspect of social identity in that culture. Historical factors shape different identities (Baumeister, 1986a).

The notion of sampling has two elements: a *universe* of units to be sampled and a *probability* of choice of a unit from that universe. The universe can be more or less complex. By complexity is meant that the number of distinguishable elements might be few versus many, the differentiation within the elements may be small or large, and the integration of the elements may be small or large. The number of nonoverlapping elements (e.g., I am bold; I am sensitive) is clearly relevant to complexity. The differentiation of the elements refers to the number of distinctions made within the element. For example, in the case of the social class element, a person may have a simple conception with little differentiation (e.g., people who are unemployed versus working versus leading the society) or a complex conception with much differentiation (e.g., rich, with new money, well educated versus rich with new money, poorly educated). *Integration* refers to the extent a change in one element changes few versus many elements. Self-structures in which changes in one element result in changes in many elements are more complex than self-structures in which such changes result in changes of only a few elements (Rokeach, 1960).

In families in which children are urged to be themselves, in which "finding yourself" is valued, or in which self-actualization is emphasized, the private self is likely to be complex. In cultures in which families emphasize "what other people will think about you," the public self is likely to be complex. In cultures in which specific groups are emphasized during socialization (e.g., "remember you are a member of this family," ". . . you are a Christian"), the collective self is likely to be complex, and the norms, roles, and values of that group acquire especially great emotional significance.

* * *

One of many methods that are available to study the self requires writing 20 sentence completions that begin with "I am . . ." (Kuhn & McPartland, 1954). The answers can be content-analyzed to determine whether they correspond to the private, public, or collective self. If a social group is part of the answer (e.g., I am a son = family; I am a student = educational institution; I am Roman Catholic = religion), one can classify the response as part of the collective self. If the generalized other is mentioned (e.g., I am liked by most people), it is part of the public self. If there is no reference to an entity outside the person (e.g., I am bold), it can be considered a part of the private self. Experience with this scoring method shows that coders can reach interrater reliabilities in the .9+ range. The percentage of the collective responses varies from 0 to 100, with sample means in Asian cultures in the 20% to 52% range and in European and North American samples between 15% and 19%. Public-

self responses are relatively rare, so sample means of private-self responses (with student samples) are commonly in the 81% to 85% range. In addition to such content analyses, one can examine the availability (how frequently a particular group, e.g., the family, is mentioned) and the accessibility (when is a particular group mentioned for the first time in the rank-order) of responses (Higgins & King, 1981).

This method is useful because it provides an operational definition of the three kinds of selves under discussion. Also, salience is reflected directly in the measure of accessibility, and the complexity of particular self is suggested by the availability measure.

Although this method has many advantages, a multimethod strategy for the study of the self is highly recommended, because every method has some limitations and convergence across methods increases the validity of our measurements. Furthermore, when methods are used in different cultures in which people have different expectations about what can be observed, asked, or analyzed, there is an interaction between culture and method. But when methods converge similarly in different cultures and when the antecedents and consequences of the self-construct in each culture are similar, one can have greater confidence that the construct has similar or equivalent meanings across cultures.

Other methods that can tap aspects of the self have included interviews (e.g., Lobel, 1984), Q-sorts of potentially self-descriptive attributes (e.g., Block, 1986), the Multistage Social Identity Inquirer (Zavalloni, 1975; Zavalloni & Louis-Guerin, 1984), and reaction times when responding to whether a specific attribute is self-descriptive (Rogers, 1981).

* * *

I have defined the self as one element of subjective culture (when it is shared by members of a culture) and distinguished the private, public, and collective selves, and indicated that the complexity of these selves will depend on cultural variables. The more complex a particular self, the more probable it is that it will be sampled. Sampling of a particular self will increase the probability that behaviors implicated in this aspect of the self will occur, when situations favor such occurrence. For example, data suggest that people from East Asia sample their collective self more frequently than do Europeans or North Americans. This means that elements of their reference groups, such as group norms or group goals, will be more salient among Asians than among Europeans or North Americans. In the next section I will describe cultural variation along certain theoretical dimensions that are useful for organizing the information about the sampling of different selves, and hence can account for differences in social behavior across cultures.

CULTURAL PATTERNS   There is evidence of different selves across cultures (Marsella et al., 1985). However, the evidence has not been linked systematically to particular dimensions of cultural variation. This section will define three of these dimensions.

Cultural complexity. A major difference across cultures is in cultural complexity. Consider the contrast between the human bands that existed on earth up to about 15,000 years ago and the life of a major metropolitan city today. According to archaeological evidence, the bands rarely included more than 30 individuals. The number of relationships among 30 individuals is relatively small; the number of relationships in a major metropolitan area is potentially almost infinite. The number of potential relationships is one measure of cultural complexity. Students of this construct have used many others. One can get reliable rank orders by using information about whether cultures have writing and records, fixity of residence, agriculture, urban settlements, technical specialization, land transport other than walking, money, high population densities, many levels of political integration, and many levels of social stratification. Cultures that have all of these attributes (e.g., the Romans, the Chinese of the 5th century B.C., modern industrial cultures) are quite complex. As one or more of the aforementioned attributes are missing, the cultures are more simple, the simplest including the

contemporary food gathering cultures (e.g., the nomads of the Kalahari desert).

Additional measures of complexity can be obtained by examining various domains of culture. Culture includes language, technology, economic, political, and educational systems, religious and aesthetic patterns, social structures, and so on. One can analyze each of these domains by considering the number of distinct elements that can be identified in it. For example, (a) language can be examined by noting the number of terms that are available (e.g., 600 camel-related terms in Arabic; many terms about automobiles in English), (b) economics by noting the number of occupations (the U.S. Employment and Training Administration's *Dictionary of Occupational Titles* contains more than 250,000), and (c) religion by noting the number of different functions (e.g., 6,000 priests in one temple in Orissa, India, each having a different function).

One of the consequences of increased complexity is that individuals have more and more potential ingroups toward whom they may or may not be loyal. As the number of potential ingroups increases, the loyalty of individuals to any one ingroup decreases. Individuals have the option of giving priority to their personal goals rather than to the goals of an ingroup. Also, the greater the affluence of a society, the more financial independence can be turned into social and emotional independence, with the individual giving priority to personal rather than ingroup goals. Thus, as societies become more complex and affluent, they also can become more individualistic. However, there are some moderator variables that modify this simple picture, that will be discussed later, after I examine more closely the dimension of individualism-collectivism.

Individualism-collectivism. Individualists give priority to personal goals over the goals of collectives; collectivists either make no distinctions between personal and collective goals, or if they do make such distinctions, they subordinate their personal goals to the collective goals (Triandis, Bontempo, Villareal, Asai, & Lucca, 1988). Closely related to this dimension, in the work of Hofstede (1980), is *power distance* (the tendency to see a large difference between those with power and those without power). Collectivists tend to be high in power distance.

Although the terms *individualism* and *collectivism* should be used to characterize cultures and societies, the terms *idiocentric* and *allocentric* should be used to characterize individuals. Triandis, Leung, Villareal, and Clack (1985) have shown that within culture (Illinois) there are individuals who differ on this dimension, and the idiocentrics report that they are concerned with achievement, but are lonely, whereas the allocentrics report low alienation and receiving much social support. These findings were replicated in Puerto Rico (Triandis et al., 1988). The distinction of terms at the cultural and individual levels of analysis is useful because it is convenient when discussing the behavior of allocentrics in individualist cultures and idiocentrics in collectivist cultures (e.g., Bontempo, Lobel, & Triandis, 1989).

In addition to subordinating personal to collective goals, collectivists tend to be concerned about the results of their actions on members of their ingroups, tend to share resources with ingroup members, feel interdependent with ingroup members, and feel involved in the lives of ingroup members (Hui & Triandis, 1986). They emphasize the integrity of ingroups over time and deemphasize their independence from ingroups (Triandis et al., 1986).

Shweder's data (see Shweder & LeVine, 1984) suggest that collectivists perceive ingroup norms as universally valid (a form of ethnocentrism). A considerable literature suggests that collectivists automatically obey ingroup authorities and are willing to fight and die to maintain the integrity of the ingroup, whereas they distrust and are unwilling to cooperate with members of outgroups (Triandis, 1972). However, the definition of the ingroup keeps shifting with the situation. Common fate, common outside threat, and proximity (which is often linked to common fate) appear to be important determinants of the ingroup/outgroup boundary. Although the family is usually the most important ingroup, tribe, coworkers, coreligionists, and members of the same political or social collective or the same aesthetic or scientific persuasion can also function as important ingroups. When the state is under threat, it becomes the ingroup.

Ingroups can also be defined on the basis of similarity (in demographic attributes, activities, preferences, or institutions) and do influence social behavior to a greater extent when they are stable and impermeable (difficult to gain membership or difficult to leave). Social behavior is a function of ingroup norms to a greater extent in collectivist than individualist cultures (Davidson, Jaccard, Triandis, Morales, and Diaz-Guerrero, 1976).

In collectivist cultures, ingroups influence a wide range of social situations (e.g., during the cultural revolution in China, the state had what was perceived as "legitimate influence" on every collective). In some cases, the influence is extreme (e.g., the Rev. Jones's People's Temple influenced 911 members of that collective to commit suicide in 1978).

* * *

As discussed earlier, over the course of cultural evolution there has been a shift toward individualism. Content analyses of social behaviors recorded in written texts (Adamopoulos & Bontempo, 1986) across historical periods show a shift from communal to exchange relationships. Behaviors related to trading are characteristic of individualistic cultures, and contracts emancipated individuals from the bonds of tribalism (Pearson, 1977).

The distribution of collectivism-individualism, according to Hofstede's (1980) data, contrasts most of the Latin American, Asian, and African cultures with most of the North American and Northern and Western European cultures. However, many cultures are close to the middle of the dimension, and other variables are also relevant. Urban samples tend to be individualistic, and traditional-rural samples tend toward collectivism within the same culture (e.g., Greece in the work of Doumanis, 1983; Georgas, 1989; and Katakis, 1984). Within the United States one can find a good deal of range on this variable, with Hispanic samples much more collectivist than samples of Northern and Western European backgrounds (G. Marin & Triandis, 1985).

The major antecedents of individualism appear to be cultural complexity and affluence. The more complex the culture, the greater the number of ingroups that one may have, so that a person has the option of joining ingroups or even forming new ingroups. Affluence means that the individual can be independent of ingroups. If the ingroup makes excessive demands, the individual can leave it. Mobility is also important. As individuals move (migration, changes in social class) they join new ingroups, and they have the opportunity to join ingroups whose goals they find compatible with their own. Furthermore, the more costly it is in a particular ecology for an ingroup to reject ingroup members who behave according to their own goals rather than according to ingroup goals, the more likely are people to act in accordance with their personal goals, and thus the more individualistic is the culture. Such costs are high when the ecology is thinly populated. One can scarcely afford to reject a neighbor if one has only one neighbor. Conversely, densely populated ecologies are characterized by collectivism, not only because those who behave inappropriately can be excluded, but also because it is necessary to regulate behavior more strictly to overcome problems of crowding.

As rewards from ingroup membership increase, the more likely it is that a person will use ingroup goals as guides for behavior. Thus, when ingroups provide many rewards (e.g., emotional security, status, income, information, services, willingness to spend time with the person) they tend to increase the person's commitment to the ingroup and to the culture's collectivism.

The size of ingroups tends to be different in the two kinds of cultures. In collectivist cultures, ingroups tend to be small (e.g., family), whereas in individualist cultures they can be large (e.g., people who agree with me on important attitudes).

Child-rearing patterns are different in collectivist and individualist cultures. The primary concern of parents in collectivist cultures is obedience, reliability, and proper behavior. The primary concern of parents in individualistic cultures is self-reliance, independence, and creativity. Thus, we find that in simple, agricultural societies, socialization is severe and conformity is demanded and obtained (Berry, 1967, 1979). Similarly, in working-class families in industrial societies, the socialization pattern leads to conformity (Kohn, 1969, 1987). In more individualist cultures such as food gatherers (Berry, 1979) and very individualistic cultures such as the United States, the child-rearing pattern emphasizes self-reliance and independence; children are allowed a good deal of autonomy and are encouraged to explore their environment. Similarly, creativity and self-actualization are more important traits and are emphasized in child-rearing in the professional social classes (Kohn, 1987).

It is clear that conformity is functional in simple, agricultural cultures (if one is to make an irrigation system, each person should do part of the job in a well-coordinated plan) and in working-class jobs (the boss does not want subordinates who do their own thing). Conversely, it is dysfunctional in hunting cultures, in which one must be ingenious, and in professional jobs, in which one must be creative. The greater the cultural complexity, the more is conformity to one ingroup dysfunctional, inasmuch as one cannot take advantage of new opportunities available in other parts of the society.

The smaller the family size, the more the child is allowed to do his or her own thing. In large families, rules must be imposed, otherwise chaos will occur. As societies become more affluent (individualistic), they also reduce the size of the family, which increases the opportunity to raise children to be individualists. Autonomy in childrearing also leads to individualism. Exposure to other cultures (e.g., through travel or because of societal heterogeneity) also increases individualism, inasmuch as the child becomes aware of different norms and has to choose his or her own standards of behavior.

* * *

Tight versus loose cultures. In collectivist cultures, ingroups demand that individuals conform to ingroup norms, role definitions, and values. When a society is relatively homogeneous, the norms and values of ingroups are similar. But heterogeneous societies have groups with dissimilar norms. If an ingroup member deviates from ingroup norms, ingroup members may have to make the painful decision of excluding that individual from the ingroup. Because rejection of ingroup members is emotionally draining, cultures develop tolerance for deviation from group norms. As a result, homogeneous cultures are often rigid in requiring that ingroup members behave according to the ingroup norms. Such cultures are *tight*. Heterogeneous cultures and cultures in marginal positions between two major cultural patterns are flexible in dealing with ingroup members who deviate from ingroup norms. For example, Japan is considered tight, and it is relatively homogeneous. Thailand is considered loose, and it is in a marginal position between the major cultures of India and China; people are pulled in different directions by sometimes contrasting norms, and hence they must be more flexible in imposing their norms. In short, tight cultures (Pelto, 1968) have clear norms that are reliably imposed. Little deviation from normative behavior is tolerated, and severe sanctions are administered to those who deviate. *Loose* cultures either have unclear norms about most social situations or tolerate deviance from the norms. For example, it is widely reported in the press that Japanese children who return to Japan after a period of residence in the West, are criticized most severely by teachers because their behavior is not "proper." Japan is a tight culture in which deviations that would be considered trivial in the West (such as bringing Western food rather than Japanese food for lunch) are noted and criticized. In loose cultures, deviations from "proper" behavior are tolerated, and in many cases there are no standards of "proper" behavior. Theocracies[1] are prototypical of tight cultures, but some contemporary relatively homogeneous cultures (e.g., the Greeks, the Japanese) are also relatively tight. In a heterogeneous culture, such as the United States, it is more difficult for people to agree on specific norms, and

---

[1]Nations run by religious rule.

even more difficult to impose severe sanctions. Geographic mobility allows people to leave the offended communities in ways that are not available in more stable cultures. Urban environments are more loose than rural environments, in which norms are clearer and sanctions can be imposed more easily. Prototypical of loose cultures are the Lapps and the Thais. In very tight cultures, according to Pelto, one finds corporate control of property, corporate ownership of stored food and production power, religious figures as leaders, hereditary recruitment into priesthood, and high levels of taxation.

* * *

The intolerance of inappropriate behavior characteristic of tight cultures does not extend to all situations. In fact, tight cultures are quite tolerant of foreigners (they do not know better), and of drunk, and mentally ill persons. They may even have rituals in which inappropriate behavior is expected. For example, in a tight culture such as Japan one finds the office beer party as a ritual institution, where one is expected to get drunk and to tell the boss what one "really" thinks of him (it is rarely her). Similarly, in loose cultures, there are specific situations in which deviance is not tolerated. For example, in Orissa (India), a son who cuts his hair the day after his father dies is bound to be severely criticized, although the culture is generally loose.

* * *

Culture and Self

Culture is to society what memory is to the person. It specifies designs for living that have proven effective in the past, ways of dealing with social situations, and ways to think about the self and social behavior that have been reinforced in the past. It includes systems of symbols that facilitate interaction (Geertz, 1973), rules of the game of life that have been shown to "work" in the past. When a person is socialized in a given culture, the person can use custom as a substitute for thought, and save time.

The three dimensions of cultural variation just described reflect variations in culture that have emerged because of different ecologies, such as ways of surviving. Specifically, in cultures that survive through hunting or food gathering, in which people are more likely to survive if they work alone or in small groups because game is dispersed, individualism emerges as a good design for living. In agricultural cultures, in which cooperation in the building of irrigation systems and food storage and distribution facilities is reinforced, collectivist designs for living emerge. In complex, industrial cultures, in which loosely linked ingroups produce the thousands of parts of modern machines (e.g., a 747 airplane), individuals often find themselves in situations in which they have to choose ingroups or even form their own ingroups (e.g., new corporation). Again, individualistic designs for living become more functional. In homogeneous cultures, one can insist on tight norm enforcement; in heterogeneous, or fast changing, or marginal (e.g., confluence of two major cultural traditions) cultures, the imposition of tight norms is difficult because it is unclear whose norms are to be used. A loose culture is more likely in such ecologies.

Over time, cultures become more complex, as new differentiations prove effective. However, once complexity reaches very high levels, moves toward simplification emerge as reactions to too much complexity. For example, in art styles, the pendulum has been swinging between the "less is more" view of Oriental art and the "more is better" view of the rococo period in Europe. Similarly, excessive individualism may create a reaction toward collectivism, and excessive collectivism, a reaction toward individualism; or tightness may result from too much looseness, and looseness from too much tightness. Thus, culture is dynamic, ever changing.

* * *

The three dimensions of cultural variation described earlier are systematically linked to different kinds of self. In this section I provide hypotheses linking culture and self.

INDIVIDUALISM-COLLECTIVISM Child-rearing patterns in individualistic cultures tend to emphasize self-reliance, independence, finding yourself, and self-actualization. As discussed earlier, such child-rearing increases the complexity of the private self, and because there are more elements of the private self to be sampled, more are sampled. Thus, the probability that the private rather than the other selves will be sampled increases with individualism. Conversely, in collectivist cultures, child-rearing emphasizes the importance of the collective; the collective self is more complex and more likely to be sampled.

* * *

Such patterns are usually associated with rewards for conformity to ingroup goals, which leads to internalization of the ingroup goals. Thus, people do what is expected of them, even if that is not enjoyable. Bontempo et al. (1989) randomly assigned subjects from a collectivist (Brazil) and an individualist (U.S.) culture to two conditions of questionnaire administration: public and private. The questionnaire contained questions about how the subject was likely to act when the ingroup expected a behavior that was costly to the individual (e.g., visit a friend in the hospital, when this was time consuming). Both of the questions How should the person act? and How enjoyable would it be to act? were measured. It was found that Brazilians gave the same answers under both the anonymous and public conditions. Under both conditions they indicated that they would do what was expected of them. The U.S. sample indicated they would do what was expected of them in the public but not in the private condition. The U.S. group's private answers indicated that the subjects thought that doing the costly behaviors was unlikely, and certainly not enjoyable. Under the very same conditions the Brazilians indicated that they thought the costly prosocial behaviors were likely and enjoyable. In short, the Brazilians had internalized[2] the ingroup norms so that conformity to the ingroup appeared enjoyable to them.

* * *

Observations indicate that the extent to which

---

[2]Made a part of themselves.

an ingroup makes demands on individuals in few or in many areas shows considerable variance. For example, in the United States, states make very few demands (e.g., pay your income tax), whereas in China during the cultural revolution, the Communist Party made demands in many areas (artistic expression, family life, political behavior, civic action, education, athletics, work groups, even location, such as where to live). It seems plausible that the more areas of one's life that are affected by an ingroup, the more likely the individual is to sample the collective self.

* * *

TIGHT-LOOSE CULTURES Homogeneous, relatively isolated cultures tend to be tight, and they will sample the collective self more than will heterogeneous, centrally located cultures. The more homogeneous the culture, the more the norms will be clear and deviation from normative behavior can be punished. Cultural heterogeneity increases the confusion regarding what is correct and proper behavior. Also, cultural marginality[3] tends to result in norm and role conflict and pressures individuals toward adopting different norms. Because rejection of the ingroup members who have adopted norms of a different culture can be costly, individuals moderate their need to make their ingroup members conform to their ideas of proper behavior. So, the culture becomes loose (i.e., tolerant of deviations from norms).

The looser the culture, the more the individual can choose what self to sample. If several kinds of collective self are available, one may choose to avoid norm and role conflict by rejecting all of them and developing individual conceptions of proper behavior. Thus, sampling of the private self is more likely in loose cultures and sampling of the collective self is more likely in tight cultures. Also, tight cultures tend to socialize their children by emphasizing the expectations of the generalized other. Hence, the public self will be complex and

will be more likely to be sampled. In other words, tight cultures tend to sample the public and collective self, whereas loose cultures tend to sample the private self.

When the culture is both collectivist and tight, then the public self is extremely likely to be sampled. That means people act "properly," as that is defined by society, and are extremely anxious [about not acting] correctly. Their private self does not matter. As a result, the private and public selves are often different. Doi (1986) discussed this point extensively, comparing the Japanese public self (*tatemae*) with the private self (*honne*). He suggested that in the United States there is virtue in keeping public and private consistent (not being a hypocrite). In Japan, proper action matters. What you feel about such action is irrelevant. Thus, the Japanese do not like to state their personal opinions, but rather seek consensus.

Consistently with Doi's (1986) arguments is Iwao's (1988) research. She presented scenarios to Japanese and Americans and asked them to judge various actions that could be appropriate responses to these situations. For example, one scenario (daughter brings home person from another race) included as a possible response "thought that he would never allow them to marry but told them he was in favor of their marriage." This response was endorsed as the *best* by 44% of the Japanese sample but by only 2% of the Americans; it was the *worst* in the opinion of 48% of the Americans and 7% of the Japanese.

Although the private self may be complex, this does not mean that it will be communicated to others if one can avoid such communication. In fact, in tight cultures people avoid disclosing much of the self, because by disclosing they may reveal some aspect of the self that others might criticize. In other words, they may be aware of the demands of the generalized other and avoid being vulnerable to criticism by presenting little of this complex self to others. Barlund (1975) reported studies of the self-disclosure to same-sex friend, opposite-sex friend, mother, father, stranger, and untrusted acquaintance in Japan and in the United States. The pattern of self-disclosure was the same—that

---

[3]Not being part of the mainstream of a culture and feeling that one or one's group is at the "margins."

is, more to same-sex friend, and progressively less to opposite-sex friend, mother, father, stranger, and least to the untrusted acquaintance. However, the amount disclosed in each relationship was about 50% more in the United States than in Japan.

CULTURAL COMPLEXITY The more complex the culture, the more confused is likely to be the individual's identity. Dragonas (1983) sampled the self-concepts of 11- and 12-year-olds in Greek small villages (simple), traditional cities (medium), and large cities (complex) cultures. She found that the more complex the culture, the more confusing was the identity. Similarly, Katakis (1976, 1978, 1984) found that the children of farmers and fishermen, when asked what they would be when they are old, unhesitatingly said "farmer" or "fisherman," whereas in the large cities the responses frequently were of the "I will find myself" variety. Given the large number of ingroups that are available in a complex environment and following the logic presented here, individuals may well opt for sampling their private self and neglect the public or collective selves.

CONTENT OF SELF IN DIFFERENT CULTURES The specific content of the self in particular cultures will reflect the language and availability of mythological constructs of that culture. Myths often provide ideal types that are incorporated in the self forged in a given culture (Roland, 1984a). For example, peace of mind and being free of worries have been emphasized as aspects of the self in India (Roland, 1984b) and reflect Indian values that are early recognizable in Hinduism and Buddhism (which emerged in India). Mythological, culture-specific constructs become incorporated in the self (Sinha, 1982, 1987). Roland (1984b) claimed that the private self is more "organized around 'we', 'our' and 'us' . . ." (p. 178) in India than in the West. But particular life events may be linked to more than one kind of self. For example, Sinha (1987b) found that the important goals of Indian managers are their own good health and the good health of their family (i.e., have both private and collective self-elements).

Sinha (personal communication, November 1985) believes the public self is different in collectivist and individualist cultures. In individualistic cultures it is assumed that the generalized other will value autonomy, independence, and self-reliance, and thus individuals will attempt to act in ways that will impress others (i.e., indicate that they have these attributes). To be distinct and different are highly valued, and people find innumerable ways to show themselves to others as different (in dress, possessions, speech patterns). By contrast, in collectivist cultures, conformity to the other in public settings is valued. Thus, in a restaurant, everyone orders the same food (in traditional restaurants, only the visible leader gets a menu and orders for all). The small inconvenience of eating nonoptimal food is more than compensated by the sense of solidarity that such actions generate. In collectivist cultures, being "nice" to ingroup others is a high value, so that one expects in most situations extreme politeness and a display of harmony (Triandis, Marin, Lisansky, & Betancourt, 1984). Thus, in collectivist cultures, the public self is an extension of the collective self. One must make a good impression by means of prosocial behaviors toward ingroup members, acquaintances, and others who may become ingroup members. At the same time, one can be quite rude to outgroup members, and there is no concern about displaying hostility, exploitation, or avoidance of outgroup members.

* * *

The collective self in collectivist cultures includes elements such as "I am philotimos" (traditional Greece, meaning "I must act as is expected of me by my family and friends"; see Triandis, 1972), "I must sacrifice myself for my ingroup," "I feel good when I display affection toward my ingroup," and "I must maintain harmony with my ingroup even when that is very disagreeable." The person is less self-contained in collectivist than in individualistic cultures (Roland, 1984b, p. 176).

Identity is defined on the basis of different elements in individualistic and collectivist cultures. Individualistic cultures tend to emphasize elements of identity that reflect possessions—what do I own, what experiences have I had, what are my accomplishments (for scientists, what is my list of publications). In collectivist cultures, identity is defined more in terms of relationships—I am the mother of X, I am a member of family Y, and I am a resident of Z. Furthermore, the qualities that are most important in forming an identity can be quite different. In Europe and North America, being logical, rational, balanced, and fair are important attributes; in Africa, personal style, ways of moving, the unique spontaneous self, sincere self-expression, unpredictability, and emotional expression are most valued. The contrast between classical music (e.g., Bach or Mozart) and jazz reflects this difference musically.

CONSEQUENCES OF SAMPLING THE PRIVATE AND COLLECTIVE SELF   In the previous section I examined the relationship between the three dimensions of cultural variation and the probabilities of differential sampling of the private, public, and collective selves. In this section I review some of the empirical literature that is relevant to the theoretical ideas just presented.

An important consequence of sampling the collective self is that many of the elements of the collective become salient. Norms, roles, and values (i.e., proper ways of acting as defined by the collective) become the "obviously" correct ways to act. Behavioral intentions reflect such processes. Thus, the status of the other person in the social interaction—for example, is the other an ingroup or an outgroup member—becomes quite salient. Consequently, in collectivist cultures, individuals pay more attention to ingroups and outgroups and moderate their behavior accordingly, than is the case in individualistic cultures (Triandis, 1972).

* * *

Who is placed in the ingroup is culture specific. For example, ratings of the "intimacy" of relationships on a 9-point scale suggest that in Japan there is more intimacy with acquaintances, coworkers, colleagues, best friends, and close friends than in the United States (Gudykunst & Nishida, 1986).

Atsumi (1980) argued that understanding Japanese social behavior requires distinguishing

relationships with benefactors, true friends, coworkers, acquaintances, and outsiders (strangers). The determinants of social behavior shift depending on this classification. Behavior toward benefactors requires that the person go out of his way to benefit them. Behavior toward true friends is largely determined by the extent the behavior is enjoyable in itself, and the presence of these friends makes it enjoyable. Behavior toward coworkers is determined by both norms and cost/benefit considerations. Finally, behavior toward outsiders is totally determined by cost/benefit ratios.

* * *

The behavioral intentions of persons in collectivist cultures appear to be determined by cognitions that are related to the survival and benefit of their collective. In individualist cultures, the concerns are personal. An example comes from a study of smoking. A collectivist sample (Hispanics in the U.S.) showed significantly more concern than an individualist sample (non-Hispanics) about smoking affecting the health of others, giving a bad example to children, harming children, and bothering others with the bad smell of cigarettes, bad breath, and bad smell on clothes and belongings, whereas the individualist sample was more concerned about the physiological symptoms they might experience during withdrawal from cigarette smoking (G. V. Marin, Marin, Otero-Sabogal, Sabogal, & Perez-Stable, 1987).

The emphasis on harmony within the ingroup, found more strongly in collectivist than in individualist cultures, results in the more positive evaluation of group-serving partners (Bond, Chiu, & Wan, 1984), the choice of conflict resolution techniques that minimize animosity (Leung, 1985, 1987), the greater giving of social support (Triandis et al., 1985), and the greater support of ingroup goals (Nadler, 1986). The emphasis on harmony may be, in part, the explanation of the lower heart-attack rates among unacculturated than among acculturated Japanese-Americans (Marmot & Syme, 1976). Clearly, a society in which confrontation is common is more likely to increase the blood pressure of those in such situations, and hence the probability of heart attacks; avoiding conflict and saving face must be linked to lower probabilities that blood pressure will become elevated. The probability of receiving social support in collectivist cultures may be another factor reducing the levels of stress produced by unpleasant life events and hence the probabilities of heart attacks (Triandis et al., 1988).

Although ideal ingroup relationships are expected to be smoother, more intimate, and easier in collectivist cultures, outgroup relationships can be quite difficult. Because the ideal social behaviors often cannot be attained, one finds many splits of the ingroup in collectivist cultures. Avoidance relationships are frequent and, in some cases, required by norms (e.g., mother-in-law avoidance in some cultures). Fights over property are common and result in redefinitions of the ingroup. However, once the ingroup is defined, relationships tend to be very supportive and intimate within the ingroup, whereas there is little trust and often hostility toward outgroup members. Gabrenya and Barba (1987) found that collectivists are not as effective in meeting strangers as are individualists. Triandis (1967) found unusually poor communication among members of the same corporation who were not ingroup members (close friends) in a collectivist culture. Bureaucracies in collectivist cultures function especially badly because people hoard information (Kaiser, 1984). Manipulation and exploitation of outgroups is common (Pandey, 1986) in collectivist cultures. When competing with outgroups, collectivists are more competitive than individualists (Espinoza & Garza, 1985) even under conditions when competitiveness is counterproductive.

In individualistic cultures, people exchange compliments more frequently than in collectivist cultures (Barlund & Araki, 1985). They meet people easily and are able to cooperate with them even if they do not know them well (Gabrenya & Barba, 1987). Because individualists have more of a choice concerning ingroup memberships, they stay in those groups with whom they can have relatively good relationships and leave groups with whom they disagree too frequently (Verma, 1985).

Competition tends to be interpersonal in individualistic and intergroup in collectivist cultures (Hsu, 1983; Triandis et al., 1988). Conflict is frequently found in family relationships in individualistic cultures and between families in collectivist cultures (Katakis, 1978).

There is a substantial literature (e.g., Berman, Murphy-Berman, & Singh, 1985; Berman, Murphy-Berman, Singh, & Kumar, 1984; Hui, 1984; G. Marin, 1985; Triandis et al., 1985) indicating that individualists are more likely to use equity, and collectivists to use equality or need, as the norms for the distribution of resources (Yang, 1981). This is consistent with the emphasis on trading discussed earlier. By contrast, the emphasis on communal relationships (Mills & Clark, 1982) found in collectivist cultures leads to emphases on equality and need. The parallel with gender differences, where men emphasize exchange and women emphasize communal relationships (i.e., equity and need; Major & Adams, 1983; Brockner & Adsit, 1986), respectively, is quite striking. * * *

*   *   *

Conclusions

Aspects of the self (private, public, and collective) are differentially sampled in different cultures, depending on the complexity, level of individualism, and looseness of the culture. The more complex, individualistic, and loose the culture, the more likely it is that people will sample the private self and the less likely it is that they will sample the collective self. When people sample the collective self, they are more likely to be influenced by the norms, role definitions, and values of the particular collective, than when they do not sample the collective self. When they are so influenced by a collective, they are likely to behave in ways considered appropriate by members of that collective. The more they sample the private self, the more their behavior can be accounted for by exchange theory and can be described as an exchange relationship. The more they sample the collective self, the less their behavior can be accounted for by exchange theory; it can be described as a communal relationship. However, social behavior is more likely to be communal when the target of that behavior is an ingroup member than when the target is an outgroup member. Ingroups are defined by common goals, common fate, the presence of an external threat, and/or the need to distribute resources to all ingroup members for the optimal survival of the ingroup. Outgroups consist of people with whom one is in competition or whom one does not trust. The ingroup-outgroup distinction determines social behavior more strongly in collectivist than in individualist cultures. When the culture is both collectivist and tight, the public self is particularly likely to be sampled. In short, a major determinant of social behavior is the kind of self that operates in the particular culture.

References

Adamopoulos, J., & Bontempo, R. N. (1986). Diachronic universals in interpersonal structures. *Journal of Cross-Cultural Psychology, 17,* 169–189.

Allport, G. W. (1943). The ego in contemporary psychology. *Psychological Review, 50,* 451–478.

Allport, G. W. (1955). *Becoming.* New Haven, CT: Yale University Press.

Atsumi, R. (1980). Patterns of personal relationships: A key to understanding Japanese thought and behavior. *Social Analysis, 6,* 63–78.

Barlund, D. C. (1975). *Public and private self in Japan and the United States.* Tokyo: Simul Press.

Barlund, D. C., & Araki, S. (1985). Intercultural encounters: The management of compliments by Japanese and Americans. *Journal of Cross-Cultural Psychology, 16,* 9–26.

Baumeister, R. F. (1986a). *Identity: Cultural change and the struggle for self.* New York: Oxford University Press.

Baumeister, R. F. (1986b). *Public self and private self.* New York: Springer.

Baumeister, R. F. (1987). How the self became a problem: A psychological review of historical research. *Journal of Personality and Social Psychology, 52,* 163–176.

Berman, J. J., Murphy-Berman, V., & Singh, P. (1985). Cross-cultural similarities and differences in perceptions of fairness. *Journal of Cross-Cultural Psychology, 16,* 55–67.

Berman, J. J., Murphy-Berman, V., Singh, P., & Kumar, P. (1984, September). *Cross-cultural similarities and differences in perceptions of fairness.* Paper presented at the International Congress of Psychology, in Acapulco, Mexico.

Berry, J. W. (1967). Independence and conformity in subsistence level societies. *Journal of Personality and Social Psychology, 7,* 415–418.

Berry, J. W. (1979). A cultural ecology of social behavior. In L. Berkowitz (Ed.), *Advances in experimental social psychology* (Vol. 12, pp. 177–207). New York: Academic Press.

Block, J. (1986, March). *Longitudinal studies of personality.* Col-loquium given at the University of Illinois, Psychology Department.

Bond, M. H., Chiu, C., & Wan, K. (1984). When modesty fails: The social impact of group effacing attributions following success or failure. *European Journal of Social Psychology, 16,* 111–127.

Bontempo, R., Lobel, S. A., & Triandis, H. C. (1989). *Compliance and value internalization among Brazilian and U.S. students.* Manuscript submitted for publication.

Brockner, J., & Adsit, L. (1986). The moderating impact of sex on the equity satisfaction relationship: A field study. *Journal of Applied Psychology, 71,* 585–590.

Cooley, C. H. (1902). *Human nature and the social order.* New York: Scribner.

Davidson, A. R., Jaccard, J. J., Triandis, H. C., Morales, M. L., & Diaz-Guerrero, R. (1976). Cross-cultural model testing: Toward a solution of the etic-emic dilemma. *International Journal of Psychology, 11,* 1–13.

Doumanis, M. (1983). *Mothering in Greece: From collectivism to individualism.* New York: Academic Press.

Doi, T. (1986). *The anatomy of conformity: The individual versus society.* Tokyo: Kodansha.

Dragonas, T. (1983). *The self-concept of preadolescents in the Hellenic context.* Unpublished doctoral dissertation, University of Ashton, Birmingham, England.

Espinoza, J. A., & Garza, R. T. (1985). Social group salience and interethnic cooperation. *Journal of Experimental Social Psychology, 231,* 380–392.

Fazio, R. H., & Williams, C. J. (1986). Attitude accessibility as a moderator of the attitude-perception and attitude-behavior relations: An investigation of the 1984 presidential election. *Journal of Personality and Social Psychology, 51,* 505–514.

Gabrenya, W. K., & Barba, L. (1987, March). *Cultural differences in social interaction during group problem solving.* Paper presented at the meetings of the Southeastern Psychological Association, Atlanta.

Geertz, C. (1973). *The interpretation of cultures.* New York: Basic Books.

Georgas, J. (1989). Changing family values in Greece: From collectivist to individualist. *Journal of Cross-Cultural Psychology, 20,* 80–91.

Gordon, C., & Gergen, K. J. (Eds.). (1968). *The self in social interaction.* New York: Wiley.

Greenwald, A. G., Carnot, C. G., Beach, R., & Young, B. (1987). Increasing voting behavior by asking people if they expect to vote. *Journal of Applied Psychology, 71,* 315–318.

Greenwald, A. G., & Pratkanis, A. R. (1984). The self. In R. S. Wyer & T. K. Srull (Eds.), *Handbook of social cognition* (Vol. 3, pp. 129–178). Hillsdale, NJ: Erlbaum.

Gudykunst, W. B., & Nishida, T. (1986). The influence of cultural variability on perceptions of communication behavior associated with relationship terms. *Human Communication Research, 13,* 147–166.

Higgins, E. T., & King, G. (1981). Accessibility of social constructs: Information-processing consequences of individual and contextual variability. In N. Cantor & J. F. Kihlstrom (Eds.), *Personality, cognition and social interaction* (pp. 69–121). Hillsdale, NJ: Erlbaum.

Hofstede, G. (1980). *Culture's consequences.* Beverly Hills, CA: Sage.

Hsu, F. L. K. (1983). *Rugged individualism reconsidered.* Knoxville: University of Tennessee Press.

Hui, C. H. (1984). *Individualism-collectivism: Theory, measurement and its relationship to reward allocation.* Unpublished doctoral dissertation, Department of Psychology, University of Illinois at Champaign-Urbana.

Hui, C. H., & Triandis, H. C. (1986). Individualism-collectivism: A study of cross-cultural researchers. *Journal of Cross-Cultural Psychology, 17,* 225–248.

Iwao, S. (1988, August). *Social psychology's models of man: Isn't it time for East to meet West?* Invited address to the International Congress of Scientific Psychology, Sydney, Australia.

James, W. (1950). *The principles of psychology.* New York: Dover. (Original work published 1890.)

Katakis, C. D. (1976). An exploratory multilevel attempt to investigate interpersonal and intrapersonal patterns of 20 Athenian families. *Mental Health and Society, 3,* 1–9.

Katakis, C. D. (1978). On the transaction of social change processes and the perception of self in relation to others. *Mental Health and Society, 5,* 275–283.

Katakis, C. D. (1984). Oi tris tautotites tis Ellinikis oikogenoias [The three identities of the Greek family]. Athens, Greece: Kedros.

Kohn, M. L. (1969). *Class and conformity.* Homewood, IL: Dorsey.

Kohn, M. L. (1987). Cross-national research as an analytic strategy. *American Sociological Review, 52,* 713–731.

Kraut, R. E. (1973). Effects of social labeling on giving to charity. *Journal of Experimental Social Psychology, 9,* 551–562.

Kuhn, M. H., & McPartland, T. (1954). An empirical investigation of self-attitudes. *American Sociological Review, 19,* 68–76.

Leung, K. (1985). *Cross-cultural study of procedural fairness and disputing behavior.* Unpublished doctoral dissertation, Department of Psychology, University of Illinois, Champaign-Urbana.

Leung, K. (1987). Some determinants of reactions to procedural models for conflict resolution: A cross-national study. *Journal of Personality and Social Psychology, 53,* 898–908.

Lobel, S. A. (1984). *Effects of sojourn to the United States. A SYMLOG content analysis of in-depth interviews.* Unpublished doctoral dissertation, Harvard University.

Major, B., & Adams, J. B. (1983). Role of gender, interpersonal orientation, and self-presentation in distributive justice behavior. *Journal of Personality and Social Psychology, 45,* 598–608.

Marin, G. (1985). Validez transcultural del principio de equidad: El colectivismo-individualismo como una variable moderatora [Transcultural validity of the principle of equity: Collectivism–individualism as a moderating variable]. *Revista Interamericana de Psichologia Occupacional, 4,* 7–20.

Marin, G., & Triandis, H. C. (1985). Allocentrism as an important characteristic of the behavior of Latin Americans and Hispanics. In R. Diaz-Guerrero (Ed.), *Cross-cultural and national studies in social psychology* (69–80). Amsterdam, The Netherlands: North Holland.

Marin, G. V., Marin, G., Otero-Sabogal, R., Sabogal, F., & Perez-Stable, E. (1987). *Cultural differences in attitudes toward smoking: Developing messages using the theory of reasoned action* (Tech. Rep.). (Available from Box 0320, 400 Parnassus Ave., San Francisco, CA 94117.)

Marmot, M. G., & Syme, S. L. (1976). Acculturation and coronary heart disease in Japanese Americans. *American Journal of Epidemiology, 104,* 225–247.

Marsella, A. J., DeVos, G., & Hsu, F. L. K. (1985). *Culture and self.* New York: Tavistock.

Mead, G. H. (1934). *Mind, self, and society.* Chicago: University of Chicago Press.

Miller, R. L., Brickman, P., & Bolen, D. (1975). Attribution versus persuasion as a means of modifying behavior. *Journal of Personality and Social Psychology, 31,* 430–441.

Mills, J., & Clark, E. S. (1982). Exchange and communal relationships. In L. Wheeler (Ed.), *Review of personality and social psychology* (Vol. 3, pp. 121–144). Beverly Hills, CA: Sage.

Murphy, G. (1947). *Personality.* New York: Harper.

Nadler, A. (1986). Help seeking as a cultural phenomenon: Differences between city and kibbutz dwellers. *Journal of Personality and Social Psychology, 51,* 976–982.

Pandey, J. (1986). Sociocultural perspectives on ingratiation. *Progress in Experimental Personality Research, 14,* 205–229.

Pearson, H. W. (Ed.). (1977). *The livelihood of man: Karl Polanyi.* New York: Academic Press.

Pelto, P. J. (1968, April). The difference between "tight" and "loose" societies. *Transaction,* 37–40.

Rogers, T. B. (1981). A model of the self as an aspect of the human information processing system. In N. Cantor & J. F. Kihlstrom (Eds.), *Personality, cognition and social interaction* (pp. 193–214). Hillsdale, NJ: Erlbaum.

Rokeach, M. (1960). *The open and closed mind.* New York: Basic Books.

Roland, A. (1984a). Psychoanalysis in civilization perspective. *Psychoanalytic Review, 7,* 569–590.

Roland, A. (1984b). The self in India and America: Toward a psychoanalysis of social and cultural contexts. In V. Kovolis (Ed.), *Designs of selfhood* (pp. 123–130). New Jersey: Associated University Press.

Rosenberg, M. (1979). *Conceiving the self.* New York: Basic Books.

Schlenker, B. R. (1985). Introduction. In B. R. Schlenker (Ed.). *Foundations of the self in social life* (pp. 1–28). New York: McGraw-Hill.

Shotland, R. L., & Berger, W. G. (1970). Behavioral validation of several values from the Rokeach value scale as an index of honesty. *Journal of Applied Psychology, 54,* 433–435.

Shweder, R. A., & LeVine, R. A. (1984). *Cultural theory: Essays on mind, self and emotion.* New York: Cambridge University Press.

Sinha, J. B. P. (1982). The Hindu (Indian) identity. *Dynamische Psychiatrie, 15,* 148–160.

Sinha, J. B. P. (1987). *Work cultures in Indian Organizations* (ICSSR Report). New Delhi, India: Concept Publications House.

Smith, M. B. (1980). Attitudes, values and selfhood. In H. E. Howe & M. M. Page (Eds.), *Nebraska Symposium on Motivation,* 1979 (pp. 305–358). Lincoln: University of Nebraska Press.

Snyder, M. (1974). Self-monitoring and expressive behavior. *Journal of Personality and Social Psychology, 30,* 526–537.

Snyder, M. (1987). *Public appearances as private realities: The psychology of self-monitoring.* New York: Freeman.

Snyder, M., Simpson, J. A., & Gangestad, S. (1986). Personality and sexual relations. *Journal of Personality and Social Psychology, 51,* 181–190.

Stryker, S., & Serpe, R. T. (1982). Commitment, identity salience, and role behavior: Theory and research example. In W. Ickes & E. S. Knowles (Eds.), *Personality, roles and social behavior* (pp. 199–218). New York: Springer.

Tajfel, H. (1978). *Differentiation between social groups.* London: Academic Press.

Triandis, H. C. (1967). Interpersonal relations in international organizations. *Journal of Organizational Behavior and Human Performance, 2,* 26–55.

Triandis, H. C. (1972). *The analysis of subjective culture.* New York: Wiley.

Triandis, H. C. (1977). *Interpersonal behavior.* Monterey, CA: Brooks/Cole.

Triandis, H. C. (1980). Values, attitudes, and interpersonal behavior. In H. Howe & M. Page (Eds.), *Nebraska Symposium on Motivation*, 1979 (pp. 195–260). Lincoln: University of Nebraska Press.

Triandis, H. C., Bontempo, R., Betancourt, H., Bond, M., Leung, K., Brenes, A., Georgas, J., Hui, C. H., Marin, G., Setiadi, B., Sinha, J. B. P., Verma, J., Spangenberg, J., Touzard, H., & de Montmollin, G. (1986). The measurement of etic aspects of individualism and collectivism across cultures. *Australian Journal of Psychology* (Special issue on cross-cultural psychology), *38,* 257–267.

Triandis, H. C., Bontempo, R., Villareal, M. J., Asai, M., & Lucca, N. (1988). Individualism and collectivism: Cross-cultural perspectives on self-ingroup relationships. *Journal of Personality and Social Psychology, 54,* 323–338.

Triandis, H. C., Leung, K., Villareal, M. J., & Clack, F. L. (1985). Allocentric versus idiocentric tendencies: Convergent and discriminant validation. *Journal of Research in Personality, 19,* 395–415.

Triandis, H. C., Marin, G., Lisansky, J., & Betancourt, H. (1984). *Simpatia* as a cultural script of Hispanics. *Journal of Personality and Social Psychology, 47,* 1363–1375.

United States Employment and Training Administration. *Dictionary of occupational titles.* Washington, DC: Government Printing Office.

Verma, J. (1985). The ingroup and its relevance to individual behaviour: A study of collectivism and individualism. *Psychologia, 28,* 173–181.

Wicklund, R. A., & Gollwitzer, P. M. (1982). *Symbolic self-completion.* Hillsdale, NJ: Erlbaum.

Yang, K. S. (1981). Social orientation and individual modernity among Chinese students in Taiwan. *Journal of Social Psychology, 113,* 159–170.

Zavalloni, M. (1975). Social identity and the recoding of reality. *International Journal of Psychology, 10,* 197–217.

Zavalloni, M., & Louis-Guerin, C. (1984). *Identité sociale et conscience: Introduction á l'égo-écologie* [Social identity and conscience: Introduction to the ego ecology]. Montréal, Canada: Les presses de l'université de Montréal.

Ziller, R. C. (1973). *The social self.* New York: Pergamon.

A Collective Fear of the Collective: Implications for Selves and Theories of Selves

Hazel Rose Markus and Shinobu Kitayama

Personality psychology generally assumes—in fact, it takes for granted—that human beings are individuals who can be meaningfully characterized, one at a time, using personality traits. This assumption "that people are independent, bounded, autonomous entities" is precisely what the authors of the next selection bring into question. The well-known American social psychologist Hazel Markus and her Japanese colleague Shinobu Kitayama describe the idea of the autonomous individual as a notion that is peculiar to Western, Euro-American culture. Japanese and other Asian cultures, they claim, have a very different view of what a person is all about.

Cultures outside Europe and North America emphasize the interdependence of the person with the larger culture, which Markus and Kitayama call "the collective." Habitual Western modes of thought as well as political ideology combine to see people as essentially separate from each other and emphasize independence, autonomy, and individual differences. However, this seemingly obvious idea may be a cultural artifact. In the East, individuals are seen as part of a greater whole, and it is not so important for one person to compete with or dominate another.

Perhaps because they are arguing against what they see as the conventional wisdom, Markus and Kitayama somewhat romanticize the Eastern view of the self. For example, they write that Asian child-rearing "places a continual emphasis on understanding and relating to others," and that the collective view is characterized by caring, responsibility, and love. But of course there is a tradeoff of advantages and disadvantages between the Eastern and Western way of life. For example, in collectivist cultures one's spouse is commonly chosen by others on the basis of a negotiation between families. Perhaps as a result of cultural conditioning, most Europeans and Americans would rather choose their own spouses! As Markus and Kitayama point out, individual rights of all sorts are not given a high priority in collectivist cultures.

Two aspects of the following article are of particular value. First, the article urges us to reexamine an assumption about human psychology held so deeply that few people in our culture are probably even aware of holding it. Second, Markus and Kitayama present, in Figure 1, a comprehensive model of the relationship between a culture's collective reality, social processes, individual reality, habitual psychological tendencies, and action. This model has the potential to be useful for the analysis of psychological differences among cultures on many different dimensions, not just collectivism vs. individualism.

From "A Collective Fear of the Collective: Implications for Selves and Theories of Selves," by H. R. Markus and S. Kitayama. In *Personality and Social Psychology Bulletin, 20,* 568–579.

Our cultural nightmare is that the individual throb of growth will be sucked dry in slavish social conformity. All life long, our central struggle is to defend the individual from the collective.

—Plath, 1980, p. 216

Selves, as well as theories of selves, that have been constructed within a European-American cultural frame show the influence of one powerful notion—the idea that people are independent, bounded, autonomous entities who must strive to remain unshackled by their ties to various groups and collectives (Bellah, Madsen, Sullivan, Swidler, & Tipton, 1985; Farr, 1991; Sampson, 1985; Shweder & Bourne, 1984). This culturally shared idea of the self is a pervasive, taken-for-granted assumption that is held in place by language, by the mundane rituals and social practices of daily life, by the law, the media, the foundational texts like the Declaration of Independence and the Bill of Rights, and by virtually all social institutions. The individualist ideal as sketched in its extreme form in the opening quotation might not be explicitly endorsed by many Americans and Europeans. Some version of this view is, however, the basis of social science's persistent belief in the person as a rational, self-interested actor, and it occasions a desire not to be defined by others and a deep-seated wariness, in some instances even a fear, of the influence of the generalized other, of the social, and of the collective.

* * *

Recent analyses of the self in cultures other than the European-American (e.g., Daniels, 1984; Derné, 1992; Markus & Kitayama, 1991; Triandis, 1990; White & Kirkpatrick, 1985) reveal some very different perspectives on the relation between the self and the collective. Japanese culture, for example, emphasizes the *inter*dependence of the individual with the collective rather than independence from it. The analysis of non–European-American views of self has two notable benefits. First, such an analysis can illuminate some central characteristics of these non-Western cultures themselves. Second, and more important for our purposes, it can help uncover some aspects of European-American social behavior that are not well captured in the current social psychological theories.

Culture and Self

INDEPENDENCE OF SELF FROM THE COLLECTIVE—A CULTURAL FRAME The model that underlies virtually all current social science views the self as an entity that (a) comprises a unique, bounded configuration of internal attributes (e.g., preferences, traits, abilities, motives, values, and rights) and (b) behaves primarily as a consequence of these internal attributes. It is the individual level of reality—the thoughts and feelings of the single individual—that is highlighted and privileged in the explanation and analysis of behavior; the collective level of reality recedes and remains secondary. The major normative task is to maintain the independence of the individual as a self-contained entity or, more specifically, to be true to one's own internal structures of preferences, rights, convictions, and goals and, further, to be confident and to be efficacious. According to this *independent* view of the self, there is an enduring concern with expressing one's internal attributes both in public and in private. Other people are crucial in maintaining this construal of the self, but they are primarily crucial for their role in evaluating and appraising the self or as standards of comparison (see Markus & Kitayama, 1991; Triandis, 1990, for a discussion of the independent or individualist self). Others do not, however, *participate* in the individual's own subjectivity.

* * *

INTERDEPENDENCE OF THE SELF AND THE COLLECTIVE—AN ALTERNATIVE FRAME The pervasive influence of the individualist ideal in many aspects of European-American social behavior has appeared in high relief as we have carried out a set of studies on the self and its functioning in a variety of Asian countries, including Japan, Thailand, and Korea (Kitayama & Markus, 1993; Kitayama, Markus, & Kurokawa, 1991; Markus & Kitayama, 1991, 1992). What has become apparent is that the European-American view of the self and its relation to the collective is only *one* view. There are other, equally powerful but strikingly different, collective notions about the self and its relation to the collective.

From one such alternative view, the self is viewed not as an independent entity separate from the collective but instead as a priori fundamentally interdependent with others. Individuals do not stand in opposition to the confines and constraints of the external collective, nor do they voluntarily choose to become parts of this external collective. Instead, the self *is* inherently social—an integral part of the collective. This interdependent view grants primacy to the *relationship* between self and others. The self derives only from the individual's relationships with specific others in the collective.

There is no self without the collective; the self is a part that becomes whole only in interaction with others (e.g., Kondo, 1990; Kumagai & Kumagai, 1985; Lebra, 1992). It is defined and experienced as inherently connected with others. In contrast to the European-American orientation, there is an abiding fear of being on one's own, of being separated or disconnected from the collective. A desire for independence is cast as unnatural and immature.

The major normative task of such a self is not to maintain the independence of the individual as a self-contained entity but instead to maintain *inter*dependence with others. Rather than as an independent decision maker, the self is cast as "a single thread in a richly textured fabric of relationships" (Kondo, 1990, p. 33). This view of the self and of the collective requires adjusting and fitting to important relationships, occupying one's proper place in the group, engaging in collectively appropriate actions, and promoting the goals of others. One's thoughts, feelings, and actions are made meaningful only in reference to the thoughts, feelings, and actions of others in the relationship, and consequently others are crucially important in the very definition of the self. (For more detailed descriptions of the interdependent self, see Hsu, 1953; Kondo, 1990; Markus & Kitayama, 1991.)

Interdependence in this sense is theoretically distinct from social identity (e.g., Tajfel & Turner, 1985; Turner & Oakes, 1989), which refers to social categorizations that define a person as a member of particular social categories (e.g., American, male, Protestant, engineer). Social identity, in the framework of Turner and colleagues, is always defined in counterpoint to personal identity, which is all the ways a person is *different* from his or her ingroups. The key feature of interdependence is not distinctiveness or uniqueness but a heightened awareness of the other, and of the nature of one's relation to the other, and an expectation of some mutuality in this regard across all behavioral domains, even those that can be designated as private or personal.

DIFFERENCES IN THE ENCULTURATION OF THE "BASIC" TASKS Although both European-American and Asian cultural groups recognize that independence from others and interdependence with others are essential human tendencies or tasks, these two tasks are weighted and organized quite differently in the two groups. The notion of the autonomous individual in continuous tension with the external collective is "natural" only from a particular cultural perspective. From an alternative perspective, such an arrangement appears somewhat unnatural and contrived. In Japan, for example, the culture in its dominant ideology, patterns of social customs, practices, and institutions emphasizes and foregrounds not independence from others but interdependence with others. Interdependence is the first goal to be taken care of; it is crafted and nurtured in the social episodes and scripted actions of everyday social life, so that it becomes spontaneous, automatic, and taken for granted. Although independence is also essential for social functioning, it remains a tacit and less culturally elaborated pursuit. It is left to the intentions and initiatives of each individual member, and so its pursuit is relatively optional and is the focus of personal and unofficial discourse because it is not strongly constrained or widely supported by socially sanctioned cultural practices.

THE CULTURAL SHAPING OF PSYCHOLOGICAL PROCESSES

In Figure 1, we have illustrated how the "reality" of independence is created and maintained in selves, as well as in theories of selves. According to this view, a cultural group's way of self-understanding is simultaneously related to a set of macrolevel phenomena, such as cultural views of personhood and their supporting collective practices, and to a set of microlevel phenomena, like individual lives and their constituent cognitive, emotional, and motivational processes.

Collective reality. Under the heading "collective reality" we have included cultural values and their related ecological, historical, economic, and sociopolitical factors. For example, the United States is a nation with a rich tradition of moral imperatives, but the most well-elaborated is the need to protect the "natural rights" of each individual. This core cultural ideal is rooted most directly in the Declaration of Independence and the Bill of Rights, which protect certain inalienable rights, including life, liberty, and the pursuit of happiness. This highlighting of individuals and their rights is objectified and reified in a variety of democratic political institutions and free-market capitalism. In Japan, as throughout Asia, the prevalent ideological and moral discourses are not tied to individual rights but to the inevitability of a strict hierarchical order and to the achievement of virtue through cultivation of the individual into a "social man" (Yu, 1992). This core cultural ideal is anchored in the works of Confucius and Mencius and finds expression in an array of economic, political, and social institutions.

Sociopsychological products and processes—transmitting the core ideas. The cultural ideals and moral imperatives of a given cultural group are given life by a diverse set of customs, norms, scripts, practices, and institutions that carry out the transformation of the collective reality into the largely personal or psychological reality. These sociopsychological products and processes objectify and make "real" the core ideas of the society (Bourdieu, 1972; D'Andrade, 1984; Durkheim, 1898/1953; Farr & Moscovici, 1984; Geertz, 1973; Oyserman & Markus, in press). For example, in the United States, the idea of human rights (including liberty from the thrall of the collective) as inherent and God-given gains its force from a large array of legal statutes protecting individual rights. In this way the individual gains superiority to the collective.

Child-rearing practices in the United States, rooted in Freudian theory and filtered through Dr. Spock and most recently the self-esteem movement, also work to develop the constituent elements of the self and to reinforce the importance of having a distinct self that the individual can feel good about. A recent study (Chao, 1993), for example, found that 64% of European-American mothers, in comparison with 8% of Chinese mothers, stressed building children's "sense of themselves" as an important goal of child-rearing. Many

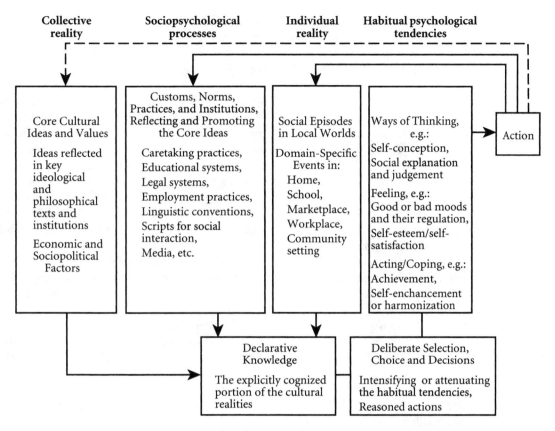

Figure 1. Cultural shaping of psychological reality.

American mothers take every opportunity to praise children and to help them realize the ways in which they are positively unique or different from their peers. Training in autonomy and the development of the appreciation of being alone also comes early. Day-old children sleep alone in their cribs, often in separate rooms from their parents (Shweder, Jensen, & Goldstein, 1995). On the playground, children are taught to stand up for themselves and fight back if necessary (Kashiwagi, 1989).

Another important quality of personhood, from the independent perspective, is the capacity to make one's own choice. In much of Western culture, but especially in North America, there are numerous examples of everyday scripts that presuppose the actor's right to make a choice. It is common for American hosts to instruct their guests, "Help yourself." With this suggestion, the host invites the guest to affirm the self by expressing some of those preferences that are thought to constitute the "real self." American children, then, are socialized to have distinct preferences. Long before the child is old enough to answer, caretakers pose questions like "Do you want the red cup or the blue cup?" With such questions, mothers signal to children that the capacity for independent choice is an important and desirable attribute. And the availability of choice gives rise to the need for preferences by which to make choices.

The practices of the media further create and foster the objectivity of the autonomous, independent self. Advertising in the United States makes appeals to nonconformity, originality, and uniqueness. A hard-sell approach is common in which the product is presented as the best or the leader of its kind, and purchasing it is claimed to reveal that the consumer has the "right" preferences or attitudes (Mueller, 1987; Zandpour, Chang, & Catalano, 1992). For example, Chanel recently marketed, in both the United States and Europe, a men's cologne with the strikingly unsubtle name of *Egoïste* and the slogan "For the man who walks on the right side of the fine line between arrogance and awareness of self-worth."

Perhaps the most powerful practice of all for the purpose of creating a shared concern with independence is that of advancing, promoting, and compensating people according to their "merit." This practice places a lifelong emphasis on inner attributes, capacities, and abilities as the "real" measure of the self and encourages people to define and develop these attributes.

In many Asian cultures, there is an equally diverse and powerful set of sociopsychological processes in each of these corresponding domains, but these practices are rooted in a view of the self as an interdependent entity. For example, in place of (or, to a certain extent, in addition to) the emphasis on human rights, there exist dense systems of rules and norms that highlight the duties of each individual to the pertinent collective, whether it is the company, school, or nation. Moreover, there are many fewer statutes protecting individual rights, and the Japanese resort to court suits to secure their rights far less readily than European-Americans (Hideo, 1988).

In the course of interpersonal interaction, the Japanese are encouraged to try to read the partner's mind and to satisfy what is taken as the partner's expectations or desires. A Japanese mother does not ask for a child's preference but instead tries to determine what is best for the child and to arrange it. Rather than asking a guest to make a choice, Japanese hosts do their best to prepare and offer what they infer to be the best possible meal for the guest, saying, for example, "Here's a turkey sandwich for you. I thought you said you like turkey better than beef last time we met."

Child rearing in many Asian cultures places a continual emphasis on understanding and relating to others, first to the mother and then to a wide range of others. The rules of interdependence are explicitly modeled, and the goal is to maintain harmonious relationships (Hsu, 1953). Interdependence can be found in all domains. In stark opposition to American practices and Freudian wisdom, cosleeping and cobathing are common in Japanese families. The emphasis is not on developing a good, private sense of self but on tuning in to and being sensitive to others. Punishing or reprimanding Japanese children often involves not the withholding of rights and privileges but a threat to the relationship. Mothers will say, "I don't like children like you" or "People will laugh at you" (Okimoto & Rohlen, 1988).

With respect to media practices, Japanese advertising often uses soft-sell appeals that focus on harmony or connection with nature or with others (Mueller, 1987). In classified ads, employers explicitly seek individuals with good interpersonal relations, as opposed to self-starters or innovators (Caproni, Rafaeli, & Carlile, 1993). A focus on relationships is also evident in all types of business practices. Japan stands out from all countries in the West because of its emphasis on durable and pervasive ties between government and industry, between banks and businesses, and among corporations. Okimoto and Rohlen (1988) contend that the emphasis on organizational networks and human relationships is so strong that Japanese capitalism can be labeled *relational capitalism*. In the pursuit of long-term relationships and mutual trust, Japanese corporations operate quite differently, often, for example, forgoing the maximization of short-term profits with the hope of gaining a long-term market share. And in contrast to the European-American emphasis on merit for promotion and compensation, wages and advancement in the majority of Japanese companies and institutions are tied to seniority in the system. In addition, employment in large corporations is typically permanent, and there is little lateral entry from the outside—all publicly scripted collective practices that foster and promote a view of the self as inherently relational and interdependent.

Beyond the caretaking, legal, business, and

media practices we have alluded to are a host of others, including educational and linguistic practices, and all the scripts and institutions that structure everyday social interactions. An important element in understanding which practices will become socially established is how the practices reflect and carry the group's underlying cultural values. Americans, for example, will be particularly susceptible to ideas and practices that directly follow from individualism (Sperber, 1985). Other practices—welfare and universal health care programs are good examples—will have a more difficult time taking hold in the United States.

Local worlds—living the core ideas. The third segment of Figure 1 represents the specific settings, circumstances, and situations of everyday life that make up an individual's immediate social environment and in which particular customs, norms, and practices become lived experience. The local worlds—home, school, the workplace, the community center, the church, the restaurant, bar, or café, the marketplace—and the specific activities or episodes they support—helping a child with homework, shopping for a gift, drinking with friends, discussing politics, playing baseball, working with others to meet a deadline—demand specific, culturally appropriate responses if a person is to become a valued member of the family, school, workplace, or community.

It is within the demands and expectations of these domain-specific, recurrent social episodes that people, often quite unknowingly, live out the core cultural values. So Americans are likely to create and live within settings that elicit and promote the sense that one is a positively unique individual who is separate and independent from others. For example, in many American schools, each child in the class has the opportunity to be a "star" or a "Very Special Person" for a week during the school year. Likewise, Japanese will create and live with situations that promote the sense of self as interdependent with others. In Japanese schools, children routinely produce group pictures or story boards, and no child leaves to go to the playground or lunch until all members of the group are ready to leave.

Habitual psychological tendencies reflecting the core ideas. As a result of efforts to respond or adjust to the set of specific episodes that constitute the individual's life space, episodes that have themselves been shaped by norms, practices, and institutions supporting the cultural group's core ideas, a set of habitual psychological tendencies is likely to develop. The final segment of Figure 1 represents the individual's "authentic" subjective experience—particular, proceduralized ways of thinking, feeling, striving, knowing, understanding, deciding, managing, adjusting, adapting, which are, in some large part, structured, reinforced, and maintained by the constraints and affordances of the particular social episodes of the individual's local worlds. In this way, people who live within a society whose daily practices and formal institutions all promote independence will come not just to believe that they are, but to experience themselves as, autonomous, bounded selves who are distinct from other members of the collective. This will be evident in many ways of thinking, feeling, and acting, but it is particularly evident when people are asked to characterize themselves.

For example, by the time they are young adults, many Americans will seek an optimal distinctiveness from others (Brewer, 1990) and will "naturally" experience an ambivalence about their collective nature and a deep concern with being categorically perceived or socially determined. The journalist Barbara Ehrenreich (1992) describes an interchange with an acquaintance who has just rediscovered her own ethnic and religious heritage and now feels in contact with her 2000-year ancestral traditions. The acquaintance asks about Ehrenreich's ethnic background. The first word to come out of Ehrenreich's mouth in answer to the question is "None." She is surprised at how natural and right her answer seems, yet slightly embarrassed. She reflects and decides that her response when asked the nature of her ethnicity was quite correct. Her identity, she claims, comes from the realization that "we are the kind of people that whatever our distant ancestors' religions—we do not believe, we do not carry on traditions, we do not do things just because someone has done them before." Her ethnicity, she contends, is rooted not in a given group but in the ideas "Think for yourself" and "Try new things." In conclusion, Ehrenreich tells of asking her own children whether they ever had any stirring of "ethnic or religious identity." "None," they all conclude, and she reports, "My chest swelled with pride as would my mother's to know that the race of 'None' marches on."

A tendency to define one's "real" self as distinct from one's social groups and obligations is characteristic of both younger and older cohorts of Americans as well. In a series of studies with young children, Hart and his colleagues (Hart, 1988; Hart & Edelstein, 1992) asked American children to imagine a "person machine" that makes the original person disappear but at the same time manufactures other people, copies of the original, which receive some but not all of the original person's characteristics. The respondent's task is to judge which new manufactured person—the one with the same physical attributes (looks like you), the one with the same social attributes (has the same friends and family), or the one with the same psychological attributes (same thoughts and feelings)—will be most like the original person. By ninth grade, Hart et al. (Hart, Fegley, Hung Chan, Mulvey, & Fischer, 1993) finds that most respondents believe it is the copy with the original's psychological characteristics that is the most similar to the original.

These findings are consistent with those of several other studies of cultural variation in self-categorization (Cousins, 1989; Triandis, 1990) and suggest that, for American students, it is the internal features of the self—the traits, attributes, and attitudes—that are privileged and regarded as critical to self-definition. From this perspective, the significant aspects of the self are those that are the inside, the private property—one's characteristic ways of behaving, one's habitual thoughts, feelings, and beliefs (e.g., think for yourself, try new things)—the elements that do not explicitly reference others or the social world. Such internal attributes are also mentioned by the Japanese, but they appear to be understood as relatively situation specific and therefore elusive and unreliable

(Cousins, 1989) as defining features of self. For the Japanese, the critical features are those attributes—social roles, duties, obligations—that connect one to the larger world of social relationships. (For other detailed examples of the cultural shaping of judgment, self, and emotion, see Kitayama & Markus, 1993, 1995; Markus & Kitayama, 1994.) In a study examining response time for self-description,[1] Kitayama et al. (1991) find that Japanese respondents are decidedly slower to characterize themselves than American respondents and that this is particularly true for positive attributes.

The top level of Figure 1 indicates feedback loops from each individual's action. The most immediate and frequent feedback occurs at the micro level. Most obviously, what an individual does influences the very nature of the situation in which he or she has acted. There are, however, people who at times contribute, through their actions, not just to the micro level but also to the more macro level. The bottom level of Figure 1 represents a more cognitive influence. Some portion of the social realities—both macro and micro—can be represented cognitively. This cognized portion of culture is shaded in each segment of the figure. The articulated, declarative knowledge of cultural values, practices, and conventions may be recruited in modulating social action, either facilitating or inhibiting the automatized psychological tendencies. Importantly, however, psychological tendencies can develop independently of this second, articulated route of cultural influence. In this way, cultural values and beliefs can cause differences in psychological processes even when these beliefs (e.g., a fear of influence by the collective) are not cognitively encoded and overtly articulated. Of course, the values and beliefs often are encoded cognitively, but this current analysis implies that cognitive representations need not be central in the

---

[1]In such a study personality adjectives are presented on a screen, and subjects must respond "me" or "not me" by pressing a key. The time taken to respond is measured in milliseconds. A slower response implies that a particular attribute is a less central aspect of the self-concept.

cultural shaping of psychological processes. Instead, we suggest that psychological processes and behavior can be best understood as an important, but only partial, element of the dynamic cultural and historical process that involves the systematic (though by no means error-free or "fax-like") transmission of cultural imperatives to shape and define the nature of the specific, immediate life space—the microlevel reality—for each individual.

Implications of a Collective Fear of the Collective for Psychological Theorizing

Using Asian cultures, particularly Japan, as a point of reference and standard, we have sketched how the European-American fear of the collective may arise and how it is naturalized, enacted, and embodied so that people rarely see or feel the collective nature or source of their behavior and instead experience themselves as separate and self-contained entities. A large set of mutually reinforcing everyday rituals, social practices, and institutions work together to elaborate and objectify the culture's view of what the self is and what it should be. Independence and autonomy are thus the "natural" mode of being—in Geertz's (1975) terms, they become "experience near" phenomena. The subjective authenticity or "naturalness" of this mode, however, is a function of the degree of fit between habitual psychological tendencies and the cultural and social systems that are grounded in these cultural imperatives.

Theorists of European-American behavior have also been extremely influenced by the prevailing ideology of individualism. They have often viewed the self as in tension, or even as in opposition, to the "ruck of society" (Plath, 1980) or the "thrall of society" (Hewitt, 1989). The source of all important behavior is typically "found" in the unique configuration of internal attributes—thoughts, feelings, motives, abilities—that form the bounded, autonomous whole. As a consequence, the ways in which the self is, in fact, quite interdependent with the collective have been under-

analyzed and undertheorized. It is our view that there are a number of important reasons for theorists to go beyond theories that are directly shaped by the cultural ideal of individualism and to consider a broader view of the self.

First, and most obviously, although current descriptions of the largely independent and autonomous self could be argued to be reasonably adequate for European-American selves, a growing body of evidence suggests that they are simply not valid for many other cultural groups (see extended discussions of this point in Markus & Kitayama, 1991; Triandis, 1990; Triandis, Bontempo, & Villareal, 1988). Second, although the cultural ideal of independence is very influential in the nature and functioning of the European-American self, it does not determine it completely. For example, with respect to the bounded or fixed nature of the self, there are a variety of studies that reveal the self as decidedly malleable and its content and functioning as dependent on the social context. Typically these studies are not integrated with the literature that suggests stability of the self (e.g., Fazio, Effrein, & Falender, 1981; James, 1993; Jones & Pittman, 1982; Markus & Kunda, 1986; McGuire & McGuire, 1982; Schlenker, 1980).

Third, at least in the United States, the analysis of the selves of those groups in society that are somewhat marginalized—women, members of nondominant ethnic groups, the poor, the unschooled, and the elderly—reveals a more obvious interdependence between the self and the collective. For example, women describe themselves in relational terms (Gilligan, 1982; Jordan, Kaplan, Miller, Stivey, & Surrey, 1991), and they do not reveal the "typical" preference for being positively unique or different from others (Josephs, Markus, & Tafarodi, 1992). Other studies reveal that those groups that are in the minority with respect to language, skin color, or religion are decidedly more likely to define themselves in collective terms (Allen, Dawson, & Brown, 1989; Bowman, 1987; Husain, 1992). Further, Americans with less schooling are more likely to describe themselves in terms of habitual actions and roles, and less likely to characterize themselves in terms of psychological attributes, than those with more schooling (Markus, Herzog, Holmberg, & Dielman, 1992). And those with low self-esteem show a marked tendency to describe themselves as similar to others (Josephs et al., 1992). These findings suggest that those with power and privilege are those most likely to internalize the prevailing European-American cultural frame to achieve Ehrenreich's "ethnicity of none" and to "naturally" experience themselves as autonomous individuals.

Fourth, a number of recent studies show many Americans to be extremely concerned about others and the public good (Bellah et al., 1985; Bellah, Madsen, Sullivan, Swidler, & Tipton, 1991; Hewitt, 1989; Withnow, 1992) and to characterize themselves in interdependent terms. For example, a recent representative sample of 1,500 adults, aged 30 or over, found that although Americans indeed characterized themselves in terms of trait attributes and not social roles or obligations, the most frequently used attributes were *caring, responsible, loved*—all terms that imply some concern with a connection to the collective (Markus et al., 1992). Even if, as we have suggested, this connection is clearly voluntary and done on one's own terms, the prevailing model of the self could be modified.

And finally, increasingly throughout social psychology, there are indications that the individualist model of the self is too narrow and fails to take account of some important aspects of psychological reality. For example, within social psychology specifically, there is a great deal of evidence that people are exquisitely sensitive to others and to social pressure. People conform, obey, diffuse responsibility in a group, allow themselves to be easily persuaded about all manner of things, and become powerfully committed to others on the basis of minimal action (Myers, 1993). Despite the powerful cultural sanctions against allowing the collective to influence one's thoughts and actions, most people are still much less self-reliant, self-contained, or self-sufficient than the ideology of individualism suggests they should be. It appears in these cases that the European-American model of self is somewhat at odds with observed individual behavior and that it might be reformulated to reflect the substantial interdependence that characterizes even Western individualists.

Alternative Views of the Self and the Collective

In trying to formulate the collective sources of the self among Europeans or Americans, models of the self and the collective "Asian style" may be particularly informative.[2] If we assume, as does Shweder (1991), that every group can be considered an expert on some features of human experience and that different cultural groups "light up" different aspects of this experience, then Asian cultures may be an important source of conceptual resources in the form of concepts, frameworks, theories, or methods that can be employed to "see" interdependence. Even though interdependence American style will doubtlessly look quite different from interdependence Japanese style, an analysis of divergent cultural groups may further any theorist's understanding of the possibilities, potential, and consequences, both positive and negative, for socialness, for engagement, for interdependence, and for the ties that bind.

* * *

We have argued here that the cultural frame of individualism has put a very strong stamp on how social psychologists view the individual and his or her relation to the collective. Although this indi-

---

[2]Some of the most important work suggesting the need for alternative models of the self comes from feminist theorists who have argued in the last 15 years that relations have a power and significance in women's lives that has gone unrecognized (Belenky, Clinchy, Goldberger, & Tarule, 1986; Gilligan, 1982; Jordan et al., 1991). The development of a psychology of women has shown that the "Lone Ranger" model of the self simply does not fit many women's experience because women's sense of self seems to involve connection and engagement with relationships and collective. In this work, being dependent does not invariably mean being helpless, powerless, or without control. It often means being interdependent—having a sense that one is able to have an effect on others and is willing to be responsive to others and become engaged with them (Jordan, 1991).—Author

vidualist view has provided a powerful framework for the analysis of social behavior, it has also, necessarily, constrained theories, methods, and dominant interpretations of social behavior. Because individualism is not just a matter of belief or value but also one of everyday practice, including scientific practice, it is not easy for theorists to view social behavior from another cultural frame, and it is probably harder still to reflect a different frame in empirical work. But the comparative approach that is characteristic of the developing cultural psychology (e.g., Cole, 1990; Stigler, Shweder, & Herdt, 1990) may eventually open new and productive possibilities for the understanding and analysis of behavior.

For example, just as social influence, from the perspective of an interdependent cultural frame, can be seen as the mutual negotiation of social reality, helping can be seen as a result of obligation, duty, or morality, rather than as voluntary or intentional (e.g., Miller, Bersoff, & Harwood, 1990). Similarly, emotion can be viewed as an enacted interpersonal process (Rosaldo, 1984) or as an interpersonal atmosphere, as it is characterized in some non-Western theories (White, 1990). Further, cognition can be seen as an internalized aspect of communication (Zajonc, 1992), and the early idea of the social and interactive nature of the mind (e.g., Asch, 1952; Bruner, 1990; Vygotsky, 1978) can be taken much more seriously than it has been. In general, viewing the self and social behavior from alternative perspectives may enable theorists to see and elaborate at least one important and powerful universal that might otherwise be quite invisible—the ways in which psychological functioning (in this case, the nature of the self), as well as theories about psychological functioning (here, theories of the nature of the self), are in many ways culture specific and conditioned by particular, but tacit and taken-for-granted, meaning systems, values, and ideals.

References

Allen, R. L., Dawson, M. C., & Brown, R. E. (1989). A schema based approach to modeling an African American racial belief system. *American Political Science Review, 83,* 421–442.

Asch, S. E. (1952). *Social psychology.* Englewood Cliffs, NJ: Prentice-Hall.

Belenky, M. F., Clinchy, B. M., Goldberger, N. R., & Tarule, J. M. (1986). *Women's ways of knowing: The development of self, voice, and mind.* New York: Basic Books.

Bellah, R. N., Madsen, R., Sullivan, W. M., Swidler, A., & Tipton, S. M. (1985). *Habits of the heart: Individualism and commitment in American life.* Berkeley: University of California Press.

Bellah, R. N., Madsen, R., Sullivan, W. M., Swidler, A., & Tipton, S. M. (1991). *The good society.* New York: Knopf.

Bourdieu, P. (1972). *Outline of a theory of practice.* Cambridge: Cambridge University Press.

Bowman, P. J. (1987). Post-industrial displacement and family role strains: Challenges to the Black family. In P. Voydanoff & L. C. Majka (Eds.), *Families and economic distress.* Newbury Park, CA: Sage.

Brewer, M. B. (1990, August). *The social self: On being the same and different at the same time.* Presidential address to the Society for Personality and Social Psychology presented at the annual meeting of the American Psychological Association, Boston.

Bruner, J. (1990). *Acts of meaning.* Cambridge, MA: Harvard University Press.

Caproni, P., Rafaeli, A., & Carlile, P. (1993, July). *The social construction of organized work: The role of newspaper employment advertising.* Paper presented at the European Group on Organization Studies conference, Paris, France.

Chao, R. K. (1993). *East and West: Concepts of the self reflected in mothers' reports of their child-rearing.* Unpublished manuscript, University of California, Los Angeles.

Cole, M. (1990). Cultural psychology: A once and future discipline? In J. J. Berman (Ed.), *Nebraska Symposium on Motivation, 1989* (Vol. 37, pp. 279–336). Lincoln: University of Nebraska Press.

Cousins, S. (1989). Culture and selfhood in Japan and the U.S. *Journal of Personality and Social Psychology, 56,* 124–131.

D'Andrade, R. (1984). Cultural meaning systems. In R. A. Shweder & R. A. LeVine (Eds.), *Cultural theories: Essays on mind, self, and emotion* (pp. 88–119). New York: Cambridge University Press.

Daniels, E. V. (1984). *Fluid signs; Being a person the Tamil way.* Berkeley: University of California Press.

Derné, S. (1992). Beyond institutional and impulsive conceptions of self: Family structure and the socially anchored real self. *Ethos, 20,* 259–288.

Durkheim, E. (1953). Individual representations and collective representations. In E. Durkheim (Ed.), *Sociology and philosophy* (D. F. Pocok, Trans.) (pp. 1–38). New York: Free Press. (Original work published 1898.)

Ehrenreich, B. (1992, March). The race of none. *Sunday New York Times Magazine,* pp. 5–6.

Farr, R. M. (1991). Individualism as a collective representation. In V. Aebischer, J. P. Deconchy, & M. Lipiansky (Eds.), *Idéologies et représentations sociales* (pp. 129–143). Cousset (Fribourg), Switzerland: Delval.

Farr, R. M., & Moscovici, S. (Eds.). (1984). *Social representations.* Cambridge: Cambridge University Press.

Fazio, R. H., Effrein, E. A., & Falender, Y. J. (1981). Self-perceptions following social interactions. *Journal of Personality and Social Psychology, 41,* 232–242.

Geertz, C. (1973). *The interpretation of cultures*. New York: Basic Books.

Geertz, C. (1975). On the nature of anthropological understanding. *American Scientist, 63,* 47–53.

Gilligan, C. (1982). *In a different voice: Psychological theory and women's development*. Cambridge, MA: Harvard University Press.

Hart, D. (1988). The adolescent self-concept in social context. In D. Lapsley & F. Power (Eds.), *Self, ego, and identity: Integrative approaches* (pp. 71–90). New York: Springer-Verlag.

Hart, D., & Edelstein, W. (1992). Self understanding development in cultural context. In T. M. Brinthaupt & R. P. Lipka (Eds.), *The self: Definitional and methodological issues*. Albany: State University of New York Press.

Hart, D., Fegley, S., Hung Chan, Y., Mulvey, D., & Fischer, L. (1993). *Judgment about personal identity in childhood and adolescence*. Unpublished manuscript.

Hewitt, J. P. (1989). *Dilemmas of the American self*. Philadelphia: Temple University Press.

Hideo, T. (1988). The role of law and lawyers in Japanese society. In D. I. Okimoto & T. P. Rohlen (Eds.), *Inside the Japanese system: Readings on contemporary society and political economy* (pp. 194–196). Stanford, CA: Stanford University Press.

Hsu, F. L. K. (1953). *Americans and Chinese: Two ways of life*. New York: H. Schuman.

Husain, M. G. (1992, July). *Ethnic uprising and identity*. Paper presented at the 11th Congress of the International Association for Cross-Cultural Psychology, Liege, Belgium.

James, K. (1993). Conceptualizing self with in-group stereotypes: Context and esteem precursors. *Personality and Social Psychology Bulletin, 19,* 117–121.

Jones, E. E., & Pittman, T. S. (1982). Towards a general theory of strategic self-preservation. In J. Suls (Ed.), *Psychological perspectives on the self* (Vol. 1, pp. 231–262). Hillsdale, NJ: Lawrence Erlbaum.

Jordan, J. V. (1991). Empathy and self boundaries. In J. V. Jordan, A. G. Kaplan, J. B. Miller, I. P. Stivey, & J. L. Surrey (Eds.), *Women's growth in connection* (pp. 67–80). New York: Guilford.

Jordan, J. V., Kaplan, A. G., Miller, J. B., Stivey, I. P., & Surrey, J. L. (Eds.). (1991). *Women's growth in connection*. New York: Guilford.

Josephs, R. A., Markus, H., & Tafarodi, R. W. (1992). Gender differences in the source of self-esteem. *Journal of Personality and Social Psychology, 63,* 391–402.

Kashiwagi, K. (1989, July). *Development of self-regulation in Japanese children*. Paper presented at the tenth annual meeting of the International Society for the Study of Behavioral Development, Jyväskylä, Finland.

Kitayama, S., & Markus, H. (1993). Construal of the self as a cultural frame: Implications for internationalizing psychology. In J. D'Arms, R. G. Hastie, S. E. Hoelscher, & H. K. Jacobson (Eds.), *Becoming more international and global: Challenges for American higher education*. Manuscript submitted for publication.

Kitayama, S., & Markus, H. (1995). A cultural perspective on self-conscious emotions. In J. P. Tangney & K. W. Fisher (Eds.), *Shame, guilt, embarrassment and pride: Empirical studies of self-conscious emotions*. New York: Guilford.

Kitayama, S., Markus, H., & Kurokawa, M. (1991, October). *Culture, self, and emotion: The structure and frequency of emotional experience*. Paper presented at the biannual meeting of the Society for Psychological Anthropology, Chicago.

Kondo, D. (1990). *Crafting selves: Power, gender, and discourses of identity in a Japanese work place*. Chicago: University of Chicago Press.

Kumagai, H. A., & Kumagai, A. K. (1985). The hidden "I" in *amae*: "Passive love" and Japanese social perception. *Ethos, 14,* 305–321.

Lebra, T. S. (1976). *Japanese patterns of behavior*. Honolulu: University of Hawaii Press.

Lebra, T. S. (1992, June). *Culture, self, and communication*. Paper presented at the University of Michigan, Ann Arbor.

Markus, H., Herzog, A. R., Holmberg, D. E., & Dielman, L. (1992). *Constructing the self across the life span*. Unpublished manuscript, University of Michigan, Ann Arbor.

Markus, H., & Kitayama, S. (1991). Culture and the self: Implications for cognition, emotion, and motivation. *Psychological Review, 98,* 224–253.

Markus, H., & Kitayama, S. (1992). The what, why and how of cultural psychology: A review of R. Shweder's *Thinking through cultures*. *Psychological Inquiry, 3,* 357–364.

Markus, H., & Kitayama, S. (1994). The cultural construction of self and emotion: Implications for social behavior. In S. Kitayama & H. R. Markus (Eds.), *Emotion and culture: Empirical studies of mutual influence* (pp. 89–130). Washington, DC: American Psychological Association.

Markus, H., & Kunda, Z. (1986). Stability and malleability in the self-concept in the perception of others. *Journal of Personality and Social Psychology, 51,* 1–9.

McGuire, W. J., & McGuire, C. V. (1982). Significant others in self space: Sex differences and developmental trends in social self. In J. Suls (Ed.), *Psychological perspectives on the self* (Vol. 1, pp. 71–96). Hillsdale, NJ: Lawrence Erlbaum.

Miller, J. G., Bersoff, D. M., & Harwood, R. L. (1990). Perceptions of social responsibilities in India and in the United States: Moral imperatives or personal decisions? *Journal of Personality and Social Psychology, 58,* 33–46.

Mueller, B. (1987, June/July). Reflections of culture: An analysis of Japanese and American advertising appeals. *Journal of Advertising Research*, pp. 51–59.

Myers, D. (1993). *Social psychology* (4th ed.). New York: McGraw-Hill.

Okimoto, D. I., & Rohlen, T. P. (Eds.). (1988). *Inside the Japanese system: Readings on contemporary society and political economy*. Stanford, CA: Stanford University Press.

Oyserman, D., & Markus, H. R. (in press). Self as social representation. In S. Moscovici and U. Flick (Eds.), *Psychology of the social*. Berlin: Rowohlt Taschenbuch Verlag Gmbh.

Plath, D. W. (1980). *Long engagements: Maturity in modern Japan*. Stanford, CA: Stanford University Press.

Rosaldo, M. (1984). Toward an anthropology of self and feeling. In R. A. Shweder & R. A. LeVine (Eds.), *Culture theory: Essays on mind, self, and emotion* (pp. 137–157). Cambridge: Cambridge University Press.

Sampson, E. E. (1985). The decentralization of identity: Toward a revised concept of personal and social order. *American Psychologist, 40,* 1203–1211.

Schlenker, B. R. (1980). *Impression management*. Pacific Grove, CA: Brooks/Cole.

Shweder, R. A. (1991). *Thinking through cultures: Expeditions in cultural psychology*. Cambridge, MA: Harvard University Press.

Shweder, R. A., & Bourne, E. (1984). Does the concept of the person vary cross-culturally? In R. A. Shweder & R. A. LeVine (Eds.), *Culture theory: Essays on mind, self, and emotion* (pp. 158–199). Cambridge: Cambridge University Press.

Shweder, R. A., Jensen, L. A., & Goldstein, W. M. (1995). Who sleeps by whom revisited: A method for extracting the moral goods implicit in practice. In J. Goodnow, P. Miller, & F. Kessel (Eds.), *Cultural practices as contexts for development.* San Francisco: Jossey-Bass.

Sperber, D. (1985). Anthropology and psychology: Towards an epidemiology of representations. *MAN, 20,* 73–89.

Stigler, J. W., Shweder, R. A., & Herdt, G. (Eds.). (1990). *Cultural psychology: Essays on comparative human development.* London: Cambridge University Press.

Tajfel, H., & Turner, J. C. (1985). The social identity theory of intergroup behavior. In S. Worchel & W. G. Austin (Eds.), *Psychology of intergroup relations* (pp. 7–24). Chicago: Nelson-Hall.

Triandis, H. C. (1990). Cross-cultural studies of individualism and collectivism. In J. J. Berman (Ed.), *Nebraska Symposium on Motivation, 1989* (Vol. 37, pp. 41–143).

Triandis, H. C., Bontempo, R., & Villareal, M. (1988). Individualism and collectivism: Cross-cultural perspectives on self-ingroup relationships. *Journal of Personality and Social Psychology, 54,* 323–338.

Turner, J. C., & Oakes, P. J. (1989). Self-categorization the-ory and social influence. In P. B. Paulus (Ed.), *The psychology of group influence* (2nd ed.). Hillsdale, NJ: Lawrence Erlbaum.

Vygotsky, L. S. (1978). *Mind in society: The development of higher psychological processes* (M. Cole, V. John-Steiner, S. Scribner, & E. Souberman, Eds.). Cambridge, MA: Harvard University Press.

White, G. M. (1990). Moral discourse and the rhetoric of emotion. In C. Lutz & L. Abu-Lughod (Eds.), *Language and the politics of emotion.* Cambridge: Cambridge University Press.

White, G. M., & Kirkpatrick, J. (Eds.). (1985). *Person, self, and experience: Exploring Pacific ethnopsychologies.* Berkeley and Los Angeles: University of California Press.

Withnow, R. (1992). *Acts of compassion.* Princeton, NJ: Princeton University Press.

Yu, A. B. (1992, July). *The self and life goals of traditional Chinese: A philosophical and cultural analysis.* Paper presented at the 11th Congress of the International Association for Cross-Cultural Psychology, Liege, Belgium.

Zajonc, R. B. (1992, April). *Cognition, communication, consciousness: A social psychological perspective.* Invited address at the 20th Katz-Newcomb Lecture at the University of Michigan, Ann Arbor.

Zandpour, F., Chang, C., & Catalano, J. (1992, January/February). Stories, symbols, and straight talk: A comparative analysis of French, Taiwanese, and U.S. TV commercials. *Journal of Advertising Research,* pp. 25–38.

VARIATION AMONG EUROPEAN AMERICANS IN EMOTIONAL FACIAL EXPRESSION

Jeanne L. Tsai and Yulia Chentsova-Dutton

Psychologists examining cultural differences usually contrast views in the East or West (such as Markus and Kitayama in the previous selection), or minority groups within larger cultures. The present article by Jeanne Tsai and Yulia Chentsova-Dutton accepts the challenge of examining cultural differences within *the apparently homogeneous European-American "ethnicity." The differences in the expression of emotion between Scandinavian and Irish-Americans suggest that cultural heritage continues to influence the behaviors of these Americans generations after their last ancestor left Europe.*

From *Journal of Cross-Cultural Psychology*, 34, 650–657, 2003.

Social scientists use the terms *European American* (EA) or *Anglo American* to refer to White, non-Hispanic individuals whose families have spent several generations in the United States and whose ancestors originally emigrated from Europe. Many social scientists view today's EAs as a homogeneous group of individuals who represent mainstream American values, norms, and practices. Therefore, researchers often focus on EAs' awareness of their majority status or their views of other racial and ethnic groups rather than their cultural ideas and practices (e.g., Dovidio, Kawakami, & Gaertner, 2002; Helms & Carter, 1991). There are several scholars, however, who would argue not only that is there considerable cultural heterogeneity among EAs but also that this variation can be traced to their different European countries of origin (Giordano & McGoldrick, 1996; Greeley & McCready, 1975). These scholars argue that although many EAs may be less aware of the ways in which they are influenced by their countries of origin, they still retain ideas and practices that originate from those cultures. These ideas and practices may be transmitted through the family as well as through local institutions without being explicitly labeled as cultural (Greeley, 1979). For example, Greeley and his colleagues found that although many EAs of Irish and Italian descent no longer identified explicitly with Irish and Italian cultures, their views of the family were consistent with Irish and Italian cultural norms, respectively (Greeley, 1979, 1981; Greeley & McCready, 1975).

In a study that compared the emotional responses of EAs and Hmong Americans (Tsai, Chentsova-Dutton, Friere-Bebeau, & Przymus, 2002), we made three observations that led us to suspect that the EAs in our sample represented different cultural heritages: (a) the variability of emotional responses in the EA sample was greater than that of the Hmong American sample; (b) while describing their cultural beliefs about emotion, some EAs emphasized emotional control, whereas others emphasized emotional expression; and (c) the occurrence rates of facial expressions in our EA sample were lower than were those reported for other EA samples from other regions of the United States using a similar task (Rosenberg & Ekman, 1994). Thus, we suspected that this variation might be associated with the unique cultural heritages of the EAs in our sample, which included Scandinavian (Norway, Denmark, Finland, and Sweden) and Irish cultures. Ethnographic accounts suggest that these particular cultures differ in their norms regarding emotional expression.

Specifically, Scandinavian cultural contexts are described as encouraging emotional moderation and control and as being more emotionally inhibited than other European cultures (Midelfort & Midelfort, 1982; Pennebaker, Rime, & Blanksenship, 1996; Rodnick, 1955). For example, Midelfort and Midelfort (1982) and Rodnick (1955) described Norwegian culture as minimizing the expression of "excessive" anger or other negative emotions because "expressing them would interfere with neighborly relationships" (Rodnick, 1955, p. 14). The same holds true for the experience of pleasure and other positive emotions (Erickson & Simon, 1996). In contrast, Irish culture has been characterized as placing a greater value on emotional expression. That is, Irish culture has been described as being more accepting of expressions of suffering and tragedy and as more encouraging of the use of laughter and humor to convey one's feelings (Greeley, 1979, 1981; McGoldrick, 1996).

In this study, we examined whether these ethnographic accounts accurately described the emotional facial expressions of EA of Scandinavian (EA-S) and Irish descent (EA-I) when these facial expressions were measured using the Facial Action Coding System, a well-established method for coding facial muscle movements (Ekman & Friesen, 1978).

Hypothesis

Based on ethnographic descriptions of Scandinavian and Irish norms regarding emotional expression, we predicted that EA-S would be less emotionally expressive than EA-I.

Method

PARTICIPANTS. EAs were recruited to participate in a larger study of emotion (Tsai et al., 2002). Participants were undergraduates from colleges and universities in Minnesota and were recruited through announcements in newspapers and flyers distributed across campuses as well as through general psychology participant pools. For this study, we selected EAs who either (a) reported having a parent or grandparent who was Scandinavian (Norwegian, Danish, Scandinavian, Finnish, or Swedish) but none that were Irish or (b) reported having a parent or grandparent who was Irish but none that were Scandinavian. A total of 14 EA-S and 11 EA-I met these criteria. The mothers, fathers, and grandparents of all participants were born in the United States; mothers, fathers, and grandparents of EA-I and EA-S varied only in the cultural heritage of their ancestors. For the EA-I group, 6 reported Irish heritage on their mother's side only, 1 reported Irish heritage on their father's side only, and 3 reported Irish heritage on both sides (1 EA-I was uncertain which parent was of Irish heritage). For the EA-S group, 4 reported Scandinavian heritage on their mother's side, 2 reported Scandinavian heritage on their father's side, and 8 reported Scandinavian heritage on both sides. Because most participants were of mixed ancestry, we conducted chi-square analyses to examine whether there were group differences in the other heritages reported (e.g., German, English, French, Polish, Italian, and Welsh); no significant group differences emerged. Therefore, we were confident that the groups differed in Scandinavian and Irish ancestry but not in any another European heritage.

* * *

RELIVED EMOTION TASK. The relived emotion task has been shown to be an effective elicitor of emotional responding in previous studies and has been widely used with both clinical and nonclinical samples (e.g., Levenson, Carstensen, Friesen, & Ekman, 1991; Oliveau & Willmuth, 1979). For each relived emotion, participants were provided with a label for the target emotion (e.g. "happiness") as well a description of the target emotion (e.g., "a time when you did something or something happened that you wanted very much, so that you felt very good") based on Lazarus (1991). Participants were asked to relive six target emotions (happiness, pride, love, anger, disgust, and sadness). The order of the emotions was randomized to avoid order effects. For each emotion, participants were asked to (a) recall and describe a time in their lives when they felt the target emotion very strongly, (b) focus on the moment at which they felt the target emotion, and (c) relive the target emotion. Participants were asked to press a button on a handheld switch to indicate when they were able to feel the emotion. They pressed the button as long as they were able to feel the emotion or until they were told to stop after 2 minutes (relived emotion period). Immediately following the relived emotion period, participants were asked to rate how intensely they felt the target emotion while they tried to relive the emotion using a 9-point Likert-type scale (0 = *not at all*, 4 = *moderately*, and 8 = *the most in my life*). Participants were also asked to rate how able they were to relive the target emotion on a 9-point Likert-type scale (0 = *not at all*, 4 = *moderately*, and 8 = *extremely*).

* * *

QUESTIONNAIRES. To ensure that the groups did not differ in their orientation to American culture, participants completed the General Ethnicity Questionnaire–American version (Tsai, Ying, & Lee, 2000), which assessed orientation to mainstream American culture in specific life domains including social affiliation (e.g., "Now, my friends are American"), activities (e.g., "I engage in American forms of recreation"), attitudes (e.g., "I am proud of American culture"), exposure (e.g., "I was raised in a way that was American"), food (e.g., "At home, I eat American food"), and language ("How fluently do you speak English?"). Participants rated 38 items on a 5-point Likert-type scale (from 1 = *very much* to 5 = *not at all*). The alpha reliability estimate for this measure was .89. To ensure that

the groups did not differ in trait affect, participants also completed a shortened version of the Positive and Negative Affect Schedule (Watson, Clark, & Tellegen, 1988), in which they are asked to rate how much they felt 14 affective states "on average." Alpha reliability estimates were .87 for positive (excited, determined, alert, enthusiastic, proud, strong, active, interested, and attention) and .72 for negative affect terms (hostile, scared, afraid, guilty, and jittery).[1] Because analyses of variance conducted on orientation to American culture and trait affect did not reveal significant group differences, observed differences in facial expression could not be attributed to these variables.

PROCEDURE. A trained female interviewer greeted the participants upon their arrival to the laboratory. Participants completed several questionnaires, including a demographic questionnaire and the cultural orientation inventory. Sensors measuring skin conductance were attached to participants' nondominant hands. Participants were then instructed to be silent and relax for 3 minutes to provide baseline measures of their facial behavior and skin conductance response.[2] Before beginning the relived emotion task, participants underwent a practice trial during which they were asked to recall and relive a past episode of surprise. Participants were allowed to ask questions about the relived emotion task at this time. Participants were then asked to relive and recall one of the target emotions. Between each emotion, participants rested for several minutes. They completed the Positive and Negative Affect Schedule at the end of the session to reduce the likelihood that the assessment of trait affect would contaminate previous assessments of emotion.

---

[1] These alpha reliabilities mean that the items on these scales were reasonably highly intercorrelated, indicating that the items on the scales tend to measure the same thing and the scales as a whole are therefore coherent.

[2] Skin conductance, described in slightly more detail later in this article, is a widely used measure of emotional arousal.

FACIAL EXPRESSIVE BEHAVIOR. Remotely controlled color video cameras recorded the participants' facial behavior during the study. Lavalier microphones clipped on participants' clothing were used to record their verbal responses. Cameras were hidden from participants' view behind darkened glass on a bookshelf. Three trained and certified coders scored participants' facial behavior using the Facial Action Coding System (FACS; Ekman & Friesen, 1978). The coders were blind to the emotion that the participants were reliving, and they coded the video segments without sound. FACS identifies visually distinguishable and anatomically based units of facial muscle movements or action units (AUs). AUs were grouped into specific emotion configurations (anger, contempt, disgust, smiles, and general negative expressions) on the basis of previous empirical findings (as cited in Tsai et al., 2002) and personal communications with Paul Ekman (May 4, 2001).

Although all AUs were coded during each emotion episode, the "target" emotional facial expressions that we examined differed for each relived emotion depending on what behavior one would expect to see during the emotional event (e.g., smiles during happiness, pride, and love)and the actual occurrence of the expressions. Thus, the behaviors included in our analyses were (a) smiles (AU6 + AU12, bilateral AU12) during happiness, pride, and love; (b) expressions of general negative emotion (AU4) and contempt (unilateral AU10, AU12, and AU14) during anger; and (c) expressions of general negative emotion and disgust (AU9 and AU10) during disgust. To demonstrate that the target emotional facial behavior occurred more frequently than did all other possible emotional facial behaviors, we conducted chi-square analyses testing each target AU combination against the other emotion-related AU combinations; these analyses revealed that the "target" emotional facial behavior occurred significantly more often than did the other emotional facial behaviors. To establish interrater reliability, three raters coded the emotional behaviors during each emotional episode of 20 participants from the larger

study. The mean agreement ratio was 0.97 (range = .70 to 1.0).[3]

PHYSIOLOGY. To ensure that hypothesized differences in facial expression were not due to differences in physiological activity, a device passed a small, constant voltage between electrodes attached to the palmar surface of the middle phalanxes of the first and third fingers of participants' nondominant hands to obtain continuous measures of skin conductance. Change in skin conductance levels was calculated by subtracting mean levels of skin conductance during baseline from mean levels during the relived period.

Results

MANIPULATION CHECK: REPORTED EMOTIONAL EXPERIENCE, ABILITY TO RELIVE EMOTIONS, AND EVENTS RECALLED To ensure that participants experienced the target emotion during the relived task and that they were able to relive their emotions, we conducted separate multivariate analyses of variance on reports of emotional experience during the relived event as well as on participants' reported ability to relive each emotion, treating Group as a between-subjects factor. There were no significant group differences for either variable. Our task was effective in eliciting moderately intense emotions * * *, and participants of both groups reported being able to relive their emotional episodes. * * *

To ensure that the types of events participants recalled were similar for the two groups, events were coded for content based on a system developed by Scherer and colleagues (see Ellgring & Banninger-Huber, 1986, for a detailed description of the coding system). Chi-square analyses revealed no significant differences in the types of events recalled for any of the emotions, with the exception

---

[3]These measures of interrater reliability indicate that the three raters of the facial expressions agreed closely in their ratings, indicating that for the larger study it was probably safe to use a single coder for each participant.

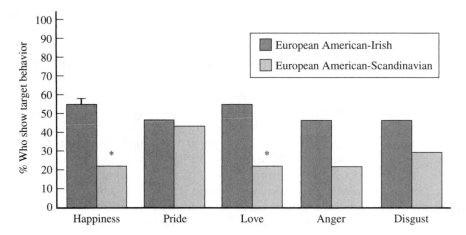

Figure 1. Percentage of participants who show target emotional behavior during each relived emotion. NOTE: EA-I = European Americans of Irish descent ($n = 11$); EA-S = European Americans of Scandinavian descent ($n = 14$). $^*p < .05$, one-tailed.

of happiness events, $\chi^2(2, 25) = 8.09$, $p < .05$).[4] The majority of participants in both groups recalled disgust events that involved another person's actions (EA-I = 72.7%, EA-S = 50%), anger events that involved another person's failure to conform to social norms (EA-I = 54.5%, EA-S = 61.5%), love events that were related to relationships (EA-I = 90.9%, EA-S = 92.9%), and pride events that were related to success in achievement situations (EA-I = 72.7%, EA-S = 78.6%). Whereas the most common (endorsed by 50% of EA-S) type of happiness event recalled by EA-S had to do with new experiences (e.g., "Parents bought me a new truck"), none of the EA-I reported such happiness events. Instead, the most common happiness event recalled by EA-I (endorsed by 72.7%) concerned success ("Found out I got the lead in the play").

GROUP DIFFERENCES IN EXPRESSIVE BEHAVIOR
Given our small sample size and the directional

nature of our hypotheses, we used a one-tailed test of significance at the $p < .05$ level to test our hypotheses.[5] To examine whether the two EA groups differed in their facial behavior, we conducted nonparametric chi-square analyses on expressive behavior (these data were categorical). Analyses revealed a significant difference in smiles during happiness, $\chi^2(1, N = 25) = 2.93$, one-tailed $p < .05$, and love, $\chi^2(1, N = 25) = 2.93$, one-tailed $p < .05$. As predicted, fewer EA-S smiled during relived happiness and love than did EA-I (see Figure 1). To ensure that the differences in facial expression during happiness were not due to differences in the types of events recalled, we conducted the same analyses excluding participants who reported "new experiences" ($n = 8$) and found that the group difference in smiles remained significant. There were no other significant differences in expressive behavior between the two EA groups, although an inspection of the odds ratios suggests

---

[4]The chi-square statistical test is used to see if frequencies of counted events (in this case the number of events recalled) differs significantly across groups. The numbers in parentheses following the Greek letter chi refer to the "degrees of freedom" for the test, which depends upon the number of groups or participants in the study.

[5]A one-tailed test at the .05 level means that only differences in the hypothesized direction will be taken seriously, and that the sizes of such differences must be sufficiently large that they would be expected to arise no more than 5 times out of 100 if there is no difference between the groups in the total population.

that the differences were in the direction of EA-S being less expressive than the EA-I (likelihood that EA-S show less behavior compared with EA-I. These differences emerged against a backdrop of no differences in skin conductance levels. * * *

Discussion

In this article, we argue that there is significant variation in the emotional expressive behavior of EA-I and EA-S, variation that is consistent with ethnographic accounts of emotion in Scandinavian and Irish cultures. EA-S showed less expressive behavior than EA-I across all of the emotions, although the differences reached significance only for happiness and love. These results are consistent with those of other studies in which cultural differences in emotional behavior appear to be more pronounced during positive than negative emotional events, although cultural norms would suggest differences in emotional behavior during both types of events (e.g., Matsumoto, 1990; Matsumoto, Takeuchi, Andayani, Kouznetsova, & Krupp, 1998; Tsai & Levenson, 1997). These findings suggest that what people would ideally like to express (or not express) may not map directly onto what they actually express.

Our study was limited in several ways that should be addressed in future research. Our sample size was small; therefore, it is possible that there were other differences that we did not have the power to detect. Our data neither address the specific ideas (e.g., beliefs about emotional expression) and practices that are responsible for these differences nor demonstrate how these ideas and practices are transmitted across generations born and raised in the same cultural context. For example, such transmission may occur via family socialization and/or via contact with local institutions. It is also unknown whether we would observe differences among EAs of other countries of origin living in different regions of the United States. Finally, our study cannot speak to the generalizability of our findings to other behaviors. It is possible that only behaviors that can be transmitted via family contact—such as emotional expression—persist across generations.

Despite these limitations, our findings do provide evidence that in the realm of emotional behavior, EAs cannot be viewed as a culturally homogeneous group. It is our hope that these results will inspire researchers to consider the diverse cultures that EAs represent and to examine whether such hetereogeneity can account for variation in psychological and social functioning in this group.

References

Dovidio, J. F., Kawakami, K., & Gaertner, S. L. (2002). Implicit and explicit prejudice and interracial interaction. *Journal of Personality and Social Psychology, 82,* 62–68.

Ekman, P., & Friesen, W. V. (1978). *Facial action coding system: A technique for the measurement of facial movement.* Palo Alto, CA: Consulting Psychologists Press.

Ellgring, H., & Banninger-Huber, E. (1986). The coding of reported emotional experiences: Antecedents and reactions. In A. B. Summerfield (Ed.), *Experiencing emotion: A cross-cultural study* (pp. 39–49). Cambridge, UK: Cambridge University Press.

Erickson, B. M., & Simon, J. S. (1996). Scandinavian families: Plain and simple. In J. K. Pearce (Ed.), *Ethnicity and family therapy* (2nd ed., pp. 595–608). New York: Guilford.

Giordano, J., & McGoldrick, M. (1996). European families: An overview. In J. K. Pearce (Ed.), *Ethnicity and family therapy* (2nd ed., pp. 427–441). New York: Guilford.

Greeley, A. M. (1979). The American Irish: A report from Great Ireland. *International Journal of Comparative Sociology, 20,* 67–81.

Greeley, A. M. (1981). *The Irish-Americans.* New York: Harper & Row.

Greeley, A. M., & McCready, W. C. (1975). The transmission of cultural heritages: The case of the Irish and Italians. In D. P. Moynihan (Ed.), *Ethnicity: Theory and experience* (pp. 209–235). Cambridge, MA: Harvard University Press.

Helms, J., & Carter, R. T. (1991). Relationships of White and Black racial identity attitudes and demographic similarity to counselor preferences. *Journal of Counseling Psychology, 38,* 446–457.

Lazarus, R. S. (1991). *Emotion and adaptation.* New York: Oxford University Press.

Levenson, R. W., Carstensen, L. L., Friesen, W. V., & Ekman, P. (1991). Emotion, physiology, and expression in old age. *Psychology and Aging, 6,* 28–35.

Matsumoto, D. (1990). Cultural similarities and differences in display rules. *Motivation and Emotion, 14,* 195–214.

Matsumoto, D., Takeuchi, S., Andayani, S., Kouznetsova, N., & Krupp, D. (1998). The contribution of individualism vs. collectivism to cross-national differences in display rules. *Asian Journal of Social Psychology, 1,* 147–165.

McGoldrick, M. (1996). Irish families. In J. K. Pearce (Ed.), *Ethnicity and family therapy* (2nd ed., pp. 544–566). New York: Guilford.

Midelfort, C. F., & Midelfort, H. C. (1982). Norwegian families. In J. Giordano (Ed.), *Ethnicity and family therapy* (pp. 438–456). New York: Guilford.

Oliveau, D., & Willmuth, R. (1979). Facial muscle electromyographyin depressed and nondepressed hospitalized subjects: A partial replication. *American Journal of Psychiatry, 136,* 548–550.

Pennebaker, J. W., Rime, B., & Blanksenship, V. (1996). Stereotypes of emotional expressiveness of northerners and southerners: A cross-cultural test of Montesquieu's hypothesis. *Journal of Personality and Social Psychology, 70,* 372–380.

Rodnick, D. (1955). *The Norwegians: A study in national culture*(1st ed.). Washington, DC: Public Affairs Press.

Rosenberg, E., & Ekman, P. (1994). Coherence between expressive and experiential systems in emotion. *Cognition & Emotion, 8,* 201–229.

Tsai, J. L., Chentsova-Dutton, Y., Friere-Bebeau, L., & Przymus, D. E. (2002). Emotional expression and physiology in European Americans and Hmong Americans. *Emotion, 2,* 380–397.

Tsai, J. L., & Levenson, R. W. (1997). Cultural influences on emotional responding: Chinese American and European American dating couples during interpersonal conflict. *Journal of Cross-Cultural Psychology, 28,* 600–625.

Tsai, J. L., Ying, Y., & Lee, P. A. (2000). The meaning of "being Chinese" and "being American": Variation among Chinese American young adults. *Journal of Cross-Cultural Psychology, 31,* 302–322.

Watson, D., Clark, L. A., & Tellegen, A. (1988). Development and validation of brief measures of positive and negative affect: The PANAS scales. *Journal of Personality and Social Psychology, 54,* 1063–1070.

HUMAN NATURE AND CULTURE: A TRAIT PERSPECTIVE

Robert R. McCrae

When most psychologists think of the relationship between culture and personality, they think of personality as something that is affected by culture. In the next article, Robert R. McCrae turns this conventional position on its head by arguing that traits help to create culture, and that different cultures may vary precisely because of the different personalities of the people who inhabit them. Because the underlying data are correlational, it becomes very difficult to test either the conventional view or McCrae's. But McCrae's article is an appropriate cautionary note that reminds us that when thinking of the relationship between culture and personality, the path from one to the other may not be a one-way street.

From *Journal of Research in Personality, 38,* 3–14, 2004.

The interaction—the intersection—of the individual with society has always been a core concern of personality psychologists. In the first half of the 20th Century, anthropologists like Ruth Benedict, Ralph Linton, and Clyde Kluckhohn pursued the study of culture and personality, with fascinating if dubious results. Sadly, anthropologists abandoned the topic in the 1960s (LeVine, 2001). Personality psychologists have also shown a recurring interest in this issue, inspiring such classics as *Childhood and Society* (Erikson, 1950), *The Authoritarian Personality* (Adorno, Frenkel-Brunswik, Levinson, & Sanford, 1950/ 1969), and *The Achieving Society* (McClelland, 1967). A survey of the major works dealing with the interrelationships between the individual and society shows that they were written by influential thinkers who were not afraid to tackle large issues and construct grand theories. And although they come from a variety of perspectives, including psy-choanalysis, learning theory, humanistic psychology, evolutionary psychology, and socioanalysis, none of these works was based on a trait approach to personality.

This body of literature on the individual and society suggests three conclusions. First, the subject matter of personality-and-culture studies—the relation of human nature to culture—is and ought to be one of the central concerns of personality psychology; personality psychologists simply cannot abandon it as anthropologists did. Second, the issues it involves are large, and must be approached with intrepid theorizing as well as rigorous research. And third, because none of the other perspectives has provided a wholly satisfactory approach, it is time to consider culture from the perspective of trait psychology.

ADVANCES IN TRAIT PSYCHOLOGY. This is an opportune time to try a trait approach, because there has been great progress in trait psychology in the past 20 years. The most celebrated achievement is a general, if not quite universal (see, e.g., Cheung & Leung, 1998), consensus on the Five-Factor Model (FFM) as a reasonably comprehensive taxonomy of personality traits. Neuroticism (N), Extraversion (E), Openness to Experience (O), Agreeableness (A), and Conscientiousness (C) appear to be the basic factors underlying both English language trait adjectives and theoretically based personality scales (McCrae & John, 1992). To the extent that this taxonomy is comprehensive, we know the range of trait variables that need to be considered in personality-and-culture studies.

We also know now that traits are not cognitive fictions, but real psychological structures. The evidence has come from studies of consensual validation (Funder, Kolar, & Blackman, 1995), the prediction of life outcomes[1] (Soldz & Vaillant, 1999), longitudinal stability (Roberts & DelVecchio, 2000), and heritability (Bouchard & Loehlin, 2001).

We have learned that traits are important for a wide range of applications. Widiger and Costa (2002) recently reviewed 56 studies that demonstrated the utility of an FFM perspective on personality disorders. Barrick and Mount (1991) revitalized I/O[2] psychology by showing the importance of personality traits for the prediction of job performance. Hoyle (2000) edited a Special Issue of *Journal of Personality* linking personality traits to problem behaviors such as drug abuse and unsafe sex.

* * *

A NEW APPROACH TO PERSONALITY-AND-CULTURE. Any attempt to revive personality-and-culture studies should not, of course, repeat the errors of the past (Bock, 2000).

---

[1]See also the selection by Ozer and Benet-Martínez earlier in this book.

[2]I/O is an abbreviation for Industrial-Organizational Psychology, the study of applications of psychology to the workplace.

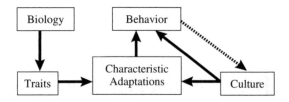

Figure 1. A simplified representation of components of the personality system and their interrelations, according to Five-Factor Theory.

The new approach I will describe applies current knowledge of trait psychology and trait assessment to problems of personality-and-culture, adopts more sophisticated statistical models, and acknowledges the fundamental role of genetics in shaping personality traits (McCrae, 2000). In the present article I will also offer as a working hypothesis the claim that culture does not affect personality, but that personality traits, in the aggregate, may in some circumstances affect culture. The claim that traits are completely unaffected by the environment is extreme, and ultimately will probably be shown to be incorrect. FFT,[3] however, offers it as a parsimonious model that explains a good deal and provides new directions for research. It can be tested in cross-cultural research.

The radical reversal of the usual causal direction between culture and personality makes sense within the framework of FFT. In simplified form, FFT can be represented by Fig. 1, in which causal pathways between biology, culture, traits, characteristic adaptations, and behavior are indicated. The only unfamiliar term here is *Characteristic Adaptations*. These are all the psychological structures that people acquire in the course of life for getting along in the world. They include knowledge, skills, attitudes, goals, roles, relationships, schemas, scripts, habits, even the self-concept. Characteristic adaptations comprise the bulk of the phenomena that psychologists are concerned with, but they do not include personality traits, which FFT depicts as deeper structures, basic tendencies that are grounded in biology. Characteristic adap-

---

[3]Five-Factor Theory.

tations are shaped by the interaction of personality traits and the environment. For example, people who are by nature extraverted are likely to be talkative, but whether they speak Danish or Telugu or Korean depends on the linguistic environment in which they live.

One distinctive feature of FFT is the postulate that the basis of traits is solely biological: there are no arrows connecting culture to personality traits. That postulate was suggested to us by two sources of evidence. First, behavior genetic studies have repeatedly shown strong heritability of adult personality traits, but virtually no influence of the shared environment (Bouchard & Loehlin, 2001). Behavior genetic studies always have another component—the non-shared environment—and it is sometimes argued that it is precisely the experiences that are unique to each child in a family that shape personality. But the most ambitious investigation to date provided "a very disappointing yield for a study designed to ferret out non-genetic, non-shared effects" (Reiss, Neiderhiser, Hetherington, & Plomin, 2000, p. 307). In fact, the non-shared environment is simply the residual that cannot be accounted for by genes or shared environment, and therefore includes not only random error (which can be assessed as unreliability), but also systematic bias that cannot be detected in mono-method studies. When Riemann, Angleitner, and Strelau (1997) supplemented self-reports with peer ratings, the estimated heritabilities of the five factors ranged from 66 to 79%.[4] FFT would attribute the remaining variance to other biological causes, such as intrauterine environment, disease, and aging.

A second basis for postulating a solely biological basis for traits is taken from longitudinal studies of adults. A large body of research shows remarkable stability of individual differences over long time periods despite a multitude of intervening life events (McCrae & Costa, 2003). These longitudinal findings make sense if one assumes that personality traits are only influenced by biology,

which changes very slowly in healthy adults. There are, to be sure, occasional reports of personality change related to life experience, but these findings are causally ambiguous. For example, Roberts, Caspi, and Moffitt (2003) showed that occupational variables at age 26 were associated with personality trait change from age 18 to age 26. But it is not clear which was cause and which effect: for all we know, the changes in personality may have occurred at age 19 and contributed to the later occupational outcomes.

In Fig. 1 there is also a path from personality traits, through characteristic adaptations and behavior, into culture. Usually the model in Fig. 1 is applied to individuals, and the pathway from traits to culture would suggest that individuals sometimes express their personality in ways that reshape society. For example, Jean-Jacques Rousseau's Openness to Experience was arguably one of the causes of the French Revolution (McCrae, 1996), with all the cultural changes that introduced.

However, the model might also be applied to social groups. One might, for example, hypothesize that a society of introverts would develop different customs and institutions than a society of extraverts. Clearly, it is not the case that personality traits are the chief or sole influences on culture, but they might, over long periods of time, leave their mark. Because this possibility is speculative at present, the link between (collective) behavior and culture is indicated by a dashed line.

Cross-cultural Tests of Five-Factor Theory

Because characteristic adaptations reflect the influence of both traits and culture, FFT predicts that the expression of traits will vary across cultures. For example, Benet-Martínez and John (2000) showed that in Spain, Openness to Experience is chiefly expressed in terms that suggest a bohemian or unconventional lifestyle. Again, the same level of dutifulness would be expressed by very different specific actions in Iran and Den-

---

[4]This means that 66–79% of the observed variation in these traits across individuals is estimated to be accounted for by genetic variation.

mark. These examples illustrate the sense in which FFT is an interactive model, in which the person and environment jointly shape psychological features and the flow of behavior.

But FFT also makes more controversial predictions. According to FFT, traits are not affected by culture, but are instead shaped solely by biology, which is the common heritage of the human species. In consequence, their characteristic properties ought to be universal. Again, FFT points to the possibility that traits may affect culture, and thus that the mean levels of traits may be associated across cultures with features of culture. FFT does not assert that traits must affect culture, or even that there will be variations in mean trait levels across cultures. Those are empirical questions, but from the perspective of FFT it is meaningful to ask them.

TESTS OF UNIVERSALITY. In 1997, McCrae and Costa reported data from six cultures—Portugal, Germany, Israel, China, Japan, and South Korea—that supported the universality of the FFM structure. Subsequent studies in Iceland, Estonia, Malaysia, the Philippines, Turkey, India, Russia, Zimbabwe, and many other cultures have continued to support this hypothesis (see McCrae & Allik, 2002). Although the case for additional, indigenous factors is still made by some writers (e.g., Cheung & Leung, 1998), it seems likely that the FFM itself can be found in any culture.

A series of cross-cultural studies have also examined adult development. In the United States, both longitudinal and cross-sectional studies have shown that between late adolescence and old age both men and women decline in levels of N, E, and O, and increase in A and C. Cross-sectional studies show similar trends in Germany, Portugal, Croatia, South Korea, Russia, Estonia, Japan, the Czech Republic, Great Britain, Spain, Turkey, and China (McCrae & Costa, 2003). Considering the very different recent histories these countries have had, it is unlikely that these age differences are due to birth cohort effects. Instead, they seem to represent intrinsic paths of human development.

Costa, Terracciano, and McCrae (2001) examined gender differences in 26 cultures. They found that women in almost every culture were higher than men in N and A, and that men were higher on a few specific facets, including Openness to Ideas, Assertiveness, and Excitement Seeking. Curiously, these effects were largest in progressive, Western cultures that emphasized equality of the sexes, perhaps because respondents attributed masculine and feminine qualities to sex roles rather than traits in traditional cultures.

Finally, a recent study extends the claim of universality to cross-observer agreement (McCrae et al., 2004). It has sometimes been proposed that traits are truly meaningful only in individualistic cultures like [that of] the U.S., where identity is defined by the individual rather than the social group. If that were true, neither self- nor external observers ought to pay much attention to traits in collectivistic cultures, and their agreement would presumably be substantially lower.

The data, however, are more consistent with FFT. Across a range of cultures, agreement between self-reports and single observer ratings ranged from about .4 to .5;[5] the same level of agreement was seen in North America and in studies from such countries as China and Russia.

ETHICAL AND SCIENTIFIC CONSIDERATIONS IN SEEKING TRAIT EFFECTS ON CULTURE. FFT allows that, in the aggregate, traits might shape cultural customs, institutions, and value systems. A clear demonstration of that process would be extremely difficult, because we cannot manipulate trait levels in a culture. But we can begin to evaluate the hypothesis by looking for associations between mean levels of personality traits and features of culture.

Before even attempting that, however, it is necessary to consider both ethical and scientific obstacles. Associations between aggregate traits and features of culture can only be found if there are cultural variations in the mean levels of traits—if, say, Norwegians are more extraverted than Hong

[5]These are correlation coefficients; the values here of .4 to .5 are reasonably high for psychological data.

Kong Chinese. But FFT claims that trait levels are determined solely by biological bases. Together, those two premises imply that there may be biological, perhaps genetic, differences in personality between different ethnic groups, and that kind of claim has a sad history as the basis of discrimination and worse.

Psychologists could deny there is even a possibility of genetic differences in personality between groups, but that does not seem scientifically defensible. We could simply avoid research on the topic to escape moral responsibility. Or we can face the issue and learn as a discipline how to deal responsibly with it. The human genome has been mapped, and there are already published reports of ethnic differences in the population frequencies of alleles purportedly related to personality traits (e.g., Gelernter, Kranzler, Coccaro, Siever, & New, 1998). Someone is going to ask about the behavioral and social implications of such findings, and we personality psychologists ought to be prepared to give thoughtful answers.

One way to deal ethically with this issue is to make sure that findings are communicated accurately. Scientists are always required to make qualified conclusions, but here we need to be especially careful. When claims for cultural differences in the mean levels of traits are made, it seems essential to:

(1) Note the magnitude of the differences, which are rather small in the present analyses;

(2) Remind readers that even at the level of the individual, traits tend to be weak predictors of specific behaviors, and that is even more likely to be true at a cultural level;

(3) Point out that there is a wide range of individual differences within all cultures, and that ascription of a single trait level to all members of a group is unjustifiable stereotyping; and

(4) Carefully specify the limitations of the research and alternative interpretations of the data.

There is a long list of the potential scientific problems that arise when researchers want to compare personality scores across cultures (van de Vijver & Leung, 1997). The translation, even if it accurately conveys the constructs, may be more or less "difficult" than the original, so raw scores could have different meanings in the two versions. Cultures may differ in their susceptibility to response biases, such as acquiescence or social desirability. They may have different rules of self-presentation, or different standards of comparison. Unless national probability samples are used, there is always concern about the comparability and representativeness of samples. There are additional concerns with the representativeness of the sample of cultures. Still, it may be possible to deal with all these issues satisfactorily (McCrae, 2002).

Before proceeding to the data, another reminder is in order. Behavior genetic studies are designed to explain the sources of variation in phenotypic traits *in a population*. They do not speak to sources of variation across populations. Even if traits were 100% heritable within a culture, it might be the case that they are substantially influenced by differences between cultures. As we will see, there is one acculturation study suggesting that this is so.

INTERCULTURAL COMPARISONS: AN EXAMPLE. The data I discuss here were provided by researchers from 36 cultures or subcultures from five continents and several language families (McCrae, 2002). In each case, the NEO-PI-R was translated and administered to samples, which were classified as student or adult in order to control for the universal age differences. All these samples are normal volunteers; data from patients and from employment screenings were omitted.

These are samples of convenience, but analyses showed that results were generalizable across age and gender subgroups, and across samples collected by different investigators in a few of the cultures. * * * I standardized the data using American norms for college-age and adult men and women and used an unweighted average across subsamples to obtain factor scores for each culture, expressed as T scores. About three-fourths of these mean values lay within the average range ($T = 45–55$),[6] but all five factors showed a range of at least one standard deviation across cultures.

These means can be used as culture-level scores on the five personality factors; with what feature of culture might they be correlated? The most influential dimensions of culture are those proposed by Geert Hofstede (2001), who extracted four factors from work value surveys completed by IBM employees around the world. Although this would not seem to be a very promising basis for divining dimensions of culture, his ratings have been used in hundreds of studies, and have an impressive list of culture-level correlates. *Power Distance* refers to attitudes toward authority and status; it contrasts hierarchical with egalitarian societies. The highest recorded levels of Power Distance were found in a sample of military recruits (Ottati, Triandis, & Hui, 1999), who had volunteered to join the bottom rung of a rigidly hierarchical organization. *Uncertainty Avoidance* describes cultures that seek to minimize the threat of unstructured situations by adopting rules and limiting innovation. *Individualism,* the most heavily researched of these dimensions, is high in countries like the U.S. where people put their own concerns ahead of their group's. *Masculinity,* as used by Hofstede, refers to egoistic work goals, based upon getting ahead rather than getting along.

Each of the five factors was significantly associated with one or more of Hofstede's dimensions. Power Distance was associated with low E ($r = -.58$), low O ($-.40$), and high C ($.52$), suggesting that most of the people in strongly hierarchical cultures report themselves to be docile and dutiful. Uncertainty Avoidance was associated with high N ($.58$) and low A ($-.56$). Individualism was associated with E ($.64$) and O ($.34$), and Masculinity with N ($.55$) and O ($r = .37$; McCrae, 2002).

It is possible to interpret these results in terms of FFT, which claims that personality can affect culture, but not vice-versa. Suppose a society consisted chiefly of people who were introverted, closed, and conscientious. What kind of social structure would they evolve? There would be few natural leaders among them, so the few would easily rise to positions of authority and keep them, and the rest would passively accept their dominance. Because most people in such a society are, *ex hypothesi,*[7] conscientious, they would dutifully obey the orders they received; the system would be stable and productive. Widespread introversion and conscientiousness could create high Power Distance cultures.

Again, suppose a group of people were by temperament anxious and quarrelsome. Every new decision would be likely to provoke stress and conflict. For such a volatile group to succeed, there would need to be strong social controls in place, rigidly maintaining the status quo. Aggregate personality traits related to high Neuroticism and low Agreeableness could thus give rise to Uncertainty Avoidance.

Although the causal ordering suggested here is arguable (Hofstede & McCrae, 2004), it does appear that there are meaningful associations between mean personality traits and dimensions of culture. NEO-PI-R scales, when translated by competent psychologists and administered to reasonably large samples, can apparently measure the personality profiles of different cultures. In theory, translation can affect trait scores, but in practice it seems not to have much effect (Piedmont, Bain, McCrae, & Costa, 2002). In theory, differences in sampling procedures could distort comparisons across nations, but experience to date suggests that this is not a major concern (McCrae, 2002). Perhaps the difficulties of comparing personality traits across cultures have been exaggerated, and we are now in a position to explore all kinds of links between personality and culture. If so, we can create new maps of the world, based not on rainfall or population density, but on personality trait levels.

---

[6]The average of a set of T scores, by definition, is 50. (Note that T is a different statistic than the commonly used t.)

[7]According to (McCrae's) hypothesis.

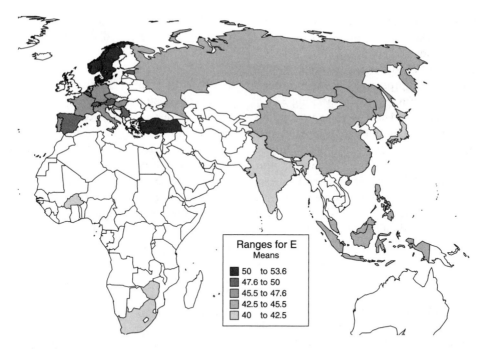

Figure 2. Distribution of mean Extraversion factor scores in Old World nations. Burkina Faso data are from 57 female and 120 male students aged 18-25 who completed the French NEO-PI-R, standardized on American college-age within-sex norms. Data from other nations are from McCrae (2002); the score for South Africa is taken from the Black South African sample; the score for India is the mean of Telugu and Marathi-speaking samples. Counties with no shading have missing data.

Fig. 2, for example, represents the Old World distribution of Extraversion. Data here are taken from McCrae (2002), with the addition of college student data from Burkina Faso (J. Rossier, personal communication, December 7, 2001).

In this Figure, the darker the shading, the higher is the Extraversion score (the US would fall between the two darkest categories). Notice the light gray in Taiwan, Korea, and Japan, in India, and in all three African nations. This map is quite clear: Asia and Africa are introverted, Europe extraverted. Europeans as a group also tend to be higher in Openness to Experience and lower in Agreeableness and Conscientiousness (Allik & McCrae, 2004).

Alternative Interpretations

But before pondering these maps too deeply, it is well to consider some cautions in interpreting the data. In this area there are still many lively disputes in progress that can stimulate research for years to come.

I have argued that mean personality scores are veridical—that Europeans really are more extraverted than Asians. But some writers, examining the same evidence, are not persuaded. Poortinga, van de Vijver, and van Hemert (2002) believe the best working hypothesis is that all cultures have the same levels of personality traits, and that observed differences are due to biases in self-report measures.

One reason to be suspicious of these culture-level scores is that they do not, in general, concur with national stereotypes. For example, Church and Katigbak (2002) found no agreement between personality judgments of the "typical" Filipino and American made by a panel of judges who had lived in both countries, and mean scores on the NEO-PI-R in those two countries.

And I myself have contributed data that complicate the interpretation of these scores (McCrae, Yik, Trapnell, Bond, & Paulhus, 1998). Working with colleagues in Vancouver in the mid-1990s, I examined personality profiles for Canadian-born Chinese, long-term immigrants from Hong Kong, and recent immigrants. There were some striking similarities in the profiles, but also noticeable differences. In particular, Canadian-born Chinese scored higher in Extraversion, Openness, and Agreeableness than did Hong Kong-born Chinese. This seems like a simple acculturation effect, but it presents a serious challenge to the ideas advanced here. If FFT is true and culture cannot affect personality, then there should be no differences in true personality scores between these groups of ethnic Chinese. Because the observed scores are different, FFT suggests that NEO-PI-R *responses* must be non-equivalent in these groups. Canadian-born Chinese may have learned that it is more socially desirable in Canada to present oneself as open and agreeable, and thus the difference is one of social desirability norms rather than personality. We can save FFT by assuming cultural biases in responding.

* * * Alternatively, perhaps FFT is wrong, and culture really can affect personality—a possibility that few would find surprising. Then one could interpret culture-level scores as accurate, and infer that growing up in Canada affects basic personality traits.

There is, however, another possibility that is consistent with both FFT and the veridicality of NEO-PI-R scores: Selective immigration. In 1996, recent immigration to Canada was fueled by the imminent take-over of Hong Kong by the People's Republic of China, and personality may have been irrelevant. But the earlier generations of Chinese immigrants—those whose descendants were our Canadian-born Chinese—may have come for personal reasons. In particular, people who voluntarily left behind a familiar world and explored a new culture may have been particularly high in Openness to Experience. If so, they may have passed on the relevant genes to their children, who then appeared more open than recent immigrants.

But before we adopt any of these interpretations, it must be noted that this seems to be the only acculturation study of its kind, and such complex and momentous issues cannot be decided on the basis of a single study. It is a simple design, using college students of a single ethnic group but different years of residence in the culture. We do not need to venture into the jungles of New Guinea to get these crucial data: surely we could do dozens of studies with Hispanics, Vietnamese, or Russians, here in the US. That would be an invaluable addition to the growing research on trait psychology and culture that would help us understand personality assessment and the origins of personality traits.

Conclusion

Acculturation studies are only one of several categories of research needed for a full understanding of trait-psychology-and-culture. Studies of culture-level correlates, longitudinal trait development, psychiatric epidemiology, and response artifacts across cultures are all obvious next steps. * * *

A trait perspective on human nature and culture offers great intellectual promise. It addresses fundamental issues with the widest possible applicability; it has already produced provocative findings; and it inspires a rich agenda for future research. In my own case, it has also led to collaborations with enthusiastic and generous colleagues all over the world, to whom I am indebted for the substance of this article. The long tradition of research and theory on culture and personality can now be sustained by trait psychology.

References

Adorno, T. W., Frenkel-Brunswik, E., Levinson, D. J., & Sanford, R. N. (1969). *The authoritarian personality.* New York: Norton (Original work published 1950)

Allik, J., & McCrae, R. R. (2004). Towards a geography of personality traits: Patterns of profiles across 36 cultures. *Journal of Cross-Cultural Psychology.*

Barrick, M. R., & Mount, M. K. (1991). The Big Five personality dimensions and job performance: A meta-analysis. *Personnel Psychology, 44,* 1–26.

Benet-Martínez, V., & John, O. P. (2000). Measuring *Los Cinco*

Grandes in Spain with indigenous Castilian markers. *American Behavioral Scientist, 44,* 141–157.

Bock, P. K. (2000). Culture and personality revisited. *American Behavioral Scientist, 44,* 32–40.

Bouchard, T. J., & Loehlin, J. C. (2001). Genes, evolution, and personality. *Behavior Genetics, 31,* 243–273.

Cheung, F. M., & Leung, K. (1998). Indigenous personality measures: Chinese examples. *Journal of Cross-Cultural Psychology, 29,* 233–248.

Church, A. T., & Katigbak, M. S. (2002). The five-factor model in the Philippines: Investigating trait structure and levels across cultures. In R. R. McCrae & J. Allik (Eds.), *The Five-Factor Model of personality across cultures* (pp. 129–154). New York: Kluwer Academic/Plenum Publishers.

Costa, P. T., Jr., Terracciano, A., & McCrae, R. R. (2001). Gender differences in personality traits across cultures: Robust and surprising findings. *Journal of Personality and Social Psychology, 81,* 322–331.

Erikson, E. H. (1950). *Childhood and society.* New York: Norton.

Funder, D. C., Kolar, D. C., & Blackman, M. C. (1995). Agreement among judges of personality: Interpersonal relations, similarity, and acquaintanceship. *Journal of Personality and Social Psychology, 69,* 656–672.

Gelernter, J., Kranzler, H., Coccaro, E., Siever, L., & New, A. (1998). Serotonin transporter protein gene polymorphism and personality measures in African American and European American samples. *American Journal of Psychiatry, 155,* 1332–1338.

Hofstede, G. (2001). *Culture's consequences: Comparing values, behaviors, institutions, and organizations across nations* (2nd ed.). Thousand Oaks, CA: Sage.

Hofstede, G., & McCrae, R. R. (2004). Personality and culture revisited: Linking traits and dimensions of culture. *Cross-Cultural Research, 38,* 52–88.

Hoyle, R. H. (Ed.) (2000). Personality processes and problem behavior [Special issue]. *Journal of Personality, 68*(6).

LeVine, R. A. (2001). Culture and personality studies, 1918–1960: Myth and history. *Journal of Personality, 69,* 803–818.

McClelland, D. C. (1967). *The achieving society.* New York: Simon & Schuster.

McCrae, R. R. (1996). Social consequences of experiential openness. *Psychological Bulletin, 120,* 323–337.

McCrae, R. R. (2000). Trait psychology and the revival of personality and culture studies. *American Behavioral Scientist, 44,* 10–31.

McCrae, R. R. (2002). NEO-PI-R data from 36 cultures: Further intercultural comparisons. In R. R. McCrae & J. Allik (Eds.), *The Five-Factor Model of personality across cultures* (pp. 105–125). New York: Kluwer Academic/Plenum Publishers.

McCrae, R. R.& Allik, J. (Eds.). (2002). T*he Five-Factor Model of personality across cultures.* New York: Kluwer Academic/ Plenum Publishers.

McCrae, R. R., & Costa, P. T., Jr. (1997). Personality trait structure as a human universal. *American Psychologist, 52,* 509–516.

McCrae, R. R., & Costa, P. T., Jr. (1999). A Five-Factor Theory of personality. In L. A. Pervin & O. P. John (Eds.), *Handbook of personality: Theory and research* (2nd ed., pp. 139–153). New York: Guilford.

McCrae, R. R., & Costa, P. T., Jr. (2003). *Personality in adulthood: A Five-Factor Theory perspective* (2nd ed.). New York: Guilford.

McCrae, R. R., Costa, P. T., Jr., Martin, T. A., Oryol, V. E. Rukavishnikov, A. A., Senin, I. G., Hrebickova, M., & Urbanek, T. (2004). Consensual validation of personality traits across cultures. *Journal of Research on Personality, 38,* 179–201.

McCrae, R. R., & John, O. P. (1992). An introduction to the Five-Factor Model and its applications. *Journal of Personality, 60,* 175–215.

McCrae, R. R., Yik, M. S. M., Trapnell, P. D., Bond, M. H., & Paulhus, D. L. (1998). Interpreting personality profiles across cultures: Bilingual, acculturation, and peer rating studies of Chinese undergraduates. *Journal of Personality and Social Psychology, 74,* 1041–1055.

Ottati, V., Triandis, H. C., & Hui, C. H. (1999). Subjective culture and the workplace: Hispanic and mainstream naval recruits. In Y.-T. Lee, C. R. McCauley, & J. G. Draguns (Eds.), *Personality and person perception across cultures* (pp. 235–253). Mahway, NJ: Erlbaum.

Piedmont, R. L., Bain, E., McCrae, R. R., & Costa, P. T., Jr. (2002). The applicability of the Five-Factor Model in a Sub-Saharan culture: The NEO-PI-R in Shona. In R. R. McCrae & J. Allik (Eds.), *The Five-Factor Model of personality across cultures* (pp. 155–173). New York: Kluwer Academic/Plenum Publishers.

Poortinga, Y. H., van de Vijver, F., & van Hemert, D. A. (2002). Cross-cultural equivalence of the Big Five: A tentative interpretation of the evidence. In R. R. McCrae & J. Allik (Eds.), *The Five-Factor Model of personality across cultures* (pp. 273–294). New York: Kluwer Academic/Plenum Publishers.

Riemann, R., Angleitner, A., & Strelau, J. (1997). Genetic and environmental influences on personality: A study of twins reared together using the self- and peer report NEO-FFI scales. *Journal of Personality, 65,* 449–475.

Reiss, D., Neiderhiser, J. M., Hetherington, E. M., & Plomin, R. (2000). *The relationship code: Deciphering genetic and social influences on adolescent development.* Cambridge, MA: Harvard University Press.

Roberts, B., Caspi, A., & Moffitt, T. E. (2003). Work experiences and personality development in young adulthood. *Journal of Personality and Social Psychology, 84,* 582–593.

Roberts, B. W., & DelVecchio, W. F. (2000). The rank-order consistency of personality traits from childhood to old age: A quantitative review of longitudinal studies. *Psychological Bulletin, 126,* 3–25.

Soldz, S., & Vaillant, G. E. (1999). The Big Five personality traits and the life course: A 45-year longitudinal study. *Journal of Research in Personality, 33,* 208–232.

van de Vijver, F. J. R., & Leung, K. (1997). Methods and data analysis of comparative research. In J. W. Berry, Y. H. Poortinga, & J. Pandey (Eds.), *Handbook of cross-cultural psychology: Vol. 1: Theory and method* (pp. 257–300). Boston: Allyn and Bacon.

Widiger, T. A., & Costa, P. T., Jr. (2002). Five-Factor Model personality disorder research. In P. T. Costa, Jr. & T. A. Widiger (Eds.), *Personality disorders and the five-factor model of personality* (2nd ed., pp. 59–87). New York: American Psychological Association.

Wiggins, J. S. (Ed.). (1996). *The five-factor model of personality: Theoretical perspectives.* New York: Guilford.

PERSONALITY *IN* CULTURE: A NEO-ALLPORTIAN VIEW

Shigehiro Oishi

It is easy and tempting when comparing cultural groups who look different, speak differently, and act differently, to see nothing but these differences. Indeed, even cultural psychology, which ought to know better, has often been guilty of treating members of large and diverse cultural groups as if they are all the same—as if no one in Asia has a Western-style sense of self, for example, or as if no North American ever puts his or her community's interest above self-interest. The present article by Shigehiro Oishi reminds us that "real culture is flexible"; i.e., the messages cultures direct toward their members are expressed at different volumes, listened to with varying degrees of attention, and sometimes are even disobeyed. As a result, even within strong cultural traditions there can remain important individual variation and room for personal expression.

From *Journal of Research in Personality, 38,* 68–74, 2004.

Introduction

"Culture and personality" is one of the fashionable slogans of contemporary social science and, by present usage, denotes a range of problems on the borderline between anthropology and sociology, on the one hand, and psychology and psychiatry, on the other. However, the phrase has unfortunate implications. A dualism is implied, whereas "culture *in* personality" and "personality *in* culture" would suggest conceptual models more in accord with the facts. Moreover, the slogan favors a dangerous simplification of the problems of personality formation. Recognition of culture as one of the determinants of personality is a great gain, but there are some indications that this theoretical advance has tended to obscure the significance of other types of determinants. "Culture and personality" is as lopsided as "biology and personality" (Kluckhohn & Murray, 1948, p. 44).

Culture and personality has a curious history similar to personality psychology itself. It was embraced as one of the most promising research topics in all social sciences in the first half of the 20th century, its participants ranging from anthropologists to sociologists, psychologists to psychiatrists (McCrae, 2000). Despite its early vitality, the field was nearly abandoned after 1960, as both anthropology and personality lost their intellectual influence on other disciplines. Although culture and personality has become a popular topic again lately, the field has been plagued by two interrelated questions: (a) Are cultural constructs merely cultural stereotypes and (b) Where are individual differences and individuality in culture and personality research?

In "The cultural background of personality," Linton (1945) already recognized the important distinction between "real culture" and "cultural constructs." For instance, we say, the Japanese culture is serene (although many Japanese are not; just look at my sisters!), or the American culture is fast-paced (although many Americans are laid back; just look at students in my personality course!). Recently, several researchers (e.g., Oyserman, Coon, & Kemmelmeier, 2002) called into question the characterization of Japanese as collectivists and Americans as individualists, and argued that these are cultural stereotypes in the mind of cross-cultural researchers rather than cultural reality. Interestingly, Gordon Allport made this exact point in his 1961 book, "Pattern and growth in personality." Although Allport is not known for his research on culture and personality, his chapter on culture offers, in my opinion, great insight into the two outstanding questions in culture and personality (see also Kluckhohn & Murray, 1948).

REAL CULTURE IS FLEXIBLE. While recognizing the importance of culture in shaping personality, Allport (1961) was quick to point out that individuals actively *select* their own way of life that suits their temperament, values, and philosophy of life. Allport believed that real culture is flexible (i.e., there are a wide range of individual differences in any given culture) because individual members like or dislike different aspects of their culture, and internalize them differently. Similarly, the effect of role or situation cannot be uniform across individuals, because some like their role (e.g., leader), actively seek it, and view it as their central self-concept, while others dislike it, actively avoid it, and do not view it as their central self-concept, even when in that role. Even when there is consistency and homogeneity in cultural messages, the individual level process of liking/disliking and internalization can lead to diverse individual differences within any given culture. An important

implication of this distinction is that the analysis of cultural products such as magazine ads might reveal larger cultural differences than the analysis of individual members' self-reported values (e.g., compare Han & Shavitt, 1994 with Oyserman et al., 2002). Thus, Allport stated that "no individual is a mirror-image of the modal or average culture pattern. We are molded by *real* culture and not by the anthropologist's distilled image of it. To apply this image directly to people is to falsify the diversity of personality found within any single culture" (p. 167). Simultaneously, Allport recognized that no matter how strong individuals' needs, temperaments, and values are, culture, role, and situation still have a substantial influence on their personality, limiting the range of its behavioral expression. Also important, culture defines and gives meaning to social roles and situations. Thus, according to Allport, personality should be understood as a product of active negotiation between biological predispositions and cultural demands.

The schematic presentation of the key processes can be seen in Fig. 1. First, individuals' temperament (e.g., fearfulness) and biological state (e.g., dopamine-inducing drug) can predispose them to feel, think, and behave in a certain way. However, this predisposition can be constrained or amplified by socio-cultural factors such as parenting (e.g., arranging lots of play dates), situation (e.g., party), role (e.g., host), and culture. Also, the degree to which individuals internalize socio-cultural demands is influenced by their liking or disliking and perception of these demands, which is in turn determined in part by individuals' temperament and biological states. Thus, individuals' feeling, thinking, and action are a function of both biological and sociocultural factors. Furthermore, individuals observe their own behaviors and others' reactions to them to form their self-concept and a unified philosophy of life over time. Self-report measures of personality, needs, and values capture this. The self-concept in turn modulates the impact of biological and socio-cultural influences on their behaviors, as many individuals strive to achieve and maintain a certain self-concept (e.g., calm). Fig. 1, therefore, delineates the

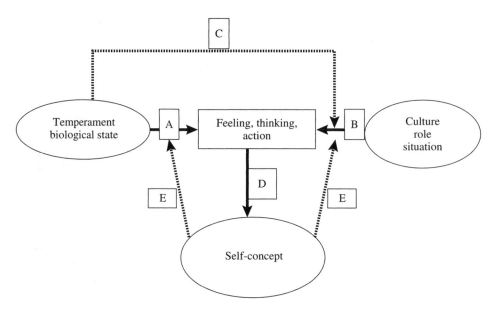

Figure 1. A neo-Allportian model of culture and personality. (A) Temperament influences observable behavior (e.g., fear). (B) Culture/role/situation also influences observable behavior. (C) However, temperament influences an individual's liking/disliking of cultural/role/situational demands and the degree of internalization of these demands (i.e., the emergence of within-cultural variation). (D) Their own behaviors and others' reaction to them lead to one's self-concept (e.g., fearful, but wants to be a less fearful person). (E/F) The self-concept in turn modulates the influence of temperament/biological factors and culture/situation/role.

dynamic interaction between personality and culture: culture plays an important role in constraining or amplifying personality expression (e.g., the experience and expression of pride in Japan vs. the US), while individuals' temperament and personality set limits on the degree to which culture influences individuals as well as the aspects of culture which individuals internalize. Conceptually, there is no contradiction in recognizing diverse cultural effects (e.g., Markus & Kitayama, 1991; Nisbett, Peng, Choi, & Norenzayan, 2001) and sizable within-culture individual differences.

In my opinion, there is one major weakness of Allport's model. That is, Allport seems to assume that individuals can consciously control most, if not all, cultural influences on their lives. However, the way we perceive certain objects and emotionally react to some events (e.g., cherry blossoms → hanami party in Japan, Labor's Day → BBQ in the US) is so deeply ingrained and automatic that our

perception, cognition, and emotion are sometimes influenced by culture outside of our conscious awareness (cf. Kitayama, Duffy, Kawamura, & Larsen, 2003). In the neo-Allportian model, therefore, it is recognized that cultural influences can be beyond one's active control. That is, because default behavioral and affective reactions to certain events and objects (e.g., cheery blossoms) are often automatic, even individuals who actively distance themselves from their culture might nevertheless be unconsciously influenced by it (see also Rozin, 2003).

WHERE ARE INDIVIDUAL DIFFERENCES IN CULTURE AND PERSONALITY RESEARCH? Although personality psychology is the science of individual differences and individuality, individual differences often take a backseat in cross-cultural research. For instance, a study that shows Americans scoring higher in extraversion than Chinese does not speak to individual differences in extraversion among Americans or Chinese. Similarly, a study that shows Americans showing more self-serving attribution than Japanese does not speak to individual differences among Americans or Japanese in these tendencies. This type of cross-cultural study including my own (e.g., Oishi, 2002), has been criticized as homogenizing culture and ignoring intra-cultural variations. However, this critique does not always apply to cross-cultural studies of personality that investigate cultural differences *in* inter-individual differences. For instance, Schimmack, Radhakrishnan, Oishi, Dzokoto, and Ahadi (2002) found that the frequency of positive emotion was highly correlated with life satisfaction among Americans and Germans, but that was not the case among Japanese, Ghanaians, and Mexicans, presumably because the latter groups did not pay attention to emotional experiences (e.g., how happy was I?) when evaluating their lives (how good is my life?). In other words, Germans and Americans who frequently experienced positive emotions evaluated their lives as more satisfying than others, whereas Japanese, Ghanaians, and Mexicans who frequently experienced positive emotions did not. Studies such as this (e.g., Suh, 2002) reveal cultural differences in the *patterns* of inter-individual differences.

A more explicit way of delineating cultural and individual differences is multi-group latent class analysis. Using this technique, Eid and Diener (2001) demonstrated the existence of a culture-specific "class" (e.g., 16% of Chinese said all positive emotions are undesirable, while this class did not exist among Americans, Australians, and Taiwanese), cultural differences in the size of a "class" (e.g., 83% of Australians and Americans indicated all positive emotions are desirable, compared with only 9% of Chinese and 32% of Taiwanese in this class), and the existence of intra-cultural variations (each sample had four to five distinct "classes"). This is an exciting development because the traditional *t* tests[1] would have shown only the mean difference in the endorsement of desirability of positive emotions across cultures (and inadvertently would have perpetuated cultural stereo-

types), whereas the latent class analyses clearly showed the existence of intra-cultural as well as inter-cultural variations. * * *

Finally, yet another type of cross-cultural study of personality investigates cultural differences in *intra*-individual process. Beginning with Allport (1937), personality psychologists have explored individual differences in intra-individual variations in mood, self-esteem, and behavior (e.g., Fleeson, 2001; Mischel & Shoda, 1995). This research paradigm can be extended to cultural differences, as well. Watson, Clark, and Tellegen (1984) conducted a 90-day daily diary study of moods, analyzed the structure of moods within each individual, and found that Americans felt sleepy when they felt other negative moods, whereas Japanese tended to feel nemui (sleepy) when they felt other positive moods. Namely, the experience of "sleepy" was qualitatively different across cultures. Similarly, we (Oishi, Diener, Scollon, & Biswas-Diener, 2004) examined intra-individual variation in moods across situations using the experience sampling method in Japan, India, and the US. We were able to examine the relationship between situation (e.g., alone, with stranger) and mood at the individual as well as at cultural levels because each participant recorded their mood in various situations when signaled at random moments. Fig. 2 indicates the positive mood of two American participants and two Japanese participants in each situation. For example, American Subject 1 felt positive moods strongly when with a romantic partner and a stranger, and moderately when with friends and co-workers. Japanese Subject 1 felt positive moods strongly only when with a romantic partner, and did not feel much positive mood when with a co-worker or a stranger. This study allowed us to look at each individual's mood profile and observe unique "if . . . then . . ." patterns of relations between situation and mood at the individual level (Mischel & Shoda,

[1]The *t* test is a widely used statistical method for assessing whether the overall means of two groups of people are significantly different.

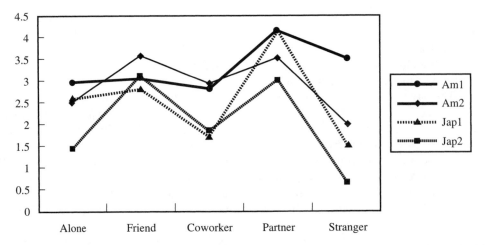

Figure 2. Average positive moods in each situation for two American and two Japanese participants in Oishi et al. (2004). They rated moods on the 7-point scale, ranging from 0 (not at all) to 6 (with maximum intensity) when signaled at random moments.

1995).[2] Using multi-level analysis, furthermore, we found that the situational effect of being with a friend on positive moods was stronger among Japanese and Hispanic participants than among Americans. Most important, our study indicates that even when two individuals from two different cultures have the same mean level of positive moods, the patterns of positive moods (when they feel good or they don't feel good) of these individuals can be quite different. These "if . . . then . . ." patterns of relations between situation and mood shed light on individuality, and provide a nuanced understanding of culture. In short, research on intra-individual processes presents a wonderful opportunity to delineate important cultural differences without losing sight of individual differences and individuality.

Conclusion

In the present paper, I argued that two inter-related issues have been central problems in culture and

personality research: within-culture heterogeneity and individual differences. Recent cross-cultural research has found compelling effects of culture on cognition and emotion. Conceptually speaking, however, the individual level processes such as liking/disliking and internalization can generate individual differences even when cultural messages are powerful. Recent data analytic techniques such as multi-group latent class analysis and multi-level analysis allow researchers to explore cultural differences while attending to individual differences and individuality. As envisioned by the pioneers of our field (e.g., Allport, Murray), the primary goal of culture and personality research should be to understand how "real culture" influences individuals who have different biological endowments, life experiences, and circumstances (e.g., how certain temperaments, traits, needs, and values might manifest themselves differently in different contexts across cultures, and to what degree and in which domains individuals can or cannot consciously control cultural influences). Such investigations will make a contribution not only to personality psychology, but also to its neighboring areas such as social, developmental, and cultural psychology.

---

[2]See the article by Mischel, later in this book, for more details on the *if . . . then* approach.

References

Allport, G. W. (1937). *Personality: A psychological interpretation.* New York: Holt.

Allport, G. (1961). *Patterns and growth in personality.* New York: Holt, Reinhart, and Winston.

Eid, M., & Diener, E. (2001). Norms for experiencing emotions in different cultures: Inter- and within-nation differences. *Journal of Personality and Social Psychology, 81,* 869–885.

Fleeson, W. (2001). Toward a structure-and process-integrated view of personality: Traits as density distributions of states. *Journal of Personality and Social Psychology, 80,* 1011–1027.

Han, S.-P., & Shavitt, S. (1994). Persuasion and culture: Advertising appeals in individualistic and collectivistic societies. *Journal of Experimental Social Psychology, 30,* 326–350.

Kitayama, S., Duffy, S., Kawamura, T., & Larsen, J. T. (2003). Perceiving an object and its context in different cultures. *Psychological Science, 14,* 201–206.

Kluckhohn, C., & Murray, H. A. (1948). *Personality in nature, society, and culture.* New York: Knopf.

Linton, R. (1945). *The cultural background of personality.* New York: Appleton-Century Crofts.

Markus, H. R., & Kitayama, S. (1991). Culture and the self: Implications for cognition, emotion, and motivation. *Psychological Review, 98,* 224–253.

McCrae, R. R. (2000). Trait psychology and the revival of personality and culture studies. *American Behavioral Scientist, 44,* 10–31.

Mischel, W., & Shoda, Y. (1995). A cognitive-affective system theory of personality: Reconceptualizing situations, dispositions, dynamics, and invariance in personality structure. *Psychological Review, 102,* 246–268.

Nisbett, R. E., Peng, K., Choi, I., & Norenzayan, A. (2001). Culture and systems of thought: Holistic versus analytic cognition. *Psychological Review, 108,* 291–310.

Oishi, S. (2002). The experiencing and remembering of well-being: A cross-cultural analysis. *Personality and Social Psychology Bulletin, 28,* 1398–1406.

Oishi, S., Diener, E., Scollon, C. N., & Biswas-Diener, R. (2004). Cross-situational consistency of affective experiences across cultures. *Journal of Personality and Social Psychology, 86,* 460–472

Oyserman, D., Coon, H. M., & Kemmelmeier, M. (2002). Rethinking individualism and collectivism: Evaluation of theoretical assumptions and meta-analyses. *Psychological Bulletin, 128,* 3–72.

Rozin, P. (2003). Five potential principles for understanding cultural differences in relation to individual differences. *Journal of Research in Personality, 37,* 273–283.

Schimmack, U., Radhakrishnan, P., Oishi, S., Dzokoto, V., & Ahadi, S. (2002). Culture, personality, and subjective well-being: Integrating process models of life satisfaction. *Journal of Personality and Social Psychology, 82,* 582–593.

Suh, E. M. (2002). Culture, identity consistency, and subjective well-being. *Journal of Personality and Social Psychology, 83,* 1378–1391.

Watson, D., Clark, L. A., & Tellegen, A. (1984). Cross-cultural convergence in the structure of mood: A Japanese replication and a comparison with US findings. *Journal of Personality and Social Psychology, 47,* 127–144.

PART VII

Process Approaches to Personality: Learning, Motivation, and the Self

The psychologist Nancy Cantor once noted that personality is not just something a person "has"; it is also something a person "does." The process approaches to personality all concern what people do, in their minds and in their lives, that leads them to be different from each other.

For example, every person learns from his or her experiences, and everyone's experiences are different. For the classic figure in the history of behaviorism, B.F. Skinner, the author of our first selection, "experience" meant the rewards and punishments that fill every moment of waking life. The answer to why any "organism"—including a person—behaves the way he or she (or it) does is found in the rewards and punishments of which behavior is always a function. For this reason, Skinner opposed trying to explain behavior in terms of neural processes, cognitive mechanisms, or anything else that could not be directly seen and manipulated. Instead, he focused on a functional analysis in which behavior is seen as a direct function of one's past experience.

Skinner's version of behaviorism had a large effect on psychology, and developed in a variety of directions including Albert Bandura's social learning theory. In the second selection, Bandura sums up the approach to personality he developed, rooted originally in behaviorism but moving far beyond it. Bandura's article reveals some fundamentally behaviorist leanings and also goes way beyond behaviorism by describing the operation of what he calls the "Self System." Through a process Bandura calls "reciprocal determinism," an individual's self system develops as a result of experience, but also determines future behavior and the future environment. Thus, the environment may determine the person, as Skinner argued, but the person also determines the environment.

The third selection is by Walter Mischel, whose influential attack on trait psychology we read in Part II. Mischel presents his "cognitive-affective personality system" (CAPS) approach to personality, which is fundamentally based on a distinctively cognitive idea, that the person's beliefs about and representations of the environment can become more important than the environment itself. Mischel also introduces his if . . . then conception of behavioral coherence, in which a person is described not in terms of global personality traits, but through the patterns of behavioral change he or she exhibits from one situation to the next.

The ideas of reward and punishment are central to the learning processes emphasized by Skinner, Bandura, and Mischel, But what a person finds rewarding or punishing depends, in large part, on his or her goals. In the fourth selection, Kennon Sheldon and his colleagues describe how the different kinds of goals people pursue, and the reasons they pursue them, are important for the development of an individual's psychological health and well-being.

A final kind of personality-relevant process considered in this section is the construction of the "self," or set of central ideas one has about the kind of person one believes oneself to be. An important thread of research on self-processes has addressed "self-esteem," the degree to which a person feels good about himself or herself. For example, to the degree one believes oneself to be attractive, or smart, or powerful, or virtuous, one's self-esteem will tend to be higher. But is this always a good thing? In the fifth selection, Roy Baumeister and his colleagues express deep doubts on this score, arguing that much evil is done in the world by people whose self-esteem is too high. Their message is countered in the subsequent article by Brent Donnellan and his colleagues, which presents evidence that excessively low self-esteem is related to a number of bad outcomes, including antisocial behavior. We recommend you read these two articles together, and look for the points of divergence and convergence. Do they really contradict each other, or are there ways in which both are right?

The final selection in this section brings together several strands of personality research. Stan Klein and his colleagues use the intensive study of a single case, a young woman they call "W.J.," to explore the neurological and psychological underpinnings of the self and personal identity. In particular, they examine the degree to which a person's self-knowledge depends on memory. In the first selection in this book Dan McAdams asks what we know when we know a person; in the last, Klein asks what we must know to know ourselves.

Why Organisms Behave

B. F. Skinner

The major historical figure in behaviorism, and one of the best-known social scientists of the twentieth century, is B. F. Skinner. Over a career that spanned more than 60 years (he died in 1990), Skinner argued strenuously and consistently that behavior was a scientific topic no different, in principle, from any other. That is, behavior is best studied through experimental methods, and the best way to demonstrate that you understand a behavior is to show that you can control it. Skinner always expressed annoyance with theories that located causes of behavior in the mind or even in the physical brain. He felt this practice merely postponed understanding, because the mind cannot be observed and the brain is poorly understood. Instead, Skinner argued, psychology should address the powerful causes of behavior that can be both seen and experimentally manipulated: the rewards and punishments in the environment of the "organism."

The first selection in this section, an excerpt from a basic text on behaviorism Skinner published at the height of his career in 1953, clearly sets forth the behaviorist manifesto. Skinner argues that locating causes of behavior in the stars, the physique, genetics, or even the nervous system offers nothing to psychological understanding. Each only misleads or—at best—distracts analysis from the causes of behavior that ought to be the real business of psychologists.

Skinner's model for a science of psychology is "functional analysis." Such an analysis entails identifying—and, in many cases, controlling—the environmental causes of which behavior is a "function." Skinner further urges that these causes be conceptualized in concrete, physical terms. Rather than abstract social forces, for example, Skinner urges us to pay attention to the specific, immediate, concrete rewards and punishments in the social environment that affect what a person does. This focus on specifics, he believed, could enable people to design environments that would elicit behaviors leading to better outcomes for all.

From *Science and Human Behavior* by B. F. Skinner (Upper Saddle River, NJ: Prentice-Hall, 1953), pp. 23–42.

We are concerned with the causes of human behavior. We want to know why men behave as they do. Any condition or event which can be shown to have an effect upon behavior must be taken into account. By discovering and analyzing these causes we can predict behavior; to the extent that we can manipulate them, we can control behavior.

There is a curious inconsistency in the zeal with which the doctrine of personal freedom has been defended,[1] because men have always been fascinated by the search for causes. The spontaneity of human behavior is apparently no more challenging than its "why and wherefore." So strong is the urge to explain behavior that men have been led to anticipate legitimate scientific inquiry and to construct highly implausible theories of causation. This practice is not unusual in the history of science. The study of any subject begins in the realm of superstition. The fanciful explanation precedes the valid. Astronomy began as astrology; chemistry as alchemy. The field of behavior has had, and still has, its astrologers and alchemists. A long history of prescientific explanation furnishes us with a fantastic array of causes which have no function other than to supply spurious answers to questions which must otherwise go unanswered in the early stages of a science.

Some Popular "Causes" of Behavior

Any conspicuous event which coincides with human behavior is likely to be seized upon as a cause. The position of the planets at the birth of the individual is an example. Usually astrologers do not try to predict specific actions from such causes, but when they tell us that a man will be impetuous, careless, or thoughtful, we must suppose that specific actions are assumed to be affected. Numerology finds a different set of causes—for example, in the numbers which compose the street address of the individual or in the number of letters in his name. Millions of people turn to these spurious

causes every year in their desperate need to understand human behavior and to deal with it effectively.

The predictions of astrologers, numerologists, and the like are usually so vague that they cannot be confirmed or disproved properly. Failures are easily overlooked, while an occasional chance hit is dramatic enough to maintain the behavior of the devotee in considerable strength. * * *

Another common practice is to explain behavior in terms of the structure of the individual. The proportions of the body, the shape of the head, the color of the eyes, skin, or hair, the marks on the palms of the hands, and the features of the face have all been said to determine what a man will do. The "jovial fat man," Cassius with his "lean and hungry look," and thousands of other characters or types thoroughly embedded in our language affect our practices in dealing with human behavior. A specific act may never be predicted from physique, but different types of personality imply predispositions to behave in different ways, so that specific acts are presumed to be affected. This practice resembles the mistake we all make when we expect someone who looks like an old acquaintance to behave like him also. When a "type" is once established, it survives in everyday use because the predictions which are made with it, like those of astrology, are vague, and occasional hits may be startling.

* * *

When we find, or think we have found, that conspicuous physical features explain part of a man's behavior, it is tempting to suppose that inconspicuous features explain other parts. This is implied in the assertion that a man shows certain behavior because he was "born that way." To object to this is not to argue that behavior is never determined by hereditary factors. Behavior requires a behaving organism which is the product of a genetic process. Gross differences in the behavior of different species show that the genetic constitution, whether observed in the body structure of the individual or inferred from a genetic history, is important. But the doctrine of "being born that

---

[1]For example, by the humanists in Part V.

way" has little to do with demonstrated facts. It is usually an appeal to ignorance. "Heredity," as the layman uses the term, is a fictional explanation of the behavior attributed to it.

Even when it can be shown that some aspect of behavior is due to season of birth, gross body type, or genetic constitution, the fact is of limited use. It may help us in predicting behavior, but it is of little value in an experimental analysis or in practical control because such a condition cannot be manipulated after the individual has been conceived. The most that can be said is that the knowledge of the genetic factor may enable us to make better use of other causes. If we know that an individual has certain inherent limitations, we may use our techniques of control more intelligently, but we cannot alter the genetic factor.[2]

The practical deficiencies of programs involving causes of this sort may explain some of the vehemence with which they are commonly debated. Many people study human behavior because they want to do something about it—they want to make men happier, more efficient and productive, less aggressive, and so on. To these people, inherited determiners—as epitomized in various "racial types"—appear to be insurmountable barriers, since they leave no course of action but the slow and doubtful program of eugenics.[3] The evidence for genetic traits is therefore closely scrutinized, and any indication that it is weak or inconsistent is received with enthusiasm. But the

practical issue must not be allowed to interfere in determining the extent to which behavioral dispositions are inherited. The matter is not so crucial as is often supposed, for we shall see that there are other types of causes available for those who want quicker results.

Inner "Causes"

Every science has at some time or other looked for causes of action inside the things it has studied. Sometimes the practice has proved useful, sometimes it has not. There is nothing wrong with an inner explanation as such, but events which are located inside a system are likely to be difficult to observe. For this reason we are encouraged to assign properties to them without justification. Worse still, we can invent causes of this sort without fear of contradiction. The motion of a rolling stone was once attributed to its *vis viva*. The chemical properties of bodies were thought to be derived from the *principles* or *essences* of which they were composed. Combustion was explained by the *phlogiston* inside the combustible object. Wounds healed and bodies grew well because of a *vis medicatrix*. It has been especially tempting to attribute the behavior of a living organism to the behavior of an inner agent, as the following examples may suggest.

NEURAL CAUSES The layman uses the nervous system as a ready explanation of behavior. The English language contains hundreds of expressions which imply such a causal relationship. At the end of a long trial we read that the *nerves* of the accused are *on edge*, that the wife of the accused is on the verge of a *nervous breakdown*, and that his lawyer is generally thought to have lacked the *brains* needed to stand up to the prosecution. Obviously, no direct observations have been made of the nervous systems of any of these people. Their "brains" and "nerves" have been invented on the spur of the moment to lend substance to what might otherwise seem a superficial account of their behavior.

---

[2]It is unclear why Skinner here portrays the inability to alter the genotype as an important limitation. In terms of Skinner's own analysis, alteration of the phenotype (overt behavior) should be a sufficient goal.

[3]Skinner is referring to writings early in the twentieth century that identified "national" or "racial" characteristics. For example, southern Europeans were held to be emotional and northern Europeans to be cold and analytical. Skinner expresses (well-taken) doubts that such descriptions are accurate, and further argues that even if they were accurate, the only prescription they offer is to "improve" the human species through selective breeding (eugenics). Skinner calls such a eugenic strategy "doubtful," surely an understatement.

The sciences of neurology and physiology have not divested themselves entirely of a similar practice. Since techniques for observing the electrical and chemical processes in nervous tissue had not yet been developed, early information about the nervous system was limited to its gross anatomy. Neural processes could only be inferred from the behavior which was said to result from them. Such inferences were legitimate enough as scientific theories, but they could not justifiably be used to explain the very behavior upon which they were based. The hypotheses of the early physiologist may have been sounder than those of the layman, but until independent evidence could be obtained, they were no more satisfactory as explanations of behavior. Direct information about many of the chemical and electrical processes in the nervous system is now available. Statements about the nervous system are no longer necessarily inferential or fictional. But there is still a measure of circularity in much physiological explanation, even in the writings of specialists. In World War I a familiar disorder was called "shell shock." Disturbances in behavior were explained by arguing that violent explosions had damaged the structure of the nervous system, though no direct evidence of such damage was available. In World War II the same disorder was classified as "neuropsychiatric." The prefix seems to show a continuing unwillingness to abandon explanations in terms of hypothetical neural damage.[4]

Eventually a science of the nervous system based upon direct observation rather than inference will describe the neural states and events which immediately precede instances of behavior. We shall know the precise neurological conditions which immediately precede, say, the response, "No, thank you." These events in turn will be found to be preceded by other neurological events, and these in turn by others. This series will lead us back to events outside the nervous system and, eventually, outside the organism. * * * We do not have and may never have this sort of neurological information at the moment it is needed in order to predict a specific instance of behavior. It is even more unlikely that we shall be able to alter the nervous system directly in order to set up the antecedent conditions of a particular instance. The causes to be sought in the nervous system are, therefore, of limited usefulness in the prediction and control of specific behavior.

PSYCHIC INNER CAUSES An even more common practice is to explain behavior in terms of an inner agent which lacks physical dimensions and is called "mental" or "psychic." The purest form of the psychic explanation is seen in the animism of primitive peoples. From the immobility of the body after death it is inferred that a spirit responsible for movement has departed. The *enthusiastic* person is, as the etymology of the word implies, energized by a "god within." It is only a modest refinement to attribute every feature of the behavior of the physical organism to a corresponding feature of the "mind" or of some inner "personality." The inner man is regarded as driving the body very much as the man at the steering wheel drives a car. The inner man wills an action, the outer executes it. The inner loses his appetite, the outer stops eating. The inner man wants and the outer gets. The inner has the impulse which the outer obeys.

It is not the layman alone who resorts to these practices, for many reputable psychologists use a similar dualistic system of explanation. The inner man[5] is sometimes personified clearly, as when delinquent behavior is attributed to a "disordered personality," or he may be dealt with in fragments, as when behavior is attributed to mental processes, faculties, and traits. Since the inner man does not occupy space, he may be multiplied at will. It has been argued that a single physical organism is controlled by several psychic agents and that its behavior is the resultant of their several wills. The Freudian concepts of the ego, superego, and id are often used in this way. They are frequently

---

[4]The current label for this syndrome, post-traumatic stress disorder, is more in line with Skinner's descriptive preference without attributing cause.

[5]Sometimes called the "homunculus."

regarded as nonsubstantial creatures, often in violent conflict, whose defeats or victories lead to the adjusted or maladjusted behavior of the physical organism in which they reside.

Direct observation of the mind comparable with the observation of the nervous system has not proved feasible. It is true that many people believe that they observe their "mental states" just as the physiologist observes neural events, but another interpretation of what they observe is possible. Introspective psychology[6] no longer pretends to supply direct information about events which are the causal antecedents, rather than the mere accompaniments, of behavior. It defines its "subjective" events in ways which strip them of any usefulness in a causal analysis. The events appealed to in early mentalistic explanations of behavior have remained beyond the reach of observation. Freud insisted upon this by emphasizing the role of the unconscious—a frank recognition that important mental processes are not directly observable. The Freudian literature supplies many examples of behavior from which unconscious wishes, impulses, instincts, and emotions are inferred. Unconscious thought-processes have also been used to explain intellectual achievements. Though the mathematician may feel that he knows "how he thinks," he is often unable to give a coherent account of the mental processes leading to the solution of a specific problem. But any mental event which is unconscious is necessarily inferential, and the explanation is therefore not based upon independent observations of a valid cause.

The fictional nature of this form of inner cause is shown by the ease with which the mental process is discovered to have just the properties needed to account for the behavior. When a professor turns up in the wrong classroom or gives the wrong lecture, it is because his *mind* is, at least for the moment, *absent*. If he forgets to give a reading assignment, it is because it has slipped his *mind* (a

hint from the class may re*mind* him of it). He begins to tell an old joke but pauses for a moment, and it is evident to everyone that he is trying to make up his *mind* whether or not he has already used the joke that term. His lectures grow more tedious with the years, and questions from the class confuse him more and more, because his *mind* is failing. What he says is often disorganized because his *ideas* are confused. He is occasionally unnecessarily emphatic because of the force of his *ideas*. When he repeats himself, it is because he has an *idée fixe*; and when he repeats what others have said, it is because he borrows his *ideas*. Upon occasion there is nothing in what he says because he lacks *ideas*. In all this it is obvious that the mind and the ideas, together with their special characteristics, are being invented on the spot to provide spurious explanations. A science of behavior can hope to gain very little from so cavalier a practice. Since mental or psychic events are asserted to lack the dimensions of physical science, we have an additional reason for rejecting them.

CONCEPTUAL INNER CAUSES The commonest inner causes have no specific dimensions at all, either neurological or psychic. When we say that a man eats *because* he is hungry, smokes a great deal *because* he has the tobacco habit, fights *because* of the instinct of pugnacity, behaves brilliantly *because* of his intelligence, or plays the piano well *because* of his musical ability, we seem to be referring to causes. But on analysis these phrases prove to be merely redundant descriptions. A single set of facts is described by the two statements: "He eats" and "He is hungry." A single set of facts is described by the two statements: "He smokes a great deal" and "He has the smoking habit." A single set of facts is described by the two statements: "He plays well" and "He has musical ability." The practice of explaining one statement in terms of the other is dangerous because it suggests that we have found the cause and therefore need search no further. Moreover, such terms as "hunger," "habit," and "intelligence" convert what are essentially the properties of a process or relation into what appear to be things. Thus we are unprepared for the properties

---

[6]A kind of psychology, prominent in the field's early days, in which trained "introspectionists" tried to observe their own mental processes.

eventually to be discovered in the behavior itself and continue to look for something which may not exist.

The Variables of Which Behavior Is a Function

The practice of looking inside the organism for an explanation of behavior has tended to obscure the variables which are immediately available for a scientific analysis. These variables lie outside the organism, in its immediate environment and in its environmental history. They have a physical status to which the usual techniques of science are adapted, and they make it possible to explain behavior as other subjects are explained in science. These independent variables are of many sorts and their relations to behavior are often subtle and complex, but we cannot hope to give an adequate account of behavior without analyzing them.

Consider the act of drinking a glass of water. This is not likely to be an important bit of behavior in anyone's life, but it supplies a convenient example. We may describe the topography of the behavior in such a way that a given instance may be identified quite accurately by any qualified observer. Suppose now we bring someone into a room and place a glass of water before him. Will he drink? There appear to be only two possibilities: either he will or he will not. But we speak of the *chances* that he will drink, and this notion may be refined for scientific use. What we want to evaluate is the *probability* that he will drink. This may range from virtual certainty that drinking will occur to virtual certainty that it will not. The very considerable problem of how to measure such a probability will be discussed later. For the moment, we are interested in how the probability may be increased or decreased.

Everyday experience suggests several possibilities, and laboratory and clinical observations have added others. It is decidedly not true that a horse may be led to water but cannot be made to drink. By arranging a history of severe deprivation we could be "absolutely sure" that drinking would

occur. In the same way we may be sure that the glass of water in our experiment will be drunk. Although we are not likely to arrange them experimentally, deprivations of the necessary magnitude sometimes occur outside the laboratory. We may obtain an effect similar to that of deprivation by speeding up the excretion of water. For example, we may induce sweating by raising the temperature of the room or by forcing heavy exercise, or we may increase the excretion of urine by mixing salt or urea in food taken prior to the experiment. It is also well known that loss of blood, as on a battlefield, sharply increases the probability of drinking. On the other hand, we may set the probability at virtually zero by inducing or forcing our subject to drink a large quantity of water before the experiment.

If we are to predict whether or not our subject will drink, we must know as much as possible about these variables. If we are to induce him to drink, we must be able to manipulate them. In both cases, moreover, either for accurate prediction or control, we must investigate the effect of each variable quantitatively with the methods and techniques of a laboratory science.

Other variables may, of course, affect the result. Our subject may be "afraid" that something has been added to the water as a practical joke or for experimental purposes. He may even "suspect" that the water has been poisoned. He may have grown up in a culture in which water is drunk only when no one is watching. He may refuse to drink simply to prove that we cannot predict or control his behavior. These possibilities do not disprove the relations between drinking and the variables listed in the preceding paragraphs; they simply remind us that other variables may have to be taken into account. We must know the history of our subject with respect to the behavior of drinking water, and if we cannot eliminate social factors from the situation, then we must know the history of his personal relations to people resembling the experimenter. Adequate prediction in any science requires information about all relevant variables, and the control of a subject matter for practical purposes makes the same demands.

Other types of "explanation" do not permit us to dispense with these requirements or to fulfill them in any easier way. It is of no help to be told that our subject will drink provided he was born under a particular sign of the zodiac which shows a preoccupation with water or provided he is the lean and thirsty type or was, in short, "born thirsty." Explanations in terms of inner states or agents, however, may require some further comment. To what extent is it helpful to be told, "He drinks because he is thirsty"? If to be thirsty means nothing more than to have a tendency to drink, this is mere redundancy. If it means that he drinks because of a state of thirst, an inner causal event is invoked. If this state is purely inferential—if no dimensions are assigned to it which would make direct observation possible—it cannot serve as an explanation. But if it has physiological or psychic properties, what role can it play in a science of behavior?

The physiologist may point out that several ways of raising the probability of drinking have a common effect: they increase the concentration of solutions in the body. Through some mechanism not yet well understood, this may bring about a corresponding change in the nervous system which in turn makes drinking more probable. In the same way, it may be argued that all these operations make the organism "feel thirsty" or "want a drink" and that such a psychic state also acts upon the nervous system in some unexplained way to induce drinking. In each case we have a causal chain consisting of three links: (1) an operation performed upon the organism from without—for example, water deprivation; (2) an inner condition—for example, physiological or psychic thirst; and (3) a kind of behavior—for example, drinking. Independent information about the second link would obviously permit us to predict the third without recourse to the first. It would be a preferred type of variable because it would be nonhistoric; the first link may lie in the past history of the organism, but the second is a current condition. Direct information about the second link is, however, seldom, if ever, available. Sometimes we infer the second link from the third: an animal is judged to be thirsty if

it drinks. In that case, the explanation is spurious. Sometimes we infer the second link from the first: an animal is said to be thirsty if it has not drunk for a long time. In that case, we obviously cannot dispense with the prior history.

The second link is useless in the *control* of behavior unless we can manipulate it. At the moment, we have no way of directly altering neural processes at appropriate moments in the life of a behaving organism, nor has any way been discovered to alter a psychic process. We usually set up the second link through the first: we make an animal thirsty, in either the physiological or the psychic sense, by depriving it of water, feeding it salt, and so on. In that case, the second link obviously does not permit us to dispense with the first. Even if some new technical discovery were to enable us to set up or change the second link directly, we should still have to deal with those enormous areas in which human behavior is controlled through manipulation of the first link. A technique of operating upon the second link would increase our control of behavior, but the techniques which have already been developed would still remain to be analyzed.

The most objectionable practice is to follow the causal sequence back only as far as a hypothetical second link. This is a serious handicap both in a theoretical science and in the practical control of behavior. It is no help to be told that to get an organism to drink we are simply to "make it thirsty" unless we are also told how this is to be done. When we have obtained the necessary prescription for thirst, the whole proposal is more complex than it need be. Similarly, when an example of maladjusted behavior is explained by saying that the individual is "suffering from anxiety," we have still to be told the cause of the anxiety. But the external conditions which are then invoked could have been directly related to the maladjusted behavior. Again, when we are told that a man stole a loaf of bread because "he was hungry," we have still to learn of the external conditions responsible for the "hunger." These conditions would have sufficed to explain the theft.

The objection to inner states is not that they do not exist, but that they are not relevant in a functional analysis.[7] We cannot account for the behavior of any system while staying wholly inside it; eventually we must turn to forces operating upon the organism from without. Unless there is a weak spot in our causal chain so that the second link is not lawfully determined by the first, or the third by the second, then the first and third links must be lawfully related. If we must always go back beyond the second link for prediction and control, we may avoid many tiresome and exhausting digressions by examining the third link as a function of the first. Valid information about the second link may throw light upon this relationship but can in no way alter it.

A Functional Analysis

The external variables of which behavior is a function provide for what may be called a causal or functional analysis. We undertake to predict and control the behavior of the individual organism. This is our "dependent variable"—the effect for which we are to find the cause. Our "independent variables"—the causes of behavior—are the external conditions of which behavior is a function. Relations between the two—the "cause-and-effect relationships" in behavior—are the laws of a science. A synthesis of these laws expressed in quantitative terms yields a comprehensive picture of the organism as a behaving system.

This must be done within the bounds of a natural science. We cannot assume that behavior has any peculiar properties which require unique methods or special kinds of knowledge. It is often argued[8] that an act is not so important as the "intent" which lies behind it, or that it can be described only in terms of what it "means" to the behaving individual or to others whom it may affect. If statements of this sort are useful for scientific purposes, they must be based upon observable events, and we may confine ourselves to such events exclusively in a functional analysis. Although such terms as "meaning" and "intent" appear to refer to properties of behavior, they usually conceal references to independent variables. This is also true of "aggressive," "friendly," "disorganized," "intelligent," and other terms which appear to describe properties of behavior but in reality refer to its controlling relations.

The independent variables must also be described in physical terms. An effort is often made to avoid the labor of analyzing a physical situation by guessing what it "means" to an organism or by distinguishing between the physical world and a psychological world of "experience." This practice also reflects a confusion between dependent and independent variables. The events affecting an organism must be capable of description in the language of physical science. It is sometimes argued that certain "social forces" or the "influences" of culture or tradition are exceptions. But we cannot appeal to entities of this sort without explaining how they can affect both the scientist and the individual under observation. The physical events which must then be appealed to in such an explanation will supply us with alternative material suitable for a physical analysis.

By confining ourselves to these observable events, we gain a considerable advantage, not only in theory, but in practice. A "social force" is no more useful in manipulating behavior than an inner state of hunger, anxiety, or skepticism. Just as we must trace these inner events to the manipulable variables of which they are said to be functions before we may put them to practical use, so we must identify the physical events through which a "social force" is said to affect the organism before we can manipulate it for purposes of control. In dealing with the directly observable data we need not refer to either the inner state or the outer force.

*   *   *

---

[7]This important clarification and qualification of Skinner's position has often been neglected by his critics over the years.

[8]For example, by humanistic, phenomenological, and cognitive psychologists.

The Self System in Reciprocal Determinism

Albert Bandura

The most prominent of the social learning theorists, Albert Bandura helped lead the way as social learning theory evolved into the cognitive approach of personality. Indeed, in some of his most recent writings, Bandura calls his approach social cognitive theory.

The following selection, published at the height of Bandura's career, could be considered one of the first important entries in this new approach. It is an ambitious effort; Bandura tackles the heavy philosophical issues that surround "basic conceptions of human nature." He points out that the behaviorists and the humanists, seemingly opposite in viewpoint, share one basic idea: the unidirectional causation of behavior. That is, behaviorists see behavior as a function of reinforcements in the environment or the situation. At the opposite end, humanists see behavior as a function of the person, of his or her characteristics and most important, his or her free choice. In the following selection, Bandura seeks a middle ground between these seemingly irreconcilable viewpoints.

Bandura does this by proposing the existence of a "self system." This cognitive system, consisting of thoughts and feelings about the self, arises as a result of experience but, once constructed, has important effects on behavior. For example, the self system sets goals and evaluates one's own progress toward those goals. Just as importantly, the self system affects one's environment by (1) administering rewards and punishments to the self (such as promising oneself an ice cream as soon as one finishes reading Bandura's chapter) and by (2) selecting the environments that one enters. For example, once a student enrolls at college he or she is buffeted by all sorts of environmental pressures—rewards and punishments—that coerce the student to study for exams, write term papers, camp out in the library, and so on. But whether to enroll in college in the first place is a choice made by the self system. Similarly, activities and self-evaluations are critically influenced by the people one is surrounded by. To an important degree, a person chooses his or her companions and so chooses who to be influenced by.

If you pushed Bandura into a corner, he would probably have to admit to being a behaviorist at heart, despite his advocacy for the self system. This is because he views the self system as being, in the final analysis, a result of the environment. But by viewing the self system as something that, once constructed, can shape behavior and even shape the environment (through a process Bandura calls "reciprocal determinism"), Bandura opens up possibilities for the analysis and prediction of behavior that go beyond anything envisaged by classical behaviorism. Furthermore, he paves the way for further research to examine implications of cognitive structures and processes for behavior.

From *American Psychologist, 33,* 344–358, 1978.

Recent years have witnessed a heightened interest in the basic conceptions of human nature underlying different psychological theories. This interest stems in part from growing recognition of how such conceptions delimit research to selected processes and are in turn shaped by findings of paradigms embodying the particular view. As psychological knowledge is converted to behavioral technologies, the models of human behavior on which research is premised have important social as well as theoretical implications (Bandura, 1974).

Explanations of human behavior have generally been couched in terms of a limited set of determinants, usually portrayed as operating in a unidirectional manner. Exponents of environmental determinism study and theorize about how behavior is controlled by situational influences. Those favoring personal determinism seek the causes of human behavior in dispositional sources in the form of instincts, drives, traits, and other motivational forces within the individual. * * *

* * * The present article analyzes the various causal models and the role of self influences in behavior from the perspective of reciprocal determinism.

Unidirectional environmental determinism is carried to its extreme in the more radical forms of behaviorism. * * * ([For example] "A person does not act upon the world, the world acts upon him," Skinner, 1971, p. 211.) The environment thus becomes an autonomous force that automatically shapes, orchestrates, and controls behavior. * * *

* * *

There exists no shortage of advocates of alternative theories emphasizing the personal determination of environments. Humanists and existentialists,[1] who stress the human capacity for conscious judgment and intentional action, contend that individuals determine what they become by their own free choices. Most psychologists find conceptions of human behavior in terms of unidirectional personal determinism as unsatisfying as those espousing unidirectional environmental determinism. To contend that mind creates reality fails to acknowledge that environmental influences partly determine what people attend to, perceive, and think. To contend further that the methods of natural science are incapable of dealing with personal determinants of behavior does not enlist many supporters from the ranks of those who are moved more by empirical evidence than by philosophic discourse.

Social learning theory (Bandura, 1974, 1977b) analyzes behavior in terms of reciprocal determinism. The term *determinism* is used here to signify the production of effects by events, rather than in the doctrinal sense that actions are completely determined by a prior sequence of causes independent of the individual. Because of the complexity of interacting factors, events produce effects probabilistically rather than inevitably. In their transactions with the environment, people are not simply reactors to external stimulation. Most external

---

[1]Such as represented in Part V.

influences affect behavior through intermediary cognitive processes. Cognitive factors partly determine which external events will be observed, how they will be perceived, whether they have any lasting effects, what valence and efficacy they have, and how the information they convey will be organized for future use. The extraordinary capacity of humans to use symbols enables them to engage in reflective thought, to create, and to plan foresightful courses of action in thought rather than having to perform possible options and suffer the consequences of thoughtless action. By altering their immediate environment, by creating cognitive self-inducements, and by arranging conditional incentives for themselves, people can exercise some influence over their own behavior. An act therefore includes among its determinants self-produced influences.

It is true that behavior is influenced by the environment, but the environment is partly of a person's own making. By their actions, people play a role in creating the social milieu and other circumstances that arise in their daily transactions. Thus, from the social learning perspective, psychological functioning involves a continuous reciprocal interaction between behavioral, cognitive, and environmental influences.

Reciprocal Determinism and Interactionism

* * *

Interaction processes have been conceptualized in three fundamentally different ways. These alternative formulations are summarized schematically in Figure 1. In the unidirectional notion of interaction, persons and situations are treated as independent entities that combine to produce behavior. This commonly held view can be called into question on both conceptual and empirical grounds. Personal and environmental factors do not function as independent determinants; rather, they determine each other. Nor can "persons" be considered causes independent of their behavior. It is largely through their actions that people produce the environmental conditions that affect their

Unidirectional

$$B = f(P, E)$$

Partially Bidirectional

$$B = f(P \rightleftharpoons E)$$

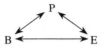

Figure 1. Schematic representation of three alternative conceptions of interaction: *B* signifies behavior, *P* the cognitive and other internal events that can affect perceptions and actions, and *E* the external environment.

behavior in a reciprocal fashion. The experiences generated by behavior also partly determine what individuals think, expect, and can do, which in turn, affect their subsequent behavior.

A second conception of interaction acknowledges that personal and environmental influences are bidirectional, but it retains a unidirectional view of behavior. In this analysis, persons and situations are considered to be interdependent causes of behavior, but behavior is treated as though it were only a by-product that does not figure at all in the causal process. * * *

* * *

In the social learning view of interaction, which is analyzed as a process of reciprocal determinism (Bandura, 1977b), behavior, internal personal factors, and environmental influences all operate as interlocking determinants of each other. As shown in Figure 1, the process involves a triadic reciprocal interaction rather than a dyadic conjoint or a dyadic bidirectional one. We have already noted that behavior and environmental conditions function as reciprocally interacting determinants. Internal personal factors (e.g., conceptions, beliefs, self-perceptions) and behavior also operate as reciprocal determinants of each other. For example, people's efficacy and outcome expectations influence how they behave, and the environmental effects created by their actions in turn alter their expectations. People activate different environmental reactions, apart from their behavior, by their physical characteristics (e.g., size, physiognomy, race, sex, attractiveness) and socially conferred attributes, roles, and status. The differential social treatment affects recipients' self-conceptions and actions in ways that either maintain or alter the environmental biases.

The relative influence exerted by these three sets of interlocking factors will vary in different individuals and under different circumstances. In some cases, environmental conditions exercise such powerful constraints on behavior that they emerge as the overriding determinants. If, for example, people are dropped in deep water they will all promptly engage in swimming activities, however uniquely varied they might be in their cognitive and behavioral repertoires. There are times when behavior is the central factor in the interlocking system. One example of this is persons who play familiar piano selections for themselves that create a pleasing sensory environment. The behavior is self-regulated over a long period by the sensory effects it produces, whereas cognitive activities and contextual environmental events are not much involved in the process.

In other instances, cognitive factors serve as the predominant influence in the regulatory system. The activation and maintenance of defensive behavior is a good case in point. False beliefs activate avoidance responses that keep individuals out of touch with prevailing environmental conditions, thus creating a strong reciprocal interaction between beliefs and action that is protected from corrective environmental influence. In extreme cases, behavior is so powerfully controlled by bizarre internal contingencies that neither the beliefs nor the accompanying actions are much affected even by extremely punishing environmental consequences (Bateson, 1961).

In still other instances, the development and activation of the three interlocking factors are all highly interdependent. Television-viewing behavior provides an everyday example. Personal preferences influence when and which programs, from among the available alternatives, individuals choose to watch on television. Although the potential televised environment is identical for all viewers, the actual televised environment that impinges on given individuals depends on what they select to watch. Through their viewing behavior, they partly shape the nature of the future televised environment. Because production costs and commercial requirements also determine what people are shown, the options provided in the televised environment partly shape the viewers' preferences. Here, all three factors—viewer preferences, viewing behavior, and televised offerings—reciprocally affect each other.

The methodology for elucidating psychological processes requires analysis of sequential interactions between the triadic, interdependent factors within the interlocking system. Investigations of reciprocal processes have thus far rarely, if ever, examined more than two of the interacting factors simultaneously. Some studies analyze how cognitions and behavior affect each other in a reciprocal fashion (Bandura, 1977a; Bandura & Adams, 1977). More often, however, the sequential analysis centers on how social behavior and environment determine each other. In these studies of dyadic exchanges, behavior creates certain conditions and is, in turn, altered by the very conditions it creates (Bandura, Lipsher, & Miller, 1960; Patterson, 1975; Raush, Barry, Hertel, & Swain, 1974; Thomas & Martin, 1976).

From the perspective of reciprocal determinism, the common practice of searching for the ultimate environmental cause of behavior is an idle exercise because, in an interactional process, one and the same event can be a stimulus, a response, or an environmental reinforcer, depending on where in the sequence the analysis arbitrarily begins.

* * *

* * * Regulatory processes are not governed solely by the reciprocal influence of antecedent and consequent acts. While behaving, people are also cognitively appraising the progression of events. Their thoughts about the probable effects of prospective actions partly determine how acts are affected by their immediate environmental consequences. Consider, for example, investigations of reciprocal coercive behavior in an ongoing dyadic interaction. In discordant families, coercive behavior by one member tends to elicit coercive counteractions from recipients in a mutual escalation of aggression (Patterson, 1975). However, coercion often does not produce coercive counteractions. To increase the predictive power of a theory of behavior, it is necessary to broaden the analysis to include cognitive factors that operate in the interlocking system. Counterresponses to antecedent acts are influenced not only by their immediate effects but also by judgments of later consequences for a given course of action. Thus, aggressive children will continue, or even escalate, coercive behavior in the face of immediate punishment when they expect persistence eventually to gain them what they seek. But the same momentary punishment will serve as an inhibitor rather than as an enhancer of coercion when they expect continuance of the aversive conduct to be ineffective. * * *

Cognitions do not arise in a vacuum, nor do they function as autonomous determinants of behavior. In the social learning analysis of cognitive development, conceptions about oneself and the nature of the environment are developed and verified through four different processes (Bandura, 1977b). People derive much of their knowledge from direct experience of the effects produced by their actions. Indeed, most theories of cognitive development, whether they favor behavioristic, information-processing, or Piagetian[2] orientations, focus almost exclusively on cognitive change through feedback from direct experimentation. However, results of one's own actions are not the sole source of knowledge. Information about the nature of things is frequently extracted from vicarious experience. In this mode of verification, observation of the effects produced by somebody else's actions serves as the source and authentication of thoughts.

There are many things we cannot come to know by direct or vicarious experience because of limited accessibility or because the matters involve metaphysical ideas that are not subject to objective confirmation. When experiential verification is either difficult or impossible, people develop and evaluate their conceptions of things in terms of the judgments voiced by others. In addition to enactive, vicarious, and social sources of thought verification, all of which rely on external influences, logical verification also enters into the process, especially in later phases of development. After people acquire some rules of inference, they can evaluate the soundness of their reasoning and derive from what they already know new knowledge about things that extend beyond their experiences.

External influences play a role not only in the development of cognitions but in their activation as well. Different sights, smells, and sounds will elicit quite different trains of thought. Thus, while it is true that conceptions govern behavior, the conceptions themselves are partly fashioned from direct or mediated transactions with the environment. A complete analysis of reciprocal determinism therefore requires investigation of how all three sets of factors—cognitive, behavioral, and environmental—interact reciprocally among themselves. Contrary to common misconception, social learning theory does not disregard personal determinants of behavior. Within this perspective, such determinants are treated as integral, dynamic factors in causal processes rather than as static trait dimensions.

Self-Regulatory Functions of the Self System

The differences between unidirectional and reciprocal analyses of behavior have been drawn most sharply in the area of self-regulatory phenomena. Exponents of radical behaviorism have always disavowed any construct of self for fear that it would usher in psychic agents and divert attention from

---

[2]Jean Piaget was a Swiss psychologist whose ideas have had an important influence on developmental psychology. The idea referred to here concerns Piaget's description of how the mind develops through an interaction between knowledge and experience.

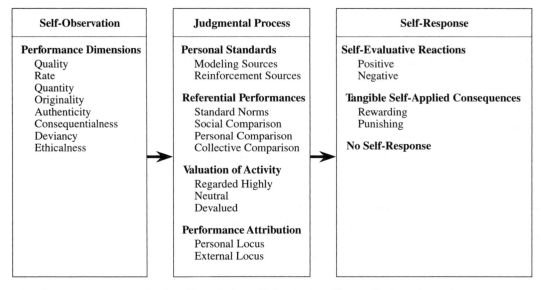

Self-Observation	Judgmental Process	Self-Response

Performance Dimensions
  Quality
  Rate
  Quantity
  Originality
  Authenticity
  Consequentialness
  Deviancy
  Ethicalness
	Personal Standards
	  Modeling Sources
	  Reinforcement Sources
	
	Referential Performances
	  Standard Norms
	  Social Comparison
	  Personal Comparison
	  Collective Comparison
	
	Valuation of Activity
	  Regarded Highly
	  Neutral
	  Devalued
	
	Performance Attribution
	  Personal Locus
	  External Locus
		Self-Evaluative Reactions
		  Positive
		  Negative
		
		Tangible Self-Applied Consequences
		  Rewarding
		  Punishing
		
		No Self-Response

Figure 2. Component processes in the self-regulation of behavior by self-prescribed contingencies.

physical to experiential reality.[3] While this approach encompasses a large set of environmental factors, it assumes that self-generated influences either do not exist or, if they do, that they have no effect upon behavior. Internal events are treated simply as an intermediate link in a causal chain. Since environmental conditions presumably create the intermediate link, one can explain behavior in terms of external factors without recourse to any internal determinants. Through a conceptual bypass, cognitive determinants are thus excised from the analysis of causal processes.

In contrast to the latter view, internal determinants of behavior are gaining increasing attention in contemporary theorizing and research. Indeed, self-referent processes occupy a central position in social learning theory (Bandura, 1977b). As will be shown later, self-generated events cannot be relegated to a redundant explanatory link. In the triadic reciprocal system, they not only operate as reciprocal determinants of behavior but they play a role in the perception and formation of the environmental influences themselves.

---

[3]We saw Skinner raise exactly this worry in the selections earlier in this section.

* * *

In social learning theory, a self system is not a psychic agent that controls behavior. Rather, it refers to cognitive structures that provide reference mechanisms and to a set of subfunctions for the perception, evaluation, and regulation of behavior. Before proceeding to a reciprocal analysis of self influences, the processes by which people exercise some control over their own behavior will be reviewed briefly.

COMPONENT PROCESSES IN SELF-REGULATION
Figure 2 summarizes the different component processes in the self-regulation of behavior through self-prescribed contingencies. Behavior typically varies on a number of dimensions, some of which are listed in the self-observation component. Depending on value orientations and the functional significance of given activities, people attend selectively to certain aspects of their behavior and ignore variations on nonrelevant dimensions.

Simply observing variations in one's performances yields some relevant information, but such data, in themselves, do not provide any basis for personal reactions. Behavior produces self-reactions through a judgmental function that includes several subsidiary processes. Whether a given performance will be regarded as commendable or dissatisfying depends upon the personal standards against which it is evaluated. Actions that measure up to internal standards are appraised favorably; those that fall short are judged unsatisfactory.

For most activities, there are no absolute measures of adequacy. The time in which a given distance is run, the number of points obtained on an achievement test, or the size of charitable contributions often do not convey sufficient information for self-appraisal even when compared with an internal standard. When adequacy is defined relationally, performances are evaluated by comparing them with those of others. The referential comparisons may involve standard norms, the performances of particular individuals, or the accomplishments of reference groups.

One's previous behavior is continuously used as the reference against which ongoing performance is judged. In this referential process, it is self-comparison that supplies the measure of adequacy. Past attainments influence performance appraisals mainly through their effects on standard setting. After a given level of performance is attained, it is no longer challenging, and new self-satisfactions are often sought through progressive improvement.

Another important factor in the judgmental component of self-regulation concerns the evaluation of the activities. People do not much care how they perform on tasks that have little or no significance for them. And little effort is expended on devalued activities. It is mainly in areas affecting one's welfare and self-esteem that favorable performance appraisals activate personal consequences (Simon, 1978).

Self-reactions also vary depending on how people perceive the determinants of their behavior. They take pride in their accomplishments when they ascribe their successes to their own abilities and efforts. They do not derive much self-satisfaction, however, when they view their performances as heavily dependent on external

factors. The same is true for judgments of failure and blameworthy conduct. People respond self-critically to inadequate performances for which they hold themselves responsible but not to those which they perceive are due to unusual circumstances or to insufficient capabilities. Performance appraisals set the occasion for self-produced consequences. Favorable judgments give rise to rewarding self-reactions, whereas unfavorable appraisals activate negative self-reactions. Performances that are judged to have no personal significance do not generate any reactions one way or another.

In the social learning view, self-regulated incentives alter performance mainly through their motivational function (Bandura, 1976). Contingent self-reward improves performance not because it strengthens preceding responses. When people make self-satisfaction or tangible gratifications conditional upon certain accomplishments, they motivate themselves to expend the effort needed to attain the desired performances. Both the anticipated satisfactions of desired accomplishments and the dissatisfactions with insufficient ones provide incentives for actions that increase the likelihood of performance attainments.

Much human behavior is regulated through self-evaluative consequences in the form of self-satisfaction, self-pride, self-dissatisfaction, and self-criticism. The act of writing is a familiar example of a behavior that is continuously self-regulated through evaluative self-reactions. Writers adopt a standard of what constitutes an acceptable piece of work. Ideas are generated and rephrased in thought before they are committed to paper. Provisional contructions are successively revised until authors are satisfied with what they have written. The more exacting the personal standards, the more extensive are the corrective improvements.

People also get themselves to do things they would otherwise put off by making tangible outcomes conditional upon completing a specified level of performance. In programs of self-directed change, individuals improve and maintain behavior on their own over long periods by arranging incentives for themselves (Bandura, 1976; Goldfried & Merbaum, 1973; Mahoney & Thoresen,

1974). In many instances, activities are regulated through self-prescribed contingencies involving both evaluative and tangible self-rewards. Authors influence how much they write by making breaks, recreational activities, and other tangible rewards contingent on completing a certain amount of work (Wallace, 1977), but they revise and improve what they write by their self-evaluative reactions.

* * *

Reciprocal Influence of External Factors on Self-Regulatory Functions

Social learning theory regards self-generated influences not as autonomous regulators of behavior but as contributory influences in a reciprocally interacting system. A variety of external factors serve as reciprocal influences on the operation of a self system. They can affect self-regulatory processes in at least three major ways: They are involved in the development of the component functions in self-regulatory systems; they provide partial support for adherence to self-prescribed contingencies; and they facilitate selective activation and disengagement of internal contingencies governing conduct.

DEVELOPMENT OF SELF-REGULATORY FUNCTIONS
The development of capabilities for self-reaction requires adoption of standards against which performances can be evaluated. These internal criteria do not emerge in a vacuum. Behavioral standards are established by precept, evaluative consequences accompanying different performances, and exposure to the self-evaluative standards modeled by others (Bandura, 1976, 1977b; Masters & Mokros, 1974). People do not passively absorb behavioral standards from the environmental stimuli that happen to impinge upon them. They extract generic standards from the multiplicity of evaluative reactions that are exemplified and taught by different individuals or by the same individuals on different activities and in different settings (Bandura, 1976; Lepper, Sagotsky, & Mailer, 1975). Peo-

ple must therefore process the divergent information and eventually arrive at personal standards against which to measure their own behavior.

Associational preferences add another reciprocal element to the acquisition process. The people with whom one regularly associates partly influence the standards of behavior that are adopted. Value orientations, in turn, exercise selective influence on choices of activities and associates (Bandura & Walters, 1959; Krauss, 1964).

EXTERNAL SUPPORTS FOR SELF-REGULATORY SYSTEMS
In analyzing regulation of behavior through self-produced consequences, one must distinguish between two different sources of incentives that operate in the system. First, there is the arrangement of self-reward contingent upon designated performances to create proximal incentives for oneself to engage in the activities. Second, there are the more distal incentives for adhering to the self-prescribed contingencies.

Adherence to performance requirements for self-reward is partly sustained by periodic environmental influences that take a variety of forms (Bandura, 1977b). First, there are the negative sanctions for unmerited self-reward. When standards are being acquired or when they are later applied inconsistently, rewarding oneself for undeserving performances is more likely than not to evoke critical reactions from others. Occasional sanctions for unmerited self-reward influence the likelihood that people will withhold rewards from themselves until their behavior matches their standards (Bandura, Mahoney, & Dirks, 1976). Personal sanctions operate as well in fostering such adherence. After people adopt codes of conduct, when they perform inadequately or violate their standards they tend to engage in self-critical and other distressing trains of thought. Anticipated, thought-produced distress over faulty behavior provides an internal incentive to abide by personal standards of performance (Bandura, 1977b).

Negative inducements, whether personal or social, are not the most reliable basis upon which to rest a system of self-regulation. Fortunately, there are more advantageous reasons for exercising some influence over one's own behavior through self-arranged incentives. Some of these personal benefits are extrinsic to the behavior; others derive from the behavior itself.

People are motivated to institute performance contingencies for themselves when the behavior they seek to change is aversive. To overweight persons, the discomforts, maladies, and social costs of obesity create inducements to control their overeating. Similarly, students are prompted to improve their study behavior when failures in course work make academic life sufficiently distressing. By making self-reward conditional upon performance attainments, individuals can reduce aversive behavior, thereby creating natural benefits for their efforts.

The benefits of self-regulated change may provide natural incentives for adherence to personal prescriptions for valued activities as well as for unpleasant ones. People often motivate themselves by conditional incentives to enhance their skills in activities they aspire to master. Here the personal benefits derived from improved proficiency support self-prescription of contingencies. Self-generated inducements are especially important in ensuring continual progress in creative endeavors, because people have to develop their own work schedules for themselves. There are no clocks to punch or supervisors to issue directives. In analyzing the writing habits and self-discipline of novelists, Wallace (1977) documents how famous novelists regulate their writing output by making self-reward contingent upon completion of a certain amount of writing each day whether the spirit moves them or not.

If societies relied solely on inherent benefits to sustain personal contingencies, many activities that are tiresome and uninteresting until proficiency in them is acquired would never be mastered. Upholding standards is therefore socially promoted by a vast system of rewards including praise, social recognition, and honors. Few accolades are bestowed on people for self-rewarding their mediocre performances. Direct praise or seeing others publicly recognized for upholding excel-lence fosters adherence to high performance standards (Bandura, Grusec, & Menlove, 1967).

* * *

Because personal and environmental determinants affect each other in a reciprocal fashion, attempts to assign causal priority to these two sources of influence reduce to the "chicken-or-egg" debate. The quest for the ultimate environmental determinant of activities regulated by self-influence becomes a regressive exercise that can yield no victors in explanatory contests, because for every ultimate environmental cause that is invoked, one can find prior actions that helped to produce it.

SELECTIVE ACTIVATION AND DISENGAGEMENT OF SELF-REACTIVE INFLUENCES   The third area of research on the role of external factors in self-regulation centers on the selective activation and disengagement of self-reactive influences (Bandura, 1977b). Theories of internalization that portray incorporated entities (e.g., the conscience or superego, moral codes) as continuous internal overseers of conduct are usually at a loss to explain the variable operation of internal control and the perpetration of inhumanities by otherwise humane people.

In the social learning analysis, considerate people perform culpable acts because of the reciprocal dynamics between personal and situational determinants of behavior rather than because of defects in their moral structures. Development of self-regulatory capabilities does not create an invariant control mechanism within a person. Self-evaluative influences do not operate unless activated, and many situational dynamics influence their selective activation.

After ethical and moral standards of conduct are adopted, anticipatory self-censuring reactions for violating personal standards ordinarily serve as self-deterrents against reprehensible acts (Bandura & Walters, 1959).[4] Self-deterring consequences are likely to be activated most strongly when the causal

---

[4]That is, you know you will feel guilty if you do it.

connection between conduct and the detrimental effects it produces is unambiguous. There are various means, however, by which self-evaluative consequences can be dissociated from reprehensible behavior. * * *

One set of disengagement practices operates at the level of the behavior. What is culpable can be made honorable through moral justifications and palliative characterizations (Gambino, 1973; Kelman, 1973). In this process, reprehensible conduct is made personally and socially acceptable by portraying it in the service of beneficial or moral ends. Such cognitive restructuring of behavior is an especially effective disinhibitor because it not only eliminates self-generated deterrents but engages self-reward in the service of the behavior.

Another set of dissociative practices operates by obscuring or distorting the relationship between actions and the effects they cause. By displacing and diffusing responsibility, people do not see themselves as personally accountable for their actions and are thus spared self-prohibiting reactions (Bandura, Underwood, & Fromson, 1975; Milgram, 1974). Additional ways of weakening self-deterring reactions operate by disregarding or obscuring the consequences of actions. When people embark on a self-disapproved course of action for personal gain, or because of other inducements, they avoid facing the harm they cause. Self-censuring reactions are unlikely to be activated as long as the detrimental effects of conduct are disregarded.

The final set of disengagement practices operates at the level of the recipients of injurious effects. The strength of self-evaluative reactions partly depends on how the people toward whom actions are directed are viewed. Maltreatment of individuals who are regarded as subhuman or debased is less apt to arouse self-reproof than if they are seen as human beings with dignifying qualities (Zimbardo, 1969). Detrimental interactions usually involve a series of reciprocally escalative actions in which the victims are rarely faultless. One can always select from the chain of events an instance of defensive behavior by the adversary as the original instigation. By blaming victims, one's own actions are excusable. The disengagement of internal control, whatever the means, is not achieved solely through personal deliberation. People are socially aided in this process by indoctrination, scapegoating, and pejorative stereotyping of people held in disfavor.

As is evident from preceding discussion, the development of self-regulatory functions does not create an automatic control system, nor do situational influences exercise mechanical control. Personal judgments operating at each subfunction preclude the automaticity of the process. There is leeway in judging whether a given behavioral standard is applicable. Because of the complexity and inherent ambiguity of most events, there is even greater leeway in the judgment of behavior and its effects. To add further to the variability of the control process, most activities are performed under collective arrangements that obscure responsibility, thus permitting leeway in judging the degree of personal agency in the effects that are socially produced. In short, there exists considerable latitude for personal judgmental factors to affect whether or not self-regulatory influences will be activated in any given activity.

Reciprocal Influence of Personal Factors on Reinforcement Effects

Reinforcement has commonly been viewed as a mechanistic process in which responses are shaped automatically and unconsciously by their immediate consequences. The assumption of automaticity of reinforcement is crucial to the argument of unidirectional environmental control of behavior. One can dispense with the so-called internal link in causal chains only if persons are conceived of as mechanical respondents to external stimuli. The empirical evidence does not support such a view (Bandura, 1977b; Bower, 1975; Mischel, 1973; Neisser, 1976). External influences operate largely through cognitive processes.

During ongoing reinforcement, respondents are doing more than simply emitting responses. They develop expectations from observed regularities about the outcomes likely to result from their actions under given situational circumstances. Contrary to claims that behavior is controlled by its immediate consequences, behavior is related to its outcomes at the level of aggregate consequences rather than momentary effects (Baum, 1973). People process and synthesize contextual and outcome information from sequences of events over long intervals about the action patterns that are necessary to produce given outcomes.

The notion that behavior is governed by its consequences fares better for anticipated than for actual consequences (Bandura, 1977b). We have already reviewed research demonstrating how the same environmental consequences have markedly different effects on behavior depending on respondents' beliefs about the nature of the relationships between actions and outcomes and the meaning of the outcomes. When belief differs from actuality, which is not uncommon, behavior is weakly influenced by its actual consequences until more realistic expectations are developed through repeated experience. But it is not always expectations that change in the direction of social reality. Acting on erroneous expectations can alter how others behave, thus shaping the social reality in the direction of the expectations.

While undergoing reinforcing experiences, people are doing more than learning the probabilistic contingencies between actions and outcomes. They observe the progress they are making and tend to set themselves goals of progressive improvement. Investigators who have measured personal goal setting as well as changes in performance find that external incentives influence behavior partly through their effects on goal setting (Locke, Bryan, & Kendall, 1968). When variations in personal goals are partialed out, the effects of incentives on performance are reduced. Performance attainments also provide an important source of efficacy information for judging one's personal capabilities. Changes in perceived self-efficacy, in turn, affect people's choices of activities, how much effort they expend, and how long they will persist in the face of obstacles and aversive experiences (Bandura, 1977a; Brown & Inouye, 1978).

Because of the personal determinants of reinforcement effects, to trace behavior back to environmental "reinforcers" by no means completes the explanatory regress. To predict how outcomes will affect behavior, one must know how they are cognitively processed. To understand fully the mechanisms through which consequences change behavior, one must analyze the reciprocally contributory influences of cognitive factors.

Reciprocal Determinism as a Generic Analytic Principle

The discussion thus far has primarily addressed issues regarding the reciprocal interactions between behavior, thought, and environmental events as they occur at the individual level. Social learning theory treats reciprocal determinism as a basic principle for analyzing psychosocial phenomena at varying levels of complexity, ranging from intrapersonal development, to interpersonal behavior, to the interactive functioning of organizational and societal systems. At the intrapersonal level, people's conceptions influence what they perceive and do, and their conceptions are in turn altered by the effects of their actions and the observed consequences accruing to others (Bandura, 1977a; Bower, 1975). Information-processing models are concerned mainly with internal mental operations. A comprehensive theory must also analyze how conceptions are converted to actions, which furnish some of the data for conceptions. In social learning theory, people play an active role in creating information-generating experiences as well as in processing and transforming informative stimuli that happen to impinge upon them. This involves reciprocal transactions between thought, behavior, and environmental events which are not fully encompassed by a computer metaphor. People are not only perceivers, knowers, and actors. They are also self-reactors with capacities for reflective self-awareness that are generally neglected in information-processing theories based on computer models of human functioning.

At the level of interpersonal behavior, we have previously examined how people reciprocally determine each others' actions (Bandura et al., 1960; Patterson, 1975; Raush et al., 1974). Although the mutuality of behavior may be the focus of study, the reciprocal processes involve cognition as well as action. At the broader societal level, reciprocal processes are reflected in the interdependence of organizational elements, social subsystems, and transnational relations (Bandura, 1973; Keohane & Nye, 1977). Here the matters of interest are the patterns of interdependence between systems, the criteria and means used for gauging systemic performances, the mechanisms that exist for exercising reciprocal influence, and the conditions that alter the degree and type of reciprocal control that one system can exert on another.

It is within the framework of reciprocal determinism that the concept of freedom assumes meaning (Bandura, 1977b). Because people's conceptions, their behavior, and their environments are reciprocal determinants of each other, individuals are neither powerless objects controlled by environmental forces nor entirely free agents who can do whatever they choose. People can be considered partially free insofar as they shape future conditions by influencing their courses of action. By creating structural mechanisms for reciprocal influence, such as organizational systems of checks and balances, legal systems, and due process and elective procedures, people can bring their influence to bear on each other. Institutional reciprocal mechanisms thus provide not only safeguards against unilateral social control but the means for changing institutions and the conditions of life. Within the process of reciprocal determinism lies the opportunity for people to shape their destinies as well as the limits of self-direction.

References

Bandura, A. (1973). *Aggression: A social learning analysis.* Englewood Cliffs, NJ: Prentice-Hall.

Bandura, A. (1974). Behavior theory and the models of man. *American Psychologist, 29,* 859–869.

Bandura, A. (1976). Self-reinforcement: Theoretical and methodological considerations. *Behaviorism, 4,* 135–155.

Bandura, A. (1977a). Self-efficacy: Toward a unifying theory of behavioral change. *Psychological Review, 84,* 191–215.

Bandura, A. (1977b). *Social learning theory.* Englewood Cliffs, NJ: Prentice-Hall.

Bandura, A., & Adams, N. E. (1977). Analysis of self-efficacy theory of behavioral change. *Cognitive Therapy and Research, 1,* 287–308.

Bandura, A., Grusec, J. E., & Menlove, F. L. (1967). Some social determinants of self-monitoring reinforcement systems. *Journal of Personality and Social Psychology, 5,* 449–455.

Bandura, A., Lipsher, D. H., & Miller, P. E. (1960). Psychotherapists' approach-avoidance reactions to patients' expression of hostility. *Journal of Consulting Psychology, 1960,* 1–8.

Bandura, A., Mahoney, M. J., & Dirks, S. J. (1976). Discriminative activation and maintenance of contingent self-reinforcement. *Behaviour Research and Therapy, 14,* 1–6.

Bandura, A., Underwood, B., & Fromson, M. E. (1975). Disinhibition of aggression through diffusion of responsibility and dehumanization of victims. *Journal of Research in Personality, 9,* 253–269.

Bandura, A., & Walters, R. H. (1959). *Adolescent aggression.* New York: Ronald.

Bateson, G. (Ed.). (1961). *Perceval's narrative: A patient's account of his psychosis, 1830–1832.* Stanford, CA: Stanford University Press.

Baum, W. M. (1973). The correlation-based law of effect. *Journal of the Experimental Analysis of Behavior, 20,* 137–153.

Bower, G. H. (1975). Cognitive psychology: An introduction. In W. K. Estes (Ed.), *Handbook of learning and cognition.* Hillsdale, NJ: Erlbaum.

Brown, I., Jr., & Inouye, D. K. (1978). Learned helplessness through modeling: The role of perceived similarity in competence. *Journal of Personality and Social Psychology, 36,* 900–908.

Gambino, R. (1973). Watergate lingo: A language of nonresponsibility. *Freedom at Issue,* No. 22.

Goldfried, M. R., & Merbaum, M. (Eds.). (1973). *Behavior change through self-control.* New York: Holt, Rinehart & Winston.

Kelman, H. C. (1973). Violence without moral restraint: Reflections on the dehumanization of victims and victimizers. *Journal of Social Issues, 29,* 25–61.

Keohane, R. O., & Nye, J. S. (1977). *Power and interdependence: World politics in transition.* Boston: Little, Brown.

Krauss, I. (1964). Sources of educational aspirations among working-class youth. *American Sociological Review, 29,* 867–879.

Lepper, M. R., Sagotsky, J., & Mailer, J. (1975). Generalization and persistence of effects of exposure to self-reinforcement models. *Child Development, 46,* 618–630.

Locke, E. A., Bryan, J. F., & Kendall, L. M. (1968). Goals and intentions as mediators of the effects of monetary incentives on behavior. *Journal of Applied Psychology, 52*(2), 104–121.

Mahoney, M. J., & Thoresen, C. E. (1974). *Self-control: Power to the person.* Monterey, CA: Brooks/Cole.

Masters, J. C., & Mokros, J. R. (1974). Self-reinforcement processes in children. In H. W. Reese (Ed.), *Advances in child development and behavior* (Vol. 9). New York: Academic Press.

Milgram, S. (1974). *Obedience to authority: An experimental view.* New York: Harper & Row.

Mischel, W. (1973). Toward a cognitive social learning reconceptualization of personality. *Psychological Review, 80,* 252–283.

Neisser, U. (1976). *Cognition and reality: Principles and implications of cognitive psychology.* San Francisco: W. H. Freeman.

Patterson, G. R. (1975). The aggressive child: Victim and architect of a coercive system. In L. A. Hamerlynck, E. J. Mash, & L. C. Handy (Eds.), *Behavior modification and families.* New York: Brunner/Mazel.

Raush, H. L., Barry, W. A., Hertel, R. K., & Swain, M. A. (1974). *Communication conflict and marriage.* San Francisco: Jossey-Bass.

Simon, K. M. (1978). *Self-evaluative reactions to one's own performances: The role of personal significance of performance attainments.* Unpublished manuscript, Stanford University.

Skinner, B. F. (1971). *Beyond freedom and dignity.* New York: Knopf.

Thomas, E. A. C., & Martin, J. A. (1976). Analyses of parent-child interaction. *Psychological Review, 83,* 141–156.

Wallace, I. (1977). Self-control techniques of famous novelists. *Journal of Applied Behavior Analysis, 10,* 515–525.

Zimbardo, P. G. (1969). The human choice: Individuation, reason, and order versus deindividuation, impulse, and chaos. In W. J. Arnold & D. Levine (Eds.), *Nebraska Symposium on Motivation* (Vol. 17). Lincoln: University of Nebraska Press.

Personality Coherence and Dispositions in a Cognitive-Affective Personality System (CAPS) Approach

Walter Mischel

Another one-time social learning theorist who is helping to develop the cognitive approach to personality is Walter Mischel, whose critique of personality traits we read in Part II. Mischel's main complaint about personality traits is that because they seek to identify average behavioral tendencies, they tend to treat an individual's distinctive reactions to particular situations as random fluctuation or measurement error. Mischel believes that the real essence of personality is not to be found in the global averages of trait assessments, but in the fine-grained analysis of how each individual changes his or her behavior according to the situation he or she is in. The present chapter summarizes Mischel's latest theoretical thinking on these issues.

The chapter begins with a reprise of Mischel's version of the person-situation debate, which is widely viewed as a debate that he started. It is interesting to compare this summary with, for example, the summary by Kenrick and Funder in Part II, and his complaints about "global traits" in these authors' rendition in Part II. Mischel's conclusion is that personality theory needs to pay increased attention to the processes that underlie each individual's distinct pattern of if . . . then responses to particular situations. The idea is that for each individual, if one thing happens, then he or she will respond in a particular way, and this pattern across situations is distinctive for each individual. He proceeds to describe his "Cognitive-Affective Personality System" (CAPS) approach, which attempts to integrate a large amount of knowledge about cognition, emotion, behavior, and even physiology.

Mischel's chapter ends on a conciliatory note, observing that the trait and cognitive approaches to personality have been split into almost warring camps, but that they really, in the final analysis, are studying the same thing. It could be observed, for example—though Mischel does not make this observation—that personality traits could themselves be construed as if . . . then patterns. If a sociable person is at a party, then he will try to meet everyone in the room; if a dominant person enters a business meeting, then she will quickly take charge, and so on. In any event, Mischel is surely correct to observe that a complete account of personality must include both average tendencies that characterize a person across contexts and throughout life as well as the distinctive patterns of how people respond to particular and ever-changing situations.

From D. Cervone and Y. Shoda (Eds.), *The coherence of personality: Social cognitive bases of consistency, organization, and variability* (pp. 37–60). New York: Guilford Press, 1999.

In the last decade, fundamental controversies and debates in the search for personality coherence have been replaced by discoveries and reconceptualizations that identify and explain its nature and structure. These efforts promise to resolve paradoxes that have long split the area of personality and to advance personality theory in line with exciting progress in other areas of social and cognitive science. In this chapter, I consider personality coherence, dispositions, dynamics, and structure from the perspective of a social-cognitive-affective processing approach (e.g., Mischel & Shoda, 1995, 1998). After quickly sketching some of the history that impacts on the present scene, I turn to the current agenda, focusing on aspects of personality coherence and personality theory that merit attention but that risk being neglected within the contemporary social-cognitive framework. * * *

* * *

My particular emphasis will be on the construct of personality dispositions and its role and potential value within a processing approach to personality in a broadly social-cognitive framework. I try to show that dispositions can readily be incorporated within such a framework at several different levels of analysis that are easily confused and need to be distinguished. A unitary approach in the study of personality that encompasses both dispositions and the processes that underlie them seems to me sorely needed given the depth of the unconstructive splits that have occurred within the area of personality, as also discussed in this chapter. But first, I consider the history that has led us here and that needs to be understood in an effort to resolve the issues that remain.

The Past: Consistency Lost?

PARADIGM PERTURBATIONS

This volume goes to press in the 70th anniversary year of the discoveries by Hartshorne and May (1928), and concurrently by Newcomb (1929), that the cross-situational consistency of behavior—which they assessed empirically in school and camp settings with such laborious care and at high cost—seemed to be grossly discrepant from the assumptions of the classical personality trait conceptions that guided their search: Namely, it was assumed that individuals are characterized by behavioral dispositions (like the tendency to be conscientious or honest or sociable) that are manifested relatively stably and consistently across many different types of situations. Their failure to find strong support for this belief only briefly perturbed the then-young field (although it did lead Newcomb to switch his career from personality to social psychology). But their studies did not challenge the traditional trait paradigm: Mainstream work within it continued and accelerated—as it still does.

The assessment needs of World War II demanded quick personality trait measurements and further stimulated work within the traditional paradigm with little time or opportunity to evaluate the utility or the theoretical implications of the results. It was not until 40 years after the discoveries of Hartshorne, May, and Newcomb, that the paradigm itself was challenged (Mischel, 1968; Peterson, 1968). That confrontation, now having its 30th anniversary, grew out of the embarrassing discrepancy between the numbers found in the extensive data that had accumulated and the still-regnant and unruffled classic trait theoretical assumptions of the field. It became apparent to quite a few personality researchers that we were ending our discussion sections with more apologies and self-criticisms than conclusions.

PARADIGM CRISIS The upsets that spiraled into a paradigm crisis converged from several directions: A core assumption of trait psychology concerning the cross-situational consistency of behavior was contradicted by the small albeit nonzero (but not by much) cross-situational consistency coefficients found when researchers actually assessed people's behavior across even seemingly similar situations. Simultaneously, analyses of the utility of the approach for the prediction of behavior in particular situations, as well as its explanatory power, cast deep doubts on both.

Classic psychodynamic theory was the major alternative available at that time and hence the tempting option. It made no assumption of cross-situational consistency in behavior (nor claimed any predictive utility) but relied crucially on clinical judgments. The theory's Achilles' heel was that the accuracy and utility of those inferences and judgments were undermined by evidence documenting the limitations of clinicians and their proneness to self-deceptive illusions of confidence (Chapman & Chapman, 1969; Mischel, 1968; Peterson, 1968). Consequently both routes to personality coherence and to personality itself—behavioral dispositions and underlying dynamics—were vulnerable.

Although *Personality and Assessment* (Mischel, 1968) was started with the intention of reviewing the state of the field, it was seen as a glove hurled to the ground. The first reactions in the early 1970s seemed devoted to arguing against the legitimacy of the critique and tried to deny its validity. (When first published, it was reviewed briefly on a back page of *Contemporary Psychology* and dismissed under the header "Personality Unvanquished.") In the next decade, the controversies and paradoxes of the field concerning the nature, locus, and even existence of personality coherence were articulated and debated and in time researched. Various routes both for continuing business as usual or for finding

constructive alternatives and solutions were outlined and pursued.

The heated disputes that then raged sharpened and often exaggerated the differences between approaches. One fallout was the warfare between social and personality psychologists. In those battles, for at least a decade, the former were seen as the champions of the situation and its power (Nisbett & Ross, 1980), and the latter felt themselves the beleaguered defenders of the person and the construct of personality (e.g., Carlson, 1971). Although that may by now seem like ancient history, it remains relevant for the current agenda as background for understanding the almost reflexive hostility that developed between two subdisciplines that previously had been unified in a constructive collaboration.

The early consequences of these confrontations included dividing the flagship *Journal of Personality and Social Psychology* into three separate unconnected sections, one for social cognition and attitudes, one for interpersonal processes, one for personality—a move virtually guaranteed to obstruct efforts to understand persons (including their minds, feelings, and relationships) in their contexts. For more than a decade in this new structure, the third part, Personality, defined its mission as welcoming articles devoted to personality "as traditionally defined," that is, in terms of broad traits, suggesting a perspective that seems more defensive than scientific. Overcoming that unfortunate way of parsing the variance and the enterprise has been perhaps the largest barrier in the search for personality coherence, in my view, and fortunately, there now are creative routes for doing so. * * *

* * *

The Present:
A Split Personality Psychology

* * * After years of debate, at last there was consensus about the state of the data—the average cross-situational consistency coefficient is nonzero but not by much (Bem, 1983; Epstein, 1983; Funder, 1983). But there was and is deep disagreement

about how to interpret the data and proceed in the field of personality psychology. Two main alternatives developed, often in seeming opposition and conflict.

The Mainstream Aggregation Solution: Remove the Situation to Find Broad Behavioral Dispositions

The most widely accepted strategy adopted within the mainstream behavioral disposition approach to personality acknowledges the low cross-situational consistency in behavior found from situation to situation: It then systematically removes the situation by aggregating the individual's behavior on a given dimension (e.g., "conscientiousness") over many different situations (or "items") to estimate an overall "true score" (as discussed in Epstein, 1979, 1980; Mischel & Peake, 1982). That approach can be extremely useful for many goals, but its limits—as well as its strengths—are seen by analogy to meteorology, as Mischel and Shoda (1995) discussed. Although overall climatic trends surely are worth knowing, if meteorologists were to focus only on the aggregate climatic trends, they would neglect the atmospheric processes that underlie the changing weather patterns, as well as give up the goal of more accurate specific weather predictions.

Thus bypassing the issues that had been raised in the "paradigm crisis," much of contemporary mainstream personality psychology proceeds in an atmosphere its advocates describe as "euphoria" within an unrevised and even more extreme global trait framework (e.g., Funder, 1991), particularly the optimistically named Big Five (e.g., Goldberg, 1993; McCrae & Costa, 1996, 1997). It focuses on identifying a few broad behavioral dispositions that will manifest themselves stably across many situations and that characterize the individual in trait terms with regard to their position on each of the five factors. It does so in coexistence with sharply critical reviews of the problems and data that continue to undermine this approach fundamentally (e.g., Block, 1995; McAdams, 1992; Pervin, 1994)—criticisms and data that seem unnervingly similar to those that stirred the crises three decades earlier—and that apparently still remain largely unheeded.

The Alternative Route: Search for Social-Cognitive-Motivational Processes Underlying Person × Situation Interactions

Social and personality psychologists who were unwilling to bypass the role of the situation and thus did not accept the field's mainstream solution—nor its sense of euphoria—have been pursuing their separate routes in a framework now called "social-cognitive" (or "cognitive-social"). Some of the main themes for this alternative route were outlined originally in the "cognitive social learning reconceptualization of personality" (Mischel, 1973). Its goal was to make clear that the 1968 critique of the state of personality required not abandoning the construct of personality but rather *reconceptualizing* it to encompass within it the complex and often subtle interactions between person and situation that characterize individuals and types.

With that aim, the proposal identified the types of social-cognitive and motivational variables and principles required for a mediating process account of person–situation interactions and personality coherence. In this account, personality is conceptualized in terms of such constructs as how the individual encodes or appraises particular types of situations, the relevant expectancies and values that become activated, and the competencies and self-regulatory strategies available (Mischel, 1973, 1990). The behavior patterns that unfold depend on the interactions among these person variables in relation to the particular type of situation (e.g., Mischel & Shoda, 1995).

The last quarter-century has seen diverse creative efforts in this general framework and in many novel directions to conceptualize and clarify personality-relevant processes and principles (e.g., Mischel, 1998). Although each has its distinctive features and focus, most share the goal of wanting to explain the nature of intraindividual coherence and the mechanisms and conditions that generate it. * * *

RECONCEPTUALIZING—AND FINDING—COHERENCE IN UNEXPECTED PLACES

Much of the research that Shoda and I and our colleagues pursued within this general framework in recent years was directed at clarifying the nature of personality consistency. Briefly, our reasoning (in accord with Mischel, 1973; Mischel & Shoda, 1995, 1998) was that if personality is a stable system that processes the information about the situations, external or internal, then it follows that, as individuals encounter different situations, their behaviors should vary across the situations. These variations should reflect important differences among the individuals in the psychologically active features for them and in the ways they process them. That is, they should reflect, in part, the structure and organization of their personality systems, for example, how they encoded the situations and the expectations, affects, and goals that became activated within them (Mischel & Shoda, 1995).

If . . . Then . . . Situation–Behavior Profiles. Over time this will generate distinctive and stable *if . . . then . . .* situation–behavior profiles of characteristic elevation and shape * * *. So that even if two people are similar in their overall average "aggressiveness," for example, they will manifest distinctive, predictable patterns of behavioral variability in their *if . . . then . . .* signatures of when and with whom and where they do and do not aggress. These expectations have been extensively supported empirically (e.g., Shoda, Mischel, & Wright, 1993a, 1993b, 1994).

These profiles provide a glimpse of the pattern of behavior variation in relation to situations that is expressive of personality invariance but that is completely bypassed in the traditional search for cross-situational consistency. Instead of searching for the traditional cross-situational consistency coefficient that has been pursued for most of the century (e.g., Hartshorne & May, 1928; Mischel, 1968; Newcomb, 1929; Peterson, 1968; Vernon, 1964), personality coherence can be found—and should be expected—in the intraindividual stable pattern of variability.

The results also make it evident that a focus on the relationships between psychological features of situations and the individual's patterns of behavior, rather than undermining the existence of personality, has to become part of the assessment and conception of personality (e.g., Mischel, 1973, 1990; Wright & Mischel, 1987; Shoda & Mischel, 1993; Shoda et al., 1994). It is obvious of course that if situation units are defined in terms of features salient for the researcher but trivial for, or irrelevant to, the individuals studied, one cannot expect their behaviors to vary meaningfully across them. In that case, the resulting pattern of behavior variation may well be unstable and meaningless. To discover the potentially predictable patterns of behavior variability that characterize individuals, one first has to identify those features of situations that are meaningful to them and that engage their important psychological qualities (e.g., their ways of encoding or construing, their expectancies, and goals). Fortunately the methodology to make that possible is now becoming available (e.g., Shoda et al., 1994; Wright & Mischel, 1987).

BEHAVIORAL SIGNATURES OF PERSONALITY: THE LOCUS OF SELF-PERCEIVED CONSISTENCY AND DISPOSITIONAL JUDGMENTS The profiles of situation–behavior relations that characterize a person constitute a sort of "behavioral signature of personality" that in turn is linked to the person's self-perceived consistency and sense of coherence (Mischel & Shoda, 1995; Shoda et al., 1993b). This was found in a reanalysis by Mischel and Shoda (1995) of the Carleton College field study (Mischel & Peake, 1982). In that study, college students were repeatedly observed on campus in various situations relevant to their conscientiousness in the college setting (such as in the classroom, in the dormitory, in the library, assessed over repeated occasions in the semester). Students who perceived themselves as consistent did not show greater overall cross-situational consistency than those who did not. But for individuals who perceived themselves as consistent, the average situation–behavior profile stability correlation was near .5,[1] whereas it was trivial for those who viewed themselves as inconsistent. So it is the stability in the situation–behavior profiles (e.g., conscientious about homework but not about punctuality), not the cross-situational consistency of behavior that underlies the perception of consistency with regard to a type of behavior or disposition.

In sum, relatively stable situation–behavior profiles reflect characteristic intraindividual patterns in how the person relates to different psychological conditions or features of situations, forming a sort of behavioral signature of personality (Shoda et al., 1994). The stability of these situation–behavior profiles in turn predicts the self-perception of consistency as well. These profiles are also linked to the dispositional judgments made about the person by others (Shoda et al., 1994). The surprise is not simply that this type of behavioral signature of personality exists, but rather that it has so long been treated as error and deliberately removed by averaging behavior over diverse situations to remove their role. Ironically, although such aggregation was intended to capture personality, it actually can delete data that reflect the individual's most distinctive qualities and unique intraindividual patterning.

These expectations and findings are congruent with classic processing theories, most notably Freud's conception of psychodynamics. In that view, people's underlying processing dynamics and qualities—the construals and goals, the motives and passions, that drive them—may be reflected not only in how often they display particular types of behavior but also in when and where, and thus also, and most importantly, *why* that behavior occurs. In short, this type of model expects that the stable patterns of situation–behavior relationships that characterize persons provide potential keys to their dynamics. They are informative roads to the underlying system that produces them, not sources of error to be eliminated systematically by aggre-

gating out the situation. Thus, in the present approach, the concept of the invariances in the expression of personality is broadened to encompass the profile of situation–behavior relations that might characterize the person, not just the overall average level of particular types of behavior aggregated across diverse situations (e.g., Shoda et al., 1993a, 1994).

Personality Reconsidered: Toward a Unifying Framework

The above findings—and the confirmation of the hypotheses that predicted them—directly violate the assumptions made if one conceptualizes personality in terms of traits as behavioral dispositions. In that classic view, the intraindividual variations in a type of behavior across situations, given that the main effects of situations are removed by standardization, should reflect only intrinsic unpredictability or measurement error. If that assumption were correct, then the stability of the intraindividual pattern of variation should on average be zero. The finding that the situation–behavior profiles reliably reflect a statistically significant, stable facet of individual differences in social behavior thus has major implications for how one thinks about personality coherence and the kind of personality model that is needed.

The data provide clear evidence at the level of *in vivo* behavior observed extensively as it unfolds across situations and over time in everyday life (Mischel & Shoda, 1995). They are consistent with parallel findings showing significant amounts of variance attributable to person × situation interaction in analysis of variance studies, based on questionnaire responses (e.g., Endler & Hunt, 1969; Endler & Magnusson, 1976; Endler, Hunt, & Rosenstein, 1962; Magnusson & Endler, 1977). Furthermore, as shown elsewhere (Shoda, 1990), the degree that an individual is characterized by stable patterns of situation–behavior relations is necessarily negatively related to the level of overall cross-situational consistency that can be expected, making it clear that the quest for higher cross-situational consistency coefficients is bound to be futile.

---

[1]This .5 is a correlation coefficient of the sort explained by Rosenthal and Rubin in their selection in Part I.

The need now is for a personality theory, or at least an approach to personality, designed to try to predict and explain these signatures of personality, rather than to eliminate or ignore them. Such an approach requires rethinking the nature of personality coherence, and of personality dispositions, structure, and dynamics, as discussed next.

PERSONALITY AS AN ORGANIZED DYNAMIC SYSTEM

A first requirement is to develop a processing model of the personality system at the level of the individual (Mischel & Shoda, 1995). In such a model, person variables, no matter how important, function not just as single, isolated variables but as components that are interconnected within an organized system of relationships that in turn interacts with the social-psychological situations in which the system is activated (e.g., Shoda & Mischel, 1998). That also requires conceptualizing the "situation" not just as a setting but in psychological terms (Shoda et al., 1994).

In short, an urgent theoretical need is to conceptualize personality as an organized system that is interactive and dynamic—a system that accounts both for intraindividual coherence and stability, on the one hand, and for plasticity and discriminativeness in behavior, on the other hand. It needs to take account of the individual's characteristic dispositions as well as of the dynamic mediating processes that underlie them. It has to consider not only social-cognitive-motivational and affective determinants and processes but also biological and genetic antecedents and levels. And it must be able to deal with the complexity of human personality and the cognitive-affective dynamics, conscious and unconscious—both 'cool' and 'hot,' cognitive and emotional, rational and impulsive— that underlie the individual's distinctive, characteristic internal states and external behavioral expressions (see Metcalfe & Jacobs, 1998; Metcalfe & Mischel, 1999).

A number of recent processing models now focus not just on how much of a particular mental representation or unit (e.g., of self-efficacy expectations, of fear of failure) a person has, but rather on how the units are related to each other within the processing system. These interconnections form a unique network that functions as an organized whole—a dynamic interacting, processing system that can operate rapidly in parallel at multiple levels of accessibility, awareness, and automaticity. Rather than conceptualizing the individual as a bundle of mediating variables or as a flow chart of discrete procedures and decision rules, this provides a more parallel and distributed (rather than serial, centralized) processing system. Particularly promising developments come from recent work in cognitive neuroscience, such as the neural network theories and connectionist models (e.g., Anderson, 1996; Kandel & Hawkins, 1992; Rumelhart & McClelland, 1986). Within such a framework, one can begin to conceptualize social information processing in terms of a dynamic organized network of interconnected and interacting represen-tations—cognitions and affects (e.g., Kunda & Thagard, 1996; Read & Miller, 1998; Shultz & Lepper, 1996)—operating at various levels of awareness (e.g., Westen, 1990). Our own attempt to move personality theory in this direction is the recently proposed cognitive-affective personality system (CAPS) (Mischel & Shoda, 1995, 1998; Shoda & Mischel, 1998).

COGNITIVE-AFFECTIVE PERSONALITY SYSTEM (CAPS)

According to CAPS, individuals differ first of all in the "chronic accessibility," that is, the ease, with which particular cognitive-affective units become activated. These units refer to the mental-emotional representations—the cognitions and affects or feelings—that are available to the person. Such mediating units were conceptualized initially in terms of five relatively stable person variables on which individuals differ in processing self-relevant information (Mischel, 1973). Over the years, these units have been modified by research (reviewed in Mischel & Shoda, 1995; Mischel, Cantor, & Feldman, 1996), and the units within the CAPS system now include affects and goals, as well as encodings, expectancies, beliefs, competencies, and self-regulatory plans and strategies.

Individual Differences in the Stable Organization of Relations among Units (Interconnections). The CAPS model goes beyond the earlier focus on person vari-

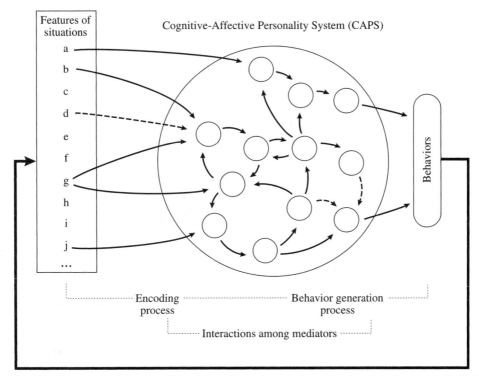

Figure 1. Simplified illustration of types of cognitive-affective mediating processes that generate an individual's distinctive behavior patterns. Situational features are encoded by a given mediating unit, which activates specific subsets of other mediating units, generating distinctive cognition, affect, and behavior in response to different situations. Mediating units become activated in relation to some situational features, deactivated (inhibited) in relation to others, and are unaffected by the rest. The activated mediating units affect other mediating units through a stable network of relations that characterize an individual. The relation may be positive (solid line), which increases the activation, or negative (dashed line), which decreases the activation. From Mischel and Shoda (1995). Copyright 1995 by the American Psychological Association, Inc. Reprinted by permission.

ables (Mischel, 1973) in emphasizing that stable individual differences reflect not only the accessibility of particular cognitions and affects but also the distinctive *organization of relationships* among them. This organization guides and constrains the activation of the particular cognitions, affects, and actions that are available within the system. It is this organization that constitutes the basic stable structure of personality and that underlies the behavioral signatures of personality described above.

CAPS is a system that interacts continuously and dynamically with the social world in which it is contextualized. It is activated in part by external situations and in part by its own internal cognitive and affective activities, including fantasy,

daydreaming, and planning (Mischel et al., 1996; Shoda & Mischel, 1996). The interactions with the external world involve a two-way reciprocal interaction: behaviors that the personality system generates impact on the social world, partly shaping and selecting the interpersonal situations the person subsequently faces and that, in turn, influence the person (e.g., Bandura, 1986; Buss, 1987).

Dynamic, Transactional System: The Active–Proactive Person. Figure 1 shows a schematic, greatly simplified CAPS system that is characterized by the available cognitive and affective units, organized in a distinctive network of interrelations. When certain features of a situation are perceived by the individual, a characteristic pattern of cognitions and affects (shown schematically as circles) becomes activated through this distinctive network of connections. The personality structure refers to the person's stable system of interconnections among the cognitive and affective units, and it is this structure that guides and constrains further activation of other units throughout the network. Ultimately the result is the activation of plans, strategies, and potential behaviors in a characteristic pattern that is situationally contextualized.

In CAPS, mediating units become activated in relation to some situation features but are deactivated or inhibited in relation to others and not affected by the rest. That is, the connections among units within the stable network that characterizes the person may be positive, which increases the activation, or negative (shown as broken lines in Figure 1), which decreases the activation.

The personality system anticipates, interprets, rearranges, and changes situations as well as reacts to them. It thus is active and indeed proactive, not just reactive. It not only responds to the environment but also may generate, select, modify, and shape situations in reciprocal transactions (Figure 2).

Activation of Personality Dynamics and Dispositions in Context. People differ characteristically in the particular situational features (e.g., being teased, being approached socially, feeling lonely) that are the salient active ingredients for them and that thus activate their characteristic and relatively predictable patterns of cognitive, affective, and behavioral reactions to those situations, that is, their distinctive processing dynamics (Mischel & Shoda, 1995). For example, some individuals readily respond aggressively to such ambiguous stimuli as having milk spilled on them in the cafeteria line (Dodge, 1986). There also are internal feedback loops within the system through which self-generated stimuli (as in thinking, fantasizing, daydreaming) activate their distinctive pathways of connections, triggering characteristic cognitive-

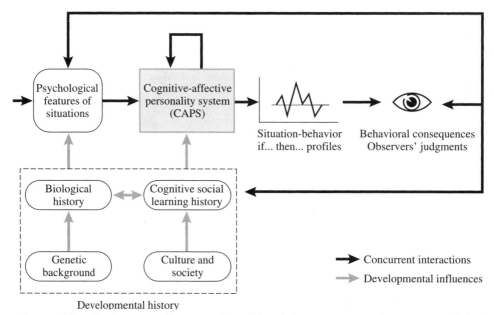

Developmental history

Figure 2. The cognitive-affective personality system (CAPS) in relation to concurrent interactions and developmental influences. From Mischel and Shoda (1995). Copyright 1995 by the American Psychological Association, Inc. Reprinted by permission.

affective-behavioral reaction patterns (e.g., Shoda & Mischel, 1998). The behaviors the person constructs may in turn affect the interpersonal environment and social ecology, which changes the situational features that are encountered subsequently (e.g., Dodge 1986, 1993, 1997a, 1997b).

Variations across Situations: Stable Individual Differences in Situation–Behavior, If . . . Then . . . Relations. It follows from the assumptions of the CAPS model that the variation in the person's behavior in relation to changing situations in part constitutes a potentially meaningful reflection of the personality system itself. Different cognitions, affects, and behaviors become activated as the situation and its features change, even when the interconnections among them remain unchanged across situations. That is, the personality system determines the *relationships* among the types of situations encountered and the cognitive, affective, and behavioral responses: Thus, as the *ifs* change, so do the *thens*, but the *relationship* between them is stable as long as the personality system remains unchanged. This assumption leads the approach to predict characteristic, predictable patterns of variation in the individual's behavior across situations— that is, the sorts of stable situation–behavior, *if . . . then . . .* profiles that were in fact found in the empirical studies summarized above (Mischel & Shoda, 1995).

Further support that CAPS generates the theoretically expected *if . . . then . . .* profiles came from a computer simulation (Mischel & Shoda, 1995; Shoda & Mischel, 1998). It was shown that individual differences in the connections (patterns of activation pathways) among the internal representations determine the links between features of situations and the outcomes generated by the system. An individual's unique configuration of person variables is manifested in the uniqueness of the *if . . . then . . .* profiles that unfold. Thus, to recapitulate, the personality system is expressed in the pattern with which a type of behavior varies over a set of situations, as well as in the average level of the behavior: Predictable variability in relation to context becomes a key to the individual's stability and

coherence, a sign of the underlying system that generates it.

The System in Action: Linking Processing Dynamics to Dispositions To illustrate such a system in action, consider a person characterized by the disposition of "rejection sensitivity" (Downey & Feldman, 1996; Downey, Freitas, Michaelis, & Khouri, 1997). When this person begins to discuss a relationship problem with a romantic partner, for example, his anxious expectations trigger the tendency to scan for evidence of imminent rejection and to focus on and encode those features of the situation most likely to provide such evidence (Downey & Feldman, 1996). These expectations, affects, and behaviors interact and combine to lead the person to readily perceive rejection even in ambiguous situations, which in turn tends to activate behavioral scripts for hostility (Ayduk, Downey, Testa, Yin, & Shoda, 1999). The hostility that is enacted can then elicit the partner rejection that is most feared, eroding the relationship in a self-defeating pattern, thereby confirming and maintaining rejection expectations (Downey et al., 1997).

Rejection sensitivity also illustrates the conditional nature of dispositions insofar as the activation of the characteristic pattern depends both on the situational features and on the cognitive-affective organization of the system. For example, the rejection-sensitive person becomes hostile specifically in relation to perceived rejection from a romantic partner but can behave exceptionally caringly and supportively in other situations (e.g., early in the relationship). Thus a characteristic and defining situation–behavior profile for this disposition may include both a tendency to become very angry and coercive and a tendency to be exceptionally sensitive and caring, each in its own distinctive context (Downey & Feldman, 1996). So the same rejection-sensitive man who coerces and abuses his partner also can behave in exceedingly tender and loving ways (e.g., Walker, 1979). He is both hurtful and kind, caring and uncaring, abusive and gentle.

Traditional analyses of such "inconsistencies" in personality raise the question "which one of these two people is the real one? What is simply the effect of the situation?" In contrast, the CAPS approach allows the same person to have contradictory facets that are equally genuine. The surface contradictions become comprehensible when one analyzes the network of relations among cognitions and affects to identify their psychological organization. The research problem becomes to understand when and why different cognitions and affects become activated predictably in relation to different features of situations, external and internal. The theory views the individual's distinctive patterns of variability not necessarily as internal contradictions but as the potentially predictable expressions of an underlying system that itself may remain quite stable in its organization. To reiterate, the stability of the disposition, which reflects the stability of the underlying system, is seen in the predictability of the *if . . . then . . .* profile, not in the consistency of behavior across different types of situations. The challenge is to discriminate, understand, and predict when each aspect will be activated and the dynamics that underlie the pattern. For example, are the caring and uncaring behaviors two scripts in the service of the same goal? If so, how are they connected to, and guided by, the person's self-conceptions and belief system in relation to the psychological features of situations that activate them?

REFINING AND REDEFINING THE CONSTRUCTS OF DISPOSITIONS, DYNAMICS, AND PERSONALITY STRUCTURE

Although it is widely asserted that process-oriented approaches to personality ignore or deny stable personality dispositions (e.g., Funder, 1991; Goldberg, 1993), in fact, in the present approach they have a significant role. The issue that does have to be addressed is just how to conceptualize "personality traits" or "dispositions" within a processing approach.

Given the depths of the splits and disputes that have occurred between the two approaches—personality as trait dispositions and personality as mediating underlying processes—it will not be a trivial task to reconcile and construct a unified theory and approach to personality. As Block (1995) and Pervin (1994) * * * make plain, the equation of the Big Five or any other set of global traits or factors with personality psychology is unacceptable and needs to be rejected. More generally, to understand intraindividual dynamics and the resultant behavioral signatures, one needs to reject making behavioral dispositions of any sort synonymous with personality. Nevertheless, it would be unwise to throw out with these false equations the concept of dispositions: That concept—a foundation stone in personality psychology—requires reanalysis and refinement rather than rejection.

Dispositional Levels. As a first step, it may be useful to distinguish some of the different levels of analysis in the study of dispositions, since at each level the definition and the relevant phenomena shift, and often the level is left unclear, easily leading to misunderstandings. Let us consider the following four levels.

Psychological processing level. At the "psychological processing level" of analysis, dispositions within the present perspective may be defined by a characteristic social cognitive-affective processing structure that underlies, and generates, distinctive processing dynamics within the personality system (Mischel & Shoda, 1995), depicted as CAPS in the solid rectangle of Figure 2. A characteristic set of cognitions, affects, and behavioral strategies in an organization of interrelations that guides and constrains their activation constitutes the processing structure of the disposition. The processing dynamics of the disposition refer to the patterns and sequences of activation among the mediating units—the mental representations—that are generated when these persons encounter or construct situations containing relevant features.

The processing dynamics are activated in relation to particular types of situational features (e.g., certain interpersonal encounters). Some of these stimuli are external, but others are internally generated in many ways, such as by thinking or ruminating about situations (e.g., Nolen-Hoeksema, Parker, & Larson, 1994), or through selective recall and reexperiences of past events and feelings, or by daydreaming, fantasies, and scenarios that are planned or imagined (e.g., Taylor & Schneider, 1989). Dynamics can also be self-activated by selective attention, such as to one's perceived strengths, resources, vulnerabilities, conflicts, ambivalences, and anticipated future (e.g., Bandura, 1986; Mischel, Ebbesen, & Zeiss, 1973, 1976; Norem & Cantor, 1986). The pattern of activation among cognitions and affects in the personality system at a given time may be defined as the *personality state*.

Behavioral level. At the level of directly observable behavior, the manifestations of a disposition and its processing dynamics are seen in the distinctive elevations and shapes of the situation–behavior profiles—the dispositional signatures—that distinguish its exemplars (see Figure 2). Individuals who have similar organizations of relations among cognitions and affects that become activated in relation to a particular distinctive set of situational features may be said to have a particular "processing disposition." These dispositions generate distinctive processing dynamics that become activated and, over time and contexts, will generate the situation–behavior profiles that have the characteristic elevations and shapes that identify the dispositional exemplars. It should be clear that, in this approach, personality psychologists do not have to choose between the study of dispositions or processes but can simultaneously analyze both the distinctive *if . . . then . . .* profiles that characterize the disposition's exemplars and illuminate the processes underlying them.

Perceived personality level: the observer's view. The behavioral manifestations of the personality system may be readily and consensually encoded by observers (the eye shown in Figure 2) as reflections of person prototypes or exemplars, (e.g., Cantor, Mischel, & Schwartz, 1982; Wright & Mischel, 1987, 1988) and of traits and types in everyday psycholexical terms, both by lay perceivers (e.g., Jones, 1990) and psychologists (e.g., John, 1990; Goldberg, 1993; McCrae & Costa, 1996).

These encodings are related not just to the mean levels of different types of behavior displayed by a person, but also to the shape of the *if . . . then . . .* profiles that express their pattern of variability

across situations. This was illustrated in a study that obtained personality prototype judgments for the sample of participants in the summer camp described in the first part of this article. As predicted, judgments by observers of how well individuals fit particular dispositional prototypes (e.g., the "friendly" child, the "withdrawn" child, the "aggressive" child) were related clearly to the shape of the observed-behavior situation profiles as well as to their average level of prototype-relevant behaviors (Shoda et al., 1993b). When the pattern of variability is changed, so are the personality judgments (Shoda, Mischel, & Wright, 1989).

Exemplars of different personality prototypes thus are characterized by distinctive patterns of stable *if . . . then . . .* profiles, as well as by the average frequency in their prototype-relevant behaviors, with high agreement. A "friendly person," for example, is seen as such not just because of her average level of friendliness but also because of the stable pattern of *if . . . then . . .* relationships, as in "friendly with people she knows personally but not with casual acquaintances at work" (Shoda & Mischel, 1993). Moreover, while perceivers often encode other people and themselves in terms of traits, they also under some conditions infer the cognitions and affects—the motives, goals, plans, and other person variables—that may underlie the behavior, functioning more like social-cognitive theorists than like trait theorists (Shoda & Mischel, 1993).

However, as discussed by Shoda and Mischel (1993), most research on the perception of personality has been constrained by sharing the traditional trait assumption that equates personality with global behavioral dispositions. It thus construes personality and situations as mutually exclusive and opposite influences. Given that assumption, information about how the target's behavior varies across different situations is usually deliberately not given to the perceiver, leaving the role of situation–behavior relationships relatively unexamined in person-perception studies. Finally, as Figure 2 also indicates, the characteristic behavior patterns generated by the system impact not only on the perceptions of others and of oneself but also modify the types of situations that will be subsequently encountered, producing a continuous reciprocal interaction between the behaviors generated and the psychological situations experienced.

Biochemical–genetic level: pre-dispositions at the biological substrate. The long-term developmental influences on the system, and the personality structures and dispositions that emerge within it, depend importantly on biological and genetic history as well as on cognitive-social learning history, and cultural–social influences (lower-left rectangle in Figure 2). Individuals differ in diverse biochemical–genetic–somatic factors that may be conceptualized as *pre*-dispositions. These *pre*-dispositions ultimately influence such personality-relevant qualities as sensory and psychomotor sensitivities and vulnerabilities, skills and competencies, temperament (including activity level and emotionality), chronic mood, and affective states. These in turn impact on the psychological system—such as CAPS—that emerges and is seen at the psychological level of analysis.

There are great individual differences within virtually every aspect of the biological human repertoire and genetic heritage that can have profound predisposing implications for the personality and behavior that ultimately develop (e.g., Plomin, DeFries, McClearn, & Rutter, 1997). These differences occur, for example, in sensory, perceptual–cognitive, and affective systems, in metabolic clocks and hormones, in neurotransmitters—in short, in the person's total biochemical–genetic–somatic heritage. These *pre*-dispositions interact with conditions throughout development and play out in ways that influence what the person thinks, feels and does. Even small differences among individuals at the biochemical–somatic level (e.g., in sensory-perceptual sensitivity, in allergy and decease proneness, in energy levels) may manifest ultimately as considerable differences in their experiences and behavior and in what comes to be perceived as their personalities.

Consequently, an adequate approach to personality coherence requires addressing not only the structure and organization of the cognitive-affective-behavioral processing system at the psychological level but also its biochemical–genetic predisposing foundations (Plomin et al., 1997; Saudino & Plomin, 1996). These genetic individual differences presumably at least indirectly affect how people construe or encode—and shape—their environments, which in turn produce important person–context interactions throughout the life course (Plomin, 1994; Saudino & Plomin, 1996).

Both biochemical and social-cognitive influences, heritable and learned, impact on the personality system at the psychological level. They influence both the cognitive-affective units that become available in the system and their organization, although the effects often are indirect. Variables of temperament or reactivity, such as activity, irritability, tension, distress, and emotional lability, visible early in life (Bates & Wachs, 1994), for example, seem to have important, albeit complexly interactive links to emotional and attentional processing and self-regulation (Rothbart, Derryberry, & Posner, 1994). These processes, in turn, should influence the organization of relations among the mediating units in the system and are likely to have important effects, for example, on the types of self-regulatory strategies and competencies that develop and that enable (or hinder) effective impulse control. Because this system, in turn, generates the specific, *if . . . then . . .* situation–behavior relations manifested, the theory predicts that individual differences in genetic–biochemical *pre*-dispositions, in the present view, will be manifested not only in the mean level of various types of behaviors, but in the behavioral signatures of personality, that is, the stable configuration of *if . . . then . . .* situation–behavior relations. When the system changes, either due to modification in the biological substrates or due to developmental changes and significant life events, the effects will also be seen at the behavioral level as a change in the relationships between the "ifs" and the "thens" in the situation–behavior profiles that characterize the person.

PURSUING DISPOSITIONS AND DYNAMICS IN A UNITARY FRAMEWORK Personality psychology has been committed since its beginnings to characterizing individuals in terms of their stable and distinctive qualities (e.g., Allport, 1937; Funder, 1991; Goldberg, 1993). Other personality theorists and researchers have focused instead on the processes that underlie these coherences and that influence how people function (e.g., Bandura, 1986; Cantor & Kihlstrom, 1987; Mischel, 1973; Pervin, 1990). These two goals—to identify and clarify personality dispositions or personality processes—have been pursued in two increasingly separated (and warring) subdisciplines with different agendas that seem to be in conflict with each other (Cervone, 1991; Cronbach, 1957, 1975; Mischel & Shoda, 1994).

The CAPS approach presented in this chapter suggests that both goals may be pursued in concert with no necessary conflict or incompatibility because, in this framework, dispositions and processing dynamics are two complementary facets of the same phenomena and of the same unitary personality system. The dispositional qualities of individuals are represented in the personality system in terms of particular enduring structures in the organization among cognitive-affective mediating units available to the person. This organization in the structure of the disposition guides and constrains the pattern of specific cognitions, affects, and potential behaviors and their interconnections that become activated by the relevant internal or external psychological features of situations. To illustrate, let us consider again the example of the disposition of rejection sensitivity. The expectations and anticipation of rejection, the readiness to encode even ambiguous experiences as rejecting, the tendency to overreact emotionally to such cues, the accessing of hostile and defensive scripts when these feelings arise—all these are characteristics of this disposition, and their activation in a distinct stable pattern defines its processing dynamics and enactment.

Misunderstandings in analyses of dispositions also can be avoided by realizing that they may be studied fruitfully at each of the four levels of analysis discussed above: at the psychological processing level of activated thoughts and feelings; at the behavioral level; at the level of the judgments of observers and of the self; and at the level of the predisposing biochemical–genetic and neural substrate. The basic caveat and crucial requirement for proceeding within a unitary framework, however, are that the construct of dispositions, and indeed of personality structure and dynamics, be revised and refined to take account of the data and theoretical developments on the nature of coherence—and thus of personality—that the last few decades have yielded. This chapter is intended as a step in that direction.

References

Allport, G. W. (1937). *Personality: A psychological interpretation.* New York: Holt, Rinehart & Winston.

Anderson, J. R. (1996). ACT: A simple theory of complex cognition. *American Psychologist, 51,* 355–365.

Ayduk, O. N., Downey, G., Testa, S., Yin, Y., & Shoda, Y. (1999). Does rejection elicit hostility in rejection sensitive women? *Social Cognition, 17,* 245–271.

Bandura, A. (1986). *Social foundations of thought and action: A social cognitive theory.* Englewood Cliffs, NJ: Prentice-Hall.

Bates, J. E., & Wachs, T. D. (1994). *Temperament: Individual differences at the interface of biology and behavior.* Washington, DC: American Psychological Association.

Bem, D. J. (1983). Further déjà vu in the search for cross-situational consistency: A response to Mischel and Peake. *Psychological Review, 90,* 390–393.

Block, J. (1995). A contrarian view of the five-factor approach to personality description. *Psychological Bulletin, 117,* 187–215.

Buss, D. M. (1987). Selection, evocation, and manipulation. *Journal of Personality and Social Psychology, 53,* 1214–1221.

Cantor, N., & Kihlstrom, J. F. (1987). *Personality and social intelligence.* Englewood Cliffs, NJ: Erlbaum.

Cantor, N., Mischel, W., & Schwartz, J. (1982). A prototype analysis of psychological situations. *Cognitive Psychology, 14,* 45–77.

Carlson, R. (1971). Where is the personality research? *Psychological Bulletin, 75,* 203–219.

Cervone, D. (1991). The two disciplines of personality psychology [Review of the *Handbook of personality: Theory and research*]. *Psychological Science, 2,* 371–376.

Chapman, L. J., & Chapman, J. P. (1969). Illusory correlations as an obstacle to the use of valid psychodiagnostic signs. *Journal of Abnormal Psychology, 74,* 271–280.

Cronbach, L. J. (1957). The two disciplines of scientific psychology. *American Psychologist, 12,* 671–684.

Cronbach, L. J. (1975). Beyond the two disciplines of scientific psychology. *American Psychologist, 30,* 116–127.

Dodge, K. A. (1986). A social information processing model of social competence in children. In M. Perlmutter (Ed.), *The Minnesota symposium on child psychology: Vol. 18. Cognitive perspectives on children's social behavioral development* (pp. 77–125). Hillsdale, NJ: Erlbaum.

Dodge, K. A. (1993). Social-cognitive mechanisms in the development of conduct disorder and depression. *Annual Review of Psychology, 44,* 559–584.

Dodge, K. A. (1997a, April). *Testing developmental theory through prevention trials.* Paper presented at the biennial meeting of the Society for Research in Child Development, Washington, DC.

Dodge, K.A. (1997b, April). *Early peer social rejection and acquired autonomic sensitivity to peer conflicts: Conduct problems in adolescence.* Paper presented at the biennial meeting of the Society for Research in Child Development, Washington, DC.

Downey, G., & Feldman, S. I. (1996). Implications of rejection sensitivity for intimate relationships. *Journal of Personality and Social Psychology, 70,* 1327-1343.

Downey, G., Freitas, A., Michaelis, B., & Khouri, H. (1997). The self-fulfilling prophecy in close relationships: Rejection sensitivity and rejection in romantic partners. *Journal of Personality and Social Psychology, 75,* 545–560.

Endler, N. S., & Hunt, J. (1969). Generalizability of contributions from sources of variance in the S-R inventories of anxiousness. *Journal of Personality, 37,* 1–24.

Endler, N.S., Hunt, J. M., & Rosenstein, A. J. (1962). An S-R inventory of anxiousness. *Psychological Monographs, 76*(536).

Endler, N. S., & Magnusson, D. (1976). Toward an interactional psychology of personality. *Psychological Bulletin, 83,* 956–974.

Epstein, S. (1979). The stability of behavior: I. On predicting most of the people much of the time. *Journal of Personality and Social Psychology, 37,* 1097–1126.

Epstein, S. (1980). The stability of behavior: II. Implications for psychological research. *American Psychologist, 35,* 790–806.

Epstein, S. (1983). The stability of confusion: A reply to Mischel and Peake. *Psychological Review, 90,* 179–184.

Funder, D. C. (1983). Three issues in predicting more of the people: A reply to Mischel and Peake. *Psychological Review, 90,* 283–289.

Funder, D. C. (1991). Global traits: a neo-Allportian approach to personality. *Psychological Science, 2,* 31–39.

Goldberg, L. R. (1993). The structure of phenotypic personality traits. *American Psychologist, 48,* 26–34.

Hartshorne, H., & May, A. (1928). *Studies in the nature of character: Vol. 1. Studies in deceit.* New York: Macmillan.

John, O. P. (1990). The big-five factor taxonomy: Dimensions of personality in the natural language and questionnaires. In L. A. Pervin (Ed.), *Handbook of personality: Theory and research* (pp. 66–100). New York: Guilford Press.

Jones, E. E. (1990). *Interpersonal perception.* New York: Macmillan.

Kandel, E. R., & Hawkins, R. D. (1992). The biological basis of learning and individuality. *Scientific American, 267*(3), 78–86.

Kunda, Z., & Thagard, P. (1996). Forming impressions from stereotypes, traits, and behaviors: A parallel-constraint-satisfaction theory. *Psychological Review, 103,* 284–308.

Magnusson, D., & Endler, N. S. (Eds.). (1977). *Personality at the crossroads: Current issues in interactional psychology.* Hillsdale, NJ: Erlbaum.

McAdams, D. P. (1992). The Five-Factor model in personality. *Journal of Personality, 60,* 329–361.

McCrae, R. R., & Costa, P. T., Jr. (1996). Toward a new generation of personality theories: Theoretical contexts for the five-factor model. In J. S. Wiggins (Ed.), *The five-factor model of personality: Theoretical perspectives* (pp. 51–87). New York: Guilford Press.

McCrae, R. R., & Costa, P. T. (1997). Conceptions and correlates of openness and to experience. In R. Hogan, J. Johnson, & S. Briggs (Eds.), *Handbook of personality psychology* (pp. 825–847). San Diego: Academic Press.

Metcalfe, J., & Jacobs W. J. (1998). Emotional memory: The effects of stress on "cool" and "hot" memory systems. In D. L. Medin (Ed.), *The psychology of learning and motivation: Vol. 38. Advances in research and theory* (pp. 187–222). San Diego, CA: Academic Press.

Metcalfe, J., & Mischel, W. (1999). A hot/cool system analysis of delay of gratification: Dynamics of willpower. *Psychological Review, 6.*

Mischel, W. (1968). *Personality and assessment.* New York: Wiley.

Mischel, W. (1973). Toward a cognitive social learning reconceptualization of personality. *Psychological Review, 80,* 252–283.

Mischel, W. (1990). Personality dispositions revisited and revised: A view after three decades. In L. A. Pervin (Ed.), *Handbook of personality: Theory and research* (pp. 111–134). New York: Guilford Press.

Mischel, W. (1998). *Introduction to personality* (6th ed.). Fort Worth, TX: Harcourt Brace.

Mischel, W., Cantor, N., & Feldman, S. (1996). Principles of self-regulation: The nature of willpower and self-control. In E. T. Higgins & A. W. Kruglanski (Eds.), *Social psychology: Handbook of basic principles* (pp. 329–360). New York: Guilford Press.

Mischel, W., Ebbesen, E. B., & Zeiss, A. R. (1973). Selective attention to the self: Situational and dispositional determinants. *Journal of Personality and Social Psychology, 27,* 129–142.

Mischel, W., Ebbesen, E. B., & Zeiss, A. R. (1976). Determinants of selective memory about the self. *Journal of Consulting and Clinical Psychology, 44,* 92–103.

Mischel, W., & Peake, P. K. (1982). In search of consistency: Measure for measure. In M. P. Zanna, E. T. Higgins, & C. P. Herman (Eds.), *Consistency in social behavior: The Ontario symposium* (Vol. 2). Hillsdale, NJ: Erlbaum.

Mischel, W., & Shoda, Y. (1994). Personality psychology has two goals: Must it be two fields? *Psychological Inquiry, 5,* 156–158.

Mischel, W., & Shoda, Y. (1995). A cognitive-affective system theory of personality: Reconceptualizing situations, dispositions, dynamics, and invariance in personality structure. *Psychological Review, 102*(2), 246–268.

Mischel, W., & Shoda, Y. (1998). Reconciling processing dynamics and personality dispositions. *Annual Review of Psychology, 49,* 229–258.

Newcomb, T. M. (1929). *Consistency of certain extrovert–introvert behavior patterns in 51 problem boys.* New York: Columbia University, Teachers College, Bureau of Publications.

Nisbett, R. E., & Ross, L. D. (1980). *Human inference: Strategies and shortcomings of social judgment. Century Psychology Series.* Englewood Cliffs, NJ: Prentice-Hall.

Nolen-Hoeksema, S., Parker, L. E. & Larson, J. (1994). Ruminative coping with depressed mood following loss. *Journal of Personality and Social Psychology, 67*, 92–104.

Norem, J. K., & Cantor, N. (1986). Anticipatory and post hoc cushioning strategies: Optimism and defensive pessimism in "risky" situations. *Cognitive Therapy and Research, 10*, 347–362.

Pervin, L. A. (Ed.). (1990). *Handbook of personality: Theory and research*. New York: Guilford Press.

Pervin, L. A. (1994). A critical analysis of trait theory. *Psychological Inquiry, 5*, 103–113.

Peterson, D. R. (1968). *The clinical study of social behavior*. New York: Appleton.

Plomin, R. (1994). *Genetics and experience: The developmental interplay between nature and nurture*. Newbury Park, CA: Sage.

Plomin, R., DeFries, J. C., McClearn, G. E., & Rutter, M. (1997). *Behavioral genetics* (3rd ed.). New York: Freeman.

Read, S. J., & Miller, L. C. (Eds.). (1998). *Connectionist models of social reasoning and social behavior*. Mahwah, NJ: Erlbaum.

Rothbart, M. K., Derryberry, D., & Posner, M. I. (1994). A psychobiological approach to the development of temperament. In J. E. Bates & T. D. Wachs (Eds.), *Temperament: Individual differences at the interface of biology and behavior* (pp. 83–116). Washington, DC: American Psychological Association.

Rumelhart, D. E., & McClelland, J. L. (1986). *Parallel distributing processing: Explorations in the microstructure of cognition: Foundations* (Vol. 1). Cambridge, MA: MIT Press/Bradford Books.

Saudino, K. J., & Plomin, R. (1996). Personality and behavioral genetics: Where have we been and where are we going? *Journal of Research in Personality, 30*, 335–347.

Shoda, Y. (1990). *Conditional analyses of personality coherence and dispositions*. Unpublished doctoral dissertation, Columbia University, New York.

Shoda, Y., & Mischel, W. (1993). Cognitive social approach to dispositional inferences: What if the perceiver is a cognitive-social theorist? *Personality and Social Psychology Bulletin, 19*, 574–585.

Shoda, Y., & Mischel, W. (1996). Toward a unified, intraindividual dynamic conception of personality. *Journal of Research in Personality, 30*, 414–428.

Shoda, Y., & Mischel, W. (1998). Reconciling processing dynamics and personality dispositions. *Annual Review of Psychology, 49*, 229–258.

Shoda, Y., Mischel, W., & Wright, J. C. (1989). Intuitive interactionism in person perception: Effects of situation–behavior relations on dispositional judgments. *Journal of Personality and Social Psychology, 56*, 41–53.

Shoda, Y., Mischel, W., & Wright, J. C. (1993a). The role of situational demands and cognitive competencies in behavior organization and personality coherence. *Journal of Personality and Social Psychology, 56*, 41–53.

Shoda, Y., Mischel, W., & Wright, J. C. (1993b). Links between personality judgments and contextualized behavior patterns: Situation–behavior profiles of personality prototypes. *Social Cognition, 4*, 399–429.

Shoda, Y., Mischel, W., & Wright, J. C. (1994). Intraindividual stability in the organization and patterning of behavior: Incorporating psychological situations into the idiographic analysis of personality. *Journal of Personality and Social Psychology, 65*, 1023–1035.

Shultz, T. R., & Lepper, M. R. (1996). Cognitive dissonance reduction as constraint satisfaction. *Psychological Review, 103*, 219–240.

Taylor, S. E., & Schneider, S. (1989). Coping and the simulation of events. *Social Cognition, 7*, 174–194.

Vernon, P. E. (1964). *Personality assessment: A critical survey*. New York: Wiley.

Walker, L. E. (1979). *The battered women*. New York: Harper & Row.

Westen, D. (1990). Psychoanalytic approaches to personality. In L. A. Pervin (Ed.), *Handbook of personality: Theory and research* (pp. 21–65). New York: Guilford Press.

Wright, J. C., & Mischel, W. (1987). A conditional approach to dispositional constructs: The local predictability of social behavior. *Journal of Personality and Social Psychology, 53*, 1159–1177.

Wright, J. C., & Mischel, W. (1988). Conditional hedges and the intuitive psychology of traits. *Journal of Personality and Social Psychology, 55*, 454–469.

The Independent Effects of Goal Contents and Motives on Well-Being: It's Both What You Pursue and Why You Pursue It

Kennon M. Sheldon, Richard M. Ryan, Edward L. Deci, and Tim Kasser

One important reason people do different things is that they are pursuing different goals. These goals may encompass life-defining choices (such as career aims or plans for one's family life) or the immediate and the mundane (such as deciding what to do over the weekend or when to change the oil in one's car). The present article by Kennon Sheldon, Richard Ryan, Edward Deci, and Tim Kasser examines how the kinds of goals that people pursue and why they pursue them affect psychological health and well-being. For example, psychological well-being is undermined by pursuing goals limited to "extrinsic" outcomes such as fame or physical attractiveness, and promoted by pursuing "intrinsic" outcomes such as emotional intimacy and personal growth.

From *Personality and Social Psychology Bulletin, 30,* 475–486, 2004.

One important aspect of motivation concerns why people perform particular behaviors—that is, their perceived reasons or motives for engaging in the behaviors. Self-determination theory (SDT) (Deci & Ryan, 1985; Ryan & Deci, 2000) has argued that it is crucial to distinguish whether people act because they are autonomous and feel volitional in doing the behavior or rather because they are controlled and feel they have to do the behavior. SDT defines autonomy as "endorsing one's actions at the highest level of reflection" (Ryan, Kuhl, & Deci, 1997, p. 708), and it defines control as feeling pressured to think, feel, or behave in specific ways. Past studies have shown that autonomy and control fall on opposite sides of a motivational continuum (Ryan & Connell, 1989) and that people can be located on this continuum via a composite measure that weights autonomy positively and control negatively (e.g., Sheldon & Elliot, 1998, 1999; Sheldon & Kasser, 1998, 2001). Research has further shown that this relative autonomy index is positively associated with a variety of performance and mental health outcomes (see Deci & Ryan, 2000, for a review).

During the past decade, SDT also has paid increasing attention to the "what" of individuals' motivations, that is, to the specific contents, targets, or referents of people's goals (Ryan & Deci,

2000). In particular, the SDT literature has focused on the distinction between intrinsic goal contents and extrinsic goal contents (Kasser & Ryan, 1993, 1996, 2001; Sheldon & Kasser, 1995, 1998, 2001). Kasser and Ryan (1996) defined intrinsic goals (such as those for personal growth, emotional intimacy, and community involvement) as ones that are inherently rewarding to pursue, presumably because they directly satisfy innate psychological needs such as belongingness (Baumeister & Leary, 1995), effectance (White, 1959), and personal causation (DeCharms, 1968), or what SDT refers to as relatedness, competence, and autonomy (Deci & Ryan, 2000). In contrast, extrinsic goals (such as those for financial success, image, and fame) are less directly satisfying of the psychological needs. Of course, extrinsic goals can be instrumental for some satisfaction of the basic needs but SDT maintains that if extrinsic goals become particularly strong such that they are out of balance with intrinsic goals, then negative well-being consequences are likely to result.

*   *   *

The Present Studies

GENERAL DESIGN AND HYPOTHESES Three studies tested the hypothesis that extrinsic versus intrinsic goal contents would contribute independent variance to the prediction of well-being, over and above the influence of autonomous versus controlled motives. This is an important issue for two reasons: First, psychological well-being is an important outcome, with many implications for mental health and adaptive functioning (Lyubomirsky, King, & Diener, 2003). Second, the "what" and "why" of motivation are two of the most important theoretical and empirical foci of motivation researchers. Thus, finding independent effects would support the broader claim that the content of goals and the dynamic motives underlying them are distinct and separable aspects of motivation.

Study 1 was a within-person study in which participants estimated how autonomous (vs. controlled) they would feel if they pursued goals of either an extrinsic or an intrinsic type, and also how happy they would be if they pursued these goals. Study 2 was a between-person cross-sectional study, examining the associations of the rated contents and motives of participants' self-generated goals with self-reports of concurrent well-being. Study 3 was between persons and longitudinal and examined both the contents and motives of college seniors' self-generated postgraduation goals as predictors of change in their well-being during their first postgraduation year. In all three studies, we expected goal contents and goal motives to have independent and distinguishable effects on well-being.

*   *   *

Study 1

Participants were provided with six personal goal statements: three representing extrinsic content domains (financial success, attractive image, and fame/popularity) and three representing intrinsic content domains (emotional intimacy, community contribution, and personal growth). Researchers have found that these six goals do indeed represent two distinct factors (Kasser & Ryan, 1996). In addition, all six types of goals appear regularly within people's idiographic listings of goals, although extrinsic goals are somewhat less frequently listed and are also somewhat less strongly endorsed (Sheldon & Kasser, 1995, 1998).

Participants first imagined that they were pursuing each goal and then rated how much each of four different reasons for pursuing the goal (two autonomous and two controlled) would contribute to their own motivation for pursuing that goal. Next, they rated how happy they thought they would be in pursuing each goal. * * * We expected that contents would predict significant independent variance in happiness ratings after motives were entered into the regression.

METHOD

Participants and Procedure. Questionnaire packets were administered in large group sessions to

802 introductory psychology students at the University of Missouri. Seven hundred and fourteen of them provided complete data and thus constituted the sample used in the analyses. These included 297 men and 417 women, 90% (643) of whom were Caucasian.

Measures. Participants first read a list of six personal goals and were asked to imagine that they were actually pursuing each goal in their own life. Three were intrinsic goals: "Having many close and caring relationships with others" (emotional intimacy), "Being fulfilled and having a very meaningful life" (personal growth), and "Helping to make the world a better place" (community contribution). The three extrinsic goals were as follows: "Being known and/or admired by many people" (fame/popularity), "Looking good and appearing attractive to others" (attractive image), and "Getting a job that pays very well and having a lot of nice possessions" (financial success). The six goals were listed in the following order: emotional intimacy, fame/popularity, attractive image, personal growth, financial success, and community contribution.

Participants were then presented with four different reasons why they might pursue goals, which were derived from self-determination theory (Ryan & Connell, 1989; Sheldon & Elliot, 1998, 1999; Sheldon & Kasser, 1995, 1998). The two autonomous reasons were "because you really identify with the goal" (identified motivation) and "because of the enjoyment or stimulation that this goal would provide you" (intrinsic motivation). The two controlled reasons were "because of the external rewards such as money, grades, or status that the goal may produce" (external motivation) and "because you would feel ashamed, guilty, or anxious if you did not have this goal" (introjected motivation). Using a 5-point scale, participants rated the degree to which they might pursue each of the six goals for the external reason, then for the introjected reason, then for the identified reason, and finally for the intrinsic reason. As in other work (e.g., Sheldon & Elliot, 1998, 1999; Sheldon & Kasser, 2001), a relative autonomy composite was

computed for each goal by adding the two autonomous motivation ratings and subtracting the two controlled motivation ratings. This procedure allowed us to evaluate the relative strength of autonomous versus controlled motivation, which has been the focus of many SDT-based studies.

* * *

Finally, participants rated "the personal happiness that you believe this goal would provide you," which served as the dependent variable. All ratings were made on a 1 (*not at all*) to 5 (*very much*) scale.

RESULTS

Preliminary Analyses. In all analyses, we focused on individual goals as the unit of analysis, with a sample of 4,284 goals composed of six goals from each of 714 participants. For the hypothesis tests, goal ratings were standardized within participants so person-level differences in scale use would be removed (Sheldon & Elliot, 1998, 2000). Thus, we were able to simultaneously evaluate both the a priori designated content of each goal (extrinsic or intrinsic) and the rated motivation of each goal (autonomous relative to controlled) as predictors of the happiness associated with the goal.

As a preliminary analysis, we examined whether the two contents of goals (extrinsic vs. intrinsic) would differ in their average levels of relative autonomy. * * * As expected, the extrinsic goals were associated with lower relative autonomy than intrinsic goals, $Ms = 1.25$ vs. 3.10, $t(4,282) = 23.76$, $p < .01$.[1]

Hypothesis Tests. The above analysis established that extrinsic goals were associated with relatively more controlled motivation, consistent with the findings of Carver and Baird (1998), Srivastava et

---

[1]The *t* statistic is commonly used to evaluate differences between groups (the numbers in parentheses are the degrees of freedom for the test); the *p* or significance level of .01 means that a difference this large would be expected only 1 time in 100 if there were no difference between these groups in the larger population.

TABLE 1

STUDY 1: RESULTS OF HIERARCHICAL REGRESSION PREDICTING EXPECTED HAPPINESS FROM RELATIVE AUTONOMY AND RELATIVE EXTRINSIC CONTENT

	R^2 Change	p Value	Beta	p Value
Step 1	.250	<.01		
Relative autonomy			.50	<.01
Step 2	.053	<.01		
Extrinsic content			−.26	<.01
Step 3	.001	>.40		
Product term			−.02	>.40

al. (2001), and past SDT research (Sheldon & Kasser, 1995, 1998). However, we hypothesized that extrinsic content would explain significant independent variance in happiness ratings despite this overlap. To test this, we used a hierarchical regression strategy in which happiness was first regressed onto motives (autonomous vs. controlled), after which content (extrinsic vs. intrinsic) was entered at the second step. We reasoned that our primary hypothesis would be supported if there were a significant change in R^2 at the second step of the regression.[2]

Table 1 contains the results. As predicted, the analysis revealed a significant main effect for relative autonomy on expected happiness at Step 1 (β = .50,[3] p < .01). More important in terms of the current argument, relative extrinsic content was significant at Step 2 (ΔR^2 = .053, p < .01, β = −.26).[4] At a third step of the equation we tested for an

interaction between the two factors and found the interaction term to be nonsignificant (ΔR^2 = .001, p > .42).[5]

As a supplemental analysis we examined the effects on happiness of only the financial success goal versus the three intrinsic goals to test more directly the Srivastava et al. (2001) assertion. In other words, we excluded the fame/popularity and attractive appearance goals, thus reducing the overall number of goals to 2,856. As in the primary analysis, happiness ratings were regressed onto motives at Step 1 and content at Step 2. In this analysis, relative autonomy was again significant at Step 1 (β = .50, p < .01) and relative financial success contributed significantly at Step 2 (ΔR^2 = .02, p < .01, β = −.16). Again, there was no interaction between motives and content (p > .15).

As a second supplemental analysis, we entered the autonomous motivation and controlled motivation variables separately to investigate whether one or the other would account for the majority of the variance. In this study, extrinsic and intrinsic content could not be entered separately into the equation because they represent a single dichotomous variable. Autonomous motivation was significant and positive (β = .69, p < .01), whereas controlled motivation was nonsignificant (β = .01, ns). Extrinsic content was again significant and negative at Step 2, as it had been in the primary analysis. Thus, in this study, the effect of the relative autonomy composite was carried primarily by the autonomy items.

BRIEF DISCUSSION Study 1 supports the hypothesis that "goal content matters" for well-being, over and above the effects of associated goal motives. Simply put, people expected to be less happy when they pursued goals that were extrinsic rather than intrinsic in content and more happy when they pursued goals for autonomous relative to controlled reasons. Thus, the goals with the highest happiness expectancies were those with both low

---

[2]This hierarchical regression analysis allows the effect of variables to be controlled, or statistically held constant, one at a time. The purpose of the present analysis is to test whether goal content would have an effect regardless of the degree to which the goal was autonomous vs. controlled.

[3]The "beta" is a measure of the strength of the association between variables in a regression analysis.

[4]The "delta R-squared" is a measure of how much more of the total variance a given predictor variable explains, holding constant the other predictors entered earlier in the hierarchical analysis.

[5]The test for the interaction is checking to see whether the effect of one of these variables (autonomy and conent) depends on the other. It doesn't.

extrinsic content and high relative autonomous motivation.

* * *

Having seen that estimations of well-being are influenced by both goal motives and contents, we next considered people's actual goal pursuits and their actual reported well-being. The question was, "Do the independent content and motive effects of Study 1 generalize to goals that are self-generated (rather than experimenter-supplied), to between-subject effects (rather than within-subject effects), and to the prediction of the person's actual concurrent (rather than estimated) well-being?"

Study 2

In this study, we used an idiographic goal-assessment technique (Emmons, 1999; Little, 1993) in which participants first listed their personal goals. A nomothetic rating procedure was then used to assess both extrinsic versus intrinsic contents and autonomous versus controlled motives for participants' goals (Sheldon & Kasser, 1995, 1998, 2001).[6] We then directly assessed participants' well-being at the time of the goal assessments.

Method

Participants and Procedure Participants were 221 entering freshmen at the University of Missouri who took part in the study in exchange for course credit and/or monetary compensation. There were 38 men and 183 women; 89% (197) were Caucasian. Participants completed a questionnaire packet containing the idiographic goal elicitation procedure and the nomothetic assessments of goal contents, motives, and subjective well-being.

---

[6]Idiographic methods allow unique data from each participant; in this case the participant can list any personal goals he or she has. Nomothetic methods require all participants' data to be rated on the same scale. The present method allows participants to generate individual goals, which then are all rated on the same scales, thus combining aspects of both idiographic and nomothetic approaches.

Measures.

Well-being. To assess subjective well-being, we administered the Positive Affect Negative Affect Schedule (PANAS) (Watson, Tellegen, & Clark, 1988). Participants were presented with 20 emotion adjectives, 10 positive and 10 negative, and they indicated the extent to which they generally feel each way using a 1 (*not at all*) to 7 (*very much*) scale. In addition, participants were administered the Satisfaction With Life Scale (SWLS) (Diener, Emmons, Larsen, & Griffin, 1985), which contains five statements such as, "In most ways my life is close to my ideal." Participants indicated their agreement with each item "in general" using a 7-point scale. Diener (1994) has referred to positive affect, the inverse of negative affect, and life satisfaction as the primary components of subjective well-being, and there is precedent in many recent studies to create a composite well-being index from these three components (e.g., Elliot & Sheldon, 1996; Sheldon & Elliot, 1999; Sheldon & Kasser, 2001).

Personal goals. Goals were defined as "projects that we think about, plan for, carry out, and sometimes (though not always) complete or succeed at." After being shown examples, participants were asked to list eight goals of their own that would last "at least through the end of the semester." Actual goals listed by participants included "Get involved in campus organizations," "Get good grades," "Get to know more people," "Don't gain weight," and "Call my parents once a week."

Motives. Participants then rated how much they were pursuing each goal for each of four reasons, using a 1 (*not at all*) to 5 (*very much*) scale. * * *

* * *

Goal contents. Participants also rated the extent to which each goal might help to bring about six "possible futures" using a 1 (*no help*) to 9 (*very much help*) scale. These possible futures mapped directly onto the six goal contents employed in Study 1: three represented intrinsic values (meaningful relationships, personal growth, and societal contribution) and three represented extrinsic values (financial success, popularity and fame, and attractive physical image). As in past research

(Sheldon & Kasser, 1995, 2001), we computed a relative extrinsic content score by summing the linkages to the three extrinsic possible futures across personal goals and then subtracting the linkages to the intrinsic possible futures. The resulting score represents the extent to which the students' personal goals concern extrinsic rather than intrinsic contents. * * *

Results

Preliminary Analyses. First, we correlated the relative extrinsic content variable and the relative autonomy variable. They were negatively correlated ($r = -.23$, $p < .01$),[7] indicating once again that people's motives tend to be more controlled when they pursue goals with more extrinsic content.

Hypothesis Tests. To test our hypothesis that goal contents would make independent contributions to well-being over and above goal motives, we used a hierarchical regression strategy similar to that in Study 1. Table 2 contains the results. At Step 1, relative autonomy was significant ($\beta = .29$, $p < .01$). Consistent with our hypothesis, at Step 2, relative extrinsic content also was significant ($\Delta R^2 = .02$, $p < .05$, $\beta = -.14$). Entering the product of these two variables at Step 3 once again revealed no significant interaction ($p > .25$).

* * *

BRIEF DISCUSSION Study 2 provided additional support for our primary hypothesis by showing the predicted relations using participants' self-generated (rather than experimenter-supplied) goals, by using reports of actual current (rather than hypothetical) well-being, and by using a between-subjects (rather than a within-subjects) design. Again, we found that motives and contents contributed independent variance to well-being, such that the individuals with the highest well-being were those

---

[7]This negative correlation (r) indicates that as the extrinsic content of a goal was larger, its relative autonomy tended to go down. The p is the standard measure of statistical significance seen in previous analyses.

	TABLE 2			

STUDY 2: RESULTS OF HIERARCHICAL REGRESSION PREDICTING CONCURRENT WELL-BEING FROM RELATIVE AUTONOMY AND RELATIVE EXTRINSIC CONTENT

	R^2 Change	p Value	Beta	p Value
Step 1	.086	<.01		
Relative autonomy			.29	<.01
Step 2	.018	<.05		
Relative extrinsic content			-.14	<.05
Step 3	.005	>.25		
Product term			-.16	>.25

who pursued intrinsic rather than extrinsic goals and who pursued goals for autonomous rather than controlled reasons. In this study, the external motivation item in the autonomy composite was modified and yielded a much higher alpha. Accordingly, both the autonomy and controlled facets of the composite predicted independent variance in well-being.

Although Study 2 added further support to our primary hypothesis, there is still an important question that has not been addressed, namely, whether the negative association between relatively strong, extrinsic goal strivings and well-being can be explained by stable individual differences rather than by people's ongoing behaviors and experiences. For example, strong extrinsic values are typically associated with higher insecurity, lower self-esteem, and lower cooperativeness, all of which are associated with poorer well-being (see Kasser, 2002a, for a review). A "third variable" explanation of the goals-to-well-being association would suggest that adopting extrinsic goals does not itself bring about diminished well-being but, rather, is just a symptom of stable personality factors that produce both the extrinsic orientation and the negative well-being. If this were true, then it might be inappropriate or irrelevant to give people recommendations concerning the kinds of goals to pursue to enhance their well-being.

To examine this issue, Study 3 employed a two-wave longitudinal design in which Time 1 goal contents and motives were used to predict change in well-being throughout the year from Time 1 to Time 2. Because Time 1 well-being was removed from Time 2 well-being, any effects of stable individual difference variables on well-being would have been removed. As such, we could assess whether characteristics of the set of goals specified by participants at Time 1 might have causal influence on changes in well-being from Time 1 to Time 2, presumably by affecting the quality of participants' experiences during that year-long period. Consistent with the earlier studies, we predicted that relative extrinsic content would have significant effects on changes in well-being, even after the effects of relative autonomous motives had been removed.

Study 3

A sample of second-semester college seniors listed five important postgraduation goals that they would be pursuing over the next couple of years. They were told that they would be asked about these goals again a year after they graduated. As in Studies 1 and 2, participants rated their autonomous and controlled reasons for pursuing each of their personal goals and, as in Study 2, they rated the linkage of each goal to the three intrinsic and the three extrinsic content domains. They also rated their current well-being at Time 1 and Time 2, allowing us to predict changes in well-being.

In addition, at Time 2, participants were reminded of the goals they had specified just before graduation and were asked how committed they were to these goals. This allowed us to determine whether the goals remained important for them at Time 2.

METHOD

Participants and Procedure. Participants were 244 graduating seniors at the University of Rochester (169) and Knox College (75). One hundred and fifty-six were women, 84 were men, and 4 did not list their gender. Again, a large majority of participants were Caucasian. One hundred and fifty-nine Time 1 participants provided complete Time 2 data 1 year later and thus constitute the final sample. * * *

At Time 1, participants completed several measures of well-being as well as some personality scales not relevant to this article. Then, they generated postgraduation personal goals and rated them both for autonomous and controlled motives and for linkages to intrinsic and extrinsic possible futures. The Time 2 assessments, conducted 1 year later, were mailed to participants at addresses they provided at Time 1. These packets contained the same well-being measures that were given at Time 1. In addition, participants were given a list of the goals they specified at Time 1 and were asked to rate their commitment to these personal goals. Participants received a $10 incentive for providing Time 1 data and a $15 incentive for providing Time 2 data.

MEASURES

Well-being. As in Study 2, we employed the PANAS and the SWLS, although in Study 3 they were administered twice, 1 year apart. As in Study 2, we created an aggregate well-being score by summing positive affect and life satisfaction and subtracting negative affect. * * *

Personal goals. During the first assessment, participants generated five postgraduation goals, defined as "behavior patterns you will try to establish in your daily life, things you will try to accomplish for yourself, or kinds of circumstances you will try to bring about." We asked participants to brainstorm a wide variety of possible goals before settling on the five that were most likely to remain important to them throughout the next year or two.

Motives and contents. Participants then used a 9-point Likert-type scale to rate their motives for these five goals using the same four reasons employed in Study 2. Again, a relative autonomy score was created for each participant by averaging the scores for each reason across the five goals and then adding the autonomous-reason averages and subtracting the controlled-reason averages. * * *

Participants also rated the extent to which each goal would be helpful for attaining the same six "possible futures" employed in Study 2 using a 1 (*no help*) to 9 (*very much help*) scale. As in Study 2, we computed a relative extrinsic content score by subtracting the three intrinsic linkage variables from the sum of the three extrinsic linkage variables. * * *

Goal commitment. To assess the continuing relevance of the goals, at Time 2, we provided each participant with a list of the five goals they had specified as their most important goals at Time 1. We then asked how committed they were to each goal: "Thinking back over the past year, how committed have you been to each of these goals?" The five responses were averaged as an indicator of whether these goals remained important to the participants over their 1st year after graduation.

Income. Finally, we asked participants to indicate their current income at the Time 1 and Time 2 assessments with a scale ranging from 1 (< $15,000) to 7 (> $150,000). This enabled us to examine whether changes in participants' income influenced the effects of goal contents and motives on changes in well-being; that is, it allowed us to examine and control for the possibility that strong, extrinsic, postgraduation goals might lead to higher incomes, which could influence well-being (Diener & Biswas-Diener, 2002).

RESULTS

Preliminary Analyses. A paired-sample *t* test revealed a significant increase in well-being, $Ms =$ 6.89 versus 6.50, $t(158) = 2.42$, $p < .05$, throughout the year-long period. Follow-up analyses revealed that this was due to significant samplewide decreases in negative affect between the end of the senior year and the assessment 1 year later. It appears that the end of these students' undergraduate careers was a stressful time compared to their lives 1 year later.

We next correlated relative autonomy with relative extrinsic content. Consistent with the results of Studies 1 and 2, they correlated negatively ($r = -.26$, $p < .01$). Once again, it appears that people

TABLE 3

STUDY 3: RESULTS OF HIERARCHICAL REGRESSION PREDICTING CHANGES IN WELL-BEING FROM RELATIVE AUTONOMY AND RELATIVE EXTRINSIC CONTENT

	R^2 Change	*p* Value	Beta	*p* Value
Step 1	.540	<.01		
Sample			−.10	<.10
Time 1 well-being			.72	<.01
Step 2	.014	<.05		
Relative autonomy			.13	<.05
Step 3	.022	<.01		
Relative extrinsic content			−.16	<.01
Step 4	.002	>.50		
Product term			−.12	>.50

tend to pursue extrinsic goals for less autonomous and more controlled reasons.

Finally, we calculated the mean for people's ratings of how committed they were to the original goals a year after specifying the goals. The mean of 6.84 on this 9-point scale was well above the midpoint of 5, suggesting that these goals in fact remained important for the participants throughout this year-long period.

Hypothesis Tests. To evaluate the relative effects of motives and content on well-being, we again used a hierarchical regression approach. At Step 1, we regressed Time 2 well-being on Time 1 well-being (to index change in well-being) and on a dummy variable representing participant subssample (0 = Rochester, 1 = Knox).[8] At Step 2, we entered relative autonomy, and at Step 3, we entered relative extrinsic content. Finally, at Step 4, we entered a Motive ¥ Content product term to probe for an interaction.

Table 3 contains the results. Step 2 revealed that relative autonomy was significant, as expected

---

[8]The "dummy variable" coding of the two colleges by assigning a value of 0 to students attending Rochester, and 1 to students attending Knox, allows any possible difference between results from the colleges to be statistically controlled.

($\Delta R^2 = .014$, $p < .05$, $\beta = .13$). Step 3 revealed that relative extrinsic content was significant, as expected ($\Delta R^2 = .022$, $p < .01$, $\beta = -.16$). Finally, Step 4 revealed no significant interaction between content and motives ($\Delta R^2 = .002$, $p > .50$).

* * *

BRIEF DISCUSSION Study 3 again demonstrated independent effects for both goal motives and goal contents on well-being using a very stringent test in which the Time 1 goal variables predicted prospective year-long change in well-being. As such, the study helps to rule out the possibility that associations among goal motives, contents, and well-being are merely a function of stable individual difference variables. Instead, results are consistent with our hypothesis that both the motives and the contents of the goals people adopt may have a causal impact on their subsequent well-being.

When we examined the separate components of the relative autonomy composite and the relative extrinsic content composite, we found that controlled motivation was significant, although autonomous motivation was not, and that extrinsic content was significant and intrinsic content was marginal. Thus, as in Study 2, both controlled motives and extrinsic contents were significant negative predictors of well-being. Autonomous motivation had been predictive of well-being in Studies 1 and 2, but not in this study. Finally, whereas intrinsic content was not a predictor of well-being in Study 2, it was marginally significant in this study.

General Discussion

SUMMARY OF RESULTS Previous research has shown, across varied samples with varied indicators of well-being, that the strong valuing of extrinsic (relative to intrinsic) goals is negatively associated with well-being (Kasser & Ryan, 1993, 1996; Sheldon & Kasser, 1995). In other words, people for whom it is highly important to amass wealth, present an attractive image, and become popular or famous tend to report ill-being, including greater anxiety, depression, narcissism, psy-

chosomatic symptoms, conduct disorder, and high-risk behaviors, as well as poorer self-actualization, self-esteem, vitality, and social functioning (see Kasser, 2002b).

Critics of the research on extrinsic goals have argued that the negative effects of extrinsic goal content are reducible to the motives people tend to have for pursuing extrinsic goals such as monetary success (e.g., Carver & Baird, 1998; Srivastava et al., 2001). These two research teams have argued that extrinsic goals are not themselves problematic for well-being, except in cases where people pursue them for the wrong reasons (e.g., with a sense of pressure, insecurity, or control). * * *

[However,] consistent with our primary hypothesis, all three studies found independent effects of goal contents on well-being after controlling for the effect of goal motives (effects that also were significant). This was true when we used three extrinsic goal contents (wealth, fame, and image) together or when we used only financial goal contents alone. * * *

When we examined the components of the relative autonomy composite separately, we found that controlled motives significantly predicted well-being in Studies 2 and 3 but not in Study 1. * * * Autonomous motives significantly predicted well-being in Studies 1 and 2 but not in Study 3, which was the most stringent test because it focused on change in well-being rather than well-being assessed at one point in time. Thus, there is evidence that both components of the autonomy composite are meaningfully involved in predicting well-being. When we examined the components of the relative extrinsic content composite, which could be done only in Studies 2 and 3, we found that the negative relation between extrinsic contents and well-being was stronger than the positive relation between intrinsic contents and well-being. This is consistent with our theoretical focus on the issue of whether extrinsic goals are out of balance with intrinsic goals and the proposition that it is the overvaluation of extrinsic goals that produces reduced well-being.

Earlier, we discussed several possible factors that could account for the unique effects of extrinsic goals on well-being, including the fact that when people strongly pursue extrinsic goals they tend to have more superficial relationships, operate with contingent self-worth, engage in more frequent social comparisons, and allow extrinsic pursuits to crowd out enjoyable and satisfying activities (Kasser, 2002a). These are all bottom-up explanations of well-being in the sense that they refer to ongoing behaviors and experiences that accumulate over time to influence global well-being (Diener, 1994; Sheldon, Ryan, & Reis, 1996). In contrast, another possible explanation for the negative relation between extrinsic goals and well-being is more top-down because it concerns stable personality factors influencing both goal importance and well-being; that is, invariant traits such as high insecurity, low self-esteem, or low cooperativeness (Kasser, 2002a) might account for both strong extrinsic goal orientations and diminished well-being.

Although more research is needed to sort out these explanations, the results of Study 3 suggest that the stable-personality-factor hypothesis is not the full story. The longitudinal design of Study 3 allowed us to remove the individuals' baseline well-being such that individual differences were controlled for and only processes occurring during the year of the study would be expected to influence Time 2 well-being. The fact that Study 3 found significant effects of extrinsic goal contents on changes in well-being (over and above the significant effect for autonomous motives) supports the idea that the less-satisfying quality of ongoing experience resulting from the strong pursuit of extrinsic goals helps explain the negative association of such goals with well-being. In other words, it does appear that people's choice of goals causally affects their subsequent well-being.

LIMITATIONS AND CONCLUSIONS Limitations of the current studies include the facts that only college student samples were employed and only self-report measures of well-being were obtained. In addition, participants were American, predominantly Caucasian, and predominantly middle class. Future research will need to investigate the extent

to which goal contents and goal motives both predict well-being in samples of different ages, ethnicities, nationalities, and socioeconomic statuses.

In conclusion, the current research provides clear evidence that "it's both what you pursue *and* why you pursue it" when it comes to predicting people's well-being, just as Ryan et al. (1996) suggested. This finding has important implications for theories of motivation because it indicates that the directive focus of goals (i.e., contents) and the dynamic processes underlying goals (i.e., motives) each makes a difference in people's lives. The finding also has important implications for theories of well-being, suggesting that people seeking greater wellbeing would be well advised to focus on the pursuit of (a) goals involving growth, connection, and contribution rather than goals involving money, beauty, and popularity and (b) goals that are interesting and personally important to them rather than goals they feel forced or pressured to pursue.

References

Baumeister, R., & Leary, M. R. (1995). The need to belong: Desire for interpersonal attachments as a fundamental human motivation. *Psychological Bulletin, 117,* 497–529.

Carver, C. S., & Baird, E. (1998). The American dream revisited: Is it what you want or why you want it that matters? *Psychological Science, 9,* 289–292.

DeCharms, R. (1968). *Personal causation: The internal affective determinants of behavior.* New York: Academic Press. Deci, E. L., & Ryan, R. M. (1985). *Intrinsic motivation and self-determination in human behavior.* New York: Plenum.

Deci, E. L., & Ryan, R. M. (2000). The "what" and "why" of goal pursuits: Human needs and the self-determination of behavior. *Psychological Inquiry, 11,* 227–268.

Diener, E. (1994). Assessing subjective well-being: Progress and opportunities. *Social Indicators Research, 31,* 103–157.

Diener, E., & Biswas-Diener, R. (2002). Will money increase subjective well-being? *Social Indicators Research, 57,* 119–169.

Diener, E., Emmons, R., Larsen, R. J., & Griffin, S. (1985). The Satisfaction With Life Scale. *Journal of Personality Assessment, 49,* 71–75.

Elliot, A. J., & Sheldon, K. M. (1996). Avoidance achievement motivation: A personal goals analysis. *Journal of Personality & Social Psychology, 73,* 171–185.

Emmons, R. A. (1999). *The psychology of ultimate concerns.* New York: Guilford.

Kasser, T. (2002a). *The high price of materialism.* Cambridge, MA: MIT Press.

Kasser, T. (2002b). Sketches for a self-determination theory of values. In E. L. Deci & R. M. Ryan (Eds.), *Handbook of self-determination research* (pp. 123–140). Rochester, NY: University of Rochester Press.

Kasser, T., & Ryan, R. M. (1993). A dark side of the American dream: Correlates of financial success as a central life aspiration. *Journal of Personality and Social Psychology, 65,* 410–422.

Kasser, T., & Ryan, R. M. (1996). Further examining the American dream: Differential correlates of intrinsic and extrinsic goals. *Personality and Social Psychology Bulletin, 22,* 80–87.

Kasser, T., & Ryan, R. M. (2001). Be careful what you wish for: Optimal functioning and the relative attainment of intrinsic and extrinsic goals. In P. Schmuck & K. M. Sheldon (Eds.), *Life goals and well-being: Towards a positive psychology of human striving* (pp. 116–131). Goettingen, Germany: Hogrefe & Huber.

Little, B. R. (1993). Personal projects and the distributed self: Aspects of a conative psychology. In J. Suls (Ed.), *The self in social perspective: Psychological perspectives on the self* (Vol. 4, pp. 157–185). Hillsdale, NJ: Lawrence Erlbaum.

Lyubomirsky, S., King, L. A., & Diener, E. (2003). *Is happiness a good thing? A theory of the benefits of positive affect.* Unpublished manuscript, Department of Psychology, University of California, Riverside.

Rokeach, T. (1973). *The nature of human values.* New York: Free Press.

Ryan, R. M., & Connell, J. P. (1989). Perceived locus of causality and internalization: Examining reasons for acting in two domains. *Journal of Personality and Social Psychology, 57,* 749–761.

Ryan, R. M., & Deci, E. L. (2000). Self-determination theory and the facilitation of intrinsic motivation, social development, and well-being. *American Psychologist, 55,* 68–78.

Ryan, R. M., Kuhl, J., & Deci, E. L. (1997). Nature and autonomy: An organizational view of social and neurobiological aspects of self-regulation in behavior and development. *Development and Psychopathology, 9,* 701–728.

Ryan, R. M., Sheldon, K. M., Kasser, T., & Deci, E. L. (1996). All goals are not created equal: An organismic perspective on the nature of goals and their regulation. In P. M. Gollwitzer & J. A. Bargh (Eds.), *The psychology of action: Linking cognition and motivation to behavior* (pp. 7–26). New York: Guilford.

Sheldon, K. M., & Elliot, A. J. (1998). Not all personal goals are "personal": Comparing autonomous and controlling goals on effort and attainment. *Personality and Social Psychology Bulletin, 24,* 546–557.

Sheldon, K. M., & Elliot, A. J. (1999). Goal striving, need satisfaction, and longitudinal well-being: The self-concordance model. *Journal of Personality and Social Psychology, 76,* 546–557.

Sheldon, K. M., & Kasser, T. (1995). Coherence and congruence: Two aspects of personality integration. *Journal of Personality and Social Psychology, 68,* 531–543.

Sheldon, K. M., & Kasser, T. (1998). Pursuing personal goals: Skills enable progress but not all progress is beneficial. *Personality and Social Psychology Bulletin, 24,* 1319–1331.

Sheldon, K. M., & Kasser, T. (2001). Getting older, getting better? Personal strivings and psychological maturity across the life span. *Developmental Psychology, 37,* 491–501.

Sheldon, K. M., Ryan, R. M., & Reis, H. T. (1996). What makes for a good day? Competence and autonomy in the day and in the person. *Personality and Social Psychology Bulletin, 22,* 1270–1279.

Srivastava, A., Locke, E. A., & Bartol, K. M. (2001). Money and subjective well-being: It's not the money, it's the motive. *Journal of Personality and Social Psychology, 80,* 959–971.

Watson, D., Tellegen, A., & Clark, L. (1988). Development and validation of brief measures of positive and negative affect: The PANAS scales. *Journal of Personality and Social Psychology, 54,* 1063–1070.

White, R. W. (1959). Motivation reconsidered: The concept of competence. *Psychological Review, 66,* 297–333.

Self-Esteem, Narcissism, and Aggression: Does Violence Result from Low Self-Esteem or from Threatened Egotism?

Roy F. Baumeister, Brad J. Bushman, and W. Keith Campbell

Is it good to have a high opinion of oneself? Parents, teachers, and the media all encourage us to feel good about ourselves and thus build "self-esteem." But is such self-esteem, encouraged by our social world but ungrounded in real accomplishment, necessarily good for us? In the present article, Roy Baumeister and his colleagues question the conventional view of self-esteem's relation to aggression and point out that an exaggerated, narcissistic sense of self can lead to hostility and violence. Sometimes thinking too well of oneself can literally be dangerous.

From *Current Directions in Psychological Science, 9*, 26–29, 2000.

For decades, the prevailing wisdom has held that low self-esteem causes aggression. Many authors have cited or invoked this belief or used it as an implicit assumption to explain their findings regarding other variables (e.g., Gondolf, 1985; Levin & McDevitt, 1993; Staub, 1989). The origins of this idea are difficult to establish. One can search the literature without finding any original theoretical statement of that view, nor is there any seminal investigation that provided strong empirical evidence that low self-esteem causes aggression. Ironically, the theory seemed to enter into conventional wisdom without ever being empirically established.

The view of low self-esteem that has emerged from many research studies does not, however, seem easily reconciled with the theory that low self-esteem causes aggression. A composite of research findings depicts people with low self-esteem as uncertain and confused about themselves, oriented toward avoiding risk and potential loss, shy, modest, emotionally labile (and having tendencies toward depression and anxiety), submitting readily to other people's influence, and lacking confidence in themselves (see compilation by Baumeister, 1993).

None of these patterns seems likely to increase aggression, and some of them seem likely to discourage it. People with low self-esteem are oriented toward avoiding risk and loss, whereas attacking someone is eminently risky. People with low self-esteem lack confidence of success, whereas aggression is usually undertaken in the expectation of defeating the other person. Low self-esteem involves submitting to influence, whereas aggression is often engaged in to resist and reject external influence. Perhaps most relevant, people with low self-esteem are confused and uncertain about who they are, whereas aggression is likely to be an attempt to defend and assert a strongly held opinion about oneself.

Painting the Picture of Violent Men

An alternative to the low-self-esteem theory emerges when one examines what is known about violent individuals. Most research has focused on violent men, although it seems reasonable to assume that violent women conform to similar patterns. Violent men seem to have a strong sense of personal superiority, and their violence often seems to stem from a sense of wounded pride. When someone else questions or disputes their favorable view of self, they lash out in response.

An interdisciplinary literature review (Baumeister, Smart, & Boden, 1996) found that favorable self-regard is linked to violence in one sphere after another. Murderers, rapists, wife beaters, violent youth gangs, aggressive nations, and other categories of violent people are all marked by strongly held views of their own superiority. When large groups of people differ in self-esteem, the group with the higher self-esteem is generally the more violent one.

When self-esteem rises or falls as a by-product of other events, aggressive tendencies likewise tend to covary, but again in a pattern precisely opposite to what the low self-esteem theory predicts. People with manic depression, for example, tend to be more aggressive and violent during their manic stage (marked by highly favorable views of self) than during the depressed phase (when self-esteem is low). Alcohol intoxication has been shown to boost self-esteem temporarily, and it also boosts aggressive tendencies. Changes in the relative self-esteem levels of African American and white American citizens have been accompanied by changes in relative violence between the groups, and again in the direction opposite to the predictions of the low-self-esteem view. Hence, it appears that aggressive, violent people hold highly favorable opinions of themselves. Moreover, the aggression ensues when these favorable opinions are disputed or questioned by other people. It there-

fore seems plausible that aggression results from threatened egotism.

Aggression, Hostility, and Self-Regard

Thus, the low-self-esteem theory is not defensible. Should behavioral scientists leap to the opposite conclusion, namely, that high self-esteem causes violence? No. Although clearly many violent individuals have high self-esteem, it is also necessary to know whether many exceptionally nonviolent individuals also have high self-esteem.

Perhaps surprisingly, direct and controlled studies linking self-esteem to aggression are almost nonexistent. Perhaps no one has ever bothered to study the question, but this seems unlikely. Instead, it seems more plausible that such investigations have been done but have remained unpublished because they failed to find any clear or direct link. Such findings would be consistent with the view that the category of people with high self-esteem contains both aggressive and nonaggressive individuals.

One of the few studies to link self-esteem to hostile tendencies found that people with high self-esteem tended to cluster at both the hostile and the nonhostile extremes (Kernis, Grannemann, & Barclay, 1989). The difference lay in stability of self-esteem, which the researchers assessed by measuring self-esteem on several occasions and computing how much variability each individual showed over time. People whose self-esteem was high as well as stable—thus, people whose favorable view of self was largely impervious to daily events—were the least prone to hostility of any group. In contrast, people with high but unstable self-esteem scored highest on hostility. These findings suggest that violent individuals are one subset of people with high self-esteem. High self-esteem may well be a mixed category, containing several different kinds of people. One of those kinds is very nonaggressive, whereas another is quite aggressive.

The view that individuals with high self-esteem form a heterogeneous category is gaining ground among researchers today. Some researchers, like Kernis and his colleagues, have begun to focus on stability of self-esteem. Others are beginning to use related constructs, such as narcissism. Narcissism is defined by grandiose views of personal superiority, an inflated sense of entitlement, low empathy toward others, fantasies of personal greatness, a belief that ordinary people cannot understand one, and the like (American Psychiatric Association, 1994). These traits seem quite plausibly linked to aggression and violence, especially when the narcissist encounters someone who questions or disputes his or her highly favorable assessment of self. Narcissism has also been linked empirically to high but unstable self-esteem, so narcissism seems a very promising candidate for aggression researchers to study.

We have recently undertaken laboratory tests of links among self-esteem, narcissism, and aggression (Bushman & Baumeister, 1998). In two studies, participants were insulted (or praised) by a confederate posing as another participant, and later they were given an opportunity to aggress against that person (or another person) by means of sounding an aversive blast of loud noise. In both studies, the highest levels of aggression were exhibited by people who had scored high on narcissism and had been insulted. Self-esteem by itself had no effect on aggression, and neither did either high or low self-esteem in combination with receiving the insult. These results confirm the link between threatened egotism and aggression and contradicted the theory that low self-esteem causes violence.

Narcissism has thus taken center stage as the form of self-regard most closely associated with violence. It is not, however, entirely fair to depict narcissists as generally or indiscriminately aggressive. In our studies (Bushman & Baumeister, 1998), narcissists' aggression did not differ from that of other people as long as there was no insulting provocation. Narcissism is thus not directly a cause of aggression and should instead be understood as a risk factor that can contribute to increasing a violent, aggressive response to provocation. The causal role of the provocation itself (in eliciting aggression by narcissists) is clearly established by the experimental findings.

Moreover, even when the narcissists were insulted, they were no more aggressive than anyone else toward an innocent third person. These patterns show that the aggression of narcissists is a specifically targeted, socially meaningful response. Narcissists are heavily invested in their high opinion of themselves, and they want others to share and confirm this opinion. When other people question or undermine the flattering self-portrait of the narcissist, the narcissist turns aggressive in response, but only toward those specific people. The aggression is thus a means of defending and asserting the grandiose self-view.

Do laboratory studies really capture what happens out in the real world, where violence often takes much more serious and deadly forms than pushing a button to deliver a blast of aversive noise? To answer this question, we conducted another study in which we obtained self-esteem and narcissism scores from incarcerated violent felons (Bushman, Baumeister, Phillips, & Gilligan, 1999). We assumed that the prisoners' responses to some items (e.g., "I certainly feel useless at times") would be affected by being in prison as well as by the salient failure experience of having been arrested, tried, convicted, and sentenced. These factors would be expected to push all scores toward low self-esteem and low narcissism.

Despite any such tendency, however, the prisoners' scores again pointed toward high narcissism as the major cause of aggression. The self-esteem scores of this group were comparable to the scores of published samples. The narcissism scores, meanwhile, were significantly higher than the published norms from all other studies. In particular, the prisoners outscored the baselines from other (nonincarcerated) groups to the largest degree on subscales measuring entitlement and superiority. (Again, though, the fact that the participants were in prison might have artificially lowered scores on some items, such as vanity, exhibitionism, and authority.) These findings suggest that the dangerous aspects of narcissism are not so much simple vanity and self-admiration as the inflated sense of being superior to others and being entitled to special privileges. It is apparently fine to love oneself quietly—instead, the interpersonal manifestations of narcissism are the ones associated with violence.

Deep Down Inside

A common question raised about these findings is whether the apparent egotism of aggressive, violent people is simply a superficial form of bluster that is put on to conceal deep-rooted insecurities and self-doubts. This question is actually an effort to salvage the low-self-esteem theory, because it suggests that aggressive people really do have low self-esteem but simply act as if they do not. For example, perhaps murderers and wife beaters really perceive themselves as inferior beings, and their aggressive assertion of superiority is just a cover-up.

The question can be handled on either conceptual or empirical grounds. Empirically, some investigators have sought to find this inner core of self-doubt and reported that they could not do so. For example, Olweus (1994) specifically rejected the view that playground bullies secretly have low self-esteem, and Jankowski (1991) likewise concluded that members of violent gangs do not carry around a load of inner insecurities or self-doubts. Likewise, a number of experts who study narcissism have reported that they could not support the traditional clinical view of an egotistical outer shell concealing inner self-loathing. Virtually all studies that have measured self-esteem and narcissism have found positive correlations between the two, indicating that narcissists have high self-esteem.

Even if such evidence could be found, though, the view that low self-esteem causes aggression would still be wrong. It is by now clear that overt low self-esteem does not cause aggression. How can hidden low self-esteem cause aggression if nonhidden low self-esteem has no such effect? The only possible response is that the hidden quality of that low self-esteem would be decisive. Yet focusing the theory on the hidden quality of low self-esteem requires one to consider what it is that is hiding it—which brings the analysis back to the surface veneer of egotism. Thus, again, it would be the

sense of superiority that is responsible for aggression, even if one could show that that sense of superiority is only on the surface and conceals an underlying low self-esteem. And no one has shown that, anyway.

Conclusion

It is time to abandon the quest for direct, simple links between self-esteem and aggression. The long-standing view that low self-esteem causes violence has been shown to be wrong, and the opposite view implicating high self-esteem is too simple. High self-esteem is a characteristic of both highly aggressive individuals and exceptionally nonaggressive ones, and so attempts at direct prediction tend to be inconclusive. Moreover, it is unwarranted to conclude that self-views directly cause aggression. At best, a highly favorable self-view constitutes a risk factor for turning violent in response to perceptions that one's favorable view of self has been disputed or undermined by others.

Researchers have started trying to look more closely at the people with high self-esteem in order to find the aggressive ones. Patterns of narcissism and instability of self-esteem have proven successful in recent investigations, although more research is needed. At present, the evidence best fits the view that aggression is more likely when people with a narcissistically inflated view of their own personal superiority encounter someone who explicitly disputes that opinion. Aggression is thus a means of defending a highly favorable view of self against someone who seeks (even unwittingly) to deflate it. Threatened egotism, rather than low self-esteem, is the most explosive recipe for violence.

Further research can benefit by discarding the obsolete view that low self-esteem causes violence and building on the findings about threatened egotism. It would be helpful to know whether a highly favorable view of self contributes to violent response by increasing the perception of insult (i.e., by making people oversensitive) or instead by simply producing a more aggressive response to the same perceived provocation. Further, research on whether narcissistic individuals would aggress against people who know bad information about them (but have not specifically asserted it themselves) would shed light on whether it is the critical view itself or the expression of it that is decisive. Another question is what exactly narcissistic people hope to accomplish by responding violently to an insult: After all, violence does not really refute criticism in any meaningful way, but it may discourage other people from voicing similar criticisms. The emotion processes involved in egotistical violence also need to be illuminated: How exactly do the shameful feelings of being criticized transform into aggressive outbursts, and does aggression genuinely make the aggressor feel better?

References

American Psychiatric Association. (1994). *Diagnostic and statistical manual of mental disorders* (4th ed.). Washington, DC: Author.

Baumeister, R. (1993). *Self-esteem*. New York: Plenum Press.

Baumeister, R. Smart, I., & Borden, J. (1996). Relation of threatened egotism to violence and aggression: The dark side of high self-esteem. *Psychological Review, 103*, 5–33.

Bushman, B. & Baumeister, R. (1998). Threatened egotism, narcissism, self-esteem, and direct and displaced aggression: Does self-love or self-hate lead to violence? *Journal of Personality and Social Psychology, 75*. 219–229.

Bushman, B., Baumeister, R., Phillips, C. & Gilligan, J. (1999). *Narcissism and self-esteem among violent offenders in a prison population*. Manuscript submitted for publication.

Gondolf, E. (1985). *Men who batter*. Holmes Beach, FL: Learning Publications.

Jankowski, M.S. (1991). *Islands in the street: Gangs and American urban society*. Berkeley: University of California Press.

Kernis, M., Grannemann, B., & Barclay, I. (1989). Stability and level of self-esteem as predictors of anger arousal and hostility. *Journal of Personality and Social Psychology, 56*. 1013–1022.

Levin, J., & McDevitt, J. (1993). *Hate crimes*. New York: Plenum Press.

Olweus, D. (1994). Bullying at school: Long-term outcomes for the victims and an effective school-based intervention program. In R. Huesmann (Ed.) *Aggressive behavior: Current perspectives* (pp. 97–130). New York: Plenum Press.

Staub, E. (1989). *The roots of evil*. New York: Cambridge University Press.

LOW SELF-ESTEEM IS RELATED TO AGGRESSION, ANTISOCIAL BEHAVIOR, AND DELINQUENCY

M. Brent Donnellan, Kali H. Trzesniewski, Richard W. Robins, Terrie E. Moffitt, and Avshalom Caspi

The title of this selection is as clear a representation of its contents as any brief summary is likely to achieve. The present article by Brent Donnellan and his colleagues contests the claims by Baumeister and his colleagues in the previous selection, that high self-esteem can cause problems, by presenting three studies that show low self-esteem to be associated with antisocial behavior. Although the controversy over the implications of self-esteem is likely to continue, the important factor may turn out not to be the level of one's self-esteem, but its basis. Self-esteem grounded in socially beneficial accomplishments is almost surely a good thing. Self-esteem that is based solely on pride may do more harm than good.

From *Psychological Science, 16,* 328–335, 2005.

The link between global self-esteem and aggression is currently being debated by researchers (Baumeister, Campbell, Krueger, & Vohs. 2003: DuBois & Tevendale, 1999) and in the popular media (e.g., Slater, 2002). Researchers on one side of the debate have argued that individuals with low self-esteem are prone to real-world externalizing problems such as delinquency and antisocial behavior (e.g., Fergusson & Horwood, 2002: Rosenberg, Schooler, & Schoenbach, 1989: Sprott & Doob, 2000). However, others have questioned this claim, noting that several studies have failed to find a relation between low self-esteem and externalizing problems (e.g., Bynner, O'Malley, & Bachman, 1981: Jang & Thornberrry, 1998: McCarthy & Hoge, 1984) or between low global self-esteem and laboratory measures of aggression (Bushman & Baumeister, 1998: Kirkpatrick, Waugh, Valencia, & Webster, 2002: Twenge & Campbell, 2003). On the basis of this research, Baumeister, Bushman, and Campbell (2000) suggested that "future research can benefit from discarding the obsolete view that low self-esteem causes violence" (p. 29). Instead, Baumeister and his colleagues have posited that any link between self-esteem and aggression probably occurs at the high end of the self-esteem continuum: that is, unrealistically high self-esteem (best captured by measures of narcissism), not low self-esteem, contributes to aggression and crime (e.g., Baumeister, Smart, & Boden, 1996).

At least three distinct traditions in the social sciences posit a link between low self-esteem and externalizing problems. Rosenberg (1965) suggested that low self-esteem weakens ties to society; according to social-bonding theory, weaker ties to society decrease conformity to social norms and increase delinquency (Hirschi, 1969). Humanistic psychologists such as Rogers (e.g., 1961) have argued that a lack of unconditional positive self-regard is linked to psychological problems, including aggression. Finally, neo-Freudians also posit that low self-regard motivates aggression. For example, Horney (1950) and Adler (1956) theorized that aggression and antisocial behavior are motivated by feelings of inferiority rooted in early childhood experiences of rejection and humiliation. More specifically, Tracy and Robins (2003) suggested that individuals protect themselves against feelings of inferiority and shame by externalizing blame for their failures, which leads to feelings of hostility and anger toward other people. Thus, three separate theoretical perspectives posit that externalizing behaviors are motivated, in part, by low self-esteem.

Despite these theoretical arguments, research on the link between low self-esteem and externalizing problems has failed to produce consistent results. An understanding of the precise nature of this relation has important theoretical implications, as well as practical implications given the media attention surrounding the issue. To bring new data to bear on this controversy, we report results from studies that extend previous research in several ways. We used a multimethod approach to assessing self-esteem and externalizing problems. Previous research has relied almost exclusively on self-report measures, so it is possible that the relations that have been observed are due to shared method variance.* * * Finally, we assessed narcissism to examine the possibility that unrealistically high self-esteem is related to aggression and to determine whether self-esteem and narcissism have independent effects.

Study 1

Study 1 investigated the relation between self-reports and teacher ratings of self-esteem and self-reports of delinquency in a sample of 11- and 14-year-olds. We also controlled for two theoretically relevant variables—supportive parenting and academic achievement—that might account for the effects of self-esteem on delinquency.

METHOD

Participants. The sample included 292 (78% response rate) 11- and 14-year-old participants (mean age = 12.66 years, $SD = 1.57$; 55% female: 56.5% European American, 4.8% Asian American or Pacific Islander, 20.5% Hispanic American, 9.2% African American, and 9.0% "other" or not reported) from two schools in northern California.

Measures. *Self-esteem* was measured with the 10-item Rosenberg (1965) Self-Esteem Scale (RSE) and the 6-item Global sub-scale of the Harter (1985) Self-Perception Profile for Children (SPPC). Teachers completed a modified teacher version of the SPPC.

Delinquency was measured using a 12-item delinquent-behaviors scale adapted from Elliott, Huizinga, and Ageton (1985).

Supportive parenting (warmth, monitoring, use of inductive reasoning, and consistent discipline) was measured using a modified scale from the Iowa Youth and Families Project (e.g., Conger et al., 1992).

Academic achievement was measured by a composite of the Math and Reading percentile scores from the Stanford Achievement Test Battery.

RESULTS AND DISCUSSION

Self-esteem was consistently negatively correlated with delinquency, regardless of whether self-esteem was assessed by the RSE ($r = -.35$), the self-report version of the SPPC ($r = -.39$), or the teacher version of the SPPC ($r = -.29$; all $ps < .05$). To explore these effects further, we compared the self-esteem scores of individuals who reported at least one delinquent act (76% of the sample) and those who reported no delinquent acts. The delinquent group had lower self-esteem than the nondelinquent group on all three self-esteem measure (Cohen's $d = 0.48$,

410 · PIECES OF THE PERSONALITY PUZZLE

0.63, and 0.35 for the RSE, self-report SPPC, and teacher SPPC, respectively; all $ps < .05$).[1]

Baumeister et al. (1996) focused their critique of the low-self-esteem hypothesis on aggression, and it was possible that our results were due to delinquent behaviors not involving aggression. To address this issue, we divided the delinquency scale into a 2-item aggression scale ("got into a fight," "beat someone up") and a 10-item nonaggression scale (e.g., "lied to parents or teachers," "used drugs or alcohol"). All the effects of self-esteem remained significant for both the aggression scale (rs ranged from $-.17$ to $-.26$. $ps < .05$) and the nonaggression scale (rs ranged from $-.28$ to $-.39$, $ps < .05$).

* * *

Study 2

The results of Study 1 provided support for the low-self-esteem hypothesis. In Study 2, we extended Study 1 in several ways. First, we used a longitudinal design to examine the prospective relation between self-esteem and externalizing problems. Second, Study 2 included non-self-report measures of externalizing problems, specifically, teacher- and parent-rated antisocial behavior. Third, Study 2 examined additional control variables, including the quality of parent-child and peer relationships, SES, and IQ. Finally, Study 2 was based on data from a representative birth cohort of New Zealanders, so the range of externalizing problems in the sample reflects the variation found in the general population.

METHOD.

Sample. Participants were members of the Dunedin Multidisciplinary Health and Development Study (for details, see Moffitt, Caspi, Rutter, & Silva, 2001), a longitudinal investigation of a complete cohort of consecutive births between April 1, 1972, and March 31, 1973, in Dunedin, New Zealand. The present study included participants who completed a measure of self-esteem at

ate 11 ($n = 812$; 48% female; 78% of the initial cohort) or at age 13 ($n = 736$; 48% female; 71% of the initial cohort).

Measures Self-esteem was measured at age 11 and age 13 with the RSE. * * *

Externalizing problems were assessed using the Rutter Child Scale (RCS; Rutter, Tizard, & Whitmore, 1970) and the Revised Behavior Problem Checklist (RBPC: Quay & Peterson, 1987). Teachers completed the RCS when the participants were ages 11 and 13; parents completed the RCS when the participants were age 11 and the RBPC when they were age 13. Information about the reliability and validity of these measures is provided by Moffitt et al. (2001).

* * *

RESULTS AND DISCUSSION

Relations Between Self-Esteem and Externalizing Problems. Results were consistent with those of Study 1: Self-esteem was negatively correlated with parent reports of externalizing problems ($r = -.18$ at age 11 and $r = -.27$ at age 13, $ps < .05$) and with teacher reports of externalizing problems ($r = -.16$ at age 11 and $r = -.18$ at age 13, $ps < .05$). Moreover, self-esteem at age 11 was prospectively related to both parent and teacher reports of externalizing problems at age 13 (both $rs = -.20$, $ps < .05$). As in Study 1, the cross-method effects were significant; individuals with low self-esteem were more likely to engage in antisocial behaviors as reported by their parents and teachers. We divided the items on the antisocial-behavior scales according to whether they involved aggressive (e.g., fighting, bullying) or nonaggressive (e.g., lying, disobedient) behaviors, and the effects of self-esteem remained significant for both the aggression items (rs ranged from $-.13$ to $-.26$, $ps < .05$) and the nonaggression items (rs ranged from $-.18$ to $-.21$, $ps < .05$).

* * *

Study 3

The results of Studies 1 and 2 support the low-self-esteem hypothesis. In Study 3, we tested the

---

[1]Cohen's *d* is a measure of effect size. Values of .2, .5, and .8 are typically interpreted as small, medium, and large coefficients.

	TABLE 1									
	RESULTS OF CORRELATIONAL AND REGRESSION ANALYSES PREDICTING AGGRESSION FROM SELF-ESTEEM AND NARCISSISM (STUDY 3)									
	Total Aggression		Physical Aggression		Verbal Aggression		Anger		Hostility	
Predictor	Zero-order correlation	β	Zero-order correlation	β	Zero-order correlation	β	Zero-order correlation	β	Zero-order correlation	β
Self-esteem	−.30*	−.39*	−.11*	−.19*	.02	−.09*	−.26*	−.33*	−.48*	−.51*
Narcissism	.18*	.30*	.21*	.27*	.31*	.34*	.14*	.24*	−.05*	.11*
Multiple R	—	.41*	—	.28*	—	.33*	—	.35*	—	.49*

Note. $N = 3.143$.
*$p < .05$.

hypothesis (Baumeister et al., 1996, 2003) that unrealistically high, not low, self-esteem predicts aggression by assessing both self-esteem and narcissism and examining their relations with reports of real-world aggression. Previous research on narcissism has used laboratory measures of aggression, and it is not clear whether the findings generalize to real-world aggression.

METHOD

Sample. The sample consisted of 3,143 undergraduate students (68.3% female; mean age = 19.6 years, $SD = 1.6$) from a large research university in northern California. They participated in exchange for course credit.

Measures. *Self-esteem* was measured with the RSE. *Narcissism* was measured by the 40-item Narcissistic Personality Inventory (Raskin & Terry, 1988). *Aggression* was assessed using the 29-item Buss-Perry Aggression Questionnaire (AQ; Buss & Perry, 1992). The AQ includes a Total Aggression scale and four subscales: Physical Aggression, Verbal Aggression, Anger, and Hostility.

RESULTS AND DISCUSSION Table 1 shows correlations of self-esteem and narcissism with aggression. Results were consistent with the findings of Studies 1 and 2: Self-esteem was negatively correlated with the Total Aggression scale of the AQ ($r = -.30$, $p < .05$) and with all of the subscales

except Verbal Aggression. Note that self-esteem was related to the Physical Aggression subscale, which has been linked to real-world displays of violence (Bushman & Wells, 1998). In contrast, narcissism was positively correlated with the Total Aggression scale ($r = .18$, $p < .05$) and with all of the subscales except Hostility. Thus, we found support for the claim that narcissistic individuals are prone to aggression.

Self-esteem and narcissism were moderately related ($r = .32$, $p < .05$), so we conducted multiple regression analyses to test whether they had independent effects on aggression (Table 1).[2] In general, the effect sizes increased in the multiple regression analyses (e.g., the zero-order relation between self-esteem and Total Aggression was −.30, whereas the regression coefficient controlling for narcissism was −.39). * * * Thus, low self-esteem and narcissism contribute independently to aggressive thoughts, feelings, and behaviors, and in fact serve as mutual suppressors.

---

[2]The multiple regression analyses permit one to examine the simultaneous effects of self-esteem and narcissism on the five dependent variables shown in Table 1. The standardized regression, or β coefficients, shown in Table 1 would be identical to the Pearson correlations shown in the Table if self-esteem and narcissism had a correlation of 0.00. The β values are, in every case, more extreme than the Pearson correlations (a phenomenon known as "suppression"), indicating that when either narcissism or self-esteem is controlled, the effect of the other variable is stronger.

General Discussion

In three studies, we found a robust relation between low self-esteem and externalizing problems. This relation held for different age groups, different nationalities, and multiple methods of assessing self-esteem and externalizing problems. * * * Moreover, our results indicate that self-esteem may foretell future externalizing problems: 11-year-olds with low self-esteem tended to increase in aggression by age 13. Finally, the effect of low self-esteem on aggression was independent of narcissism; in fact, when healthy self-regard was disentangled from narcissistic self-perceptions, the relation between low self-esteem and aggression became even stronger. Thus, our results support the concern (Baumeister et al., 1996) about the dangers of narcissism but do not support the conclusion that low self-esteem is unrelated to externalizing problems. In this section, we discuss conceptual and methodological issues that may help explain the inconsistencies in the literature on the association between low self-esteem and externalizing problems.

Baumeister et al. (1996) suggested that inflated high self-esteem (as captured by measures of narcissism) is a better predictor of aggression than low self-esteem. This suggestion seems to be based on the assumption that low self-esteem and narcissism are opposite ends of the same continuum (self-hate v. self-love). For example, Baumeister et al. noted that "an effective and valid [self-esteem scale would identify the arrogant, conceited narcissist just as well as the person who holds an unbiased appreciation of his or her own well-recognized good qualities" (pp. 28–29). Accepting this view may result in the need to pit the low-self-esteem hypothesis against the narcissism hypothesis; that is, antisocial individuals have either low self-esteem or its antithesis, narcissism. Moreover, conceptualizing low self-esteem and narcissism as opposite ends of the same continuum leads to the concern that "the societal pursuit of high self-esteem for everyone may literally end up doing considerable harm" (Baumeister et al., 1996, p. 29).

However, this concern may not be warranted because it is possible to draw a distinction between healthy self-regard and narcissistic self-views. For example, Rosenberg (1965) noted that "when we deal with self-esteem, we are asking whether the individual considers himself adequate—a person of worth—not whether he considers himself superior to others" (p. 62). In contrast, narcissists describe themselves as special, extraordinary people who are better and more deserving than others. Empirically, measures of self-esteem and narcissism typically correlate only in the .20s to low .30s, which is far below the level of convergent validity one would expect between two self-report measures of the same construct. Thus, the precise relation between self-esteem and narcissism remains an open question.

Several conceptualizations are currently being debated in the self-esteem literature, including whether narcissism is an exaggerated form of high self-esteem, a particular facet of self-esteem, a highly contingent and unstable form of self-esteem, a need to feel superior to others, or a defensive shell of inflated self-esteem that compensates for unconscious feelings of inadequacy (e.g., Campbell, Rudich, & Sedikides, 2002: Kirkpatrick et al., 2002: Morf & Rhodewalt, 2001: Tracy & Robins, 2003). Although resolving this issue is beyond the scope of this article, our results indicate that self-esteem and narcissism have independent effects on externalizing problems, thus demonstrating their discriminant validity. Moreover, when narcissism is partialed out of self-esteem, the regression coefficient for self-esteem more closely captures Rosenberg's (1965) conceptualization of self-esteem and provides clear support for the low-self-esteem hypothesis.

Another way to reconcile the inconsistent results in the literature is to consider methodological differences between our work and previous laboratory research on self-esteem and aggression. Although experimental measures of aggression have a great deal of external validity (Anderson & Bushman, 1997), they do not necessarily have the same correlates as measures of real-world aggression and antisocial behavior. In fact, in their review of the literature, Anderson and Bushman (1997) noted that lab and real-world studies sometimes produce discrepant results, and suggested that "rather than take the perspective that one 'side' or the other is wrong, it may be more prudent to try to locate the source of the discrepancies in psychological processes that may differ in the two settings" (p. 33).

There are several possible sources of the discrepancy between our findings and those of the previous lab studies. First, lab studies typically examine a specific form of aggression, namely, aggression provoked by a competitive task in which self-evaluative processes have been activated. In contrast, real-world externalizing problems occur in a wide range of contexts, and these other forms of aggression may have distinct correlates.

Second, aggressive behavior in the lab does not lead to any serious harm to the other person, whereas real-world aggression often does: blasting someone with white noise does not have the same consequences as hitting someone. The correlates of milder forms of aggression, particularly those that have no clear negative repercussions, may differ from the correlates of other forms of aggression.

Third, aggressive behaviors occurring in the lab are not antisocial to the same extent as real-world aggression. One could argue that it is socially appropriate to blast one's opponent with white noise in the context of an experiment that has been sanctioned by the university. In contrast, the externalizing behaviors assessed in the present research are explicitly socially undesirable, antisocial, and in most cases illegal. Thus, the discrepancy between our findings and those of previous lab studies may reflect the fact that individuals with narcissistically high self-esteem are more likely to be aggressive when it is socially desirable (e.g., lab paradigms for assessing aggression, athletic events, some corporate settings), whereas individuals with low self-esteem are more likely to be aggressive when it is socially undesirable and contrary to social norms. Future research should examine the specific motivational processes underlying different forms of aggressive behavior in individuals with low versus high self-esteem.

Finally, the relation between low self-esteem and aggression was generally small to moderate in the present studies. This result might provide the simplest explanation for inconsistencies in the literature. If the true effect size is small, then it is not surprising that some studies have reported null findings because of lack of power and fluctuations in observed effect sizes across samples due to systematic and random factors. Moreover, from a meta-analytic perspective, variation in effect sizes across studies indicated the presence of moderator variable. Thus, researchers need to develop theoretical models that generate testable predictions about the boundary conditions on the effect of low self-esteem.

Although much work on these exciting and controversial topics remains to be completed, we believe it is reasonable to conclude that both low self-esteem and narcissism contribute to externalizing problems. Our findings provide strong support for a replicable link between low self-esteem and externalizing problems, and we recommend that the low-self-esteem hypothesis not be discarded prematurely.

REFERENCES

Adler, A. (1956). *The individual psychology of Alfred Adler: A systematic presentation in selections from his writings* (H.L. Ansbacher & R.R. Ansbacher. Eds.). New York: Harper.

Anderson, C.A., & Bushman, B.J. (1997). External validity of "trivial" experiments: The case of laboratory aggression. *Review of General Psychology, 1.* 19–41.

Baumeister, R.F., Bushman, B.J., & Campbell, W.K. (2000). Self-esteem, narcissism, and aggression: Does violence result from low self-esteem or from threatened egotism? *Current Directions in Psychological Science, 9.* 26–29.

Baumeister, R.F., Campbell, J.D., Krueger, J.I., & Vohs, K.E. (2003). Does high self-esteem cause better performance, interpersonal success, happiness, or healthier lifestyles? *Psychological Science in the Public Interest. 4* (1).

Baumeister, R.F., Smart, L., & Boden, J.M. (1996). Relation of threatened egotism to violence and aggression: The dark side of high self-esteem. *Psychological Review. 103.* 5–33.

Bushman, B.J., & Baumeister, R.F. (1998). Threatened egotism, narcissism, self-esteem, and direct and displaced aggression: Does self-love or self-hate lead to violence? *Journal of Personality and Social Psychology, 75.* 219–229.

Bushman, B.J., & Wells, G.L. (1998). Trait aggressiveness and hockey penalties: Predicting hot tempers on the ice. *Journal of Applied Psychology, 83.* 969–974.

Buss, A.H., & Perry, M. (1992). The aggression questionnaire. *Journal of Personality and Social Psychology, 63.* 452–459.

Bynner, J.M., O'Malley, P., & Bachman, J.G. (1981). Self-esteem and delinquency revisited. *Journal of Youth and Adolescence, 10.* 407–441.

Campbell, W.K., Rudich, E.A., & Sedikides, C. (2002). Narcissism, self-esteem, and the positivity of self-views: Two portraits of self-love. *Personality and Social Psychology Bulletin, 28.* 358–368.

Conger, R., Conger, K., Elder, G.H., Lorenz, F., Simons, R., & Whitebeck, L.B. (1992). A family process model of economic hardship and adjustment of early adolescent boys. *Child Development, 63.* 526–541.

DuBois, D.I., & Tevendale, H.D. (1999). Self-esteem in childhood and adolescence: Vaccine or epiphenomenon? *Applied and Preventive Psychology, 8.* 103–117.

Elliot, D.S., Huizinga, D., & Ageton, S. (1985). *Explaining delinquency and drug use.* Beverly Hills, CA: Sage.

Fergusson, D.M., & Horwood, L.J. (2002). Male and female offending trajectories. *Development and Psychopathology, 14.* 159–177.

Harter, S. (1985).*The self-perception profile for adolescents.* Unpublished manuscript. University of Denver. Denver, CO.

Hirschi, T. (1969). *Causes of delinquency.* Berkeley: University of California Press.

Horney, K. (1950). *Neurosis and human growth.* New York: Norton.

Jang, S.J., & Thornberry, T.P. (1998). Self-esteem, delinquent peers, and delinquency: A test of the self-enhancement thesis. *American Sociological Review, 63.* 586–598.

Kirkpatrick, L.A., Waugh, C.E., Valencia, A., & Webster, G.D. (2002). The functional domain specificity of self-esteem and the differential prediction of aggression. *Journal of Personality and Social Psychology, 82.* 756–767.

McCarthy, J.D., & Hoge, D.R. (1984). The dynamics of self-esteem and delinquency. *American Journal of Sociology, 90.* 396–410.

Moffitt, T.E., Caspi, A., Rutter, M., & Silva, P.A. (2001). *Sex differences in antisocial behavior: Conduct disorder, delinquency, and violence in the Dunedin Longitudinal Study.* Cambridge, England: Cambridge University Press.

Morf, C.C., & Rhodewalt, F. (2001). Expanding the dynamic self-regulatory processing model of narcissism: Research directions for the future. *Psychological Inquiry, 12.* 243–251.

Quay, H.C., & Peterson, D.R. (1987). *Manual for the Behavior Problem Checklist.* Miami, FL: Author.

Raskin, R., & Terry, H. (1988). A principal-components analysis of the Narcissistic Personality Inventory and further evidence of its construct validation. *Journal of Personality and Social Psychology, 54.* 890–902.

Rogers, C.R. (1961). *On becoming a person.* Boston: Houghton Mifflin.

Rosenberg, M. (1965). *Society and adolescent self-image.* Princeont, NJ: Princeton University.

Rosenberg, M. Schooler, C., & Schoenbach, C. (1989). Self-esteem and adolescent problems: Modeling reciprocal effects. *American Sociological Review, 54.* 1004–1018.

Rutter, M., Tizard, J., & Whitmore, K. (1970). *Education, health, and behavior.* London: Longman.

Slater, L. (2002, February 3). The trouble with self-esteem: Maybe thinking highly of yourself is the real problem. *New York Times Magazine.* Section 6, p. 44.

Sprott, J.B., & Doob, A.N. (2000). Bad, sad, and rejected: the lives of aggressive children. *Canadian Journal of Criminology, 42.* 123–133.

Tracy, J.L., & Robins, R.W. (2003). "Death of a (narcissistic) salesman": An integrative model of fragile self-esteem. *Psychological Inquiry, 14.* 57–62.

Twenge, J.M., & Campbell, W.K. (2003). "Isn't it fun to get the respect that we're going to deserve?" Narcissism, social rejection, and aggression. *Personality and Social Psychology Bulletin, 29.* 261–272.

Self-Knowledge of an Amnesic Patient: Toward a Neuropsychology of Personality and Social Psychology

Stanley B. Klein, Judith Loftus, and John F. Kihlstrom

The final selection in this section and this book brings together nearly every tradition in personality psychology. For example, Freud's original intention was to develop a neuropsychological understanding of personality by closely studying individual cases. That is also the intention of the following article, but it goes much further than that. The thorough assessment of "W.J." conducted by Stanley Klein and his colleagues also includes tests of cognitive ability akin to those used in trait assessment, along with self-report personality tests and personality descriptions rendered by people who know her well. The goal is to better understand the basis of self-knowledge. For example, if you forgot everything you ever did and that ever happened to you, would you still know something about who you are?

In the first selection in this book, Dan McAdams asks, "What do we know when we know a person?" In this selection, Klein and colleagues ask, "What do you really know when you know yourself—and how do you know it?"

From *Journal of Experimental Psychology: General, 125,* 250–260, 1996.

* * *

* * * In this article we offer the case of W.J., who suffered profound retrograde amnesia following a head injury, as a demonstration of the way in which questions of interest to social personality psychologists can be addressed with neurological data. Specifically, our tests of W.J. have provided us with data, unobtainable from individuals with no memory loss, that is pertinent to the debate over the relation between knowledge of traits and memory for specific personal events relevant to those traits.

The Role of Episodic and Semantic Memory in Trait Self-Knowledge

Does a person's knowledge of his or her own traits depend on an ability to recall his or her own past behavior? Is it possible for a person who cannot recall any personal experiences—and therefore cannot know how he or she behaved—to know what he or she is like? Questions such as these have stimulated debate among philosophers (e.g., Grice, 1941; Hume, 1739/1817; Locke, 1690/1731;

Shoemaker, 1963) and psychologists (e.g., Buss & Craik, 1983; James, 1890; Klein & Loftus, 1993; Locksley & Lenauer, 1981) for more than 300 years. Unfortunately, as evidenced by the number of years that debate on this topic has persisted, the question of whether trait knowledge is inseparable from memory for past behavior has proven difficult to answer. In this article we make a modest contribution to this debate by demonstrating that an individual can have detailed and accurate knowledge of her traits despite having little if any conscious access to behavioral memories from which she could infer that knowledge.

Knowledge of personality traits and recollections of specific personal events involving those traits can be considered examples of two types of knowledge about the self: semantic personal knowledge and episodic personal knowledge. * * * Semantic personal knowledge is information that has been abstracted from memories of the self in specific events. * * * Thus, semantic personal knowledge of traits might include the facts that a person is kind, outgoing, and lazy. Episodic personal knowledge, by contrast, consists of memories of specific events involving the self. * * * Thus, episodic personal knowledge of traits could include memories of instances in which behavior was kind, outgoing, or lazy.

Our previous research with individuals with no memory loss used a number of techniques to examine the relation between these two types of trait knowledge about the self. Our data consistently have supported the view that in the realm of trait knowledge, semantic personal memory and episodic personal memory are functionally independent, by which we mean that the operations of semantic personal memory do not require the operations of episodic personal memory (for reviews, see Kihlstrom & Klein, 1994, 1997; Klein & Loftus, 1993).

In our initial investigations of the relation between semantic and episodic memory for traits, we used a priming paradigm. In a series of studies, we found that participants who made self-descriptiveness judgments about trait words were no faster than participants who performed a control task to

then perform a second task that required them to retrieve personal episodic memories about the same traits. * * * We concluded from this that the semantic personal knowledge required for a self-descriptiveness judgment was accessed without activating episodic personal memories. If episodic memories had been activated during the self-descriptiveness judgments, then participants who made those judgments should have had an advantage over participants who performed the control task in the speed with which they subsequently retrieved episodic memories.

We have conducted several other studies of trait self-knowledge that also support the independence of semantic and episodic personal memory. Klein, Loftus, and Plog (1992), for example, made use of the phenomenon of transfer-appropriate processing (e.g., Roediger & Blaxton, 1987; Roediger, Weldon, & Challis, 1988) in a study of recognition memory for traits to show that different processes are involved in accessing the two types of memory. In addition, Klein et al. (1989, Experiment 4) applied the principle of encoding variability (e.g., Bower, 1972; Martin, 1971, 1972) in a study of recall for traits and found that the type of information made available by accessing semantic personal memory was different from that made available by accessing episodic personal memory.

However, although this research converges in support of the functional independence of semantic and episodic trait knowledge of self, a number of theorists have noted a problem inherent in trying to infer the functional independence of semantic and episodic memory from the performance of individuals with no memory loss (e.g., Parkin, 1993; Tulving, Hayman, & Macdonald, 1991). Specifically, experiments that attempt to demonstrate such independence must be able to show that each of these memory systems can operate without the other—that participants can perform a task involving one memory system without activating the other. However, when participants have access to both episodic and semantic memory, it is difficult to rule out interplay between the two systems in the performance of experimental tasks and therefore difficult to compellingly demonstrate that the two systems are independent. For example, although Klein et al. (1989, Experiment 2; see also Klein et al., 1992, Experiments 2, 3, & 4) found that participants appeared to make self-descriptiveness judgments without retrieving episodic memories, it is possible that episodes were retrieved but that the tests used to detect retrieval were not sufficiently sensitive. * * *

However, amnesic memory impairment offers an opportunity to overcome this problem. Amnesic patients provide a particularly effective method for testing the independence of semantic and episodic personal memory, because these patients typically display intact semantic memory with impaired access to episodic memory. * * * Therefore, it is possible with amnestic patients to test semantic self-knowledge of traits with assurance that episodic memory for traits is not involved. If the two systems are indeed functionally independent, then amnesic patients should be able to make trait self-descriptiveness judgments despite their inability to recall personal events.

This hypothesis has been tested by Tulving (1993). Tulving found that the patient K.C., whose entire fund of episodic memory was permanently lost following a motorcycle accident, was able to describe his personality with considerable accuracy. Tulving asked K.C. on two occasions to rate a list of trait adjectives for self-descriptiveness. Tulving also asked K.C.'s mother to rate K.C. on the same traits. Tulving's findings revealed that K.C.'s ratings were both reliable (K.C.'s trait self-ratings showed 78% agreement across sessions) and consistent with the way he is perceived by others (there was 73% agreement between K.C.'s and his mother's ratings of K.C.'s traits). K.C. thus appears to have accurate and detailed knowledge about his personality despite the fact that he has no conscious access to any behavioral episodes from which he could infer this knowledge.

The fact that K.C., without access to episodic self-knowledge, can access semantic self-knowledge to make trait self-descriptiveness judgments confirms that semantic personal memory is functionally independent of episodic personal memory in the realm of trait knowledge. Having established this, however, a question still remains. Although K.C.'s case shows that semantic personal memory can function without episodic personal memory, does this mean that under ordinary circumstances the two types of memory do not interact? K.C. can make trait judgments: but perhaps his judgments would be different if his episodic memory were intact. * * *

To this question we bring the case of W.J., who, as a result of a head injury, suffered temporary retrograde amnesia. Retrograde amnesia is the inability to recall events that precede the onset of the amnesia. Typically, it entails loss of episodic memory with sparing of semantic memory. * * * When it occurs following a closed-head injury, retrograde amnesia typically has the additional feature of being temporary, resolving in the days or weeks following the injury. * * *

Because W.J.'s amnesia was temporary, it was possible to test her semantic personal memory both without and with access to episodic personal memory. We asked W.J. to make trait judgments about herself during the time when she was amnesic for events pertaining to those judgments and again when her episodic memory had returned. In this way, we were able to look for differences in her semantic memory performance as a function of the accessibility of episodic memory. Performance differences would tell us that semantic and episodic personal memory, although functionally independent, do interact in some way. However, consistent performance without and with episodic memory would point toward a stronger form of independence between the two memory types.

Method

PARTICIPANTS

Patient W.J. The patient, W.J., is an 18-year-old female undergraduate. During the first week of her second quarter at college she sustained a concussional head injury as a result of a fall. After complaining of a headache and difficulty in concentration and memory, she was taken to a hospital emergency room where a computerized tomography brain scan was performed. No signs of neurological abnormality were observed.

W.J. was interviewed by Stanley B. Klein on several occasions. In a meeting 5 days after her head injury, she complained of great difficulty remembering events that occurred before the accident. Questioned informally, she was unable to bring to mind a single personal event or experience from the last 6–7 months of her life—a period of time covering approximately her first quarter at college. Her memory for more remote personal events was patchy, with amnesic gaps dating back to about 4 years before her injury.

Despite her dense retrograde amnesia for events from the preceding 6–7 months, W.J.'s memory for general facts about her personal life during that period seemed largely intact. She knew, for example, which classes she attended during her first quarter at college, although she could not remember a specific occasion when she attended class or a specific event that happened during a class; she knew the names of teachers and friends from college, although she could not remember particular experiences shared with them.

W.J. also showed a moderate degree of anterograde memory impairment, which seemed limited to the period of approximately 45 min following her fall. Although her boyfriend reported that she was conscious and coherent, W.J. had no recollection of events that occurred during that time.

Eleven days after the accident, W.J.'s retrograde amnesia had cleared considerably. Her memory impairment appeared limited to events from the last 6 months, and within that period she was able to clearly recollect a number of incidents. For example, she could describe in great detail a visit to the home of her boyfriend's parents 3 months earlier. Her anterograde amnesia, on the other hand, remained unchanged.

When interviewed 3 weeks later, W.J. appeared to have completely recovered her memory for events preceding her fall. She still, however, was unable to recall events that occurred immediately afterward.

Control Participants with No Memory Loss.

Control group for memory testing. Three female undergraduates, whose mean age (19 years, 4 months) was closely matched to W.J.'s age (18 years, 3 months), were tested on the same battery of memory tests that was administered to W.J.

Control group for personality testing. Two opposite-sex couples, whose arrival at college coincided with W.J.'s (6 months prior to testing) and whose mean time as a couple (4.2 years) closely matched that of W.J. and her boyfriend (3.5 years), completed the same personality trait questionnaire that was completed by W.J. and her boyfriend.

PROCEDURE

Memory Testing. Memory performance following closed-head injury follows a fairly consistent pattern of preserved and impaired function. * * * Immediate memory span and access to semantic knowledge typically are intact, whereas episodic memories of events preceding and following the injury are likely to be impaired. In most cases, the retrograde component of the amnesia shrinks in the days following the injury, with memories returning in a roughly chronological order from the most distant to the most recent events.

To evaluate W.J.'s memory function, we administered the following battery of memory tests to her and to three female control participants. Except where indicated, all testing was conducted 5 days after W.J. had sustained her head injury. Participants were tested individually.

Digit span. W.J.'s immediate memory was assessed using a digit-span technique. * * * An experimenter read aloud to the participant a list of digits, at a rate of one digit every 2 s, beginning with a list of two digits. The participants then were to immediately repeat the digits back to the experimenter in correct order. If the list was repeated correctly, the experimenter read another list of digits, increasing the length of the list by one digit.

Testing continued until the participant failed to repeat a list correctly. The procedure then was repeated with new lists and a change in instructions so that participants repeated the digits in reverse order, rather than in presentation order.

Free recall. W.J.'s ability to retain information beyond the span of immediate memory was examined using a free-recall paradigm. Participants were presented with five lists of 16 unrelated nouns. Each list was read aloud by the experimenter at the rate of 1 noun every 2 s. Immediately after presentation of the last item in a list, participants were given 1 min to write as many of the items from that list as possible, in any order. Each participant's recall performance was plotted as a serial-position curve, which shows the probability of an item being correctly recalled as a function of its serial position in the input list. * * *

Semantic memory. To investigate W.J.'s access to semantic knowledge, we selected two tasks—verbal fluency and category judgment—from the battery of semantic memory tests used by Wilson & Baddeley (1988).

In the verbal fluency task, participants were required to generate as many items as possible from each of six semantic categories: animals, fruits, furniture, girls' names, birds, and metals. Participants were allowed 1 min per category in which to write responses.

In the category judgment task, participants were shown 24 pairs of words and, for each pair, were asked to decide whether the words belonged to the same semantic category (e.g., fruits, animals). Half of the pairs contained words from the same semantic category (e.g., *grape–apple*), and half contained words from different categories (e.g., *tiger–boat*). Participants were asked to state their decisions as quickly as possible, and their decision latencies were recorded.

Episodic memory. We used the autobiographical memory-cueing task originated by Galton (1879) and later modified by Crovitz and Schiffman (1974) and Robinson (1976) to test memory for personal episodes. In this task, participants were presented with cue words. For each cue, they were asked to recall a specific personal event and to provide as precise a date as possible for that event. For example, a participant might respond to the cue *dog* by recalling that she walked her dog that morning or that she received a dog as a gift for her 10th birthday.

Our study examined episodic memory under two cueing conditions: unconstrained and constrained (e.g., Schacter, Kihlstrom, Kihlstrom, & Berren, 1989; Schacter, Wang, Tulving, & Freedman, 1982). In the unconstrained condition, participants were read a list of 24 cue words, 1 word at a time. They were instructed to recall for each cue a specific personal event related to the cue from any time in their past. The 24 cues were common English words, randomly selected from the set of 48 cue words presented by Robinson (1976). The cues included 8 affect words (e.g., *lonely, surprised*), 8 object words (e.g., *car, river*) and 8 activity words (e.g., *run, visit*). All participants received the same set of 24 cue words in a fixed-random order.

At the beginning of the session, participants were told that we were interested in studying memory for personal events. They were informed that a series of words would be read to them and that they should try to think of a specific personal event that was related to each word. They were instructed to provide a brief verbal description of each memory and to date the memory as accurately as possible. If on any trial a participant was unable to retrieve a memory within 60 s, the trial was terminated and the participant was read the next cue.

After a short rest break, the constrained-cueing task was administered. This task was identical to the unconstrained task, except that participants were instructed to restrict their recall to events that had occurred within the last 6 months. The same cues were used in the constrained and unconstrained conditions.

In a second session, conducted 4 weeks after the first session, participants were tested again using only the unconstrained-cueing condition.

Personality Testing. A list of 80 trait adjectives was selected from Kirby & Gardner's (1972) norms to create a personality questionnaire. The adjectives selected were close to the norm means on the dimensions of familiarity, imagery, and behavioral specificity and spanned the range of social desirability. The questionnaire consisted of four sheets of paper with 20 traits per sheet. Beside each trait were four choices: *not at all, somewhat, quite a bit,* and *definitely.*

Personality testing was conducted in two sessions. The first session took place 5 days after W.J.'s accident. W.J. was provided with a personality questionnaire and was instructed to indicate, by circling the appropriate choice, the extent to which each trait described her since her arrival at college. Her boyfriend also completed the questionnaire, indicating for each trait how well it described W.J. since her arrival at college. After a brief break, W.J. filled out the questionnaire a second time, this time indicating for each trait the extent to which it described her during high school.

Two control couples also completed the questionnaire. For each couple, the woman indicated how well each of the 80 trait adjectives on the questionnaire described her since her arrival at college, and the man indicated the extent to which the traits described his partner since her arrival at college.

A second session was conducted four weeks later. W.J. and the two women of the control couples again were given the personality questionnaire and asked, for each trait, to indicate how well it described them since their arrival at college.

Results

MEMORY TESTING

Digit Span. Immediate memory, as measured by the digit span, typically is normal in patients who have suffered closed-head injuries. * * * W.J.'s digit-span performance (5 digits forward and 5 digits backward) was comparable to that of the control participants (Ms = 5.3 digits forward and 5.7 digits backward).[1] This suggests that W.J. can

hold as much information in immediate memory as can control participants with no memory loss.

Free Recall. Figure 1 shows two serial-position curves: one for W.J. and one representing the mean performance of the control participants. As can be seen, there is little difference between the curves. For both, items from the beginning and end of the list were better recalled than were items in the middle, resulting in the U-shaped curve characteristic of normal free-recall performance. * * *

Semantic Memory. Amnestic patients usually perform normally or near normally on tasks requiring access to knowledge contained in semantic memory. * * * W.J.'s performance * * * was within the range established by the control participants, indicating that the speed and accuracy with which she could access material from semantic memory was unimpaired.

Episodic Memory. Retrograde amnesia for personal episodes commonly is observed in cases of closed-head injury. * * * Figure 2 presents the proportion of episodic memories produced from four different time periods: from within the previous 12 months, from more than a year but less than 5 years ago, from more than 5 but less than 10 years ago, and from more than 10 years ago.

The temporal distributions of memories produced during the first unconstrained-cueing session are shown in Figure 2A. As can be seen, there is a marked difference between the performance of W.J. and that of the controls. Paralleling previous studies of participants with no memory loss (e.g., * * * Rubin, Wetzler, & Nebes, 1986), control participants showed a pronounced recency bias in their recall: The majority of memories came from the most recent 12-month period (65%), with increasingly smaller proportions recalled from each of the more distant past periods.

By contrast, W.J.'s recall was characterized by a strong primacy bias: She had considerable difficulty retrieving memories from the previous 12 months (she could recall only a single episode from the last year and none from the last 6

---

[1]M is the mean.

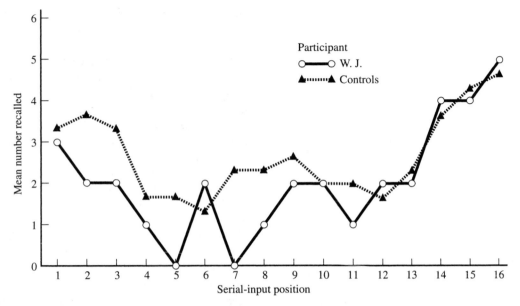

Figure 1. Serial-position curve, showing mean number of nouns recalled by W.J. and control participants with no memory loss as a function of serial-input position.

months) and progressively less difficulty retrieving memories from earlier periods. The temporal gradient found in W.J.'s recall fits nicely with a growing body of evidence showing that following closed-head injury, disruption of memory retrieval is more likely to be seen for recently acquired memories than for older memories (e.g., * * * Lucchelli et al., 1995; MacKinnon & Squire, 1989). * * *

Although W.J.'s performance on the first unconstrained autobiographical cueing task indicates that she was densely amnesic for recent personal episodes, several investigators have noted that caution must be exercised when interpreting results from this task (e.g., Evans et al., 1993; Kopelman, 1994 * * *). Because W.J. was not required to produce memories from specified time periods, it is difficult to know whether her failure to retrieve personal memories from the last 6 months reflects an inability to do so or, rather, a bias to sample from more remote time periods.

The constrained autobiographical cueing task allowed us to distinguish between these alternatives by requiring participants to restrict their recall to

memories of events occurring in the previous 6 months. In this condition, W.J. was unable to retrieve a single memory. By contrast, control participants produced memories in response to 96% of the cues. These data clearly suggest that W.J.'s failure to produce recent episodic memories in the unconstrained-cueing task represents a retrieval impairment rather than a bias in sampling.

Figure 2B presents the results from the second unconstrained-cueing session, conducted 4 weeks after the first. As noted previously, informal questioning indicated that W.J.'s retrograde amnesia largely had cleared at this point. Consistent with this observation, W.J. and control participants produced virtually identical temporal distributions of memories, characterized by pronounced recency biases (83% and 77% of the memories retrieved by W.J. and the controls, respectively, came from the 12 months preceding the test). It should be noted that W.J.'s recency bias was not due to recall of events occurring during the 4-week period following initial testing: Only 2 of the 20 memories she dated as having occurred during the last year were drawn from that period. These data, then, demon-

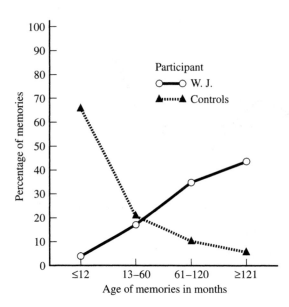

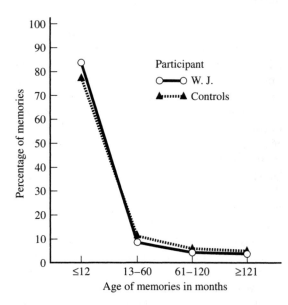

Figure 2. Percentage of episodic memories in four age periods produced by W. J. and control participants with no memory loss with unconstrained cueing during Session 1 (A) and Session 2 (B).

strate a substantial recovery of W.J.'s episodic memory by the second testing session.

PERSONALITY TESTING The central question for the present research is whether semantic self-knowledge is independent of episodic self-knowledge. To examine this question, we had W.J. make trait ratings of herself at college both during her amnesia and following its resolution. We reasoned that if semantic knowledge of one's traits is not dependent on access to trait-related episodic memories, then W.J.'s trait self-ratings should be unaffected by changes in the accessibility of her episodic memories.

We asked W.J. on two occasions to provide ratings of herself at college. The first rating session took place while she was densely amnesic for personal events that had occurred during college; the second session occurred after her memory for her experiences at college had fully recovered. Two female controls provided trait ratings of themselves at college during the same two sessions.

W.J.'s ratings of herself at college showed considerable consistency across testings: The Pearson product–moment correlation coefficient between ratings produced in the first and second session was significant ($r = .74$, $p < .05$) and virtually identical to that for the control participants ($r = .78$, $p < .05$)[2] Thus, despite a dramatic change in the accessibility of her episodic memories of herself at college across testings. W.J.'s test–retest reliability was comparable to that of participants who had access to episodic memories at both testings. It appears that W.J.'s loss of episodic memory did not affect access to her trait self-knowledge.

It is, of course, possible that W.J.'s ratings agreed over sessions because she simply endorsed positive traits and rejected negative traits on both trials. * * * To address this concern, we compared W.J.'s self-ratings from the first session with ratings of her made by her boyfriend. Research has shown that the social desirability of traits is far less

---

[2]The *r* is the correlation coefficient, and *p* is the probability that a correlation as large as reported would have been found if its real value were 0.

likely to influence ratings made by an external assessor who knows the person well (e.g., McCrae, 1982; Wiggins, 1973). Therefore, if W.J. were basing her ratings on social desirability, we would not expect a strong correlation between her ratings and ratings of her provided by her boyfriend. However, the correlation between W.J.'s self-ratings and those made by her boyfriend was significant ($r = .65$, $p < .05$) and did not differ from that obtained from control couples ($r = .65$, $p < .05$). Thus, we conclude that W.J.'s self-ratings could not be based purely on social desirability.

*　*　*

Another concern is whether W.J.'s ratings of herself at college were, in fact, based on knowledge of herself during her 6 months at college. It is conceivable, for example, that during initial testing W.J. was unable to access any self-knowledge from the last 6–7 months. Under these circumstances, she may have adopted a strategy of retrieving memories from the most recent period for which she had accessible self-knowledge (i.e., high school) to make reasonable guesses about what she was like at college. Since trait self-descriptions tend to be relatively stable by adolescence (e.g., Engel, 1959; Mortimer & Lorence, 1981; O'Malley & Bachman, 1983), some agreement between ratings based on knowledge of the self in the high-school and college contexts would not be surprising.

To address this concern, we asked W.J. during the first test session to rate how she saw herself during high school. We then computed the correlation between her ratings of herself at high school and her postamnesia ratings of herself at college. We compared this correlation with the correlation between her ratings of herself at college across sessions.

We predicted that if W.J. had access to knowledge of herself at college during her amnesia, then the correlation between her ratings of herself at high school and her postamnesia ratings of herself at college would be lower than the correlation between her ratings of herself at college across testings. By contrast, if, during her amnesia, W.J. actually based her trait ratings of herself at college on knowledge of what she was like in high school,

then the correlation between her ratings of herself at high school and her postamnesia ratings of herself at college should be comparable to that obtained between her ratings of herself at college across sessions.

Statistical analyses revealed that the correlation between her ratings of herself at high school and her postamnesia ratings of herself at college was significant ($r = .53$, $p < .05$), meaning that some degree of reliability in W.J.'s ratings of her college self could have been achieved by reliance on her memories of her precollege behavior and experiences. However, this figure was significantly lower than the correlation obtained between W.J.'s ratings of herself at college across sessions ($r = .74$), $t(158) = 1.71$, $p < .05$, one-tailed.[3] So, there is reliable variability in her college self that is not accounted for by her high-school self. Put another way, while she was amnesic. W.J. knew something about what she had been like at college, which was different from what she was like in high school; but she knew this despite the fact that she could not recall anything from her time in college.

Discussion

This experimental case study illustrates some of the ways in which theoretical issues of concern to personality and social psychologists, especially those surrounding the self, can be addressed with neurological data.

W.J., a college freshman, suffered a concussive blow to the head in the winter quarter of 1995. As a result of this injury, she showed a profound retrograde amnesia for events that had transpired over the 6 months immediately prior to the accident. Over the next month, this amnesia remitted completely. W.J.'s amnesic deficit in episodic personal memory was documented by the Crovitz–Robinson technique of cued autobiographical recall. When tested 5 days after the accident, under both free and constrained conditions. W.J.'s performance was clearly impaired compared with that of

---

[3]The t is a statistic used to evaluate the difference between means.

a group of participants with no memory loss. Four weeks later, W.J.'s performance had improved considerably and was indistinguishable from that of controls.

In contrast to the impairment and recovery of episodic memory, W.J.'s self-ratings of personality did not change at all over the same period of time: Her self-ratings made during the amnesic period agreed with those she made afterward.

The fact that W.J.'s episodic personal memories were affected by the concussion, but her semantic personal memories were not, is evidence that these two types of self-knowledge are represented independently and perhaps mediated by separate cognitive systems. Admittedly, it remains possible that W.J.'s ratings of her personality were based on episodic memories from high school (or earlier) that were not covered by the amnesia or on knowledge of what her personality was like before she entered college. Additionally, it is possible that the trait cues used for personality testing may have retrieved some episodic memories that were not retrieved by means of the affect, object, and activity cue words from the autobiographical memory-cueing task. One problem with neuropsychological evidence, from the investigator's point of view, is that the deficits in question rarely are complete. Still, the evidence obtained in this case is consistent with the results from K.C., the amnesic patient studied by Tulving (1993) and with evidence from intact participants derived from several different paradigms (for reviews, see Kihlstrom & Klein, 1994; Klein & Loftus, 1993). Moreover, this evidence about the self is consistent with conclusions derived from studies of person memory (* * * for a recent review, see Kihlstrom & Hastie, 1997). We believe that when considered as a whole, the evidence we have presented compels one to seriously entertain the possibility that semantic personal knowledge is represented in a manner that is independent of episodic personal knowledge.

A NEUROPSYCHOLOGICAL APPROACH TO ISSUES IN SOCIAL AND PERSONALITY PSYCHOLOGY

Over and above this specific theoretical question, we hope that this case study will stimulate other personality and social psychologists to consider the theoretical promise of patients with neuropsychological impairments. Consider, as an example, the classic case of Phineas Gage, the 19th-century railway worker who underwent profound personality changes following traumatic injury to the anterior portion of his cerebral cortex. * * * For more than a century, this case has served as the source of speculations about the role of the frontal lobes in emotion, personality, and social relations (e.g., Damasio & Anderson, 1993), and it may be that data from frontal-lobe patients will help resolve the vexing question of the relations between cognition and emotion (e.g., Lazarus, 1984; Zajonc, 1980, 1984).

* * *

Neuropsychological evidence also is relevant to questions of the self. For example, the patient H.M., who received a bilateral resection of his temporal lobes, has suffered a gross anterograde amnesia since the day of his operation in 1953 (Milner, Corkin, & Teuber, 1968; Scoville & Milner, 1957). Despite the physical changes wrought by 40 years of aging and the fact that he remembers nothing of what he has done or experienced in all that time, H.M. has preserved a continuity of identity. Studies of amnesic patients' interpersonal, emotional, and motivational lives promise to provide new perspectives on the relations of these functions with memory.

CONCLUSIONS

In the past, cognitive psychologists have made good use of neuropsychological case material in developing theories about mental function (Gazzaniga, 1995; Heilman & Valenstein, 1993; Kolb & Whishaw, 1990). With rare exceptions, however (e.g., K. Goldstein, 1934/1995; Luria, 1966; Sacks, 1974, 1985, 1995), neuropsychologists have seldom inquired into their patients' personal and social lives. And, whether for lack of interest or lack of access, personality and social psychologists have rarely studied the victims of brain damage. We hope that this situation changes, for it would seem that neurological patients have much to teach us about the psychological processes involved in forming, maintaining, and using mental representations of ourselves and other people.

References

Bower, G. H. (1972). Stimulus-sampling theory of encoding variability. In A. W. Melton & E. Martin (Eds.), *Coding processes in human memory* (pp. 85–123). Washington, DC: Winston.

Buss, D. M., & Craik, K. H. (1983). The act frequency approach to personality. *Psychological Review, 90*, 105–126.

Crovitz, H. F., & Schiffman, H. (1974). Frequency of episodic memories as a function of their age. *Bulletin of the Psychonomic Society, 4(5B)*, 517–518.

Damasio, A. R., & Anderson, S. W. (1993). The frontal lobes. In K. M. Heilman & E. Valenstein (Eds.), *Clinical neuropsychology* (pp. 409–560). New York: Oxford University Press.

Engel, M. (1959). The stability of the self-concept in adolescence. *Journal of Abnormal and Social Psychology, 58*, 211–215.

Evans, J., Wilson, B., Wraight, E. P., & Hodges, J. R. (1993). Neuropsychological and SPECT scan findings during and after transient global amnesia: Evidence for the differential impairment of remote episodic memory. *Journal of Neurology, Neurosurgery, and Psychiatry, 56*, 1227–1230.

Galton, F. (1879). Psychometric experiments. *Brain, 2*, 149–162.

Gazzaniga, M. S. (Ed.), (1995). *The cognitive neurosciences.* Cambridge, MA: MIT Press.

Goldstein, K. (1995). *The organism.* New York: Zone Books. (Original work published 1934.)

Grice, H. P. (1941). Personal identity. *Mind, 50*, 330–350.

Heilman, K. M., & Valenstein, E. (1993). *Clinical neuropsychology* (3rd ed.). New York: Oxford University Press.

Hume, D. A. (1817). *A treatise of human nature.* London: Thomas & Joseph Allman. (Original work published 1739.)

James, W. (1890). *The principles of psychology* (Vol. 1). New York: Holt.

Kihlstrom, J. F., & Hastie, R. (1997). Mental representations of self and others. In S. R. Briggs, R. Hogan, & W. H. Jones (Eds.), *Handbook of personality psychology.* San Diego, CA: Academic Press.

Kihlstrom, J. F., & Klein, S. B. (1994). The self as a knowledge structure. In R. S. Wyer & T. K. Srull (Eds.), *Handbook of social cognition: Vol. 1. Basic processes* (pp. 153–208). Hillsdale, NJ: Erlbaum.

Kihlstrom, J. F., & Klein, S. B. (1997). Self-knowledge and self-awareness. In J. G. Snodgrass & R. L. Thompson (Eds.), *Annals of the New York Academy of Sciences. The self across psychology: Self-recognition, self-awareness, and the self concept.* New York: New York Academy of Sciences.

Kirby, D. M., & Gardner, R. C. (1972). Ethnic stereotypes: Norms on 208 words typically used in their assessment. *Canadian Journal of Psychology, 26*, 140–154.

Klein, S. B., & Loftus, J. (1993). The mental representation of trait and autobiographical knowledge about the self. In T. K. Srull & R. S. Wyer (Eds.), *Advances in social cognition* (Vol. 5, pp. 1–49). Hillsdale, NJ: Erlbaum.

Klein, S. B., Loftus, J., & Burton, H. (1989). Two self-reference effects: The importance of distinguishing between self-descriptiveness judgments and autobiographical retrieval in self-referent encoding. *Journal of Personality and Social Psychology, 56*, 853–865.

Klein, S. B., Loftus, J., & Plog, A. E. (1992). Trait judgments about the self: Evidence from the encoding specificity paradigm. *Personality and Social Psychology Bulletin, 18*, 730–735.

Kolb, B., & Whishaw, I. Q. (1990). *Fundamentals of human neuropsychology* (3rd ed.). San Francisco: Freeman.

Kopelman, M. D. (1994). The autobiographical memory interview (AMI) in organic and psychogenic amnesia. *Memory, 2*, 211–235.

Lazarus, R. S. (1984). On the primacy of cognition. *American Psychologist, 39*, 124–129.

Locke, J. (1731). *An essay concerning human understanding.* London: Edmund Parker. (Original work published 1690.)

Locksley, A., & Lenauer, M. (1981). Considerations for a theory of self-inference processes. In N. Cantor & J. F. Kihlstrom (Eds.), *Personality, cognition, and social interaction* (pp. 263–277). Hillsdale, NJ: Erlbaum.

Lucchelli, F., Muggia, S., & Spinnler, H. (1995). The "Petites Madeleines" phenomenon in two amnesic patients: Sudden recovery of forgotten memories. *Brain, 118*, 167–183.

Luria, A. R. (1966). *Human brain and psychological processes.* New York: McGraw-Hill.

MacKinnon, D. F., & Squire, L. R. (1989). Autobiographical memory and amnesia. *Psychobiology, 17*, 247–256.

Martin, E. (1971). Verbal learning theory and independent retrieval phenomena. *Psychological Review, 78*, 314–332.

Martin, E. (1972). Stimulus encoding in learning and transfer. In A. W. Melton & E. Martin (Eds.), *Coding process in human memory* (pp. 59–84). New York: Wiley.

McCrae, R. R. (1982). Consensual validation of personality traits: Evidence from self-reports and ratings. *Journal of Personality and Social Psychology, 43*, 293–303.

Milner, B., Corkin, S., & Teuber, H. L. (1968). Further analysis of the hippocampal amnesic syndrome: 14-year follow-up study of H. M. *Neuropsychologia, 6*, 215–234.

Mortimer, J. T., & Lorence, J. (1981). Self-concept stability and change from late adolescence to early childhood. *Research in Community and Mental Health, 2*, 5–42.

O'Malley, P., & Bachman, J. (1983). Self-esteem: Change and stability between the ages 13 and 23. *Developmental Psychology, 19*, 257–268.

Parkin, A. J. (1993). *Memory.* Cambridge, MA: Blackwell.

Robinson, J. A. (1976). Sampling autobiographical memory. *Cognitive Psychology, 8*, 578–595.

Roediger, H. L., & Blaxton, T. A. (1987). Retrieval modes produce dissociations in memory for surface information. In D. Gorfein & R. R. Hoffman (Eds.), *Memory and cognitive processes: The Ebbinghaus centennial conference* (pp. 349–379). Hillsdale, NJ: Erlbaum.

Roediger, H. L., Weldon, M. S., & Challis, B. H. (1988). Explaining dissociations between implicit and explicit measures of retention: A processing account. In H. L. Roediger & F. I. M. Craik (Eds.), *Varieties of memory and consciousness: Essays in honor of Endel Tulving* (pp. 3–41). Hillsdale, NJ: Erlbaum.

Rubin, D. C., Wetzler, S. E., & Nebes, R. D. (1986). Autobiographical memory across the life span. In D. C. Rubin (Ed.), *Autobiographical memory* (pp. 202–221). New York: Cambridge University Press.

Sacks, O. (1974). *Awakenings.* Garden City, NY: Doubleday.

Sacks, O. (1985). *The man who mistook his wife for a hat.* New York: Doubleday.

Sacks, O. (1995). *An anthropologist on Mars: Seven paradoxical tales.* New York: Knopf.

Schacter, D. L., Kihlstrom, J. F., Kihlstrom, L. C., & Berren, M. B. (1989). Autobiographical memory in a case of multiple personality disorder. *Journal of Abnormal Psychology, 98,* 508–514.

Schacter, D. L., Wang, P. L., Tulving, E., & Freedman, M. (1982). Functional retrograde amnesia: A quantitative case study. *Neuropsychologia, 20,* 523–532.

Scoville, W. B., & Milner, B. (1957). Loss of recent memory after bilateral hippocampal lesions. *Journal of Neurology, Neurosurgery, and Psychiatry, 20,* 11–21.

Shoemaker, S. (1963). *Self-knowledge and self-identity.* Ithaca, NY: Cornell University Press.

Tulving, E. (1993). Self-knowledge of an amnesic is represented abstractly. In T. K. Srull & R. S. Wyer (Eds.), *Advances in social cognition* (Vol. 5, pp. 147–156). Hillsdale, NJ: Erlbaum.

Tulving, E., Hayman, C. A. G., & Macdonald, C. A. (1991). Long-lasting perceptual priming and semantic learning in amnesia: A case experiment. *Journal of Experimental Psychology: Learning, Memory, and Cognition, 17,* 595–617.

Wiggins, J. S. (1973). *Personality and prediction: Principles of personality assessment.* Reading, MA: Addison-Wesley.

Wilson, B., & Baddeley, A. D. (1988). Semantic, episodic, and autobiographical memory in a postmeningitic amnesic patient. *Brain and Cognition, 8,* 31–46.

Zajonc, R. B. (1980). Feeling and thinking: Preferences need no inferences. *American Psychologist, 35,* 151–175.

Zajonc, R. B. (1984). On the primacy of affect. *American Psychologist, 39,* 117–123.

REFERENCES FOR EDITORS' NOTES

Allport, G. W. (1937). *Personality: A psychological interpretation*. New York: Henry Holt.

Allport, G. W., & Odbert, H. S. (1936). Trait-names: A psycho-lexical study. *Psychological Monographs: General and Applied, 47*, 171. (1, Whole No. 211).

American Psychological Association. *Publication Manual of the American Psychological Association* (5th ed.) 2001. Washington, DC: American Psychological Association.

Bem, D. J., & Allen, A. (1974). On predicting some of the people some of the time: The search for cross-situational consistencies in behavior. *Psychological Review, 81*, 506–520.

Block, J. (1995). A contrarian view of the five-factor approach to personality description. *Psychological Bulletin, 117*, 187–215.

Funder, D. C. (2007). *The personality puzzle* (4th ed.). New York: Norton.

Gay, P. (1988). *Freud: A life for our time*. New York: Norton.

Mischel, W. (1968). *Personality and assessment*. New York: Wiley.

Mischel, W., & Peake, P. K. (1982). Beyond *déjà vu* in the search for cross-situational consistency. *Psychological Review, 90*, 730–755.

Myers, I. B., & McCaulley, M. H. (1985). *Manual: A guide to the development and use of the Myers-Briggs Type Indicator*. Palo Alto, CA: Consulting Psychologists Press.

Ozer, D. J., & Reise, S. P. (1994). Personality assessment. *Annual Review of Psychology, 45*, 357–388.

Ross, L. (1977). The intuitive psychologist and his shortcomings. In L. Berkowitz (Ed.), *Advances in experimental social psychology* (Vol. 10, pp. 174–214). New York: Academic Press.

CREDITS

Allport, G. W. (1931). Except from "What is a trait of personality?" *Journal of Abnormal and Social Psychology, 25,* 368–371. Copyright © 1931 by the Educational Publishing Foundation (American Psychological Association). Adapted with permission.

Bandura, A. (1978). Excerpt from "The self system in reciprocal determinism." *American Psychologist, 33,* 344–358. Copyright © 1978 by the Educational Publishing Foundation (American Psychological Association) Adapted with permission.

Baumeister, Roy F. (2000). Self-esteem, narcissism, and aggression. *Current Directions in Psychological Science,* 26–29. Reprinted with permission from Blackwell Publishers.

Baumeister, et al. (1998). Excerpt from "Freudian defense mechanisms and empirical findings in modern social psychology: Reaction formation, projection, displacement, un-doing, isolation, sublimation, and denial." *Journal of Personality, 66,* 1081–1124. Reprinted with permission from Blackwell Publishers.

Borkenau, P. et al. (2001). Excerpt from "Genetic and environmental influences on observed personality." *Journal of Personality and Social Psychology, 80,* 655–668. Copyright © 2001 by the Educational Publishing Foundation (American Psychological Association). Adapted with permission.

Buss, et al. (1992). Sex differences in jealousy: Evolution, physiology and psychology. *Psychological Science, 3,* 251–255. Reprinted with permission from Blackwell Publishers.

Canli, Turhan. (2004). Functional brain mapping of extraversion and neuroticism. *Journal of Personality, 72,* 6, 1105–1132. Reprinted with permission of Blackwell Publishers.

Caspi, et al. (2003). Influence of life stress on depression. *Science Magazine.* 301, 386–389. Reprinted with permission from Science Magazine. Copyright © 2003 AAAS.

Chronbach, L. J., & Meehl, P. E. (1955). Construct validity in psychological tests. *Psychological Bulletin, 52,* 281–301.

Csikszentmihalyi, Mihaly. (1999). Excerpt from "If we are so rich, why aren't we happy?" *American Psychologist, 54,* 821–827. Copyright © 1999 by the Educational Publishing Foundation (American Psychological Association). Adapted with permission.

Dabbs, J. M. Jr. Reprinted from *Personality and Individual Differences, 20,* Testosterone differences among college fraternities: Well-behaved vs. rambunctious, pp.157–161. Copyright © 1996, with permission from Elsevier.

Dahlsgaard, Katherine. (2005). Shared virtue. *Review of General Psychology, 9,* 203–213. Copyright © 2005 by the Educational Publishing Foundation (American Psychological Association). Reprinted with permission.

Donnellan, M. Brent. (2005). Low self-esteem is related to aggression, antisocial behavior, and delinquency. *Psychological Science, 16, 1,* 328–335. Reprinted with permission from Blackwell Publishing.

Eagly and Wood. (1999). The origins of sex differences in human behavior. *American Psychologist, 54,* 408–423. Copyright © 1999 by the Educational Publishing Foundation (American Psychological Association). Reprinted with permission.

Erikson, Erik H. (1950). Eight Stages of Man. From *Childhood and Society* by Erik H. Erikson. Copyright 1950, © 1963 by W. W. Norton & Company, Inc., renewed © 1978, 1991 by Erik H. Erikson. Used by permission of W. W. Norton & Company, Inc.

Farah, Martha J. Reprinted from *Trends in Cognitive Science, 9,* Neuroethics: The practical and the philosophical, pp. 34–37. Copyright © 2005, with permission from Elsevier.

Freud, Sigmund. Lecture XXXI. From *Introductory Lectures of Psycho-Analysis* by Sigmund Freud, translated by James Strachey. Copyright © 1965, 1964, 1963 by James Strachey. Used by permission of Liveright Publishing Corporation.

Freud, Sigmund. Lecture XXXI. From *Introductory Lectures of Psycho-Analysis* by Sigmund Freud, translated by James Strachey. Sigmund Freud © Copyrights, The Institute of Psycho-Analysis and The Hogarth Press for permission to quote from The Standard Edition of the Complete Psychological Works of Sigmund Freud translated and edited by James Strachey. Reprinted by permission of The Random House Group Ltd.

Gosling, Samuel D., John, Oliver P., Craik, Kenneth H., & Robbins, Richard W. (1998). Excerpt from "Do people know how they behave? Self-reported act frequencies compared with on-line codings by observers." *Journal of Personality and Social Psychology, 74,* 1337–1349. Copyright © 1998 by the Educational Publishing Foundation (American Psychological Association). Adapted with permission.

Horney, Karen. (1967). The Distrust Between Sexes. pp. 104–116. From *Feminine Psychology* by Karen Horney. Copyright © 1967 by W. W. Norton & Company, Inc. Used by permission of W. W. Norton & Company, Inc.

Jung, C. G.; Psychological Types–Volume 6, The Collected Works of C. G. Jung. © 1971 Princeton University Press, 1999 renewed PUP. Reprinted by permission of Princeton University Press.

Kenrick and Funder. (1988). Excerpt from "Profiting from controversy: Lessons from the person-situation debate." *American Psychologist, 43,* 23–34. Copyright © 1988 by the Educational Publishing Foundation (American Psychological Association). Adapted with permission.

Klein, Loftus, et al. (1996). Excerpt from "Self-knowledge of an amnesic patient." *Journal of Experimental Psychology: General, 125,* 250–260. Copyright © 1996 by the Educational Publishing Foundation (American Psychological Association). Adapted with permission.

Lyubormirsky, Sonja. (2005). Pursuing Happiness: The architecture of sustainable change. *Review of General Psychology, 9,* 111–113. Copyright © 2005 by the Educational Publishing Foundation (American Psychological Association). Reprinted with permission.

Markus & Kitayama. (1994). A collective fear of the collective: Implications for selves and theories of selves. *Personality and Social Psychology Bulletin, 20,* 568–579. Copyright © 1994 by the Society for Personality and Social Psychology, Inc. Reprinted by permission of Sage Publications, Inc.

Maslow, A. H. A theory of human motivation. *Motivation and Personality*, pp. 80–106. Copyright © 1954 by Harper & Brothers. Copyright © 1970 by Abraham H. Maslow. Reprinted by permission of Addison-Wesley Educational Publishers.

McAdams, Dan. (1995). Excerpt from "What do we know when we know a person?" *Journal of Personality, 63*, 365–396. Reprinted with permission of Blackwell Publishing.

McCrae & Costa. (1999). Excerpt from "A five-factor theory of personality." In Pervin & John (eds.), *Handbook of Personality*. pp. 139–153. New York: Guilford. Copyright © 1999 by Guilford Press. Reprinted with permission.

McCrae, R. R. Reprinted from *Journal of Research in Personality, 38*, 1, Human nature and culture: A trait perspective, figure 2, pg.11, Copyright © 2004, with permission from Elsevier.

Mischel, Walter. (1968). Consistency and specificity in behavior. In *Personality and Assessment*, 13–39. New York: Wiley. © 1968 by John Wiley & Sons, Inc. This material is used by permission of John Wiley & Sons, Inc.

Mischel, Walter. (1999). Personality coherence and dispositions in cognitive-affective personality approach. In D. Cervone and Y. Shoda (eds.) *The Coherence of Personality*. New York: Guilford. Copyright © 1999 by Guilford Press. Reprinted with permission.

Oishi, Shigehiro. Personality in culture: A non-Allportian view. Reprinted from *Journal of Research in Personality, 38*, pp. 68–74. Copyright © 2004, with permission from Elsevier.

Ozer, Daniel. (2006). Personality and the prediction of consequential outcomes. *Annual Review of Psychology, 57*, 401–421. Reprinted with permission of Annual Reviews, Inc.

Rogers, C. (1947). Excerpt from "Some observations on the organization of personality." *American Psychologist, 2*, 358–368.

Rosenthal & Rubin. (1982). *Journal of Educational Psychology, 74*, pp. 166–69. Table 1, p. 167 (adapted). Copyright © 1982 by the Educational Publishing Foundation (American Psychological Association). Adapted with permission.

Steinem, Gloria. (1994). Womb envy, testyria, and breast castration: What if Freud were female? *Ms. Magazine*, 49–56. Reprinted with permission of Gloria Steinem.

Skinner, B. F. (1953). Why organisms behave. *Science and Human Behavior*, 23–42. Reprinted with permission of the B. F. Skinner Foundation.

Triandis, H. C. (1989). Excerpt from "The self and social behavior in differing cultural contexts." *Psychological Review, 96*, 506–520. Copyright © 1989 by the Educational Publishing Foundation (American Psychological Association). Adapted with permission.

Tsai, Jeanne. (2003). Variation among European Americans in emotional facial expression. *Journal of Cross-Cultural Psychology, 34*:6, 650–657. Copyright © 2003 International Association for Cross-Cultural Psychology. Reprinted by permission of Sage Publications, Inc.